Coastal Queensland & the Great Barrier Reef

Cairns & the
Daintree Rainforest
p228

Townsville to
Mission Beach
p207

Whitsunday Coast
p181

Capricorn Coast & the
Southern Reef Islands
p167

Fraser Island & the
Fraser Coast p147

Noosa & the
Sunshine Coast p124

Brisbane
& Around
p50

The Gold Coast p107

Paul Harding, Cristian Bonetto, Charles Rawlings-Way,
Tamara Sheward, Tom Spurling, Donna Wheeler

Contents

MATT MUNRO / LONELY PLANET IMAGES ©

DINGO, FRASER ISLAND
P166

AUSTRALIANCAMERA / SHUTTERSTOCK ©

THE DAINTREE RAINFOREST
P261

Contents

DIVING, GREAT BARRIER REEF P32

BANKSIA

Welcome to Coastal Queensland

*Let it all hang out in Queensland:
Australia's holiday haven offers
beaches, reefs, jungles, uptempo locals
and a laid-back tropical pace of life.*

Landscape Diversity

Queensland's most famous 'landscape' is actually underwater: the astonishing 2000km-long Great Barrier Reef. Also offshore are hundreds of islands, harbouring giant dunes and surreal forests growing in the sand. Back on the mainland, bewitching national parks protect lush rainforests, sparkling lakes and wildlife that ranges from cute and cuddly (koalas) to downright fearsome (crocs). Skyscrapers define the landscape in Surfers Paradise and Brisbane: everywhere else you'll find laid-back beach towns and sugar-cane fields rattling under the Queensland sun.

Big Adventures

Outdoor Queensland is truly 'great'. Take the Great Barrier Reef for starters: slip on some goggles and ogle one of the most amazing underwater landscapes on earth. There's also white-water river rafting and easygoing kayaking along the coast. Bushwalking here is first-rate: propel yourself along a multiday 'Great Walk', or take a shorter hike through a rainforest gorge or up a mountainside. Sail across the azure Whitsunday waters, or tackle a 4WD adventure along Fraser Island's 'beach highway'. There's also great surfing, skydiving, mountain biking, fishing and hang-gliding to be had.

On Your Plate & in Your Glass

With a hip caffeine scene, rambling farmers markets and fabulous riverside restaurants, Brisbane has reinvented itself as a foodie destination. The city's alter ego shows up at sunset, when clubs, pubs and small city bars light up the night. Elsewhere in the state – including foodie haunts such as Noosa, Cairns and Port Douglas – you'll find culinary rewards great and small, from fish and chips to sizzling steaks. Wash it down with Queensland's ubiquitous XXXX beer, or hunt down some fine wine from the little-known Granite Belt wine region.

Urban Enticements

Wrapped around river bends, boom town Brisbane is a glamorous patchwork of neighbourhoods, each with a distinct cultural flavour: bohemian West End; party-central Fortitude Valley; affluent Paddington; exclusive New Farm...explore and soak up the vibes. The Gold Coast should also be high on your list: nightclubs and surf clubs in equal measure. Other hubs include Cairns (gateway for the Daintree and Great Barrier Reef), Noosa (on the Sunshine Coast) and Airlie Beach (to access the Whitsundays). Urban essentials abound: cafes, bars, restaurants, galleries, shops and more.

Why I Love Coastal Queensland

By Charles Rawlings-Way, Writer

Growing up in a chilly southern Australian city, the very notion of Queensland – with its beaches, islands, sunshine and swaying palms – was irresistible in my imagination. Towns like Mission Beach, Noosa and Port Douglas assumed near-mythical status, demanding to be investigated at the first opportunity. Then, when the time came to actually explore the Sunshine State, the reality didn't disappoint. And I haven't stopped exploring since! From the tropical north to the booming southeast, Queensland is an essential Australian destination.

For more about our writers, see p320

Above: Hill Inlet, Whitsunday Island

Coastal Queenland & the Great Barrier Reef

ELEVATION

| 1000m |
| 750m |
| 500m |
| 250m |
| 0 |

0 — 200 km
0 — 100 miles

PAPUA NEW GUINEA

SOUTH PACIFIC OCEAN

CORAL SEA

Daintree Rainforest
Butterflies, beaches and tropical jungle (p261)

Kuranda
Hilltop hippie haven (p249)

Cairns
Snorkel by day, dance on tables by night (p229)

Hinchinbrook Island
Hike the rugged Thorsborne Trail (p220)

Great Barrier Reef
Snorkel or scuba through kaleidoscopic coral (p201)

Rafting the Tully River
A white-water adrenaline rush (p220)

Great Barrier

Thursday Island
Horn Island
Prince of Wales Island
Cape York
Bamaga
Jardine River National Park
Shelburne Bay
Iron Range National Park
Lockhart River
Weipa
Mungkan Kandju National Park
Coen
Aurukun
Princess Charlotte Bay
Cape Melville National Park
Barrow Point
Lizard Island
Lakefield National Park
Hope Vale
Cooktown
Cape York Peninsula
Staaten River National Park
Mitchell River
Wujal Wujal
Daintree National Park
Pormpuraaw
Kowanyama
Mossman
Port Douglas
Kuranda
Atherton Tableland
Mareeba
Cairns
Mt Bartle Frere (1657m)
Babinda
Innisfail
Mission Beach
Ravenshoe
Wooroonooran National Park
Tully
Dunk Island
Hinchinbrook Island
Hinchinbrook National Park
Cardwell
Ingham
Magnetic Island
Bulleringa National Park
Mt Surprise
Undara Volcanic National Park
Lumholtz National Park
Paluma Range National Park
Townsville
Bowling Green Bay National Park
Normanton
Croydon
Georgetown
Great

15°S
10°S
145°E
150°E
155°E

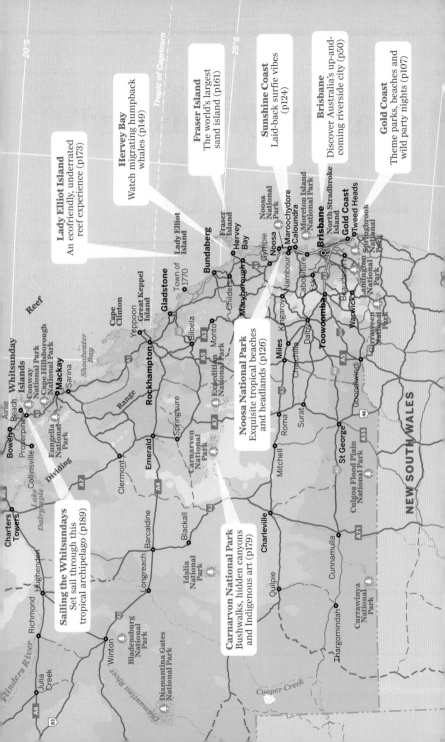

Lady Elliot Island
An ecofriendly, underrated reef experience (p173)

Hervey Bay
Watch migrating humpback whales (p149)

Fraser Island
The world's largest sand island (p161)

Sunshine Coast
Laid-back surfie vibes (p124)

Brisbane
Discover Australia's up-and-coming riverside city (p50)

Gold Coast
Theme parks, beaches and wild party nights (p107)

Sailing the Whitsundays
Set sail through this tropical archipelago (p189)

Carnarvon National Park
Bushwalks, hidden canyons and Indigenous art (p179)

Noosa National Park
Exquisite tropical beaches and headlands (p126)

Coastal Queensland's
Top 15

1

Great Barrier Reef

1 The Great Barrier Reef (p201) lives up to its reputation. Stretching more than 2000km along the Queensland coastline, it's a complex ecosystem populated with dazzling coral, languid sea turtles, gliding rays, timid reef sharks and 1500 species of colourful tropical fish. Whether you dive on it, snorkel over it, explore it via scenic flight or glass-bottom boat, linger in an island resort or camp on a remote coral-fringed atoll, this vivid undersea kingdom and its 900 coral-fringed islands are unforgettable.

Daintree Rainforest

2 Lush green rainforest tumbles down towards brilliant white-sand coastline in the ancient, World Heritage–listed Daintree Rainforest (p261). Upon crossing the Daintree River and entering this extraordinary wonderland – home to 3000 or so plant species including fan palms, ferns and mangroves – you'll be enveloped by birdsong, the buzz of insects and the constant commentary of frogs. Continue exploring via wildlife-spotting tours, mountain treks, interpretive boardwalks, tropical-fruit orchard tours, canopy walks, 4WD trips, horse riding, kayaking and cruises. Cassowary (p255)

TORORO REACTION / SHUTTERSTOCK ©

DAWI88888 / SHUTTERSTOCK ©

Brisbane

3 Once considered little more than a provincial sidekick to Sydney and Melbourne, Brisbane (p52) has reinvented itself as one of Asia Pacific's hippest hubs. No longer happy to settle for 261 days of sunshine a year, Queensland's new, improved capital is smashing it on the cultural front, with an ever-expanding booty of ambitious street art and galleries, boutique bookshops, secret cocktail bars and award-winning microbreweries. The result: big-city Australian cool with a laid-back, subtropical twist. Street art, South Bank Parkands (p57)

Kuranda

4 You can drive or catch a bus from Cairns to the hinterland rainforest village of Kuranda (p249) in around half an hour. But that would be missing the point! Kuranda is as much about the journey as it is the destination. Hop into a gondola on the 7.5km-long Skyrail Rainforest Cableway, browse Kuranda's markets for arts, crafts and gourmet goodies, then wind your way back down to Cairns through picturesque mountains, via 15 tunnels and across 37 bridges on the Kuranda Scenic Railway. Kuranda Original Rainforest Markets

5

6

Noosa National Park

5 Cloaking the headland beside the stylish resort town of Noosa itself, Noosa National Park (p126) features a string of perfect bays fringed with sand and pandanus trees. Surfers come here for the long, rolling waves; walkers make the trip for the unspoiled natural vibes. Lovely hiking trails criss-cross the park: our pick is the scenic coastal trail to Hell's Gates on which you might spy sleepy koalas in the trees around Tea Tree Bay, and dolphins swimming off the rocky headland. Koala mother and joey, Noosa National Park

Whale Watching at Hervey Bay

6 For most of the year, Hervey Bay (p149) is a soporific seaside village with a long beach and a flat, shallow sea. That all changes in mid-July, when migrating humpback whales cruise into the bay, and tourists cruise out to see them. It's one of the world's top whale-watching regions, and witnessing these aqua-acrobats blowing and breaching is a guaranteed breath-taker. Do some research and choose an eco-accredited operator: humanity owes these great creatures a little peace and privacy.

Gold Coast

7 Brash, trashy, hedonistic, overhyped... Queensland's Gold Coast (p107) is all of these things, but if you're looking for a party, bring it on! Beyond the bling is a rapidly growing food, bar and craft brew scene, and the beach – an improbably gorgeous coastline of clean sand, warm water and peeling surf breaks. Bronzed surf life-savers patrol the sands and pit their skills against one another in gruelling surf carnivals, putting the rest of us to shame. Also here are Australia's biggest theme parks – roller-coaster nirvana. Surfers Paradise (p109)

Lady Elliot Island

8 This ecofriendly resort island (p173) is one of the loveliest and most peaceful places to experience the Great Barrier Reef. Snorkel straight off Lady Elliot's white sands – the living reef that surrounds the tiny coral cay is teeming with tropical fish, turtles and the island's resident manta rays. At hatching time (January to April) you can see baby turtles scamper across the sand, and humpback whales pass by from June to October. Getting to the island is equally memorable – with a scenic flight over the turquoise reef. Sea turtle

Sunshine Coast

9 The endless summers and surfer-chic culture of the Sunshine Coast (p124) bewitch all who step on to its sandy shores. There's a wholesomeness here that's as natural and unaffected as the idyllic local surf beaches and balmy sea breezes. Early mornings see a steady flow of surfers, joggers, cyclists and walkers making the most of the beach scene and surfside cafes. Noosa, the coast's boutique resort town, where barefoot surfers mingle effortlessly with the designer-clad beach elite, is the elegant yet unpretentious star of this sandy crown.

Hiking Hinchinbrook Island

10 Queensland has plenty of resort islands where you can sprawl on a sunlounger and do very little. But if you're up for something more active, consider hiking the Thorsborne Trail on Hinchinbrook Island (p220). Tracking north–south along the island, the Thorsborne isn't for the faint-hearted – prepare to cross creeks, draw water and protect your food from ravenous rats. End-to-end, allow three nights at bush camp sites along the ungraded 32km-long track. Hiker numbers are limited, so book ahead. Thorsborne Trail

ANDREW BAIN / GETTY IMAGES ©

Carnarvon National Park

11 Carnarvon National Park (p179), with its magnificent gorge, is a magnet for bushwalkers, birdwatchers and nature lovers. The 30km-long gorge is a diverse ecosystem offering a huge range of walks, hidden canyons, and clifftop views. Pretty-faced wallabies scamper about the gorge floor, while at night, spotlights reveal gliders soaring from tree to tree. Indigenous Australians have been visiting this sacred place for at least 20,000 years, and have left remarkable galleries of stencil art that can be admired in several of the area's caves. The Art Gallery, Carnarvon Gorge

Sailing the Whitsundays

12 You can hop around an entire archipelago of tropical islands in this seafaring life and never find anywhere with the sheer tropical beauty of the Whitsundays (p189). Travellers of all monetary persuasions launch yachts from party town Airlie Beach and drift between these lush green isles in a slow search for paradise (you'll probably find it in more than one place). Wish you were here? Whitehaven Beach, Whitsunday Island (p199)

Rafting the Tully River

13 You won't find a wilder ride in all of Australia than down the Tully River (p220), smack bang in the wettest part of the country (check out the towering gumboot at the entrance to Tully town: its 7.9m represent the amount of rain that fell in 1950). Rafting trips are timed to coincide with the release of the river's hydroelectric floodgates, so even if it's not raining, adrenaline hounds are guaranteed thrills – and possibly spills – on Grade IV rapids all year round.

Fraser Island

14 Fraser Island (p161) is an ecological wonderland created by drifting sand, where wild dogs roam free and lush rainforest grows in the sand. It's a primal island utopia, home to a profusion of wildlife including the purest strain of dingo in Australia. The best way to explore the island is in a 4WD – cruising up the seemingly endless Seventy-Five Mile Beach and bouncing along sandy inland tracks. Tropical greenery, pristine freshwater pools and beach camping under the stars will bring you back to nature.

Cairns

15 It's early morning in Cairns (p229) and you're boarding a boat out to the reef. By midmorning you're snorkelling or diving around the colourful coral; by late afternoon you're heading back to shore after an action-packed day. But it's not over yet: you order a cold sundowner and decide on one of Cairns' myriad restaurants for an alfresco dinner. Then you're ready to hit this hedonistic city's bars, pubs and clubs, and you dance till 4am. Suddenly, the sun is coming up. Do it all again? Nudey Beach (p245), Fitzroy Island, near Cairns

Need to Know

For more information, see Survival Guide (p291)

Currency
Australian dollar ($)

Language
English

Visas
All visitors to Australia need a visa. Apply online through the Department of Immigration and Border Protection (p301).

Money
ATMs widely available. Credit cards accepted at most hotels, restaurants and shops.

Mobile Phones
European phones will work on Australia's network, but most American or Japanese phones will not. Use global roaming or a local SIM card and prepaid account.

Time
Australian Eastern Standard Time (AEST; GMT/UCT plus 10 hours)

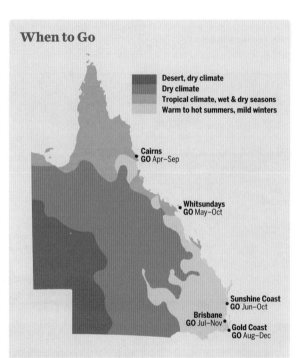

When to Go

Desert, dry climate
Dry climate
Tropical climate, wet & dry seasons
Warm to hot summers, mild winters

Cairns GO Apr–Sep

Whitsundays GO May–Oct

Sunshine Coast GO Jun–Oct

Brisbane GO Jul–Nov

Gold Coast GO Aug–Dec

High Season (Jun–Sep)
→ Crowds and lofty accommodation prices in the north; a bit more wintry in the southeast, but still fine and mild.
→ Best time to see migrating whales.
→ Good visibility on the Great Barrier Reef.

Shoulder Season (Apr–May & Oct–Nov)
→ Warm, pleasant temperatures, with long beach days.
→ Fewer crowds, and resort prices come down slightly.

Low Season (Dec–Mar)
→ The wet season: hot and humid with torrential rain in the north.
→ Party season on the Gold Coast; accommodation books out quickly.
→ Unsafe swimming north of Agnes Water from November to May (jellyfish).

Useful Websites

Lonely Planet (www.lonely planet.com/australia/queens land) Destination information, hotel bookings, traveller forum and more.

Queensland Tourism (www. queenslandholidays.com.au) Extensive Queensland coverage: accommodation and attractions.

Courier Mail (www.couriermail. com.au) Brisbane's daily paper: current affairs and rugby league.

Queensland Department of National Parks, Sport & Racing (www.nprsr.qld.gov.au) National parks info.

Coastalwatch (www.coastal watch.com) Surf reports and surf-cams.

Important Numbers

Australian landline phone numbers have a two-digit STD area code followed by an eight-digit number. Drop the initial 0 in the area code if calling from abroad.

Emergency	☎000
Country Code	☎61
International Access Code	☎0011
Queensland STD Area Code	☎07
Directory Assistance	☎1223

Exchange Rates

Canada	C$1	$1.02
Euro Zone	€1	$1.42
Japan	¥100	$1.16
New Zealand	NZ$1	$0.96
UK	UK£1	$1.69
USA	US$1	$1.34

For current exchange rates see www.xe.com.

Daily Costs

Budget: Less than $150

➡ Hostel dorm bed: $25–35

➡ Double room in a hostel: $80–100

➡ Budget pizza or pasta meal: $15–20

➡ Short bus or tram ride: $4

Midrange: $150–300

➡ Double room in a motel or B&B: $130–250

➡ Breakfast or lunch in a cafe: $20–30

➡ Car hire per day: from $35

➡ Short taxi ride: $25

Top End: More than $300

➡ Double room in a top-end hotel: from $250

➡ Three-course meal in a classy restaurant: from $80

➡ Adventure activities: sailing the Whitsundays from $300 per night, diving course $650

➡ Domestic flight Brisbane to Cairns: from $120

Opening Hours

Banks 9.30am to 4pm Monday to Friday; some also 9am to noon Saturday

Bars 4pm to late

Cafes 7am to 5pm

Nightclubs 10pm to 4am Thursday to Saturday

Post Offices 9am to 5pm Monday to Friday; some also 9am to noon Saturday

Pubs 11am to midnight

Restaurants noon to 2.30pm and 6pm to 9pm

Shops 9am to 5pm Monday to Saturday

Supermarkets 7am to 8pm

Arriving in Queensland

Brisbane Airport (p303) Air-train trains to central Brisbane every 15 to 30 minutes, 5am to 10pm. Prebooked shuttle buses service city hotels. A taxi into the city costs $35 to $45 (25 minutes).

Gold Coast Airport (p303) Prebooked shuttle buses service Gold Coast hotels. Public bus 777 runs from the airport along the coast to Broadbeach. A taxi to Surfers Paradise costs around $35 (25 minutes).

Cairns Airport (p303) Sun Palm shuttles meet arriving flights and can deliver you to Cairns, Mission Beach or Port Douglas. A taxi into central Cairns costs around $25 (15 minutes).

Getting Around

Queensland is a massive state: getting from A to B requires some thought.

Car Explore remote areas and visit regions with no public transport. Hire cars in major towns; drive on the left.

Plane Fast-track your holiday with affordable, frequent, fast domestic flights. Carbon offset your flights if you're feeling guilty.

Bus Reliable, frequent long-haul services around the state (not always cheaper than flying).

Train Reliable, regular services up and down the coast. Opt for a sleeper carriage rather than an 'overnighter' seat if you want to actually sleep.

For much more on **getting around**, see p304

What's New

Brouhaha Brewery
Small-town Maleny is making waves on the craft-beer scene with the opening of Brouhaha Brewery, a svelte new micro-brewery producing a rotating selection of competent IPAs, stouts, saisons and sours. (p146)

Cooking School Noosa
Queensland's chicest surf town isn't short on culinary hot spots. Some of the region's most respected chefs are now sharing their kitchen skills at Cooking School Noosa. (p128)

Gold Coast Breweries
A craft-beer revolution is going on in Goldie, with a crop of back-block breweries arriving on the scene. Currumbin's Balter (p120) and Burleigh's Black Hops Brewing (p119) join stalwart Burleigh Brewing Company (p119) with stylish taprooms.

Trans North
It's now a heckuva lot easier to get from Cairns to Cooktown, with Trans North running a three-times-weekly bus along the coastal route. (p244)

Just Tuk'n Around
Just Tuk'n Around runs half-hour rickshaw tours around the Whitsundays' unstoppable party town, Airlie Beach, with a real 'local secrets' vibe. (p192)

G:link (Gold Coast Light Rail)
This long-awaited tram system has revolutionised public transport on the car-centric Gold Coast, shunting people between Southport and Broadbeach. (p109)

First Coat Art & Music Festival
Home-grown and foreign aerosol artists hit Toowoomba in May for First Coat Art & Music Festival, a trio of days celebrating street art, tunes and contemporary creativity. (p105)

Jet-Boating Airlie Beach
Pioneer Jet Whitsundays is now running heart-starting/stopping jet-boat rides around the coast off Airlie Beach. Don't wear your best suit. (p192)

Riverboarding on the Tully
Come face to face with foaming Tully River rapids on an eye-level riverboard – the Rapid Boarders expedition is unlike anything you'll find elsewhere in Australia. (p235)

Townsville History Walking Tour
Not too humid? Sign up for a Townsville History Walking Tour with a new operation, which also offers a City Day Tour or a Palmer St Wine and Dine Tour. (p210)

For more recommendations and reviews, see lonelyplanet.com/queensland

If You Like...

Beaches

Surfers Paradise The brash, buzzy heart of the Gold Coast is a beacon for sun-worshippers and party kids (and the sand and surf are heavenly; p109)

Rainbow Beach This aptly named surf spot dazzles with its ancient, multicoloured sand cliffs and dunes. (p154)

Whitehaven Beach The jewel of the Whitsundays, with powdery white sand and gin-clear waters. (p189)

Four Mile Beach Reach for your camera: backed by palms, this long, photogenic Port Douglas beach is one for the holiday album. (p255)

Cape Tribulation The rainforest sweeps down to smooch the reef at these empty stretches of sand. (p262)

Fraser Island The world's largest sand island is basically one big beach. (p161)

The Spit A long, wild stretch of pristine Gold Coast sand and dunes, beyond the high-rises and the crowds. (p113)

Yeppoon A long sweep of Queensland sand where locals and Rockhampton folk come to cool off. (p176)

Rose Bay One of little Bowen's best bays. Sit on the sand and eat a mango. (p200)

Islands

North Stradbroke Island Take a quick trip from Brisbane for whale watching, surfing, long beach walks and swimming in forest-ringed lakes. (p96)

The Whitsundays Book in at one of the archipelago's top resorts, or board a sailing boat and explore as many of these pristine islands as you can. (p189)

Lady Musgrave Island Ringed by reef, this secluded island is a great place to play castaway. (p171)

Fraser Island Rev-up your 4WD: the world's largest sand island has giant sand dunes, freshwater lakes and wildlife. (p161)

Lady Elliot Island Ringed by reef and reachable by light aircraft, Lady Elliot has the best snorkelling in the southern Great Barrier Reef. (p173)

Fitzroy Island A lovely island off Cairns, with enticing beaches, rich coral and a hilly interior. Prime day-trip terrain. (p245)

Lizard Island Pitch a tent or check into the plush resort on this far-north island. (p263)

Frankland Islands These five uninhabited, coral-fringed isles are custom-made for adventurers and beach bums alike. (p245)

Dunk Island Recent cyclones didn't spare gorgeous Dunk and its butterflies, bushwalks and

bird life, but take a day trip or camp overnight and see how the rebuild is shaping up. (p226)

St Helena Island Engaging convict history a short hop from Brisbane in Moreton Bay. (p95)

Indigenous Culture

Kuku-Yalanji Dreamtime Walks Walks through Queensland's Mossman Gorge with knowledgeable Indigenous guides. (p261)

Ingan Tours Aboriginal-operated rainforest tours from Mission Beach or Tully. (p222)

Tjapukai Aboriginal Cultural Park Interactive tours and vibrant performances in Cairns by local Tjapukai people. (p233)

Gallery of Modern Art Brisbane's must-see GOMA includes a significant collection of fibre art from contemporary Indigenous artists. (p57)

Food & Drink

Jan Powers Farmers Market Next to the Brisbane Powerhouse, this fabulous farmers market is the place for brilliant local food. (p95)

Noosa Food & Wine Salubrious, surfside Noosa serves up four gluttonous days of feasting and workshops in May. (p128)

Kuranda Koala Gardens (p249),

Granite Belt Wineries Surprise! Queensland has vineyards! Tour the low-key cellar doors in this cool mountainous region and sample some top drops. (p100)

Atherton Tablelands The volcanic soil of the Tablelands yields exotic fruits, strong coffee, surprising wines and lush dairy products. (p249)

Bundaberg Rum Distillery Visit the home of Queensland's iconic firewater, squeezed from local sugar cane. (p159)

Burleigh Brewing Company Burleigh Brewing Company and newcomer Black Hops Brewing have been brewing up a storm of late. (p119)

Wildlife Encounters

Noosa National Park Koalas, dolphins and seasonal whales are easy to spot at this highly accessible pocket of green. (p126)

Lone Pine Koala Sanctuary Swoon over a one-on-one with Australia's best-loved soft, furry icon. (p61)

Currumbin Wildlife Sanctuary A low-key alternative to Australia Zoo. (p119)

Hartley's Crocodile Adventures Come face-to-toothy-snout with a prehistoric predator near Port Douglas. (p248)

Kuranda Koala Gardens Birds, bats, butterflies and – of course – koalas – await at Kuranda, near Cairns. (p249)

Fraser Island The wild dingoes here are the purest-bred in Australia. (p166)

Wildlife Habitat Port Douglas See some koalas, kangaroos, crocs, lorikeets and cassowaries in natural habitats. (p255)

Cassowaries in Mission Beach The road signs are here for a reason: cassowaries are out there! (p221)

Eungella National Park Never seen a duck-billed platypus? Here's your chance. (p187)

Scenic Journeys

Sailing the Whitsundays Set sail in this magical Queensland archipelago. (p195)

Cairns to Kuranda Sail above the rainforest on a cable car to Kuranda, then take the scenic old-fashioned railway back. (p250)

Cairns to Port Douglad One of Australia's most spectacular drives cuddles the coastline to provide watercolour vistas of the Coral Sea. (p253)

Month by Month

TOP EVENTS

Noosa Food & Wine, May

Cairns Festival, August

Brisbane Festival, September

NRL Grand Final, September

Woodford Folk Festival, December

January

January yawns into action as Queensland recovers from its Christmas hangover, but then everyone realises: 'Hey, it's summer!' Heat and humidity all along the coast; monsoonal rains up north. The Daintree region virtually shuts down at this time of year.

✪ Australia Day

Australia Day is the nation's 'birthday' – marking the landing of the First Fleet on 26 January 1788. Expect picnics, barbecues, fireworks and, increasingly, nationalistic chest-beating. In less mood to celebrate are Indigenous Australians, who refer to it as 'Invasion Day'.

February

High temperatures and frown-inducing humidity continue. It's still the cyclone season (from December to April) anywhere north of the tropic line. Brisbanites flock to Gold Coast or Sunshine Coast beaches on weekends.

✪ Chinese New Year

Brisbane's sizeable Chinese community celebrates the new year in Fortitude Valley's Chinatown Mall (Duncan St). Expect cacophonous firecrackers, gyrating dragons, martial-arts displays and (of course) fabulous food. (p59)

✪ Brisbane Street Art Festival

Welcome to the Brisbane Street Art Festival: live music, theatre, exhibitions and cred-heavy street artists turning Brisbane walls into epic artworks each February. (p67)

March

Heat and humidity ease in Queensland's south – crowds dissipate and resort prices drop. Meanwhile, high temperatures and general irritability prevail in the north.

☆ Brisbane Comedy Festival

Feeling blue? Check yourself into this month-long laugh-fest at the energised Brisbane Powerhouse arts hub on the banks of the Brisbane River. Local and international acts. (p67)

April

April is arguably the best time to visit Queensland. The weather is fine north and south, crowds are thin on the ground, and you can usually land a decent deal on accommodation.

✪ Bleach Festival

Over two weeks in early April, the Bleach Festival injects a much-needed shot of arts and culture into the Gold Coast's arty arteries. (p111)

☆ Gold Coast Film Festival

Around 75% of the Queensland film industry centres on the Gold Coast...so let's throw a festival! Independent, local and international films all get screen time, plus there are free outdoor flicks and film-making workshops. Hey look, is that Angelina Jolie? (p111)

May

Up north, the end of the Wet brings folks outdoors, while in the southeast they get their last full beach days before cooler weather rolls in. You can find good deals on accommodation all around.

✕ Noosa Food & Wine Festival

One of Australia's best regional culinary fests, with cooking demonstrations, wine tastings, cheese exhibits, feasting on gourmet fare and live concerts at night. Over three days in mid-May. (p128)

☆ Wintermoon Folk Festival

On the edge of Eungella National Park, 70km north of Mackay, Wintermoon is a family-friendly folk- and world-music fest. Most people camp, and impromptu performances happen all around the grounds. It takes place on the Labour Day long weekend. (p183)

✰ Port Douglas Carnivale

Port Douglas, an hour north of Cairns, is so darned pleasant...why not have a party? Over 10 days (OK, a big party), the Port Douglas Carnivale features live music, food, wine and a fab street parade. (p257)

Top: Coolangatta Gold surf life-saving competition
Bottom: Australia Day celebrations, Brisbane

⭐ First Coat Art & Music Festival

Home-grown and foreign aerosol artists hit Toowoomba in May for First Coat Art & Music Festival, a trio of days celebrating street art, tunes and contemporary creativity. (p105)

☞ Whale-Watching Season

Between May and November, right along the eastern Australian coast, migrating southern right and humpback whales come close to shore to feed, breed and calve. Take an eco-accredited tour from Hervey Bay (p149) or North Stradbroke Island (p96) to see them.

June

The tourist season kicks into gear as visitors from southern states head to Queensland's warm, stinger-free waters. Prices are higher and accommodation fills quickly. Southeast Queensland has cooler, mild temperatures.

⭐ Mary Poppins Festival

Did you know that Mary Poppins author PL Travers was born in Maryborough in Queensland? Celebrate this fact and the art of storytelling at this bookish, two-week school-holiday event. (p157)

July

July sees even bigger numbers of out-of-state visitors coming to Queensland, fleeing the cold southern drear. Expect crowded markets, tours and accommodation in the far north.

August

Peak season continues in northern Queensland, where temperatures remain mild and rainfall is minimal. In the south, cooler weather continues, making for brisk, sunny days on the beach.

⭐ 'Ekka' Royal Queensland Show

The Royal Queensland Show – formerly the Brisbane Exhibition, shortened to 'Ekka' – brings the country to Brisbane in a festive 10-day event. Fireworks, concerts, fashion parades, theme-park rides, show bags, junk food and prize-winning livestock by the truckload. (p69)

⭐ Cairns Festival

Running for two weeks from late August into September, the massive art-and-culture Cairns Festival delivers a stellar program of music, theatre, dance, comedy, film, Indigenous art and public exhibitions. Lots of outdoor events. (p237)

☆ Gympie Music Muster

We like both kinds of music: country *and* western! The Gympie Music Muster is a charity-based music event, with more boots and banjos than seems plausible. Bring your tent. (p157)

September

Peak northern tourist season begins to tail off in September, as the weather generally remains mild across the country. September brings out some well-known festivals, including the superb Brisbane Festival.

⭐ Brisbane Festival

One of Australia's largest, most diverse arts fiestas, the Brisbane Festival runs for 22 days in September. An impressive schedule includes concerts, plays, dance and fringe events. It finishes off with 'Riverfire', an elaborate fireworks show over the Brisbane River. (p69)

⭐ Wallaby Creek Festival

In late September, this three-day festival features blues, roots and world sounds, plus kids' activities, workshops, performance artists and acrobats. It all happens in a lush tropical setting near Rossville, 77km north of Cape Tribulation.

⭐ Carnival of Flowers

This 10-day flora-fest in Toowoomba (p103) celebrates the return of spring to southeast Queensland. The highlight is the Floral Parade, featuring flower-bedecked floats. There's also a food-and-wine component, concerts, garden tours, open-air cinema and blooming displays all over the 'garden city'.

⭐ Swell Sculpture Festival

Interesting sculpted things come to Currumbin (p119) in September, along with guided walks, artist talks, yoga sessions, live tunes, workshops, good food...

☆ NRL Grand Final

The culmination of the annual National Rugby League competition – which features the Brisbane Broncos, North Queensland Cowboys and Gold Coast Titans among 13 other teams – is the bone-crunching Grand Final in late September. Get to a barbecue, drink some beer and yell at the TV with the locals.

☆ Caloundra Music Festival

The Caloundra Music Festival is a huge four-day, family-friendly serving of rock, blues and more by gorgeous Kings Beach every September/October. (p136)

October

October brings the tail end of the dry season in the north, with temperatures on the rise. Warmer weather blankets the south, though beach days remain few and nights cool.

🏃 Coolangatta Gold

The epic Coolangatta Gold is a gruelling test of surf life-saving endurance: a 23km surf-ski paddle, a 3.5km swim and various beach runs = 41.5km of arduousness. Anyone can enter: see the B-grade 1984 movie of the same name for inspiration. (p120)

⭐ Valley Fiesta

Fortitude Valley, Brisbane's buzzing nocturnal hub, hosts this weekend-long arts event with free outdoor concerts, craft and designer markets, fashion parades and art exhibitions showcasing the city's creative side.

⭐ Gold Coast 600

VROOM!! The Gold Coast 600 is a three-day petrol fest on the streets of Surfers Paradise, with big Supercars carving up the tarmac. (p111)

November

Northern beaches may close due to 'stingers' (jellyfish) in the shallows north of Agnes Water. The surf life-saving season flexes its muscles on beaches along the state's south coast.

☆ Airlie Beach Music Festival

The Airlie Beach Music Festival entails three days of letting it all hang out in this famous party town, with loads of live tunes to rock out to. (p193)

☆ Brisbane Asia Pacific Film Festival

An eclectic 16-day showcase of cinema from across the Asia Pacific region in November/December. (p71)

December

Ring the bell, school's out! Holidays begin two weeks before Christmas. Cities are packed with shoppers and the weather hots up. North of Townsville, monsoon season is under way: afternoon thunderstorms bring pelting rain. The beaches are busy down south.

☆ Woodford Folk Festival

On the Sunshine Coast, the Woodford Folk Festival stages a diverse collection of performers playing folk sounds from across the globe. Runs from 27 December to 1 January. (p144)

Itineraries

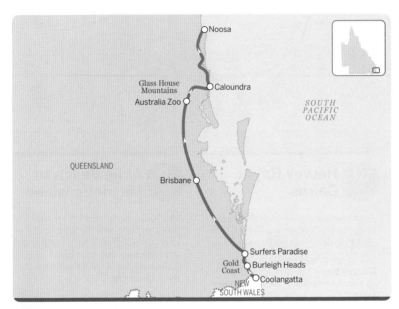

 5 DAYS Coolangatta to Noosa

The perfect Queensland introduction, this short-on-time tour delivers the best of the state's southeast: beaches, cities, coastal towns and wildlife encounters.

Kick-start your trip on the Gold Coast, beginning in laid-back **Coolangatta** on the New South Wales border, moving through beachy, gently hipster **Burleigh Heads** – great beer and coffee – to the party-prone pleasure dome of **Surfers Paradise**. If you have a couple of days to spare, let loose your inhibitions (and your stomach) at the Gold Coast theme parks. To sample some culture head north to **Brisbane**, taking in the superb Gallery of Modern Art, some craft-beer bars and live tunes in the West End or emerging Teneriffe and Newstead, and a night on the tiles in ever-changing Fortitude Valley.

Truck north to the **Glass House Mountains** for some breathtaking panoramas and rock climbing. Nearby is the superb **Australia Zoo** – brilliant if you have the kids in tow (and even if you don't). Next up is the laid-back Sunshine Coast: sunny **Caloundra** is fast evolving, with great cafes, eateries, street art and fantastic beaches. A short hop north is **Noosa**, a classy resort town with sublime beaches, a lush national park (home to sometimes-sighted koalas) and a first-class foodie scene.

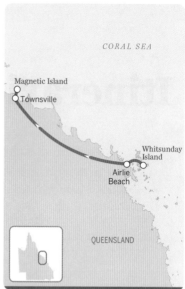

10 DAYS Hervey Bay to Cairns

Track north along the central section of Queensland's eastern seaboard, with plenty of islands to visit en route.

Two hours north of Noosa is amiable **Hervey Bay**: from here, explore the huge dunes and crystalline lakes on **Fraser Island**. Not far north, sip Australia's favourite rum in **Bundaberg**.

Sample Queensland's coral wonders at **Lady Musgrave Island** or **Lady Elliot Island**, then devour a steak at 'beef city' **Rockhampton**. Offshore, unwind for a few days on the trails and beaches on **Great Keppel Island** – pure tropical-beach bliss.

Spot a platypus in peaceful **Eungella National Park**, then wheel into buzzy **Airlie Beach**, gateway to the azure waters and powdery white-sand beaches of the **Whitsunday Islands**: sail, dive, snorkel, chill-out at a resort or camp on an uninhabited atoll.

Vibrant **Townsville** is next. Don't miss hiking the Thorsborne Trail on magnificent **Hinchinbrook Island**. Recover at super-chilled **Mission Beach**, where the rainforest meets the sea. End your road trip in **Cairns**: shout yourself a trip to the Great Barrier Reef and a seafood feast.

10 DAYS Airlie Beach to Magnetic Island

This 10-day jaunt takes in party town Airlie Beach, party remedy the Whitsunday Islands, the urban enticements of Townsville and chilled-out Magnetic Island – a quick-fire summation of our favourite things about Queensland.

Fly into **Airlie Beach** where there are two must-dos: cut loose after dark with other travellers, and book a boat trip to the **Whitsunday Islands**. There are myriad day-trip options, but a multiday sail lets you explore remote islands with no one else on them. Ensure your itinerary includes Whitsunday Island for a swim off sublime Whitehaven Beach. After cruising the islands, book a night at a swish island resort. Feeling more adventurous? Sign up for an overnight kayaking trip to one of the islands.

Back in Airlie, track north to **Townsville**, Queensland's third-biggest city. Walk along the waterfront, check out the Reef HQ Aquarium, clamber up Castle Hill and enjoy the local dining scene. Experienced divers might want to book a dive on the famous wreck of the SS *Yongala*. Wind up your journey on **Magnetic Island**, an unpretentious isle with easygoing beach villages, plenty of wildlife and scenic bushwalking tracks.

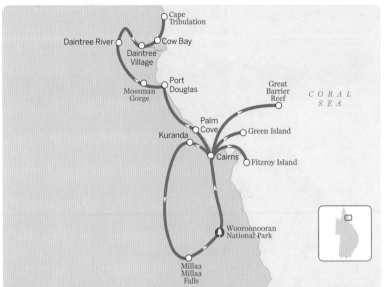

 ## Cairns to Cape Tribulation

Far North Queensland is like nowhere else on earth – a dizzying array of coral reefs, tropical atolls, rainforests and interesting towns.

Australia's reef-diving capital, **Cairns** is an obligatory east-coast destination. Spend a few days pinballing between botanic gardens, hip restaurants and buzzy watering holes. A short hop offshore, reef-trimmed **Green Island** and **Fitzroy Island** have verdant vegetation and lovely beaches, without too many folks competing for patches of sand. Further afield, a snorkelling or diving trip to the **Great Barrier Reef** is an essential experience, or plan a few days on a liveaboard expedition to Cod Hole, one of Australia's best dive spots.

Next up, head inland via gondola cableway or scenic railway to **Kuranda** for rainforest walks and a wander around the town's famous markets. If you have your own wheels, you can explore further: swing by the picturesque **Millaa Millaa Falls** and take a rainforest hike in spectacular **Wooroonooran National Park**.

Back down at sea level, treat yourself to a night in a plush resort at **Palm Cove**, just north of Cairns. An hour further north is **Port Douglas**, an uptempo holiday hub with fab eateries, bars and a beaut beach. It's also a popular base for boat trips to the outer reef. Next stop is **Mossman Gorge**, where lush lowland rainforest surrounds the photogenic Mossman River. Take a guided walk and cool off in a waterhole.

Further north is the **Daintree River**, where you can go on a crocodile-spotting cruise, then stop for lunch at the low-key **Daintree Village**. Afterwards, continue back to the river, where you'll cross by vehicle ferry to the northern side. From here, continue driving north (easy does it – this is cassowary country!) to the Daintree Discovery Centre – a great place to learn about this magnificent jungle wilderness. The beach at nearby **Cow Bay** is perfect for a few hours of beachcombing among the seashells and driftwood.

Last stop on your tropical tour is **Cape Tribulation**, a magnificent natural partnership between rainforest and reef. Spend a few nights taking in the splendour at one of the camping or backpacker places nooked into the rainforest.

Top: Glass House
Mountains (p133)

Bottom: Fraser Island

Plan Your Trip

Your Reef Trip

The Great Barrier Reef, stretching over 2000km from just south of the Tropic of Capricorn (near Gladstone) to just south of Papua New Guinea, is the most extensive reef system in the world. There are numerous ways to experience this magnificent spectacle. Diving and snorkelling are the best methods of getting close to the menagerie of marine life and dazzling corals. You can also surround yourself with fabulous tropical fish without getting wet on a semi-submersible or a glass-bottomed boat, or see the macro perspective on a scenic flight.

When to Go

High season on the reef is from June to December. The best overall underwater visibility is from August to January.

From December to March, **northern Queensland** (north of Townsville) has its wet season, bringing oppressive heat and abundant rainfall (it's cooler from July to September). Stinger (jellyfish) season is between November and May; most reef operators offer Lycra stinger suits to snorkellers and divers, or bring your own.

Anytime is generally good to visit the **Whitsundays**. Winter (June to August) can be pleasantly warm, but you will occasionally need a jumper. South of the Whitsundays, summer (December to March) is hot and humid.

Southern and central Queensland experience mild winters (June to August) – pleasant enough for diving or snorkelling in a wetsuit.

Picking Your Spot

There are many popular and remarkable spots from which to access the 'GBR', but bear in mind that individual areas change over time, depending on the weather or recent damage.

Best for...

Wildlife
Sea turtles around Lady Elliot Island or Heron Island. (p173)

Looking for reef sharks and rays while kayaking off Green Island. (p245)

Spotting wild koalas on Magnetic Island. (p214)

Snorkelling
Getting underwater at Knuckle, Hardy and Fitzroy Reefs. (p33)

Offshore at Magnetic Island (p214) or the Whitsunday Islands (p189).

Views from Above
Scenic chopper or plane rides from Cairns (p236) or the Whitsunday Islands (p190).

Skydiving over Airlie Beach. (p191)

Sailing
Sailing from Airlie Beach through the Whitsunday Islands. (p195)

Exploring Agincourt Reef from Port Douglas. (p253)

Mainland Gateways

There are several mainland gateways to the reef, all offering slightly different experiences and activities. Here's a brief overview, ordered from south to north.

Agnes Water & Town of 1770 Small towns and good choices if you want to escape the crowds. Tours head to Fitzroy Reef Lagoon, one of the most pristine sections of the reef, where visitor numbers are still limited. The lagoon is excellent for snorkelling, but also spectacular viewed from the boat.

Gladstone A bigger town but still a relatively small gateway. It's an excellent choice for avid divers and snorkellers, being the closest access point to the southern or Capricorn reef islands and innumerable cays, including Lady Elliot Island.

Airlie Beach A small town with a full rack of sailing outfits. The big attraction here is spending two or more days aboard a boat and seeing some of the Whitsunday Islands' fringing coral reefs. Whether you're a five- or no-star traveller, there'll be a tour to match your budget.

Townsville Renowned among divers. Whether you're learning or experienced, a four- or five-night diving safari around the numerous islands and pockets of the reef is a great choice. Kelso Reef and the wreck of the SS *Yongala* are teeming with marine life. There are also a couple of day-trip options on glass-bottomed boats, but for more choice you're better off heading to Cairns. The gigantic Reef HQ Aquarium is also here.

Mission Beach Closer to the reef than any other gateway destination, this small town offers a few boat and diving tours to sections of the outer reef. The choice isn't huge, but neither are the crowds.

Cairns The main launching pad for reef tours, with a staggering number of operators offering everything from relatively inexpensive day trips on large boats to intimate five-day luxury charters. Tours cover a wide section of the reef, with some operators going as far north as Lizard Island. Inexpensive tours are likely to travel to inner, less pristine reefs. Scenic flights also operate out of Cairns.

Port Douglas A swanky resort town and a gateway to the Low Isles and Agincourt Reef, an outer ribbon reef featuring crystal-clear water and stunning corals. Diving, snorkelling and cruising trips tend to be classier, pricier and less crowded than in Cairns. You can also take a scenic flight from here.

Cooktown Close to Lizard Island, but most tour operators here shut down between November and May for the wet season.

Islands

Speckled throughout the reef is a profusion of islands and cays that offer some of the most stunning access. Here is a list of some of the best islands, travelling from south to north.

Lady Elliot Island The coral cay here is twitcher heaven, with 57 resident bird species. Sea turtles also nest here and it's possibly the best spot on the reef to see manta rays. It's also a famed diving location. There's a resort here, but you can also visit Lady Elliot on a day trip from Bundaberg.

Heron Island A tiny, tranquil coral cay sitting amid a huge spread of reef. It's a diving mecca, but the snorkelling is also good and it's possible to do a reef walk from here. Heron is a nesting ground for green and loggerhead turtles and home to 30 bird species. The sole resort on the island charges accordingly.

Hamilton Island The big daddy of the Whitsundays, Hamilton is a sprawling, family-friendly resort laden with infrastructure. While the atmosphere isn't exactly intimate, there's a wealth of tours going to the outer reef. It's also a good place to see patches of the reef that can't be explored from the mainland.

Hook Island An outer Whitsunday island surrounded by fringing reefs. There's excellent swimming and snorkelling here, and the island's sizeable bulk provides plenty of good bushwalking. There's affordable accommodation on Hook and it's easily accessed from Airlie Beach, making it a top choice for those on a modest budget.

Orpheus Island A national park and one of the reef's most exclusive, tranquil and romantic hideaways. Orpheus is particularly good for snorkelling – you can step right off the beach and be surrounded by colourful marine life. Clusters of fringing reefs also provide plenty of diving opportunities.

Green Island Another of the reef's true coral cays. The fringing reefs here are considered to be among the most beautiful surrounding any island, and the diving and snorkelling are spectacular. Covered in dense rainforest, the entire island is national park. Bird life is abundant. Accessible as a day trip from Cairns.

Lizard Island Remote, rugged and the perfect place to escape civilisation, Lizard has a ring of talcum-white beaches, remarkably blue water and few visitors. It's home to the Cod Hole, arguably Australia's best-known dive site, where you can swim with docile potato cod weighing as much as 60kg. Accommodation here has no grey areas: it's either five-star luxury or bush camping.

Reef Highlights

0 — 200 km
0 — 100 miles

Lizard Island

Cooktown

CORAL SEA

PORT DOUGLAS
Book yourself onto an upmarket catamaran day-trip out to Agincourt Reef. (p253)

PORT DOUGLAS

Green Island
Fitzroy Island

CAIRNS

CAIRNS
Hop over from Cairns for a luxurious sojourn on Green Island, with its rainforest and fringing coral. On a budget? Take a day trip to Fitzroy and/or Green Island. (p229)

Innisfail

Tully MISSION BEACH
Dunk Island

Hinchinbrook Island

GREAT BARRIER REEF

Ingham

MISSION BEACH
Unwind on Mission Beach with rainforest walks, and overnight on nearby Dunk Island which has good swimming, kayaking and hiking. (p221)

Magnetic Island

TOWNSVILLE

Charters Towers

Bowen

Airlie Beach

Hamilton Islnd
Lindeman Island

Whitsunday Islands

TOWNSVILLE
In Townsville, visit the excellent Reef HQ Aquarium for a dry-land reef encounter. If you're an experienced diver, book a trip on a live-aboard boat to dive the SS *Yongala* wreck. And don't miss the koalas on Magnetic Island. (p209)

Mackay

THE WHITSUNDAYS
From party-prone Airlie Beach, explore some white-sand Whitsundays beaches and encircling coral reefs via a tour or sailing cruise. (p189)

Tropic of Capricorn

Great Keppel Island

Rockhampton

Emerald

Gladstone

TOWN OF 1770

TOWN OF 1770
Head to the Town of 1770 and day-trip out to Lady Musgrave Island for semisubmersible coral-viewing, plus snorkelling or diving in the definitive blue lagoon. (p169)

Bundaberg

Fraser Island

Hervey Bay
Maryborough

Miles

Noosa

Diving & Snorkelling the Reef

Much of the diving and snorkelling on the reef is boat-based, although there are some excellent reefs accessible by walking straight off the beach of some islands. Free use of snorkelling gear is usually part of any day cruise to the reef – you can typically fit in around three hours of underwater wandering. Overnight or liveaboard trips obviously provide a more in-depth experience and greater coverage of the reefs. If you don't have a diving certificate, many operators offer the option of an introductory dive, where an experienced diver conducts an underwater tour. A lesson in safety and procedure is given beforehand and you don't require a five-day Professional Association of Diving Instructors (PADI) course or a 'buddy'.

Key Diving Details

Your last dive should be completed 24 hours before flying – even in a balloon or for a parachute jump – in order to minimise the risk of residual nitrogen in the blood that can cause decompression injury. It's fine to dive soon after arriving by air.

Find out whether your insurance policy classifies diving as a dangerous-sport exclusion. For a nominal annual fee, the Divers Alert Network (www.diversalertnetwork.org) provides insurance for medical or evacuation services required in the event of a diving accident. DAN's hotline for emergencies is ☎+1 919 684 9111.

Visibility for coastal areas is 1m to 3m, whereas several kilometres offshore visibility is 8m to 15m. The outer edge of the reef has visibility of 20m to 35m and the Coral Sea has visibility of 50m and beyond.

In the north, the water is warm all year round, from around 24°C to 30°C. Going south it gradually gets cooler, dropping to a low of 20°C in winter.

Top Reef Dive Spots

The Great Barrier Reef is home to some of the world's best diving sites. Here are a few of our favourite spots to get you started:

SS Yongala A sunken shipwreck that has been home to a vivid marine community for more than 90 years.

Cod Hole Go nose-to-nose with a potato cod.

Heron Island Join a crowd of colourful fish straight off the beach.

Lady Elliot Island With 19 highly regarded dive sites.

Wheeler Reef Massive variety of marine life, plus a great spot for night dives.

MAKING A POSITIVE CONTRIBUTION TO THE REEF

The Great Barrier Reef is incredibly fragile and it's worth taking some time to educate yourself on responsible practices while you're there.

➡ No matter where you visit, take all litter with you – even biodegradable material such as apple cores – and dispose of it back on the mainland.

➡ It is an offence to damage or remove coral in the marine park.

➡ If you touch or walk on coral you'll damage it and get some nasty cuts.

➡ Don't touch or harass marine animals.

➡ If you have a boat, be aware of the rules in relation to anchoring around the reef, including 'no anchoring areas' to avoid coral damage.

➡ If you're diving, check that you are weighted correctly before entering the water and keep your buoyancy control well away from the reef. Ensure that equipment such as secondary regulators and gauges aren't dragging over the reef.

➡ If you're snorkelling (especially if you're a beginner), practise your technique away from coral until you've mastered control in the water.

➡ Hire a wetsuit rather than slathering on sunscreen, which can damage the reef.

➡ Watch where your fins are – try not to stir up sediment or disturb coral.

➡ Do not enter the water near a dugong, whether you're swimming or diving.

➡ Note that there are limits on the amount and types of shells that you can collect.

TOP SNORKELLING SITES

Some nondivers may wonder if it's really worth going to the Great Barrier Reef 'just to snorkel'. The answer is a resounding yes! Much of the rich, colourful coral lies just underneath the surface (coral needs bright sunlight to flourish) and is easily viewed by snorkellers. Here's a round-up of some top snorkelling sites.

➡ Fitzroy Reef Lagoon (Town of 1770)

➡ Heron Island (Capricorn Coast)

➡ Keppel Island (Capricorn Coast)

➡ Lady Elliot Island (Capricorn Coast)

➡ Lady Musgrave Island (Capricorn Coast)

➡ Hook Island (Whitsundays)

➡ Hayman Island (Whitsundays)

➡ Border Island (Whitsundays)

➡ Lizard Island (Cairns)

➡ Hardy Reef (Whitsundays)

➡ Knuckle Reef (Whitsundays)

➡ Michaelmas Reef (Cairns)

➡ Hastings Reef (Cairns)

➡ Norman Reef (Cairns)

➡ Saxon Reef (Cairns)

➡ Opal Reef (Port Douglas)

➡ Agincourt Reef (Port Douglas)

➡ Mackay Reef (Port Douglas)

Boat Excursions

Unless you're staying on a coral-fringed island, you'll need to join a boat excursion to experience the reef's real beauty. Day trips leave from many places along the coast, as well as from island resorts, and typically include the use of snorkelling gear, snacks and a buffet lunch, with scuba diving an optional extra. On some boats, naturalists or marine biologists give talks on the reef's ecology.

Boat trips vary dramatically in passenger numbers, type of vessel and quality – which is reflected in the price – so get all the details before committing. When selecting a tour, consider the vessel (motorised catamaran or sailing ship), the number of passengers (from six to 400), what extras are offered and the destination. The outer reefs are usually more pristine. Inner reefs often show signs of damage from humans and coral-eating crown-of-thorns starfish. Coral bleaching is a major issue in far northern sections of the reef.

Many boats have underwater cameras for hire, although you'll save money by hiring these on land (or using your own waterproof camera or underwater housing). Some boats also have professional photographers on board who will dive and take high-quality shots of you in action.

Liveaboards

If you're eager to do as much diving as possible, a liveaboard is an excellent option as you'll do three dives per day, plus some night dives, all in more remote parts of the Great Barrier Reef. Trip lengths vary from one to 12 nights. The three-day/three-night voyages, which allow up to 11 dives (nine day and two night dives), are the most common.

It's worth checking out the various options as some boats offer specialist itineraries, following marine life and events such as minke whales or coral spawning, or offer trips to less-visited spots like the far northern reefs, Pompey Complex, Coral Sea Reefs or Swain Reefs.

It's recommended to go with operators who are Dive Queensland (www.dive-queensland.com.au) members: this ensures they follow a minimum set of guidelines. Ideally, they'll also be accredited by Ecotourism Australia (www.ecotourism.org.au).

REEF RESOURCES

Dive Queensland www.dive-queens
land.com.au

Tourism Queensland www.queens
landholidays.com.au

**Great Barrier Reef Marine Park
Authority** www.gbrmpa.gov.au

**Department of National Parks,
Sport & Racing** www.nprsr.qld.gov.au

Australian Bureau of Meteorology
www.bom.gov.au

Popular departure points for liveaboard dive vessels, along with the locales they visit are:

Bundaberg The Bunker Island group, including Lady Musgrave and Lady Elliot Islands, possibly Fitzroy, Llewellyn and the rarely visited Boult Reefs or Hoskyn and Fairfax Islands.

Town of 1770 Bunker Island group.

Gladstone Swains and Bunker Island group.

Mackay Lihou Reef and the Coral Sea.

Airlie Beach The Whitsundays, Knuckle Reef and Hardy Reef.

Townsville SS *Yongala* wreck, plus canyons of Wheeler Reef and Keeper Reef.

Cairns Cod Hole, Ribbon Reefs, the Coral Sea and possibly far northern reefs.

Port Douglas Osprey Reef, Cod Hole, Ribbon Reefs, Coral Sea and possibly the far northern reefs.

Dive Courses

In Queensland, there are numerous places where you can learn to dive, take a refresher course or improve your skills. Courses here are generally of a high standard, and all schools teach either PADI or Scuba Schools International (SSI) qualifications. Which certification you choose isn't as important as choosing a good instructor, so be sure to seek recommendations and meet with the instructor before committing to a program.

One of the most popular places to learn is Cairns, where you can choose between courses for the budget-minded (four-day courses cost between $520 and $765) that combine pool training and reef dives, to longer, more intensive courses that include reef diving on a liveaboard (five-day courses, including three-day/two-night liveaboard, cost between $800 and $1000).

Other places where you can learn to dive, and then head out on the reef, include Bundaberg, Mission Beach, Townsville, Airlie Beach, Hamilton Island, Magnetic Island and Port Douglas.

Camping on the Great Barrier Reef

Pitching a tent on an island is a hugely fun and affordable way to experience the Great Barrier Reef. Campers enjoy an idyllic tropical setting at a fraction of the cost of the five-star island resort down the road. Campsite facilities range from extremely basic (read: nothing) to fairly flash, with showers, flush toilets, interpretive signage and picnic tables. Most islands are remote, so ensure you're adequately prepared for medical and general emergencies.

Wherever you stay, you'll need to be self-sufficient, bringing your own food and drinking water (5L per day per person is recommended). Weather can prevent planned pick-ups, so have enough supplies to last an extra few days in case you get stranded.

Camp only in designated areas, keep to marked trails and take out all that you brought in. Fires are banned, so you'll need a gas stove or similar. National park camping permits must be booked in advance online through the Queensland government's Department of National Parks, Sport & Racing (p36). Here are our top camping picks:

Whitsunday Islands Nearly a dozen beautifully sited camping areas, scattered on the islands of Hook, Whitsunday and Henning.

Capricornia Cays Camping available on three separate coral cays – Masthead Island, North West Island and Lady Musgrave Island, a fantastic, uninhabited island with a maximum limit of 40 campers.

Dunk Island Easy to get to, with good swimming, kayaking and hiking.

Fitzroy Island Resort and national park with walking trails through bush, and coral off the beaches.

Frankland Islands Coral-fringed islands with white-sand beaches off Cairns.

Lizard Island Eye-popping beaches magnificent coral and abundant wildlife; visitors mostly arrive by plane.

Girraween National Park (p101)

Plan Your Trip

Queensland Outdoors

A cavalcade of ancient rainforests, magnificent islands, point breaks and the amazing Great Barrier Reef: Queensland is tailor-made for outdoor action. Scuba diving and snorkelling are daily indulgences, while the surfing in the southeast is world-class. There's also sailing, kayaking and loads of other watery pursuits. Back on dry land, you can bushwalk, try hang-gliding or spot wildlife. For an adrenaline rush, hire a 4WD, try white-water rafting or go skydiving.

Best Outdoor Experiences

Best Wildlife Spotting

Koalas on Magnetic Island (p214)

Cassowaries in the Daintree Rainforest (p261) and Mission Beach (p221)

Platypuses in Eungella National Park (p187)

Crocodiles in the Daintree River (p261)

Dingoes on Fraser Island (p166)

Best Aquatic Activities

Diving and snorkelling on the Great Barrier Reef (p32)

Surfing at Burleigh Heads (p116) and Noosa (p126)

Kayaking at North Stradbroke Island (p96), Noosa Everglades (p144) and Airlie Beach (p191)

Sailing around the Whitsundays (p189)

Fishing on Lake Tinaroo (p253)

Best National Parks for Bushwalking

Wooroonooran National Park (p248)

D'Aguilar National Park (p64)

Lamington National Park (p123)

Springbrook National Park (p123)

Girraween National Park (p101)

For Daredevils

Skydiving over Mission Beach (p223)

Bungee jumping in Cairns (p233)

White-water rafting on the Tully River (p236)

Rock climbing in the Glass House Mountains (p60)

On the Land

Bushwalking

Despite the heat and humidity, bushwalking happens in Queensland year-round, from short 1km ambles to multiday treks with camping along the way.

There are some celebrated, rugged tracks for experienced walkers in Queensland: one of the most famous is the 32km ungraded Thorsborne Trail on Hinchinbrook Island in northern Queensland. With limited walker numbers, the Thorsborne traverses a range of environments – including remote beaches, rainforests and creeks – amid spectacular mountain scenery. Other prime spots include Springbrook National Park and D'Aguilar National Park. For peak baggers, Wooroonooran National Park, south of Cairns, contains Queensland's highest peak, the eccentrically named Mt Bartle Frere (1622m).

When to Walk

The accommodating climate in southeast Queensland makes hiking feasible year-round. But regardless of the season, you should always take plenty of drinking water with you: the Queensland sun kicks like a mule.

North of the Capricorn Coast, the best time to hike is from April to September – things can get pretty hot and sticky during the summer season (November to March). Longer walking tracks are often closed over summer, and even shorter tracks require advance planning to take into account the harsher conditions. Summer is also the most dangerous period for bushfires: the **Department of National Parks, Sport & Racing** (☑13 74 68; www. nprsr.qld.gov.au) in Queensland can advise on current alerts.

Resources

Pick up Lonely Planet's *Walking in Australia,* which details 60 countrywide walks of varying lengths. The *Take a Walk* series (www.takeawalk.com. au) includes titles covering southeast Queensland. *Tropical Walking Tracks* by Kim Dungey and Jane Whytlaw covers dozens of walks outside Cairns, Kuranda and Cooktown, in the Daintree area and in the Atherton Tableland.

Bushwalking clubs and information:

Brisbane Bushwalkers www.brisbanebushwalkers. org.au

Bushwalking Queensland www.bushwalking queensland.org.au

Cairns Bushwalkers Club www.cairnsbushwalkers.org.au

Tablelands Bushwalking Club www.tablelandsbushwalking.org

Cycling & Mountain Biking

Queensland gets hot and humid, but during the winter plenty of two-wheelers go touring for days, weekends or even weeks. Or you can just rent a bike for a few hours and wheel around a city. The landscape is (mostly) low-lying and mountain-free, and the sun is usually shining.

Rates charged by rental outfits for road or mountain bikes range from $15 to $20 per hour and $30 to $50 per day. Security deposits range from $50 to $200, depending on the rental period. For more information, contact Bicycle Queensland (www.bq.org.au) or see Lonely Planet's *Cycling Australia*.

Paragliding, Hang-Gliding & Parasailing

You'll see **paragliders** circling the skies over plenty of places along the Queensland coast. One of the best spots is above the Carlo Sandblow at Rainbow Beach, where championship competitions happen every January. Tandem paragliding flights there generally last around 20 to 30 minutes and cost around $180.

If you're keen to try **hang-gliding**, South East Queensland Hanggliding (www.hangglidequeensland.com.au) runs tandem flights at Mt Tamborine in the Gold Coast hinterland. Flights last around 20 minutes and cost $275. Paragliding is also offered from the same steep launchpad by Paragliding Queensland (www.pgqld.com.au): tandem flights here cost $290.

Parasailing (dangling below a parachute-like canopy while being dragged

PLAN YOUR TRIP QUEENSLAND OUTDOORS

GREAT WALKS OF QUEENSLAND

Great Walks of Queensland is a $16.5-million project that has created a world-class set of 10 walking tracks. For complete track descriptions, maps and camp-site bookings, visit www.nprsr.qld.gov.au/experiences/great-walks.

WALK	DIFFICULTY	DISTANCE	DURATION	SCENERY
Carnarvon	Hard	86km	6-7 days	Dramatic sandstone gorges, Aboriginal rock paintings, panoramic ridgelines
Conondale Range	Hard	56km	4 days	Valleys, gorges, forests, waterfalls, ridges and 360-degree views inside Conondale National Park
Cooloola	Moderate	102km	5 days	Rainforest, tall eucalyptus forest, dry coastal woodland, heath plains and sea views in Cooloola Recreation Area
Fraser Island	Hard	90km	up to 8 days	Rainforests, coloured sands, picturesque lakes, towering sand dunes
Gold Coast Hinterland	Moderate	55km	3 days	Palm-filled valleys, mist-covered mountains, clifftop views, waterfalls, crystal-clear rivers
Mackay Highlands	Moderate	50km	4-6 days	Rainforest, gorges, steep escarpments, rolling farmlands
Sunshine Coast Hinterland	Moderate	58km	4 days	Winds through the scenic Blackall Range with waterfalls, eucalyptus forest, subtropical rainforest and fine views
Wet Tropics	Moderate	100km	6 days	Waterfalls, gorges, views and World Heritage–listed rainforest at Girringun National Park
Whitsunday	Hard	30km	3 days	Lowland tropical rainforest, rocky creeks, lush palm valleys and views, amid rugged Conway Range inside Conway National Park
Whitsunday Ngaro Sea Trail	Moderate	200m to 7km	up to 4 days	Series of walking and sea-kayaking trails around Whitsunday, South Molle and Hook Islands in the Whitsunday archipelago

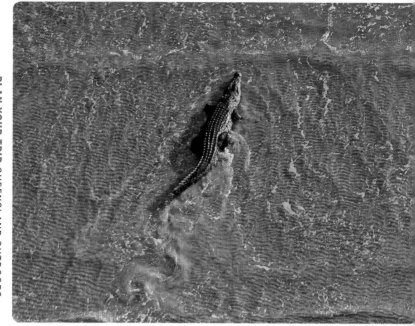

Saltwater crocodile

along by a boat) is another heart-starting way to get the most from the coast. There are beachside operators on the Gold Coast and at many other beach resorts along the coast.

Wildlife-Watching

Native wildlife is one of Queensland's (and indeed Australia's) top selling points. National parks are your best bet for the greatest concentrations of species, although many native critters are nocturnal (bring a torch). Queensland is also a birdwatching nirvana, with a wide variety of habitats and species, particularly waterbirds.

As well as national parks, wildlife hot spots include Cape Tribulation and the Mareeba Wetlands for birds; Magnetic Island for koalas; Fraser Island for dingoes; Hervey Bay for whales; North Stradbroke Island for dolphins, sea turtles and rays; Eungella National Park for platypuses; and the Daintree for crocodiles and cassowaries. And, as the road signs attest, the rainforest around Mission Beach is also home to cassowaries.

On the Water
Diving & Snorkelling

The Queensland coast boasts enough spectacular dive sites to make you blow bubbles and gasp for breath. The Great Barrier Reef offers some of the world's best diving and snorkelling, and there are dozens of operators vying to teach you how to scuba dive or provide you with the ultimate dive safari. There are also around 1600 shipwrecks along the Queensland coast, putting a man-made spin on the marine metropolis concept.

You can snorkel just about everywhere along Queensland's coast, which requires minimum effort and no experience. Many dive spots are also popular snorkelling sites.

Diving is generally good year-round, although during the wet season – December to March – floods can wash a lot of mud out into the ocean and visibility is sometimes poor. Aside from the myriad diving and snorkelling reef tours available in Cairns and Port Douglas, other top dive spots include the following:

Daintree National Park (p261)

Bundaberg Wreck dives, gropers, turtles and rays.

Hervey Bay Shallow caves, schools of large fish, wreck dives, turtles, sea snakes, stonefish, rays and trevally.

Mooloolaba Pristine reefs and wreck diving on the sunken warship HMAS *Brisbane*.

Moreton Island Tangalooma wrecks, nudibranches, urchins, sponges and coral, plus good snorkelling.

North Stradbroke Island Manta rays, leopard and grey nurse sharks, humpback whales, turtles, dolphins, and hard and soft corals.

Rainbow Beach One of Australia's top diving destinations, with grey nurse sharks, turtles, manta rays and giant gropers amid volcanic pinnacles.

Southport Abundant marine life including rays, sharks, turtles and 200 fish species.

Diving Courses & Prices

Every major town along the Queensland coast has a dive school, but standards and dive options vary – it's worthwhile doing some research before signing up. Many budget courses only offer shore dives, which can be less interesting than open-water dives out on far-flung sections of the reef. At the other end of the scale, some of the more expensive courses enable you to live aboard a boat or yacht for several days far from the mainland, with all your meals included in the price.

Multiday PADI open-water courses cost anywhere from $520 to $770; one-off introductory dives cost between $120 and $520. Normally, you have to show that you can tread water for 10 minutes and swim 200m before you can start a course. Many schools will also require that you undertake a medical, which usually costs extra (around $80).

For certified divers, renting gear and going on a two-tank day dive generally costs between $180 and $250. You can also hire mask, snorkel and fins from a dive shop for around $30 to $50.

Surfing

From a surfer's perspective, Queensland's Great Barrier Reef is one of nature's tragic errors – it's effectively a 2000km-long breakwater! Mercifully, there are some pumping surf beaches along the coast in southeast Queensland. The Gold Coast has great breaks, as does virtually the entire shoreline of the Sunshine Coast. Get your hands on a copy of Mark Warren's definitive *Atlas of Australian Surfing* for the low-down on the best breaks.

You can hire boards from almost any surf shop along the coast, and op shops in surf towns are usually full of used boards. But unless you're taking lessons, it's probably best to start off with a boogie board (aka

STINGER WARNING

All water activities, including diving and snorkelling, are affected by stingers (box jellyfish), which can be found at any time of year off the Queensland coast and in river mouths, from Agnes Water north. They are dangerous and should not be taken lightly. Look for the stinger-resistant enclosures at beaches during the peak stinger season, which runs from November to May. Never enter the water at beaches that have been closed due to stingers, and consider using a full-body Lycra suit if you must swim in the water during stinger season.

DAE PHOTO / SHUTTERSTOCK ©

Top: Shipwrecks, Moreton Island (p99)

Bottom: Rainbow lorikeet

bodyboard) and work your way up – surfing isn't as easy as it looks! Always ask locals and life-savers about the severity of breaks, rips and hazards – broken boards, noses and egos are not uncommon, particularly among inexperienced surfers with lofty ambitions.

Top Surf Spots

Agnes Water & Town of 1770 Pretty much the last place on the coast heading north where you can catch a wave (north of here the Great Barrier Reef intercepts the ocean swells). The breaks here are strictly for old hands, though: the waves can get fast and steep, you have to paddle well out from shore, and you may be sharing your personal space with the odd reef shark.

Burleigh Heads The point break here is magnificent, peeling in from the national park on the headland to the main beach – but it does require some experience.

Caloundra to Mooloolaba A very popular strip of sandy suburban shoreline with fine beach breaks.

Coolangatta An essential surf haunt for Gold Coasters, particularly Kirra Beach. The Superbank is here, too – a 2km-long sandbar stretching from Snapper Rocks to Kirra Point.

Noosa Popular with longboarders, with good wave action at Sunshine Beach and the point breaks around the national park, especially during the cyclone swells of summer (December to February).

North Stradbroke Island Harder to get to, but has fabulous surf beaches that are always less crowded than the Gold Coast and Sunshine Coast beaches.

Surfing Lessons

If you're new to the beach, the best way to find your feet is with a few lessons, and there are dozens of surf schools in south-east Queensland. Two of the best spots to learn – mostly because the waves are kind to beginners – are Surfers Paradise and Noosa. Two-hour group lessons typically cost around $60, with five-day courses for the super-keen costing around $250.

White-Water Rafting

The mighty cascades of the Tully, North Johnstone and Russell Rivers between Townsville and Cairns are renowned white-water-rafting locations, benefiting from extraordinarily high rainfall in the area (the town of Tully received 7.9m of rain in 1950!). The Tully is the most popular of the three with moderate Grade III

BUNGEE JUMPING & SKYDIVING

Brave? Lose a bet? Just plain crazy? Cairns is the place to try bungee jumping, with multiperson 'jungle swings' for those not willing to go it alone. If you'd rather jump out of a plane, sign up for some skydiving at Caloundra, Surfers Paradise, Brisbane, Airlie Beach, Mission Beach or Cairns. Most folks start with a 9000ft jump, with around 30 seconds of free fall – or up the ante to 14,000ft with up to a minute of pant-wetting plummeting. Prices start at around $300 for a skydive, and $100 for a bungee jump.

---

to IV rapids, which means the rapids are moderate but rafts require continuous manipulation to stay upright. The Tully also receives regular hydroelectric dam water releases, with rafting trips timed to coincide with the increased flow.

Most of the guides who operate tours here have internationally recognised qualifications and safety is high on their list of priorities. This said, you don't need any experience to take part, just a need for speed. You also need to be older than 13 on the Tully (or age 10 on the Russell). Rafting day trips cost around $250, including transfers.

Kayaking & Canoeing

Kayaking and canoeing are brilliant in Queensland. Numerous outfits along the coast offer paddling expeditions along calm waterways and lakes, or out through the protected Barrier Reef waters – sometimes from the mainland to offshore islands. There are also companies that operate guided tours off the Gold and Sunshine Coasts. Two-hour paddles cost around $70.

North Stradbroke Island Straddie Adventures (p97); mangroves and lovely coastline, dolphins, sea turtles, rays.

Whitsunday Islands Salty Dog Sea Kayaking (p189); one-day and multiday trips exploring Molle Islands, amid coral reefs, dolphins, turtles and sea eagles.

Noosa Kayak Noosa (p127); sea kayak tours around Noosa National Park.

Magnetic Island Magnetic Island Sea Kayaks (p216); exploring the picturesque bays of the island.

Mission Beach Coral Sea Kayaking (p223); day paddles to and around Dunk Island, multiday trips to stunning Hinchinbrook Island.

Sailing

Queensland's waters are pure utopia for salty sea dogs of all levels of ability, with some of the most spectacular sailing locations in the world. The hands-down winner of the state's many picture-postcard sailing spots is the Whitsunday Islands – 74 idyllic gems surrounded by a translucent blue sea that, at times, has a seamless and uninterrupted horizon. There are myriad charters, tours and boat operators based at Airlie Beach, the gateway to the archipelago. There's also a sizeable local sailing scene around Manly, just outside Brisbane, or you can explore some of the islands off the Far North Queensland coast on board a chartered boat or cruise from Port Douglas.

Tours

You'll find plenty of day tours that hop between two or three islands, but three-day/two-night all-inclusive cruises are better value and provide a deeper appreciation of the area's assets. You can also choose between tours that sleep their passengers on board, and ones that dock at island resorts for the night.

The main benefit of joining a tour is that you don't require any sailing expertise – some outfits will get you to participate under guidance, but you can be a complete landlubber and still enjoy a true sailing experience. The range of tours is huge and, as with most activities, the smaller the number of passengers the greater the price. As a general guide, day

tours cost around $170 for adults and $70 for children. Three-day, two-night sailing packages typically start from around $600 per person.

Chartering a Boat

It's fairly easy to charter your own boat at Airlie Beach, but be warned: that glassy sea has the potential to turn nasty and, regardless of what operators say, braving the ocean solo should only be attempted by sailors with some experience.

If you're lacking the skills, but still want a far more intimate experience than a tour, consider chartering your own boat and hiring a skipper to do the hard work for you. The cost of a 'bareboat' (unskippered) charter will set you back somewhere between $600 and $1200 per day, depending on the size of the boat. With a skipper you're looking at upwards of $1500 per day.

Fishing

Fishing in all its formats is incredibly popular in Queensland, especially in coastal areas. More than a few Queensland families spend entire summers living out of the back of their 4WDs while trying their luck in the surf breaks. There are also plenty of dams, rivers, lakes and jetties that are perfect for dangling a line. Top fishing spots include North Stradbroke Island, Fraser Island, Rainbow Beach, Lake Tinaroo and Lakefield National Park.

There are local fishing shops in most coastal towns for advice on what's biting where, and to get yourself set up with a rig. Fishing charters are also big-business in Queensland: hook yourself on to a tour in places like North Stradbroke Island, Caloundra, Rainbow Beach, Port Douglas, Hamilton Island and Maroochydore. The heavy-tackle game-fishing season runs from September to December.

Plan Your Trip
Travel with Children

If you can survive the long-haul distances between cities, travelling around Queensland with the kids can be a real delight. There's oodles of interesting stuff to see and do, both indoors and out, including beaches, zoos, theme parks and adventures on the Great Barrier Reef. Lonely Planet's *Travel with Children* contains buckets of useful information for travel with little 'uns.

Queensland for Kids

Accommodation

Many Queensland motels and the better-equipped caravan parks have playgrounds and swimming pools, and can supply cots and baby baths – some motels also have in-house children's movies and child-minding services.

Top-end hotels and many (but not all) midrange hotels are well versed in the needs of guests with children. B&Bs and some exclusive resorts, on the other hand, often market themselves as child-free. Check when you book.

Babysitting

Some of Queensland's licensed child-care agencies have places set aside for casual care: phone local councils for a list of child-care providers. Avoid unlicensed operators.

Day-care or babysitting options with rates starting at around $25 per hour include the following:

Babysitters R Us (📞0400 860 767; www.babysittersrus.com.au) Brisbane, Gold Coast, Caboolture and Noosa.

Best Regions for Kids

Brisbane & Around
Big-city kiddie adventures: ferry rides, an artificial riverside swimming beach, hands-on museums and galleries, and a koala sanctuary.

The Gold Coast
The beaches here are beaut, and there are five massive roller-coaster-wrapped theme parks just north of Surfers Paradise.

Noosa & the Sunshine Coast
Don't miss Noosa National Park, the native critters at Australia Zoo, and a visit to Mooloolaba's bedazzling Sea Life Sunshine Coast Aquarium.

Fraser Island & the Fraser Coast
Check out the colourful sand cliffs at Rainbow Beach, or careen around the sand in a 4WD on Fraser Island.

Cairns & the Daintree Forest
Rainforest walks, a swimming lagoon, playgrounds and boat trips to the reef or islands. Don't miss the scenic railway to Kuranda in the hinterland.

Busy Bees Babysitting (☑0417 794 507; www. busybeesbabysitting.com.au) Gold Coast, Cairns, Palm Cove and Port Douglas.

Dial an Angel (☑07-3498 6341, 1300 721 111; www.dialanangel.com) Brisbane.

Change Rooms & Breastfeeding

Queenslanders are relaxed about breast-feeding and nappy (diaper) changing in public. All cities and most major towns also have centrally located public rooms (often in shopping centres) where parents can go to nurse their baby or change a nappy; check with the local tourist office.

Discounts

Child concessions (and family rates) often apply to accommodation, tours, admission fees and transport around the state, with some discounts as high as 50% of the adult rate. However, the definition of 'child' varies from under-fives to under 18 years. Accommodation concessions generally apply to children under 12 years sharing the same room as adults. Kids under two years old receive discounts on many flights across Australia (they are seat-belted on to a parent's lap and thus don't occupy a seat).

Eating Out

Many cafes, restaurants, surf clubs and pubs around Queensland offer kids' meals, or will provide small serves from the main menu. Some also supply high chairs. Many fine-dining restaurants, however, don't welcome small children. If all else fails, grab some fish and chips and head for the beach. There are also plenty of free or coin-operated barbecues in parks around the state.

Necessities

Queensland has high-standard medical services and facilities, and items such as baby formula and disposable nappies are widely available.

Major hire-car companies will supply and fit child-safety seats, charging a one-off fee of around $25. Taxi companies aren't legally required to supply child seats, but may be able to organise one if you call in advance.

Wet 'n' Wild, Gold Coast (p115)

Children's Highlights

Outdoor Adventure

➡ Sea kayaking along the Noosa River (p127) or around Dunk Island (p223) off Mission Beach.

➡ Horse riding on Magnetic Island (p216) or along the beach near Noosa (☑0438 710 530; www.noosahorseriding.com.au; 22 Wills Rd, Weyba Downs; 1hr/2hr ride $75/110).

➡ Snorkelling the Great Barrier Reef on a boat trip from Port Douglas (p256).

➡ Taking a 4WD camping adventure on Fraser Island (p161).

Theme Parks

➡ Braving the roller coasters, IMAX movies and Bengal tigers: Dreamworld (p115) is hard to beat!

➡ Hitting Warner Bros Movie World (p115) for movie-themed rides and wandering VIP cartoon characters.

➡ Flinging yourself into pools, down slides and into aquatic mayhem: it's wet, it's wild, it's Wet'n'Wild (p115).

Feeding kangaroos

➡ Cooling off on a humid Gold Coast afternoon at WhiteWater World (p115).

➡ Talking with the animals at Australia Zoo (p133) – OK, so it's not technically a theme park, but the kids will love it just as much.

Rainy-Day Activities

➡ Exploring museums and galleries in Brisbane: the hands-on Queensland Museum & Sciencentre (p57); the Queensland Maritime Museum (p57), where you can clamber through the corridors of a Navy frigate; and the kids' galleries and installations at the Gallery of Modern Art (p57).

➡ Watching sharks, seals and other marine life at Sea Life Sunshine Coast (p137) in Mooloolaba.

➡ Visiting Townsville's Reef HQ Aquarium (p209) for a look at the wonders of the Great Barrier Reef.

➡ Riding the zipline and clambering over obstacle courses inside the recreated rainforest at the indoor Cairns Zoom & Wildlife Dome (p234), complete with resident crocs and koalas.

When to Go

The southeast (Brisbane, Gold Coast, Sunshine Coast) can be great fun any time of year, though it does get a little chilly during the winter (June to August), making for unpredictable beach days.

Winter, on the other hand, is the best (but busiest) time to visit tropical Far North Queensland, with clear nights, stinger-free beaches and an absence of summer's oppressive heat, humidity and monsoonal downpours.

Travelling during school holidays can be maddening and expensive – particularly on the Gold Coast and Sunshine Coast.

Regions at a Glance

The Gold Coast

Surfing
Nightlife
National Parks

Surfers Paradise

They don't call it Surfers Paradise for nothing! The beach here is one of the best places in Australia to learn to surf, or head for the more challenging breaks around Burleigh Heads and Kirra.

Clubs, Pubs & Bars

All along the Gold Coast – from the throbbing clubs in Surfers Paradise to the surf-side pubs and surf life-saving clubs in Coolangatta – you'll never be far from a cold après-surf beer (or tequila, champagne or poolside daiquiri).

Hinterland Greenery

Ascend into the Gold Coast hinterland to discover some brilliant national parks: Springbrook, Lamington and Tamborine feature waterfalls, hikes and constant native birdsong.

p107

Brisbane & Around

Neighbourhoods
Food
Islands

Inner-City Hip

Brisbane is a tight-knit web of distinct enclaves: check out the bohemian West End, and postindustrial neighbours Newstead and Teneriffe, with their ever-growing number of on-point cafes, brew-bars and music rooms.

Cafe & Culture

Brisbane is hot and humid, but that doesn't mean the locals can't enjoy a steaming cup of java. Cool cafes abound, well supplied by a clutch of quality local bean roasters.

Nearby Islands

In Moreton Bay you'll find the underrated North Stradbroke Island, with excellent surfing, sea-kayaking and beach walks, and Moreton Island, which has a full-kit resort and loads of activities. You can also visit the former prison island of St Helena. Overnight if you can – day trips can be rushed.

p50

Noosa & the Sunshine Coast

Surfing
Food
Nature

Sunshine Coast Surf

The relaxed surfer ethos of the Sunshine Coast permeates the backstreets and the beaches, with surf shops aplenty, and reliable breaks and warm waves right along the coast.

Noosa Dining Scene

You know you're *really* on holiday when you wake up and the choice of where to have breakfast, lunch and dinner is the most important item on the day's agenda. Welcome to Noosa!

Noosa National Park

Bathed by the South Pacific, with photogenic beaches reaching up to hillsides awash with dense subtropical bush – accessible Noosa National Park is perfect for bushwalking, swimming or just chilling out in the sun.

p124

Fraser Island & the Fraser Coast

Islands
Small Towns
Marine Life

Fraser Island

Sandy Fraser Island hosts a unique subtropical ecosystem that's pretty darn close to paradise. A day tour merely whets the appetite; camp overnight and wish upon a thousand shooting stars.

Rainbow Beach & Childers

One on the coast and one inland, these two little towns are absolute beauties: Rainbow Beach for its magnificent cliffs, and Childers for its country vibe and historic architecture.

Whale Watching

Off Hervey Bay, migrating humpback whales breach, blow and tail-slap. Controversy enshrouds the whale-watching business worldwide, but eco-accredited tours give these amazing creatures the space they need.

p147

Capricorn Coast & the Southern Reef

Diving & Snorkelling
Islands
Accessible Outback

Southern Reef Encounters

From the Town of 1770, book a snorkelling cruise out to the reef or a bunk on a liveaboard dive vessel. Or base yourself on an island for full immersion in this Technicolour underwater world.

Lady Elliot Island

Tiny, coral-ringed Lady Elliot is superb for snorkelling, with reefs directly off the beach. The resort is eco-attuned, and the flight here is a scenic tour in itself.

Rockhampton

Just 40km from the coast, Australia's 'beef capital' gives visitors a true taste of the bush, with buckin' broncos and big hats. Further west, cattle-station stays offer full immersion into outback livin'.

p167

Whitsunday Coast

Islands
Sailing
Nightlife

The Whitsundays

With 74 tropical beauties to choose from, the Whitsunday Islands archipelago is truly remarkable. There are plenty of ways to experience the islands: bushwalking, kayaking or just lounging around on a yacht.

Island-Hopping

The translucent seas around the Whitsundays would seem incomplete without billows of snow-white sails in the picture. The wind, the sea, the beckoning sandy bays... Climb aboard a yacht and find your perfect island.

Airlie Beach

The main jumping-off point for trips around the Whitsundays, Airlie Beach is a party town full of party people. Join the thirsty throngs in the bars after dark.

p181

Townsville to Mission Beach

Coastline
Nature
Architecture

Beautiful Beaches

Between Townsville's palm-shaded Strand and Flying Fish Point near Innisfail, this stretch of coastline shelters vast, sandy expanses such as the namesake shore at Mission Beach, through to intimate coves like Etty Bay. Offshore, you'll find standout beaches on wild Hinchinbrook Island and lovable Dunk.

National Parks

Hiking, camping, swimming and picnicking opportunities abound in the region's national parks, with prehistoric-looking cassowaries roaming the rainforest. Top picks include the bushwalking paradise Hinchinbrook Island and the rainforest-cloaked peaks of Paluma Range National Park.

Historic Buildings

Architectural hits in the region include the gold-rush era streetscapes of Charters Towers, beautiful 19th-century buildings in Townsville, and Australia's highest concentration of art deco edifices in Innisfail.

p207

Cairns & the Daintree Rainforest

Diving & Snorkelling
Nightlife
Indigenous Culture

Reef Trips

Every day, from Cairns and Port Douglas, a flotilla of boats ferries passengers out to experience the bedazzling underwater world of the Great Barrier Reef. Sidestep the crowds on a liveaboard vessel and explore remote sections of the reef.

Cairns After Dark

There are so many backpackers and tourists in Cairns, it's sometimes hard to spot a local. You can usually find one or two in the city's boisterous pubs and bars.

Daintree Tours

Several excellent Aboriginal-led tour companies can take you on a cultural journey through the timeless Daintree Rainforest and Mossman Gorge, offering an insight into the area's rich Indigenous heritage.

p228

On the Road

Brisbane & Around

Best Places to Eat

➡ Urbane (p75)

➡ Gauge (p76)

➡ Barrelroom (p102)

➡ Zev's Bistro (p104)

➡ Island Fruit Barn (p98)

Best Places to Sleep

➡ New Inchcolm Hotel & Suites (p72)

➡ Next (p71)

➡ Spicers Balfour Hotel (p73)

➡ Allure (p98)

➡ Vacy Hall (p104)

Why Go?

Sophisticated city galleries and rooftop bars, desolate subtropical beaches, cool-climate vineyards: the greater Brisbane region deals in Queensland's most gasp-inducing contrasts. Star of the show is Brisbane itself, a lush, sultry metropolis with flourishing restaurant, bar and cultural scenes that attest to its coming of age. Lapping at the city's eastern fringe is Moreton Bay, home to low-lying sandy isles that beckon with their turquoise waves, sparkling forests and passing parade of sea life.

Head west from Brisbane and you'll hit lofty Toowoomba, an underrated university town where heritage architecture and well-pruned gardens share the streets with smashing street art, specialist coffee shops and a growing number of fashionable eateries and bars. Things get even cooler (literally) further south in the vineyard-laced Granite Belt, a corner of the state where surf clubs, mojitos and palm trees are ditched for elegant reds, crackling fires and the occasional mid-year snowman.

When to Go
Brisbane

Jan Sweltering heat means summer is the perfect time to cool off in the North Stradbroke Island surf.

May–Aug Cooler temperatures and clear blue skies make sightseeing a breeze.

Sep Spring has sprung. Warmer temperatures and the hot-ticket Brisbane and Bigsound festivals.

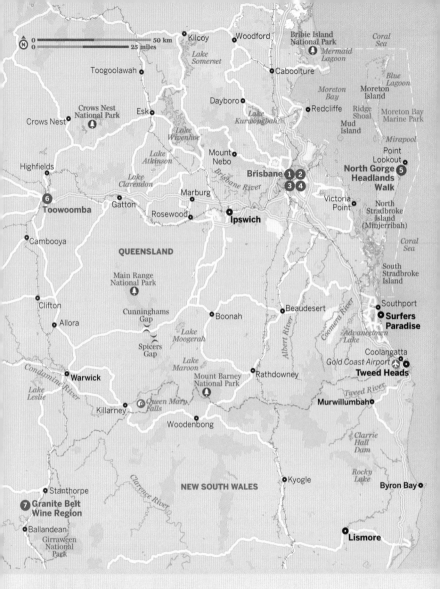

Brisbane & Around Highlights

1 **Gallery of Modern Art** (p57) Finding your muse at one of Australia's hottest galleries of contemporary art.

2 **South Bank Parklands** (p57) Picnicking, strolling or simply sunning by an inner-city beach.

3 **West End** (p56) Roaming bookshops, microbreweries and band venues in Brisbane's boho heartland.

4 **Brisbane Powerhouse** (p59) Catching a show in a converted power station.

5 **North Gorge Headlands Walk** (p96) Experiencing one of North Stradbroke Island's most beautiful walks.

6 **Toowoomba** (p103) Hunting down street-art murals and cool little cafes in Queensland's largest inland town.

7 **Granite Belt Wine Region** (p100) Sniffing, swilling and savouring award-winning drops in Queensland's very own wine region.

BRISBANE

POP 2.3 MILLION

No longer satisfied in the shadow of Sydney and Melbourne, Brisbane is subverting stereotypes and surprising the critics. Welcome to Australia's new subtropical 'It kid'.

⊙ Sights

Most of Brisbane's major sights lie in the city centre (CBD) and South Bank directly across the river. While the former offers colonial history and architecture, the latter is home to Brisbane's major cultural institutions and the South Bank Parklands.

⊚ Central Brisbane

★ City Hall   LANDMARK

(Map p58; ✏07-3339 0845; www.brisbane.qld. gov.au; King George Sq; ⊙8am-5pm Mon-Fri, 9am-5pm Sat & Sun, clock tower tours 10.15am-4.45pm, City Hall tours 10.30am, 11.30am, 1.30pm & 2.30pm; ₪Central) **FREE** Fronted by a row of sequoia-sized Corinthian columns, this sandstone behemoth was built between 1920 and 1930. The foyer's marble was sourced from the same Tuscan quarry as that used by Michelangelo to sculpt his *David*. The Rolling Stones played their first-ever Australian gig in the building's auditorium in 1965, a magnificent space complete with a 4300-pipe organ, mahogany and blue-gum floors and free concerts every Tuesday at noon. Free tours of the 85m-high clock tower run every 15 minutes; grab tickets from the excellent on-site Museum of Brisbane.

★ Museum of Brisbane   MUSEUM

(Map p58; ✏07-3339 0800; www.museumofbrisbane.com.au; Level 3, Brisbane City Hall, King George Sq; ⊙10am-5pm; ₪Central) **FREE** Delve into the city's highs and lows at this forward-thinking museum, tucked away inside City Hall. The current hero exhibition is 100% Brisbane. An innovative collaboration between the museum and Berlin-based theatre company Rimini Protokoll, the interactive project explores the lives of 100 current Brisbane residents, who accurately reflect the city's population based on data from the Australian Bureau of Statistics (ABS). The result is a snapshot of a metropolis much more complex than you may have expected.

City Botanic Gardens   PARK

(Map p58; www.brisbane.qld.gov.au; Alice St; ⊙24hr; 🚢QUT Gardens Point, ₪Central) **FREE** Originally a collection of food crops planted by convicts in 1825, this is Brisbane's favourite green space. Descending gently from the Queensland University of Technology campus to the river, its mass of lawns, tangled Moreton Bay figs, bunya pines, macadamia trees and tai chi troupes are a soothing elixir for frazzled urbanites. Free, one-hour guided tours leave the rotunda at 11am and 1pm daily, and the gardens host the popular Brisbane Riverside Markets (p90) on Sunday. Ditch the gardens' average cafe for a picnic.

Parliament House   HISTORIC BUILDING

(Map p58; www.parliament.qld.gov.au; cnr Alice & George Sts; ⊙tours 1pm, 2pm, 3pm & 4pm nonsitting days; 🚢QUT Gardens Point, ₪Central) **FREE** With a roof clad in Mt Isa copper, this lovely blanched-white stone, French Renaissance–style building dates from 1868 and overlooks the City Botanic Gardens. The only way to peek inside is on one of the free tours, which leave on demand at the listed times (2pm only when parliament is sitting). Arrive five minutes before tours begin; no need to book.

Roma Street Parkland   PARK

(Map p58; www.visitbrisbane.com.au/Roma-Street-Parkland-and-Spring-Hill; 1 Parkland Blvd; ⊙24hr; ₪Roma St) **FREE** This beautifully maintained, 16-hectare downtown park is one of the world's largest subtropical urban gardens. Formerly a market and a railway yard, the park opened in 2001 and is a showcase for native Queensland vegetation, complete with a rainforest and fern gully, waterfalls, skyline lookouts, a playground, barbecues and no shortage of frangipani. It's something of a maze: easy to get into, hard to get out of.

Adjacent to the Roma Street Parkland is the Old Windmill (Map p58; Wickham Tce; 🚌30, ₪Central) – reputedly the oldest surviving building in Queensland (1828). Due to a design flaw, the windmill sails were too heavy for the wind to turn, and a convict-powered treadmill was briefly employed before the mill was abandoned. The building was converted into a signal post and later a TV broadcast site and meteorological observatory.

Shrine of Remembrance   LANDMARK

(Map p58; Anzac Sq, Ann St; ₪Central) Designed in the Greek Revival style, this graceful monument honours the Australian men and women who have served in conflicts around the world. Its 18 columns symbolise 1918, the end of WWI, while the structure itself is made of

BRISBANE'S GALLERY SCENE

While the Gallery of Modern Art (p57), aka GOMA, and the Queensland Art Gallery (p57) might steal the show, Brisbane also has a growing array of smaller, private galleries and exhibition spaces where you can mull over both the mainstream and the cutting-edge.

The Pillars Project (Map p58; www.thepillarsproject.com; Merrivale St, South Brisbane; ⊘24hr; ➋198, ➌South Bank Terminals 1 & 2, ➍South Brisbane) One of Brisbane's most unexpected art spaces. A series of pillars under the South Brisbane Rail Underpass have been transformed into arresting street-art murals by numerous artists. Among these is the internationally acclaimed, Brisbane-raised Fintan Magee.

Institute of Modern Art (IMA; Map p68; ➋07-3252 5750; www.ima.org.au; 420 Brunswick St, Fortitude Valley; ⊘noon-6pm Tue, Wed, Fri & Sat, to 8pm Thu; ➍Fortitude Valley) Located in the Judith Wright Centre of Contemporary Arts in Fortitude Valley is this excellent noncommercial gallery with an industrial vibe and regular showings by both local and international names working in mediums as diverse as installation art, photography and painting.

TW Fine Art (Map p68; ➋0437 348 755; www.twfineart.com; 181 Robertson St, Fortitude Valley; ⊘10am-5pm Tue-Sat, to 3pm Sun; ➋470, ➍Fortitude Valley) Easy-to-miss, this Fortitude Valley gallery eschews the 'keep it local' mantra for intellectually robust, critically acclaimed contemporary art from around the world. It also runs an innovative online gallery of limited-edition prints, which you can browse at the gallery and have couriered straight to your home.

Fireworks Gallery (Map p54; ➋07-3216 1250; www.fireworksgallery.com.au; 52a Doggett St, Newstead; ⊘10am-6pm Tue-Fri, to 4pm Sat; ➋300, 302, 305, 306, 322, 393, 470) A fabulous warehouse space showcasing mainly painting and sculpture by both Indigenous and non-Indigenous contemporary Australian artists. It's just a short stroll from James St in Fortitude Valley.

Milani (Map p54; ➋07-3391 0455; www.milanigallery.com.au; 54 Logan Rd, Woolloongabba; ⊘11am-6pm Tue-Sat; ➋174, 175, 204) FREE A superb gallery with cutting-edge Aboriginal and confronting contemporary artwork. It's in an industrial corner of Woolloongabba, surrounded by car yards and hairdressing equipment suppliers – if it looks closed, simply turn the door handle.

Suzanne O'Connell Gallery (Map p68; ➋07-3358 5811; www.suzanneoconnell.com; 93 James St, New Farm; ⊘11am-4pm Wed-Sat; ➋470) FREE This New Farm gallery specialises in Indigenous art, with brilliant works from artists all across Australia. Check the website for regular exhibition openings.

Jan Murphy Gallery (Map p68; ➋07-3254 1855; www.janmurphygallery.com.au; 486 Brunswick St, Fortitude Valley; ⊘10am-5pm Tue-Sat; ➋195, 196, 199, ➍Fortitude Valley) Fronted by a strip of Astroturf, this charcoal-grey gallery is another leading exhibition space for contemporary Australian talent in the thick of Fortitude Valley's gallery district.

Philip Bacon Galleries (Map p68; ➋07-3358 3555; www.philipbacongalleries.com.au; 2 Arthur St, Fortitude Valley; ⊘10am-5pm Tue-Sat; ➋195, 196, 199, ➍Fortitude Valley) A pioneer on the Brisbane art scene, this gallery represents some of the country's most revered artists.

prized Queensland sandstone from Helidon, a town to the west of Brisbane.

Customs House   HISTORIC BUILDING
(Map p58; ➋07-3365 8999; www.customs house.com.au; 399 Queen St; ⊘9am-5pm; ➌Riverside, ➍Central) FREE It might be crowded out by skyscrapers these days, but Brisbane's Customs House (1889) continues to cut a very fine figure with its elegant Corinthian columns and copper dome. For almost a century, this was where ships heading into Brisbane's port were required to pay duties. Its current tenants include the University of Queensland and an elegant restaurant. Check out the fascinating old port photos in the foyer.

Greater Brisbane

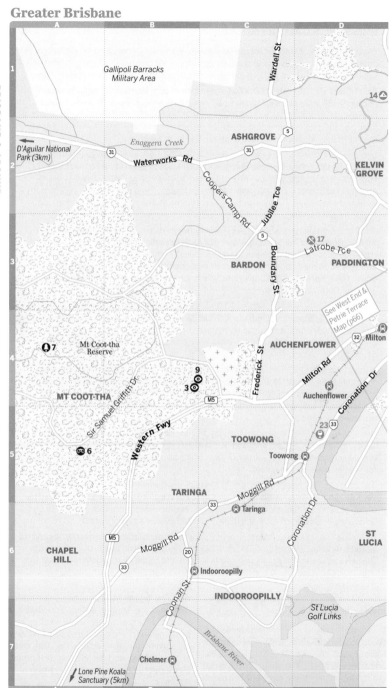

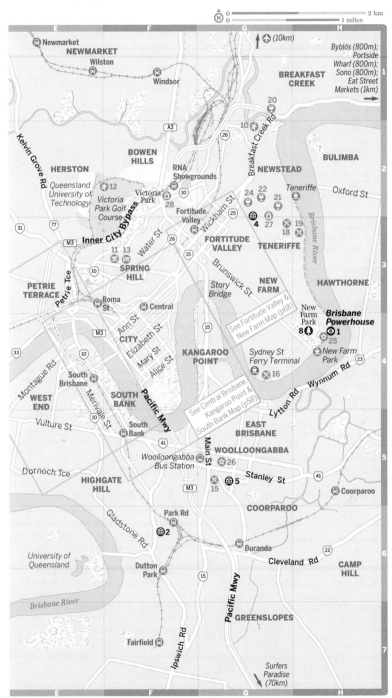

BRISBANE & AROUND

(10km)

Newmarket

NEWMARKET

Wilston

Windsor

Byblós (800m);
Portside
Wharf (800m);
Sono (800m);
Eat Street
Markets (1km)

BREAKFAST
CREEK

20

10

BOWEN
HILLS

HERSTON

RNA
Showgrounds

NEWSTEAD

BULIMBA

Teneriffe

Oxford St

Queensland
University of
Technology

12

Victoria
Park Golf
Course

Victoria
Park

28

24

22

21

Wickham St

Fortitude
Valley

4

27

19

18

Inner City Bypass

Water St

FORTITUDE
VALLEY

TENERIFFE

HAWTHORNE

Brisbane River

11

13

SPRING
HILL

Brunswick St

Story
Bridge

NEW
FARM

New
Farm
Park

Brisbane
Powerhouse

PETRIE
TERRACE

Petrie Tce

Roma
St

Central

Ann St

CITY

Elizabeth St

Mary St

Alice St

See Fortitude Valley &
New Farm Map (p68)

8

1

25

New Farm
Park

23

KANGAROO
POINT

Sydney St
Ferry Terminal

16

Pacific Mwy

South
Brisbane

WEST
END

Montague Rd

Merivale St

SOUTH
BANK

Vulture St

South
Bank

See Central Brisbane,
Kangaroo Point &
South Bank Map (p58)

Lytton Rd

Wynnum Rd

EAST
BRISBANE

Dornoch Tce

HIGHGATE
HILL

Woolloongabba
Bus Station

WOOLLOONGABBA

Main St

26

Stanley St

15

5

Coorparoo

COORPAROO

Gladstone Rd

Park Rd

2

University of
Queensland

Dutton
Park

15

Buranda

Cleveland Rd

22

CAMP
HILL

Brisbane River

Pacific Mwy

GREENSLOPES

Fairfield

Ipswich Rd

Surfers
Paradise
(70km)

N 0 — 2 km
0 — 1 miles

Greater Brisbane

Old Government House   HISTORIC BUILDING
(Map p58; ☎07-3138 8005; www.ogh.qut.edu.au; 2 George St; ⏱9am-4pm, 1hr guided tours 10.30am Tue-Thu; 🚌QUT Gardens Point, 🚆Central) FREE Hailed as Queensland's most important historic building, this 1862 showpiece was designed by estimable government architect Charles Tiffin as a plush residence for Sir George Bowen, Queensland's first governor. The lavish innards were restored in 2009 and the property now offers free podcast and guided tours; the latter must be booked by phone or email.

The building also houses the William Robinson Gallery, dedicated to the Australian artist and home to an impressive collection of his works, including two Archibald Prize–winning paintings.

St John's Cathedral   CHURCH
(Map p58; ☎07-3835 2222; www.stjohnscathedral.com.au; 373 Ann St; ⏱9.30am-4.30pm; 🚆Central) A magnificent fusion of stone, carved timber and stained glass just west of Fortitude Valley, St John's Cathedral is a beautiful example of 19th-century Gothic Revival architecture. The building is a true labour of love: construction began in 1906 and wasn't finished until 2009, making it one of the world's last cathedrals of this architectural style to be completed.

Commissariat Store Museum   MUSEUM
(Map p58; www.queenslandhistory.org; 115 William St; adult/child/family $6/3/12; ⏱10am-4pm Tue-Fri; 🚌North Quay, 🚆Central) Built by convicts in 1829, this former government storehouse is the oldest occupied building in Brisbane. Inside is an immaculate little museum devoted to convict and colonial history. Don't miss the convict 'fingers' and the exhibit on Italians in Queensland.

🔵 South Bank & West End

While Brisbane's CBD obsesses with trade and governance, cross-river South Bank dedicates itself to the finer things in life. It's here that you'll find many of the city's major cultural institutions, conveniently strung together along the waterfront. Adding a deep shade of green are the South Pank Parklands, a riverside oasis of lurid bougainvillea, beachside lounging and weekend market stalls. Further south lies West End, a (rapidly gentrifying) enclave of cool laced with arty cafes, indie bookshops, record peddlers, microbreweries, music venues and side streets lined with sleepy, peeling Queenslander abodes.

★ **Queensland
Cultural Centre**   CULTURAL CENTRE
(Map p58; Melbourne St, South Bank; ⬛ South Bank Terminals 1 & 2, 🚆 South Brisbane) On South Bank, just over Victoria Bridge from the CBD, the Queensland Cultural Centre is the epicentre of Brisbane's cultural confluence. Surrounded by subtropical gardens, the sprawling complex of architecturally notable buildings includes the Queensland Performing Arts Centre (p87), the Queensland Museum & Sciencentre, the Queensland Art Gallery, the State Library of Queensland, and the particularly outstanding Gallery of Modern Art (GOMA).

★ **Gallery of Modern Art**   GALLERY
(GOMA; Map p58; www.qagoma.qld.gov.au; Stanley Pl, South Bank; ⊙10am-5pm; ⬛ South Bank Terminals 1 & 2, 🚆 South Brisbane) **FREE** All angular glass, concrete and black metal, must-see GOMA focuses on Australian art from the 1970s to today. Continually changing, and often confronting, exhibits range from painting, sculpture and photography to video, installation and film. There's also an arty bookshop, children's activity rooms, a cafe (p76), a Modern Australian restaurant (☑07-3842 9916; mains $39-47; ⊙noon-2pm Wed-Sun, plus 5.30-8pm Fri), as well as free guided gallery tours at 11am, 1pm and 2pm.

South Bank Parklands   PARK
(Map p58; www.visitbrisbane.com.au; Grey St, South Bank; ⊙dawn-dusk; 👶; ⬛ South Bank Terminals 1, 2 & 3, 🚆 South Brisbane, South Bank) **FREE** Should you sunbake on a sandy beach, chill in a rainforest, or eye-up a Nepalese peace pagoda? You can do all three in this 17.5-hectare park overlooking the city centre. Its canopied walkways lead to performance spaces, lush lawns, eateries and bars, public art and regular free events ranging from yoga sessions to film screenings. The star attractions are Streets Beach (p61), an artificial, lagoon-style swimming beach (packed on weekends); and the near-60m-high Wheel of Brisbane, delivering 360-degree views on its 10-minute rides.

Queensland Art Gallery   GALLERY
(QAG; Map p58; www.qagoma.qld.gov.au; Melbourne St, South Bank; ⊙10am-5pm; ⬛ South Bank Terminals 1 & 2, 🚆 South Brisbane) **FREE** While current construction works (due for completion in September 2017) have temporarily limited its gallery space, QAG is home to fine a permanent collection of Australian and international works. Australian art dates from the 1840s to the 1970s: check out works by celebrated masters including Sir Sidney Nolan, Arthur Boyd, William Dobell and George Lambert.

**Queensland Museum &
Sciencentre**   MUSEUM
(Map p58; ☑07-3840 7555; www.southbank.qm.qld.gov.au; cnr Grey & Melbourne Sts, South Bank; Queensland Museum admission free, Sciencentre adult/child/family $14.50/11.50/44.50; ⊙9.30am-5pm; ⬛ South Bank Terminals 1 & 2, 🚆 South Brisbane) **FREE** Dig deeper into Queensland history at the state's main historical repository, where intriguing exhibits include a skeleton of the state's own dinosaur *Muttaburrasaurus* (aka 'Mutt'), and the *Avian Cirrus,* the tiny plane in which Queenslander Bert Hinkler made the first England-to-Australia solo flight in 1928. Also on-site is the Sciencentre, an educational fun house with a plethora of interactive exhibits delving into life science and technology. Expect long queues during school holidays.

Queensland Maritime Museum   MUSEUM
(Map p58; ☑07-3844 5361; www.maritimemuseum.com.au; Stanley St; adult/child/family $16/7/38; ⊙9.30am-4.30pm, last admission 3.30pm; ⬛ Maritime Museum, 🚆 South Bank) On the southern edge of the South Bank Parklands is this sea-salty museum, the highlight of which is the gigantic HMAS *Diamantina,* a restored WWII frigate that you can clamber aboard and explore.

Wheel of Brisbane   FERRIS WHEEL
(Map p58; ☑07-3844 3464; www.thewheelofbrisbane.com.au; Grey St, South Bank; adult/child/family $19/13.50/55; ⊙10am-10pm Sun-Thu, to 11pm Fri & Sat; ⬛ South Bank Terminals 1 & 2, 🚆 South Brisbane) Don't have wings but pining for a lofty view of the city? Then consider a ride on the riverside Wheel, a few steps from the Queensland Performing Arts Centre (p87). The enclosed gondolas rise to a height of nearly 60m, which, while not spectacularly high, still offers a revealing, 360-degree panorama of the booming skyline. Rides last 10 to 12 minutes and include audio commentary of Brisbane sights. Online bookings offer a nominal discount.

Central Brisbane, Kangaroo Point & South Bank

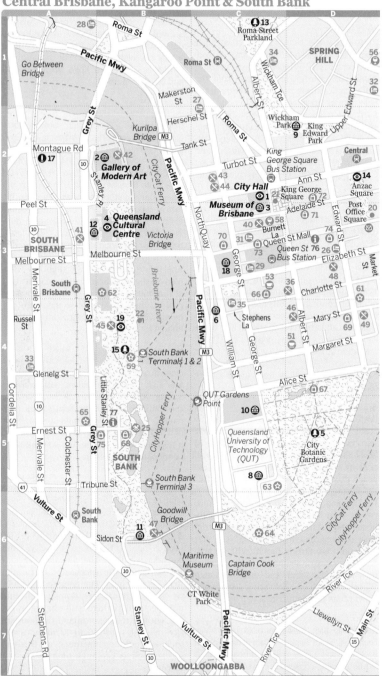

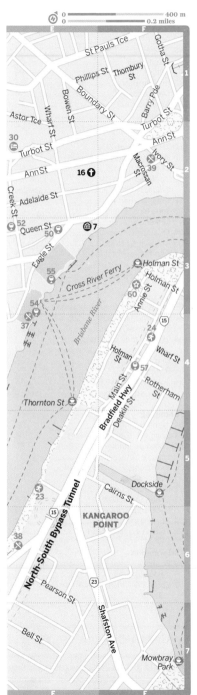

Fortitude Valley & New Farm

Brisbane Riverwalk   BRIDGE
(Map p68; 📖195, 196, 🚢Sydney St) Jutting out over the city's big, brown waterway, the Brisbane Riverwalk offers a novel way of surveying the Brisbane skyline. The 870m-long path – divided into separate walking and cycling lanes – runs between New Farm and the Howard St Wharves, from where you can continue towards central Brisbane itself. The Riverwalk replaces the original floating walkway, sadly washed away in the floods of 2011.

★**Brisbane Powerhouse**   ARTS CENTRE
(Map p54; ☎box office 07-3358 8600, reception 07-3358 8622; www.brisbanepowerhouse.org; 119 Lamington St, New Farm; ⏱9am-9pm Tue-Sun; 📖195, 196, 🚢New Farm Park) On the eastern flank of New Farm Park stands the Powerhouse, a once-derelict power station superbly transformed into a contemporary arts centre. Its innards pimped with graffiti remnants, industrial machinery and old electrical transformers-turned-lights, the centre hosts a range of events, including art exhibitions, theatre, live music and comedy. You'll also find two buzzing riverside restaurants. Check the website to see what's on.

Chinatown   AREA
(Map p68; Duncan St, Fortitude Valley; ⏱24hr; 🚉Fortitude Valley) Punctuated by a replica Tang dynasty archway at its western end, Duncan St is Brisbane's rather modest Chinatown. The pedestrianised strip (and the stretch of Ann St between Duncan St and Brunswick St Mall) is home to a handful of Chinatown staples, including glazed flat ducks hanging behind steamy windows, Asian grocery stores and the aromas of Thai, Chinese, Vietnamese and Japanese cooking. The area is at it most rambunctious during Chinese New Year (www.chinesenewyear.com.au; ⏱Jan/Feb) festivities.

New Farm Park   PARK
(Map p54; www.newfarmpark.com.au; Brunswick St, New Farm; ⏱24hr; 📖195, 196, 🚢New Farm Park) On the tail end of Brunswick St by the river, New Farm Park will have you breathing deeply with its jacaranda trees, rose gardens and picnic areas. It's a perfect spot to spend a lazy afternoon, with gas barbecues and free wi-fi (near the rotunda at the river end of the park). Younger kids will especially love the

Central Brisbane, Kangaroo Point & South Bank

playground – a Crusoe-esque series of platforms among vast Moreton Bay fig trees. Jan Powers Farmers Market (p91) and the Moonlight Cinema (p85) happen here, too.

◉ Greater Brisbane

Brisbane Botanic Gardens GARDENS
(Map p54; ☏ 07-3403 2535; www.brisbane.qld.gov.
au/botanicgardens; Mt Coot-tha Rd, Mt Coot-tha;
⊙8am-5.30pm, to 5pm Apr-Aug; 🚍471) **FREE**

At the base of Mt Coot-tha, this 52-hectare garden houses a plethora of mini-ecologies, from cactus, bonsai and herb gardens, to rainforests and arid zones. Free guided walks are held at 11am and 1pm Monday and Saturday, and self-guided tours can be downloaded from the website. To get here via public transport, take bus 471 from Adelaide St in the city, opposite King George Sq ($4.60, 25 minutes).

Mt Coot-tha Reserve   NATURE RESERVE
(Map p54; www.brisbane.qld.gov.au; Mt Coot-tha Rd, Mt Coot-tha; ⊘24hr; ⊟471) FREE A 15-minute drive or bus ride from the city, this huge bush reserve is topped by 287m Mt Coot-tha, Brisbane's highest point. On the hillsides you'll find the Brisbane Botanic Gardens, the **Sir Thomas Brisbane Planetarium** (Map p54; ☑07-3403 2578; www.brisbane.qld.gov. au/planetarium; admission free, shows adult/child/family/concession $15.80/9.60/43/13; ⊘10am-4pm Tue-Fri, 11am-8.15pm Sat, 11am-4pm Sun; ⊟471), walking trails and the eye-popping **Mt Coot-tha Lookout** (Map p54; ☑07-3369 9922; www.brisbanelookout.com; 1012 Sir Samuel Griffith Dr, Mt Coot-tha; ⊘24hr; ⊟471), the latter offering a bird's-eye view of the city skyline and greater metro area. On a clear day you'll even spot the Moreton Bay islands.

Lone Pine Koala Sanctuary   WILDLIFE RESERVE
(☑07-3378 1366; www.koala.net; 708 Jesmond Rd, Fig Tree Pocket; adult/child/family $36/22/85; ⊘9am-5pm; ⊟430) About 12km south of the city centre, Lone Pine Koala Sanctuary occupies a patch of parkland beside the river. It's home to over 130 koalas, plus kangaroos, possums, wombats, birds and other Aussie critters. The koalas are undeniably cute – most visitors readily cough up the $18 to have their picture snapped hugging one. There are animal presentations scheduled throughout the day.

🏃 Activities

You'll find a plethora of excellent art and heritage walking trails around town at www. brisbane.qld.gov.au/facilities-recreation/sports-leisure/walking/walking-trails.

CityCycle   CYCLING
(☑1300 229 253; www.citycycle.com.au; hire per hr/day $2.20/165, 1st 30min free; ⊘24hr) To use Brisbane's bike-share, subscribe via the website ($2/11 per day/week), then hire a bike (additional fee) from any of the 150 stations around town. It's pricey to hire for

more than an hour, so make use of the free first 30 minutes per bike and ride from station to station, swapping bikes as you go. Only a quarter of bikes include a helmet (compulsory to wear) so you may need to purchase one from shops such as Target or Kmart.

Spring Hill Baths   SWIMMING
(Map p54; ☑1300 332 583; www.cityaquatics andhealth.com.au; 14 Torrington St, Spring Hill; adult/child/family $5.40/3.90/16.40; ⊘6.30am-7pm Mon-Thu, to 6pm Fri, 8am-5pm Sat, 8am-1pm Sun; ⊟30, 321) Opened in 1886, this quaint heated 25m pool was the city's first in-ground pool. Still encircled by its cute timber change rooms, it's one of the oldest public baths in the southern hemisphere.

Streets Beach   SWIMMING
(Map p58; ☑07-3156 6366; ⊘daylight hours; ⊠South Bank Terminals 1, 2 & 3, ⊠South Bank) A central spot for a quick (and free) dip is Australia's only artificial, inner-city beach at South Bank. Lifeguards, hollering kids, beach babes, strutting gym-junkies, palm trees, ice-cream carts – it's all here.

Urban Climb   CLIMBING
(Map p66; ☑07-3844 2544; www.urbanclimb. com.au; 2/220 Montague Rd, West End; adult/child $20/18, once-off registration fee $5; ⊘noon-10pm Mon-Fri, 10am-6pm Sat & Sun; ⊟60, 192, 198) A large indoor climbing wall with one of the largest bouldering walls in Australia. Suitable for both beginners and advanced climbing geeks.

Pinnacle Sports   CLIMBING
(☑07-3368 3335; www.pinnaclesports.com.au; 2hr abseiling from $80, 3hr climbing from $90) Climb the Kangaroo Point Cliffs or abseil down them: either way it's a lot of fun! Options include a two-hour sunset abseil, as well as full-day rock-climbing trips to the Glass House Mountains.

Indooroopilly Golf Club   GOLF
(☑07-3721 2121; www.indooroopillygolf.com.au; Meiers Rd, Indooroopilly; 18 holes Mon-Fri & Sun from $65, cart hire $45; ⊘6am-5pm Mon-Fri & Sun; 🏌; ⊟411, 417) Indooroopilly Golf Club is located about 8km south of the city centre. Saturday is members-only.

Victoria Park Golf Course   GOLF
(Map p54; ☑07-3252 0666; www.victoriapark.com. au; Herston Rd, Herston; 18 holes Mon-Fri $31, Sat & Sun $37, club hire from $20; ⊘6am-10pm Sun-Thu, to 11pm Fri & Sat; ⊟330, 361, 375) Brisbane's

1. Surfing
Catch some of Queensland's best waves on the Gold Coast. (p107)

2. North Stradbroke Island
Point Lookout (p96) offers eye-popping views and a chance to spot humpback whales, dolphins and turtles.

3. Noosa National Park
Crystalline waters are just part of the stunning coastal scenery at this headland park. (p126)

4. South Bank Parklands
Streets Beach lies at the heart of this 17.5-hectare park (p57) right next to Brisbane city centre.

OZBEACHES / GETTY IMAGES ©

MARTIN VALIGURSKY / SHUTTERSTOCK ©

3

DARREN TIERNEY / SHUTTERSTOCK ©

WORTH A TRIP

D'AGUILAR NATIONAL PARK

Suburban malaise? Slake your wilderness cravings at this 36,000-hectare national park (www.nprsr.qld.gov.au/parks/daguilar; 60 Mount Nebo Rd, The Gap), just 10km northwest of the city centre but worlds away (it's pronounced 'dee-ag-lar'). At the park's entrance, the Walkabout Creek Visitor Information Centre (07-3164 3600; www.walkabout-creek.com.au; wildlife centre adult/child/family $7.20/3.50/18.25; 9am-4.30pm) has maps. There's an on-site wildlife centre, home to a number of local critters, including reptiles and nocturnal marsupials.

Walking trails in the park range from a few hundred metres to a 24km-long loop. Among them is the 6km-return Morelia Track at the Manorina day-use area and the 4.3km Greenes Falls Track at Mt Glorious. Mountain biking and horse riding are also options. You can camp in the park too, in remote, walk-in bush camp sites (137 468; www.npsr.qld.gov.au/parks/daguilar/camping.html; per person/family $6.15/24.60). There are a couple of walks (1.5km and 5km return) kicking off from the visitor centre, but other walks are a fair distance away (so you'll need your own wheels).

To get here, catch bus 385 ($5.70, 25 minutes) from Roma St Station to The Gap Park 'n' Ride, then walk a few hundred metres up the road.

most central public course, immediately north of Spring Hill. The floodlit driving range is open late and there's an 18-hole Putt Putt course to boot.

Story Bridge
Adventure Climb   ADVENTURE SPORTS
(Map p58; 1300 254 627; www.sbac.net.au; 170 Main St, Kangaroo Point; climb from $100; 234, Thornton St, Holman St) Scaling Brisbane's most famous bridge is nothing short of thrilling, with unbeatable views of the city – morning, twilight or night. The two-hour climb scales the southern half of the structure, taking you 80m above the twisting, muddy Brisbane River below. Dawn climbs are run on the last Saturday of the month. Minimum age 10 years.

Riverlife   ADVENTURE SPORTS
(Map p58; 07-3891 5766; www.riverlife.com.au; Naval Stores, Kangaroo Point Bikeway, Kangaroo Point; hire bikes/in-line skates per 4hr $35/40, kayaks per 2hr $35; 9am-5pm; Thornton St) Based at the bottom of the Kangaroo Point Cliffs, Riverlife offers numerous active city thrills. Rock climb (from $55), abseil ($45) or opt for a kayak river trip (from $45). The latter includes a booze-and-food 'Paddle and Prawns' option ($85) on Friday and Saturday nights. Also rents out bikes, kayaks and in-line skates.

Q Academy   MASSAGE
(Map p68; 1300 204 080; www.qacademy.com.au; 20 Chester St, Newstead; 1hr massage $30; 300, 302, 305, 306, 322, 470) Q Academy offers one of Brisbane's best bargains: one-hour

relaxation or remedial massage for $30. Although the practitioners are massage students at the accredited academy, all have extensive theoretical training and enough experience to leave you feeling a lot lighter. It's a very popular spot, so book online at least a week in advance.

Skydive Brisbane   SKYDIVING
(1300 663 634; www.skydive.com.au; from $300) Offers tandem skydives over Brisbane, landing on the beach in Redcliffe. See the website for specials.

Fly Me to the Moon   BALLOONING
(07-3423 0400; www.brisbanehotairballooning.com.au; adult/child incl transfers from $250/330) One-hour hot-air balloon trips over the hinterland. Flights are followed by a champagne breakfast at a vineyard in the Scenic Rim region west of the Gold Coast. Return transfers to Brisbane are available.

Tours

CityCat   BOATING
(13 12 30; www.translink.com.au; one-way $5.60; 5.25am-11.25pm) Ditch the car or bus and catch a CityCat ferry along the Brisbane River for a calmer perspective. Ferries run every 15 to 30 minutes between the Northshore Hamilton terminal northeast of the city to the University of Queensland in the southwest, stopping at 16 terminals in between, including Teneriffe, New Farm Park, North Quay (for the CBD) and South Bank (also handy for West End).

Brisbane Explorer   TOURS
(Map p58; ☑ 02-9567 8400; www.brisbane
cityexplorer.com.au; day tickets per adult/child/
family $40/25/110; ⊗ 9am-5.15pm) This hop-on,
hop-off shuttle bus wheels past 15 Brisbane
landmarks (in 1½ hours if you don't jump
off), including the CBD, Mt Coot-tha, Chinatown, South Bank and Story Bridge. Tours
depart every 45 minutes from Post Office Sq
on Queen St. Buy tickets online or from the
driver. A second, five-stop tour is also offered,
taking in the Brisbane Botanic Gardens and
Mt Coot-tha.

Brisbane Greeters   TOURS
(Map p58; ☑ 07-3156 6364; www.brisbane
greeters.com.au; Brisbane City Hall, King George Sq;
⊗ 10am) Free, small-group, hand-held introductory tours of Brizzy with affable volunteers. Book at least three days in advance,
either online or by phone. Booking online
allows you to opt for a 'Your Choice' tour,
based on your personal interests and schedule. Note that 'Your Choice' tours should be
booked at least five days in advance.

River City Cruises   CRUISE
(Map p58; ☑ 0428 278 473; www.rivercitycruises.
com.au; South Bank Parklands Jetty A; adult/child/
family $29/15/65) River City runs 1½-hour
cruises with commentary from South Bank
to New Farm and back. They depart from
South Bank at 10.30am and 12.30pm (plus
2.30pm during summer).

XXXX Brewery Tour   TOURS
(Map p66; ☑ 07-3361 7597; www.xxxx.com.au;
cnr Black & Paten Sts, Milton; adult/child $32/18;
☑ 375, 433, 475) Feel a XXXX coming on?
This 1½-hour brewery tour includes a few
humidity-beating ales (leave the car at
home). Tours run four times daily Monday
to Friday and nine times Saturday; check the
website. Also on offer are combined brewery
and Suncorp Stadium (p88) tours (adult/
child $48/28) at 10.30am Thursday. Book
tours in advance, and wear enclosed shoes.
There's also an alehouse here if you feel like
kicking on.

Lucy Boots Bushwalking Tours   WALKING
(☑ 0499 117 199; www.lucybootsbushtours.com.
au; tour incl lunch $120) Take a guided hike
through some easily accessible wilderness
on a day trip from Brisbane: Lamington
National Park, Tamborine Mountain, the
Glass House Mountains, Bribie Island or
Springbrook National Park. Price includes
lunch and Brisbane pick-up/drop-off.

Brisbane Ghost Tours   TOURS
(☑ 07-3344 7265; www.brisbaneghosttours.com.
au; walking tours adult/child/family $20/13/55, bus
tours adult/child $50/40) 'Get creeped' on these
1½-hour guided walking tours or 2½-hour
bus tours of Brisbane's haunted heritage:
murder scenes, cemeteries, eerie arcades and
the infamous **Boggo Road Gaol** (Map p54;
☑ 07-3844 0059, 0411 111 903; www.boggoroadgaol.
com; Annerley Rd, Dutton Park; history tour adult/
child/family $26.50/13.75/52, ghost tour adult/child
over 12yr $45/30; ⊗ 1½hr historical tours 11am Thu-
Sun, 10am Sun, 2hr ghost tours 7.30pm Wed & Fri-
Sun, 8.30pm Fri; ☑ 112, 116, 202). Offers several
tours a week; bookings essential.

🎓 Courses

**Golden Pig Cooking
School & Cafe**   COOKING
(Map p54; ☑ 07-3666 0884; www.goldenpig.
au; 38 Ross St, Newstead; 4hr cooking class $165;
⊗ cafe 7.30am-noon Mon, to 2pm Tue-Fri; ☑ 300,
302, 305) In a warehouse on the edge of Newstead, chef Katrina Ryan runs a series of popular cooking classes, with themes ranging
from modern Greek, Vietnamese and South
American, to Middle Eastern, brunch and
sourdough baking. Ryan's background is impressive, having worked at some of Australia's top restaurants. See the website for class
times and types, which also include 'singles'
classes for foodies sick of Tinder.

James St Cooking School   COOKING
(Map p68; ☑ 07-3252 8850; www.jamesstcooking
school.com.au; 22 James St, Fortitude Valley; 3hr class
$145-160; ☑ 470, ☑ Fortitude Valley) Nurture your
inner Jamie Oliver at this fantastic cooking
school, aptly located above the gut-rumbling
James Street Market (p77). The school offers
both hands-on and demonstration classes, its
three-hour courses covering themes as varied
as sausage making; Middle Eastern, Indian
and Modern French cooking; even 'beer and
BBQing'. Expect to play with lots of fresh produce from the market downstairs.

🎊 Festivals & Events

Brisbane International   SPORTS
(www.brisbaneinternational.com.au; ⊗ Jan) Running over eight days in early January, this
pro tennis tournament is a prologue to Melbourne's Grand Slam Australian Open, held
later in the month. Featuring the world's
top players, it takes place at the Queensland Tennis Centre in the riverside suburb
of Tennyson.

West End & Petrie Terrace

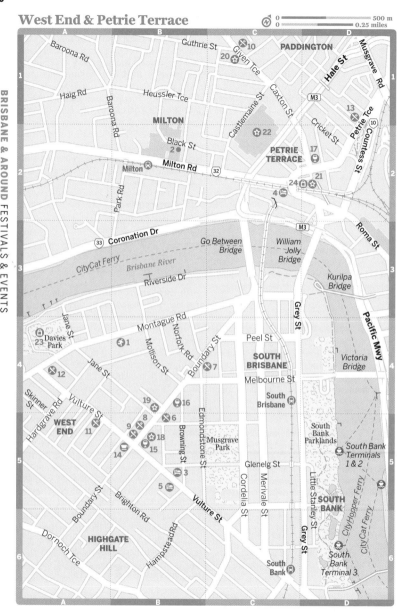

BrisAsia Festival   CULTURAL
(www.brisbane.qld.gov.au) Running for three weeks in late January and February, the BrisAsia Festival celebrates both traditional and modern Asian cultures with over 80 events across the city. The festival program includes dance, music and theatre performances, film screenings, interactive community events and no shortage of Asian cuisines.

West End & Petrie Terrace

BRISBANE & AROUND FESTIVALS & EVENTS

Brisbane Street Art Festival   ART
(www.bsafest.com.au; ☺ Feb) The hiss of spray cans underscores this booming two-week festival, which sees local and international street artists transform city walls into arresting art works. Live mural art aside, the program includes exhibitions, music, theatre, light shows, workshops and street-art masterclasses.

Brisbane Comedy Festival   COMEDY
(www.briscomfest.com; ☺ Feb/Mar) Feeling blue? Check yourself into this month-long laugh-fest, usually running from late February to March. Showcasing almost 70 comedy acts from Australia and beyond, festival gigs take place at the riverside Brisbane Powerhouse (p87) arts hub as well as at Brisbane City Hall (p52).

CMC Rocks Queensland   MUSIC
(www.cmcrocks.com; ☺ Mar) The biggest country and roots festival in the southern hemisphere, taking place over three days and nights in March at Willowbank Raceway in the southwest outskirts of Brisbane. Expect big-name international acts like Dixie Chicks, Little Big Town and Kip Moore as well as home-grown country A-listers.

Anywhere Theatre Festival   PERFORMING ARTS
(www.anywherefest.com; ☺ May) For over two weeks in May, all of Brisbane becomes a stage as hundreds of performances pop up across the city in the most unexpected places. Expect anything from theatre in laneways to cabaret in antique shops and bellowing sopranos in underground reservoirs.

**Queensland Cabaret
Festival**   PERFORMING ARTS
(www.queenslandcabaretfestival.com.au; ☺ Jun) Come June, the Brisbane Powerhouse (p87) cranks up the sass and subversion for the 10-day Queensland Cabaret Festival. Expect a mix of both local and international acts, with past performers including US actor and singer Molly Ringwald and British *chansonnière* Barb Jungr.

Out of the Box   ART
(www.outoftheboxfestival.com.au; ☺ Jun) Eight-day biennial festival of performing and visual arts for kids eight years and under, with lots of interactive and free events. Held in June in even-numbered years at the Queensland Performing Arts Centre (p87).

Queensland Music Festival   MUSIC
(QMF; www.queenslandmusicfestival.org.au; ☺ Jul) Renowned singer-songwriter Katie Noonan is the current artistic director of this biennial statewide festival, which serves up an eclectic program of music ranging from classical to contemporary. Held over three weeks in July in odd-numbered years. Most events are free.

Queensland Poetry Festival   LITERATURE
(www.queenslandpoetryfestival.com; ☺ Aug) One of Australia's main literary festivals, featuring four eloquent days of readings, spoken word,

Fortitude Valley & New Farm

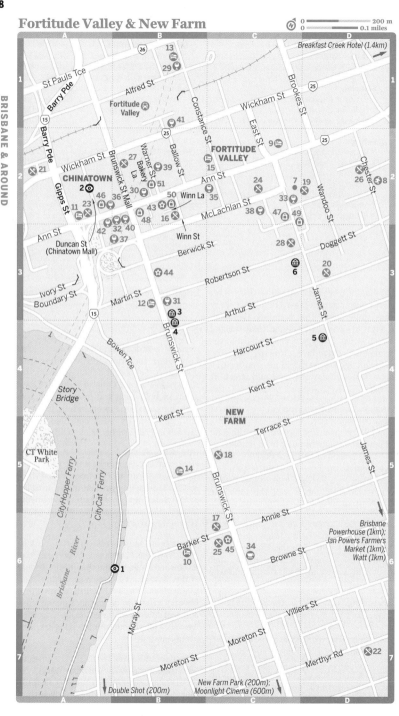

0 — 200 m
0 — 0.1 miles

Breakfast Creek Hotel (1.4km)

St Pauls Tce
Barry Pde
Alfred St
Fortitude Valley
Wickham St
Brookes St
Barry Pde
Wickham St
CHINATOWN
Gipps St
Brunswick St Mall
Warner St
Bakery La
Ballow St
Constance St
FORTITUDE VALLEY
East St
Wandoo St
Chester St
Ann St
McLachlan St
Winn La
Winn St
Berwick St
Duncan St (Chinatown Mall)
Ann St
Robertson St
Doggett St
Ivory St
Boundary St
Martin St
Arthur St
James St
Brunswick St
Harcourt St
Bowen Tce
Story Bridge
Kent St
Kent St
NEW FARM
Terrace St
James St
CT White Park
CityHopper Ferry
CityCat Ferry
Brunswick St
Annie St
Brisbane Powerhouse (1km); Jan Powers Farmers Market (1km); Watt (1km)
Barker St
Browne St
Brisbane River
Moray St
Villiers St
Moreton St
Moreton St
Merthyr Rd

Double Shot (200m)
New Farm Park (200m); Moonlight Cinema (600m)

Fortitude Valley & New Farm

slams, performance, music, ekphrastic poetry, installations, collaborations, cross-platform creations, screenings, workshops and interviews with local and visiting creatives. Held at the Judith Wright Centre of Contemporary Arts (p87).

'Ekka' Royal Queensland Show　CULTURAL
(www.ekka.com.au; ⊙ Aug) Country and city collide at this epic 10-day event in August. Head in for fireworks, showbags, theme-park rides, concerts, shearing demonstrations and prize-winning livestock by the truckload. There's also a cooking stage, with demonstrations and the odd celebrity chef.

Bigsound Festival　MUSIC
(www.bigsound.org.au; ⊙ Sep) Held over three huge days in September, Australia's premier new music festival draws buyers, industry

experts and fans of fresh Aussie music talent. With the Judith Wright Centre of Contemporary Arts (p87) as its heart, the fest features around 150 up-and-coming artists playing around 15 venues.

Brisbane Festival　PERFORMING ARTS
(www.brisbanefestival.com.au; ⊙ Sep) One of Australia's largest and most diverse arts festivals, running for three weeks in September and featuring an impressive schedule of concerts, plays, dance and fringe events. The festival ends with the spectacular 'Riverfire', an elaborate fireworks show over the Brisbane River.

Brisbane Pride Festival　LGBT
(www.brisbanepride.org.au; ⊙ Sep) Spread over four weeks, Australia's third-largest LGBT festival includes the popular Pride March

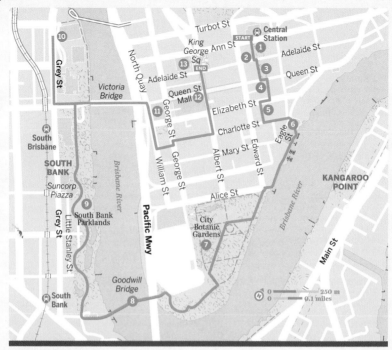

City Walk
CBD to Southbank

START CENTRAL STATION
END KING GEORGE SQ
DISTANCE/DURATION 5KM; TWO HOURS

Cross Ann St south of Central Station to the elegant ❶ **Shrine of Remembrance** (p52) above the northern edge of ❷ **Anzac Square**, with its bulbous boab trees and wandering ibises. At the southern side of the square, scale one of the pedestrian bridges over Adelaide St, which lead to the elevated, manicured ❸ **Post Office Square**. The square is fronted at its southern end by Brisbane's stately stone ❹ **GPO**. Take the alley between the wings of the post office through to Elizabeth St. Cross the road and stick your head into beautiful white-stone ❺ **St Stephen's Cathedral**.

Walk through the courtyard behind the cathedral until reaching Charlotte St. Take a left, cross Eagle St and duck through ❻ **Eagle Street Pier** on the river. Check the Story Bridge views to your left, then go down the steps to the riverside boardwalk and truck south.

At Edward and Alice Sts, detour through the ❼ **City Botanic Gardens** (p52). Cast an eye across the river to the Kangaroo Point cliffs, then skirt around the back of the Brisbane Riverstage to the pedestrian-only ❽ **Goodwill Bridge**: check out HMAS *Diamantina* in the Queensland Maritime Museum to your left. From here, jag north into the ❾ **South Bank Parklands** (p57).

If time is your friend, duck into the outstanding ❿ **Gallery of Modern Art** (p57). Otherwise, cross Victoria Bridge back into central Brisbane. Just south of the gorgeous ⓫ **Treasury Building** on William St, an unnamed alley cuts through to George St. Dogleg across George into Charlotte St, continue along Charlotte then turn left into Albert St in Brisbane's rapidly changing CBD.

Continue along Albert St, cross ⓬ **Queen Street Mall** and then Adelaide St into King George Sq, where the towering ⓭ **City Hall** (p52) beckons with its commanding clock-tower views.

and Fair Day, which sees thousands march from Fortitude Valley to New Farm Park in a celebration of diversity. Pride's fabulous Queen's Ball takes place in June.

Brisbane Writers Festival LITERATURE
(BWF; www.uplit.com.au; ☺Sep) Queensland's premier literary event has been running for over five decades. Expect a five-day program of readings, discussions and other thought-provoking events featuring both Australian and international writers and thinkers.

Oktoberfest CULTURAL
(www.oktoberfestbrisbane.com.au; ☺Oct) Brisbanites don their *lederhosen* and *dirndl* for Australia's biggest German shindig, held at the Brisbane Showgrounds over two weekends in October. It's a sud-soaked blast, with traditional German grub, yodellers, oompah bands and a dedicated 'Kinder Zone' with rides, Deutsch lessons and more for little aspiring Germans.

Park Sounds MUSIC
(www.parksounds.com.au; ☺Nov) Hip-hop rules at Brisbane's newest music festival, held at Pine Rivers Park in suburban Strathpine. The 2016 line-up included ARIA-winning A-listers Bliss n Eso, as well as other of-the-moment Aussie acts like Drapht and Pon Cho (of Thundamentals). Held over an afternoon in November.

Brisbane Asia Pacific Film Festival FILM
(BAPFF; brisbaneasiapacificfilmfestival.com; ☺Nov/Dec) A 16-day celebration of cinema from Oceania and Asia, with around 80 films from countries as diverse as Australia, New Zealand, China, Korea, the Philippines, Afghanistan, India, Russia and Iran. The program includes feature films, shorts and documentaries, as well as panel discussions and other special events.

🛏 Sleeping

Prices do not generally abide by any high- or low-season rules; wavering rates usually reflect demand. Rates are often higher midweek, as well as during major events and holiday periods.

Central Brisbane

Base Brisbane Embassy HOSTEL $
(Map p58; ☎07-3014 1715; www.stayatbase.com; 214 Elizabeth St; dm/d/tw from $35/100/130; ❄@☎; ⛟Central) A city branch of the Base

chain, this spruced-up place is quieter than other hostels despite being just behind the bustling Queen St Mall. While it feels a little soulless, it does have its draws, among them a large screening room for films, and a sun deck with barbecue and city views. Slurp craft beers at the **Embassy Hotel** (Map p58; www.embassybar.com.au; ☺11am-10pm Mon-Wed, to 11pm Thu, to late Fri, noon-late Sat) downstairs.

Base Brisbane Uptown HOSTEL $
(Map p58; ☎07-3238 5888; www.stayatbase.com; 466 George St; dm/tw & d from $21/145; ❄@☎; ⛟Roma St) This purpose-built hostel near Roma St Station flaunts its youth with mod interiors, decent facilities and overall cleanliness. Each room has air-con, a bathroom and individual lockers, and it's wheelchair-accessible. The bar downstairs is a party palace, with big-screen sports, DJs and open-mic nights.

Soho Motel MOTEL $
(Map p58; ☎07-3831 7722, 1800 46 76 46; www.sohobrisbane.com.au; 333 Wickham Tce, Spring Hill; r from $100; ❄❄☎; ⛟30, ⛟Roma St) A short hop from Roma St Station, this red-brick, 50-room joint is better inside than it looks from the street, with tasteful, compact rooms featuring little balconies. The owners are friendly and savvy, and pay attention to the little things: free wi-fi, 11am check-out, free (limited) parking, custom-made furniture and plush linen. Good value for money.

★Next HOTEL $$
(Map p58; ☎07-3222 3222; www.snhotels.com/next/brisbane; 72 Queen St; r from $180; ❄☎❄; ⛟Central) Right above the Queen St Mall, Next delivers stylish, central, affordable accommodation. Rooms are generic though svelte and contemporary, with high-tech touchscreen technology and decent beds. The outdoor lap pool flanks a buzzing bar, itself adjacent to a handy traveller lounge (complete with massage chairs and showers) for guests who check-in early or want a place to relax before a late flight. There's an on-site gym too.

Ibis Styles HOTEL $$
(Map p58; ☎07-3337 9000; www.ibisstyles brisbaneelizabeth.com.au; 40 Elizabeth St; d from $140; ❄@☎; ⛟Central) Smart, contemporary, budget digs is what you get at the world's largest Ibis hotel. Multicoloured carpets and striking geometric shapes set a playful tone in the lobby, and while the standard rooms

are smallish, all are comfortable and fresh, with fantastic mattresses, smart TVs and impressive river and South Bank views. Property perks include a small gym with quality equipment and guest laundry facilities.

Punthill Brisbane HOTEL **$$**
(Map p58; ☑07-3055 5777, 1300 731 299; www.punthill.com.au/property/brisbane/punthill-brisbane; 40 Astor Tce, Spring Hill; 1-/2-bedroom apt from $150/185; P✦🌐🕸; ☑Central) Its lobby graced with retro bicycles (for hire), Punthill offers smart, contemporary suites in muted colours. Digs include comfy king beds, kitchenette or full kitchen, balcony and millennial details like flat-screen TV and iPod dock. On-site facilities include a small pool, gym and guest laundry. A good all-round option, with competitive rates and a central location. Parking $25.

★**New Inchcolm**
Hotel & Suites HISTORIC HOTEL **$$$**
(Map p58; ☑07-3226 8888; www.inchcolm.com.au; 73 Wickham Tce; d from $210; P✦🌐🕸; ☑Central) Built in the 1920s as doctors' suites, the heritage-listed Inchcolm (complete with oak-clad vintage elevator) is fabulously plush and intimate. Rooms in the newer wing have more space and light; in the heritage wing there's more character. All feature thoughtful touches, including coffee machines, Riedel stemware and minibars with locally sourced treats. There's also an in-house restaurant. Parking $40.

Treasury LUXURY HOTEL **$$$**
(Map p58; ☑07-3306 8888; www.treasurybrisbane.com.au; 130 William St; r from $200; P✦🌐🕸; 🛎North Quay, ☑Central) Nostalgic slumber awaits inside the ostentatious former Land Administration Building, steps away from the Queen St Mall and a quick walk from South Bank museums and galleries. Rooms are graced with heritage features, from lofty ceilings, tie-back drapes and classic wooden furniture, to framed architectural prints and the odd fireplace. The best rooms have river views. Efficient staff, twice-daily housekeeping and on-site gym. Parking $30.

🛏 South Bank & West End

GoNow Family Backpacker HOSTEL **$**
(Map p66; ☑0434 727 570, 07-3472 7570; www.gonowfamily.com.au; 147 Vulture St, West End; dm $19-30, d $70; P✦🌐🕸; ☑198, 199) These have to be the cheapest beds in Brisbane, and

GoNow is doing a decent job of delivering a clean, respectful, secure hostel experience despite the bargain-basement pricing. It's not a party place: you'll be better off elsewhere if you're looking to launch into the night with drunken forays. The upstairs rooms have more ceiling height.

Brisbane Backpackers HOSTEL **$**
(Map p66; ☑1800 626 452, 07-3844 9956; www.brisbanebackpackers.com.au; 110 Vulture St, West End; dm $21-34, d/tw/tr from $100/110/135; P✦@🌐🕸; ☑198, 199) If you're looking to party, you're in the right place. This hulking hostel comes with a great pool and bar area, and while rooms are basic, they're generally well maintained. An easy walk from West End's buzzing eateries, bars and live-music venues.

Rydges South Bank HOTEL **$$**
(Map p58; ☑07-3364 0800; www.rydges.com; 9 Glenelg St, South Brisbane; r from $180; ✦🌐🕸; ☑South Brisbane) Fresh from a recent refurbishment, this 12-floor winner is within walking distance of South Bank Parklands and major galleries. In rich hues of silver, grey and purple, standard rooms are large and inviting (try to get one facing the city), with sublimely comfortable beds, smart TVs, free wi-fi, motion-sensor air-con and small, but modern, bathrooms.

🛏 Fortitude Valley & New Farm

Bunk Backpackers HOSTEL **$**
(Map p68; ☑07-3257 3644, 1800 682 865; www.bunkbrisbane.com.au; 11-21 Gipps St, Fortitude Valley; dm from $25, s $60, tw/apt from $85/190; P✦@🌐🕸; ☑Fortitude Valley) This old arts college was reborn as a backpackers over a decade ago – and the party hasn't stopped! It's a huge, five-level place with dozens of rooms (mostly eight-bed dorms), just staggering distance from the Valley nightlife. Facilities include a large communal kitchen, pool and jacuzzi, and in-house bar, **Birdees** (Map p68; ☑07-3852 5000; www.katarzyna.com.au/venues/birdees; 608 Ann St; ⊙3pm-late Mon-Wed, noon-late Thu-Sun), as well as a few great five-bed apartments. Not for bed-by-10pm slumberers. Parking $12.

Bowen Terrace GUESTHOUSE **$**
(Map p68; ☑07-3254 0458; www.bowenterrace.com.au; 365 Bowen Tce, New Farm; dm from $34, s/d without bathroom from $70/80, d/f with bathroom from $95/145; P@🌐🕸; ☑196, 195, 199) In a restored, century-old Queenslander,

Bowen Terrace offers modestly priced lodging in a real-estate hot spot. Simple rooms include TV, bar fridge, quality linen and lofty ceilings with fans (no air-con). There's a communal kitchen, as well as laundry facilities and a pool. Soundproofing between the rooms isn't great, but the place is good value for money, with more class than your average hostel.

Tryp　　　　　　　　　　　BOUTIQUE HOTEL **$$**
(Map p68; ☎07-3319 7888; www.trypbrisbane. com; 14-20 Constance St, Fortitude Valley; r $160-340; ❋ ☎; ☒ Fortitude Valley) Fans of street art will appreciate this hip 65-room slumber pad, complete with a small gym, a rooftop bar and a glass-panelled elevator affording views of the graffiti-strewn shaft. Each of the hotel's four floors features work by a different Brisbane street artist, and while standard rooms are small, all are comfy and feature coffee machines and fab marshmallow beds.

Limes　　　　　　　　　　BOUTIQUE HOTEL **$$**
(Map p68; ☎07-3852 9000; www.limeshotel. com.au; 142 Constance St, Fortitude Valley; d from $180; P ❋ ☎; ☒ Fortitude Valley) Although the rooms at trendy Limes are tight, they do make good use of limited space, with plush bedding, kitchenette and work space. Thoughtful extras include coffee machines, free wi-fi and gym passes. While we love the rooftop hot tub, bar and cinema, it can make for noisy nights; bring ear plugs if you're a light sleeper. Parking nearby for $20.

Central Brunswick Apartments　　　　　　　　APARTMENT **$$**
(Map p68; ☎07-3852 1411; www.centralbrunswickhotel.com.au; 455 Brunswick St; studio from $110, 1-bedroom apt from $130; P ❋ ☎; ☒195, 196, 199, ☒ Fortitude Valley) Emerging from the husk of an old brick brewery building, Central Brunswick Apartments offers modern, hotel-style studio rooms with double bed and en suite bathroom (with older-style showers over bath), as well as larger one-bedroom apartments with double bed, fully equipped kitchen and laundry facilities. There's an on-site gym, jacuzzi and sauna, free wi-fi (download limits apply) and rooftop BBQ. Parking $10.

★**Spicers Balfour Hotel**　BOUTIQUE HOTEL **$$$**
(Map p68; ☎1300 163 054; www.spicers retreats.com/spicers-balfour-hotel; 37 Balfour St, New Farm; r from $280, ste from $430; P ❋ ☎;

☒195, 196, 199) Sophisticated Spicers occupies two renovated heritage buildings on the same street. Slumber in one of the small, plush rooms in the old Queenlander or upgrade to a spacious, deco-inspired suite in the 1920s villa, four of which come with free-standing bath. All rooms and suites feature gorgeous beds, Bose sound system and free wi-fi. The hotel houses a reputable restaurant, and breakfast is included.

Alpha Mosaic Brisbane　　　　HOTEL **$$$**
(Map p68; ☎07-3332 8888; www.alphamosaic hotelbrisbane.com.au; 12 Church St, Fortitude Valley; d from $115, 1-/2-bedroom ste from $150/280; P ❋ ☎; ☒300, 302, 305, 306, 322, 470, ☒ Fortitude Valley) The slick, 18-level Alpha Mosaic is well suited to its surroundings, with oh-so-fashionable James St a quick sashay away. While the rooms aren't quite as svelte as the lobby, they are contemporary and comfortable, in muted hues and featuring comfortable king-sized beds and good soundproofing. The one- and two-bedroom suites come with fully equipped kitchen and laundry facilities. Wi-fi is free. Parking is $25.

🛏 Greater Brisbane

Brisbane City YHA　　　　　　HOSTEL **$**
(Map p66; ☎07-3236 1004; www.yha.com.au; 392 Upper Roma St; dm from $34, tw & d with/without bathroom from $125/107, f from $145; P ❋ @ ☎ ☒; ☒375, 380, ☒ Roma St) This immaculate, well-run hostel has a rooftop pool and a sun deck with eye-popping river views. The maximum dorm size is six beds (not too big); most have bathrooms. Big on security, kitchen space (lots of fridges) and activities, the place runs film nights as well as weekly city walking tours and barbecues. That said, this is a YHA, not a nonstop party palace. Parking $12.

Brisbane City Backpackers　　　HOSTEL **$**
(Map p58; ☎07-3211 3221, 1800 062 572; www. citybackpackers.com; 380 Upper Roma St; dm $19-33, d/tr from $80/105; P ❋ @ ☎ ☒; ☒375, 380, ☒ Roma St) On the Upper Roma St hostel row, this hyperactive, low-frills party palace makes good use of its limited outdoor space, including a viewing tower and pool. The on-site bar has something happening every night: DJs, pool comps, quiz nights, karaoke... Free wi-fi, too. Cheaper rooms have no air-con. If you came to party, you're in the right place.

Newmarket Gardens Caravan Park

CAMPGROUND $

(Map p54; ☑07-3356 1458; www.newmarket gardens.com.au; 199 Ashgrove Ave, Newmarket; powered/unpowered sites $43/41, on-site vans $57, budget r $68, cabins $135-160; P ❄ @ 🛜; ☷390, ☷Newmarket) Just 4km north of the city and dotted with mango trees, this place offers a row of five simple budget rooms (no air-con), five tidy cabins (with air-con) and a sea of van and tent sites. Not much in the way of distractions for kids. From central Brisbane, bus 390 stops around 200m east of the caravan park (alight at stop 20).

Art Series – The Johnson

HOTEL $$

(Map p54; ☑07-3085 7200; www.artseries hotels.com.au/johnson; 477 Boundary St, Spring Hill; r from $165; P ❄ 🛜 ⛟; ☷301, 321, 411) Opened in 2016, this is Brisbane's first Art Series hotel. It's dedicated to abstract artist Michael Johnson, whose big, bold brushstrokes demand attention in the svelte lobby. Framed works by Johnson also grace the hotel's uncluttered contemporary rooms, each with heavenly AH Beard mattresses, designer lighting and free wi-fi. There's an on-site gym as well as a sleek 50m rooftop pool designed by Olympic gold-medallist Michael Klim.

✖️ Eating

Brisbane's food scene is flourishing – a fact not lost on the nation's food critics and switched-on gluttons. From Mod Oz degustations to curbside food trucks, the city offers an increasingly competent, confident array of culinary highs.

✖️ Central Brisbane

Miel Container

BURGERS $

(Map p58; ☑07-3229 4883; www.facebook.com/ mielcontainer; cnr Mary & Albert Sts; burgers from $12; ⏰11am-10pm Mon-Thu & Sat, to 11pm Fri; ☷Central) Planted in a nook below Brisbane's skyscrapers, this rude-red shipping container flips outstanding burgers. Choose your bun, your burger, your veggies, cheese and sauces, then search for a spare seat by the footpath. If it's all too hard, opt for the classic Miel grass-fed beef-pattie burger with onion jam, bacon and bush tomato. Succulent, meaty bliss.

Felix for Goodness

CAFE $

(Map p58; ☑07-3161 7966; www.felixforgoodness. com; 50 Burnett Lane; mains lunch $12-22, dinner $23-24; ⏰7am-2.30pm Mon & Tue, to 9.30pm Wed-Fri, 8am-2pm Sat; 🛜 ✍; ☷Central) 🌿 Felix channels Melbourne with its arty laneway locale, industrial fit-out and effortlessly cool vibe. Sip espresso or chow down decent brunch grub like spelt poppy seed pikelets with vanilla cream, saffron cardamom and poached pears, or pumpkin, ricotta and caramelised onion frittata. A short evening menu focuses on bar bites (best paired with a creative cocktail), with the odd pasta or risotto main.

Strauss

CAFE $

(Map p58; ☑07-3236 5232; www.straussfd. com; 189 Elizabeth St; dishes $6.50-13.50; ⏰6.30am-3pm Mon-Fri; 🛜; ☷Central) Strauss bucks its corporate surrounds with low-key cool and a neighbourly vibe. Head in for pastries or a short, competent, locavore menu of creative salads, thick-cut toasted sandwiches (go for the pastrami, sauerkraut, cheese and pickle combo) and upgraded classics like French toast paired with lemon curd and labne. The place takes its coffee seriously, with cold brew and rotating espresso and filtered options.

AJ Vietnamese Noodle House

VIETNAMESE $

(Map p58; ☑07-3229 2128; www.aj-vietnamese-noodle-house.com.au; 70 Charlotte St; mains $11-15; ⏰11.30am-3pm & 5-9pm Mon-Fri, 11.30am-9pm Sat; ☷Central) When it all gets too much, find solace in a steaming bowl of *pho* (Vietnamese noodle soup) at this cheap, humble bolt-hole. AJ's broth is fragrant and delicate, and there's a number of variations, including spicy beef noodle soup and a BBQ pork wonton noodle with veggies. If you're especially hungry, devour a side of rice paper rolls.

Govinda's

VEGETARIAN $

(Map p58; ☑07-3210 0255; www.brisbane govindas.com.au; 358 George St; all-you-can-eat $12.90; ⏰7am-8pm Mon-Fri, from 11am Sat; ✍; ☷Roma St) Grab a plate and pile it high with the likes of vegetarian curry, koftas (veggie puffs), salads, pappadams, chutneys and semolina fruit pudding at this no-frills budget eatery, run by the Hare Krishnas. You'll find another branch at West End (Map p66; ☑0404 173 027; 82 Vulture St, all-you-can-eat $12; ⏰11am-3pm & 5-8pm Mon-Fri, 11am-3pm Sat; ☷199).

Greenglass

FRENCH $$

(Map p58; www.facebook.com/greenglass336; 336 George St; lunch $12-30, dinner mains $18-35; ⏰7am-9pm Mon-Fri; ☷Roma St) Up a flight of stairs wedged between a discount chemist

FOOD TRUCKS & NIGHT MARKETS

When it comes to food trucks and street food, Brisbane's crush has turned into a full-blown affair. There's an ever-growing number of food vans roaming city streets, serving up good-quality fast food, from tacos, ribs, wings and burgers, to wood-fired pizza, Brazilian hot dogs and Malaysian saté. You'll find a list of Brisbane food trucks (with respective menus) at www.bnefoodtrucks.com.au, a website that also includes a handy, interactive map showing the current location of food trucks across town.

From Tuesday to Sunday, Fish Lane (opposite the Queensland Museum & Sciencentre on Grey St) is the setting for Eating at Wandering Cooks (www.facebook.com/wandering cooks), a rotating mix of quality food trucks and stalls open for lunch and dinner.

Further east along the Brisbane River, in suburban Hamilton, is the hugely popular Eat Street Markets (p80). Easily reached on the CityCat (alight at Bretts Wharf), it's the city's hipsterish take on the night street-food market, with a maze of upcycled shipping containers pumping out everything from freshly shucked oysters to smoky American barbecue and Turkish gözleme, all to the sound of live, rocking bands.

and a topless bar is this pared-back, loft-style newcomer. Head up for novel breakfast items like charcoal bun filled with fried egg, avocado and thinly sliced pork belly, French-centric bistro lunch dishes and an enlightened wine list that favours small-batch Australian drops.

★ **Urbane** MODERN AUSTRALIAN $$$
(Map p58; ☑07-3229 2271; www.urbane restaurant.com; 181 Mary St; 5-course menu $110, 7-course menu $145; ⊙6-10.30pm Tue-Sat; ☑; ⊕Eagle St Pier, ⊠Central) Argentinian chef Alejandro Cancino heads intimate Urbane, the apotheosis of Brisbane fine dining. If the budget permits, opt for the eight-course degustation, which does more justice to Cancino's talents. Needless to say, dishes intrigue and delight, whether it's corn 'snow' (made by dropping corn mousse into liquid nitrogen) or pickled onion petals filled with tapioca pearls and regional macadamia nuts. The wine list is smashing.

Cha Cha Char STEAK $$$
(Map p58; ☑07-3211 9944; www.chachachar.com. au; 5/1 Eagle St Pier; mains $35-90; ⊙noon-11pm Mon-Fri, 6-11pm Sat & Sun; ⊕Eagle St Pier, ⊠Central) Fastidious carnivores drool at the mere mention of this linen-tabled steakhouse, famed for its wood-fired slabs of premium Australian beef. Rib, rump and T-bone aside, the kitchen also offers first-rate seafood and roast game dishes like paperbark-smoked duck breast with roasted mushrooms, pomme fondant, grilled baby zucchinis and pomegranate jus. Part of the Eagle St Pier complex, the dining room's floor-to-ceiling windows come with river views.

✕ South Bank & West End

Plenty West End CAFE $
(Map p66; ☑07-3255 3330; www.facebook.com/ plentywestend; 284 Montague Rd, West End; dishes $5.50-23.50; ⊙6.30am-3pm, kitchen closes 2.25pm; ☜☑; ⊠60, 192, 198) 🍽 In the far west of West End lies this graphics-factory-turned-cafe, a rustic, industrial backdrop for farm-to-table edibles. Scan the counter for freshly made panini and cakes, or the blackboard for headliners like caramelised Brussels sprouts with pumpkin purée, feta, raisins and pumpkin seeds. Libations include fresh juices, kombucha on tap and fantastic, organic coffee. When you're done, pick up some pineapple hot sauce at the in-store providore.

Morning After CAFE $
(Map p66; ☑07-3844 0500; www.morningafter. com.au; cnr Vulture & Cambridge Sts, West End; breakfast $9-19, lunch mains $15-21; ⊙7am-4pm; ☜☑; ⊠199) Decked out in contemporary blonde-wood furniture, gleaming subway tiles and bold green accents, this new-school West End cafe is crisper than an apple. Join the effortlessly cool for vibrant, revamped cafe fare such as zucchini fritters with fried eggs, carrot and ginger purée and Vietnamese salad, and bucatini pasta with kale pesto, spinach purée and pistachio. Alas, the coffee is a little less consistent.

Kiss the Berry HEALTH FOOD $
(Map p58; ☑07-3846 6128; www.kisstheberry. com; 65/114 Grey St, South Bank; bowls $10.50-16; ⊙7am-5pm; ☑; ⊕South Bank Terminals 1 & 2, ⊠South Brisbane) Overlooking South Bank Parklands is this youthful, upbeat açaí bar

serving fresh, tasty bowls of the organic super food in various combinations. Our favourite is the naughty-but-nice Snickers Delight (with banana, strawberries, raw cacao powder, peanut butter, coconut water, almond milk, granola, raw cocoa nibs and coconut yoghurt and flakes). For a liquid açaí fix, opt for one of the meal-in-a-cup smoothies.

Beach Burrito Company   MEXICAN $
(Map p66; ☑ 07-3846 6286; www.beachburrito company.com; 100 Boundary St, West End; mains $12-21; ⊙ 11.30am-10pm Sun-Thu, to 10pm Fri & Sat; ⎕ 198, 199) Beach-shack style and a predictable Mex repertoire of tacos, burritos, quesadillas and margaritas.

★ Gauge   MODERN AUSTRALIAN $$
(Map p58; ☑ 07-3852 6734; www.gaugebrisbane. com.au; 77 Grey St, South Brisbane; breakfast $12-19, mains $26-33; ⊙ 7am-3pm Mon-Wed, 7am-3pm & 5.30-9pm Thu & Fri, 8am-3pm & 5.30-9pm Sat, 8am-3pm Sun; ⎘ South Bank Terminals 1 & 2, ⎗ South Brisbane) All-day, cafe-style Gauge is so hot right now. In a crisp, sparse space punctuated by black-spun aluminium lamps, native flora and a smashing wine list, clean, contemporary dishes burst with Australian confidence. Signatures include a provocative 'blood taco' packed with roasted bone marrow, mushroom and native thyme, and a brilliant twist on banana bread – garlic bread with burnt vanilla and brown butter.

Julius   ITALIAN $$
(Map p58; ☑ 07-3844 2655; www.juliuspizzeria. com.au; 77 Grey St, South Brisbane; pizzas $21-24.50; ⊙ noon-9.30pm Sun, Tue & Wed, to 10pm Thu, to 10.30pm Fri & Sat; ⎘ South Bank Terminals 1 & 2, ⎗ South Brisbane) Suited up in polished concrete and the orange glow of Aperol, this svelte Italian fires up superlative pizzas, divided into *pizze rosse* (with tomato sauce) or *pizze bianche* (without). The former includes a simple, beautiful marinara, cooked the proper Neapolitan way (sans seafood). The pasta dishes are also solid, with *fritelle di ricotta* (fried ricotta dumplings filled with custard) making a satisfying epilogue.

GOMA Cafe Bistro   CAFE $$
(Map p58; ☑ 07-3842 9906; www.qagoma.qld.gov. au; Gallery of Modern Art, Stanley Pl, South Bank; lunch $15-34; ⊙ 10am-3pm Mon-Fri, from 8.30am Sat & Sun; ⎘ South Bank Terminals 1 & 2, ⎗ South Brisbane) The casual, indoor-outdoor GOMA Cafe Bistro serves high-quality burgers, salads and modern bistro mains, and it serves both breakfast and lunch served on the weekends.

Billykart West End   MODERN AUSTRALIAN $$
(Map p66; ☑ 07-3177 9477; www.billykart.com.au; 2 Edmondstone St, West End; breakfast $6-23.50, dinner mains $26-36; ⊙ restaurant 7am-2.30pm Mon & Sun, 7am-9.30pm Tue-Sat, shop 11am-5pm Mon, 11am-9pm Tue-Fri, 9am-9pm Sat, 9am-5pm Sun; ⎕ 192, 196, 198, 199) Brisbane-based celeb chef Ben O'Donoghue heads Billykart, a slick yet casual eatery where billy-kart blueprints and faux Queenslander veneers salute local childhood memories. Dishes are beautifully textured and flavoured, from the cult-status breakfast Aussie-Asian eggs (tiger prawn, bacon, deep fried egg, oyster sauce, chilli and shizu cress) to a smashing lunch-and-dinner spanner crab spaghettini. Weekend breakfast is especially popular; head in by 9am.

Sea Fuel   FISH & CHIPS $$
(Map p66; ☑ 07-3844 9473; www.facebook.com/ seafuel; 57 Vulture St, West End; meals $14-26; ⊙ 11.30am-8.30pm; ▤; ⎕ 199) The only thing missing is a beach at Sea Fuel, one of Brisbane's best fish-and-chip peddlers. It's a polished, modern spot, with distressed timber tabletops and blown-up photos of coastal scenes. The fish is fresh and sustainably caught in Australian and New Zealand waters, and the golden chips flawlessly crisp and sprinkled with chicken salt. Alternatives include fresh oysters, Thai fish cakes and sprightly salads.

Chop Chop Chang's   ASIAN $$
(Map p66; ☑ 07-3846 7746; www.chopchop changs.com.au; 185 Boundary St, West End; mains $18-32, banquet menus $38-55; ⊙ 11.30am-3pm & 5.30-9.30pm; ⎕ 199) 'Happiness never decreases by being shared.' So said the Buddha. And the hungry hordes at Chop Chop Chang's seem to concur, passing around bowls of flavour-packed, pan-Asian street food like caramelised pork with tamarind, star anise and cassia bark, Isaan-style *larb* (ground-pork with pak chi farang, hot mint and dry chilli) and cooling watermelon and pomelo salad. Open later on Friday and Saturday nights.

★ Stokehouse Q   MODERN AUSTRALIAN $$$
(Map p58; ☑ 07-3020 0600; www.stokehouse.com. au; River Quay, Sidon St, South Bank; mains $36-42; ⊙ noon-late Mon-Thu, 11am-late Fri-Sun; ⎘ South Bank Terminal 3, ⎗ South Bank) Sophisticated Stokehouse guarantees a dizzying high,

its confident, locally sourced menu paired with utterly gorgeous river and city views. At crisp, linen-clad tables, urbanites toast to inspired creations like chicken liver and Madeira brûlée with fruit toast, pear and native cranberry chutney. Next door, Stoke Bar offers similar views for a more casual (albeit pricey) drinking session.

Bacchus   MODERN AUSTRALIAN $$$

(Map p58; ☑ 07-3364 0837; www.bacchus southbank.com.au; Rydges South Bank, 9 Glenelg St, South Brisbane; high tea $38, with glass of champagne from $53; ☻ high tea 2.30-4.30pm Tue-Thu & Sun, 1.30-4.30pm Fri & Sat; ☻ South Bank Terminals 1 & 2, ☒ South Brisbane) Indulge in a little afternoon delight at Bacchus, a plush, gold-accented restaurant well-known for its afternoon high teas. Nibble elegantly from three-tiered stands laden with bite-sized cucumber sandwiches, ham croissants, scones, fruit tartlets, macarons and more. Pair with top-tier teas from Harney & Sons or, better still, a glass of bubbles. Book a day or two ahead, especially on weekends.

✖ Fortitude Valley

★ King Arthur Cafe   MODERN AUSTRALIAN $

(Map p68; ☑ 07-3358 1670; www.kingarthur cafe.com; 164c Arthur St, Fortitude Valley; meals $11.50-21; ☻ 7am-3pm Tue-Fri, to 2pm Sat-Mon; ☎; ☒ 470, ☒ Fortitude Valley) Just off James St, King Arthur is never short of eye-candy creatives, guzzling gorgeous coffee (including batch brew), nibbling on just-baked goods and tucking into revamped cafe classics like scrambled eggs with kale, broccoli, fermented chilli and goats curd, or warm smoked local fish with horseradish cream, potato hash and pickled seasonal veggies. Best of all, it's all made using local produce and ethically sourced meats.

Nodo Donuts   CAFE $

(Map p68; ☑ 07-3852 2230; www.nodo.com.au; 1 Ella St, Newstead; dishes $7.50-16; ☻ 7am-3pm Tue-Fri, from 8am Sat & Sun; ☎; ☒ 300, 302, 305, 306, 322, 470) Light-washed, hip-kid Nodo serves up Brisbane's poshest doughnuts (usually sold out by 2pm), with combos like blueberry and lemon and Valrhona chocolate with beetroot. They're baked (not fried), gluten-free and even include a raw variety, dehydrated for nine hours. The rest of the cafe menu is equally focused on natural, unrefined ingredients, from the green breakfast bowl right through to the

activated almond-milk Magic Mushroom shake. Great coffee, too.

Ben's Burgers   BURGERS $

(Map p68; ☑ 07-3195 3094; www.bensburgers. com.au; Winn Lane, 5 Winn St; burgers $11; ☻ 7am-late; ☒ Fortitude Valley) Prime ingredients drive Ben's, a small, pumping joint in the Valley's coolest laneway. Roll out of bed for a breakfast Elvis (bacon, peanut butter, banana, maple syrup), or head in later for the trio of lunch and dinner burgers, among them a meat-free option. Sides are straightforward – fries or chilli cheese fries – with brownies and pecan pie making for a fitting epilogue.

Thai Wi-Rat   THAI, LAOTIAN $

(Map p68; ☑ 07-3257 0884; 270-292 Brunswick St, Fortitude Valley; dishes $12-19; ☻ 11am-3pm & 5-9.30pm Mon-Thu, to 10pm Fri-Sun; ☒ Fortitude Valley) Under the watchful eyes of Thai royalty, locals sit at easy-wipe tables and tuck into chilli-heavy Thai and Laotian dishes at this lo-fi Chinatown eatery. Ditch the lunch specials for main-menu items like crunchy, tangy *som tum* (green paw paw salad) or classic *larb*. The wines on offer aren't great, so consider bringing your own bottle of plonk. Takeaway available.

James Street Market   MARKET $

(Map p68; www.jamesst.com.au/james-st-market; 22 James St, Fortitude Valley; 8-piece sashimi $17, hot dishes $10-28; ☻ 8.30am-7pm Mon-Fri, 8am-6pm Sat & Sun; ☒ 470, ☒ Fortitude Valley) Local gourmands drop by this small, contemporary, lavishly stocked market for sophisticated fridge and pantry fare, including pesto-stuffed olives, stinky cheeses, dips, freshly baked bread, pastries and tubs of homemade gelato. If you're feeling a little peckish, the fresh-seafood counter serves good sushi, sashimi and warming dishes like Japanese noodle soup with Moreton Bay bugs.

★ Longtime   THAI $$

(Map p68; ☑ 07-3160 3123; www.longtime.com.au; 610 Ann St; mains $15-45; ☻ 5.30-10pm Tue-Thu & Sun, to 10.30pm Fri & Sat; ☎; ☒ Fortitude Valley) Blink and you'll miss the alley leading to this dim, kicking hot spot. The menu is designed for sharing, with a banging repertoire of sucker-punch, Thai-inspired dishes that include a must-try soft shell crab *bao* (steamed bun) with Asian slaw. Reservations are only accepted for 5.30pm, 6pm and 6.30pm sittings, after which it's walk-ins only (Tuesday and Sunday are the easiest nights to score a table).

Les Bubbles
STEAK $$

(Map p68; ✆07-3251 6500; www.lesbubbles.com. au; 144 Wickham St, Fortitude Valley; steak frites $30; ⏱noon-11pm Sun-Thu, to midnight Fri & Sat; ⛋Fortitude Valley) From the red-neon declaration – 'Quality meat has been served here since 1982' – to the photos of crooks and cops, this sassy steakhouse relishes its former brothel days. Today the only thing on the menu is superb steak frites, served with unlimited fries and salad. Simply choose your sauce (try the green peppercorn and cognac option) and your libation.

Tinderbox
ITALIAN $$

(Map p68; ✆07-3852 3744; www.thetinderbox. com.au; 7/31 James St, Fortitude Valley; pizzas $20-24, mains $28; ⏱5pm-late Tue-Sun; ⛋470, ⛋Fortitude Valley) Popular with on-point James St peeps, this modern, mosaic-clad bistro straddles a leafy laneway by the Palace Centro cinemas. The menu is a share-friendly, Italian affair, spanning spicy 'nduja (spreadable pork salumi) arancini and seared cuttlefish with chilli and rocket, to perfectly charred wood-fired pizzas like a standout *funghi* (porcini mushrooms, mozzarella and roasted onion). Wash it all down with an innovative cocktail.

★E'cco
MODERN AUSTRALIAN $$$

(Map p58; ✆07-3831 8344; www.eccobistro.com. au; 100 Boundary St; mains $36-42, 5-course tasting menu $89; ⏱noon-2.30pm Tue-Fri, 6pm-late Tue-Sat; ⛋; ⛋174, 230, 300) Years on, E'cco remains one of the state's gastronomic highlights. Polished yet personable staff deliver beautifully balanced, visually arresting dishes, which might see cured ocean trout flavoured with oyster emulsion or perfect suckling pig meet its match in smoked carrot purée, kimchi and spicy 'nduja. The kitchen offers a smaller, dedicated vegetarian menu (mains $30 to $38) as well as a highly recommended, good-value tasting menu for the full effect.

Madame Rouge
FRENCH $$$

(Map p68; ✆07-3252 8881; www.madame rougebistro.com.au; 100 McLachlan St, Fortitude Valley; mains $30-36; ⏱5pm-midnight Tue-Thu & Sat, noon-midnight Fri, noon-5pm Sun; ⛋Fortitude Valley) Dark and sexy, Madame Rouge sets a very Parisian scene with her red-velvet curtains, tasselled table lamps and Toulouse-Lautrec prints. The menu –

co-designed by powerhouse chef Philip Johnson of E'cco fame – reads like a greatest hits of French gastronomy: gratinated goats cheese souffle; slow-cooked duck leg with puy lentils and black cabbage; crème brûlée. A beautiful, skilful ode to classic Gallic decadence.

🍴 New Farm

New Farm Confectionery
SWEETS $

(Map p68; ✆07-3139 0964; www.newfarm confectionery.com.au; 14 Barker St, New Farm; sweets from $3; ⏱10am-6pm Wed & Thu, to 9.30pm Fri & Sat; ⛋195, 196, 199) For a locavore sugar rush, squeeze into this tiny confectioner, located on the side of the New Farm Six Cinemas. From the macadamia brittle and chocolate-coated Madagascan vanilla marshmallow, to the slabs of blackberry-infused white chocolate, all of the products are made using natural, top-tier ingredients. Nostalgic types shouldn't miss the sherbet powder, made with actual fruit and paired with lollipops for gleeful dipping.

Sourced Grocer
MODERN AUSTRALIAN $

(Map p54; ✆07-3852 6734; www.sourced grocer.com.au; 11 Florence St, Teneriffe; dishes $7-23; ⏱7am-3pm Mon-Sat, 8am-3pm Sun, shop 7am-8pm Mon-Thu, to 7pm Fri, to 5pm Sat, to 4pm Sun; ⛋199, 393, ⛋Teneriffe) You can have your avocado on sourdough (with smoked labna, naturally) *and* buy your local Bee One Third honey at Sourced Grocer, an understatedly cool warehouse turned cafe-providore. Decked out with cushioned milk crates, a vertical garden and native flora in recycled tins, its open kitchen smashes it with seasonal, locavore dishes like standout cabbage pancakes with crispy Brussels sprout leaves, soft egg and shaved goats-milk cheese.

Little Loco
CAFE $

(Map p68; ✆07-3358 5706; www.facebook.com/ littlelococafe; 121 Merthyr Rd, New Farm; breakfast $8-17, lunch $14.50-17; ⏱6am-3pm Mon-Fri, 6.30am-2.30pm Sat & Sun; ⛋; ⛋196, 199, 195) A white space speckled green with plants, this little New Farm local keeps peeps healthy with dishes like the Green Bowl, a tasty, feel-great combo of kale, spinach, broccolini, feta, pomegranate seeds, avocado and dukkah. There's no shortage of vegetarian and paleo bites, as well as dairy- and gluten-free options. Such salubrious credentials make sense given that the cafe's owner is Brisbane soccer player Daniel Bowles.

Double Shot CAFE $

(Map p54; ☑07-3358 6556; www.facebook.com/doubleshotnewfarm; 125 Oxlade Dr, New Farm; mains $11.50-19.50; ⊙7am-3pm Wed, Thu & Sat, to 9pm Fri, 8am-3pm Sun; ⊒196, ⊛Sydney St) With its button-cute wooden porch, manicured hedge and upbeat furniture, petite Double Shot is a hit with brunching mums, dog-walkers and polished, suit-clad realtors. Join the New Farm crew for good coffee, coconut bread with whipped ricotta, Spanish sardines on sourdough or refreshing green papaya, coconut and chicken salad. Tapas served from 3pm on Friday.

Chouquette BAKERY $

(Map p68; ☑07-3358 6336; www.chouquette. com.au; 19 Barker St, New Farm; items $2.50-11; ⊙6.30am-4pm Wed-Sat, to 12.30pm Sun; ☑; ⊒195,196,199) The best patisserie this side of Toulouse? Something to think about as you grab a nutty coffee and a bag of the namesake *chouquettes* (small choux pastries topped with granulated sugar), a shiny slice of *tarte au citron* (lemon tart), or a filled baguette. Charming French-speaking staff are the glacé cherry on the torte.

Wilde Kitchen HEALTH FOOD $

(Map p54; ☑07-3252 2595; www.wildekitchen. com.au; cnr Macqaurie & Florence Sts, Teneriffe; dishes $9.50-19.50; ⊙6.30am-2.30pm; ☎☑; ⊒199, ⊛Teneriffe) 🖉 Chow guilt-free at this lean, low-key cafe, where everything on the menu is paleo, vegetarian, gluten-free or dairy-free. Kickstart the AM with warm coconut and kaffir lime rice, or lunch on the especially popular sticky pork. Wholesome snacks include date truffles and Jaffa slices, best paired with a spicy, caffeine-free 'golden latte' (made with turmeric, cinnamon, honey, coconut oil, pepper and saffron).

Balfour Kitchen MODERN AUSTRALIAN $$

(Map p68; ☑1300 597 540; www.spicers retreats.com/spicers-balfour-hotel/dining; Spicers Balfour Hotel, 37 Balfour St, New Farm; breakfast $14-25, dinner mains $32-38; ⊙6.30-11am, noon-2.30pm & 5.30-8.30pm Mon-Fri, from 7.30am Sat & Sun; ⊒195, 196, 199) Should you nosh in the dining room, on the verandah or among the frangipani in the courtyard? This polished cafe-restaurant creates a very Queensland conundrum. Wherever you may land a linen-covered table, swoon over nuanced, sophisticated dishes, from morning brioche French toast with hazelnut, chocolate ganache and sour cherries, to evening hot-smoked barramundi paired with charred cauliflower and pil-pil sauce. Live tunes accompany Sunday lunch.

Himalayan Cafe NEPALI $$

(Map p68; ☑07-3358 4015; 640 Brunswick St, New Farm; mains $16-27; ⊙5.30-9.30pm Tue-Thu & Sun, to 10.30pm Fri & Sat; ☑; ⊒195, 196, 199) Awash with prayer flags, this free-spirited, karma-positive restaurant pulls in the punters with authentic Tibetan and Nepalese dishes like tender *fhaiya deakau* (lamb with veggies, coconut milk, sour cream and spices). Repeat the house mantra: 'May positive forces be with every single living thing that exists'.

Watt MODERN AUSTRALIAN $$

(Map p54; ☑07-3358 5464; www.wattbrisbane. com.au; Brisbane Powerhouse, 119 Lamington St, New Farm; bar food $10-29, restaurant $25-34; ⊙10.30am-6pm Mon, to 10pm Tue-Fri, 8am-10pm Sat & Sun; ⊒195, 196, ⊛New Farm Park) On the riverbank level of the Brisbane Powerhouse is Watt, a breezy, contemporary space made for long, lazy vino sessions and people watching. Keep it casual with bar bites like Cuban fish tacos and manchego croquettes, or book a table in the restaurant for farm-to-table options like wild Bendigo rabbit pappardelle with smoked speck, hazelnut, watercress pesto and parmesan.

Bar Alto ITALIAN $$$

(Map p54; ☑07-3358 1063; www.baralto.com. au; Brisbane Powerhouse, 119 Lamington St, New Farm; mains $27-33; ⊙restaurant 11.30am-9pm Tue-Thu & Sun, to 10pm Fri & Sat, bar 9.30am-late Tue-Sun; ⊒195, 196, ⊛New Farm Park) At the arts-pumping Brisbane Powerhouse, this snappy upstairs bar-restaurant draws culture vultures and general bon vivants with its enormous balcony, at the ready with gorgeous river view. Local ingredients sing in Italian-inspired dishes like spanner-crab gnocchi, while the solid wine list includes a good number of interesting Italian drops. Book ahead if dining Friday to Sunday (Sunday lunch can book out weeks in advance in summer).

🍴 Kangaroo Point & Woolloongabba

Cliffs Cafe CAFE $

(Map p58; ☑07-3391 7771; www.cliffscafe.com. au; 29 River Tce, Kangaroo Point; dishes $6.50-19.50; ⊙7am-5pm; ⊒234) Looking straight out at the river, skyline and City Botanic Gardens, lofty Cliffs offers what is arguably the best view of Brisbane. It's a casual, open-air pavilion, serving big breakfasts, panini, burgers, fish and chips, salads and sweet treats. While the food won't necessarily blow your socks off, the unobstructed, postcard panorama will. Kick back with a coffee or beer and count your blessings.

Pearl Cafe
CAFE $$

(Map p54; ☑ 07-3392 3300; www.facebook.com/pearl.cafe.brisbane; 28 Logan Rd, Woolloongabba; mains $16-34; ⊙ 7am-8pm Tue-Sat, to 3pm Sat & Sun; ⊑ 125, 175, 204, 234) Channelling Melbourne and Paris with its Euro flair, Pearl is one of Brisbane's best-loved weekend brunch spots. There are freshly baked cakes on the counter, a sophisticated selection of spirits on the shelf, and beautiful cafe dishes on the menu. Snub the underwhelming avocado on toast for more inspiring options, among them the popular daytime pork cotoletta. Sandwiches are chunky and generously filled.

★1889 Enoteca
ITALIAN $$$

(Map p54; ☑ 07-3392 4315; www.1889enoteca.com.au; 10-12 Logan Rd, Woolloongabba; pasta $21-42, mains $32-49; ⊙ noon-2.30pm & 6-10pm Tue-Fri, 6-10pm Sat, noon-2.30pm Sun; ⊑ 125, 175, 204, 234) Italian purists rightfully adore this moody, sophisticated bistro and wine store, where pasta is *not* served with a spoon (unless requested) and a Roman-centric menu delivers seductive dishes like *carciofi alla Giuda* (Jewish-Roman-style fried artichoke with parsley and lemon mascarpone) and melt-in-your-mouth gnocchi with pork and fennel sausage, parmesan cream and black truffle tapenade. Superlative wines include drops from lauded, smaller Italian producers.

✖ Greater Brisbane

Eat Street Markets
STREET FOOD $

(☑ 07-3358 2500; www.eatstreetmarkets.com; 99 MacArthur Ave, Hamilton; admission adult/child $2.50/free, meals from $10; ⊙ 4-10pm Fri & Sat; ▣ Bretts Wharf) What was once a container wharf is now Brisbane's hugely popular take on the night food market. Its maze of shipping-containers-turned-kitchens peddle anything from freshly shucked oysters to smoky American barbecue and Turkish gözleme. Add craft brews, festive lights and live music and you have one of Brisbane's coolest nights out. To get here, catch the CityCat ferry to Bretts Wharf.

Scout
CAFE $

(Map p66; ☑ 07-3367 2171; www.scoutcafe.com.au; 190 Petrie Tce, Petrie Terrace; mains $14-18; ⊙ 7am-3pm; ⊑ 375, 380) This vintage neighbourhood shopfront was vacant for 17 years before Scout showed up and started selling bagels. The vibe is downbeat, affable and creative, with a short, clean menu of healthy salads and bagels stuffed with combos like roasted rosemary potatoes, gorgonzola, mozzarella and chilli jam.

★Shouk Cafe
MIDDLE EASTERN $$

(Map p54; ☑ 07-3172 1655; www.shoukcafe.com.au; 14 Collingwood St, Paddington; dishes $15.50-22; ⊙ 7.30am-2.30pm; ☎ ✍; ⊑ 375) Shouk wins on many levels: affable staff, laid-back vibe, verdant views from the backroom and – most importantly – generous portions of fresh, gorgeous dishes inspired by the Middle East. Swoon over sardines on toasted rye with roasted capsicum, chopped olives, raisins, orange-pickled fennel and labna, or the beautiful *kusheri* (spiced brown rice with lentils, chickpeas and caramelised onion on a beetroot and tahini purée).

Kettle & Tin
CAFE $$

(Map p66; ☑ 07-3369 3778; www.kettleandtin.com.au; 215 Given Tce, Paddington; mains $14-32; ⊙ 7am-4pm Mon & Sun, to 9pm Tue-Thu, to 10pm Fri & Sat; ⊑ 375) Behind its picket fence, cute-as-a-button Kettle & Tin serves up solid, scrumptious cafe grub. Breakfast standouts include thick-cut Kassler bacon with sautéed kale, white beans, celeriac purée and roasted apple, while Paddo's lunching ladies fawn over the daikon and carrot salad with toasted sesame, nori seaweed and puffed rice. Come dinner, cross the Pacific with the ever-popular smoked-duck-breast fajitas.

Byblós
MIDDLE EASTERN $$$

(☑ 07-3268 2223; www.byblosbar.com.au; Portside Wharf, 39 Hercules St, Hamilton; mains $28-34, banquet per person $60; ⊙ 11.30am-late; ▣ Bretts Wharf) A slice of contemporary Beirut by the Brisbane River, Byblós specialises in Lebanese and Mediterranean edibles. While service can be a little hit-and-miss, the menu delivers a solid selection of vibrant, mostly sharing-style dishes like *makanek* (homemade spiced sausages finished with roasted nuts), *shanklish* (soft aged cheese mixed with aniseed and chilli) and *salmon kebbi nayeh* (salmon minced with burghal and traditional spices).

Sono
JAPANESE $$$

(☏ 07-3268 6655; www.sonorestaurant.com.au; Portside Wharf, 39 Hercules St, Hamilton; mains $19-58; ⏱ noon-2.30pm Wed-Sun, plus 6-9.30pm Tue-Thu, to 10pm Fri & Sat, to 9pm Sun; 🚢 Bretts Wharf) One of Brisbane's best Japanese restaurants – hushed, muted and polite – is hidden unexpectedly at Portside Wharf, a few ferry stops downriver from the CBD.

🍷 Drinking & Nightlife

Brisbane's bar scene has evolved into a sophisticated entity, with sharp, competent drinking holes pouring everything from natural wines and locally made saisons, to G&Ts spiked with native ingredients. The city's live-music scene is equally robust, with cult-status venues in Fortitude Valley, West End and the city itself pumping out impressive local and international talent. Tip: always carry some photo ID.

🍸 Central Brisbane

★ Super Whatnot
BAR

(Map p58; ☏ 07-3210 2343; www.superwhatnot.com; 48 Burnett Lane; ⏱ 3-11pm Mon-Thu, noon-1am Fri, 3pm-1am Sat, 3-8pm Sun; 🚇 Central) Trailblazing Super Whatnot remains one of Brisbane's coolest drinking holes, an industrial, split-level playpen in a former beauty school. Slip inside for cognoscenti craft beers, decent vino and crafty cocktails, served to a pleasure-seeking mix of indie kids and thirsty suits. Bar bites include cheeky hot dogs and nachos.

Coffee Anthology
CAFE

(Map p58; ☏ 07-3210 1881; www.facebook.com/coffeeanthology; 126 Margaret St; ⏱ 7am-3.30pm Mon-Fri, to noon Sat; ☎; 🚇 Central) True to its name, Coffee Anthology keeps caffeine geeks hyped with a rotating selection of specialist blends from cult-status roasters like Padre and Industry Beans. Tasting notes guide the indecisive, and you can even buy a bag or two if you like what's in your cup. Friendly, breezy and contemporary, the place also serves simple breakfast and lunch bites, from porridge and muffins to bagels.

Brooklyn Standard
BAR

(Map p58; ☏ 0405 414 131; www.facebook.com/brooklynstandardbar; Eagle Lane; ⏱ 4pm-late Mon-Fri, 6pm-late Sat; 🚢 Riverside, 🚇 Central) The red neon sign sets the tone: 'If the music is too loud, you are too old'. And loud, live, nightly tunes are what you get in this rocking cellar bar, decked out in NYC paraphernalia and buzzing with a mixed-age crowd. Stay authentic with a Brooklyn lager or knock back a kooky cocktail (either way, the pretzels are on the house).

Gresham Bar
BAR

(Map p58; www.thegresham.com.au; 308 Queen St; ⏱ 7am-3am Mon-Fri, 4pm-3am Sat & Sun; 🚇 Central) Tucked into one corner of a noble, heritage-listed bank building, the Gresham evokes the old-school bars of New York; we're talking pressed-metal ceiling, Chesterfields and a glowing cascade of spirit bottles behind a handsome timber bar (complete with library-style ladder). It's a dark, buzzing, convivial spot, with an especially robust selection of whiskies and a snug side room you'll find difficult to leave.

John Mills Himself
CAFE, BAR

(Map p58; ☏ bar 0421 959 865, cafe 0434 064 349; www.johnmillshimself.com.au; 40 Charlotte St; ⏱ cafe 6.30am-3.30pm Mon-Fri, bar 4-10pm Tue-Thu, to midnight Fri; 🚇 Central) No doubt Mr Mills would approve of this secret little coffee shop, occupying the very building in which he ran a printing business last century. Accessible from both Charlotte St and an alley off Elizabeth St, its marble bar and penny-tile floors set a very Brooklyn scene for top third wave coffee. Later in the day, cafe becomes intimate bar, pouring craft Australian beers and spirits.

Coop Espresso Bar
COFFEE

(Map p58; www.facebook.com/coopespresso; Eagle Lane; ⏱ 6am-4pm Mon-Fri; 🚢 Riverside, 🚇 Central) In the shadow of looming towers, cool-kid Coop brews some of the best coffee in town. It's a hole-in-the-wall operation, its inked baristas, hypnotic beats and expert brews providing brief respite for corporate types. Order an espresso (or cold-press filtered coffee), a slice of banana bread (especially good toasted) and devour both on a wooden bench in the street art-pimped laneway.

Mr & Mrs G Riverbar
BAR

(Map p58; ☏ 07-3221 7001; www.mrandmrsg.com.au; Eagle St Pier, 1 Eagle St; ⏱ 3-10pm Mon & Tue, noon-11pm Wed & Thu, noon-midnight Fri & Sat, noon-10pm Sun; 🚢 Eagle St Pier, 🚇 Central) Mr & Mrs G spoils guests with curving floor-to-ceiling windows overlooking the river, skyline and Story Bridge. It's a casually chic affair, with vibrantly coloured bar stools, cushy slipper chairs and

GLBTI BRISBANE

While Brisbane's GLBTI scene is significantly smaller than its Sydney and Melbourne counterparts, the city has an out-and-proud queer presence.

Major events on the calendar include **Melt** (www.brisbanepowerhouse.org/festivals; ☉ Jan/Feb), a 12-day feast of queer theatre, cabaret, dance, comedy, circus acts and visual arts held at the Brisbane Powerhouse in January and February. In March, the Powerhouse also hosts the **Queer Film Festival** (www.brisbanepowerhouse.org/festivals/brisbane-queer-film-festival; ☉ Mar), a showcase for gay, lesbian, bisexual and transgender films. September heralds the Brisbane Pride Festival (p69), which peaks during Pride Fair Day, held at New Farm Park.

Fortitude Valley's **Wickham Hotel** (Map p68; ☑ 07-3852 1301; www.thewickham.com.au; 308 Wickham St; ☉ 6.30am-late Mon-Fri, 10am-late Sat & Sun; ☒ Fortitude Valley) attracts a mainly mixed crowd these days, though it remains a staunchly queer-friendly pub. The Valley is also home to gay-friendly clubs **Beat MegaClub** (Map p68; www.thebeatmegaclub.com.au; 677 Ann St, Fortitude Valley; ☉ 8pm-5am Mon-Sat, from 5pm Sun; ☒ Fortitude Valley) and the scenier Family (p83); on Sunday the latter hosts 'Fluffy', Brisbane's biggest gay dance party. Closer to the city centre, the **Sportsman Hotel** (Map p58; ☑ 07-3831 2892; www.sportsmanhotel.com.au; 130 Leichhardt St, Spring Hill; ☉ 1pm-1am Sun-Thu, to 2.30am Fri & Sat; ☒ Central) is another perennially busy gay venue: a blue-collar, orange-brick pub with pool tables, drag shows and a rather eclectic crowd. In general, you'll find a significant local gay presence in the inner suburbs of Fortitude Valley, New Farm, Newstead, West End and Paddington.

For current entertainment and events listings, interviews and articles, check out *Q News* (www.qnews.com.au) and *Blaze* (www.gaynewsnetwork.com.au). Tune in to *Queer Radio* (9pm to 11pm every Wednesday; www.4zzzfm.org.au), a radio show on 4ZZZ (aka FM102.1) – another source of Brisbane info. For lesbian news and views, *Dykes on Mykes* precedes it (7pm to 9pm Wednesday).

hand-painted Moroccan side tables on which to rest your glass of chenin blanc. If you're feeling peckish, generous tapas dishes include succulent *keftethes* (Greek-style meatballs), cheese and charcuterie.

Riverbar & Kitchen　　　　BAR
(Map p58; ☑ 07-3211 9020; www.riverbarandkitchen.com.au; 71 Eagle St; ☉ 7am-11.30pm; ☒ Riverside, ☒ Central) A chilled-out spot for an afternoon ale or barrel-aged cocktail, Riverbar & Kitchen is true to its name, down by the muddy Brisbane River at the base of the Eagle St Pier complex. Decked-out like a boat shed, with coiled ropes, white-painted timber and booths, the vibe is casual, breezy and free-flowing. Decent food too, from morning staples to burgers, pizzas and surf-and-turf bistro mains.

South Bank

Maker　　　　COCKTAIL BAR
(Map p58; ☑ 0437 338 072; 9 Fish Lane, South Brisbane; ☉ 4pm-midnight Tue-Sun; ☒ South Bank Terminals 1 & 2, ☒ South Brisbane) Intimate, black-clad and spliced by a sexy brass bar,

Maker crafts seamless, seasonal cocktails using house liqueurs, out-of-the-box ingredients and a splash of whimsy. Here, classic negronis are made with house-infused vermouth, while gin and tonics get Australian with native quandong and finger lime. Other fortes include a sharp edit of boutique wines by the glass and beautiful bar bites prepared with award-winning restaurant Gauge (p76).

Cobbler　　　　BAR
(Map p66; www.cobblerbar.com; 7 Browning St, West End; ☉ 5pm-1am Mon, 4pm-1am Tue-Thu & Sun, 4pm-2am Fri & Sat; ☒ 60, 192, 198, 199) Whisky fans will weep tears of joy at the sight of Cobbler's imposing bar, graced with over 400 whiskies from around the globe. Channelling a speakeasy vibe, this dimly lit West End wonder also pours a cognoscenti selection of rums, tequilas and liqueurs, not to mention a crafty selection of cocktails that add modern twists to the classics. Bottoms up!

Catchment Brewing Co　　　　BREWERY
(Map p66; ☑ 07-3846 1701; www.catchmentbrewingco.com.au; 150 Boundary St, West End; ☉ 4-10pm Mon, 11am-10pm Tue-Thu & Sun, 11am-1am Fri

& Sat; 📖199) Sink local suds at Catchment, a hip, two-level microbrewery with notable, seasonal nosh and live music in the courtyard. House brews include Pale Select, a nod to the signature beer of the defunct West End Brewery, while guest taps showcase other local beers. The best seats in the house are the two, tiny, 1st-floor balconies, serving up afternoon sun and Boundary St views.

Jungle
BAR

(Map p66; 📞0449 568 732; www.facebook. com/junglewestend; 76 Vulture St, West End; ⏱noon-midnight Thu-Sun; 📖199) Aloha and welcome to paradise... Well, at least to Brisbane's only proper tiki bar. An intimate, hand-built bamboo hideaway pimped with wood-carved stools, a green-glowing bar and DJ-spun Hawaiian tunes, it's an apt place to cool down with a tropical libation. Keep it classic with a rumalicious piña colada (served in a pineapple, naturally), or neck a Red Stripe lager from Jamaica.

Blackstar Coffee Roasters
CAFE

(Map p66; www.blackstarcoffee.com.au; 44 Thomas St, West End; ⏱7am-5pm; 📶; 📖199) One of Brisbane's top coffee roasters, laid-back Blackstar is never short of West End hipsters, hippies and laptop-tapping creatives. Slurp a single-origin espresso or cool down with a bottle of cold-pressed coffee. Food options (lunch dishes $10 to $17) include brownies, eggs and spanakopita, while its string of special events includes a ukulele night on the last Friday of the month.

Archive Beer Boutique
BAR

(Map p66; 📞07-3844 3419; www.archivebeer boutique.com.au; 100 Boundary St, West End; ⏱11am-late; 📖198,199) A foaming juggernaut, Archive serves up a dizzying choice of craft suds. Whether you're hankering for a Brisbane chilli-choc porter, a Melbourne American IPA or a Sydney guava gose, chances are you'll find it pouring here. There are over 20 rotating beers on tap, as well as hundreds of Aussie and imported bottled brews. Decent bar grub includes grilled meats, burgers and pizzas.

🍸 Fortitude Valley

⭐ Gerard's Bar
WINE BAR

(Map p68; 📞07-3252 2606; www.gerardsbar.com.au; 13a/23 James St; ⏱3-10pm Mon-Thu, noon-late Fri & Sat; 📖470, 📵Fortitude Valley) A stylish, grown-up bar that's one of Brisbane's best. Perch yourself at the polished concrete bar, pick an

unexpected drop from the sharply curated wine list, and couple with standout bar snacks that include flawless croquettes and prized Jamón Iberico de Belotta. If you're craving a cocktail, try the signature 'Gerard The Drunk', an intriguing, climate-appropriate medley of vodka, passionfruit, pomegranate and rose water.

APO
COCKTAIL BAR

(Map p68; 📞07-3252 2403; www.theapo.com.au; 690 Ann St; ⏱3pm-1am Tue, noon-1am Wed, Thu & Sun, noon-3am Fri & Sat; 📵Fortitude Valley) A smart, quality-driven establishment, the APO was once an apothecary (hence the name). It's a dark, moody, two-level space, where Victorian brickwork contrasts with polished concrete floors and the odd marble feature wall. Drinks are sharp, sophisticated and include bottled single-batch cocktails such as a rhubarb-and-vanilla negroni. Topping it off is a smashing menu of French-Lebanese-inspired bites, including a not-to-be-missed Lebanese taco.

Eleven
ROOFTOP BAR

(Map p68; 📞07-3067 7447; www.elevenrooftop bar.com.au; 757 Ann St; ⏱noon-midnight Tue-Thu & Sun, to 3am Fri & Sat; 📵Fortitude Valley) Slip into your slinkiest threads for Brisbane's finest rooftop retreat, its marble bar pouring a competent list of libations, including pickled-onion-pimped martinis and high-flying French champagnes. Drink in the multi-million-dollar view, which takes in the city skyline and Mt Coot-tha beyond, and schmooze to DJ-spun tunes later in the week. The dress code is especially strict on Friday and Saturday evenings; see the website.

Cloudland
BAR

(Map p68; 📞07-3872 6600; www.katarzyna.com. au/venues/cloudland; 641 Ann St; ⏱4pm-late Tue-Thu, 11.30am-late Fri-Sun; 📵Fortitude Valley) Jaws hit the floor at this opulent, multilevel bar, club and Pan-Asian restaurant. Named for a much-loved, long-demolished 1940s Brisbane dance hall, Cloudland has birdcage booths, lush foliage and vast chandeliers that are best described as enchanted forest meets sheikh palace meets Addams Family gothic. Free salsa lessons on Thursday from 9pm.

Family
CLUB

(Map p68; 📞07-3852 5000; www.thefamily.com. au; 8 McLachlan St; ⏱9pm-3.30am Fri-Sun; 📵Fortitude Valley) Queue up for one of Brisbane's biggest and mightiest clubs. The music here is phenomenal, pumping through four levels with myriad dance floors, bars, themed booths and elite DJs from home and away. Running on Sunday, the 'Fluffy' dance party is a big hit with Brisbane's younger, hotter gay party peeps.

Holey Moley Golf Club COCKTAIL BAR
(Map p68; ☏ 1300 727 833; www.holeymoley. au; 25 Warner St; 9-hole mini golf game per person $16.50; ⊙ noon-late Mon-Fri, 10am-late Sat & Sun; ☒ Fortitude Valley) Mini golf, in a church, with cocktails is what awaits at Holey Moley (best booked ahead). Order a Putty Professor (rum, milk, chocolate sauce, peanut butter, Reese's Peanut Butter Cup, crushed Maltesers) and tee off on one of two courses. Each of the 18 holes is themed; the standout *Game of Thrones*–themed Iron Throne is by local artist Cezary Stulgis. Kids welcome until 5pm.

Bloodhound Corner Bar & Kitchen BAR
(Map p68; ☏ 07-3162 6402; www.bloodhound cornerbar.com.au; 454 Brunswick St; ⊙ 3pm-late Mon-Wed, noon-late Thu-Sun; ☒ Fortitude Valley) Starting its life as a grocery store, this 19th-century pile is now a new-school Valley bar. Vintage brick walls, mottled floorboards and open fireplaces share the space with street art, a pinball machine and plenty of hipster beards. Guzzle international beers, well-mixed cocktails, or get experimental with one of the craft spirit flights. Decent bar snacks nod to South America, with live music upstairs on Saturday.

Woolly Mammoth Alehouse BAR
(Map p68; ☏ 07-3257 4439; www.woollymam moth.com.au; 633 Ann St; ⊙ 4pm-late Tue-Thu, from noon Fri-Sun; ☒ Fortitude Valley) The combination of craft beer, giant Jenga and 4m shuffleboard table is not lost on Millennials, who stream into this big, polished playpen to let the good times roll. Brew types include IPAs, saisons and goses, most of which hail from Australian microbreweries. Check the website to see what's playing on the Mane Stage, which could be anything from comedy to UK hip-hop.

Elixir ROOFTOP BAR
(Map p68; ☏ 07-3363 5599; www.elixirrooftop.com. au; 646 Ann St; ⊙ 4pm-late Wed-Fri, 1pm-late Sat & Sun; ☒ Fortitude Valley) What rooftop Elixir lacks in views it makes up for in ambience. Hurry up the stairs for a sultry, tropical playpen of lush leaves, flickering tealights, DJ-spun beats and languid day beds. Refresh

with craft beers or Elixir's Fresh Market martini, a twist on the classic using hand-picked market fruits. Check the website for weekly drinks and food promotions.

Alfred & Constance BAR
(Map p68; ☏ 07-3251 6500; www.alfredand constance.com.au; 130 Constance St; ⊙ 7am-late; ☒ Fortitude Valley) Eccentric A&C occupies two old weatherboard houses away from the main Valley action. Suits, surfies and fluoro-clad ditch diggers roam between the cafe, tiki bar and beer garden, eyeing up a kooky jumble of chandeliers, skeletons, surfboards and old hi-fi equipment. Beneath it all is the Fever Club (open from 9pm Friday and Saturday), an intimate, Berlin-inspired discotheque with flashing LED lights and a pop/disco playlist.

Press Club COCKTAIL BAR
(Map p68; ☏ 07-3852 5000; www.pressclub.net. au; 339 Brunswick St; ⊙ 7pm-2.30am Tue-Thu, 6pm-3am Fri & Sat, 6pm-2am Sun; ☒ Fortitude Valley) Looking more like a hang-out for aliens than journos (picture sci-fi bar stools and glowing chandeliers), Press Club sets an offbeat scene for cocktails, ciders and smooth live tunes. Head in Tuesday and Saturday for R&B, Wednesday for jazz, Thursday for swing, or Friday for funk and soul. Tuesday nights are especially huge while Sunday's DJ sets are popular with local 'hospo' (hospitality) peeps.

Cru Bar & Cellar WINE BAR
(Map p68; ☏ 07-3252 1744; www.crubar.com; 22 James St; ⊙ bar 11am-late, wine shop 9am-7pm Sat-Thu, 9am-8pm Fri; ☒ 470, ☒ Fortitude Valley) A sassy enoteca with fold-back windows, Cru seduces oenophiles with a ferocious wine list. A hefty number of drops by the glass span all price points, while the wine shop out back stocks an impressive selection, including a robust booty of French wines, blue-blooded Italian amarone, even Queensland tempranillo. The food is a little hit and miss; stick to the oysters and cheese.

🍷 New Farm

★ The Triffid BAR
(Map p54; ☏ 07-3171 3001; www.thetriffid.com.au; 7-9 Stratton St, Newstead; ☒ 300, 302, 305, 306, 322, 393) Not only does the Triffid have an awesome beer garden (complete with shipping-container bars and a cassette-themed mural honouring Brisbane bands), it's also one of the city's top live-music venues. Music

acts span local, Aussie and international talent, playing in a barrel-vaulted WWII hangar with killer acoustics. It's hardly surprising given that the place is owned by former Powderfinger bassist John Collins.

★ **Green Beacon Brewing Co**   MICROBREWERY
(Map p54; ☑07-3252 8393; www.greenbeacon. com.au; 26 Helen St, Teneriffe; ☺noon-late; ☏; ☐393, 470, ☒Teneriffe) In a cavernous warehouse in post-industrial Teneriffe, Green Beacon brews some of Brisbane's best beers. The liquid beauties ferment in vast stainless-steel vats behind the long bar before flowing through the taps and onto your grateful palate. Choose from six core beers or seasonal specials like blood-orange IPA. Peckish? Decent bites include fresh local seafood, and there's always a guest food truck parked out front.

Newstead Brewing Co   MICROBREWERY
(Map p54; ☑07-3172 2488; www.newstead brewing.com.au; 85 Doggett St, Newstead; ☺11am-midnight; ☐60, 393, 470, ☒Teneriffe) What was once a bus depot is now a pumping microbrewery, its 12 taps pouring six standard house brews, one cider and five seasonal beers (dubbed the 'fun stuff' by one staffer). For an enlightening overview, order the paddle board of four different brews. If beer doesn't rock your boat, knock back cocktails, craft spirits or wine from a small, engaging list of smaller producers.

On the food front, ditch the so-so pizzas for the deliciously spicy, tangy buffalo wings.

Death Before Decaf   COFFEE
(Map p68; 3/760 Brunswick St; ☺24hr; ☐195, 196, 199) Kick-ass speciality coffee, brewed all day and all through the night: this ink-loving, headbanging legend is a godsend for people craving a decent cup after 4pm. Death Before Decaf, we salute you.

Kangaroo Point & Woolloongabba

Canvas Club   COCKTAIL BAR
(Map p54; ☑07-3891 2111; www.canvas club.com.au; 16b Logan Rd, Woolloongabba; ☺noon-midnight Tue-Fri, from 10am Sat & Sun; ☐125, 175, 204, 234) Slap bang on Woolloongabba's main eating, drinking and shopping strip, Canvas sets a hip, arty scene for cheeky cocktail sessions. Debate the symbolism of the street-art mural while downing seasonal libations like the Don Pablo (rum, amaro

and apple-and-cinnamon foam) or the silky smooth Bangarang (tequila, watermelon, chilli, coriander, lime and condensed milk). Smashing.

Story Bridge Hotel   PUB
(Map p58; ☑07-3391 2266; www.storybridge hotel.com.au; 200 Main St, Kangaroo Point; ☺6.30am-midnight Sun-Thu, to 1.30am Fri & Sat; ☐234, ☒Thornton St, Holman St) Beneath the bridge at Kangaroo Point, this beautiful 1886 pub and beer garden is perfect for a pint after a long day exploring. Regular live music (see the website for upcoming acts) and a good choice of drinking and eating areas.

Greater Brisbane

★ **Lefty's Old Time Music Hall**   BAR
(Map p66; www.leftysoldtimemusichall.com; 15 Caxton St, Petrie Tce; ☺5pm-late Tue-Sun; ☐375) Paint the town and the front porch too, there's a honky-tonk bar in Brisvegas! Tarted up in chandeliers and mounted moose heads (yep, those are bras hanging off the antlers), scarlet-hued Lefty's keeps the good times rolling with close to 200 whiskies and the sweet twang of live country-and-western. A short, star-spangled food menu includes chilli cheese fried and southern fried chicken.

Regatta Hotel   PUB
(Map p54; ☑07-3871 9595; www.regattahotel. com.au; 543 Coronation Dr, Toowong; ☺6.30am-1am; ☒Regatta) Dressed in iron lacework and prettier than a wedding cake, this 1874 pub is a Brisbane institution. Directly opposite the Regatta CityCat ferry terminal, its revamped drinking spaces include a polished, contemporary main bar, a chi-chi outdoor courtyard and a basement speakeasy called The Walrus Club (open 5pm to late Thursday to Saturday). Check the website for weekly events, which often include live music.

Breakfast Creek Hotel   PUB
(Map p54; ☑07-3262 5988; www.breakfast creekhotel.com; 2 Kingsford Smith Dr, Albion; ☺10am-late; ☐300, 302, 305) Built in 1889 and sporting an eclectic French-Renaissance style, the Breakfast Creek Hotel is a Brisbane icon. The pub offers various bars and dining areas, including a beer garden and an art deco 'private bar' where the wooden kegs are spiked daily at noon. A converted electricity substation on-site is now home to

Substation No 41, an urbane bar with over 400 rums in its inventory.

 Entertainment

Most big-ticket international bands have Brisbane on their radar, and the city regularly hosts top-tier DJ talent. World-class cultural venues offer a year-round program of theatre, dance, music and comedy.

Qtix (☑13 62 46; www.qtix.com.au) is a booking agency, usually for more high brow entertainment.

Live Music

Underground Opera
OPERA

(Map p58; ☑07-3389 0135, 0429 536 472; www.undergroundopera.com.au; Spring Hill Reservoir, Wickham Tce, Spring Hill; ⊙hours vary; ☐30, ☒Central) A professional, Brisbane-based performing-arts company running annual seasons of opera and Broadway musical recitals in the subterranean Spring Hill Reservoir, built between 1871 and 1882. See the website for season dates and prices.

Riverstage
LIVE MUSIC

(Map p58; ☑07-3403 7921; www.brisbane.qld.gov.au/facilities-recreation/arts-and-culture/riverstage; 59 Gardens Point Rd; ☒QUT Gardens Point, ☒Central) Evocatively set in the Botanic Gardens, this outdoor arena hosts no shortage of prolific national and international music acts. Past performers include U2, 5 Seconds of Summer, Ellie Goulding and Flume.

Lock 'n' Load
LIVE MUSIC

(Map p66; ☑07-3844 0142; www.locknloadbistro.com.au; 142 Boundary St, West End; ⊙3pm-late Mon-Thu, from noon Fri, from 7am Sat & Sun; ☎; ☐199) Ebullient and woody, this two-storey gastropub lures an upbeat crowd of music fans, here to watch jazz, acoustic, roots, blues and soul acts take to the small front stage. Catch a gig, then show up for breakfast or lunch the next day (the brekkie of craft-beer baked beans with fat bacon, sour cream, jalapeños and corn bread tames a hangover). Check the website for upcoming gigs.

Max Watt's House of Music
LIVE MUSIC

(Map p66; ☑1300 762 545; www.maxwatts.com.au/brisbane; 125 Boundary St, West End; ☐199) Unobstructed sight lines and an eclectic line-up of local and international talent underscore this intimate music room. Past guests include Toronto post-bop outfit BadBadNotGood, DC-based progressive metal heads Periphery

and LA rapper Kid Ink. Check the website for upcoming gigs.

The Zoo
LIVE MUSIC

(Map p68; ☑07-3854 1381; www.thezoo.com.au; 711 Ann St, Fortitude Valley; ⊙7pm-late Wed-Sun; ☒Fortitude Valley) Going strong since 1992, the Zoo has surrendered a bit of musical territory to Brightside, but it is still a grungy spot for indie rock, folk, acoustic, hip-hop, reggae and electronic acts, with no shortage of raw talent. Recent acts have included Gold Coast garage rockers Bleeding Knees Club and American indie pop artist Toro y Moi.

Brightside
LIVE MUSIC

(Map p68; www.thebrightsidebrisbane.com.au; 27 Warner St, Fortitude Valley; ⊙noon-late Tue-Fri, 5pm-5am Sat; ☎; ☒Fortitude Valley) The foundation stone of this 1906 church says 'To the glory of God'. But it's the god of live alternative rock the faithful are here to worship these days: heavy, impassioned, unhinged and unfailingly loud. Acts usually hit the stage Thursday to Saturday, playing anything from punk, hardcore and metal to indie, alternative and pop. Just like 1991, minus the cigarettes.

Brisbane Jazz Club
JAZZ

(Map p58; ☑07-3391 2006; www.brisbanejazzclub.com.au; 1 Annie St, Kangaroo Point; adult/under 18yr $31/11; ⊙6.30-11pm Thu-Sat, 5.30-10pm Sun; ☒Holman St) Straight out of the bayou, this tiny riverside jazz shack has been Brisbane's jazz beacon since 1972. Anyone who's anyone in the scene plays here when they're in town.

Cinemas

South Bank Cineplex
CINEMA

(Map p58; ☑07-3829 7970; www.cineplex.com.au; cnr Grey & Ernest Sts, South Bank; adult/child from $6.50/4.50; ⊙10am-late; ☒South Bank Terminals 1, 2 & 3, ☒South Bank) The cheapest complex for mainstream releases: wade through a sea of popcorn aromas and teenagers.

Palace Centro
CINEMA

(Map p68; ☑07-3852 4488; www.palacecinemas.com.au; 39 James St, Fortitude Valley; adult/child $18/12; ⊙9am-late; ☐470, ☒Fortitude Valley) On see-and-be-seen James St, Palace Centro screens quality mainstream releases as well as independent films. It also hosts a French film festival in March/April. Discounted tickets are offered on Monday.

New Farm Six Cinemas CINEMA
(Map p68; ☑ 07-3358 4444; www.newfarm
cinemas.com.au; 701 Brunswick St, New Farm;
adult/child $16/10; ⊙ 10am-late; ☐ 195, 196, 199)
When those subtropical heavens open up,
take refuge at New Farm's historic movie
palace. Recently remodelled and restored,
its six, state-of-the-art screening rooms
show mostly mainstream new releases.
Tuesday is popular with penny-pinching
film buffs, with all tickets a bargain $8.

Theatre & Performing Arts

Queensland Performing
Arts Centre PERFORMING ARTS
(QPAC; Map p58; ☑ guided tours 07-3840 7444, tickets 136 246; www.qpac.com.au; Queensland Cultural
Centre, cnr Grey & Melbourne Sts, South Bank; tours
adult/child $15/10; ⊙ box office 9am-8.30pm Mon-
Sat; ☒ South Bank Terminals 1 & 2, ☒ South Brisbane) Brisbane's main performing arts centre
comprises four venues and a small exhibition
space focused on aspects of the performing
arts. The centre's busy calendar includes bal-
let, concerts, theatre and comedy, from both
Australian and international acts. One-hour
backstage tours run on Friday from 10.30am;
book tickets by phone or email, or purchase
them on the day from the ground-floor QPAC
cafe.

Metro Arts Centre ARTS CENTRE
(Map p58; ☑ 07-3002 7100; www.metroarts.com.
au; Level 2, 109 Edward St; ⊙ gallery 10am-4.30pm
Mon-Fri, 2-4.30pm Sat, performance times vary;
☒ Eagle St Pier, ☒ Central) This downtown venue
hosts community theatre, local dramatic pieces, dance and art shows. It's an effervescent
spot for a taste of Brisbane's creative talent,

be it offbeat, quirky, fringe, progressive or just
downright weird. The on-site gallery hosts
thought-provoking temporary art exhibitions
and associated artist talks. See the website for
upcoming exhibitions, performances and special events.

QUT Gardens Theatre THEATRE
(Map p58; ☑ 07-3138 4455; www.gardenstheatre.
qut.edu.au; 2 George St, Queensland University of
Technology; ⊙ box office 10am-4pm Mon-Fri; ☒ QUT
Gardens Point, ☒ Central) Despite the theatre's
location on a city university campus, productions here are anything but amateur. Expect
to see some of Australia's best professional
stage actors here.

Judith Wright Centre
of Contemporary Arts PERFORMING ARTS
(Map p68; ☑ 07-3872 9000; www.judithwright
centre.com; 420 Brunswick St, Fortitude Valley; ⊙ box
office 11am-4pm Mon-Fri; ☎; ☒ Fortitude Valley)
Home to both a medium-sized and intimate
performance space, this free-thinking arts
incubator hosts an eclectic array of cultural
treats, including contemporary dance, circus
and visual arts. It's also the hub for the hugely
popular Bigsound Festival (p69), a three-day
music fest in September. Scan the website for
upcoming performances and exhibitions.

Brisbane Powerhouse PERFORMING ARTS
(Map p54; ☑ box office 07-3358 8600; www.brisbane
powerhouse.org; 119 Lamington St, New Farm;
☐ 195, 196, ☒ New Farm Park) What was a 1920s
power station is now a buzzing hub of na-
tionally and internationally acclaimed theatre, music, comedy, dance and more. There
are loads of happenings at the Powerhouse –
some free – as well as popular in-house bars

OUTDOOR CINEMA

One of the best ways to spend a warm summer night in Brisbane is with a picnic basket
and some friends at an outdoor cinema. **Moonlight Cinema** (Map p54; www.moonlight.
com.au; Brisbane Powerhouse, 119 Lamington Rd, New Farm; adult/child $17/12.50; ⊙ 7pm Wed-
Sun; ☐ 195, 196, ☒ New Farm Park) runs between December and early March at New Farm
Park near the Brisbane Powerhouse. Films, which include current mainstream releases
and the odd cult classic, screen from Wednesday to Sunday, flickering into life around
7pm.

A parallel option is **Ben & Jerry's Openair Cinemas** (Map p58; www.openaircinemas.
com.au; Rainforest Green, South Bank Parklands, South Bank; adult/child online $17/12, at the gate
$22/17; ⊙ from 5.30pm Tue-Sat, from 5pm Sun; ☒ South Bank Terminals 1 & 2, ☒ South Brisbane)
at South Bank, where from late September to mid-November you can watch big-screen
classics and recent releases under the stars (or clouds) at the Rainforest Green at South
Bank Parklands. Hire a beanbag or deckchair, or bring a picnic rug. Note that most sessions
sell out online prior to the night of the screening, so book in advance. Live music (which
sometimes includes prolific Australian acts) runs beforehand.

and restaurants with standout views over the Brisbane River. See the website for upcoming events.

Sport

Suncorp Stadium
STADIUM

(Map p66; www.suncorpstadium.com.au; 40 Castlemaine St, Milton; 375, 379) In winter, rugby league is the big spectator sport here and local team the Brisbane Broncos call this stadium home.

The Gabba
STADIUM

(Brisbane Cricket Ground; Map p54; www.thegabba.com.au; 411 Vulture St, Woolloongabba; 174, 175, 184, 185, 200) You can cheer both AFL football and interstate and international cricket at the Gabba in Woolloongabba, south of Kangaroo Point. If you're new to cricket, try and get along to a Twenty20 match, which sees the game in its most explosive form. The cricket season runs from late September to March; the football from late March to September.

Comedy

Paddo Tavern
COMEDY

(Map p66; 07-3369 4466; www.standup.com.au; 186 Given Tce, Paddington; pub 10am-late, comedy shows vary; 375) If a car wash married its supermarket cousin, their first-born would probably look like this ugly Paddington pub, which has incongruously adopted a pseudo Wild West theme inside. But it's one of the best places in Brisbane to see stand-up comedy: check the website for listings.

Shopping

Brisbane's retail landscape is deliciously eclectic, stretching from *Vogue*-indexed high-end handbags to weekend-market arts and craft.

Central Brisbane

Noosa Chocolate Factory
FOOD

(Map p58; www.noosachocolatefactory.com.au; 144 Adelaide St; 8am-7pm Mon-Thu, to 9pm Fri, 9am-6pm Sat, 10am-5pm Sun; Central) Don't delude yourself: the small batch, artisanal chocolates from this Sunshine Coast Willy Wonka will override any self-control. Best sellers include generous, marshmallowy Rocky Road and a very Queensland concoction of unroasted macadamias covered in Bowen mango–flavoured chocolate. Best of all, the chocolate here is palm-oil free. A second branch at No 156 also serves speciality coffee and hot chocolate.

Maiocchi
FASHION & ACCESSORIES

(Map p58; 07-3012 9640; www.maiocchi.com.au; Brisbane Arcade, 117 Adelaide St; 9am-5.30pm Mon-Thu, 8.30am-8pm Fri, 9am-4pm Sat, 11am-4pm Sun; Central) Home-grown label Maiocchi is well known for its gorgeous, vintage-inspired frocks, simple in cut but rich in little details and quirks. Expect custom prints, '50s silhouettes and the Japanese influences. Your next summery cocktail dress aside, the boutique also stocks tops, pants and shoes, as well as a thoughtfully curated selection of Australian-made jewellery, bags and homewares. You'll find it in the heritage-listed Brisbane Arcade.

Jan Powers Farmers Market
MARKET

(Map p58; www.janpowersfarmersmarkets.com.au; Reddacliff Place, George St; 8am-6pm Wed; North Quay, Central) Central Brisbane lives out its bucolic village fantasies when local growers and artisans descend on Reddacliff Place to sell their prized goods. Fill your shopping bags with just-picked fruit and vegetables, meats and seafood, fresh pasta, fragrant breads, pastries and more. Stock up for a picnic in the City Botanic Gardens, or simply grab a coffee and a ready-to-eat, multiculti bite.

Archives Fine Books
BOOKS

(Map p58; 07-3221 0491; www.archivesfinebooks.com.au; 40 Charlotte St; 9am-6pm Mon-Thu, to 7pm Fri, to 5pm Sat; Central) Rickety bookshelves and squeaky floorboards set a nostalgic scene at this sprawling repository of pre-loved pages. While the true number of books on offer is a little less than the one million claimed (our little secret), the place is a veritable sea of engaging titles. The oldest book on our last visit – by the canonised Roberto Francesco Romolo Bellarmino – dated back to 1630.

Folio Books
BOOKS

(Map p58; 07-3210 0500; www.foliobooks.com.au; 133 Mary St; 8.30am-6pm Mon-Thu, to 7pm Fri, to 5pm Sat, 10am-4pm Sun; Eagle St Pier, Central) Bibliophiles flock to Folio for an eclectic, sophisticated collection of titles covering everything from Canberra politics and Queensland modernism, to international art, gastronomy, design and fiction. Staff are helpful, and the place is utterly dangerous for those skilled at losing track of time.

RM Williams
CLOTHING

(Map p58; 07-3229 3354; www.rmwilliams.com.au; Lower Ground, Wintergarden, 171-209 Queen St

THE BARRACKS

Across a footbridge from Roma St Station or a short walk away from Caxton St in Petrie Terrace, the **Barracks** (Map p66; ☑ 07-3011 9022; www.thebarracks.info; 61 Petrie Tce, Petrie Terrace; ☐ 375, 379) once served as a jail (1860 to 1883), then as a police depot (until the 1940s), and then sat derelict for decades before reopening as a mixed-use development in 2008, following a $120 million overhaul.

Comprising three big heritage-listed buildings from its former days, the development was hailed an immediate success (and garnered national awards) in the realm of urban renewal, and Brisbanites have embraced it as their own – noir history and all.

The Barracks houses the six-screen **Palace Barracks** (Map p66; ☑ 07-3367 1954; www.palacecinemas.com.au; 61 Petrie Tce, Petrie Terrace; adult/concession/child $19/14.50/13; ⏰ 10am-late; ☐ 375, 379) cinema as well as a major supermarket, liquor store and a small handful of shops and casual eateries.

Mall; ⏰ 9am-6pm Mon-Thu, to 9pm Fri, to 5pm Sat, 10am-4.30pm Sun; ☒ Central) An iconic manufacturer of stylish Aussie bush/farm gear, RM Williams stocks high-quality leather boots, hats, oilskin jackets, belts, jumpers and shirts; the kind of stuff your wealthy agricultural uncle would wear when he makes the trip into town.

Record Exchange   MUSIC
(Map p58; ☑ 07-3229 4923; www.therecordexchange.com.au; Level 1, 65 Adelaide St; ⏰ 9am-5pm Mon-Thu, to 9pm Fri, 9.30am-5pm Sat, 10am-4pm Sun; ☒ Central) This jam-packed upstairs shop is home to an astounding collection of vinyl, CDs, DVDs, posters and other rock memorabilia. 'Brisbane's most interesting shop' (self-professed).

South Bank & West End

Where The Wild Things Are   BOOKS
(Map p66; ☑ 07-3255 3987; www.wherethewildthingsare.com.au; 191 Boundary St, West End; ⏰ 8.30am-6pm Mon-Sat, to 5pm Sun; ☝ ; ☐ 199) Little brother to Avid Reader next door, Where The Wild Things Are stocks a whimsical collection of books for toddlers, older kids and teens. The bookshop also runs regular activities, from weekly story-time sessions to book launches, signings and crafty workshops covering themes like book illustration. Scan the bookshop's website and Facebook page for upcoming events.

Jet Black Cat Music   MUSIC
(Map p66; ☑ 0419 571 299; www.facebook.com/jetblackcatmusic; 72 Vulture St, West End; ⏰ 10.30am-5pm Tue-Fri, 10am-4pm Sat; ☐ 199) Serious music fans know all about Shannon Logan and her little West End record shop. She's usually behind the piano-cum-counter, chatting with a loyal fan base who drop in for an in-the-know, hard-to-find booty of indie vinyl and CDs. Logan only sells what she's passionate about, and the place also hosts occasional in-store gigs showcasing well-known local and international indie talent.

Junky Comics   BOOKS
(Map p66; ☑ 07-3846 5456; www.junkycomicsbrisbane.com; 93 Vulture St, West End; ⏰ 10am-5.30pm Tue-Fri, to 5pm Sat, to 4pm Sun; ☐ 199) Indie Junky stocks comics with cred, from classic DC, Dark Horse and Marvel titles, to female-, queer- and child-orientated works. You'll also find locally produced zines, graphic novels, art and prints, not to mention cool tees.

Fortitude Valley

Camilla   FASHION & ACCESSORIES
(Map p68; ☑ 07-3852 6030; www.camilla.com.au; 1/19 James St; ⏰ 9.30am-5pm Mon-Wed, Fri & Sat, to 7pm Thu, 10am-4pm Sun; ☐ 470, ☒ Fortitude Valley) Fans of Camilla's statement-making silk kaftans include Beyoncé and Oprah Winfrey. And while the label may be Bondi based, its wildly patterned, resort-style creations – which also include frocks, tops, jumpsuits and swimwear – are just the ticket for languid lounging in chi-chi Brisbane restaurants and bars. Fierce and fabulous, these pieces aren't cheap, with kaftans starting from $500 and bikinis at around $300.

Libertine   PERFUME
(Map p68; ☑ 07-3216 0122; www.libertineparfumerie.com.au; 181 Robertson St; ⏰ 10am-5pm Mon-Fri, 9.30am-5pm Sat, 10am-4pm Sun; ☐ 470,

TO MARKET, TO MARKET

Beyond the weekly farmers markets that feed the masses in central Brisbane (p88), New Farm and West End is a string of other fantastic local markets, peddling anything from handmade local fashion and bling, to art, skincare and out-of-the-box giftware. Hit the stalls at the following options.

Young Designers Market (Map p58; www.youngdesignersmarket.com.au; Little Stanley St, South Bank; ⊙10am-4pm, 1st Sun of the month; ᎏSouth Bank Terminal 3, ⺁South Bank) Explore the work of up to 80 of the city's best emerging designers and artists, selling fashion and accessories, contemporary jewellery, art, furniture and homewares. Held beside South Bank Parklands, the market generally runs on the first Sunday of the month.

Collective Markets South Bank (Map p58; www.collectivemarkets.com.au; Stanley St Plaza; ⊙5-9pm Fri, 10am-9pm Sat, 9am-4pm Sun; ᎏSouth Bank Terminal 3, ⺁South Bank) It might draw the tourist hordes, but this thrice-weekly event by South Bank Parklands peddles some great items, from artisan leather wallets and breezy summer frocks, to handmade jewellery, skincare, homewares and art.

Finders Keepers Markets A biannual market with over 100 art and design stalls held in a 19th-century museum that's now a concert hall in inner-suburban Bowen Hills. Complete with live music and food, it's a great spot to score high-quality, one-off fashion pieces, jewellery and more from local and interstate design talent.

Brisbane Riverside Markets (Map p58; ☑07-3870 2807; www.facebook.com/brisbane riversidemarkets; City Botanic Gardens, Alice St; ⊙8am-3pm Sun; ᎏQUT Gardens Point, ⺁Central) Come Sunday, chilled-out crowds gather at the northern end of the City Botanic Gardens for this weekly city-centre market. Scan the stalls for pretty, handmade frocks, scented candles, colourful ceramics and a plethora of street food from all corners of the globe. Live music keeps the mood festive and the peeps grooving.

⺁Fortitude Valley) While you won't stumble across any celeb-endorsed eau de toilettes at Libertine, you will discover some of the world's most coveted and hard-to-find perfume and skincare brands for women and men. Among them is Amouage (established for the Sultan of Oman), Santa Maria Novella and Creed, the latter's in-store offerings including the very fragrance created for Princess Grace on her wedding day.

Fallow
FASHION & ACCESSORIES

(Map p68; ☑07-3854 0155; www.fallow.com.au; Level 1, 354 Brunswick St; ⊙11am-5pm Mon-Fri, 10am-5pm Sat, 11am-4pm Sun; ⺁Fortitude Valley) Up a flight of stairs is this brooding chamber of avant-garde men's fashion. The focus is on sculptural, androgynous pieces from cult-status ateliers not usually stocked in Australia (think Germany's Pal Offner and Denmark's Aleksandr Manamis). Accessories include handmade fragrances from France's Mad et Len and an exquisite collection of handmade jewellery, including Gothic- and Edwardian-inspired pieces by Brisbane-based Luke Maninov.

Tym Guitars
MUSIC

(Map p68; ☑07-3161 5863; www.tymguitars.com.au; 5 Winn St; ⊙10am-5pm Tue-Thu & Sat, to 7pm Fri, 11am-4pm Sat; ⺁Fortitude Valley) Cult-status music store Tym stocks everything from vintage guitars and amps to handmade guitar pedals. (It's the kind of place where you might find a limited-edition pedal made by the likes of American alt-rocker J Mascis of Dinosaur Jr.) Tym's vinyl selection includes an especially notable collection of punk, stoner and psychedelic rock records, and the space hosts monthly alt-rock gigs.

Miss Bond
JEWELLERY

(Map p68; ☑0410 526 082; www.facebook.com/ missbond.com.au; 5g Winn Lane; ⊙10am-4pm Wed-Sat, to 3pm Sun; ⺁Fortitude Valley) Her name is Bond. Kerrie Bond. And if it isn't handmade, she won't sell it. What you will find in Miss Bond's driveway-turned-studio is a curated selection of fetching, locally made jewellery. The pieces here are striking and imaginative, many made using recycled silver, gold, pearls and op-shop materials. Wearables aside, the space also sells beautiful ceramics.

Outpost FASHION & ACCESSORIES
(Map p68; ☑07-3666 0306; www.theoutpost
store.com.au; 5 Winn St; ⊙10am-6pm Tue-Thu & Sat,
to 8pm Fri, 9.30am-4.30pm Sun; ℝFortitude Valley)
Hipsters and urban lumberjacks hit Outpost
for cool, workwear-inspired threads from the
likes of Japan's Edwin, Australia's Invicta Venture and Station Stripes and America's Car-
hartt. The store stocks its own retro-print tees,
as well as an eclectic mix of designer flasks,
backpacks, cow- and kangaroo-leather wallets, artwork and beautifully crafted knives
from France's Opinel. There's an in-house bar-
ber on Sunday.

Stock & Supply FASHION & ACCESSORIES
(Map p68; ☑07-3061 7530; www.stockand
supply.com.au; 4/694 Ann St; ℝFortitude Valley)
Technically on Bakery Lane, just off Ann St,
this youthful, unisex bolthole serves up a
cool selection of smaller surf and streetwear
brands. Pick up anything from graphic tees
to beachwear from the likes of skater outfit
Crawling Death and surf-meets-art label The
Critical Slide Society. The store also stocks
wallets, jewellery, caps and footwear.

James Street FASHION & ACCESSORIES
(Map p68; www.jamesst.com.au; James St; ☐470,
ℝFortitude Valley) Channelling LA with its
low-slung architecture, sports cars and chic
eateries is the Valley's glamtastic stretch
of James St. Slip under its colonnade of
fig trees for high-end boutiques, including
celebrated Aussie fashion labels Scanlan &
Theodore and Sass & Bide, home-grown designer Camilla Franks and Melbourne skincare brand Aesop.

Winn Lane FASHION & ACCESSORIES
(Map p68; www.winnlane.com.au; Winn Lane;
ℝFortitude Valley) Duck behind Ann St (off
Winn St) and discover this arty congrega-
tion of boutiques, bookshops, jewellers and
casual eats. Spangled with street art, the
lane has a vibe that is emerging and quirky.
Don't miss Miss Bond for contemporary,
locally designed jewellery, Outpost for in-
the-know men's labels and accessories and,
just off Winn Lane, Tym Guitars, famed for
its handmade guitar pedals, vintage guitars
and punk-heavy vinyl collection.

Butter Beats MUSIC
(Map p68; ☑07-3257 3257; www.butterbeats
recordstore.com; 11/8 Duncan St; ⊙11am-5pm;
ℝFortitude Valley) Rare and collectable records in the Valley, including old-school

Aussie indie. If they don't have it, they'll find
it for you. Also stocks street-art supplies if
you're in the mood for some tagging.

🛍 New Farm

Commercial Road Antiques ANTIQUES
(Map p54; ☑07-3852 2352; 85 Commercial Rd,
Teneriffe; ⊙10am-5pm; ☐393, 470, ⛴Teneriffe)
Whether you're on the prowl for a Victorian dresser, a mid-century armchair or a '60s
beatnik frock, chances are you'll find it in
this warren of eclectic antiques and retro.
It's especially great for vintage glassware,
and there's usually a good selection of tribal
and Asian decorative objects.

Jan Powers Farmers Market MARKET
(Map p54; www.janpowersfarmersmarkets.com.au;
Brisbane Powerhouse, 119 Lamington St; ⊙6am-
noon Sat; ☐195, 196, ⛴New Farm Park) Hankering for some purple heirloom carrots or
blue bananas? Chances are you'll find them
at this abundant, appetite-piquing farmers
market. Grab a croissant and coffee and
soak up the spectacle of buxom fruit and
vegetables, cheeses, fish, silky olives, coffee
and colourful flowers. Best of all, the CityCat
will take you straight there.

🛍 Greater Brisbane

Finders Keepers Markets MARKET
(Map p54; www.thefinderskeepers.com/brisbane-
markets; Old Museum, 480 Gregory Tce, Bowen
Hills; adult/child $2/free; ⊙hours vary; ☐370,
375, ℝFortitude Valley) A biannual market
with over 100 art and design stalls held in
a 19th-century museum that's now a concert
hall in inner-suburban Bowen Hills. Complete with live music and food, it's a great
spot to score high-quality, one-off fashion
pieces, jewellery and more from local and
interstate design talent.

Paddington Antique Centre ANTIQUES
(Map p54; ☑07-3369 8088; www.paddington
antiquecentre.com.au; 167 Latrobe Tce, Paddington; ⊙10am-5pm Mon-Sat, to 4pm Sun; ☐375)
Built in 1929, this former theatre is now
a sprawling antiques emporium. Over 50
dealers sell all manner of treasure and trash
under a peeling, midnight-blue ceiling,
from flouncy English crockery, to retro fashion, lamps, toys, film posters, even the odd
17th-century Chinese vase. Take your time
and pay attention – you never know what
you might find.

BRISBANE & AROUND INFORMATION

Davies Park Market MARKET
(Map p66; www.daviesparkmarket.com.au; Davies Park, West End; ⊙6am-2pm Sat; 🚌199, 192, 198) Under a grove of huge Moreton Bay fig trees, this popular, laid-back Saturday market heaves with fresh produce, not to mention a gut-rumbling booty of multicultural food stalls. Grab an organic coffee from the Gyspy Vardo, sip it on a milk crate, then scour the place for organic fruit and veggies, artisanal provisions, herbs, flowers, handmade jewellery and even the odd bonsai.

Portside Wharf SHOPPING CENTRE
(🕿07-3907 4111; www.portsidewharf.com.au; 39 Hercules St, Hamilton; 🚢Bretts Wharf) A few ferry stops downriver from New Farm is Portside Wharf, Brisbane's cruise-ship terminal, which has spawned a shopping-and-eating complex and a copse of apartment towers. The vibe is a little contrived, but some of the restaurants here are beautifully sited overlooking the river. To get here, take the CityCat ferry to Bretts Wharf, and follow the riverside path 500m further east.

ⓘ Information

EMERGENCY

Ambulance, Fire, Police	🕿000
International Access Code	🕿0011
Reverse Charges	🕿1800-REVERSE (738 3773)

INTERNET ACCESS

Brisbane City Council offers free wi-fi access in much of central Brisbane (the CBD), and you will also find free wi-fi hot spots at South Bank Parklands, Roma Street Parkland, the State Library of Queensland, James St in Fortitude Valley and New Farm Park.

Brisbane Square Library (www.brisbane.qld. gov.au; 266 George St; ⊙9am-6pm Mon-Thu, to 7pm Fri, 10am-3pm Sat & Sun; 🛜; 🚌North Quay, 🚉Central) Free wi-fi access.

MEDICAL SERVICES

CBD Medical Centre (🕿07-3211 3611; www. cbdmedical.com.au; Level 1, 245 Albert St; ⊙7am-7pm Mon-Fri, 8.30am-5pm Sat, 9.30am-5pm Sun; 🚉Central) General medical services and vaccinations.

Royal Brisbane & Women's Hospital (🕿07-3646 8111; www.health.qld.gov.au/rbwh; Butterfield St, Herston; 🚌370, 375, 333) Located 3km north of the city centre. Has a 24-hour casualty ward.

Travellers' Medical & Vaccination Centre (TMVC; 🕿07-3815 6900; www.traveldoctor. com.au; 75a Astor Tce, Spring Hill; ⊙8.30am-4.30pm Mon-Fri; 🚉Central) Travellers' medical services.

MONEY

American Express (🕿1300 139 060; www. americanexpress.com; 261 Queen St; ⊙9am-5.30pm Mon-Fri; 🚉Central) Foreign exchange bureau.

Travelex (🕿07-3210 6325; www.travelex. com.au; Shop 149F, Myer Centre, Queen St Mall; ⊙8am-6pm Mon-Thu, to 8pm Fri, 9am-5pm Sat, 10am-4pm Sun; 🚉Central) Money exchange.

POST

Main Post Office (GPO; Map p58; 🕿13 13 18; www.auspost.com.au; 261 Queen St; ⊙7am-6pm Mon-Fri, 10am-1.30pm Sat; 🚉Central) Brisbane's main post office.

TOURIST INFORMATION

Brisbane Visitor Information & Booking Centre (Map p58; 🕿07-3006 6290; www. visitbrisbane.com.au; The Regent, 167 Queen St Mall; ⊙9am-5.30pm Mon-Thu, to 7pm Fri, to 5pm Sat, 10am-5pm Sun; 🚉Central) Terrific one-stop info counter for all things Brisbane.

South Bank Visitor Information Centre (Map p58; 🕿07-3156 6366; www.visitbrisbane.com. au; Stanley St Plaza. South Bank; ⊙9am-5pm; 🚢South Bank Terminal 3, 🚉South Bank) One of Brisbane's official tourist information hubs, with brochures, maps and festival guides, plus tour and accommodation bookings, and tickets to entertainment events.

ⓘ Getting There & Away

AIR

Sixteen kilometres northeast of the city centre, Brisbane Airport (p303) is the third-busiest airport in Australia and the main international airport serving Brisbane and southeastern Queensland.

It has separate international and domestic terminals about 2km apart, linked by the Airtrain (p93), which runs every 15 to 30 minutes from 5am (6am on weekends) to 10pm (between terminals $5/free per adult/child).

It's a busy hub, with frequent domestic connections to other Australian capital cities and regional towns, as well as nonstop international flights to New Zealand, the Pacific islands, North America and Asia (with onward connections to Europe and Africa).

BUS

Brisbane's main bus terminus and booking office for long-distance buses is the **Brisbane Transit Centre** (Roma St Station; www.brisbane transitcentre.com.au; Roma St), about 500m northwest of the city centre. It also incorporates Roma St train station, which services both long-distance and suburban trains.

Booking desks for **Greyhound** (📱1300 473 946, 07-4690 9850; www.greyhound.com.au) and **Premier Motor Service** (📱13 34 10; www. premierms.com.au) are here.

Long-haul routes include Cairns, Darwin and Sydney, though it's usually just as affordable to fly, not to mention a lot quicker.

CAR & MOTORCYCLE

Brisbane has an extensive network of motorways, tunnels and bridges (some of them tolled) run by **Transurban Queensland** (📱13 33 31; www.govianetwork.com.au). The Gateway Motorway (M1) runs through Brisbane's eastern suburbs, shooting north towards the Sunshine Coast and northern Queensland and south towards the Gold Coast and Sydney. See the Transurban Queensland website for toll details and fees.

Major car-rental companies have offices at Brisbane Airport and in the city. Smaller rental companies with branches near the airport (and shuttles to get you to/from there) include **Ace Rental Cars** (📱1800 620 408; www.acerental cars.com.au; 330 Nudgee Rd, Hendra), Apex Car Rentals (p306) and **East Coast Car Rentals** (📱1800 327 826; www.eastcoastcarrentals. com.au; 504 Nudgee Rd, Hendra).

TRAIN

Brisbane's main station for long-distance trains is Roma St Station (essentially the same complex as the Brisbane Transit Centre). For reservations and information contact **Queensland Rail** (📱13 16 17; www.queenslandrail.com.au).
NSW TrainLink Brisbane to Sydney.
Spirit of Queensland Brisbane to Cairns.
Spirit of the Outback Brisbane to Longreach via Bundaberg, Gladstone and Rockhampton.
Tilt Train Brisbane to Rockhampton via Bundaberg and Gladstone.
Westlander Brisbane to Charleville.

ℹ Getting Around

Brisbane's excellent public transport network – bus, train and ferry – is run by TransLink, which runs a Transit Information Centre at Roma St Station (Brisbane Transit Centre). The tourist offices in the city centre and South Bank can also help with public transport information. Complementing the network is a nifty network of bike paths.

TO/FROM THE AIRPORT

Airtrain (📱1800 119 091; www.airtrain.com. au; adult one-way/return $17.50/33) services run every 15 to 30 minutes from 5am (6am on weekends) to 10pm, connecting Brisbane airport's two terminals to central Brisbane. Handy stops include Fortitude Valley, Central Station, Roma St Station (Brisbane Transit Centre), South Brisbane and South Bank (one-way/ return $17.50/33). Trains continue to the Gold Coast (one-way from $33.70).

Con-X-ion (📱1300 370 471; www.con-x-ion. com) runs regular shuttle buses between the airport and hotels in the Brisbane city centre (one-way/return $20/36). It also connects Brisbane Airport to Gold Coast hotels and private residences (one-way/return $49/92), as well as to Sunshine Coast hotels and private residences (one-way/return from $52/96). Book tickets online.

A taxi to central Brisbane costs $50 to $60.

CAR & MOTORCYCLE

Ticketed two-hour parking is available on many streets in the CBD and the inner suburbs. Heed the signs: Brisbane's parking inspectors are pretty ruthless. During the day, parking is cheaper around South Bank and the West End than in the city centre, but it's free in the CBD in the evening from 6pm weekdays (from noon on Saturday). For more detailed information on parking, see www.visitbrisbane.com.au/parking.

PUBLIC TRANSPORT

Buses, trains and ferries operate on an eight-zone system: all of the inner-city suburbs are in Zone 1, which translates into a single fare of $4.60/2.30 per adult/child. If travelling into Zone 2, tickets are $5.70/2.85.

If you plan to use public transport for more than a few trips, you'll save money by purchasing a **Go Card** (www.translink.com.au/tickets-and-fares/go-card; starting balance adult/child $10/5). Purchase the card, add credit and then use it on city buses, trains and ferries, and you'll save more than 30% off individual fares. Go Cards are sold (and can be recharged) at transit stations, 7-Eleven convenience stores, newsagents, by phone or online. You can also top-up on CityCat ferry services (cash only).

Boat

CityCat (p64) catamarans service 18 ferry terminals between the University of Queensland in St Lucia and Northshore Hamilton. Handy stops include South Bank, the three CBD terminals, New Farm Park (for Brisbane Powerhouse) and Bretts Wharf (for Eat Street Markets). Services run roughly every 15 minutes from 5.20am to around midnight. Tickets can be bought on board or, if you have one, use your Go Card.

Free CityHopper ferries zigzag back and forth across the water between North Quay, South Bank, the CBD, Kangaroo Point and Sydney St in New Farm. These additional services start around 6am and run till about 11pm.

TransLink also runs Cross River Ferries, connecting Kangaroo Point with the CBD, and New Farm Park with Norman Park on the adjacent shore (and also Teneriffe and Bulimba further north). Ferries run every 10 to 30 minutes from around 6am to around 11pm. Fares/zones apply as per all other Brisbane transport.

For more information, including timetables, see www.brisbaneferries.com.au.

Bus

Brisbane's bus network is extensive and especially handy for reaching West End, Kangaroo Point, Woolloongabba, Fortitude Valley, Newstead, as well as Paddington.

In the city centre, the main stops for local buses are the underground **Queen Street Bus Station** (Map p58) and **King George Square Bus Station** (Map p58). You can also pick up many buses from the stops along Adelaide St, between George and Edward Sts.

➡ Buses generally run every 10 to 30 minutes, from around 5am (around 6am Saturday and Sunday) till about 11pm.

➡ CityGlider and BUZ services are high-frequency services along busy routes. Tickets cannot be purchased on board CityGlider and BUZ services; use a Go Card (p93).

➡ Free, hop-on, hop-off City Loop and Spring Hill Loop bus services circle the CBD and Spring Hill, stopping at key spots like QUT, Queen St Mall, City Botanic Gardens, Central Station and Roma Street Parkland. Buses run every 10 minutes on weekdays between 7am and 6pm.

➡ Brisbane also runs dedicated nocturnal NightLink bus, train and fixed-rate taxi services (the latter from specified taxi ranks) from the city and Fortitude Valley. See translink.com.au for details.

Train

TransLink's Citytrain network has six main lines, which run as far north as Gympie on the Sunshine Coast and as far south as Varsity Lakes on the Gold Coast. All trains go through Roma St Station, Central Station and Fortitude Valley Station; there's also a handy South Bank Station.

The Airtrain (p93) service integrates with the Citytrain network in the city centre and along the Gold Coast line.

Trains run from around 4.30am, with the last train on each line leaving Central Station between 11.30pm and midnight (later on Friday and Saturday). On Sunday the last trains run at around 11pm or 11.30pm.

Single train tickets can be bought at train stations, or use your Go Card (p93).

For timetables and a network map, see www.translink.com.au.

Taxi

There are numerous taxi ranks in the city centre, including at Roma St Station, Treasury (corner of George and Queen Sts), Albert St (corner of Elizabeth St) and Edward St (near Elizabeth St). You might have a tough time hailing one late at night in Fortitude Valley: there's a rank near the corner of Brunswick St and Ann St, but expect long queues. The main taxi companies are Black & White (p308) and Yellow Cab Co (p308).

NightLink flat-fare taxis run on Friday and Saturday nights, with dedicated ranks at Elizabeth Street (corner of George St) in the city and on Warner St in Fortitude Valley.

AROUND BRISBANE

Redcliffe

POP 51,180

As the site of Queensland's first European settlement (1824), the Redcliffe Peninsula, jutting into Moreton Bay about 35km north of central Brisbane, talks up its historical credentials. In reality, there are not a whole lot of historic relics to see here. Locals focus squarely on maintaining a relaxed pace of life and a laid-back, beachy suburban vibe permeates the shoreline and backstreets. The area has plenty of unpolished fish-and-chip joints and calm beaches that are right up kids' alleys.

Redcliffe is also the childhood home of the brothers Gibb – Barry, Robin and Maurice. Better known as the Bee Gees, the trio is honoured with an interactive, eponymous laneway.

⊙ Sights & Activities

Redcliffe Museum   MUSEUM

(☑ 07-3883 1898; www.moretonbay.qld.gov.au/ redcliffe-museum; 75 Anzac Ave; ⊙ 10am-4pm Tue-Sun) FREE Inside a converted church, the spick-and-span Redcliffe Museum details the peninsula's history through information boards, a nifty short film, artefacts and a series of personal accounts from locals.

Brisbane Whale Watching WHALE WATCHING
(☑07-3880 0477; www.brisbanewhalewatching.com.au; Redcliffe Jetty, Redcliffe Pde; adult/child incl lunch $135/95) From June to November, Brisbane Whale Watching corrals passengers onto a high-speed catamaran and whizzes them out to see humpback whales as they pass by on their annual migration. Trips depart Redcliffe Jetty. Brisbane pick-ups are available for an extra $30 per person.

Dolphin Wild ADVENTURE
(☑07-3880 4444; www.dolphinwild.com.au; adult/child/family incl lunch $95/65/255, snorkelling tour per adult/child additional $20/10) For a scenic trip around Moreton Bay, sign up for a one-day Moreton Island cruise with Dolphin Wild. Tours include boating around the bay, snorkelling at the Tangalooma wrecks on Moreton Island, lunch and a bit of beach time. Oh, and some dolphins! Tours depart Newport Marina in the suburb of Scarborough, just north of Redcliffe. Brisbane pick-ups available.

🛏 Sleeping

Scarborough Holiday Village CARAVAN PARK $
(☑07-3203 8864; www.scarboroughholidayvillage.com.au; Reef Point Esplanade, Scarborough; powered sites/cabins from $40/150; ❄) Mainly set up for campervans and caravans, this grassy spot occupies the northern tip of Redcliffe Peninsula, near Scarborough's marina. Nab one of the dinky pastel-coloured villas if you're tired of life on the road.

Mon Komo Hotel HOTEL $$
(☑07-32839300;www.oakshotelsresorts.com/mon komo; 99 Marine Pde; d from $160, 1-/2-/3-bedroom apt from $190/260/350; ❄ 🌐 ☳) Much of the accommodation around Redcliffe is a little 'daggy', to use an Australianism. Thankfully, the polished, multistorey Mon Komo remedies this with stylish, contemporary hotel rooms and apartments in soothing, natural hues. On-site perks include an (unheated) swimming pool and buzzing dining-and-drinking terrace out the front, right across from Suttons Beach. Less appealing is the cheeky wi-fi charge ($18 per 24 hours).

ℹ Information

Redcliffe Visitor Information Centre (☑07-3283 3577; Redcliffe Jetty, Redcliffe Pde; ⊙9am-4pm; 🛜) The main visitor centre is in the heart of town, wedged between Redcliffe Pde and the Redcliffe jetty. Pick up brochures, maps, information on the nearby Bee Gees Way and the interesting *Redcliffe Heritage Trail*

brochure. A second **branch** (☑1800 667 386; www.moretonbay.qld.gov.au; Pelican Park, Hornibrook Esplanade, Clontarf; ⊙9am-4pm) is located in Clontarf at the southern base of the peninsula.

ℹ Getting There & Away

Translink (☑13 12 30; www.translink.com.au) bus route 696 connects Redcliffe to Kippa-Ring train station (15 minutes). From Kippa-Ring station, CityTrain services depart for central Brisbane ($8.60, 55 minutes).

Some vehicle ferries to Moreton Island leave from Scarborough Marina, at the northern tip of the headland. Bus route 699 connects Kippa-Ring station to both Newport Marina and Scarborough Marina (seven and 15 minutes, respectively).

Manly & St Helena Island
POP 3700

Just a few kilometres south of the mouth of the Brisbane River, seaside Manly has a busy marina that makes a good base for trips out onto Moreton Bay. Bunched-up at the base of a hillside, the suburb itself is an affluent, self-contained delight, with sunny seaside lawns, a Saturday farmers market and the opportunity to stroll, jog or simply sit back and gaze out at the mangrove-fringed bay.

Manly is also the gateway to little St Helena Island, about 6km from the Brisbane River mouth. A grim high-security prison from 1867 till 1932, St Helena still has the remains of several prison buildings, plus parts of Queensland's first tramway, built in 1884. The old trams were pulled by horses, but these days a tractor drags the coaches along as part of the island tour.

◉ Sights & Activities

St Helena Island TOURS
(☑1300 438 787; www.sthelenaisland.com.au; William Gunn Jetty, Wyvernleigh Cl, Manly; tour adult/child/family $80/45/200) To visit St Helena Island, take a trip from Manly Harbour on the *Cat-O'-Nine-Tails* boat. The five-hour day tour includes a tramway ride and a 'dramatised tour' of the prison, complete with floggings if you so desire. This is the only way you can visit the island.

Jan Powers Farmers Market MARKET
(www.janpowersfarmersmarkets.com.au; Esplanade, btwn Cambridge & Cardigan Pdes, Manly; ⊙6am-noon 1st & 3rd Sat of the month) Down by the shore at Manly, this is an offshoot of the

much-loved Brisbane market of the same name. Grab a takeaway coffee and pique your appetite eyeing-up stalls packed with fresh fruit and veggies, crusty bread, local olive oil, glistening seafood, meats, spices, honey, jams and more.

Royal Queensland Yacht Squadron
BOATING

(RQYS; ☑ 07-3396 8666; www.rqys.com.au; 578 Esplanade, Manly) The estimable Royal Queensland Yacht Squadron, south of the town centre, runs yacht races every Wednesday afternoon, and many of the skippers are happy to take visitors on board for the ride (for free!). Sign on at the club before noon. Ask about sailing lessons if you're interested in learning how to hoist a spinnaker.

🛏 Sleeping & Eating

Manly Marina Cove Motel
MOTEL $$

(☑ 07-3348 1000; www.manlymarinacove.com; 578a Royal Esplanade, Manly; d/f from $170/220; P ❋ 🛜 ⊠) Down by the namesake marina, a short walk along the foreshore from Manly's main street, this motel raises the bar with its wonderfully clean, upbeat, nautically themed rooms. North-facing rooms get the most light while south-facing rooms on the 1st floor come with water views. There's a small plunge pool on-site and the option of breakfast (continental/cooked $13/22).

Tide Wine Bar
CAFE $

(☑ 07-3396 8962; www.tidewinebar.com.au; William Gunn Jetty, 1 Wyvernleigh Cl, Manly; lunch dishes $14-21, dinner mains $18-28; ⊙ 7am-10pm Sun-Thu, to late Fri & Sat, kitchen closes 9pm) Right over the water, modern, breezy Tide Wine Bar will have you sipping smooth lattes and well-priced vino while gazing out at envy-inducing yachts. Food options cover all bases: morning bircher, pancakes and corn fritters; lunchtime salads and burgers; graze-friendly tapas and platters; and a short, decent dinner menu that includes risotto, steak and fresh, locally caught fish.

Dramanti Artisan Roaster
CAFE

(☑ 07-3108 8338; www.dramanti.com; 94 Tingal Rd, Wynnum; ⊙ 6am-3pm Mon-Fri, to 2pm Sat & Sun; 🛜) Easy to miss, this competent micro-roastery-cafe lies at the back of a car park, a quick walk from Wynnum Central train station. The place brews superlative coffee in a head-spinning number of ways, including espresso, Aeropress, V60, Kalita Wave and cold drip. Tasty bites include muffins, paleo snacks and bagels. Don't forget to buy a few bags of beans to take home.

ℹ️ Information

Wynnum Manly Tourism & Visitor Information Centre (☑ 07-3348 3524; www.manlyharbourvillage.com; William Gunn Jetty, 1 Wyvernleigh Cl, Manly; ⊙ 9am-3pm) The helpful tourist information office is located on William Gunn Jetty.

ℹ️ Getting There & Away

If you're not driving, the easiest way to reach Manly is to catch the train, which departs from central Brisbane's Roma St Station and Central Station, as well as from the inner-city stations of South Bank, South Brisbane and Fortitude Valley ($5.70, 40 minutes) every 30 minutes or so.

North Stradbroke Island
POP 2030

An easy 30-minute ferry chug from the Brisbane suburb of Cleveland, this unpretentious holiday isle is like Noosa and Byron Bay rolled into one. There's a string of glorious powdery white beaches, great surf and some quality places to stay and eat. It's also a hot spot for spying dolphins, turtles, manta rays and, between June and November, hundreds of humpback whales. 'Straddie' also offers freshwater lakes and 4WD tracks.

At Point Lookout, the eye-popping North Gorge Headlands Walk is an absolute highlight. It's an easy 20-minute loop around the headland along boardwalks, with the thrum of cicadas as your soundtrack. Keep an eye out for turtles, dolphins and manta rays offshore. The view from the headland down Main Beach is a show-stopper.

About 8km east of Dunwich on Alfred Martin Way is the car park for **Naree Budjong Djara National Park** (www.nprsr.qld.gov.au/parks/naree-budjong-djara). From here, take the 2.6km walking track to Straddie's glittering centrepiece, Blue Lake (Kaboora): keep an eye out for forest birds, skittish lizards and swamp wallabies along the way. There's a wooden viewing platform at the lake, which is encircled by a forest of paperbarks, eucalypts and banksias. You can cool off in the water, if you don't mind the spooky unseen depths.

North Stradbroke Island Historical Museum (☑ 07-3409 9699; www.stradbrokemuseum.com.au; 15-17 Welsby St, Dunwich; adult/child $5/1; ⊙ 10am-2pm Tue-Sat, 11am-3pm Sun)

Point Lookout

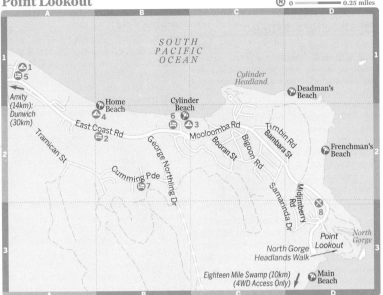

Point Lookout

⊕ Activities, Courses & Tours
Manta Lodge & Scuba
Centre ....(see 5)

⭙ Sleeping
1 Adder Rock Campground A1
2 Allure...B2
3 Cylinder Beach Campground.............B2
4 Home Beach Campground B2
5 Manta Lodge YHA A1
6 Stradbroke Island Beach Hotel B2
7 Straddie Views.....................................B2

⊗ Eating
8 Blue Room Cafe.....................................D3

describes shipwrecks and harrowing voyages, and gives an introduction to the island's rich Aboriginal history (the Quandamooka are the traditional owners of Minjerribah, aka Straddie).

🏃 Activities

Manta Lodge & Scuba Centre   DIVING
(☑ 07-3409 8888; www.mantalodge.com.au; 132 Dickson Way, Point Lookout; wetsuit/surfboard hire $20/30, diving course from $500) Based at the YHA (p98), Manta Scuba Centre offers a broad range of options. You can hire a wetsuit, mask, snorkel and fins ($25 for 24 hours) or a surfboard, or take the plunge with a diving course. Snorkelling trips (from $60) include a boat trip and all gear.

**North Stradbroke
Island Surf School**   SURFING
(☑ 07-3409 8342; www.northstradbrokeislandsurf-school.com.au; lessons from $50) Small-group, 1½-hour surf lessons in the warm Straddie waves. Solo lessons available if you're feeling bashful.

Straddie Super Sports   CYCLING
(☑ 07-3409 9252; www.straddiesupersports.com.au; 18 Bingle Rd, Dunwich; hire per hr/day mountain bikes $10/50, kayaks $15/60, SUP board $10/50; ⊗ 8am-4.30pm Mon-Fri, to 3pm Sat, 9am-2pm Sun) Friendly Straddie Super Sports hires out mountain bikes, kayaks and stand up paddleboards, surfboards (per day $50) and bodyboards (per day $15). The place also sells fishing gear and camping accessories.

Straddie Adventures   KAYAKING
(☑ 0433 171 477; www.straddieadventures.com.au; adult/child sea-kayaking trips from $75/40, sand-boarding $35/30) Operated by the area's traditional Aboriginal owners, this outfit runs insightful sea-kayaking trips with an

Indigenous cultural bent. Sand-boarding sessions are also offered.

🛏 Sleeping & Eating

Straddie Camping CAMPGROUND $

(☑ 07-3409 9668; www.straddiecamping.com.au; 1 Junner St, Dunwich; 4WD sites from $16.55, powered/unpowered sites from $39/32, cabins from $120; ⊙ booking office 8am-4pm Mon-Sat) There are eight island campgrounds operated by this outfit, including two 4WD-only foreshore sites (permits required – $43.75). The best of the bunch are grouped around Point Lookout: Cylinder Beach, Adder Rock and Home Beach all overlook the sand. Amity Point campground has new eco-cabins. Good weekly rates; book well in advance.

Manta Lodge YHA HOSTEL $

(☑ 07-3409 8888; www.mantalodge.com.au; 132 Dickson Way, Point Lookout; dm/d/tw/f from $35/90/90/115; @ �widehat🞄) This affable, three-storey hostel has clean (if unremarkable) rooms and a great beachside location. There's a communal firepit out the back, a curfew-free kitchen, cosy communal spaces, plus a dive school (p97) downstairs. Rental options include surfboards, bodyboards, stand-up paddleboards, bikes and snorkelling gear. Wi-fi is free in communal areas and $5 for 24 hours in the dorms.

Straddie Views B&B $$

(☑ 04-5950 2257; 26 Cumming Pde, Point Lookout; s/d from $125/150) There are two spacious downstairs suites at this B&B, run by friendly Straddie local Jan. Each is inviting and sophisticated, with queen-sized bed, private bathroom, earthy hues and thoughtful extras like chocolates on the bed and port in the decanter. Cooked breakfasts are served on the upstairs deck (the ocean views are free).

★ Allure APARTMENT $$$

(☑ 07-3415 0000, 1800 555 200; www.allurestradbroke.com.au; 43-57 East Coast Rd, Point Lookout; bungalows/villas from $175/250; ✻ 🞄🞄) Set in a leafy compound with a pool, a gym and a kitchen garden for guests, Allure offers large, spotless, contemporary bungalows and villas. Bungalows are studio-style affairs with kitchenettes and mezzanine bedrooms, while villas offer full kitchens and separate bedrooms. All have private laundry facilities and outdoor deck with barbecues. While there isn't much space between the shacks, they're cleverly designed with privacy in mind.

Cheaper rates for stays of more than one night.

Stradbroke Island Beach Hotel HOTEL $$$

(☑ 07-3409 8188; www.stradbrokehotel.com.au; East Coast Rd, Point Lookout; d $180-325; ✻ 🞄🞄) Straddie's only pub has 13 cool, inviting rooms with shell-coloured tiles, blonde timbers and balconies. Walk to the beach, or get distracted by the open-walled bar downstairs en route (serves breakfast, lunch and dinner; pizzas $15 to $19, mains $18 to $38). Flashy three- and four-bed apartments are also available for multinight stays. Wi-fi is charged ($5 per gigabyte).

★ Island Fruit Barn CAFE $

(☑ 07-3409 9125; 16 Bingle Rd, Dunwich; mains $10-16; ⊙ 7am-5pm Mon-Fri, to 4pm Sat, 8am-4pm Sun; 🞄) On the main road in Dunwich, Island Fruit Barn is a casual little congregation of tables with excellent breakfasts, smoothies, salads, sandwiches, winter soups and cakes, many gluten free or vegan, and all made using top-quality ingredients. Order the scrumptious spinach-and-feta roll, then stock up on fresh produce and gourmet condiments in the super-cute grocery section.

Blue Room Cafe CAFE $

(☑ 0438 281 666; 27 Mooloomba Rd, Point Lookout; dishes $10-18; ⊙ 7.30am-2.30pm, providore to 5.30pm Mon-Sat, to 2pm Sun; 🞄) A youthful, beach-shack-chic cafe, with a small alfresco terrace and fresh, feel-good dishes like red papaya filled with kiwi fruit and strawberries and topped with granola and cacao crunch; organic-egg omelette with spinach and goats-milk cheese; and generous fish tacos jammed with grilled fish and housemade Mexican black-bean corn salsa. Small bites include cookies and yummy vegan snacks. The adjoining providore is aptly named the Green Room.

❶ Getting There & Away

The hub for ferries to North Stradbroke Island is the Brisbane seaside suburb of Cleveland. From here, **Stradbroke Ferries** (☑ 07-3488 5300; www.stradbrokeferries.com.au; return per vehicle incl passengers from $110, walk-on adult/child $10/5; ⊙ 5.30am-8pm) offers passenger/vehicle services to Dunwich and back (45 minutes, 12 to 17 times daily). Cheaper online fares are available for vehicles. **Gold Cats Stradbroke Flyer** (☑ 07-3286 1964; www.flyer.com.au; Middle St, Cleveland; return adult/child/family $19/10/50; ⊙ 5am-7.30pm) runs passenger-only trips daily between Cleveland and One Mile Jetty at Dunwich (30 minutes, 13 to 14 daily). A free Stradbroke Flyer courtesy bus picks up water-taxi passengers from the Cleveland train station 10 minutes prior to most water-taxi departures (see the website for exclusions).

Regular **Citytrain** (www.translink.com.au) services run from Brisbane's Central and Roma St Stations (as well as the inner-city stations of South Bank, South Brisbane and Fortitude Valley) to Cleveland station ($8.60, one hour). Buses to the ferry terminal meet the trains at Cleveland station (seven minutes).

ⓘ Getting Around

Straddie is big: it's best to have your own wheels to explore it properly. If you plan to go off-road, you can get information and buy a 4WD permit ($43.75) from Straddie Camping.

Alternatively, **Stradbroke Island Buses** (☑ 07-3415 2417; www.stradbrokeislandbuses.com.au) meet the ferries at Dunwich and run to Amity and Point Lookout (one-way/return $4.70/9.40). Services run roughly every hour and the last bus to Dunwich leaves Point Lookout at 6.20pm. Cash only.

There's also the **Stradbroke Cab Service** (☑ 0408 193 685), which charges around $60 from Dunwich to Point Lookout.

Straddie Super Sports (p97) in Dunwich hires out mountain bikes (per hour/day $10/50).

Moreton Island

POP 300

If you're not going further north in Queensland than Brisbane but want a fix of tropical bliss, sail over to Moreton Island. Its prelapsarian beaches, dunes, bushland and lagoons are protected, with 95% of the isle comprising the **Moreton Island National Park & Recreation Area** (www.nprsr.qld.gov.au/parks/moreton-island). Apart from a few rocky headlands, it's all sand, with Mt Tempest, the highest coastal sand hill in the world, towering high at a lofty 280m. Off the west coast are the rusty, hulking Tangalooma Wrecks, which provide excellent snorkelling and diving.

The island has a rich history, from early Aboriginal settlements to the site of Queensland's first and only whaling station at Tangalooma, which operated between 1952 and 1962.

⊙ Sights & Activities

Around half a dozen dolphins swim in from the ocean and take fish from the hands of volunteer feeders each evening. You have to be a guest of the Tangalooma Island Resort to participate, but onlookers are welcome. Also at the resort is the **Tangalooma Marine Education & Conservation Centre** (☑ 1300 652 250; www.tangalooma.com; Tangalooma Island Resort; ⊙ 10am-noon & 1-4pm), which has a display on the diverse marine and bird life of Moreton Bay.

Island bushwalks include a desert trail (two hours) leaving from **Tangalooma Island Resort** (☑ 1300 652 250, 07-3637 2000; www.tangalooma.com; Tangalooma; d from $210, 2-/3-/4-bedroom apt from $480/510/550; ✳ @ � 🛒), as well as the strenuous trek up Mt Tempest, 3km inland from Eagers Creek – worthwhile, but you'll need transport to reach the start.

Cape Moreton Lighthouse offers great views when the whales are passing by.

Moreton Bay Escapes (☑ 1300 559 355; www.moretonbayescapes.com.au; 1-day tour adult/child from $200/140, 2-day camping tours from $360/250) ⚓ runs informative one-, two- and three-day 4WD tours that will have you snorkelling or kayaking, sand-boarding, marine wildlife-watching and hiking. **Adventure Moreton Island** (☑ 07-3410 6927; www.adventuremoretonisland.com; 1-day tours from $145) runs a handful of day tours, among them an Island Adrenaline Tour ($189), allowing you to choose four activities from a list that includes quad-bike riding, sand-boarding, and snorkelling at the Tangalooma Wrecks.

Tangalooma hosts the island's sole resort. There are also five national park **camping areas** (☑ 13 74 68; www.nprsr.qld.gov.au/experiences/camping; sites per person/family $6.15/24.60) on Moreton Island, all with water, toilets and cold showers. Book online or by phone before you get to the island.

ⓘ Getting There & Away

Several ferries operate from the mainland. To explore once you get to the island, bring a 4WD or take a tour. Most tours are ex-Brisbane, and include ferry transfers.

Amity Trader (☑ 07-3820 6557; www.amitytrader.com; 4WD/walk-on passengers return $270/40) Runs vehicle barges for 4WD vehicles and walk-on passengers from the Brisbane suburb of Victoria Point to Kooringal on Moreton Island several times monthly. See the website for the current timetable.

Micat (☑ 07-3909 3333; www.micat.com.au; Tangalooma; return adult/child from $52/35, standard 4WD incl 2 people $200-300) Vehicle ferry services from Port of Brisbane to Tangalooma around eight times weekly (75 to 90 minutes); see the website for directions to the ferry terminal.

Tangalooma Flyer (☑07-3637 2000; www.tangalooma.com; return adult/child $80/45) Fast passenger catamaran operated by Tangalooma Island Resort. It makes the 75-minute trip to the resort three to four times daily from Holt St Wharf in the Brisbane suburb of Pinkenba (see the website for directions).

Granite Belt

Dappling the western flanks of the Great Dividing Range about 210km southwest of Brisbane, the Granite Belt subverts the southeast Queensland clichés of sun, surf and palms. Here, rolling hillsides are lined with cool-climate vineyards, olive grows and orchards growing apples, pears, plums and peaches. This is Queensland's only real wine region of any size – the only place in the state where it's cool enough to grow commercial quantities of grapes.

Stanthorpe & Ballandean

POP 5385 (STANTHORPE), 470 (BALLANDEAN)

Queensland's coolest town (literally), Stanthorpe is one of the state's lesser-known tourist drawcards. With its distinct four-season climate, the town is a winter retreat where normally sweltering Queenslanders can cosy up with a bottle of vino rosso from one of the numerous local wineries. In 1860 an Italian priest planted the first grapevines here, but it wasn't until the influx of Italian immigrants in the 1940s that the wine industry really took off. Today, functional Stanthorpe and the tiny village of Ballandean, about 20km to the south, claim a flourishing wine industry, with cellar-door sales, on-site dining, vineyard events and boutique accommodation.

But it's not all wine and song: the Granite Belt's changing seasons also make it a prime fruit-growing area, with plenty of fruit picking available for backpackers who don't mind chilly mornings.

◉ Sights & Activities

Weekenders come not only for the wine, but also the food: across the Granite Belt region you'll find a number of food artisans selling (and often serving) everything from olive oils and chutneys, to cheeses, fudge, cider and craft beer.

Granite Belt Brewery BREWERY
(☑07-4681 1370; www.granitebeltbrewery.com.au; 146 Glenlyon Dr, Stanthorpe; ◉10am-midnight, restaurant noon-2.30pm & 5.30pm-late) It's not just about the wine around here – there are some local breweries too! Swing into the bar at the Happy Valley accommodation-restaurant to sample some local suds. A $12 tasting paddle (or the driver-friendly $7 version) gives you a sample of four current offerings, which might include the Granite Pilsner, Poziers Porter or Irish Red Ale.

Stanthorpe Regional Art Gallery GALLERY
(☑07-4681 1874; www.srag.org.au; cnr Lock & Marsh Sts, Stanthorpe; ◉10am-4pm Tue-Fri, to 1pm Sat & Sun) It may be small, but this is one of Queensland's better regional art galleries, with a permanent collection that includes works by Australian greats like Margaret Olley and Charles Blackman, as well as one piece by Pablo Picasso. While these works are not always on display, you can expect interesting rotating exhibitions of mostly canvases and ceramics. Check the website or call for info on Sunday afternoon live music.

☞ Tours

Wine Discovery Tours WINE
(☑0412 579 341; www.winediscoverytours.com.au; tours incl lunch from $120) Winery tours in a flashy Volkswagen People Mover, with detours to wilderness areas.

Filippo's Tours WINE
(☑07-4681 3130; www.filippostours.com.au; day tours ex-Stanthorpe/Brisbane from $100/145) Runs tours of Granite Belt wine country, including lunch or dinner. Also offers overnight and multi-day packages (per person from $305).

Granite Highlands Maxi Tours WINE
(☑0417 192 179, 1800 852 969; www.maxitours.com.au; half-/full-day tour from $75/85) 'You drink, we drive'. Good-value half- and full-day tours, plus overnight packages ex-Brisbane for groups (per person $280).

✯ Festivals & Events

Brass Monkey Season WINE, MUSIC
(www.granitebeltwinecountry.com.au/events/four-seasons-of-events/brass-monkey-season) The main event in the Granite Belt spans an entire season: winter (June to August) is Brass Monkey Season, with a parade of music events, exhibitions and Christmas in July.

BRISBANE & AROUND GRANITE BELT

GIRRAWEEN NATIONAL PARK

A short drive east of Ballandean, Girraween National Park (www.nprsr.qld.gov.au/parks/girraween) is home to some astonishing granite boulders, pristine forests and brilliant blooms of springtime wildflowers (Girraween means 'place of flowers'), all of which make a marvellous setting for a bushwalk. Wildlife is abundant and there are 17km of trails to take you around and to the top of some of the surreal granite outcrops. Although winter nights here can be cold, it's hot work scaling the boulders, so take plenty of water with you.

Although Ballandean and Stanthorpe are a short drive away, there are a couple of excellent places to stay in the area. Girraween Environmental Lodge (☑ 07-4684 5138; www.girraweenlodge.com.au; Pyramids Rd, Wyberba; d $250, extra adult/child $40/20; ❋) ⟋ is a fantastic bushland retreat with 10 smart, self-contained timber cabins, while nearby Wisteria Cottage (☑ 07-4684 5121; www.wisteriacottage.com.au; 2117 Pyramids Rd, Wyberba; d incl breakfast from $210) comprises three simple, tasteful cottages. There are two good drive-in camping grounds (☑ 13 74 68; www.qpws.usedirect.com; per person/family $6.15/24.60) in the park – Castle Rock and Bald Rock Creek – each with drinking water, barbecues and showers. Book online or via phone before arriving.

Stanthorpe Rocks　　　　MUSIC
(www.stanthorperocks.com.au; ☺ Nov) An annual bash at Ballandean Estate (p102) winery, on the second weekend in November. Head in for a rocking weekend of food, wine and Aussie music stalwarts like the Black Sorrows, Hoodoo Gurus and Wendy Matthews.

Apple & Grape
Harvest Festival　　　FOOD & DRINK
(www.appleandgrape.org; ☺ Feb-Mar) Running in even-numbered years, this harvest festival is one of Australia's largest, running for 10 days from late February to early March. The main part of the festival takes place on the last weekend, with a street parade, fireworks and wine fiesta in Stanthorpe.

Vintage Lunch　　　　FOOD & DRINK
(www.goldengroveestate.com.au; ☺ Feb) Celebrate the start of the vintage Siciliano-style at Golden Grove Estate (p102). Held annually in February, the shindig includes the blessing and stomping of the grapes, hypnotic Tarantella music and a Mediterranean buffet lunch. *Viva il vino!*

Opera in the Vineyard　　　MUSIC
(www.ballandeanestate.com/operainthevineyard.aspx; ☺ May) A hugely popular charity event, held at Ballandean Estate (p102) on the first weekend in May. Book ahead to enjoy top-tier talent from Opera Queensland taking to the stage at one of Queensland's most celebrated wineries.

🛏 Sleeping

⭐ **Diamondvale B&B Cottages**　COTTAGE **$$**
(☑ 07-4681 3367; www.diamondvalecottages.com.au; 26 Diamondvale Rd, Stanthorpe; 1-/2-/4-bedroom from $160/320/650; 🐾) In atmospheric bushland outside of Stanthorpe (expect to see kangaroos, koalas and echidnas), Diamondvale consists of four lovely private cottages and a four-bedroom lodge, each with old-fashioned details, a wood-burning fireplace, kitchen and verandah. The communal barbecue hut is a winner, as is the hospitality of owners Tony and Kerryn. Walk 2km along the creek into town or simply jump in for a swim.

Sippers at Ballandean　RENTAL HOUSE **$$**
(☑ 0409 788 772; www.ballandean.net.au; 2655 Eukey Rd, Ballandean; per night weekdays/weekends $400/660, up to 6 people; ❋) ⟋ This contemporary, two-level house is ideal for larger groups wanting a base close to Granite Belt wineries. All four bedrooms feature super-comfy king beds or twins as well as en suite bathroom with spacious shower (one room has a jacuzzi) and access to the native garden. The upstairs living area is huge, with a fireplace, games table and well-equipped kitchen complete with quality appliances.

Azjure Studio Retreat　APARTMENT **$$$**
(☑ 0405 127 070; www.azjure.com.au; 165 Sundown Rd, Ballandean; 1-/2-bedroom studios from $300/430; ❋ 🐾) This multi-award-winning retreat features three modern, free-standing

TOP FIVE GRANITE BELT WINERIES

Winery-hopping is a must-do in this neck of the woods, and numerous wineries have cellar doors that allow visitors to sample and purchase their drops.

Boireann Wines (☑07-4683 2194; www.boireannwinery.com.au; 26 Donnellys Castle Rd, The Summit; ☉10am-4pm Fri-Mon) Awarded five stars by Aussie wine guru James Halliday, Boireann grows French and Italian grape varieties, used to craft handmade, premium reds that are arguably the finest in Queensland.

Ravens Croft Wines (☑07-4683 3252; www.ravenscroftwines.com.au; 274 Spring Creek Rd, Stanthorpe; ☉10.30am-4.30pm Fri-Sun) Highly respected winemaker Mark Ravenscroft produces superb reds, including petit verdot, Tempranillo and pinotage. The latter varietal hails from South Africa, like Ravenscroft himself.

Golden Grove Estate (☑07-4684 1291; www.goldengroveestate.com.au; 337 Sundown Rd, Ballandean; 9am-4pm Mon-Fri & Sun, to 5pm Sat; ☉10am-3pm) Established in 1946, this third-generation family-run estate has established a solid reputation for its many unique varieties, among them Spanish Tempranillo and Italian Barbera, Vermentino and Nero d'Avola.

Ballandean Estate (☑07-4684 1226; www.ballandeanestate.com; 354 Sundown Rd, Ballandean; ☉9am-5pm) The Puglisi family have been making vino here since 1931 and their estate is Queensland's oldest family-owned and operated winery. Free winery tours at 11am.

Robert Channon Wines (☑07-4683 3260; www.robertchannonwines.com; 32 Bradley Lane, Stanthorpe; ☉11am-4pm Mon, Tue & Fri, 10am-5pm Sat & Sun) Located 11km west of Stanthorpe, Robert Channon Wines is not short of trophy-winning wines (try the Verdehlo or chardonnay).

studios for two people (plus a villa for four) with a sweeping panorama across the vines. Each has a spacious open-plan layout, with fully equipped kitchen, laundry, huge windows, a verandah with barbecue and spa tub with bucolic views. Pop open a bottle of local Nebbiolo and swill as kangaroos hop past in the twilight.

✗ Eating & Drinking

L'Aquila   ITALIAN $
(☑07-4681 0356; 130 High St, Stanthorpe; pizzas $16-24, pasta $15; ☉restaurant 8.30am-5pm Mon-Thu, to 9pm Fri, 5-9pm Sat, pizza takeaway 5-8pm Tue-Thu & Sun, 5-9pm Fri & Sat) While the space may lack warmth or charm, this is a handy spot if you're hankering for Italian flavours. Tuck into quick-and-easy focaccias and panini, bowls of pasta or salads. Eat-in pizzas are only available at lunch (11.30am to 2pm).

Yim Thai   THAI $$
(☑07-4681 0155; www.diningonthebelt.com.au/yim-thai-menu; 137a High St, Stanthorpe; mains $14-28; ☉11am-2.30pm Tue-Sat, plus 5.30pm-late daily) A surprising find on Stanthorpe's main street: Yim Thai's (relatively) authentic Thai curries, soups and stir-fries bring some

Southeast Asian culinary life to agricultural, inland Queensland.

★ Barrelroom   MODERN AUSTRALIAN $$$
(☑07-4684 1326; www.barrelroom.com.au; Ballandean Estate, 354 Sundown Rd, Ballandean; mains $34-36, 7-course tasting menu $90; ☉noon-2.30pm & 6-8.30pm Thu-Mon) Located at Ballandean Estate winery and suitably flanked by massive 150-year-old wine barrels, Barrelroom is one of the Granite Belt's top dining destinations. Using seasonal regional produce, the kitchen creates sophisticated yet soulful dishes like miso-cured tuna with brown rice curd, salt-baked beetroot and bottarga, or free-range pork with beautifully braised onion, pickled mushroom, white bean and sprouts. Book ahead, especially on weekends.

Brass Monkey Brew House   MICROBREWERY
(☑0488 967 401; www.brassmonkeybrewhouse ptyltd.com; 106 Donges Rd, Severnlea; ☉10am-6pm Thu-Mon) Just south of Stanthorpe is this award-winning, family-run microbrewery. Occupying a humble tin shed scattered with communal tables and a fireplace, its small-batch beers (made using local hops) are listed on blackboards along the wall. Slurp on anything from German pilsner to English brown ale, best paired with the family's celebrated

Bratwurst sausage. Other bites might include decent beef-cheek pie and a stout-soaked burger (naturally).

ℹ️ Information

Stanthorpe Visitor Information Centre (📋 07-4681 2057, 1800 762 665; www.granitebelt winecountry.com.au; 28 Leslie Pde, Stanthorpe; ⊙ 9am-4pm) You can get a winery-trail map and the *Stanthorpe to Ballandean Bike Trail* brochure from the Stanthorpe visitor centre, just south of the creek.

ℹ️ Getting There & Away

Crisps Coaches (📋 07-4661 8333; www. crisps.com.au) runs services from Brisbane to Stanthorpe ($69, 3¼ hours, one to three daily) via Warwick. One daily service continues on to Tenterfield in NSW (except on Saturday), stopping in Glen Alpin and Ballandean en route. The company also runs three daily services from Toowoomba to Stanthorpe ($49, two to 3½ hours) on weekdays, reduced to one service daily on weekends.

To tour the Granite Belt wineries, either take a guided tour or bring your own set of wheels (plus a sober friend to do the driving).

Toowoomba

POP 114,620

Not only is the 'Garden City' Queensland's largest and oldest inland city, it is also the birthplace of two national icons: the archetypal Aussie cake, the lamington, and Oscar-winner Geoffrey Rush. Squatting on the edge of the Great Dividing Range, 700m above sea level, Toowoomba is a sprawling country hub with wide tree-lined streets and stately homes.

⊙ Sights

Toowoomba's stately late-19th-century sandstone buildings include the neoclassical old post office (138 Margaret St) and the courthouse (cnr Margaret & Neil Sts). The visitor centre (p105) publishes a series of themed brochures, including the *Historic Walking Tour*.

Cobb & Co Museum   MUSEUM
(📋 07-4659 4900; www.cobbandco.qm.qld.gov.au; 27 Lindsay St; adult/child/family $12.50/6.50/32; ⊙ 10am-4pm) Immediately north of Queens Park, this engaging, child-friendly museum houses Australia's finest collection of horse-drawn vehicles, including beautiful 19th-century Cobb & Co Royal Mail coaches and an

omnibus used in Brisbane until 1924. Hands-on displays depict town life and outback travel during the horse-powered days, and the museum also houses a blacksmith forge and an interesting Indigenous section, with shields, axe heads, boomerangs, plus animated films relating Dreaming stories. Look for the spinning windmills out the front.

Ju Raku En Japanese Garden   GARDENS
(📋 guided tours 07-4631 2627; www.toowoombarc. qld.gov.au; West St; ⊙ 7am-dusk) FREE Australia's largest and most traditional Japanese garden, Ju Raku En is located circa 4km south of the centre at the University of Southern Queensland. The 5-hectare oasis was designed by a Japanese professor in Kyoto and contains all the expected elements, from rippling lake and carefully aligned boulders, to conifers, bamboo stands, cherry blossom trees and photogenic bridges.

Picnic Point   PARK
(www.picnic-point.com.au; Tourist Rd; ⊙ 24hr, cafe-restaurant 8.30am-5pm Mon-Thu, to 9pm Fri, 8am-9pm Sat, 8am-5pm Sun) FREE Riding high on the rim of the Great Dividing Range and strung along the eastern edge of town are Toowoomba's Escarpment Parks, the pick of which is Picnic Point. You'll find walking trails, plenty of namesake picnic spots, a playground for kids, as well as a cafe-restaurant (mains $14 to $35). That said, what everyone really comes for are the eye-popping views over the Lockyer Valley. It's from here that you can really appreciate just how lofty Toowoomba really is.

Toowoomba Regional Art Gallery   GALLERY
(📋 07-4688 6652; www.tr.qld.gov.au/facilities-recreation/theatres-galleries/galleries; 531 Ruthven St; ⊙ 10am-4pm Tue-Sat, 1-4pm Sun) FREE Toowoomba's modestly sized art gallery houses an interesting collection of paintings, ceramics and drawings. Its permanent exhibition of Australian art includes works by late-19th- and early-20th-century greats such as Tom Roberts, Arthur Streeton and Rupert Bunny, while the adjacent room showcases mainly European decorative arts from the 17th to 19th centuries. Call ahead to view the gallery's notable library, a treat of rare books, maps and manuscripts. The venue also hosts regular touring exhibitions.

Queens Park Botanic Gardens   GARDENS
(www.tr.qld.gov.au; cnr Lindsay & Campbell Sts; ⊙ 24hr) FREE Toowoomba's showpiece botanical gardens are a blaze of colour in the

spring and autumn. Graced with parterre gardens, neat English flower beds, palms and conifers, they're a perfect spot for a picnic or a lazy read-and-snooze. You'll find the gardens in the northeast corner of Queens Park, across the street from the Cobb & Co Museum.

🛏 Sleeping & Eating

Toowoomba Motor Village　　CARAVAN PARK $
(☎1800 675 105; www.toowoombamotorvillage. com.au; 821 Ruthven St; powered/unpowered sites $38/32, cabins & units $72-130; ❀🛜) This trim-and-tidy hillside park is a 2.5km hike south of the centre, but it is well equipped and offers views over the suburbs.

★ Vacy Hall　　GUESTHOUSE $$
(☎07-4639 2055; www.vacyhall.com.au; 135 Russell St; d $135-245; 🛜) Uphill from the town centre, this magnificent 1873 mansion (originally a wedding gift from a cashed-up squatter to his daughter) offers 12 heritage-style rooms with no shortage of authentic charm. A wide verandah wraps around the house, all rooms have en suites or private bathrooms, and most have working fireplaces. Super-high ceilings make some rooms taller than they are wide. Free wi-fi.

Ecoridge Hideaway　　CHALET $$
(☎07-4630 9636; www.ecoridgehideaway.com. au; 712 Rockmount Rd, Preston; r from $145; 🅿🛜) Ecoridge is an excellent alternative to the often unremarkable accommodation in central Toowoomba. Around 15km from the city on a back road to Gatton, the three self-contained cabins here are simple yet smart, with wood heaters, gas cooking and gorgeous sunrise views across the Great Dividing Range. Cheaper for longer stays. Free wi-fi available at reception office only.

Highlander Motel　　MOTEL $$
(☎07-4638 4955; www.highlandermotorinn.com.au; 226-228 James St; d/f from $130/170; 🅿❀🛜🏊) A stock-standard but clean, well-maintained motel with firm beds, kitchenettes and a few thoughtful extras like shaving cream in the bathrooms. The property includes a saltwater pool and guest laundry facilities. Wi-fi is free, though the signal is not especially strong in some of the rooms.

Quality Hotel Platinum International　　MOTEL, APARTMENTS $$$
(☎07-4634 0400; www.platinuminternational.com. au; 326 James St; d/apt from $165/180; ❀@🛜🏊) Top of the motel tree in Toowoomba is this

impeccable, two-tier corporate operation. In hues of charcoal, grey and red, rooms are sharp and contemporary, with high-quality mattresses, coffee pod machines and crisp, slick bathrooms. Other pluses include an inviting pool, a decent restaurant-bar and genuine, friendly staff. While the location is a bit bleak, double glazing keeps much of the traffic noise at bay.

Junk Asian　　ASIAN $
(☎0474 744 425; www.junkboat.com.au; 5/476 Ruthven St; dishes $10-20; ⊙11am-10pm) One of several trendy eateries at the Walton Stores redevelopment, this casually hip Pan-Asian eatery is the brainchild of two-hatted chef Tony Kelly. Under a slithering Chinese dragon, young and old get chin and fingers messy over street-food staples like ramen with slow-cooked egg and pork, green papaya salad, and addictive Chinese *bao* stuffed with soft shell crab, chipotle, burnt lime kewpie and pickled slaw.

Phatburgers　　BURGERS $
(☎07-4638 4738; www.phatburgers.com.au; 520 Ruthven St; burgers mini $9-11, large $13-22; ⊙10am-9pm) Using local, grass-fed beef, chipper Phat plates up brilliant, juicy burgers. Hardcore carnivores, prepare to drool over the Raw Muscle, packed with 240g of succulent rib-eye steak. Herbivores aren't overlooked, with a satisfying Grasseater burger jammed with a lentil patty, eggplant, minted rocket, feta, hummus and house-made chutney. Burgers aside, Phat also peddles hot dogs, fish and chips and salt-and-pepper squid.

Firefly　　CAFE $$
(☎07-4564 9197; www.thefireflycafe.com.au; 100 Russell St; mains lunch $16.50-22, dinner $26-29; ⊙7am-3pm Tue-Sat, plus 5.30-8pm Fri; 🍴) With street art on the wall and plastic farm animals on the tables, warm, kooky Firefly occupies a former car-detailing workshop on the edge of the city centre. High-quality, seasonal produce drives generous, honest dishes like toasted brioche with grilled peaches, sweet dukkah and whipped coconut cream, not to mention a lusty Brekky Burger (with bacon, fried eggs, spinach and onion jam). Great coffees too.

★ Zev's Bistro　　MODERN AUSTRALIAN $$$
(☎07-4564 8636; www.facebook.com/zevsbistro; 517 Ruthven St; mains $34; ⊙5pm-late Tue & Wed, 11.30am-late Thu-Sun) Up-and-coming chef Kyle Zevenbergen has catapulted Toowoom-

TOOWOOMBA STREET ART

LA, Mexico City, Berlin, Melbourne, Toowoomba. No, that's not a typo. As surprising as it may seem, Toowoomba is now one of Australia's hottest hubs for street art, with dozens of murals created by some of the scene's most prolific street artists.

Propelling the boom is the town's **First Coat Art & Music Festival** (www.firstcoat. com.au; ☺May), an annual three-day event that sees both local and global talent transform laneways, walls, warehouses and car parks into bold, arresting works. Many of the murals dot the centre of town, especially around Ruthven and Margaret Sts, as well as near the train station.

While there's no shortage of engaging pieces, undisputed standouts include Matt Adnate's haunting depiction of a young **Indigenous boy** (49 Neil St) and, a quick walk west, Fintan Magee's surreal **elephant and treehouse** (488 Ruthven St). Further north on Neil St is Lisa King's Bowie-inspired **triple portrait** (cnr Neil & Bowen Sts). Further north still is a pop-tastic depiction of the late, croc-wrestling Steve Irwin by artist Mark Paul Deren (aka Madsteez).

You'll find a comprehensive list of works around town mapped on the First Coat website. Alternatively, drop by art lab **Kontraband Studios** (☑0410 804 205; www.kontra bandstudios.com.au; 6 Laurel St; ☺10am-5pm Mon-Fri, to 2pm Sat) for some face-to-face insight into a scene that has put this high-altitude town on the world street-art map.

---

ba's dining scene to a whole new level with his eponymous bistro, a burnt orange-and-charcoal space pimped with his brother's modern artworks. Dishes range from very good to excellent, packed with ingenuity, local accents and texture; think sous-vide kangaroo finished on a coal barbecue and served with a potato and wattleseed purée, braised fennel and wild berries lactose-fermented with eucalyptus.

🍷 Drinking & Nightlife

Ground Up Espresso Bar CAFE
(www.facebook.com/grounduptoowoomba; 501 Ruthven St; ☺6.30am-3.30pm Mon-Fri, 7am-3pm Sat & Sun) Cool staffers, a rustic-industrial fit-out and a setting on an aerosol-pimped laneway off Ruthven St: you'd be forgiven for thinking you're in Brisbane or Melbourne at Ground Up. Affable and relaxed, the cafe peddles rotating house blends, single origins and filtered coffees, as well as irresistible pastries from revered local bakery, the Baker's Duck (look out for the fig danish).

Bunker Records & Espresso COFFEE
(www.facebook.com/bunkerrecords.au; 229 Margaret St; ☺10am-4.30pm Tue-Fri, 9am-2pm Sat) Top-notch specialist coffee in a record shop is what you get at Bunker. Slurp a (weekly changing) single origin at the front espresso bar then scour the wooden crates at the back for a varied mix of old and new vinyl spanning a range of genres, from funk, jazz and hip-hop, to pop (limited-edition 45"

Japanese release of Madonna's *True Blue,* anyone?).

Spotted Cow PUB
(www.spottedcow.com.au; cnr Ruthven & Campbell Sts; ☺11am-late; 🛜) A friendly, family-owned pub with regular live bands (think indie acts like Australia's The Rubens and the US's Sheer Mag), the Spotted Cow is a Toowoomba institution. Choose from 20 rotating beers on tap (including five craft brews) and tuck into decent pub grub (mains $15 to $49), from burgers and steaks to a finger-licking 1kg pot of mussels ($28). Trivia on Wednesday night.

⭐ Entertainment

Empire Theatre THEATRE
(☑1300 655 299; www.empiretheatre.com.au; 56 Neil St; tour $5; ☺box office 9am-5pm Mon-Fri, to 1pm Sat, tours 10am Tue & Thu) Toowoomba's cultural heart beats stridently inside the magnificent Empire Theatre, sections of which date back to 1911 (the Moderne facade is from 1933). The venue plays hosts to a variety of performances, from touring prolific musical acts, to musicals, theatre, comedy, kids' concerts, opera and even ballet from the likes of the Russian National Ballet Theatre. Book a tour (30 to 45 minutes), or just stick your head into the lobby and ogle the deco details.

ℹ️ Information

Toowoomba Visitor Information Centre
(☑1800 331 155, 07-4639 3797; www.southern

queenslandcountry.com.au; 86 James St;
⊙9am-5pm; 🛜) The comprehensive visitor
centre is located southeast of town, at the junction with Kitchener St. Drop by for an extensive
selection of brochures and maps, as well as local
gifts and artisanal food products.

ⓘ Getting There & Away

Toowoomba is 126km west of Brisbane on the
Warrego Hwy. Greyhound (p93) services run
eight times daily between Brisbane Airport,
central Brisbane and Toowoomba ($35, two
hours), and once daily to Stanthorpe ($47, 2½
hours) further south. **Murrays** (⊉132 251;
www.murrays.com.au) also runs services between Brisbane Airport, central Brisbane and
Toowoomba (from $24, four daily), though less
frequently. Toowoomba's **main bus station**
(cnr Neil St & Bell St Mall) serves both city and
long-distance routes.

From Brisbane Airport, the **Airport Flyer**
(⊉1300 304 350, 07-4630 1444; www.theair
portflyer.com.au; one-way/return $75/140)
runs six daily door-to-door services to/from
Toowoomba. The cost is cheaper for more than
one passenger.

Around Toowoomba

Highfields & Crows Nest

North of Toowoomba the New England
Hwy travels the ridges of the Great Dividing Range. The route passes through the
nondescript Toowoomba satellite town of
Highfields on its way north to the cute if
uneventful town of Crows Nest. The latter
town – circulating around a village green
about 50km north of Toowoomba – plays
host to the World Worm Races every October. Far more impressive is the Crows
Nest National Park (www.nprsr.qld.gov.au/
parks/crows-nest), 6km east of town. Here,

eucalyptus forest and a seasonal waterfall
are punctuated by craggy granite outcrops,
sheer cliffs and shy but curious wallabies.

Cowboy Up Trail Riding (⊉07-4698 4772;
www.cowboyup.com.au; 160 Rocky Gully Rd, Emu
Creek; 2hr trail ride $90, 4hr muster $180) will
help you channel your inner drover on their
fantastic horse-riding adventures.

In a wooden cottage that's over a century
old, the helpful Hampton visitor information centre (⊉1800 009 066, 07-4697 9066;
www.crowsnest.info; 8623 New England Hwy, Hampton; ⊙9am-5pm; 🛜) stocks both local and
statewide brochures and maps.

Jondaryan

Northwest of Toowoomba on the Warrego
Hwy, the huge Woolshed at Jondaryan
(⊉07-4692 2229; www.jondaryanwoolshed.com.au;
264 Jondaryan-Evanslea Rd, Jondaryan; adult/child/
family $10/5/30; ⊙8.30am-4.30pm) showcases
the rich pastoral traditions of Queensland.
Built in 1859, the heritage-listed place offers
an engaging time-trip back to simpler (though
more strenuous) days on the farm.

The woolshed played a pivotal role in the
history of the Australian Labor Party: it was
here in 1890 that the first of the legendary
shearers' strikes began. Today the woolshed
is the centrepiece of a sprawling tourist
complex with an interesting collection of
rustic old buildings, antique farm and industrial machinery (including a mighty,
steam-driven 'roadburner' which applied
the first tarmac to many of Australia's roads)
and regular blacksmithing and shearing
demonstrations. Wagon rides, sheepdogs
working, wool spinning and the like happen
throughout the day.

Jondaryan also hosts a string of annual events, including New Year's Eve bashes
(book accommodation well in advance).

The Gold Coast

Best Places to Eat

➡ Rick Shores (p118)

➡ Bstow (p119)

➡ Harry's Steak Bistro (p118)

➡ Glenelg Public House (p116)

➡ BSKT Cafe (p116)

Best Places to Sleep

➡ La Costa Motel (p121)

➡ Burleigh Break (p117)

➡ Island (p111)

➡ Sheraton Grand Mirage Resort (p113)

➡ QT (p111)

Why Go?

Built for pleasure and remaining a place utterly dedicated to sun, surf and the body beautiful, this strip of coast is possibly Australia's most iconic holiday destination. Its shimmering high-rises can, when glimpsed from afar, appear like a make-believe city, and its reputation for tackiness is occasionally deserved. But this is far outstripped by a booming, youthful spirit and startling physical beauty: some 52km of pristine sand and countless epic surf breaks, heartbreakingly hazy sunsets, blissful water temperatures and 300 sunny days a year.

While Surfers Paradise's malls and mega-clubs let the party-hard kids have their fun, the other neighbourhoods have a distinct charm of their own. Main Beach and Broadbeach corner coastal chic; Burleigh Heads, Mermaid and Palm Beach have a retro charm and booming culinary scene; while Coolangatta pleases with its pro-surfer vibe. Not to be overlooked is the lush, misty subtropical rainforest of the hinterland.

When to Go
Surfers Paradise

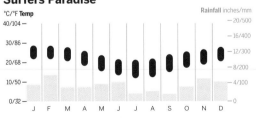

Dec–Feb Sunshine, high temperatures and busy beaches.

Jun–Aug Winter brings tourists from cooler climes, chasing the sun and still-swimmable water.

Oct & Nov Perfect weather, lower prices; time your visit to miss Schoolies week.

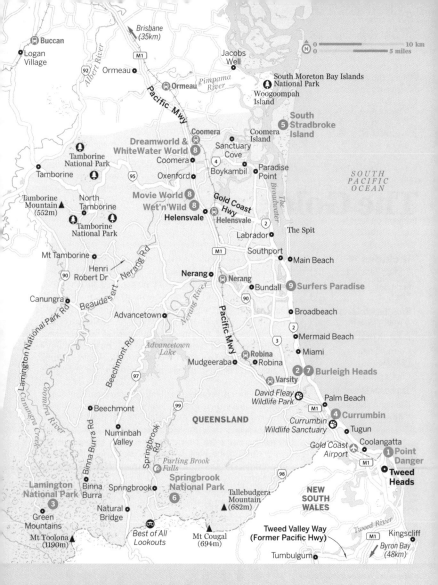

The Gold Coast Highlights

1 **Point Danger** (p120)
Braving a dawn surf at this legendary break.

2 **Burleigh Heads** (p116)
Eating your way around the young, fun and creative culinary scene.

3 **Lamington National Park** (p123) Bushwalking through craggy gorges and densely canopied rainforests.

4 **Balter** (p120) Talking beer and breaks with surfing legends at Currumbin's fabulous brewery.

5 **South Stradbroke Island** (p118) Retreating from the crowds to a long stretch of sand.

6 **Springbrook National Park** (p123) Taking in the view at the aptly named Best of All Lookout.

7 **Burleigh Social** (p118)
Grabbing a 6am macadamia-milk latte before a soft-sand beach run to Miami.

8 **Theme parks** (p115)
Testing your nerve (and your digestive system) on the Gold Coast's roller coasters.

9 **Surfers Paradise** (p109)
Drinking, dancing and watching the sun come up at the beach.

ⓘ Getting There & Away

AIR

Gold Coast Airport (p303) is in Coolangatta, 25km south of Surfers Paradise. All the main Australian domestic airlines fly here. **Scoot** (www.flyscoot.com), **Air Asia** (☑1300 760 330; www.airasia.com) and **Air New Zealand** (☑13 24 76; www.airnewzealand.com.au) fly in from overseas.

Brisbane Airport (p303) is 16km northeast of Brisbane city centre and accessible by train. It is a useful arrival point for the Gold Coast, especially for international visitors.

BUS

Greyhound (www.greyhound.com.au) Has frequent services to/from Brisbane ($23, 1½ hours), Byron Bay ($35, 2½ hours) and beyond.

Premier Motor Service (☑13 34 10; www.premierms.com.au) A couple of daily services head to Brisbane (from $21, 1½ hours), Byron Bay (from $29, 2½ hours) and other coastal areas.

TRAIN

TransLink (☑13 12 30; https://translink.com.au) Citytrain services connect Brisbane with Nerang, Robina and Varsity Lakes stations on the Gold Coast (75 minutes) roughly every half hour. The same line extends north of Brisbane to Brisbane Airport.

ⓘ Getting Around

TO/FROM THE AIRPORT

Byron Bay Xcede (www.byronbay.xcede.com.au) Transfers from Gold Coast Airport to hotels and private addresses in Byron Bay; prebooking advised (adult/child $37/18.50).

Con-X-ion Airport Transfers (☑1300 266 946; www.con-x-ion.com) Transfers to/from Gold Coast Airport (one way adult/child from $22/13), Brisbane Airport (one way from adult/child $49/25) and Gold Coast theme parks.

Gold Coast Tourist Shuttle (☑1300 655 655, 07-5574 5111; www.gcshuttle.com.au; one way per adult/child $22/13) Meets flights into Gold Coast Airport and transfers to most Gold Coast accommodation. Also runs to Gold Coast theme parks.

BUS

Surfside Buslines (☑13 12 30; www.surfside.com.au), a subsidiary of Brisbane's main TransLink operation, runs regular buses up and down the Gold Coast, plus shuttles from the Gold Coast train stations into Surfers Paradise and beyond (including the theme parks).

Surfside, in conjunction with Gold Coast Tourist Shuttle also offers a Freedom Pass, which includes return Gold Coast Airport transfers, unlimited theme-park transfers and local bus travel for $78/39 per adult/child. It's valid for three days; five-, seven- and 10-day passes also available.

TRAM

G:link (Gold Coast Light Rail; ☑13 12 30; http://translink.com.au; tickets from $4.80, Go Explore day pass adult/child $10/5) is a handy if rather pricey light rail and tram service connecting Southport and Broadbeach with stops along the way. It's worth buying a Go Explore day pass (adult/child $10/5; available only from 7-Eleven shops) if you're doing more than one very short trip. Otherwise, you can buy single-trip tickets (from $4.80) from a machine on the tram platform.

Surfers Paradise

POP 22,150

Some may mumble that paradise has been lost, but there's no denying that Surfers' frenetic few blocks and its glorious strip of sand attracts a phenomenal number of visitors – 20,000 per day at peak. Party-hard teens and early-20-somethings come here for a heady dose of clubs, bars, malls and perhaps a bit of beachtime as a hangover remedy before it all starts again. Families like the ready availability of big apartments, loads of kid-friendly eating options and, yes, that beautiful beach.

⊙ Sights & Activities

SkyPoint Observation Deck   VIEWPOINT
(www.skypoint.com.au; Level 77, Q1 Bldg, Hamilton Ave; adult/child/family $24/14/62; ⊗7.30am-8.30pm Sun-Thu, to 11.30pm Fri & Sat) Surfers Paradise's best sight is best observed from your beach towel, but for an eagle-eye view of the coast and hinterland, zip up to this 230m-high observation deck near the top of Q1, one of the world's notably tall buildings. You can also tackle the SkyPoint Climb up the spire to a height of 270m (adult/child from $74/54).

Cheyne Horan School of Surf   SURFING
(☑1800 227 873; www.cheynehoran.com.au; 2hr lessons $49; ⊗10am & 2pm) Learn to carve up the waves at this school, run by former pro surfer Cheyne Horan. Multilesson packages reduce the cost.

Balloon Down Under   BALLOONING
(☑07-5500 4797; www.balloondownunder.com; 1hr flights adult/child $279/225) Up, up and away on sunrise flights over the Gold Coast, ending with a champagne breakfast.

Surfers Paradise

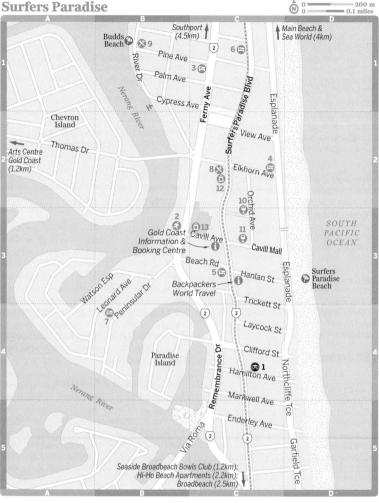

Surfers Paradise

Whales in Paradise
WHALE WATCHING

(✆07-5538 2111; www.whalesinparadise.com. au; cnr Cavill & Ferny Aves; adult/child/family $99/69/267; ⊙ Jun-Nov) Leaves central Surfers three times a day for 3½ hours of whale watching.

⚝ Festivals & Events

★ Bleach Festival
CULTURAL

(www.bleachfestival.com.au; ⊙ early Apr) Visual-art shows, contemporary dance, music of all genres, theatre and performances feature, held in a variety of indoor and outdoor spaces. There's a late-summer party vibe, with the occasional superstar performer heading the bill, as well as some edgy and provocative work.

Gold Coast Film Festival
FILM

(www.gcfilmfestival.com; ⊙ Apr) Mainstream and art-house flicks from all over the world feature in mid- to late April on outdoor screens, including SIPFest, two nights of short films screened right on the beach.

Gold Coast 600
SPORTS

(www.v8supercars.com.au; ⊙ Oct) For three days in October the streets of Surfers are transformed into a temporary race circuit for high-speed racing cars.

🛏 Sleeping

Budds in Surfers
HOSTEL $

(✆07-5538 9661; www.buddsinsurfers.com.au; 6 Pine Ave; dm $32-34, d $95-110; @🛜🏊) Laidback Budds features tidy bathrooms, clean tiles, a sociable bar and a nice pool, all just a short hop from calm Budds Beach. Bike hire available. Female-only dorms are available on request and there's one double with en suite.

Sleeping Inn Surfers
HOSTEL $

(✆07-5592 4455, 1800 817 832; www.sleepinginn. com.au; 26 Peninsular Dr; dm $30-34, d $78-92; @🛜🏊) This backpackers occupies an old apartment block away from the centre, so, as the name suggests, there's a chance you may get to sleep in. Larger dorms come with their own kitchen and bathroom and most have a private living area. Note, no children allowed, and guests in dorm rooms must have an international passport. An adjoining apartment block offers some renovated private rooms.

Chateau Beachside Resort
APARTMENT $

(✆07-5538 1022; www.chateaubeachside.com.au; cnr Elkhorn Ave & Esplanade; studio/1-bedroom apt

> **ℹ SCHOOLIES ON THE LOOSE**
>
> Every year in November, thousands of teenagers flock to Surfers Paradise to celebrate the end of their high-school education in a three-week party known as Schoolies Week. Although local authorities have stepped in to regulate excesses, boozed-up and drug-addled teens are still the norm. It's not pretty.
>   For more info, see www.schoolies.com.

$99/119; ❄@🛜🏊) Less Loire Valley, more Las Vegas, this seaside 'chateau' (actually an 18-storey tower) has studios and apartments that are individually furnished, and all but the very cheapest have ocean views. The 18m pool is a bonus. Minimum two-night stay.

★ Island
HOTEL $$

(✆07-5538 8000; www.theislandgoldcoast. com.au; 3128 Surfers Paradise Blvd; d $180-250; P❄🛜🏊) The fabulously faded Islander Hotel has been reborn as the Island and it's indeed an island of contemporary style in this corner of Surfers. Rooms have standard low ceilings but their natural timber, whitewash and monochromatic palette make for a soothing bolt-hole. Plus they're spacious – doubles are 27 sq metres, suites 45 sq metres – and have king-sized beds.

★ QT
HOTEL $$

(✆07-5584 1200; www.qtgoldcoast.com.au; 7 Staghorn Ave; d $185-280; ❄🛜🏊) Acapulco chairs, retro bikes and preppy-styled staff are a deliberate take on the mid-century-design glory days of Surfers. The clever transformation of what was yet another bland '80s tower really does work, with an airy lobby you'll be happy to hang about in. Room interiors are less nostalgic, but have plenty of colour pops.

Moorings on Cavill
APARTMENT $$

(✆07-5538 6711; www.mooringsoncavill.com.au; 63 Cavill Ave; 1-/2-bedroom apt from $135/185; ❄🛜🏊) This roomy 73-apartment tower at the river end of Cavill Ave is great for families: the vibe is quiet and respectful. The location is hard to beat too: close to the beach, shops and restaurants. Super-clean and managed with a smile.

Q1 Resort
APARTMENT $$$

(📞07-5630 4500, 1300 792 008; www.q1.com.au; Hamilton Ave; 1-bedroom apt $189-259, 2-bedroom $276-375; 🌀@🛜🏊) Spend a night in Australia's tallest residential tower, which features white-on-white interiors and fabulous wrap-around views. There's a lagoon-style pool and a fitness centre if the beach hasn't exhausted you. Prices fluctuate, with good specials for five-night, no-housekeeping stays.

✕ Eating

Self-caterers will find supermarkets in the **Chevron Renaissance Shopping Centre** (www.chevronrenaissanceshoppingcentre.com.au; cnr Elkhorn Ave & Surfers Paradise Blvd; ⏰9am-5.30pm Mon-Sat, 10am-4pm Sun) and **Circle on Cavill** (www.circleoncavill.com.au; cnr Cavill & Ferny Aves; ⏰9am-5.30pm Mon-Sat, 10am-4pm Sun).

★Bumbles Café
CAFE $$

(📞07-5538 6668; www.bumblescafe.com; 21 River Dr, Budds Beach; mains $14-24; ⏰7.30am-4pm) This gorgeous spot – a converted house (actually, at one stage, a brothel) – is the place for breakfast, sweet treats and coffee. It comprises a series of rooms, from the pink Princess Room (perfect for afternoon tea) to a library. Serves up some very desirable cakes.

Surfers Sandbar
MODERN AUSTRALIAN $$

(📞07-5526 9994; www.facebook.com/sandbargc; 52 Esplanade; mains $18-29; ⏰6.30am-midnight) After a staggering 19 years in beachside business, the owners here handed over the reins to their son. Back from serious hospitality work in Bali, he transformed Sandbar into a Riviera-meets-Canggu hot spot, full of intriguing interior details, happy locals and creative, globally inflected dishes.

Baritalia
ITALIAN $$

(📞07-5592 4700; www.baritaliagoldcoast.com.au; Shop 15, Chevron Renaissance Centre, cnr Elkhorn Ave & Surfers Paradise Blvd; pizzas $20-28, lunch specials $14-16, mains $20-38; ⏰8am-late; 🛜) A thoroughly Italian place with a fab outdoor terrace and friendly, European staff. Go for the Byron Bay slow-roasted pork belly, or excellent pastas, pizzas and risotto (including gluten-free choices). Decent Australian and Italian wines by the glass and good coffee.

🍷 Drinking & Nightlife

★Elsewhere
CLUB

(📞07-5592 6880; www.elsewherebar.com; 23 Cavill Ave.; ⏰9pm-4am Thu-Sun) A Saturday Night Fever–style dance floor always bodes well for good times, and this little bar-to-club venue features DJs who know their electronica, including cracking live sets from the soon-to-be-famous. Crowds are cooler than elsewhere, but it's a friendly, conversation-filled place, until DJs seriously turn up the volume.

Black Coffee Lyrics
BAR, CAFE

(📞0402 189 437; www.facebook.com/blackcoffeelyrics; 40/3131 Surfers Paradise Blvd, Surfers Paradise; ⏰5pm-late Tue-Fri, from 8am Sat & Sun) Upstairs and hidden in an unexpected location – within a nondescript arcade – this is the antithesis to Surfers shiny. Filled with vintage furniture and bordering on grungy, it's a dark oasis where locals come for coffee and tapas-style dishes, for steaks, and for bourbon, boutique brews and espresso martinis until late. Weekend breakfasts are hearty and there's the option of beer or bloody Marys from 10am.

☆ Entertainment

Arts Centre Gold Coast
THEATRE, CINEMA

(📞07-5588 4000; www.theartscentregc.com.au; 135 Bundall Rd; ⏰box office 8am-9pm Mon-Fri, to 9pm Sat, 11am-7pm Sun) A bastion of culture and civility beside the Nerang River, the Arts Centre has two cinemas, a restaurant, a bar, the Gold Coast City Gallery and a 1200-seat theatre, which regularly hosts impressive productions (comedy, jazz, opera, kids' concerts etc).

❶ Information

Backpackers World Travel (📞07-5561 0634; www.backpackerworldtravel.com; 3063 Surfers Paradise Blvd; ⏰10am-4pm; 🛜) Accommodation, tour and transport bookings and internet access.

Gold Coast Information & Booking Centre (📞1300 309 440, 07-5536 4709; www.visitgoldcoast.com; 2 Cavill Ave; ⏰8.30am-5pm Mon-Fri, 9am-6pm Sat, 9am-4pm Sun) The main Gold Coast tourist information booth; also sells theme-park tickets and has public transport info.

Surfers Paradise Day & Night Medical Centre (📞07-5592 2299; www.daynightmedical.com.au; 3221 Surfers Paradise Blvd; ⏰7am-11pm) General medical centre and pharmacy. Make an appointment, or just walk in.

Main Beach & The Spit

POP 3970

North of Surfers Paradise, the apartment towers are slightly less lofty and the pace eases up. Main Beach makes for a serene base if you're here for views, beach time and generally taking it easy. Tedder Ave may no longer possess place-to-be cache, but it still has a pleasantly village-like atmosphere, with enjoyable eating options alongside its chichi shops.

Further north the Spit separates the Southport Broadwater from the Pacific Ocean, stretching 5km to almost meet South Stradbroke Island. Its southern end is home to Marina Mirage, another upmarket shopping and eating zone, along with Mariner's Cove, a base for aquatic activities.

The beach up here, backed as it is with dunes and native parkland, has a startling sublimity. It also has some very uncrowded surf breaks that deliver when nothing else does.

◉ Sights & Activities

Main Beach Pavilion   ARCHITECTURE
(Macarthur Pde; ⊙9am-5pm) FREE The lovely Spanish Mission–style Main Beach Pavilion (1934) is a remnant from pre-boom days. Inside are some fabulous old photos of the Gold Coast before the skyscrapers.

★ Federation Walk   WALKING
(www.federationwalk.org) This pretty 3.7km trail takes you through patches of fragrant littoral rainforest, flush with beautiful bird life, and runs parallel to one of the world's most beautiful strips of surf beach. Along the way, it connects to the Gold Coast Oceanway, which heads 36km to Coolangatta. Federation Walk begins and finishes at the entrance to Sea World, in the car park of Phillip Park.

Australian Kayaking Adventures   KAYAKING
(☑0412 940 135; www.australiankayakingadventures.com.au; half-day tours adult/child $85/75, sunset tours $55/45) Paddle out to underrated South Stradbroke Island, or take a dusk paddle around Chevron Island in the calm canals behind Surfers.

Island Adventures   WHALE WATCHING
(☑07-5532 2444; www.goldcoastadventures.com.au; Mariner's Cove, 60-70 Sea World Dr, Main Beach; cruises incl lunch adult/child $129/69) Alternatively, gawp at wildlife and the Broadwater's sprawling McMansions on this catamaran cruise that includes water sports and a BBQ lunch on McLaren's Landing Eco Resort.

🛏 Sleeping & Eating

**Surfers Paradise YHA
at Main Beach**   HOSTEL $
(☑07-5571 1776; www.yha.com.au; 70 Sea World Dr, Main Beach; dm $33-36, d & tw $85; @ 🛜) Despite the Surfers Paradise of the name, this is a great 1st-floor position overlooking the marina. There's a free shuttle bus, BBQ nights every Friday, and the hostel is within wobbling distance of the Fisherman's Wharf Tavern. Sky-blue dorms; very well organised. Can also arrange tours and activities.

Main Beach Tourist Park   CARAVAN PARK $
(☑07-5667 2720; www.goldcoasttouristparks.com.au; 3600 Main Beach Pde, Main Beach; powered sites $62, cabins & villas from $165; P ﹡ 🛜 ﹡) Just across the road from the beach and surrounded by a phalanx of high-rise apartments, this caravan park is a family favourite. It's a tight fit between sites, but the facilities are good and the location is iconic.

Pacific Views   APARTMENT $$
(☑07-5527 0300; www.pacificviews.com.au; cnr Main Beach Pde & Woodroffe Ave, Main Beach; 1-bedroom apt $140-210; P ﹡ 🛜 ﹡) If you can cope with decor surprises, these individually owned and furnished apartments have amazing floor-to-ceiling views, living-room sized balconies and helpful staff. They're just one block back from the beach, and there's a cafe downstairs that will make you coffee at 5.30am if you're up for an early beach wander.

**★ Sheraton Grand Mirage
Resort**   RESORT $$$
(☑07-5577 0000; www.sheratongrandmiragegoldcoast.com; 71 Sea World Dr, Main Beach; d $280-400) This 270-room absolute-beachfront hotel recently received a light and lovely makeover. It has a relaxed glamour, and rooms are nicely low-slung and set among 6 hectares of tropical gardens. The large guest-only pool has a swim-up bar, and a delicious strip of Spit beach is accessible down a little path. The upstairs bar, open to nonguests, has ocean views.

Peter's Fish Market   SEAFOOD $
(☑07-5591 7747; www.petersfish.com.au; 120 Sea World Dr, Main Beach; meals $9-16; ⊙9am-7.30pm) A no-nonsense fish market–cum–fish and chip shop selling fresh and cooked seafood. It's fresh from the trawlers, in all shapes and sizes, and at great prices. Kitchen opens at noon.

Main Beach & The Spit

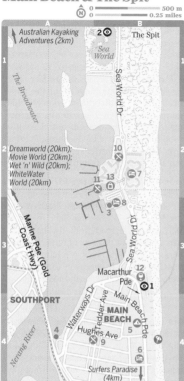

★ **Gourmet Farmers Market** MARKET **$**
(☑ 07-5555 6400; www.facebook.com/Marina MirageFarmersMarket; Marina Mirage, 74 Sea World Dr, Main Beach; ⊙ 7-11am Sat) On Saturday mornings, the open spaces of the Marina Mirage mall fill with stalls selling seasonal fruit and veg, baked goods, pickles, oils, vinegars, seafood, pasta and more, all from small-scale producers and makers.

★ **Pier** MODERN AUSTRALIAN, PIZZA **$$**
(☑ 07-5527 0472; www.piermarinamirage.com. au; Ground fl, Marina Mirage, Sea World Dr, Main Beach; pizzas $18-24; ⊙ noon-11.30pm) An easy but super-stylish marina-side spot, with upstairs and downstairs seating, both perfect for yachtie views. The mostly European staff is winning and the menu is flexible. Wood-fired pizzas can be combined with arancini (which get their own menu), or there are small and large dishes that tick a number of culinary boxes without being faddish.

★ **Bar Chico** MODERN AUSTRALIAN **$$**
(☑ 07-5532 9111; www.barchico.com.au; 26-30 Tedder Ave, Main Beach; dishes $12-22; ⊙ 4pm-midnight Mon-Wed, from noon Thu-Sun) A welcome addition to the Tedder strip, this dark and moody European-style bar does fabulous cheese and charcuterie plates, fish or meat tapas-style dishes and big, beguiling salads. Displays a chef-like attention to detail, with in-house fermenting and curing, and lots of high-end ingredients. Wine is similarly thoughtful, with some particularly nice Spanish drops.

Providore CAFE **$$**
(☑ 07-5532 9390; www.providoremirage.com.au; Marina Mirage, 74 Sea World Dr, Main Beach; mains $16-29; ⊙ 7am-6pm) Floor-to-ceiling windows rimmed with Italian mineral-water bottles, inverted desk lamps dangling from the ceiling, good-looking Euro tourists, wines by the glass, perfect patisserie goods, cheese fridges, and baskets overflowing with fresh produce: this excellent deli-cafe gets a lot of things right.

🍷 Drinking & Nightlife

Southport Surf Lifesaving Club CLUB
(www.sslsc.com.au; Macarthur Pde; ⊙ 6.30am-midnight) This beautiful, airy pavilion-style club

GOLD COAST THEME PARKS

The gravity-defying rollercoasters and water slides at the Gold Coast's American-style parks offer some seriously dizzying action and, although recently beset with a number of accidents, still attract huge crowds. Discount tickets are sold in most of the tourist offices on the Gold Coast or can be bought online (☑13 33 86; www.themeparks.com.au). The Mega Pass ($110 per person for 14-day entry) grants unlimited entry to Sea World, Warner Bros Movie World, Wet'n'Wild and the little-kid-friendly farm-park Paradise Country (all owned by Village Roadshow). Dreamworld and WhiteWater World have a Summer Season Pass giving unlimited entry (adult/child $99/79).

A couple of tips: the parks can get insanely crowded, so arrive early or face a long walk from the far side of the car park. Also note that the parks don't let you bring your own food or drinks.

Dreamworld (☑07-5588 1111, 1800 073 300; www.dreamworld.com.au; Dreamworld Pkwy, Coomera; adult/child $65/55; ⊙10am-5pm) Touts itself as Australia's 'biggest' theme park. There are the 'Big 9 Thrill Rides', plus Wiggles World and the DreamWorks experience, both for younger kids. Other attractions include Tiger Island, and a range of interactive animal encounters. A one-day pass (adult/child $65/55) gives you entry to both Dreamworld and WhiteWater World.

Sea World (www.seaworld.com.au; adult/child $80/70; ⊙9.30am-5pm) Continues to attract controversy for its marine shows, where dolphins and sea lions perform tricks for the crowd. While Sea World claims the animals lead a good life, welfare groups argue that keeping such sensitive sea mammals in captivity is harmful, and is especially exacerbated when mixed with human interaction. The park also displays penguins and polar bears, and has water slides and rollercoasters.

Movie World (☑07-5573 3999, 13 33 86; www.movieworld.com.au; Pacific Hwy, Oxenford; adult/child $79/69; ⊙9.30am-5pm) Movie-themed shows, rides and attractions, including the Batwing Spaceshot, Justice League 3D Ride and Scooby-Doo Spooky Coaster. Batman, Austin Powers, Porky Pig et al roam through the crowds.

Wet'n'Wild (☑07-5556 1660, 13 33 86; www.wetnwild.com.au; Pacific Hwy, Oxenford; adult/child $79/69; ⊙10am-5pm) The ultimate water slide here is the Kamikaze, where you plunge down an 11m drop in a two-person tube at 50km/h. This vast water park also has pitch-black slides, white-water rapids and wave pools.

WhiteWater World (☑1800 073 300, 07-5588 1111; www.dreamworld.com.au/whitewater-world; Dreamworld Pkwy, Coomera; adult/child $65/55; ⊙10am-4pm Mon-Fri, to 5pm Sat & Sun) This park features the Cave of Waves, Pipeline Plunge and more than 140 wet and watery activities and slides.

has spectacular views. The deck is open early for coffee, or head here for lazy beery afternoons. It's one of the only places open late north of Surfers.

Broadbeach, Mermaid & Nobby Beach

POP 19,890

Directly south of Surfers Paradise, Broadbeach may be all about apartment towers and pedestrian malls, but it's decidedly more upmarket than its neighbour, with carefully landscaped streets and smart places to eat, drink and shop.

Miami Marketta (www.miamimarketta.com; 23 Hillcrest Pde, Miami; ⊙cafe 6am-2pm Tue-Sat, street food 5-10pm Wed, Fri & Sat) is a permanent street market with food, fashion and live music, a smidge south of Mermaid in just-as-cool Miami.

🛏 Sleeping & Eating

Hi-Ho Beach Apartments APARTMENT $$
(☑07-5538 2777; www.hihobeach.com.au; 2 Queensland Ave, Broadbeach; 1-/2-bedroom apt $175/275; P❄🖥🔊) A top choice for location, close to the beach and cafes. You're not paying for glitzy lobbies here, but rooms are comfortable and it's well managed, clean and quiet. And, hey, the Vegas-esque sign!

Peppers Broadbeach
APARTMENT $$$

(www.peppers.com.au/broadbeach; 21 Elizabeth Ave, Broadbeach; 1-/3-bedroom apt $500/800; ❄ ☎ ❄) When you want flawless, if unexciting, comfort, this Peppers apartment hotel is for you. Think marble dining tables, European kitchen appliances, wrap-around balconies, high-thread-count linen. The three bedroom 'sky homes' really take the luxury to town. The day spa has heated indoor and outdoor pools.

★Sparrow Eating House
MODERN AUSTRALIAN $

(☑ 07-5575 3330; www.sparroweatinghouse.com. au; 2/32 Lavarack Rd, Nobby Beach; sharing dishes $11-22; ⊙ 5pm-midnight Wed-Fri, from 7am Sat & Sun) This lovely, clean-lined monochrome industrial space with green accents has a low-key glamour and a kitchen that loves what it does. Come for a casual lunch of spring gnocchi with hazelnuts and herbs; enjoy a blood-orange margarita and some tequila prawns; or pop in for a glass of small-producer wine.

Cardamom Pod
VEGETARIAN $

(www.cardamompod.com.au; 1/2685 Gold Coast Hwy, Broadbeach; 1/2/3/4 dishes with rice $10/16/24/31; ⊙ 11.30am-9.30pm; ♫) 🍃 Vegetarians rejoice! This magical Krishna-inspired, vegan-friendly eatery conjures up some of the best vegetarian cuisine around. Choose from curry, vegan bake or cheesy bake of the day. Finish off with a trademark dessert: raw, gluten- and sugar-free (and delicious). Everything is made from scratch on the premises.

★Glenelg Public House
STEAK $$

(☑ 07-5575 2284; www.theglenelgpublichouse.com. au; 2460 Gold Coast Hwy, Mermaid Beach; mains $22-32; ⊙ 5pm-midnight Mon-Thu, from noon Fri-Sun) This atmospheric little place uses premium produce and a sparing accompaniments. The epic steak list ($22 to $68, sharing $80 to $90) takes in local breeds, the best of New Zealand and New South Wales tablelands and both grass- and grain-fed cuts. There's also an 'early tea' dinner special before 6.30pm.

★BSKT Cafe
MODERN AUSTRALIAN $$

(☑ 07-5526 6565; www.bskt.com.au; 4 Lavarack Ave, Mermaid Beach; mains $10-27; ⊙ 7am-4pm Mon-Thu, to 10pm Fri & Sat, to 5pm Sun; ♫ ♿) This satisfyingly industrial cafe is 100m from the beach, but that's far from its only charm: focused on organic produce, the dishes and service punch well above cafe level. Vegans and paleos will be at home here, as will kids, in the fenced play area, and yogis, in the upstairs yoga school.

🍷 Drinking & Nightlife

★Cambus Wallace
COCKTAIL BAR

(www.thecambuswallace.com.au; 4/2237 Gold Coast Hwy, Nobby Beach; ⊙ 5pm-midnight Tue-Thu, from 4pm Fri-Sun) Dark, moody, maritime-themed bar that attracts a good-looking but relaxed local crew. Settle in with something from its long, long list of bottled beer and cider, or try a Gold Coast take on cocktail classics (a coconut, lime and rum Maiden Voyage could not be better suited to the climate).

Seaside Broadbeach Bowls Club
CLUB

(☑ 07-5531 5913; www.broadbeachbowlsclub. com; 169 Surf Pde, Broadbeach; ⊙ 11.30am-8pm) Home to the best bowling greens in Australia – some say, the world. Far from a tired old space, this traditional club has had a modern makeover with its bars and restaurants bright, breezy and beachy. Come for a sunset beer on the huge terrace, and barefoot bowls.

Burleigh Heads

POP 9580

The super-chilled surfie enclave of Burleigh (drop the 'Heads', you're already fond friends, right?) has long been a family favourite, but is now having its moment in the sun. The town's retro vibe and youthful energy epitomise both the Gold Coast's timeless appeal and its new, increasingly interesting, spirit. You'll find some of the region's best cafes and restaurants here and, yes, that famous right-hand point break still pumps while the pine-backed beach charms everyone who lays eyes on it.

👁 Sights

Burleigh Head National Park
PARK

(www.npsr.qld.gov.au/parks/burleigh-head; Goodwin Tce, Burleigh Heads; ⊙ 24hr) FREE Walk the headland through this 27-hectare rainforest reserve, with its abundent bird life and walking trails. Great views of the Burleigh surf.

★Village Markets
MARKET

(☑ 0487 711 850; www.thevillagemarkets.co; Burleigh Heads State School, 1750 Gold Coast Hwy, Burleigh Heads; ⊙ 8.30am-1pm 1st & 3rd Sun of month) A long-running market that highlights local creators and collectors, with fashion and lifestyle stalls, live music and a strong local following.

David Fleay Wildlife Park
WILDLIFE RESERVE

(☑ 07-5576 2411; www.npsr.qld.gov.au/parks/david-fleay; cnr Loman Lane & West Burleigh Rd, West Burleigh; adult/child/family $22/10/55; ⊙ 9am-5pm) Opened by the doctor who first succeed-

Burleigh Heads

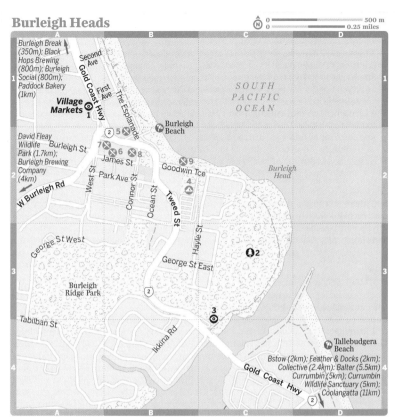

0   500 m
0   0.25 miles

ed in breeding platypuses, this wildlife park has 4km of walking tracks through mangroves and rainforest, and plenty of informative native wildlife shows throughout the day. It's around 3km inland from Burleigh Heads.

Jellurgal Cultural Centre   CULTURAL CENTRE
(☑07-5525 5955; www.jellurgal.com.au; 1711 Gold Coast Hwy, Burleigh Heads; ☺8am-3pm Mon-Fri) 🌿**FREE** This Aboriginal cultural centre at the base of Burleigh's headland sheds some light on life here hundreds and thousands of years ago. There's a collection of artefacts and a number of different tours (various prices) available – all include walks to the headland (Jellurgal, the Dreaming Mountain), past middens and important Aboriginal sites.

🛏 Sleeping & Eating

Burleigh Break   MOTEL $
(www.burleighbreak.com.au; 1935 Gold Coast Hwy, Burleigh Heads; d $120-160; ℗ 🛜) A progressive

Burleigh Heads

renovation has seen one of the Gold Coast's beloved mid-century motels transformed into a friendly and great-value place to stay. Classic motel design means highway views,

THE GOLD COAST BURLEIGH HEADS

SOUTH STRADBROKE ISLAND

This narrow, 21km-long sand island is largely undeveloped – the perfect antidote to the Gold Coast's busyness. At its northern end, the narrow channel separating it from North Stradbroke Island is a top fishing spot; at its southern end, where the Spit is only 200m away, you'll find breaks so good they have Gold Coast's surfers braving the swim over.

South Stradbroke was once attached to North Stradbroke, until a huge storm in 1896 blasted through the isthmus that joined them. South Stradbroke's isolation since has been a boon for its natural habitat. There are wallabies aplenty and pristine bush, sand and sea to explore. And, of course, no cars. If you don't wish to overnight (accommodation choices are limited), you can charter a boat or do a day tour with **Water'bout** (☑ 0401 428 004; www.waterbout.com. au; Waterways Dr Boat Ramp, Proud Park, Main Beach; tours per adult $125).

Campers should head to North Currigee, South Currigee or Tipplers campgrounds.

but you're still just a minute's amble from the beach. Rooms have retained vintage features where possible, but otherwise are fresh and simple. Ask about long-stay discounts.

Burleigh Beach Tourist Park
CARAVAN PARK $

(☑ 07-5667 2750; www.goldcoasttouristparks.com. au; 36 Goodwin Tce, Burleigh Heads; powered sites $46-60, cabins $140-210; ❋ @ � ⛲) This council-owned park is snug, but it's well run and in a great spot near the beach. Aim for one of the three blue cabins at the front of the park. There's a minimum two-night stay for cabins.

★ Borough Barista
CAFE $

(14 Esplanade, Burleigh Heads; mains $5-19; ◷ 5.30am-2.30pm) It's all cool tunes and friendly vibes at this little open-walled espresso shack. Join local surfers for their dawn piccolo lattes and post-surf for a chia bowl or breakfast salad on a footpath bench. Lunches revolve around good proteins with burgers or big salads.

Paddock Bakery
BAKERY $

(☑ 0419 652 221; www.paddockbakery.com; Hibiscus Haven, Miami; dishes $9-17; ◷ 7.30am-2.30pm) An antique wood-fired oven sits in the heart of this beautiful old weatherboard cottage and turns out wonderful bread, croissants, granola and pastries. The semi-sourdough doughnuts have a devoted fan base, as do the Nutella doughboats – spherical shaped so as to fit more goo. There's a full breakfast and lunch menu, too, as well as top coffee and cold-pressed juices.

Burleigh Social
CAFE $

(2 Hibiscus Haven, Burleigh Heads; dishes $12-19; ◷ 6am-2pm) This backstreet cafe has a party vibe from early morning at its picnic-table seating. There's paleo granola or the big paleo breakfast (salmon, bacon or ham with kale, eggs and avocado) or nicely done versions of Australian cafe staples such as smashed avocado, eggs on sourdough and bacon-and-egg rolls. Brisket subs and veggie burgers take it into lunch.

★ Rick Shores
MODERN ASIAN $$

(☑ 07-5630 6611; www.rickshores.com.au; 43 Goodwin Tce, Burleigh Heads; mains $32-52; ◷ noon-11pm Tue-Sun) Feet-in-the-sand dining can often play it safe, and while this Modern Asian newcomer sends out absolute crowd-pleasing dishes, it's also pleasingly inventive. The space is all about the view, the sound of the nearby waves, the salty breeze and communal-table conviviality. Serves are huge, which can allay the menu price if you're not dining solo and are into sharing.

★ Harry's Steak Bistro
STEAK $$

(☑ 07-5576 8517; www.harryssteakbistro.com. au; 1744 Gold Coast Hwy, Burleigh Heads; mains $20-40; ◷ 5-11pm Wed & Thu, noon-11pm Fri-Sun) Don't misread the menu – a mix and match steak-and-sauce affair, plus unlimited fries – as belonging to a chain restaurant. Harry's, a stylish, sparse paean to 'beef, booze and banter', is super-serious about its steaks, with each accredited the name of its farm and region.

★ Justin Lane Pizzeria & Bar
PIZZA $$

(☑ 07-5576 8517; www.justinlane.com.au; 1708 Gold Coast Hwy, Burleigh Heads; pizzas $19-24; ◷ 5pm-late) One of the seminal players in Burleigh's food and drinking scene, Justin Lane has now colonised most of an old shopping arcade. Yes, the fun stretches upstairs, downstairs and across the hall. Great pizzas, simple but flavour-packed pasta dishes and possibly the coast's best regional Italian wine list make it a must, even if you're not here for the party vibe.

Finders Keepers MODERN AUSTRALIAN **$$**
(☑ 07-5659 1643; www.finderskeepersbar.com.au; 49 James St; mains $16-29; ⊘ 4-10pm Tue-Fri, 7am-11pm Sat & Sun) This dark, stylish restaurant feels like it's been transported from Sydney's Woollahra or Melbourne's South Yarra, but the friendly young staff is pure Burleigh. Similarly, the tapas-style dishes are a mix of sophistication (foie gras parfait and poached scallop mornay) and health-conscious coastal casual (ancient grain salad, and salmon on buckwheat and seasonal greens with a sea-vegetable butter sauce).

🍷 Drinking & Nightlife

Black Hops Brewing BREWERY
(www.blackhops.com.au; 15 Gardenia Grove, Burleigh Heads; ⊘ 10am-6pm Mon-Fri, noon-4pm Sat) The Black Hops boys run a friendly and fun tap room where you can enjoy a paddle or whatever craft delight they've currently got on tap. There are eight poetically named beers – from the Bitter Fun pale ale to the Flash Bang white IPA – to choose from, or you can purchase whatever they have bottled.

Burleigh Brewing Company BREWERY
(☑ 07-5593 6000; www.burleighbrewing.com.au; 17a Ern Harley Dr, Burleigh Heads; monthly tours $50; ⊘ 3-6pm Wed & Thu, to 8.30pm Fri, 2-8pm Sun) Hang out in this light, woody and blokey space with fellow beer lovers. There's live music and local food trucks, not to mention a 24 tap line-up of Burleigh brews, including their main line and pilot project beers. Tours run on Wednesday nights mid-month and need to be booked through the website.

Currumbin & Palm Beach

POP 16,310

Around the point from Burleigh, Palm Beach has a particularly lovely stretch of sand, backed with a few old-style beach shacks. Its numbered streets are also home to some great coffee stops and dining ops. Further south again, Currumbin is a sleepy family-focused town, with a beautiful surf beach, safe swimming in Currumbin Creek and some evocative mid-century architecture worth clocking. It's also home to the iconic eponymous wildlife sanctuary.

◉ Sights & Activities

Kids will enjoy a summer swim at **Currumbin Rock Pools** (Currumbin Creek Rd, Currumbin Valley).

★ Currumbin Wildlife
Sanctuary WILDLIFE RESERVE
(☑ 07-5534 1266, 1300 886 511; www.cws.org.au; 28 Tomewin St, Currumbin; adult/child/family $49/35/133; ⊘ 8am-5pm) This nicely restrained, old-style operation includes Australia's biggest rainforest aviary, where you can hand-feed a technicolour blur of rainbow lorikeets. There's also kangaroo feeding, photo ops with koalas and crocodiles, reptile shows and Aboriginal dance displays. Entry is reduced after 3pm, and there's often an adults-at kids-prices special during school holidays.

🍴 Eating & Drinking

Feather & Docks CAFE **$**
(☑ 07-5659 1113; www.featheranddocks.com.au; 1099 Gold Coast Hwy, Palm Beach; dishes $12-18; ⊘ 5.30am-3pm; 🍴) Given the witness-the-fitness early-to-rise lifestyle round these parts, the notion of breakfast burgers and lunch that starts at 10.30am makes a lot of sense. That said, most things on the menu work for either breakfast or lunch, from the French toast to the brekky tortilla to the stacked pastrami melts.

★ Bstow MODERN AUSTRALIAN **$$**
(☑ 0410 033 380; www.bstow.com.au; 8th Ave Plaza, 1176 Gold Coast Hwy, Palm Beach; mains $18-24) Best-of-both-worlds Bstow is somewhere you'll want to hang with a drink – it does very special cocktails; think house-infused gin and freshly pressed, muddled or juiced mixers – but also warrants a leisurely dinner – the sharing-plate-style dishes are seriously considered, easy on the eye and a creative mix of tastes and textures.

Collective MODERN AUSTRALIAN **$$**
(www.thecollectivepalmbeach.com.au; 1128 Gold Coast Hwy, Palm Beach; mains $17-24; ⊘ noon-9pm) Locals' favourites come together here, with five kitchens serving one great, rambling indoor-outdoor communal dining space, strung with fairy lights, flush with pot plants and packed with up to 300 happy eaters. There are two bars, one of them a balmy rooftop affair. Choose from burgers, pizza, tapas, Asian fusion, Mexican and Mod Oz share plates. You can even head here for a post-surf breakfast at 7am.

★ **Balter** BREWERY
(☑ 07-5525 6916; www.balter.com.au; 14 Traders Way, Currumbin; tasting paddles $12; ⊙ 3-9pm Fri, 1-8pm Sat & Sun) Local surf star Mick Fanning (the man who punched a shark, right?) and his fellow circuit legends Joel Parkinson, Bede Durbidge and Josh Kerr are all partners in this wonderful new brewery, hidden away at the back of a Currumbin industrial estate. Come and sample the already sought-after Balter XPA or a special such as the German-style Keller pilsner.

Coolangatta

POP 5710

A down-to-earth beach town on Queensland's far southern border, 'Coolie' has quality surf beaches, including the legendary Superbank, and a tight-knit, very real community that makes it feel less touristy than it otherwise could. The legendary Coolangatta Gold (www.sls.com.au/coolangattagold; ⊙ Oct) surf-life-saving comp happens here every October and the Quiksilver & Roxy Pro (www.aspworldtour.com; ⊙ Mar) kicks off surfing's most prestigious world tour at Snapper Rocks each March. Follow the boardwalk north around Kirra Point for another beautiful long stretch of beach, sometimes challenging surf, and locally loved indie-atmosphere cafes and bars.

Point Danger Light, the lighthouse on the headland between Coolangatta and Tweed Heads, marks the border between Queensland and NSW and offers amazing views along the coast.

For local surfing lessons, try Gold Coast Surfing Centre (☑ 0417 191 629; www.gold coastsurfingcentre.com; group lessons $45) or Cooly Surf (☑ 07-5536 1470; 25 Griffith St; 2hr surfing lessons $45; ⊙ 9am-5pm).

🛏 Sleeping & Eating

Coolangatta Sands Backpackers HOSTEL $
(☑ 07-5536 7472; www.taphousegroup.com.au/coolangatta-sands-backpackers; cnr Griffith & McLean Sts, Coolangatta; dm $17-25, d $68-80; ❄ @ 🛜) Above the boozy Coolangatta Sands Hotel, this hostel is a warren of rooms and corridors, but there's a fab wraparound balcony above the street (no booze allowed, unfortunately – go downstairs to the pub) and red chesterfields in the TV room for when it's raining.

Kirra Beach Tourist Park CARAVAN PARK $
(☑ 07-5667 2740; www.goldcoasttouristparks.com.au; 10 Charlotte St, Kirra; powered/unpowered sites $39/35, s/d $65/140, cabins $125-140; ❄ @ 🛜 🏊) A large council-run park with

Coolangatta

plenty of trees, wandering ibises and a camp kitchen and heated swimming pool. Good-value self-contained cabins (with or without bathroom), all a few hundred metres from the beach.

★ La Costa Motel
MOTEL **$$**

(☎07-5599 2149; www.lacostamotel.com.au; 127 Golden Four Dr, Bilinga; d $130-185; ❊ 🛜) One of the few motels of 1950s 'highway heritage', this mint-green weatherboard, located just off the Gold Coast Hwy, has stayed true to its roots on the outside, while the interiors are neat, comfortable and include kitchenettes. A lovely apartment with a private deck suits longer stays. Prices are significantly lower outside high season.

★ Hotel Komune
HOTEL, HOSTEL **$$**

(☎07-5536 6764; www.komuneresorts.com; 146 Marine Pde, Coolangatta; dm $38-45, 1-bedroom apt $140-180, 2-bedroom apt $185-300; 🛜 ▨) With a palm-laden pool area and an ultra laid-back vibe, this 10-storey converted apartment tower is the ultimate surf retreat. It has budget dorms, apartments and a hip penthouse begging for a party. That said, the party is usually to be found downstairs, at the on-site bar (well, nightclub) from around 9pm, with music Fridays to Sundays.

★ Black Sheep Espresso Baa
CAFE **$**

(☎07-5536 9947; www.tbseb.com.au; 72-80 Marine Pde, Coolangatta; ⏰5am-3pm) A passionate crew of coffee obsessives run this cute little cafe right in the heart of the Marine Pde shopping strip. Perfect espresso, filter coffee and that Gold Coast necessity, iced lattes, are joined by a small but creative breakfast and lunch menu.

Cafe Dbar
MODERN AUSTRALIAN **$$**

(☎07-5599 2031; www.cafedbar.com.au; 275 Boundary St, Coolangatta; mains $19-27; ⏰11.15am-3pm Mon-Thu, to 8pm Fri-Sun) This lovely spot is perched above the cliffs of Point Danger, at the easternmost point of two states, almost on top of the NSW–Queensland border. You can deliberate on any number of fabulous breakfast options, grab a good takeaway coffee, or stay for share plates and salads. There's also a stylish little shop attached for a postprandial browse.

Bellakai
MODERN AUSTRALIAN **$$$**

(☎07-5599 5116; www.facebook.com/bellakai.coolangatta; 82 Marine Pde, Coolangatta; mains $30-40; ⏰5am-9.30pm) From 5am (yes, 5am) until late, Bellakai plates up casual but spot-on dishes. The menu changes seasonally, but it will go something like this: fish of the day with red curry and wilted greens, or house-made parpadelle with prawns. Mornings mean coffee and Coolie locals catching up.

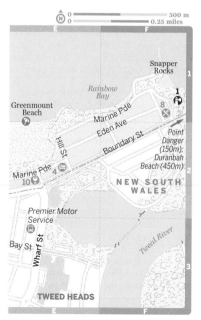

GOLDIE'S BEST SURF BREAKS

The Gold Coast possesses some of the longest, hollowest and best waves in the world, and is lauded for its epic consistency. The creation of the 2km Superbank sand bar has made for a decade of even better waves, even more often.

Snapper Rocks A highly advanced point break at Coolangatta's far south; home to the Quiksilver Pro World Surfing League, and home break to Australian pro surfers Stephanie Gilmore and Joel Parkinson.

Duranbah Universally known as D-bah, this point and peaky beach break is good for those who like their waves technical and punchy.

Greenmount Classic beach break that benefits from a southerly swell.

Kirra Beautiful beach break that doesn't work that often, but, oh when it does.

Burleigh Heads Strong currents and boulders to watch out for, but a perfect break that's more often on than not.

The Spit One of north Goldie's stalwarts, this peaky beach break can work even when the surf is small.

Drinking & Nightlife

★ Eddie's Grub House   BAR
(07-5599 2177; www.eddiesgrubhouse.com; 171 Griffith St, Coolangatta; noon-10.30pm Tue-Thu & Sun, to midnight Fri & Sat) A totally old-school rock-and-roll bar, with dirty blues and best-of rock soundtrack, Eddie's is emblematic of the new Gold Coast: indie, ironic and really fun. Yes, there's grub to be had, and Eddie's 'dive bar comfort food' is exactly that. But this is a place for drinking, dancing, chatting and chilling (as they say themselves).

Coolangatta Hotel   PUB
(www.thecoolyhotel.com.au; cnr Marine Pde & Warner St, Coolangatta; 10am-late) The hub of Coolangatta's sometimes boisterous nocturnal scene, this huge pub, across from the beach, pumps with live bands (Grinspoon, The Rubens), sausage sizzles, pool comps, trivia nights, acoustic jam nights, surprisingly sophisticated pub-meal deals (pasta and rosé, anyone?) – basically, the works. Big Sunday sessions.

Getting There & Away

Greyhound (1300 473 946; www.greyhound.com.au) runs to Brisbane and beyond, while **Premier Motor Service** (13 34 10; www.premierms.com.au) heads as far north as Cairns. Coaches stop on Wharf St.

GOLD COAST HINTERLAND

Inland from the surf, sand and half-nakedness of the Gold Coast, the densely forested mountains of the McPherson Range feel a million miles away. There are some brilliant national parks here, with subtropical jungle, waterfalls, lookouts and rampant wildlife.

Tamborine Mountain

The squat, mountain-top rainforest community of Tamborine Mountain – comprising Eagle Heights, North Tamborine and Mt Tamborine – is 45km inland from the Gold Coast beaches, and has cornered the arts-and-craft, Germanic-kitsch, package-tour, chocolate-fudge-liqueur market in a big way. If this is your bag, Gallery Walk (07-5545 2006; 197 Long Rd, Eagle Heights) in Eagle Heights is the place to stock up.

Tamborine National Park (www.nprsr.qld.gov.au/parks/tamborine) comprises 13 sections stretching across the 8km plateau, offering waterfalls and super views of the Gold Coast. Accessed via easy-to-moderate walking trails are Witches Falls, Curtis Falls, Cedar Creek Falls and Cameron Falls. Pick up a map at the visitor centre in North Tamborine.

With Skywalk (07-5545 2222; www.rainforestskywalk.com.au; 333 Geissman Dr, North Tamborine; adult/child/family $20/10/49; 9.30am-4pm) you can take a 1.5km walk descending down into the forest floor to pretty Cedar Creek, with spectacular elevated steel viewpoints and bridges cutting through the upper canopy along the way. Look out for rare Richmond birdwing butterflies en route.

🛏 Sleeping & Eating

⭐**Songbirds Rainforest Retreat** HOTEL $$$
(☑07-5545 2563; www.songbirds.com.au; Lot 10,
Tamborine Mountain Rd, North Tamborine; villas
$270-498; 🅿🛜) By far the classiest outfit on
the hill. Each of the six Southeast Asian–
inspired villas has a double spa with rain-
forest views; rates drop for stays of two
nights or more. The award-winning restau-
rant, also on-site, is worth visiting for a long
lunch.

⭐**Long Road Bistro** MODERN AUSTRALIAN $$
(☑07-5545 0826; www.witcheschasecheese.com.
au/bistro; 165/185-187 Long Rd, Eagle Heights;
mains $21-29; ⊙10am-4pm Mon-Fri, from 7am
Sat & Sun) Pop in for a big Sunday roast (say,
pork belly with a beetroot and green-apple
relish) or grab a lentil burger or cookies-and-
cream-pimped iced coffee. It's part of the
Witches Chase Cheese Company (☑07-
5545 2032; www.witcheschasecheese.com.au; 165
Long Rd, Eagle Heights; ⊙10am-4pm) so, as you
might imagine, the cheese board is a winner.
There's also live music and something of a
party vibe on weekends.

Lamington National Park

Australia's largest remnant of subtropical
rainforest cloaks the deep valleys and steep
cliffs of the McPherson Range, reaching ele-
vations of 1100m on the Lamington Plateau.
Here, the 200-sq-km **Lamington National
Park** (www.nprsr.qld.gov.au/parks/lamington) is
a Unesco World Heritage Site and has more
than 160km of walking trails.

The two most accessible sections of the
park are Binna Burra and Green Mountains, both reached via long, narrow, winding roads from Canungra (not great for big
campervans). Binna Burra can also be accessed from Nerang.

🛏 Sleeping & Eating

At the end of Lamington National Park
Rd,**Green Mountains Campground** (☑13
74 68; www.nprsr.qld.gov.au/parks/lamington/
camping.html; Green Mountains; site per person/
family $6.15/24) is adjacent to the day-use vis-
itor car park. There are plenty of spots for
tents and caravans (and a toilet-and-show-
er block); book in advance.

Binna Burra Mountain Lodge (☑1300
246 622, 07-5533 3622; www.binnaburralodge.
com.au; 1069 Binna Burra Rd, Beechmont;

powered/unpowered sites $35/28, safari tents
$105, d with/without bathroom $290/175; 🅿)
is an atmospheric mountain retreat; the
closest thing to a ski lodge in the bush. You
can stay in rustic log cabins, well-appoint-
ed apartments (known as 'sky lodges') with
spectacular scenic rim views, or in a tent
surrounded by forest. There's a good restaurant and teahouse.

The famous 1926 **O'Reilly's Rainforest
Retreat** (☑07-5502 4911, 1800 688 722; www.
oreillys.com.au; Lamington National Park Rd, Green
Mountains; s $80-99, d $149-188, 1-bedroom villas
$360-375; @🛜🏊) has lost much of its orig-
inal grandeur but retains a rustic charm –
and sensational views! There are plenty of
organised activities, plus a day spa, a cafe, a
bar and a restaurant.

Springbrook National Park

About a 40-minute drive west of Burleigh
Heads, **Springbrook National Park** (☑13
74 68; www.nprsr.qld.gov.au/parks/springbrook) is
a steep remnant of the huge Tweed Shield
volcano that centred on nearby Mt Warning
in NSW more than 20 million years ago. It's
a wonderland for hikers, with excellent trails
through cool-temperate, subtropical and eucalypt forests offering a mosaic of gorges,
cliffs and waterfalls.

Excellent viewpoints in the park include
the appropriately named **Best of All Lookout** (Repeater Station Rd), **Canyon Lookout**
(Canyon Pde), whch is also the start of a 4km
circuit walk to Twin Falls and the superb
lookout beside the 60m **Goomoolahra
Falls** (Springbrook Rd), giving views across the
plateau and all the way back to the coast.

🛏 Sleeping & Eating

There are 11 grassy sites at the pretty **Settlement Campground** (☑13 74 68; www.
nprsr.qld.gov.au/parks/springbrook/camping.html;
52 Carricks Rd, Springbrook; sites per person/fam-
ily $6/24), the only campground at Spring-
brook. There are toilets and gas BBQs but
no showers. Book ahead.

Mouses House (☑07-5533 5192; www.
mouseshouse.com.au; 2807 Springbrook Rd,
Springbrook; d $270-320; ❄🛜) hides 12 cedar
chalets, linked by softly lit boardwalks, in
the magical misty woods. Each has a spa
and a wood fire, and some are by a cascad-
ing stream.

Noosa &
the Sunshine Coast

Best Places to Eat

➜ Spirit House (p145)

➜ Wasabi (p131)

➜ Noosa Beach House (p131)

➜ Embassy XO (p143)

Best Places to Sleep

➜ Oceans (p139)

➜ Monaco (p136)

➜ YHA Halse Lodge (p128)

➜ Glass House Mountains Ecolodge (p134)

Why Go?

The Sunshine Coast – the 100 golden kilometres stretching from the tip of Bribie Island to the Cooloola Coast – is aglow with perfect beaches, coveted surf and a laid-back, sun-kissed populace who will quickly tell you how lucky they are. Resort towns dot the coast, each with its own appeal and vibe, from upmarket, cosmopolitan Noosa to newly hip, evolving Caloundra.

Further inland is the lush, cool hinterland. It's here that you'll find the ethereal Glass House Mountains, looming over the land- and seascapes, and the iconic Australia Zoo. Further north, the Blackall Range offers a change of scenery with thick forests, lush pastures and quaint villages dotted with artisan food shops, cafes and crafty boutiques.

When to Go
Noosa

May Gourmands and gluttons nosh and slosh at the four-day Noosa Food & Wine.

Aug Postholiday lull means fewer crowds, solitary beach walks and warm, unsticky weather.

Sep Up-and-coming Caloundra draws music fans with its rocking surfside Caloundra Festival.

Noosa & the Sunshine Coast Highlights

1 **Noosa National Park** (p126) Hiking and wildlife spotting in Noosa's beautiful, easily accessible slice of Eden.

2 **Noosa's food scene** (p130) Feasting on local produce and culinary ingenuity at a string of foodie-approved restaurants.

3 **Great Sandy National Park** (p143) Cruising up one of Australia's most spectacular natural highways, the Great Beach Drive.

4 **Caloundra** (p134) Riding waves, slurping local beers and checking out the street art in the Sunshine Coast's new hub of cool.

5 **Glass House Mountains** (p133) Soaking up the grandiose vistas of (and from) the hinterland's most geologically surreal landmarks.

ℹ Getting There & Around

AIR

Sunshine Coast Airport (p303) is at Marcoola, 10km north of Maroochydore and 26km south of Noosa. **Jetstar** (☑13 15 38; www.jetstar. com) and **Virgin Australia** (☑13 67 89; www. virginaustralia.com) have daily direct flights from Sydney and Melbourne; **Qantas** (☑13 13 13; www.qantas.com.au) flies direct from Sydney eight times weekly. Jetstar also runs direct flights from Adelaide three times weekly.

From July to October, **Air New Zealand** (www. airnewzealand.com) flies direct from Auckland three to four times weekly.

BUS

Greyhound Australia (☑1300 473 946; www.greyhound.com.au) has several daily services from Brisbane to Caloundra (from $19, two hours), Maroochydore (from $23, two hours) and Noosa (from $24, 2½ to 3¼ hours). **Premier Motor Service** (☑13 34 10; www.premierms.com.au) also runs buses to Maroochydore ($23, 1½ to 1¾ hours) and Noosa ($23, 2½ hours) from Brisbane.

Several companies offer transfers from Sunshine Coast Airport and Brisbane to points along the coast. Fares from Brisbane cost from around $40 to $60 and from Sunshine Coast Airport between $25 and $35. (Fares are around half-price for children.)

Con-X-ion (☑1300 370 471; www.con-x-ion. com) does airport transfers from the Sunshine Coast and Brisbane Airports.

Henry's (☑07-5474 0199; www.henrys.com. au) runs a door-to-door service from Sunshine Coast Airport to points north as far as Noosa Heads and Tewantin.

Sunbus (TransLink; ☑13 12 30; www.sunbus. com.au) is a local TransLink-operated bus that buzzes between Caloundra and Noosa, and from Noosa to the train station at Nambour ($8.60, 1¼ hours) via Eumundi.

Noosa

POP 39,380

Noosa is one of Australia's most fashionable resort towns, a salubrious hub backing onto crystalline waters and pristine subtropical rainforest. The town is located within the Noosa Biosphere Reserve, a Unesco-recognised area famous for its highly diverse ecosystem.

While the designer boutiques, polished restaurants and canal-side villas draw the beach-elite sophisticates, the beach and bush are free, leading to a healthy intermingling of urbane fashionistas and laid-back surfers

and beach bods. Noosa encompasses three main zones: upmarket Noosa Heads (around Laguna Bay and Hastings St), the more relaxed Noosaville (along the Noosa River) and the administrative hub of Noosa Junction.

On long weekends and school holidays, the main shopping and dining strip of Hastings St becomes a slow-moving file of traffic; the rest of the time, it's delightfully low(er) key.

◉ Sights & Activities

Covering the headland, **Noosa National Park** (www.noosanationalpark.com;) is one of Noosa's top sights; the most scenic way to reach it is to follow the boardwalk along the coast from town. The park's walking tracks lead to stunning coastal scenery, idyllic bays and great surfing. Pick up a walking-track map from the Noosa National Park Information Centre (p132) at the park's entrance.

For a panoramic view that takes in Noosa, its densely wooded national park, the ocean and distant hinterland, walk or drive up to **Laguna Lookout** (Map p127; Viewland Dr, Noosa Junction) from Viewland Dr.

Merrick's Learn to Surf   SURFING
(☑0418 787 577; www.learntosurf.com.au; Beach Access 14, Noosa Main Beach, Noosa Heads; 2hr lessons $65; ⊙9am & 1.30pm) Merrick's is one of the most popular surf schools on the Sunshine Coast, offering super-fun, two-hour group lessons twice daily, as well as the option of private tutorials. Kids aged seven and over are welcome, and the outfit runs special five-day kids' lessons during the school holidays, to boot. Lessons can be conducted in French, too – *très bien!*

Foam and Resin   SURFING, WATER SPORTS
(Map p127; 53 Hastings St, Noosa Heads; surfboard rental 2hr/full-day $25/35, stand-up paddleboard rental 2hr $30; ⊙9am-5pm) Owned and run by a Kiwi expat, this open-air surf rental kiosk sits opposite the visitor centre in Noosa Heads. It's generally cheaper than its competitor on the beach and offers good-quality equipment, including longboards and shortboards. Opening times can vary.

**Adventure
Sports Noosa**   KITESURFING, WATER SPORTS
(☑07-5455 6677; www.kitesurfaustralia.com.au; 136 Eumundi Noosa Rd, Noosaville; 2½hr kitesurfing lesson $275; ⊙9am-5pm Mon-Fri, to 2pm Sat Aug-Apr, 10am-5pm Mon & Tue, 9am-5pm Thu & Fri, 9am-2pm Sat May-Jul) As well as running kitesurfing lessons, Adventure Sports hires out

Noosa Heads

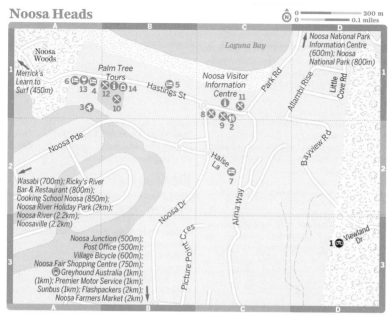

Noosa Heads

kayaks (half-day $35), bikes (two hours $19, full day $25) and stand-up paddle boards (half-day from $35, full day from $55).

Noosa Ocean Rider   BOATING
(Map p129; ☑ 0438 386 255; www.facebook.com/NoosaOceanrider; Jetty 17, 248 Gympie Tce, Noosaville; 1hr per person/family $70/250) Thrills and spills on a very fast and powerful speedboat. Standard tours will have you zipping around the ocean side of Noosa National Park.

Kayak Noosa   KAYAKING
(Map p129; ☑ 07-5455 5651; www.kayaknoosa.com; 194 Gympie Tce, Noosaville; 2hr sunset kayak adult/child $60/45) Tours around Noosa National Park. Also hires out kayaks (two hours from $25) and stand-up paddle boards (one/two hours $20/30).

Noosa Ferry   CRUISE
(Map p127; ☑ 07-5449 8442; www.noosaferry.com) This excellent ferry service runs an informative hop-on, hop-off Classic Tour (all-day pass adult/child $25/7) between Tewantin and the Sofitel Noosa Pacific Resort jetty in Noosa Heads. It also offers an Eco Cruise (great for birdwatchers; adult/child $49/22.50) on Tuesdays and Thursdays, and a wonderful one-hour Sunset Cruise (BYO

alcoholic drinks; per adult/child $25/10) Tuesday to Saturday.

👉 Tours

Noosa Woody Hire
DRIVING

(📱 0475 587 385; www.noosawoodyhire.com; driving tour 1/2/4hr $190/290/590) Cruise around in an attention-stealing 1946 Ford Woody. Accommodating four to five passengers, the vehicle was lovingly restored by young, affable local Tim Crabtree. With his wife, Kim, the surfboard shaper offers tailored tours; all include refreshments. The four-hour tour includes a gourmet picnic lunch and can take in hinterland foodie stops; they can also visit the Eumundi Markets (p145).

Discovery Group
DRIVING

(Map p129; 📱 07-5449 0393; www.thediscovery group.com.au; 186 Gympie Tce, Noosaville; 1-day Fraser Island tour adult/child $175/120, 4hr Everglades tour $79/65) Runs wonderful one- and two-day 4WD truck tours of Fraser Island. Also offers trips through the Everglades (full-day guided canoe trip adult/child $129/90).

Bike On Australia
MOUNTAIN BIKING

(📱 07-5474 3322; www.bikeon.com.au; guided mountain-bike tours from $65, bike hire per day $25) Runs a variety of tours, including self-guided and adventurous eco-jaunts. The fun, half-day Off the Top Tour – downhill on a mountain bike – costs $79. Also rents out road bikes (three/seven days from $120/250).

🍴 Courses

Cooking School Noosa
COOKING

(📱 07-5449 2443; www.thecookingschoolnoosa. com; 2 Quamby Pl, Noosa Heads; ⏱ 5½hr session incl lesson, lunch & wine $250) Lauded restaurant Wasabi (p131) also runs hands-on cooking courses, helmed by in-house chefs as well as special guest chefs from around the country. Regular options include Japanese, Southeast Asian and French courses, all of which use seasonal local produce and conclude with lunch and sommelier-picked accompanying wines.

🎉 Festivals & Events

Noosa Festival of Surfing
SURFING

(www.noosafestivalofsurfing.com; ⏱ Mar) A week of wave-riding action in March. There's a huge range of competition divisions, from invite-only pros to amateur competitions spanning all age brackets – there's even a dog surfing category! Water action aside, events include surf talks and workshops as well as film screenings and live music.

Noosa Food & Wine
FOOD & DRINK

(www.noosafoodandwine.com.au; ⏱ May) A four-day tribute to all manner of gastronomic delights, featuring prolific chefs, masterclasses, special lunches and dinners, as well as themed food and wine tours.

Noosa Long Weekend
CULTURAL

(www.noosalongweekend.com; ⏱ Jul) A 10-day festival of music, dance, theatre, film, visual arts, literature and food in July.

🛏 Sleeping

For an extensive list of short-term holiday rentals, try Noosa Visitor Information Centre (p132) and the privately run **Accom Noosa** (Map p127; 📱 07-5447 3444, 1800 072 078; www.accomnoosa.com.au; Shop 5/41 Hastings St, Noosa Heads).

⭐ YHA Halse Lodge
HOSTEL $

(Map p127; 📱 07-5447 3377; www.halselodge.com. au; 2 Halse Lane, Noosa Heads; dm $33.50, d $88; @ 🛜) This splendid, colonial-era Queenslander is a legendary backpacker stopover and well worth the clamber up its steep drive. There are four to six-bed dorms, twins, doubles and a lovely wide verandah. Popular with locals, the bar is a mix-and-meet bonanza, offering great meals (mains $16.50 to $26.50), cheap happy-hour beers, and live music on Thursdays. Close to the Main Beach action.

Flashpackers
HOSTEL $

(📱 07-5455 4088; www.flashpackersnoosa. com; 102 Pacific Ave, Sunshine Beach; mixed dm from $38, female dm $45, d from $100; ❄ 🛜 🏊) Flashpackers challenges the notion of hostels as flea-bitten dives. Thoughtful touches to its neat dorms include full-length mirrors, personal reading lights, ample wall sockets and the free use of surfboards and bodyboards.

Noosa River Holiday Park
CARAVAN PARK $

(Map p129; 📱 07-5449 7050; www.noosaholiday parks.com.au; 4 Russell St, Noosaville; unpowered/ powered sites $38/46; 🛜) This park is especially appealing for its location on the banks of the Noosa River, right between Noosa Heads and Noosaville. The latter's eateries and bars are within walking distance and the site itself has lovely spots to take a dip in the river. It's a seriously popular place: reservations

Noosaville

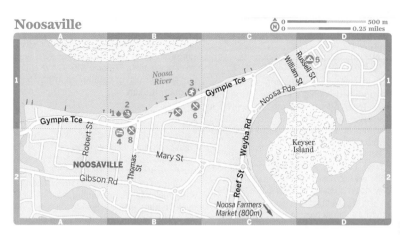

Noosaville

😊 Activities, Courses & Tours
1 Discovery Group......................................B1
2 Kayak Noosa..B1
3 Noosa Ocean Rider B1

🛏 Sleeping
4 Islander Noosa Resort............................B2
5 Noosa River Holiday Park D1

😊 Eating
6 Bordertown BBQ & Taqueria B1
7 Little Humid...B1
  Noosa Boathouse ....(see 2)
8 Thomas Corner B2

open nine months in advance and it usually books out soon after.

⭐10 Hastings   MOTEL $$
(Map p127; ☑07-5455 3350; www.10hastings street.com.au; 10 Hastings St, Noosa Heads; studio from $199, studio ste from $250, 2-bedroom apt from $400; 🅿❄🛜🏊) A rarity along Noosa's central Hastings St, this renovated boutique motel is a refreshing alternative to the resorts. Clean, fresh, beach-chic rooms come as compact two-person studios and larger studio suites (sleeping two adults and two children). Larger still are the two-bedroom apartments (sleeping up to six). Perks include complimentary beach towels and mini-bar items. Check for minimum stays.

Hotel Laguna   APARTMENT $$
(Map p127; ☑07-5447 3077; www.hotellaguna.com. au; 6 Hastings St, Noosa Heads; studios/ste from $165/230; 🅿❄🛜🏊) Neatly wedged between the river and Hastings St, Hotel Laguna consists of self-contained apartments and smaller studios. All apartments are privately owned and each is individually decorated, but all are smart and pleasant (if not always spotless). There's a communal guest laundry

and courtyard-style pool area. The location means you are only a roll-out-of-bed to the beach and a coffee whiff from great cafes.

Islander Noosa Resort   RESORT $$
(Map p129; ☑07-5440 9200; www.islandernoosa. com.au; 187 Gympie Tce, Noosaville; 2-/3-bedroom villas $220/270; 🅿❄🛜🏊) Set on 1.6 hectares of tropical gardens, with a central lagoon-style pool area and wooden boardwalks meandering through the trees, this is a good family option in the heart of Noosaville. On-site facilities includes jacuzzis, saunas, gym and two tennis courts. Apartments are a little dated and not always as clean as they could be, but are comfy and pleasant.

⭐Fairshore   APARTMENT $$$
(Map p127; ☑07-5449 4500; www.fairshore noosa.com.au; 41 Hastings St, Noosa Heads; 4-person apt from $495; 🅿❄🛜🏊) A smart, family-friendly apartment resort with direct access to Noosa Main Beach and buzzing Hastings St, Fairshore comes with a magazine-worthy, palm-fringed pool area. Two-bedroom apartments offer one or two bathrooms; though each apartment varies in style, all have laundry facilities and most

are airy and contemporary. There's also a small gym. Parking is free (vehicle height restriction 1.85m).

✕ Eating

Noosa prides itself on being a culinary destination, with global and local flavours on offer from fine restaurants to beachside takeaways. In Noosa Heads, eateries clutter Hastings St; in Noosaville, head to Thomas St and Gympie Tce.

Self-caterers can stock up on groceries at **Noosa Fair Shopping Centre** (📞07-5447 3788; www.noosafairshopping.com.au; 3 Lanyana Way, Noosa Junction; ⊙supermarket 8am-9pm Mon-Fri, to 5.30pm Sat, 9am-6pm Sun) in Noosa Junction. Altogether more atmospheric is the Sunday **Noosa Farmers Market** (📞0418 769 374; www.noosafarmersmarket.com.au; Noosa Australian Football Club Grounds, 155 Weyba Rd, Noosaville; ⊙7am-noon Sun).

Betty's Burgers & Concrete Co BURGERS $
(Map p127; 📞07-5455 4378; www.bettysburgers. com.au; 2/50 Hastings St, Noosa Heads; burgers $10-16; ⊙10am-9pm) Betty's has achieved cult status all the way down Australia's east coast, which explains the queues at its lush, semi-alfresco Noosa outlet – but the burgers are worth the wait for pillowy soft buns and flawlessly grilled, premium-meat patties (veggie option available). The perfect fries are wonderfully crispy and the moreish concretes (frozen custard drinks) come in flavours like lemon-raspberry cheesecake. Bliss.

Bordertown
BBQ & Taqueria AMERICAN, MEXICAN $
(Map p129; 📞07-5442 4242; www.facebook.com/ bordertownbarbeque; 1/253 Gympie Tce, Noosaville; burgers $12-17, tacos $7-9; ⊙8am-9pm Sun-Thu, to 10.30pm Fri & Sat; 🚭🍴) Pimped with murals by Queensland artists Mitch 13 and Thom Stuart, clued-in Bordertown rocks great burgers and succulent tacos (with authentic shells made by a Mexican family in Melbourne). Libations at the concrete bar include craft beers, creative cocktails and an alcoholic Bordertown Cola, made in-house using sassafras, vermouth and Fernet-Branca. Check their Facebook page for DJ sessions.

Hard Coffee CAFE $
(Map p127; 📞0410 673 377; 18 Hastings St, Noosa Heads; mains $10-16; ⊙7am-3pm) One of the cheaper options on Hastings St, super-casual

Hard Coffee lurks inside a nondescript food court. The food is simple but tasty, with options like smoked-salmon focaccia, steak sandwich BLAT, and a basic but satisfying avo smash for a bargain $10. Good coffee and no shortage of regulars chatting about the morning surf.

Tanglewood Organic
Sourdough Bakery BAKERY $
(📞07-5473 0215; www.facebook.com/tanglewood organicsourdough; Belmondos Organic Market, 59 Rene St, Noosaville; pastries from $5; ⊙8am-5pm Mon-Fri, to 4pm Sat; 🚭) Part of the upmarket Belmondos Organic Market, Tanglewood will have you oohing and aahing over its just-made, buttery pastries, artfully displayed on timber logs. If you can't make up your mind, opt for the standout pecan tart or their famous bread-and-butter pudding. Then there are the chocolate sea-salt cookies, not to mention those gorgeous loaves of artisan bread...

Massimo's GELATO $
(Map p127; 75 Hastings St, Noosa Heads; gelato from $5; ⊙9.30am-9.30pm Sun-Thu, to 10pm Fri & Sat) Both tourists and loyal locals queue here for Massimo's icy treats. Whether this is one of Queensland's best *gelaterias* is debatable, but there's no doubting the gelati's creamy texture and fresh, natural flavours. Cash only.

★**Thomas Corner** MODERN AUSTRALIAN $$
(Map p129; 📞07-5470 2224; www.thomas corner.com.au; cnr Thomas St & Gympie Tce, Noosaville; mains $16-33; ⊙11.30am-8pm Mon-Fri, 8am-8pm Sat & Sun; 🚭) Lunching ladies rightfully adore this casually chic, alfresco nosh spot. It's run by locally renowned chef David Rayner, whose vibrant, beautifully plated creations might see locally smoked fish paired with endive, apple, labne and pancetta crumbs, or parmesan-and-sage gnocchi happily married with mushrooms, spinach, truffle paste and poached egg. The popular weekend breakfast menu is equally as inspired.

El Capitano PIZZA $$
(Map p127; 📞07-5474 9990; www.elcapitano.com. au; 52 Hastings St, Noosa Heads; pizzas $22-25; ⊙5-9.30pm) Down an easy-to-miss path and up a set of stairs is Noosa's best pizzeria, a hip, swinging hot spot with bar seating (good for solo diners), louvred windows and marine-themed street art. The light, fluffy pizzas here are gorgeous, made with sour-

dough bases and topped with artisan ingredients. Check the blackboard for pizza and cocktail specials – and always book ahead.

Noosa Boathouse   MODERN AUSTRALIAN **$$**
(Map p129; ☑07-5440 5070; www.noosaboathouse.com.au; 194 Gympie Tce, Noosaville; mains $20-38; ☺restaurant 11.30am-3pm & 5-8pm Tue-Sun, cafe 6am-6pm daily, rooftop bar 4.30-7pm Tue-Sun) This modern, floating nosh spot has numerous sections: cafe, fish-and-chip kiosk, rooftop bar (open for sunset drinks) and a Cape Cod–style restaurant. While the latter's menu – think Mod Oz with Italian and Asian touches – isn't quite as ambitious as it sounds, the place is a fantastic option for great-tasting food and killer views sans the eye-watering price tag.

Kaali   INDIAN **$$**
(Map p127; ☑07-5474 8989; www.kaaligourmetindian.com; 2/2 Hastings St, Noosa Heads; mains $21-32.50; ☺11am-9pm Mon-Fri, 5-10pm Sat & Sun; ☑) After all the Mod Oz cuisine on offer in Noosa Heads, this touch of India offers some spicy relief. At the western end of Hastings St, it's a casual spot, cooking up excellent curries and great tandoori breads.

★**Noosa Beach House**   MODERN AUSTRALIAN **$$$**
(Map p127; ☑07-5449 4754; www.noosabeachhousepk.com.au; 16 Hastings St, Noosa Heads; dinner mains $39-46, 6-course tasting menu $100; ☺6.30-10.30am & 5.30-9.30pm daily, also noon-2.30pm Sat & Sun) An uncluttered mix of white walls, glass and timber, this effortlessly chic restaurant belongs to globe-trotting celebrity chef Peter Kuravita. Seasonal ingredients and fresh local seafood underscore a contemporary menu whose deeply seductive Sri Lankan snapper curry with tamarind and *aloo chop* (potato croquette) nods to Kuravita's heritage. Weekends see a good-value five-curry lunch, served family-style for $38 per person.

★**Wasabi**   JAPANESE **$$$**
(☑07-5449 2443; www.wasabisb.com; 2 Quamby Pl, Noosa Heads; 3 courses $80, 7-/9-course omakase menu $134/157; ☺5-9.30pm Wed, Thu & Sat, noon-9.30pm Fri & Sun) An award-winning, waterside destination restaurant, Wasabi is on the lips of every local gourmand. Premium produce from the region and Wasabi's own farm sings in delicate yet thrilling dishes like handmade duck-egg noodles and fresh fish in burnt-onion broth with fish-crackling and legumes, or tempura-style spanner crab

and *yama imo* (mountain potato) dumpling with kombu salt and *yuzu* (a small citrus fruit) zest.

★**Ricky's River Bar & Restaurant**   MODERN AUSTRALIAN **$$$**
(☑07-5447 2455; www.rickys.com.au; Noosa Wharf, 2 Quamby Pl, Noosa Heads; mains $35-45, 6-course tasting menu $105, with matching wines $165; ☺noon-late) Perched on the Noosa River, elegant Ricky's is the darling of business folk discussing deals over long lunches. Reserve a table for lunch (the view is half the experience) and swoon over dishes like chargrilled calamari with almond cream, curry leaf, heirloom tomato and quinoa, or Coral Coast barramundi with cauliflower and macadamia *skordalia* (dip), preserved lemon, rhubarb and couscous.

Little Humid   MODERN AUSTRALIAN **$$$**
(Map p129; ☑07-5449 9755; www.humid.com.au; 2/235 Gympie Tce, Noosaville; mains $27-42; ☺noon-2pm & 6-8.30pm Wed-Sun; ☑) This deservedly popular eatery serves up beautiful bistro fare with subtle twists: seasonal dishes like crispy-skin duck with liquorice and orange glaze; herb- and pine-nut-crusted ocean trout; and a decent range of vegetarian options, like creamed broccoli with caramelised fennel and baby spinach, field mushrooms and crushed kipfler potatoes. Book for dinner (up to a week ahead during holiday periods).

🍸 Drinking & Nightlife

★**Clandestino Roasters**   COFFEE
(☑1300 656 022; www.clandestino.com.au; Belmondos Organic Market, 59 Rene St, Noosaville; ☺7am-4pm Mon-Fri, to 3pm Sat; ☜) It might be off the tourist radar, but this trendy warehouse microroastery packs in hipsters, surfers and suits, all here for Noosa's top coffee. Choose from two blends and eight single origins served a number of ways, including espresso-style, cold-drip, clover, V60 pour-over and siphon. Communal tables and free wi-fi make it a popular spot with the laptop brigade.

★**Village Bicycle**   BAR
(☑07-5474 5343; 2/16 Sunshine Beach Rd, Noosa Junction; ☺4pm-midnight Mon-Sat, from 12.30pm Sun) Noosa's coolest local drinking spot by far, Village Bicycle is run by young mates Luke and Trevor. Splashed with street art, it's a convivial space, packed nightly with loyal regulars here to knock back some

beers, tuck into quality bar grub – think tacos and burgers – and listen to live tunes.

Miss Moneypenny's COCKTAIL BAR
(Map p127; 07-5474 9999; www.missmoney pennys.com; 6 Hastings St, Noosa Heads; 11.30am-midnight;) Dashing, award-winning Miss Moneypenny's sets a sophisticated scene for languid toasts. Well-crafted cocktails fall into numerous categories, from Seasonals and Sours to tongue-in-cheek '80s Cruise Ship Drinks. Not that irony gets in the way of quality: even the piña colada is shaken with original Coco Lopez coconut cream. Nosh includes posh bar bites and pizzas ($16 to $30).

Shopping

Noosa Longboards SPORTS & OUTDOORS
(Map p127; 07-5447 4776; www.noosalong boards.com; 20 Hastings St, Noosa Heads; 9am-5pm) Established in 1994, this iconic brand was one of the first to sell traditional-style longboards at the beginning of the longboard renaissance in Oz. Two decades on, it's famous for handcrafting them with a contemporary twist. Boards aside, the shop stocks its own beachwear label, threads from veteran Aussie label Okanui, as well as authentic, vintage Hawaiian shirts.

ⓘ Information

POST

Post Office (13 13 18; www.auspost.com. au; 91 Noosa Dr, Noosa Junction; 9am-5pm Mon-Fri, to 12.30pm Sat)

TOURIST INFORMATION

Noosa National Park Information Centre (07-5447 3522; 8.45am-4.15pm) At the entrance to Noosa National Park.

Noosa Visitor Information Centre (Map p127; 07-5430 5000; www.visitnoosa.com; 61 Hastings St, Noosa Heads; 9am-5pm;) Official tourist office.

Palm Tree Tours (Map p127; 07-5474 9166; www.palmtreetours.com.au; Bay Village Shopping Centre, 18 Hastings St, Noosa Heads; 9am-5pm) Long-standing tour desk.

ⓘ Getting There & Away

Long-distance bus services stop at the **Noosa Junction Bus Station** on Sunshine Beach Rd in Noosa Junction. **Greyhound Australia** (1300 473 946; www.greyhound.com.au) has several daily bus connections from Brisbane to Noosa (from $24, 2½ to 3¼ hours), while **Premier Motor Service** (p93) has one ($23, 2½ hours).

Most hostels have courtesy pick-ups.

Sunbus (TransLink; 13 12 30; www.sunbus. com.au) operates frequent services from Noosa to Maroochydore ($10.50, one hour to 1¼ hours) and Nambour train station ($10.50, 1¼ hours).

ⓘ Getting Around

BICYCLE

Bike On Australia (p128) Rents out bicycles from several locations in Noosa, including **Flashpackers** (p128) in Sunshine Beach. Alternatively, bikes can be delivered to and from your door for $35 (or free if the booking is over $100).

BOAT

Noosa Ferry (p127) operates ferries between Noosa Heads and Tewantin several times a day (all-day pass adult/child $25/7). **Noosa Water Taxi** (0411 136 810; www.noosawatertaxi. com; one-way per person $10) operates a water-taxi service around Noosa Sound (Friday to Sunday), and is also available for private charters and water-taxi hire by appointment.

BUS

Sunbus has local services that link Noosa Heads, Noosaville, Noosa Junction and Tewantin.

CAR & MOTORCYCLE

All the major car-rental brands can be found in Noosa; rentals start at about $55 per day.

Noosa Car Rentals (0429 053 728; www. noosacarrentals.com.au)

Scooter Hire Noosa (07-5455 4096; www. scooterhirenoosa.com; 13 Noosa Dr, Noosa Heads; 4/24hr $39/59; 8.30am-5pm)

Bribie Island

POP 18,135

This slender island at the northern end of Moreton Bay is linked to the mainland by bridge and is popular with young families, retirees and those with a cool million (or three) to spend on a waterfront property. While it's far more developed than Stradbroke or Moreton Islands, there are still secluded spots to be found.

The **Abbey Museum** (07-5495 1652; www.abbeymuseum.com; 63 The Abbey Pl, off Old Toorbul Point Rd, Caboolture; adult/child $12/7, family from $19.80; 10am-4pm Mon-Sat) houses an extraordinary collection of art and archaeology, once the private collection of Englishman 'Reverend' John Ward. The Abbey Medieval Festival is held here in June or July.

The **Caboolture Warplane Museum** (☑ 07-5499 1144; www.caboolturewarplanemuseum. com; Hangar 104, Caboolture Airfield, McNaught Rd, Caboolture; adult/child/family $10/5/30; ☺ 9am-3pm) houses a booty of restored WWII planes, including a P51D Mustang, CAC Wirraway and Cessna Bird Dog.

Pick up maps and information at **Bribie Island Visitor Information Centre** (☑ 07-3408 9026; www.tourismbribie.com.au; Benabrow Ave, Bellara; ☺ 9am-4pm).

🛏 Sleeping & Eating

Bribie Island National Park Camping   CAMPGROUND **$**
(☑ 13 74 68; www.npsr.qld.gov.au/parks/bribie island; camp sites per person/family $6.15/24.60) On the island's west coast, **Poverty Creek** is a large, grassy camping site. Facilities here include toilets, a portable toilet/waste disposal facility and screened cold showers. Just south, **Ocean Beach** offers similar facilities. On the east coast, the **Gallagher Point** camping area harbours a limited number of bush camping sites, with no toilets or other facilities. All three sites are accessible by 4WD.

On The Beach Resort   APARTMENT **$$$**
(☑ 07-3400 1400; www.onthebeachresort.com. au; 9 North St, Woorim; 2-/3-bedroom apt from $215/300; ❄ ⊛) On The Beach out-luxes anything else on the island, with superb service and great facilities, including a salt-water pool and huge sun-deck. Apartments are modern, bright and breezy, with fully equipped kitchens and laundry facilities. There's a four-night minimum stay during the Christmas and Easter holiday periods.

Bribie Island SLSC   PUB FOOD **$$**
(☑ 07-3408 2141; www.thesurfclubbribieisland. au; First Ave, Woorim; mains $18-30; ☺ 11.30am-2.30pm & 5.30pm-late) While the pub grub here won't blow you away, it's tasty enough and comes with a beachside deck for chilled wave-watching sessions. Expect all the surf-club staples, from garlic prawns and beer-battered barramundi to pasta dishes and golden schnitzel.

❶ Getting There & Away

There is no 4WD hire on Bribie, and you'll need a vehicle access permit ($46.25 per week) for the island's more off-track spots. Pick up one at **Gateway Bait & Tackle** (☑ 07-5497 5253; www.gatewaybaitandtackle.com.au; 1383 Bribie Island Rd, Ningi; ☺ 5.30am-5pm Mon,

AUSTRALIA ZOO

Just north of Beerwah is one of Queensland's, if not Australia's, most famous tourist attractions. **Australia Zoo** (☑ 07-5436 2000; www.australiazoo. com.au; 1638 Steve Irwin Way, Beerwah; adult/child/family $59/35/172; ☺ 9am-5pm) is a fitting homage to its founder, zany wildlife enthusiast Steve Irwin. The park has an amazing menagerie, with a Cambodian-style Tiger Temple, the famous Crocoseum and a dizzying array of critters, including native dingoes, Tasmanian devils and hairy-nosed wombats.

Various companies offer tours from Brisbane and the Sunshine Coast. The zoo operates a free bus to/from the Beerwah train station.

Tue, Thu & Fri, to 2pm Wed, 4.30am-5pm Sat, 4.30am-3pm Sun) or online (www.npsr.qld. gov.au).

Frequent Citytrain services run from Brisbane to Caboolture, from where **Bribie Island Coaches** (☑ 07-3408 2562; www.bribiecoaches.com. au) route 643 runs to Bribie Island via Ningi and Sandstone Point. Buses run roughly every hour, stopping in Bongaree and continuing through to Woorim. Regular Brisbane Translink fares apply (one-way from central Brisbane $11.40).

Glass House Mountains

The breathtaking volcanic plugs of the Glass House Mountains rise abruptly from the sub-tropical plains 20km northwest of Caboolture. In Dreaming legend, these curious rocky peaks belong to a family of mountain spirits. To British explorer James Cook, their shapes recalled the industrial, conical glass-making furnaces of his native Yorkshire. It's worth diverting off the Bruce Hwy onto the slower Old Gympie Rd to snake your way through dense bush, scattered with old Queenslander shacks and offering arresting views of these spectacular magma intrusions.

The Glass House Mountains National Park is broken into several sections (all within in cooee of Beerwah), with picnic grounds and lookouts but no camping grounds. The peaks are reached by a series of sealed and unsealed roads that head inland from Steve Irwin Way, which itself is home to the blockbuster Australia Zoo, founded by the world-famous Crocodile Hunter himself.

Hikers are spoilt for choice here. A number of signposted walking tracks reach several of the peaks, but be prepared for some steep and rocky trails. A new track, the 6km Soldier Settlers Walk, has wonderful views and plants plus a crossing over a recently opened timber bridge. The moderate walk up Ngungun (253m) has sensational views, while Tibrogargan (364m) offers a challenging scramble. The steepish Beerburrum (278m) is also open. Note – at the time of research, the Tibrogargan walk was closed due to rock falls; contact the Glass House Mountains **tourist office** (☑07-5458 8848; www.visitsunshinecoast.com.au; cnr Bruce Pde & Reed St; ⊙9am-4pm) for updates.

Rock climbers can usually be seen scaling Tibrogargan and Ngungun. Mt Coonowrin (aka 'crook-neck'), the most dramatic of the volcanic plugs, is closed to the public.

Glass House Mountains Ecolodge (☑07-5493 0008; www.glasshouseecolodge.com; 198 Barrs Rd; r $125-220; ❉🐾) 🖊, near Australia Zoo, offers a range of wonderful, good-value sleeping options, including cosy Orchard Rooms ($125), the reformed Church Loft ($220), and converted railway carriages. Mt Tibrogargan can be seen from the gorgeous garden.

The **Glasshouse Mountains Tavern** (www.glasshousemountainstavern.com.au; 10 Reed St; mains $14-32.50; ⊙10am-9pm Sun-Thu, to midnight Fri, to 9.30pm Sat, kitchen closes around 8pm) cooks up tasty, no-nonsense pub nosh, including steaks, bangers (sausages), burgers and salads.

Caloundra

POP 77,600

Straddling a headland at the southern end of the Sunshine Coast, Caloundra has shaken off the quaint 'Valium Coast' clichés and reinvented itself as an unexpected centre of cool. Beyond its golden beaches, water sports and beautiful Coastal Pathway walking track is a burgeoning creative scene, spanning everything from top-notch speciality coffee shops and bars to impressive street art and a microbrewery, not to mention the coast's most sharply curated regional art galleries. The cherry on the proverbial cake is the Caloundra Music Festival (p136), one of Queensland's biggest, best-loved annual music events.

◉ Sights & Activities

On Sunday mornings, crowds flock to Bulcock St to browse the market stalls at **Caloundra Street Fair** (www.caloundrastreet fair.com.au; Bulcock St; ⊙8am-1pm Sun).

Caloundra Regional Gallery   GALLERY
(☑07-5420 8299; http://gallery.sunshinecoast. qld.gov.au; 22 Omrah Ave; ⊙10am-4pm Tue-Fri, to 2pm Sat & Sun) FREE When you're done with catching rays and waves, sidestep to this small, sophisticated gallery. Rotating exhibitions showcase quality local and national artists, with a number of outstanding Art Prize shows each year. The gallery stays up late for Friday[3]Live on the third Friday of the month, with music, talks, performances, drinks and bites.

Queensland Air Museum   MUSEUM
(☑07-5492 5930; www.qam.com.au; 7 Pathfinder Dr; adult/child/family $13/7/30; ⊙10am-4pm) Occupying two hangars beside Caloundra Airport, the volunteer-run QAM houses circa 70 civilian and military aircraft, including a mid-century Douglas DC-3 (the world's first mass-produced all-metal airliner) and a supersonic F-111 fighter jet belonging to the Royal Australian Air Force. Displays shed light on various aspects of Australian and international aviation history, including wartime battles and women in aviation, and there's a small collection of fabulously retro brochures, cabin bags and in-flight crockery from Australian airlines past and present.

Mind and Body
PT & Adventures   HEALTH & FITNESS
(☑0401 286 200; www.mabpersonaltraining. com.au; tours per person (minimum 2) from $199) Sprightly personal trainer Melinda Bingley runs these pulse-racing fitness and adventure tours, which include hiking and kayaking excursions. Among them is a Glass House Mountains Discovery Adventure, which follows the expedition path of early English explorer Matthew Flinders. Running from Golden Beach in Caloundra to Mount Tibrogargan, the six-hour tour includes kayaking, bushwalking, driving and lunch.

Caloundra Surf School   SURFING
(☑0413 381 010; www.caloundrasurfschool.com. au; 1½hr lessons from $50) The pick of the local surf schools, with board hire also available.

Caloundra Jet Ski   OUTDOORS
(☑0434 330 660; www.caloundrajetski.com.au; cnr Esplanade & Otranto Ave) Affable, joke-cracking

Caloundra

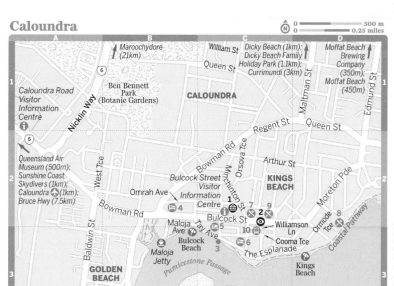

Caloundra

⦿ Sights
1 Caloundra Regional Gallery C2
2 Caloundra Street Fair C2

⦿ Activities, Courses & Tours
3 Caloundra Jet Ski C3

⦿ Sleeping
4 Caloundra Backpackers B2
5 Monaco C3
6 Rumba Resort C3

⦿ Eating
7 Baci Gelati C2
8 Cptn D2
9 Green House Cafe C2
   Stormie D's Cupcakery .... (see 9)

⦿ Drinking & Nightlife
   26 Degrees .... (see 6)
   Lamkin Lane Espresso Bar .... (see 9)

⦿ Transport
10 Caloundra Transit Centre C3

local Ken Jeffrey owns and operates these thrilling jet-ski tours of the Pumicestone Passage, the narrow waterway separating Caloundra and the northern tip of Bribie Island. Tours offer interesting insight into the

area's ecosystem and are suitable for both novice and experienced jet-skiers (even the most nervous newbies will end up zipping across the blue like pros).

Deluxe Kombi Service   DRIVING
(☑ 07-5491 5432, 0402 615 126; www.deluxekombi service.com.au; ⦿ 1hr tour $77) What better way to explore the area than in a 1960s Kombi with a cool surfer dude? Local Michael Flocke has meticulously restored two rare vans (complete with sunroof and seating for eight), which he uses for insightful, anecdote-rich tours of the town and surrounding region. Book a one-hour town tour or longer, bespoke tours of the Sunshine Coast hinterland.

Sunshine Coast Skydivers   SKYDIVING
(☑ 07-5437 0211; www.sunshinecoastskydivers. com.au; Caloundra Aerodrome, Pathfinder Dr; tandem jumps from $279) Send your adrenalin into overdrive as you scan Caloundra and the Pacific Ocean from a brain-squeezing 4570m up (or even just 2130m, if you prefer).

Blue Water Kayak Tours   KAYAKING
(☑ 07-5494 7789; www.bluewaterkayaktours. com; half-day tours minimum 4 people $100, twilight tours $55; ⦿ half-day tours 8.30am Tue-Sun, twilight tours Wed-Sun) Energetic kayak tours across the channel to the northern tip of

Bribie Island National Park; single and double kayaks are available. All tours must be booked in advance.

✯✯ Festivals & Events

Caloundra Music Festival   MUSIC
(www.caloundramusicfestival.com; ☺Sep-Oct) A four-day, family-friendly music festival held at Kings Beach, with 40,000-strong crowds and a diverse line-up of entertainment, featuring prolific current and veteran Australian rock and indie pop acts, as well as international guests.

🛏 Sleeping & Eating

Dicky Beach
Family Holiday Park   CARAVAN PARK $
(☑07-5491 3342; www.sunshinecoastholidayparks.com.au; 4 Beerburrum St; powered/unpowered site $46/41, cabins from $118; ✲🛜☒) You can't get any closer to Dicky, one of Caloundra's most popular beaches. The brick cabins are as ordered and tidy as the grounds and there's a small swimming pool for the kids.

Caloundra Backpackers   HOSTEL $
(☑07-5499 7655; www.caloundrabackpackers.com.au; 84 Omrah Ave; dm from $26, d with/without bathroom from $75/60; 🛜) Caloundra's only hostel is a no-nonsense budget option with a sociable courtyard, book exchange, and weekly BBQ, pizza and wine-and-cheese nights. Dorms won't inspire, but they're clean and peaceful.

Monaco   APARTMENT $$
(☑07-5490 5490; www.monacocaloundra.com.au; 12 Otranto Ave; 1-/2-/3-bedroom apt from $159/240/329; P✲🛜☒) Modern, good-sized apartments one block from Bulcock Beach. Apartments are individually owned, so styles vary; the more expensive apartments offer full water vistas. Wi-fi is free but capped, and apartments are serviced every eight days. Property perks include a stylish, heated lap pool, separate kids' pool, spa, sauna, gym and games rooms. Minimum two-night stay, with cheaper rates for longer stays.

Rumba Resort   RESORT $$$
(☑07-5492 0555; www.rumbaresort.com.au; 10 Leeding Tce; r from $200; ✲🛜☒) This sparkling, resort-white playground is the slickest slumber pad in town. Studio rooms are light, spacious and modern, each with two-person jacuzzi, home-theatre system and espresso machine. The pool area is worthy of a photo

shoot and flanked by one of Caloundra's coolest new bars. Easy walking access to beachfront eateries, to boot.

★ Baci Gelati   GELATO $
(49 Bulcock St; gelato from $4.50; ☺9am-5pm Mon-Fri, 9.30am-5pm Sat, 10am-4pm Sun) Baci scoops out some of the best gelati in Queensland, made by an Italian expat, his Hungarian wife and a fellow Italian mate. The secret: top-quality ingredients, from fresh fruit and Bronte pistachios to Belgian chocolate and local Maleny milk. Creative flavours include ginger beer, chai, salted caramel and an extraordinary Sicilian hazelnut. Take-home packs are available (0.5/1L $12/23).

Stormie D's Cupcakery   BAKERY $
(☑07-5491 5812; www.stormiedscupcakery.com.au; 17a Bulcock St; mini/regular cupcakes $2.50/4.80; ☺10am-4pm Mon-Fri, 9am-1pm Sat) Stormie Dutton could easily front an indie rock group, but she's too busy baking in her pink sugar temple. Her cupcakes are local legends, selling out quickly and offered in combos like strawberries and cream and orange with cranberry and pistachio. Be reckless and order the salted caramel milkshake, which comes with pretzels stuck to the rim with Nutella.

Green House Cafe   VEGETARIAN $
(☑07-5438 1647; www.greenhousecafe.com.au; 5/8 Orumuz Ave; mains $13-17; ☺8am-3pm Mon-Fri, to 2pm Sat & Sun; 🌱) A showcase for local ingredients, this chilled, light-filled laneway spot serves up fresh, organic and filling vegetarian grub such as avocado on toast with cashew cheese, *shakshouka* (spiced, poached) eggs and *nasi goreng* (spiced fried rice). For a serious health kick, down a smoothie with kale and seasonal greens paired with banana, coconut-milk yoghurt, kiwi, chia seeds, coconut water and supergreens powder. Mama will approve.

Cptn   INTERNATIONAL $$
(☑07-5341 8475; www.cptnkingsbeach.com.au; 1/8 Levuka Ave, Kings Beach; mains lunch $18-29, dinner $26-29; ☺6am-6pm Mon-Thu, to 9.30pm Fri-Sun, kitchen to 3pm Mon-Thu, to 8pm Fri-Sun; 🛜) Beachside Cptn beats the competition with its crisp, contemporary fit-out and beautiful, honest nosh. Don't expect culinary acrobatics, just well-executed, thoughtful dishes like barramundi fish and chips, grilled halloumi with roasted vegetables, or grilled chicken breast with mixed Mediterranean vegetables, roast potatoes, goats cheese and red-wine

jus. Good coffee, well-priced wines by the glass and a young, friendly team.

Drinking & Nightlife

Lamkin Lane Espresso Bar CAFE
(www.facebook.com/lamkinlane; 31 Lamkin Lane;
⏱6am-4pm Mon-Fri, 7am-noon Sat & Sun) The hearts of coffee snobs will sing at Lamkin Lane, where affable, knowledgeable baristas like nothing better than chatting about the week's pair of special blends and trio of single-origins. The team here have a strong relationship with their coffee farmers, which means your brew is as ethical as it is smooth and aromatic. Cash only.

**Moffat Beach
Brewing Company** MICROBREWERY
(☑07-5491 4023; 12 Seaview Tce, Moffat Beach;
⏱7am-4pm Mon & Tue, to late Wed-Sat, to 8pm Sun) Just up from hipster-staple Moffat Beach, this cafe-cum-microbrewery has both guest and house brews on tap (look out for the cult-status double IPA Iggy Hop). Bottled beers span Oz and the globe; the four-brew paddle ($20) will help the indecisive. Nod away to live tunes on Fridays from 5pm and on weekends from 3pm (the latter sessions are especially pumping).

26 Degrees COCKTAIL BAR
(☑07-5492 0555; www.facebook.com/26degrees Bar; 10 Leeding Tce, Rumba Beach Resort; ⏱10am-late; 🛜) Twenty-six degrees is both the average temperature in Caloundra and the town's degree of latitude – it's now also one of Caloundra's most fashionable spots to imbibe. Located inside the Rumba Resort, the poolside bar is a beach-chic affair, with white louvres, whitewashed timber bar and lush green foliage. Dirty martini lovers will appreciate its funky version, made with marinated olives.

ℹ Information

Sunshine Coast Visitor Centre (☑07-5458 8846; www.visitsunshinecoast.com; 7 Caloundra Rd; ⏱9am-4pm Mon-Fri, to 3pm Sat & Sun; 🛜) On the roundabout at the town's entrance; there's also a centrally located kiosk on **Bulcock Street** (☑07-5458 8847; www.visitsunshine coast.com; 77 Bulcock St; ⏱9am-3pm; 🛜). Both branches offer free wi-fi.

ℹ Getting There & Away

Greyhound Australia (☑1300 473 946; www.greyhound.com.au) buses run one daily morning service from Brisbane to Noosa,

stopping in Caloundra (from $19, two hours) en route. There is also one morning service to Brisbane.

Sunbus (TransLink; ☑13 12 30; www.sunbus. com.au) has frequent services to Maroochydore ($5.70, one hour). Transfer in Maroochydore for buses to Noosa.

The **Caloundra Transit Centre** (23 Cooma Tce) is the main bus station for both long-distance and local buses, located a quick walk south of Bulcock St. (At the time of research the building itself was closed, though buses continue to stop here.)

Mooloolaba & Maroochydore

POP 12,550 & 18,300

Mooloolaba has seduced many with its sublime climate, golden beach and laid-back lifestyle. Eateries, boutiques and pockets of resorts and apartments have spread along Mooloolaba Esplanade, transforming this once-humble fishing village into one of Queensland's most popular destinations.

Further north, booming Maroochydore takes care of the business end, with a brand-new city centre under construction and a string of buzzing eateries, as well as its own stretch of sandy beachfront.

◉ Sights & Activities

Sea Life Sunshine Coast AQUARIUM
(Map p138; ☑1800 618 021; www.underwaterworld. com.au; Wharf Marina, Parkyn Pde, Mooloolaba; adult/child/family $39/26/130; ⏱9am-5pm) Kids will love this popular tropical oceanarium, complete with an 80m-long transparent underwater tunnel for close-up views of rays, reef fish and eight species of shark. There's a touch tank, live shows, presentations and – during school holidays – the option of sleeping at the aquarium overnight ($90 per person).

While visitors can also swim with seals and dive with sharks, it's worth considering that animal-welfare groups believe captivity is debilitating and stressful for marine animals and exacerbated by human interaction.

Wildlife HQ ZOO
(☑0428 660 671; www.whqzoo.com; adult/child/ family $29/15/79; ⏱9am-4pm) Located at the **Big Pineapple** (www.bigpineapple.com.au; 76 Nambour Connection Rd, Woombye) FREE, this 8-hectare zoo houses native Australian, African, South American and rare Asian critters, among them red pandas and tahrs (Himalayan mountain goats).

Mooloolaba

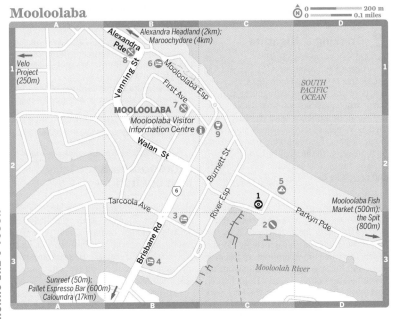

Mooloolaba

◉ Sights
1 Sea Life Sunshine Coast C2

✈ Activities, Courses & Tours
Coastal Cruises Mooloolaba..........(see 2)
Hire Hut ....(see 2)
2 Sunreef...C3
Whale One...(see 2)

🛌 Sleeping
3 Dockside Apartments............................B3
4 Mooloolaba Beach Backpackers...........B3

5 Mooloolaba Beach Caravan Park C2
6 Oceans B1

🍴 Eating
7 Char B1
Good Bar...(see 7)
8 Spice Bar..B1

🍸 Drinking & Nightlife
9 Taps@Mooloolaba C2

Sunreef · DIVING
(Map p138; ☎ 07-5444 5656; www.sunreef.com.au; Wharf Marina, Parkyn Pde, Mooloolaba; dives from $165; ⊙8am-5pm Mon-Sat, to 4pm Sun) Offers two dives (from $165) on the wreck of sunken warship HMAS *Brisbane*. Also runs a day trip to Flinders Reef (from $229), including two dives, equipment, lunch and snacks. A PADI Open Water Diver course is $495.

Hire Hut · WATER SPORTS
(Map p138; ☎ 07-5444 0366; www.hirehut.com.au; Wharf, Parkyn Pde, Mooloolaba) Hires out kayaks (two hours $25), giant stand-up paddle boards (two hours $350, up to 10 people per board), jet skis (one hour $180) and boats

(per hour/half-day from $42/75). Also hires out bicycles (two/four hours $19/25).

Robbie Sherwell's XL Surfing Academy · SURFING
(☎ 07-5478 1337, 0423 039 505; www.xlsurfing academy.com; 1hr private/group lessons $95/45) Dip a toe into Aussie surf culture at this long-established school, which caters to all levels, from rookie to advanced.

☞ Tours

Coastal Cruises Mooloolaba · CRUISE
(Map p138; ☎ 0419 704 797; www.cruisemooloolaba. com.au; Wharf Marina, Parkyn Pde, Mooloolaba) Sunset ($25) and seafood lunch cruises ($35)

through Mooloolaba Harbour, the river and canals.

Whale One WILDLIFE
(Map p138; ☑1300 942 531; www.whaleone. com.au; Wharf Marina, Parkyn Pde, Mooloolaba; whale-watching tours adult/child/family $59/39/196) Between June and November, Whale One runs cruises that get you close to the spectacular acrobatic displays of humpback whales, which migrate north from Antarctica to mate and give birth.

✪ Festivals & Events

Big Pineapple Music Festival MUSIC
(www.bigpineapplemusicfestival.com; ☺May) The one-day 'Piney Festival' is one of the region's top music events, with four stages showcasing titans of the current Aussie music scene. Past acts have included alternative rockers John Butler Trio and Birds of Tokyo, alt-electronica acts Rüfüs and Hermitude, and even Brisbane's own progressive-pop twins The Veronicas. Camp sites are available and sell out quickly.

**Maroochy Music
& Visual Arts Festival** MUSIC
(www.mmvaf.com; ☺Sep; ☎) Headliners at this annual, one-day fest in Maroochydore have included of-the-moment Australian music acts Peking Duk and Matt Corby; alt-indie talent such as Boo Seeka, George Maple and Ngaiire have also taken the stage. The visual-arts side of the fest includes specially commissioned works from local and international artists.

🍴 Sleeping & Eating

Cotton Tree Holiday Park CAMPGROUND $
(Map p140; ☑07-5459 9070; www.sunshinecoast holidayparks.com.au; Cotton Tree Pde, Cotton Tree, Maroochydore; powered/unpowered sites from $48/41, villas from $157) In Cotton Tree, a popular area of Maroochydore, this holiday park enjoys direct access to the beach and Maroochy River.

**Mooloolaba Beach
Caravan Park** CARAVAN PARK $
(Map p138; ☑07-5444 1201; www.sunshinecoast holidayparks.com.au; Parkyn Pde, Mooloolaba; powered sites from $42) The park runs two sites: one fronting the lovely Mooloolaba Beach, and a smaller one at the northern end of the Esplanade, with the best location and views of any accommodation in town.

Mooloolaba Beach Backpackers HOSTEL $
(Map p138; ☑07-5444 3399; www.mooloolaba backpackers.com; 75 Brisbane Rd, Mooloolaba; dm with/without bathroom $34/30, d $75; ℗⑤☀) Some dorms have en suites, and although the rooms are a little drab, the number of freebies (bikes, surfboards, stand-up paddleboards and breakfast) more than compensates. Besides, it's only 500m from beachside activities and nightlife.

Dockside Apartments APARTMENT $$
(Map p138; ☑07-5478 2044; www.dockside mooloolaba.com.au; 50 Burnett St, Mooloolaba; 2-/3-bedroom apt from $290/375; ℗✳⑤☀) While the fully equipped apartments here are all different (all are privately owned and rented out), each is neat, clean and comfortable. The property sits in a quiet spot away from the hubbub, but is an easy walk from Mooloolaba's main restaurant and bar strip, surf club, beach and wharf precinct. Discounted rates for longer stays.

Maroochydore Beach Motel MOTEL $$
(Map p140; ☑07-5443 7355; www.maroochydore beachmotel.com; 69 Sixth Ave, Maroochydore; s/d/f from $120/135/180; ℗✳⑤☀) A quirky, spotless, themed motel with 18 different rooms, including the Elvis Room (naturally), the Egyptian Room, and the Aussie Room (complete with toy wombat). Although on a main road, it's less than a 200m walk to the beach.

★**Oceans** RESORT $$$
(Map p138; ☑07-5444 5777; www.oceansmooloolaba. com.au; 101-105 Mooloolaba Esplanade, Mooloolaba; 2-bedroom apt from $500; ℗✳⑤☀) Cascading water and contemporary art greet guests at this upmarket apartment resort directly across from the beach. Ocean views are de rigueur in the apartments, which are sleek and immaculately clean, with Nespresso machines, stand-alone spa and quality appliances. Apartments are serviced daily and there are also adults' and children's pools, a gym and a sauna. Parking and wi-fi are free.

★**Velo Project** CAFE $
(☑07-5444 8693; www.theveloproject.com.au; 19 Careela St, Mooloolaba; dishes $6-22.50; ☺7am-2pm; ☎) In-the-know Velo sits on a Mooloolaba side street. A mishmash of recycled furniture and vintage ephemera, it's an easy, breezy affair, where locals play retro board games while munching on smashed avo with red onion, roasted garlic, corn and fresh herbs, or house-made toasted banana, macadamia and date bread with mascarpone and

Maroochydore

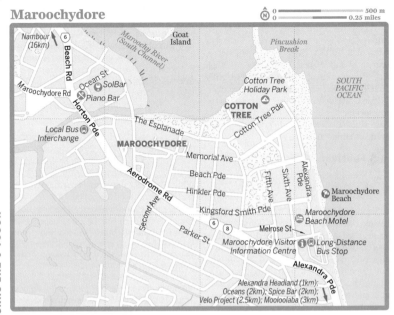

an orange-cardamom syrup. Great, locally roasted coffee, too.

Good Bar
AMERICAN **$**

(Map p138; ☑ 07-5477 6781; www.thegoodbar. com.au; 5/19-23 First Ave, Mooloolaba; burgers $12-20, hot dogs $12-16; ⊙ 11am-late Tue-Sun, kitchen closes 10.30pm) Clad in concrete floors and red-and-black tiles, trendy Good Bar serves quality American grub, including succulent burgers and epic *haute dawgs* with combos like house-smoked Weiner with Asian slaw, peanuts, crispy noodles and *nam jim* (dipping sauce). Other standouts include a 20-hour smoked Cape Grim brisket. There's a French-Mex breakfast menu on weekends, plus craft spirits and beers behind the bar.

Piano Bar
MEDITERRANEAN **$$**

(Map p140; ☑ 0422 291 249; www.thepianobar. com.au; 22-24 Ocean St, Maroochydore; bar snacks $4-9, tapas $9-20; ⊙ 5-10pm Mon & Tue, to 11pm Wed & Thu, noon-11pm Fri-Sun) Bohemian down to its tasselled lampshades, Liberace tomes and fedora-clad barkeeps, Piano Bar peddles generously sized, pan-Mediterranean tapas (order one or two at a time). The charred marinated octopus is pillow-soft, while the glazed beetroot with feta is beautifully textured. Less ubiquitous wine varietals and

live blues, funk or jazz Wednesday to Monday seal the deal.

★ Spice Bar
FUSION **$$$**

(Map p138; ☑ 07-5444 2022; www.spicebar.com. au; 1st fl, 123 Mooloolaba Esplanade, Mooloolaba; small plates $7-18, large plates $28-36; ⊙ 6pm-late Tue, noon-3pm & 6pm-late Wed-Sun) Local gourmands swoon over this slick, contemporary eatery dishing up superb Asian-fusion fare. The menu is a share-plates affair, with options ranging from Hervey Bay scallops with a soy-ginger *sabayon* to butter-soft beef cheek *rendang* (curry) with sweet potato, snake beans and curry leaf. For the best experience, opt for one of the fantastic degustation menus (five/seven/10 courses $55/75/90).

Char
STEAK, SEAFOOD **$$$**

(Map p138; ☑ 07-5477 7205; www.charmooloolaba. com.au; 19 First Ave, Mooloolaba; mains $29-91; ⊙ 5-9pm) Char is owned and proudly run by ex-Melburnian Brett Symons, who wanted to create a restaurant he would personally eat in. It's a smart yet relaxed space, with crisp white linen, tealights and a menu of simple yet elegant dishes. The secret? Top-tier produce, from ridiculously fresh Australian oysters to Wagyu beef from Cape Grim in northwest Tasmania. Book ahead.

Drinking & Nightlife

Pallet Espresso Bar COFFEE
(☑0487 342 172; www.facebook.com/thepallet espressobar; 2/161-163 Brisbane Rd, Mooloolaba; ⊙6.30am-3pm Mon-Fri, to 1pm Sat) You'll find (upcycled) pallets here, along with chatty locals, a communal table and a couple of soccer balls, in case you feel the urge to have a kick on the lawn. Not a lot of food options (think raisin toast and some sweet baked treats), but what it does well is full-bodied, velvety, espresso-based coffee. Just off Brisbane Rd.

Taps@Mooloolaba BAR
(Map p138; ☑07-5477 7222; www.tapsaustralia. com.au; cnr Esplanade & Brisbane Rd, Mooloolaba; ⊙noon-late) A beer fiend's nirvana, Taps lets you pull your own suds. Seriously. It may sound gimmicky, but it's serious business: there are around 20 craft and other brews to quench the most serious of post-surf thirsts. Beer-friendly bites include cream-cheese-stuffed jalapeños, burgers, loaded fries and a taco salad.

SolBar CLUB
(Map p140; ☑07-5443 9550; www.solbar.com. au; 10/12-20 Ocean St, Maroochydore; ⊙7.30am-late) SolBar is a godsend for city-starved indie fans. A constantly surprising line-up takes to the stage here, and budding singer-songwriters can try their own luck at the open-mic night on Wednesdays. The venue doubles as a swinging cafe-bar-restaurant, serving everything from smashed avo, pancakes and zucchini-and-corn fritters at brekkie to lunch and dinner grub such as burgers, pizzas and salads.

ⓘ Information

The **Mooloolaba Visitor Information Centre** (Map p138; ☑07-5458 8844; www.visitsun shinecoast.com.au; cnr Brisbane Rd & First Ave, Mooloolaba; ⊙9am-3pm; 🕾) is located a block away from the Esplanade in the heart of town. The **Maroochydore Visitor Information Centre** (Map p140; ☑07-5458 8842; www. visitsunshinecoast.com.au; cnr Sixth Ave & Melrose St, Maroochydore; ⊙9am-4pm Mon-Fri, to 3pm Sat & Sun; 🕾) also lies one block from the beach.

Further north in Marcoola, Sunshine Coast Airport also houses a **tourist information centre** (☑07-5448 9088; www.visitsunshinecoast.com.

au; Sunshine Coast Airport, Friendship Dr, Marcoola; ⊙9am-3pm).

ⓘ Getting There & Away

AIR

Sunshine Coast Airport (p303) Gateway airport for the Sunshine Coast, with direct daily flights to Sydney and Melbourne and thrice-weekly direct flights to Adelaide. Seasonal nonstop flights to Auckland, New Zealand.

BUS

Long-distance buses (Map p138) stop in front of the Sunshine Coast Visitor Information Centre in Maroochydore and beside Underwater World – Sea Life in Mooloolaba. **Greyhound** (☑1300 473 946; www.greyhound.com.au) buses stop in both Maroochydore and in Mooloolaba, running several times daily to Brisbane (one-way departing Mooloolaba/Maroochydore from $21/22, around two hours). **Premier Motor Services** (☑13 34 10; www.premierms. com.au) runs buses once daily to and from Brisbane (one-way $23, 1½ to 1¾ hours).

Sunbus (TransLink; ☑13 12 30; www.sunbus. com.au) has frequent services between Mooloolaba and Maroochydore ($4.60, 15 minutes) and on to Noosa ($8.60, one to 1½ hours). The **local bus interchange** (Map p138; Horton Pde, Maroochydore) is at Sunshine Plaza shopping centre.

Coolum

POP 7905
Rocky headlands create a number of secluded coves before spilling into the fabulously long stretch of golden sand and rolling surf of Coolum Beach. Like much of the coast along here, the backdrop is spreading suburbia, but thanks to a reasonable cafe society and easy access to the coast's hot spots, it's a useful escape from the more popular and overcrowded holiday scenes at Noosa, Mooloolaba and Maroochydore.

🏃 Activities

Skydive Ramblers (☑07-5448 8877; www.sky divefordive.com; Sunshine Coast Airport, Kittyhawk Cl, Marcoola; jump from 1830/4570m $299/429) will throw you out of a plane at a ridiculous height. Soak up the coastal view before a spectacular beach landing.

Coolum Surf School (☑0438 731 503; www. coolumsurfschool.com.au; 2hr lesson $60, 5-lesson package $225) will have you riding the waves in no time with surfing lessons; it also hires out surfboards/bodyboards ($50/25 for 24 hours).

🛏 Sleeping & Eating

Coolum Beach Caravan Park   CARAVAN PARK $
(✆ 07-5446 1474; www.sunshinecoastholidayparks.com.au; 1827 David Low Way, Coolum Beach; powered sites $46, cabins from $157; 🐾) Location, location, location: the park not only has absolute beach frontage, but is also just across the road from Coolum's main strip.

Villa Coolum   MOTEL $
(✆ 07-5446 1286; www.villacoolum.com; 102 Coolum Tce, Coolum Beach; 1-bedroom units $99-159, 2-bedroom units $129-180; 🐾🅿🖥) Hidden behind a verandah, these good-value '70s-style units offer a warm, friendly welcome. While they show signs of wear and tear, they're spacious and upbeat, with tropical accents and comfy beds. Adding appeal is a pool, pleasant garden and walking distance to one of the area's in-the-know beaches, First Bay.

Element on Coolum Beach   APARTMENT $$$
(✆ 07-5455 1777; www.elementoncoolumbeach.com.au; 1808 David Low Way, Coolum Beach; 1-2-3-bedroom apt from $224/230/359; 🅿🖥🐾🖥) Coolum Beach's smartest slumber spot, with heated pool, central location and 49 huge, stylish apartments. Each apartment is individually owned, so interiors will vary. That said, you can expect spotless, fully equipped, contemporary digs in soothing neutral tones, with full-sized kitchens, tall windows and balconies. Rates come down for week-long stays.

The Caf   CAFE $
(✆ 07-5446 3564; www.thecafcoolum.com; 21 Birtwill St, Coolum Beach; mains $14-19; ⊘ 6.30am-4pm; 🐾) Complete with cable-reel-turned-table, cockatoo wallpaper and laid-back vibe, this is arguably Coolum's coolest little cafe. The place whips up great gourmet salads and sandwiches, pies, fresh juices and feel-good smoothies.

Castro's Bar & Restaurant   ITALIAN, MODERN AUSTRALIAN $$
(✆ 07-5471 7555; cnr Frank St & Beach Rd, Coolum Beach; pizzas $21-26, mains $24-34; ⊘ 5-8.30pm Mon-Thu, to 9pm Fri & Sat, to 8pm Sun) Not even vaguely Cuban, but this popular, casual spot does enjoy a Fidel-like longevity thanks to its mouth-watering menu. Tuck into satisfying wood-fired pizzas, gorgeous risottos (if it's available, order the sweetcorn, pumpkin, chicken and caramelised onion option), or surrender to Castro's smashing, slow-cooked confit duck, wood-fired and served with golden roast potatoes and poached pear stuffed with date chutney.

Peregian Beach & Sunshine Beach

POP 3530 & 2290

Fifteen kilometres of uncrowded, unobstructed beach stretch north from Coolum to Sunshine Beach and the rocky northeast headland of Noosa National Park.

Peregian is the place to indulge in long, solitary beach walks, surfing excellent breaks, and the not-so-uncommon spotting of whales breaking offshore. Locals will tell you that the place is popular with 'yummy mummies' catching up at breezy local cafes with strollers and yoga mats in tow.

A little further north, the laid-back-latte ethos of Sunshine Beach attracts Noosa locals and surfies escaping the summer hordes. Beach walks morph into bush trails over the headland; a stroll through the Noosa National Park takes an hour to reach Alexandria Bay and two hours to Noosa's Laguna Bay. Road access to the park is from McAnally Dr or Parkedge Rd.

🍴 Eating & Drinking

Le Bon Delice   CAFE $
(✆ 07-5471 2200; www.lebondelice.com.au; cnr Heron St & David Low Way, Peregian Beach; cakes from $3, meals $9-14; ⊘ 7am-4pm Mon & Wed-Sat, to 3pm Sun) From the *mille feuille* (French vanilla slice), tarts and pillowy mousse cakes to the *dacquoises* (a dessert cake made with almond and hazelnut meringue) and eclairs, the calorific concoctions from French-born owner and *pâtissier* Jean Jacques at this corner patisserie are as beautiful to look at as they are to devour. If you're hankering for something savoury, nibble on the quiche. Also opens on Tuesdays during the school holidays.

Hand of Fatima   CAFE $$
(✆ 0434 364 328; www.facebook.com/handoffatima cafe; 2/4 Kingfisher Dr, Peregian Beach; mains $17-18.50; ⊘ 5.30am-2.30pm) A friendly, lo-fi cafe where barefoot beach-goers banter with the staff while waiting for their impeccable macchiatos. In one corner is the tiny open kitchen, pumping out Middle Eastern–inspired dishes like breakfast Persian rice pudding with roasted fruits and nuts, or lunchtime braised *cotechino* (pork) sausage with lentils, caramelised onion and Turkish bread. Cash only.

★ **Embassy XO** CHINESE $$$
(☑ 07-5455 4460; www.embassyxo.com.au; 56 Duke
St, Sunshine Beach; mains $29-42; ☺ restaurant
6-9pm Wed-Sun, also noon-2pm Fri & Sat, noon-3pm
Sun, bar menu 3-6pm Wed-Sun) Smart, sophisti-
cated Embassy XO is not your average sub-
urban Chinese joint. Local produce drives
smashing Asian dishes like Hinterland zuc-
chini flowers stuffed with tofu and Sichuan
chilli caramel and Moreton Bay bug wontons
with *tobiko* (flying fish roe) and coconut
miso bisque. Other options include gorgeous
banquets (vegetarian/nonvegetarian $55/80),
yum cha lunch Friday to Sunday and moreish
bar snacks from 3pm to 6pm.

Pitchfork MODERN AUSTRALIAN $$$
(☑ 07-5471 3697; www.pitchforkrestaurant.com.
au; 5/4 Kingfisher Dr, Peregian Beach; mains
$32-45; ☺ noon-2pm & 5pm-late Tue-Sun) The
award-winning chefs at this bright, summery restaurant pump out a concise, contemporary menu where crispy soft-shell
crab might get fresh peppercorn *nam jim*
and green apple, or where roasted pork belly goes sultry in a smoked pork *jus*. Allow
time for a meal here: sip on an Italian *soave*
and soak up the action on the lush, green
square.

Marble Bar Bistro BAR
(☑ 07-5455 3200; www.marblebarbistro.com; 40
Duke St, Sunshine Beach; ☺ noon-9pm Sun-Thu,
to midnight Fri & Sat; ☎) Kick back in a cush-
ioned lounge or perch at one of the concrete bar tables at this sheltered, alfresco
bar. Bites include hit-and-miss tapas ($8
to $22.50) and pizzas ($17.50 to $18.50),
though the place is best for a toast rather
than a memorable feed.

Cooloola Coast

Stretching for 50km between Noosa and
Rainbow Beach, the Cooloola Coast is a remote strip of long sandy beach backed by
the Cooloola Section of the Great Sandy National Park. Although it's undeveloped, the
4WD and tin-boat set flock here in droves,
so it's not always as peaceful as you might
imagine. If you head off on foot or by canoe
along one of the many inlets or waterways,
however, you'll soon escape the crowds. The
coast is famous for the Teewah coloured
sand cliffs, estimated to be about 40,000
years young.

Great Sandy National Park:
Cooloola Section

Extending from Lake 'Cootharaba north to
Rainbow Beach, this 54,000-hectare section
of national park offers wide ocean beaches,
soaring cliffs of richly coloured sands, pristine bushland, heathland, mangroves and
rainforest, all of which are rich in bird life,
including rarities such as the red goshawk
and the grass owl. One of the most extraordinary experiences here is driving along the
beach from Noosa North Shore to Double
Island Point, around 50km to the north.

The route is only accessible to 4WDs
with a vehicle permit (available from www.
npsr.qld.gov.au) and forms part of the Great
Beach Drive, a spectacular coastal touring
route linking Noosa and Hervey Bay. At
Double Island Point, a 1.1km-long walking
trail leads up to spectacular ocean views
and a lighthouse dating back to 1884. From
June to October, it's also a prime place for
spotting majestic humpback whales.

From the Double Island Point section of
the beach, a 4WD track cuts across the point
to the edge of a large tidal lake (perfect for
kids and less-confident swimmers) and then
along Rainbow Beach to the town of Rainbow Beach, passing along the way spectacular coloured cliffs made of ancient, richly
oxidised sands in over 70 earthy shades.
According to local Indigenous legend, the
sands obtained their hues when Yininigie
(a spirit represented by a rainbow) plunged
into the cliffs after fighting an evil tribes-
man. The black sand is rutile, once locally
mined to make titanium for American space
technology.

Great Beach Drive 4WD Tours (☑ 07-
5486 3131; www.greatbeachdrive4wdtours.com;
full-day tour adult/child/family $165/95/475) of-
fers intimate, eco-centric 4WD tours of the
spectacular Great Beach Drive from Noosa
to Rainbow Beach. **Epic Ocean Adventures**
(☑ 0408 738 192; www.epicoceanadventures.com.
au; 1/6 Rainbow Beach Rd, Rainbow Beach; 3hr surf-
ing/kayaking trip $65/75; ☺ shop 8am-5pm) runs
adventure tours departing both Rainbow
Beach and Noosa, and including dolphin-
and turtle-spotting kayaking trips.

Hoof it along the beach with **Rainbow
Beach Horse Rides** (☑ 0412 174 337; www.
rainbowbeachhorserides.com.au; Clarkson Dr, Rainbow Beach; 90min beach ride $140), including an
evocative, two-hour Full Moon Ride ($200).

WOODSTOCK DOWNUNDER

The famous Woodford Folk Festival (www.woodfordfolkfestival.com; ⊙ Dec/Jan) features a huge diversity of over 2000 national and international performers playing folk, traditional Irish, Indigenous and world music, as well as buskers, belly dancers, craft markets, visual-arts performances, environmental talks and Tibetan monks. The festival is held on a property near the town of Woodford from 27 December to 1 January each year. Camping grounds are set up on-site with toilets, showers and a range of foodie marquees, but prepare for a mud bath if it rains. The festival is licensed, so leave your booze at home. Tickets cost $137 per day ($168 with camping) and can be bought online or at the gate. Check online for updated programs.

Woodford is 35km northwest of Caboolture. Shuttle buses run regularly from the Caboolture train station to and from the festival grounds.

The most popular (and best-equipped) camping grounds (☑ 13 74 68; www.npsr.qld. gov.au; sites per person/family $6.15/24.60) are Fig Tree Point (at the northern end of Lake Cootharaba), Harry's Hut (about 4km upstream) and Freshwater (about 6km south of Double Island Point) on the coast. You can also camp at designated zones on the beach if you're driving up to Rainbow Beach.

Rainbow Beach Ultimate Camping (☑ 07-5486 8633; www.rainbow-beach-hire-a-camp.com.au; 2-/3-/5-night camping experience for 1-4 people from $580/690/820) takes all the hard work out of camping by providing most of the equipment and setting it up for you, from the tent, mattresses, stretchers and crockery, to the dining table, BBQ, private toilet and shower.

For park information, contact the QPWS Great Sandy Information Centre (☑ 07-5449 7792; 240 Moorindil St, Tewantin; ⊙ 8am-4pm).

Lake Cooroibah

A couple of kilometres north of Tewantin, the Noosa River widens into Lake Cooroibah. Surrounded by lush bushland, the glassy lake feels a world away from the bustle of Noosa and makes for a soothing day trip.

From the end of Moorindil St in Tewantin, cash-only Noosa North Shore Ferries (☑ 07-5447 1321; www.noosanorthshoreferries.com. au; one-way per pedestrian/car $1/7; ⊙ 5.30am-10.20pm Sun-Thu, to 12.20am Fri & Sat) shuttles across the river to Noosa North Shore. Ferries depart roughly every 10 minutes.

The refreshingly feral Gagaju Bush Camp (☑ 07-5474 3522; http://gagaju.tripod.com; 118 Johns Rd, Cooroibah; dm $15; @) is a riverside eco-wilderness camp with basic dorms constructed out of recycled timber.

Noosa North Shore Retreat (☑ 07-5447 1225; www.noosanorthshoreretreat.com.au; Beach Rd, Noosa North Shore; powered/unpowered camp sites from $42/32, cottages/r from $170/220; ✳ @ ☒) has everything from camping and vinyl 'village tents' to shiny motel rooms and cottages, and the Great Sandy Bar & Restaurant (mains $19 to $28).

Lake Cootharaba & Boreen Point

Cootharaba is the largest lake in the Cooloola Section of Great Sandy National Park, measuring about 5km across and 10km in length. On the western shores of the lake and at the southern edge of the national park, Boreen Point is a relaxed little community and home to one of Queensland's oldest and most atmospheric pubs. The lake is the gateway to the glassy Noosa Everglades, which lure with the offer of bushwalking, canoeing and bush camping.

From Boreen Point, a road leads another 5km to Elanda Point (unsealed for half the way).

Kanu Kapers (☑ 07-5485 3328; www.kanu kapersaustralia.com; 11 Toolara St, Boreen Point; guided tour adult/child from $155/80, 2-/3-day kayaking & camping tour $395/595) offers fantastic half-day and full-day guided tours of the Noosa Everglades, as well as two- and three-day kayaking and camping adventures to Cooloola National Park. Self-guided tours are also available.

On Lake Cootharaba, stunning little Boreen Point Camping Ground (☑ 07-5485 3244; www.noosaholidayparks.com.au; Esplanade, Boreen Point; powered/unpowered sites from $31/25) is crowd-free and provides your own secluded patch of lake-front, native bush.

Framed by palms, jacarandas, quandong trees and the odd bush turkey, the adorable old **Apollonian Hotel** (☑ 07-5485 3100; www.apollonianhotel.com.au; 19 Laguna St, Boreen Point; mains $18-28; ☺ kitchen 10am-8pm Sun-Thu, to 10pm Fri & Sat, bar 10am-10pm Sun-Thu, to midnight Fri & Sat; ⊛) – complete with shady verandahs and a beautifully preserved interior – dates back to the late 19th century. It's famous for its Sunday spit-roast lunch.

Eumundi

POP 3560

Adorable Eumundi is a quaint highland village with a quirky New Age vibe that's greatly amplified during its famous market days. Fig trees, weatherboard pubs and tin-roof cottages line its historic streetscape, which is dotted with cafes, galleries, eclectic boutiques and crafty folk.

Eumundi Markets (☑ 07-5442 7106; www.eumundimarkets.com.au; 80 Memorial Dr; ☺ 8am-1.30pm Wed, 7am-2pm Sat) is one of Australia's most famous and atmospheric artisan markets, attracting over 1.6 million visitors a year to its 600-plus stalls. Dive into a leafy, bohemian wonderland of hand-crafted furniture, jewellery, clothing and accessories, art, fresh local produce, gourmet provisions and more.

The shamelessly charming **Majestic Theatre** (☑ 07-5485 2330; www.themajestictheatre.com.au; 3 Factory St, Pomona; tickets adult/child $14/7; ☺ screening 7.30pm Tue-Fri), in Pomona, 10km northwest of Eumundi, is Australia's longest-running commercial theatre. The venue screens films from the silent era around four to 12 times a month.

Book lovers should check out **Berkelouw Books** (☑ 07-5442 8366; www.facebook.com/BerkelouwBooksEumundi; 87 Memorial Dr; ☺ 9am-5pm Mon, Tue, Thu & Fri, 8am-5pm Wed & Sat, 9am-4pm Sun), packed with fascinating new, rare and secondhand books.

Internationally renowned surfboard shaper **Tom Wegener** (www.tomwegenersurfboards.com; Cooroy) offers homestays where you can spend a day or two learning about the craft of surfboard shaping. (You can also have him make a board for you.) The homestay costs $500 per day (excluding materials) and includes eight hours in the studio, plus meals and surfing sessions.

🛏 Sleeping & Eating

Harmony Hill Station   B&B $$

(☑ 0418 750 643, 07-5442 8685; www.harmonyhillaccom.com.au; 81 Seib Rd; carriages from $145, lodge per night $550; ⊛) Perched on a hilltop in a 5-hectare property, Harmony Hill will have you slumbering in a restored, fully self-contained 1912 railway carriage. Sleeping up to four people, it's the perfect place to relax or romance, with grazing kangaroos and sunset-gazing from Lover's Leap. For groups, there's also a beautifully appointed, self-contained lodge with three queen-sized bedrooms. Minimum stays apply.

Bohemian Bungalow   INTERNATIONAL $$

(☑ 07-5442 8679; www.bohemianbungalow.com.au; 69 Memorial Dr; pizzas $19-25, mains $20-38; ☺ 11.30am-9pm Wed-Fri, 8am-9pm Sat, 8am-3pm Sun) The fare in this gorgeous white Queenslander is outdone only by its whimsical interiors – postmodern bohemian with peacocks, candles and ceramic horses on every ledge and corner. The menu is equally mood-lifting, whether it's local eggs with *vincotto*-roasted Noosa tomatoes or banana-and-buckwheat pancakes or post-brekkie items like smoked-salmon fish cakes and gourmet sourdough pizzas.

Imperial Hotel   PUB FOOD $$

(☑ 07-5442 8811; www.imperialhoteleumundi.com.au; 1 Etheridge St, Eumundi; mains $18-34; ☺ 10am-late) A gorgeous colonial-style pub with kooky bohemian touches, the Imperial is much-loved for its beer garden and live music acts. The tasty menu covers all bases, from fish tacos and Turkish-spiced zucchini fritters to pasta dishes, burgers, surf-and-turf mains and interesting salads.

★ **Spirit House**   THAI $$$

(☑ 07-5446 8994; www.spirithouse.com.au; 20 Nindery Rd, Yandina; share plates $14-49; ☺ noon-3pm daily & 6-9pm Wed-Sat) One of Queensland's top dining destinations (book three weeks ahead for weekends), Spirit House evokes the deep jungles of Southeast Asia with Thai flavours propelling confident dishes like fried soft-shell crab with curry powder and garlic, and braised duck leg with fish sauce, watermelon, ginger and mint. Also home to a cooking school (four-hour classes are $150). It's 11km south of Eumundi.

ℹ Information

Discover Eumundi Heritage & Visitor Centre (☑ 07-5442 8762; www.discovereumundi.com; 73 Memorial Dr, Eumundi; ☺ 10am-3pm Mon-Fri, to 2pm Sat, to 1pm Sun) Also houses the town's modest **local history museum** (admission free).

Sunshine Coast Hinterland

Inland from Nambour, the Blackall Range forms a stunning backdrop to the Sunshine Coast's beaches a short 50km away. A relaxed half- or full-day circuit drive from the coast follows a winding road along the razorback line of the escarpment, passing through quaint mountain villages and offering spectacular views of the coastal lowlands.

Maleny

POP 3440

Perched high in the rolling green hills of the Blackall Range, Maleny offers an intriguing melange of artists, musicians and other creative souls; ageing hippies; rural 'tree-changers' and co-op ventures. Its bohemian edge underscores a thriving commercial township that has moved on from its timber and dairy past without yielding to the tacky 'ye olde' tourist-trap developments of nearby mountain villages.

The stunning **Mary Cairncross Scenic Reserve** (②07-5429 6122; www.mary-cairncross.com.au; 148 Mountain View Rd; by donation; ◎7am-6pm) allows visitors to experience the subtropical rainforests that once blanketed the Blackall Range. Spread over 55 hectares southeast of central Maleny, the reserve includes walking tracks that snake through the rainforest, an oasis that's home to over 120 species of bird life, unbearably cute pademelons (rainforest wallabies) and fine examples of red cedar trees.

Maleny Botanic Gardens (②07-5408 4110; www.malenybotanicgardens.com.au; 233 Maleny-Stanley River Rd; adult/child $16/free, incl aviary $26/7; ◎9am-4.30pm) are a mind-clearing oasis of hedges, lawns and ponds, soaking up a natural tapestry of rare cycads, orchids, roses, azaleas and annuals, as well as a massive aviary.

🍴 Sleeping & Eating

Morning Star Motel   MOTEL **$**

(②07-5494 2944; www.morningstarmotel.com; 2 Panorama Pl, Maleny; r $110-150; ❄🐾) Run by an affable couple, the rooms at this comfy motel have outstanding coastal views. The decor might be a little '80s but the bathrooms are immaculate and modern, and the rooms cosy and spotless. Deluxe suites even come with their own corner spa. Weekend prices are highest.

Sweets on Maple   SWEETS **$**

(②07-5494 2118; www.sweetsonmaple.com.au; 39 Maple St, Maleny; homemade fudge 100g from $5; ◎9.30am-4.30pm Mon-Fri, to 4pm Sat & Sun) There are many ye olde lolly shops in this neck of the woods, but Sweets on Maple licks them all. The old-fashioned sweets parlour lures in passers-by with the crazy-making smell of fresh-baking fudge, and keeps them there with flavours like chocolate chilli and Frangelico with lime. Succumb – your secret is safe with us.

🍷 Drinking & Nightlife

Brouhaha Brewery   MICROBREWERY

(②07-5435 2018; www.brouhahabrewery.com.au; 6/39 Coral St, Maleny; ◎10am-9pm Wed & Thu, to 11.30pm Fri & Sat, to 7pm Sun) Maleny is on the craft-beer radar thanks to this hip microbrewery sporting an industrial fit-out and outdoor deck. Its nine rotating brews include IPAs, stouts, saisons and sours, some made with local produce. Can't choose? Order the well-priced tasting paddle ($14). Quality grub (11am to 8pm) includes baked cob loaf with blue cheese and spinach, and Aussie bush–spiced squid.

Big Barrel   MICROBREWERY

(②07-5429 6300; www.malenymountainwines.com.au; 787 Landsborough-Maleny Rd, Maleny; ◎10am-5pm) Scotsman Ryan McLeod distilled whisky in Tasmania before buying this Maleny Mountain Wines cellar door and adding a microbrewery. Wines at Big Barrel include a smooth Maleny rosé (made using locally grown Chambourcin grapes), while the microbrewery uses local rainwater to produce some unusual drops, from malt-forward Scotch ale to a mango cider.

Fraser Island & the Fraser Coast

Best Places to Eat

➡ Coast (p153)

➡ Paolo's Pizza Bar (p153)

➡ Waterview Bistro (p155)

➡ Pop In (p157)

➡ Oodies Cafe (p161)

➡ Alowishus Delicious (p160)

Best Places to Sleep

➡ Eliza Fraser Lodge (p165)

➡ Debbie's Place (p155)

➡ Torquay Beachfront Tourist Park (p152)

➡ Colonial Lodge (p151)

➡ Standy's B&B (p157)

➡ Inglebrae (p160)

Why Go?

North of the much vaunted Sunshine Coast is this little pocket of quintessential Queensland which takes in World Heritage–listed Fraser Island and some mellow coastal communities, such as Hervey Bay and Rainbow Beach, the agricultural centre of Bundaberg, and numerous old-fashioned country towns never too far from the ocean.

Fraser is the world's largest sand island, home to ancient rainforests and luminous lakes, moody ocean swells and a beach shipwreck – few leave here unimpressed. Across the waters of the Great Sandy Strait, Hervey Bay appeals to retirees and young travellers alike, and from July to October, migrating humpback whales stream into the bay. Further south, tiny Rainbow Beach is a backpacker hot spot with decent surfing.

Bundaberg, the largest city in the region, is a friendly, sunny urban centre overlooking the sea of cane fields that fuels its eponymous rum, a fiery spirit guaranteed to scramble a few brain cells.

When to Go
Bundaberg

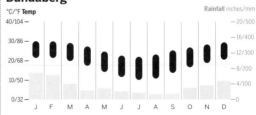

Aug Scoot your boots at the Gympie Music Muster.

Jul–Nov Watch humpback whales – optimal sighting time is August to October.

Nov–Mar Spy on turtles laying eggs in the sand at Mon Repos.

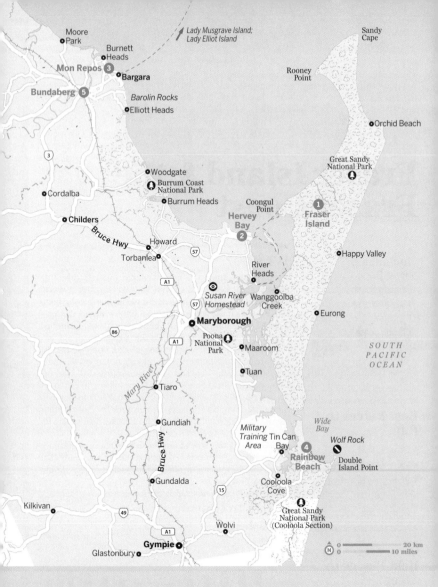

Fraser Island & the Fraser Coast Highlights

1 Fraser Island (p161) Cruising up the beach 'highway', swimming in Lake McKenzie and camping under the stars.

2 Hervey Bay (p149) Watching the whales play.

3 Mon Repos (p159) Witnessing turtles take their first flipper-stumble down the beach.

4 Rainbow Beach (p154) Gazing over the rainbow cliffs from atop the Carlo Sandblow and diving with sharks at Wolf Rock.

5 Bundaberg Rum Distillery (p159) Sampling 'liquid gold' at this distillery in Bundaberg.

Hervey Bay

POP 52,288

Hervey Bay is an unassuming seaside community with an endless beachfront esplanade ideal for extensive lingering – Pialba, Torquay and Scarness all claim a section. Here patrons of beer gardens and cafes dust off their sandy feet after a dip in the warm, gentle waters surrounding the town. Young travellers with an eye on Fraser Island rub shoulders with grey nomads passing languidly through camp sites and serious fisherfolk recharging in pursuit of the one that got away. Throw in the chance to see majestic humpback whales frolicking in the water and the town's convenient access to the World Heritage–listed Fraser Island, and it's easy to understand how Hervey Bay has become an unflashy, yet undeniably appealing, tourist hot spot.

Fraser Island shelters Hervey Bay from the ocean surf and the sea here is shallow and completely flat – perfect for kiddies and summer holiday pics.

◉ Sights

Reef World　　　　　　　　　　　AQUARIUM
(☑ 07-4128 9828; Pulgul St, Urangan; adult/child $20/10, shark dives $55; ☺ 9.30am-4pm) In operation since 1979, this small aquarium is popular with families for its interactive feeding sessions at 11am and 2.30pm. You can also take a dip with lemon, whaler and other nonpredatory sharks.

Fraser Coast Discovery Sphere　　MUSEUM
(☑ 07-4191 2610; www.frasercoastdiscoverysphere.com.au; 166 Old Maryborough Rd, Pialba; gold-coin donation; ☺ 10am-4pm) The stalwart of family-centred Hervey Bay tourism is a little tired, but still a very informative way to learn about the region's geography and marine life.

Wetside Water Park　　　　　　　　PARK
(☑ 1300 79 49 29; www.frasercoast.qld.gov.au/Wetside; The Esplanade, Scarness; ☺ 10am-6pm Wed-Sun, daily during school holidays) On hot days, this wet spot on the foreshore can't be beaten. There's plenty of shade, fountains, tipping buckets and a boardwalk with water infotainment. Opening hours vary so check the website for updates.

⚡ Activities

Whale Watching

Whale-watching tours operate out of Hervey Bay every day (weather permitting) during the annual migrations between late July and early November. Sightings are guaranteed from August to the end of October (with a free subsequent trip if the whales don't show). Outside of the peak season, many boats offer dolphin-spotting tours. Boats cruise from Urangan Harbour out to Platypus Bay and then zip around from pod to pod to find the most active whales. Most vessels offer half-day tours for around $120 for adults and $60 for children, and most include lunch and/or morning or afternoon tea. Tour bookings can be made through your accommodation or the information centres.

Spirit of Hervey Bay　　WHALE WATCHING
(☑ 1800 642 544; www.spiritofherveybay.com; Urangan Harbour; adult/child $120/60; ☺ 8.30am & 1.30pm) The largest whale-watching vessel with the greatest number of passengers.

Freedom Whale Watch　　WHALE WATCHING
(☑ 1300 879 960; www.freedomwhalewatch.com.au; Urangan Harbour) Watch the whales from three levels on a 58m catamaran (adult/child $130/90). This large business can also arrange well-regarded fishing charters and scuba-diving trips to Lady Elliot.

Blue Dolphin Marine Tours　　WHALE WATCHING
(☑ 07-4124 9600; www.bluedolphintours.com.au; Urangan Harbour; adult/child $150/120) One of the more experienced outfits scouting for whale and whatever else the ocean can throw up in Hervey Bay. Smaller groups (24 maximum) aboard the speedy *Blue Dolphin* ensure an intimacy that is difficult to replicate on larger vessels.

Tasman Venture　　WHALE WATCHING
(☑ 1800 620 322; www.tasmanventure.com.au; Urangan Harbour; whale-watching adult/child $115/60; ☺ 8.30am & 1.30pm) One of the best, with underwater microphones and viewing windows. Sightings are guaranteed during the season; you get a free subsequent trip if the whales don't show. Throw in a Fraser Island day trip (adult/child $279/175) and you've knocked over 48 hours in style from the luxury of your Hervey Bay lodging.

Fishing

MV Princess II　　　　　　　　FISHING
(☑ 07-4124 0400; adult/child $160/100) Wet your hook with an experienced crew who've been trolling these waters for more than two decades.

Hervey Bay

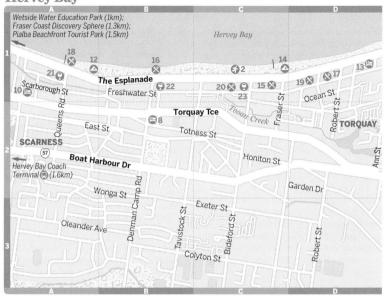

MV Fighting Whiting FISHING
(☎07-4124 3377; www.fightingwhiting.com.au; adult/child/family $70/35/175) Keep your catch on these calm-water tours. Sandwiches, bait and all fishing gear included.

Other Activities

Hervey Bay Ecomarine Tours CRUISE
(☎07-4124 0066; www.herveybayecomarinetours.com.au; Urangan Marina; 5hr tours adult/child $85/45) Cruise on a 12m glass-bottomed boat, the only one in Hervey Bay. Includes snorkelling, coral viewing and an island barbecue. It's a wonderful day out with family or friends. The new owners also run peaceful 90-minute cruises at 7am and 5pm daily.

Air Fraser Island SCENIC FLIGHTS
(☎1300 172 706; www.airfraserisland.com.au) Air Fraser's 'Day Away' ($150) is terrific value for those looking to land on the island and explore a little on foot. Add a 4WD on arrival

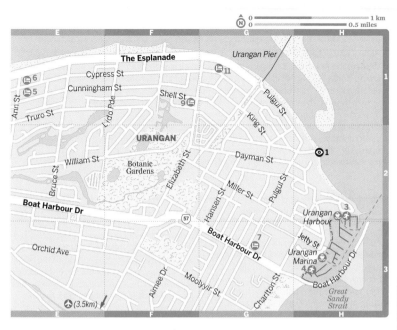

for another $100. Price includes return flight from Hervey Bay or Sunshine Coast.

Aquavue   WATER SPORTS

(☑07-4125 5528; www.aquavue.com.au; 415a The Esplanade, Torquay) In the prime spot on the Torquay foreshore is this long-running aquatic-sports operator. They hire out paddle boards and kayaks ($20 per hour), catamarans ($50 per hour) and jet skis ($50 per 15 minutes). More adventurous souls who perhaps don't have time to visit Fraser properly can take a very fun 90-minute run to gorgeous Moon Point, which includes lunch ($260).

Susan River Homestead   HORSE RIDING

(☑07-4121 6846; www.susanriver.com; Maryborough–Hervey Bay Rd) Horse-riding packages (adult/child $250/160) including accommodation, all meals and use of the on-site swimming pool and tennis courts. Day trippers can canter off on two-hour horse rides (adult/child $85/75).

Skydive Hervey Bay   SKYDIVING

(☑0458 064 703; www.skydiveherveybay.com.au) Tandem skydives from $325 at 4270m, with up to 45 mouth-flapping seconds of free fall, the highest legal altitude in Australia. Or get a taste of the plummet from 1830m for $189.

🧭 Tours

Fraser Experience   TOURS

(☑07-4124 4244; www.fraserexperience.com; adult/child from $180/130) Small group tours of Fraser Island; offers some freedom with the itinerary, though only one departure per day. Also available is a somewhat conspicuous Hummer tour.

Fraser Explorer Tours   TOURS

(☑07-4194 9222; www.fraserexplorertours.com.au; 1-/2-day tours from $179/330) Very experienced drivers; lots of departures to Fraser Island.

🎊 Festivals & Events

Hervey Bay Ocean Festival   CULTURAL

(www.herveybayoceanfestival.com.au; ☉Aug) The newly crowned Ocean Festival blesses boats and croons to the whales.

🛏 Sleeping

⭐**Colonial Lodge**   APARTMENT **$**

(☑07-4125 1073; www.herveybaycoloniallodge.com.au; 94 Cypress St, Torquay; 1-/2-bedroom apt $95/140; ✳🛜☒) Only nine apartments at this hacienda-style lodge in the middle of Torquay mean that guests can hang out by the pool with a level of exclusivity. Staff are friendly and the apartments are bigger than average,

A WHALE OF A TIME

Every year, from July to early November, thousands of humpback whales cruise into Hervey Bay's sheltered waters for a few days before continuing their arduous migration south to the Antarctic. Having mated and given birth in the warmer waters off northeastern Australia, they arrive in Hervey Bay in groups of about a dozen (known as pulses), before splitting into smaller groups of two or three (pods). The new calves utilise the time to develop the thick layers of blubber necessary for survival in icy southern waters by consuming around 600L of milk daily.

Viewing these majestic creatures is simply awe-inspiring. You'll see these showy aqua-acrobats waving their pectoral fins, tail slapping, breaching or simply 'blowing', and many will roll up beside the whale-watching boats with one eye clear of the water...making those on board wonder who's actually watching whom.

with a lovely place to sit out front. It's a short walk to the shallows across the road.

Emeraldene Inn INN $
(07-4124 5500; www.emeraldene.com.au; 166 Urraween Rd, Urraween; d from $110) The Emeraldene has been around for a while, but the 10 rooms deserve more attention given the very reasonable price tag and the lovely bush setting just a few blocks from the shore.

Colonial Village YHA HOSTEL $
(07-4125 1844; www.yha.com.au; 820 Boat Harbour Dr, Urangan; dm/d/cabins from $22.50/52/81; @) This excellent YHA is set on 8 hectares of tranquil bushland, close to the marina and only 50m from the beach. It's a lovely spot, thick with ambience, possums and parrots. Facilities include a pool, tennis and basketball courts, and a sociable bar-restaurant. All dorm rooms come with their own dining tables and desks, and stand-alone single beds.

Torquay Beachfront Tourist Park CARAVAN PARK $
(07-4125 1578; www.beachfronttouristparks.com.au; The Esplanade, Torquay; unpowered/powered sites from $26/31;) Fronting Hervey Bay's exquisitely long sandy beach, all of Beachfront's three shady parks live up to their name, with fantastic ocean views. This Torquay site is in the heart of the action. Other branches are at Pialba (07-4128 1399; The Esplanade, Pialba; unpowered/powered sites from $33.50/41;) and Scarness (07-4128 1274; The Esplanade, Scarness; powered/unpowered sites from $41/34;). Prices have jumped recently, but don't let that deter you; these are some of the East Coast's top sites.

Flashpackers HOSTEL $
(07-4124 1366; www.flashpackersherveybay.com; 195 Torquay Tce, Torquay; dm $26-32, d $80; @) Very hospitable staff keep the guests happily engaged with activities, contests and movies when they are not lounging by the excellent pool, or fixing a snack from the walk-in fridge. The dorm rooms are decent enough and the en-suite rooms are quite posh by hostel standards. It's set just back from the beach, but this is a positive as the street has ample parking and there's a little more discretion for late-night revelers stumbling back to bed.

Mango Tourist Hostel HOSTEL $
(07-4124 2832; www.mangohostel.com; 110 Torquay Rd, Scarness; dm/d $28/60; @) Small and discerning hostel run by knowledgeable local Phil, who communicates clearly and directly, and his lovely wife, who balances the act. Intimate and loaded with character (and geckos), the old Queenslander, set on a quiet street away from the beach, sleeps guests in a four-bed dorm room and two very homey doubles.

Shelly Bay Resort APARTMENT $$
(07-4125 4533; www.shellybayresort.com.au; 466 The Esplanade, Torquay; 1-/2-bedroom units $139/170; @) The bright, breezy beach-facing apartments at Shelly Bay Resort are some of the best value in town, especially the two-bedroom ones, which have prime corner locations overlooking the pool. Customer service is first class, whether staying for work or pleasure; there's a lot to like about this one.

Pier One RESORT $$
(07-4125 4965; www.herveybaywaterfrontapts.com.au; 569 The Esplanade, Urangan; 1-/2-bedroom apt $189/259) The latest large-scale project on the Esplanade, Pier One sits alongside Pier Apartments and suits travellers looking for a view of the sea in the background and the pool in the foreground. The apartments are bigger than most, come with two bathrooms, Ikea furniture and a very reasonable price tag.

Arlia Sands Apartments
APARTMENT $$

(🖉07-4125 4360; www.arliasands.com.au; 13 Ann St, Torquay; 1-/2-bedroom apt from $135/145; ❄️ ⚲) Excellent value, if a little less than stylish, these self-contained units have recently been upgraded just enough to make a difference. It's off the main drag yet close to the beach and shops and is *très* quiet.

Grange Resort
RESORT $$$

(🖉07-4125 2195; www.thegrange-herveybay.com. au; 33 Elizabeth St, Urangan; 1-/2-bedroom villas from $235/305; ❄️ 🛜 ⚲) Reminiscent of a stylish desert resort with fancy split-level condos and filled with life's little luxuries, the Grange is thriving under new management and is close to the beach and to town. Pets are very welcome – a rarity in these parts – except in the fabulous pool bar where amphibious creatures sink beers until the sun goes down.

✖️ Eating

Bayaroma Cafe
CAFE $

(🖉07-4125 1515; 428 The Esplanade, Torquay; breakfast $10-22, mains $9.50-20; ⊘6.30am-3.30pm; 🖉) Famous for its coffee, all-day breakfasts and people-watching position, Bayaroma has a jam-packed menu that truly has something for everyone – even vegetarians! Attentive, chirpy service is an added bonus.

Enzo's on the Beach
CAFE $

(www.enzosonthebeach.com.au; 351a The Esplanade, Scarness; mains $8-20; ⊘6.30am-5pm) This shabby-chic beachside cafe is the place to go to fill up on sandwiches, wraps, salads and coffees before working them off on a hired kayak or kitesurfing lesson.

Simply Wok
ASIAN $

(🖉07-4125 2077; 417 The Esplanade, Torquay; mains $14-23; ⊘7am-10pm) Noodles, stir-fries, seafood and curries will satisfy any cravings for Asian cuisine, and there's a nightly (from 5pm to 9pm) all-you-can-eat hot buffet for $16.90. Surprisingly good breakfast.

★Paolo's Pizza Bar
ITALIAN $$

(🖉07-4125 3100; www.paolospizzabar.com.au; 2/446 The Esplanade, Torquay; mains $14-27; ⊘5-9pm) Hordes of locals come for a slice of Naples from the pizza oven or in the form of fine pasta (the spaghetti marinara at $22 was amazing), and relish the attentive family-run service. It's the best Italian in the region, but you can't book, so get here early to avoid the shoulder shrug.

★Coast
FUSION $$

(🖉07-4125 5454; 469 The Esplanade, Torquay; mains $21-60; ⊘5pm-late Tue & Wed, 11.30am-late Thu-Sun) A local restaurateur and a red-hot English chef have teamed up to deliver an outstanding Australian venture in the unlikely locale of Hervey Bay. Almost all meals are prepared to be shared, and span the Asian–Middle Eastern cuisine range. Not hungry? Share a cocktail pitcher (from $30) and nibble on bar snacks more akin to hors d'oeuvres.

Black Dog Café
MODERN AUSTRALIAN $$

(🖉07-4124 3177; 381 The Esplanade, Torquay; mains $12-35; ⊘lunch & dinner) Black Dog delivers a wide variety of contemporary Australian staples to all parts of Hervey Bay. Its relaxed diner down the Torquay end of the Esplanade serves up burgers, seafood, salads and the like without fuss and at very fair prices.

Eat at Dan & Steph's
CAFE $$

(449 The Esplanade, Torquay; Mains $16-24; ⊘6am-4pm Wed-Mon) Former TV cooking show winners Dan and Steph have kicked on from their public success with a popular restaurant with an informal vibe. Most meals take an interesting spin on familiar dishes. The smoked beef salad ($18) and the pumpkin and pomegranate black rice ($18) were both a big tick. Breakfast looks good, too.

🍷 Drinking & Nightlife

Beach House Hotel
PUB

(344 The Esplanade, Scarness) The Beach House has been reborn, thanks to a shed load of cash, a prime viewpoint on Scarness Beach and a willingness to give the people what they want: beer taps at every turn, gambling dens, a huge courtyard, decent food and accessible live music most nights of the week.

Hoolihan's
PUB

(382 The Esplanade, Scarness; ⊘11am-2am) Like all good Irish pubs, Hoolihan's is wildly popular, especially with the backpacker crowd. This one is pretty basic, but the kerbside seating is ideal for people-watching, or for being watched by people, whichever comes first.

Viper
CLUB

(410 The Esplanade, Torquay; ⊘10pm-3am Wed, Fri & Sat) Viper is the kind of club everyone rolls their eyes at when its name is mentioned early in the night, but you can't keep the dancers out come midnight, especially in summer. Music varies wildly between God-awful bad and actually pretty good.

ⓘ Information

Hervey Bay Visitor Information Centre
(☎1800 811 728; www.visitfrasercoast.com;
cnr Urraween & Maryborough Rds) Helpful and
well-stocked with brochures and information.
On the outskirts of town.

Marina Kiosk (☎07-4128 9800; Buccaneer Ave,
Urangan Boat Harbour, Urangan; ⊙6am-6pm)

ⓘ Getting There & Away

AIR

Hervey Bay airport is on Don Adams Dr, just off
Booral Rd. **Qantas** (☎13 13 13; www.qantas.
com.au) and **Virgin** (☎13 67 89; www.virginaus-
tralia.com.au) have daily flights to/from destinations around Australia.

BOAT

Boats to Fraser Island leave from River Heads,
about 10km south of town, and from Urangan
Marina. Most tours leave from Urangan Harbour.

BUS

Buses depart **Hervey Bay Coach Terminal**
(☎07-4124 4000; Central Ave, Pialba). **Greyhound** (☎1300 473 946; www.greyhound.com.
au) and **Premier Motor Service** (☎13 34 10;
www.premierms.com.au) have several services
daily to/from Brisbane ($72, 6½ hours), Ma-
roochydore ($91, six hours), Bundaberg ($29,
two hours) and Rockhampton ($92, six hours).

Tory's Tours (☎07-4128 6500; www.torys-
tours.com.au) has twice daily services to Brisbane airport (adult/child $80/68). **Wide Bay
Transit** (☎07-4121 3719; www.widebaytransit.
com.au) has hourly services from Urangan Marina (stopping along the Esplanade) to Maryborough ($8, one hour) every weekday, with fewer
services on weekends.

ⓘ Getting Around

Hervey Bay is the best place to hire a 4WD for
Fraser Island.

Aussie Trax (☎07-4124 4433; www.fraseris-
land4wd.com.au; 56 Boat Harbour Dr, Pialba)

Fraser Magic 4WD Hire (☎07-4125 6612; www.
fraser4wdhire.com.au; 5 Kruger Ct, Urangan)

Hervey Bay Rent A Car (☎07-4194 6626;
www.herveybayrentacar.com.au; 5 Cunningham
St, Torquay)

Safari 4WD Hire (☎07-4124 4244; www.safa-
ri4wdhire.com.au; 102 Boat Harbour Dr, Pialba)

Rainbow Beach

POP 1142

Rainbow Beach is an idyllic Australian beach
town at the base of the Inskip Peninsula,

which is best known for its colourful sand
cliffs and easy access by barge to Fraser
Island. It's a decidedly low-key place, half-
secret to non-4WD lovers who know little
of the dramatic approach possible along the
Cooloola Section of the Great Sandy National Park. It's a great place to try your hand
at different outdoor activities, tap into the
backpacker party scene, or just chill out with
family and friends.

🏃 Activities

Rainbow Paragliding   PARAGLIDING
(☎07-5486 3048, 0418 754 157; www.paragliding
rainbow.com; glides $200) If ever there was a
place worthy of leaping from, then the colourful cliffs of Rainbow Beach may just be it.
Jean Luc has been paragliding here with ex-
hilarated customers for 20 years. Better value than skydiving and a more mellow thrill.

Wolf Rock Dive Centre   DIVING
(☎07-5486 8004, 0438 740 811; www.wolfrockdive.
com.au; 20 Karoonda Rd; double dive charters from
$240) Wolf Rock, a congregation of volcanic
pinnacles off Double Island Point, is regarded as one of Queensland's best scuba-diving
sites. The endangered grey nurse shark is
found here all year.

Epic Ocean Adventures   SURFING
(☎0408 738 192; www.epicoceanadventures.com.
au; 3hr surf lessons $65, 3hr kayak tours $75) Rainbow Beach can throw up some challenging
breaks for beginners, but the instructors here
are first class. They also offer dolphin-spotting
sea-kayak tours.

Fraser's on Rainbow   ADVENTURE SPORTS
(☎07-5486 8885; www.frasersonrainbow.com)
Rainbow Beach is a smart alternative to
Hervey Bay as a gateway to Fraser Island.
These three-day tag-along tours cost $479
and are seriously fun.

Surf & Sand Safaris   ADVENTURE SPORTS
(☎07-5486 3131; www.surfandsandsafaris.com.
au; half-day tours adult/child $75/40) Half-day
4WD tours through the Great Sandy National Park and along the beach to the coloured
sands and lighthouse at Double Island Point.
Full-day trips can also be arranged through
a partner operator.

Skydive Ramblers   SKYDIVING
(☎0418 218 358; www.skydiveforfun.com.au;
10,000/14,000ft dives $350/399) Soft landings
on the beach; hard flying through the air.

Pippies Beach House DRIVING
(☑07-5486 8503; www.pippiesbeachhouse.com.
au) Departs Rainbow Beach; well-organised,
small convoys to Fraser Island ($417) with
high safety standards. Maximum of 34 guests
and highly recommended by the party set
filling out Pippies' dorm rooms.

🛏 Sleeping

Rainbow Beach Hire-a-Camp CAMPGROUND $
(☑0419 464 254, 07-5486 8633; all-inclusive
camping 4 people $145) Camping on the beach
is one of the best ways to experience this
part of the coast; if you don't have camping
gear, Rainbow Beach Hire-a-Camp can hire
out equipment, set up your tent, provide
food and cooking equipment and camp site,
organise camping permits and break camp
for you when you're done. Too easy!

Dingo's Backpacker's Resort HOSTEL $
(☑1800 111 126; www.dingosresort.com; 20 Spectrum St; dm $30; ❄@🛜🏊) This party hostel
with a busy public bar is not for those in
need of a good rest. It has loud music (live
or otherwise) and karaoke most nights, a
chill-out gazebo for a temporary escape, free
pancake breakfasts and cheap meals nightly.
Dorms are clean and adequate, while excellent tours can be arranged.

Rainbow Beach
Holiday Village CARAVAN PARK $
(☑07-5486 3222; www.rainbowbeachholiday
village.com; 13 Rainbow Beach Rd; powered/unpow-
ered sites from $43/36, villas from $120; ❄🛜)
Popular beachfront park with a range of villas if you want the vibe but not the hassle.

Pippies Beach House HOSTEL $
(☑07-5486 8503; www.pippiesbeachhouse.com.
au; 22 Spectrum St; dm/d $24/65; ❄@🛜🏊)
This five-bedroom beach house has been
converted into a relaxed hostel – the party
is elsewhere in Rainbow – where you can
catch your breath between outdoor pursuits.
Free breakfast, wi-fi and boogie boards, and
lots of organised group activities, sweeten
the stay. Pippies has expanded, but insist on
staying in the main house if you can.

★ Debbie's Place B&B $$
(☑07-5486 3506; www.rainbowbeachaccom-
modation.com.au; 30 Kurana St; d/ste from
$150/180, 3-bedroom apt from $340; ❄🛜🏊)
Greenery abounds at Debbie's meticulously
kept Queenslander, which has become the
standard bearer for Rainbow Beach holiday
accommodation. The charming rooms are
fully self-contained, with private entrances
and verandahs. The effervescent Debbie is a
mine of information and makes this a cosy
home away from home. You can leave your
car here if taking a tour to Fraser.

Plantation Resort RESORT $$$
(☑07-5486 9600; www.plantationresortatrainbow.
com.au; 1 Rainbow Beach Rd; d from $250) The
high-end option in Rainbow is still shining
brightly enough to warrant the price tag.
Try to stretch the budget for an ocean-view
penthouse (from $380) to get the maximum
effect. Popular with conferences and out-of-
towners, the Plantation also has a smart bar-
restaurant, **Arcobaleno on the Beach** (pizzas $15-25; ⊙9am-10pm), where the beautiful
people gather for happy hour, live tunes and
audacious seafood delights.

🍴 Eating

Rainbow Fruit CAFE $
(☑07-5486 3126; 2 Rainbow Beach Rd; wraps from
$9; ⊙8am-5pm) Rainbow fresh fruit and
vegetables are sliced, diced and puréed for
a range of juices, wraps and salads at this
humble cafe on the main strip.

★ Waterview Bistro MODERN AUSTRALIAN $$
(☑07-5486 8344; Cooloola Dr; mains $26-35;
⊙11.30am-11.30pm Wed-Sat, to 6pm Sun) Sunset
drinks are a must at this swish restaurant
with sensational views of Fraser Island from
its hilltop perch. Get stuck into the signature
seafood chowder, steaks and seafood, or have
fun cooking your own meal over hot stones.

Rainbow Beach
Surf Lifesaving Club PUB FOOD $$
(☑07-5486 3249; Wide Bay Esplanade; mains from
$15; ⊙11am-10pm) The food is fairly standard
pub fare, served quickly, with huge slabs of
meat, pasta and sides of chips, but the view
and the accompanying beer are the reason
you come to places like Rainbow Beach in
the first place. The strong community spirit
is palpable, even if the odd resident boozer
makes for a sad mid-afternoon.

ℹ Information

Rainbow Beach Visitor Centre (☑07-5486
3227; www.rainbowbeachinfo.com.au; 8 Rainbow Beach Rd; ⊙7am-5.30pm) Despite the
posted hours, it's open sporadically.
Shell Tourist Centre (36 Rainbow Beach Rd;
⊙6am-6pm) At the Shell service station;
arranges tour bookings and barge tickets for
Fraser Island.

ℹ Getting There & Away

Greyhound (☑1300 473 946; www.greyhound. com.au) has several daily services from Brisbane ($51, five hours), Noosa ($34, three hours) and Hervey Bay ($28, two hours). **Premier Motor Service** (☑13 34 10; www.premierms.com. au) has less expensive services. **Active Tours and Transfers** (☑07 5313 6631; www.active-transfers.com.au) runs a shuttle bus to Rainbow Beach from Brisbane Airport ($135, three hours) and Sunshine Coast Airport ($95, two hours).

Most 4WD-hire companies will also arrange permits and barge costs to Fraser Island ($100 per vehicle return), and hire out camping gear. Try **All Trax** (☑07-5486 8767; www.fraserisland4x4. com.au; Rainbow Beach Rd, Shell service station; per day from $165) or **Rainbow Beach Adventure Centre** (☑07-5486 3288; www.adventurecentre. com.au; 13 Spectrum St; per day from $180).

Maryborough

POP 23,113

Founded in 1847, Maryborough is one of Queensland's oldest towns, and its port saw the first shaky step ashore for thousands of 19th-century free settlers looking for a better life in the new country. Heritage and history are Maryborough's specialities; the pace of yesteryear is reflected in its beautifully restored colonial-era buildings and gracious Queenslander homes.

This charming old country town is also the birthplace of Pamela Lyndon (PL) Travers, creator of the umbrella-wielding Mary Poppins. The award-winning film *Saving Mr Banks* tells Travers' story, with early-1900s Maryborough in a starring role. There's a life-sized statue of Ms Poppins on the corner of Richmond and Wharf Sts. Mary Poppins groupies should schedule their trips for the Mary Poppins Festival in June/July.

◉ Sights

Brennan & Geraghty's Store   MUSEUM
(☑07-4121 2250; 64 Lennox St; adult/family $5.50/13.50; ⊗10am-3pm) This National Trust-classified store traded for 100 years before closing its doors. The museum is crammed with tins, bottles and packets, including early Vegemite jars and curry powder from the 1890s. It's a nostalgic wonderland for Australian/British oldies and anyone interested in the tastes of times gone by.

Portside   HISTORIC SITE
(101 Wharf St; ⊗10am-4pm Mon-Fri, to 1pm Sat & Sun) In the historic area beside the Mary River, Portside has 13 heritage-listed buildings, parkland and museums. The **Portside Centre** (☑07-4190 5730; cnr Wharf & Richmond Sts; ⊗10am-4pm), located in the former Customs House, has interactive displays on Maryborough's history. Part of the centre, but a few doors down, the Bond Store Museum also highlights key periods in Maryborough's history. Downstairs is the original packed-earth floor and even some liquor barrels from 1864.

Maryborough Heritage City Markets   MARKET
(cnr Adelaide & Ellena Sts; ⊗8am-1.30pm Thu) Market fun made all the more entertaining by the firing (1pm) of the historic Time Cannon, a town crier and rides on the *Mary Ann* steam loco (adult/child $3/2) through Queen's Park.

Heritage Centre   NOTABLE BUILDING
(☑07-4123 1842; cnr Wharf & Richmond Sts; ⊗9am-4pm) If tracing your genealogical tree is a priority, head to the Heritage Centre where you'll find colonial immigration records from ships logs; and if dear old great-great-granddaddy arrived in Australia courtesy of Her Majesty's prison system, you'll find convict records as well.

Maryborough Military & Colonial Museum   MUSEUM
(☑07-4123 5900; www.maryboroughmuseum. org; 106 Wharf St; adult/couple/family $5/8/10; ⊗9am-3pm) Check out the only surviving three-wheeler Girling car, originally built in London in 1911. There's also a replica Cobb & Co coach and one of the largest military libraries in Australia.

☞ Tours

Free **guided walks** (⊗9am Mon-Sat) depart from the City Hall and take in the town's many sites.

Tea with Mary   TOURS
(☑1800 214 789; per person $20; ⊗9.30am Thu & Fri) Tour of the historic precinct with a Mary Poppins–bedecked guide who spills the beans on the town's past; book through the visitor centre (p157).

Ghostly Tours & Tales   WALKING
(☑1800 811 728; tours incl dinner $75; ⊗6pm last Saturday of the month) Get spooked on a torch-lit tour of the city's grisly murder sites, opium dens, haunted houses and cemetery. Tours begin from the Maryborough Post Office in Bazaar St.

✪✦ Festivals & Events

Mary Poppins Festival   CULTURAL
(www.marypoppinsfestival.com.au; ⊙ Jun-Jul) A supercalifragilisticexpialidocious festival celebrating PL Travers and the famous Miss Poppins every June/July over the school holidays.

🛏 Sleeping & Eating

Ned Kelly's Motel   MOTEL $
(☑ 07-4121 0999; www.nedkellymotel.com.au; 150 Gympie Rd; s/d $45/75, cabins from $89; ✱ ☒) The fabled Victorian bushranger Ned Kelly never made it this far north, so his statue on the side of the road may hold you up momentarily. Don't be alarmed, it's just a budget motel bearing his name. Rooms are basic, but there's a pool and laundry. Very cheap rates.

★ Standy's B&B   B&B $$
(50 Ferry Rd; 1-/2-bedroom studios $150/180) Named after two retired Standardbred racehorses who now enjoy the lush riverside surrounds, this pristine new homestay on the outskirts of Maryborough offers an accessible piece of high-class rural living. The house itself is a white beauty on the banks of the Mary River and is set on 6 hectares of prime land. Guests can choose from two spacious, country-style studios, with white walls and polished floorboards. The food, service and surrounds are all excellent.

Eco Queenslander   BOUTIQUE HOTEL $$
(☑ 0438 195 443; www.ecoqueenslander.com; 15 Treasure St; per couple from $140) 🍴 Lovely Cecile, the French adventurer who fell in love with Maryborough, is an enthusiastic host to the house she gleefully restored. The old Queenslander has a comfy lounge, full kitchen, laundry and cast-iron bathtub. Sustainable features include solar power, rainwater tanks, energy-efficient lighting and bikes for you to use. Minimum two-night stay.

★ Pop In   CAFE $
(203 Bazaar St; sandwiches $8.50; ⊙ 7am-3pm Mon-Fri, to 1pm Sat) Very popular local cafe with a rotating fresh salad menu and a reputation for fine sandwiches and cakes. Service is efficient and friendly – it's the place to go for a quick meal if you're passing through Maryborough.

Toast   CAFE $
(☑ 07-4121 7222; 199 Bazaar St; dishes $6-12; ⊙ 6am-4pm Mon-Sat, 6am-2.30pm Sun) Stainless-steel fittings, polished cement floors and coffee served in paper cups stamp the

metro-chic seal on this groovy cafe. The best coffee we found for some distance.

ℹ Information

Maryborough/Fraser Island Visitor Centre
(☑ 1800 214 789; www.visitfrasercoast.com; Kent St; ⊙ 9am-5pm Mon-Fri, to 1pm Sat & Sun)

ℹ Getting There & Away

Queensland Rail (☑ 1800 872 467; www.queenslandrail.com.au) has two services: the Spirit of Queensland ($75, five hours) and the Tilt Train ($75, 3½ hours) connecting Brisbane with Maryborough West station. The station is 7km west of the centre, and is connected via a shuttle bus.

Greyhound (☑ 1300 473 946; www.greyhound.com.au) and **Premier Motor Service** (☑ 13 34 10; www.premierms.com.au) have buses to Gympie ($30, one hour), Bundaberg ($40, three hours) and Brisbane ($64, 4½ hours).

Wide Bay Transit (☑ 07-4121 4070; www.widebaytransit.com.au) has hourly services (fewer on weekends) between Maryborough and Hervey Bay ($8, one hour), departing from outside City Hall in Kent St.

Gympie
POP 18,359

Gympie is a pleasant former gold-rush town with some fine heritage architecture, lush parkland and a good ol' country feel. Come in August for the **Gympie Music Muster** (www.muster.com.au), one of the finest country music festivals in Australia.

The **Gympie Gold Mining & Historical Museum** (☑ 07-5482 3995; www.gympiegoldmuseum.com.au; 215 Brisbane Rd; adult/child/family $10/5/25; ⊙ 9am-4pm) holds a diverse collection of mining equipment and steam engines, while the **Woodworks Forestry & Timber Museum** (☑ 07-5483 7691; www.woodworksmuseum.com.au; cnr Fraser Rd & Bruce Hwy; $5; ⊙ 10am-4pm Mon-Sat) displays memorabilia and equipment from the region's old logging days.

If you can't muster up the energy to drive any further, the **Gympie Muster Inn** (☑ 07-5482 8666; www.gympiemusterinn.com.au; 21 Wickham St; d from $140) is a friendly motel.

Childers
POP 1570

Surrounded by lush green fields and rich red soil, Childers is a charming little town, its main street lined with tall, shady trees and lattice-trimmed historical buildings.

The lovely, 100-year-old Federal Hotel has swingin' saloon doors, while a bronze statue of two romping pig dogs sits outside the Grand Hotel. Backpackers flock to Childers for fruit-picking and farm work.

There's a moving memorial to the 15 backpackers who were tragically killed in a hostel fire in 2000, and fantastic art at the Childers Palace Memorial & Art Gallery (☑07-4130 4660; 72 Churchill St; ☺9am-5pm Mon-Fri, to 3pm Sat & Sun) FREE.

The Old Pharmacy (☑0400 376 359; 90 Churchill St; adult/child $5/3; ☺9am-3.30pm Mon-Fri, 9am-1pm Sat) was an operational apothecary's shop from 1894 to 1982, and also functioned as the town dentist, vet, optician and local photographer.

🛏 Sleeping & Eating

Sugarbowl Backpackers　　　CARAVAN PARK $
(☑07-4126 1521; www.sugarbowlchilders.com; Bruce Hwy; powered site $29, cabin $90; @ ≋) This proxy backpacker employment agency is well-maintained and welcoming for those seeking farm labour. A 10-minute walk out of town, Sugarbowl is a clean and green spot favoured by many seasonal pickers. Rates are for two people; prices drop for longer stays. Camping sites are also available.

Mango Hill B&B　　　B&B $$
(☑1800 816 020, 0408 875 305; www.mangohill cottages.com; 8 Mango Hill Dr; d incl breakfast from $150; ≋) For warm, country hospitality, the cute cane-cutter cottages at Mango Hill B&B, 4km south of town, are decorated with handmade wooden furniture, country decor and comfy beds that ooze charm and romance. There's an organic winery on-site called Hill of Promise. Perfect to break up your East Coast road trip, especially if you're travelling with a loved one.

Mammino's　　　ICE CREAM $
(115 Lucketts Rd; ice-cream cups $5; ☺9am-5pm) On your way out of town, take a detour to Mammino's for wickedly delicious, homemade macadamia ice cream. Lucketts Rd is off the Bruce Hwy just south of Childers. Don't worry about the faded signs; this place is amazing.

Drunk Bean　　　CAFE $
(☑07-4126 1118; Childers Shopping Centre, Bruce Hwy; mains $8-14; ☺7am-4pm) Near the Woolworths supermarket is this excellent cafe that doubles as an arts-and-craft store. Breakfast, smoothies, light lunches and a stretch of the legs. Well worth pulling over for.

Federal Hotel　　　PUB FOOD $$
(☑07-4126 1438; 71 Churchill St; mains from $17) This grand old federal-era pub is a ripper for hearty pub food and an ice-cold lager to wash it down. Take in a cross-section of Childers society over your parmigiana or steak.

❶ Information

Childers Visitor Information Centre (☑07-4126 3886; 72 Churchill St; ☺9am-4pm Mon-Fri, to 3pm Sat & Sun) Beneath the Childers Palace Memorial & Art Gallery.

❶ Getting There & Away

Childers is 50km south of Bundaberg. **Greyhound Australia** (☑1300 473 946; www.greyhound.com.au) and **Premier Motor Service** (☑13 34 10; www.premierms.com.au) both stop at the Shell service station north of town and have daily services to/from Brisbane ($91, 6½ hours), Hervey Bay ($19, one hour) and Bundaberg ($27 1½ hours).

Burrum Coast National Park

Shifting between a lowland vegetation of stringybark trees, dense mangroves and flat coastal dunes, Burrum Coast National Park feels wonderfully remote. It's a popular spot for knowledgeable campers, birdwatchers, fishers, canoeists and hikers. The park covers two sections of coastline on either side of the little holiday community of Woodgate, 37km east of Childers. The Woodgate section of the park begins at the southern end of the Esplanade, and has attractive beaches and abundant fishing. The more isolated Kinkuna section of the park is thick bush and only for the serious explorer, but it does boast a fine, secluded beach with decent surf.

The NPRSR camping ground (www.nprsr.qld.gov.au; per person/family $6.75/24.60) at Burrum Point is reached by a 4WD-only track. Several walking tracks start at the camping ground or Acacia St in Woodgate.

Woodgate Beach Tourist Park (☑07-4126 8802; www.woodgatebeachtouristpark.com; 88 The Esplanade; unpowered/powered site $30/35, cabin $60-115, beachfront villa $140; ❄ @) is right on the beach.

Bundaberg

POP 70,588

Bundaberg is the largest town in the Fraser Coast region and is known across the land more for its eponymous dark rum and fruit-farming backpackers than its coral-fringed beach hamlets. The town proper is an agricultural centre with some friendly pubs and a decent regional art gallery. However, in many people's eyes, the beach hamlets around Bundaberg are more attractive than the town itself. Some 25km north of the centre is Moore Park with wide, flat beaches. To the south is the very popular Elliott Heads with a nice beach, rocky foreshore and good fishing.

◉ Sights & Activities

★ **Bundaberg Rum Distillery**   DISTILLERY
(☑ 07-4131 2999; www.bundabergrum.com.au; Hills St; adult/child self-guided tours $19/9.5, guided tours $28.50/14.25; ☉10am-3pm Mon-Fri, to 2pm Sat & Sun) Bundaberg's biggest claim to fame is the iconic Bundy Rum: you'll see the Bundy Rum polar bear on billboards and bumper stickers all over town. Choose from either a self-guided tour through the museum, or a guided tour of the distillery – tours depart on the hour. Both include a tasting for the over-18-year-olds. Wear closed shoes.

Bundaberg Barrel   BREWERY
(☑ 07-4154 5480; www.bundaberg.com; 147 Bargara Rd; adult/child $12/5; ☉ 9am-4.30pm Mon-Sat, 10am-3pm Sun) Bundaberg's nonalcoholic ginger beer and other soft drinks aren't as famous as Bundy Rum, but they are very good. Visit the Barrel to take an audio tour of the small museum. Tastings are included and it's geared toward families.

Bundaberg Regional Arts Gallery   GALLERY
(☑ 07-4130 4750; www.bundabergregionalgalleries.com.au; 1 Barolin St; ☉10am-5pm Mon-Fri, 11am-3pm Sat & Sun) FREE This small (and vividly purple) gallery has surprisingly good exhibitions.

Hinkler Hall of Aviation   MUSEUM
(☑ 07-4130 4400; www.hinklerhallofaviation.com; Mt Perry Rd, Botanic Gardens; adult/child $18/10, family $28-40; ☉9am-4pm) This modern museum has multimedia exhibits, a flight simulator and informative displays chronicling the life of Bundaberg's famous son Bert Hinkler, who made the first solo flight between England and Australia in 1928.

TURTLE TOTS

Mon Repos, 15km northeast of Bundaberg, is one of Australia's most accessible turtle rookeries. From November to late March, female loggerheads lumber laboriously up the beach to lay eggs in the sand. About eight weeks later, the hatchlings dig their way to the surface, and, under cover of darkness, emerge en masse to scurry as quickly as their little flippers allow down to the water.

The Bundaberg Visitor Centre (p161) has information on turtle conservation and organises nightly tours (adult/child $12/6.25) from 7pm during the season. Bookings are mandatory and need to be made through the visitor centre or online at www.bundabergregion.org. The Bundaberg Visitor Centre also has reports of how many turtles have been seen through the season.

Alexandra Park & Zoo   PARK
(Quay St) FREE Lovely sprawling park with plenty of shady trees, flower beds and swaths of green lawn for a lazy picnic, right beside the Burnett River. There's also a small zoo for the littlies.

Anzac Park Pool   SWIMMING
(☑ 07-4151 5640; 19 Quay St; adult/child $4/3; ☉5.30am-6pm Mon-Thu, 5.30am-9pm Fri, 6am-6pm Sat, 9am-5pm Sun) This friendly public swimming pool is a Bundaberg institution on a lazy summer's day. Good management, yummy lolly (candy) selection and a glorious Olympic-sized pool.

Bundaberg Aqua Scuba   DIVING
(☑ 07-4153 5761; www.aquascuba.com.au; 239 Bourbong St; diving courses from $349) Leads dives to nearby sites around Innes Park.

★ **Lady Elliot Island**   TOURS
(☑ 07-5536 3644, toll-free 1800 072 200; www.lady elliot.com.au; adult/child $365/210) Fly to Lady Elliot Island, spend five hours on the Great Barrier Reef and use the resort's facilities.

Burnett River Cruises   CRUISE
(☑ 0427 099 009; www.burnettrivercruises.com.au; School Lane, East Bundaberg; 2½hr tours adult/child $26.50/10) The *Bundy Belle*, an old-fashioned ferry, chugs at a p]leasant pace to the mouth of the Burnett River. See website or call for tour times.

Bundaberg

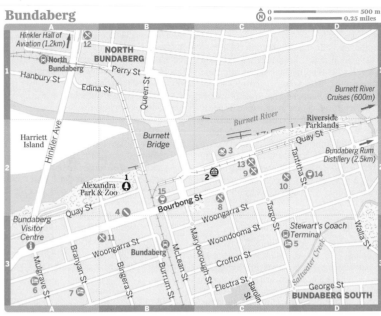

Bundaberg

🛏 Sleeping & Eating

Bigfoot Backpackers   HOSTEL $
(☎07-4152 3659; 66 Targo St; dm from $24; 🅿❄) Pretty grim, bare-bones dorm rooms at this central hostel, but it's an excellent place to arrange fruit-picking jobs and to meet other travellers in the spacious games-room area.

Bundaberg Spanish Motor Inn   MOTEL $
(☎07-4152 5444; www.bundabergspanishmotorinn. com; 134 Woongarra St; s/d $115/120; ❄🛜🏊) A Spanish hacienda-style motel doesn't feel out of place in the Bundaberg climate, and this old-fashioned motel in a quiet street off the main drag is *muy bueno* (very good). Spotless units are self-contained and all rooms overlook the central pool. Breakfast is *deliciosa*.

★**Inglebrae**   B&B $$
(☎07-4154 4003; www.inglebrae.com; 17 Branyan St; r incl breakfast $130-150; ❄) For old-world English charm in a glorious Queenslander, this delightful B&B is just the ticket. Polished timber and stained glass seep from the entrance into the rooms, which come with high beds and small antiques.

★**Alowishus Delicious**   CAFE $
(☎07-4154 2233; 176 Bourbong St; coffees from $3, mains $10-22; ⊙7am-5pm Mon-Wed, 7am-9pm Thu, 7am-11pm Fri, 8am-11pm Sat, 8am-5pm Sun) Finally! A cafe open at night! This creative catering company is a great place to type that blog, meet a friend for a late-night pastry, or bang in a coffee between shifts picking mangoes.

Spicy Tonight FUSION $
(☑07-4154 3320; 1 Targo St; dishes $12-20; ⊙11am-2.30pm & 5-9pm Mon-Sat, 5-9pm Sun) What do you get when you cross Thai and Indian? Spices you never knew could coexist. Bundaberg's saucy little secret serves hot curries, vindaloo, tandoori and a host of vegetarian dishes.

Indulge CAFE $
(80 Bourbong St; dishes $9-18; ⊙8.30am-4.30pm Mon-Fri, 7.30am-12.30pm Sat) Much of the local Bundaberg sugar must go into the incredible cakes and pastries at this cafe, which promotes local produce.

★**Oodies Cafe** CAFE $$
(☑07-4153 5340; www.oodies.com.au; 103 Gavin St; ⊙6.30am-4pm) A double garage on the edge of Bundaberg's CBD is the unlikely venue for the town's coolest cafe. Oodies is an oddity where you can lounge on leather armchairs with the hipcats sipping chai lattes, or dine from the healthy, well-priced breakfast and lunch menus. Sandwiches, burgers, cakes and more are served.

Cool Banana's Cafe CAFE $$
(☑07-4198 1182; 91 Bourbong St; meals from $10; ⊙8am-8.30pm) Cheap and cheerful cafe run by the same crowd as **Les Chefs** (☑07-4153 1770; 238 Bourbong St; mains $27; ⊙lunch Tue-Fri, dinner Mon-Sat). Daily specials include fish and chips, kebabs and lamb roasts. Coffee and breakfast is decent too.

🍺 Drinking & Nightlife

Spotted Dog Tavern BAR
(☑07-4198 1044; 217 Bourbong St) Bundaberg's most popular bar-restaurant is busy all day. Food is nothing special – standard pub fare without much fuss – but the music, live sports, and air of permanent celebration on the spacious patio make it a local favourite.

Bargara Brewing Company CRAFT BEER
(☑07-4152 1675; 10 Tantitha St; ⊙11am-10pm Wed-Sat, 5-10pm Sun) Bundaberg has a buzzing new rival to the rum monopoly in the form of a craft brewery that serves fine platters of nibbles to accompany pints of Drunk Fish, Great Barrier Beer and Hip Hop.

ℹ Information

Bundaberg Visitor Centre (☑07-4153 8888, 1300 722 099; www.bundabergregion.org; 271 Bourbong St; ⊙9am-5pm) This reliable information centre serves the region admirably. Definitely stop by if you are driving through the area.

ℹ Getting There & Away

AIR
Bundaberg is served daily by **Virgin** (☑13 67 89; www.virginaustralia.com.au) and **Qantas** (☑13 13 13; www.qantas.com.au).

BUS
The **coach terminal** (☑07-4153 2646; 66 Targo St) is on Targo St. Both **Greyhound** (☑1300 473 946; www.greyhound.com.au) and **Premier Motor Service** (☑13 34 10; www.premierms.com.au) have daily services connecting Bundaberg with Brisbane ($94, seven hours), Hervey Bay ($29, two hours) and Rockhampton ($54, five hours).

Duffy's Coaches (☑1300 383 397) has numerous services every weekday to Bargara ($5, 35 minutes), leaving from the back of Target on Woongarra St.

TRAIN
The **Queensland Rail** (p157) Tilt Train stops at Bundaberg train station en route to Brisbane ($49, 4½ hours, Sunday to Friday). Queensland Rail's Spirit of Queensland ($89, seven hours, three weekly) also travels from Brisbane to Bundaberg on its route to Cairns and Rockhampton.

Bargara
POP 6893

16km east of Bundaberg, Bargara is a popular beachside holiday destination for Queenslanders due to its surf beach, long esplanade and quiet, family-friendly atmosphere.

Kacy's Bargara Beach Motel (☑07-4130 1100; www.bargaramotel.com.au; 63 Esplanade; d from $139, 2-bedroom apt from $199; ❋ 🐾 🥘) has a great location opposite the esplanade, and a range of accommodation from pleasant motel rooms to self-contained apartments.

At **Windmill at Bargara** (☑07-4130 5906; 12 See St; mains from $13; ⊙6.30am-5pm; 🐾 🍴) there's lots of space for the kids to play on the grass and sip chai lattes while smiling parents nibble on fresh gelato and bask in the afternoon glow of exhaustion.

Fraser Island

The local Butchulla people call it K'Gari – paradise – and for good reason. Sculpted from wind, sand and surf, the striking blue freshwater lakes, crystalline creeks, giant dunes and lush rainforests of this gigantic sandbar form an enigmatic island paradise unlike anywhere else. Fraser Island is the largest sand island in the world (measuring

Fraser Island

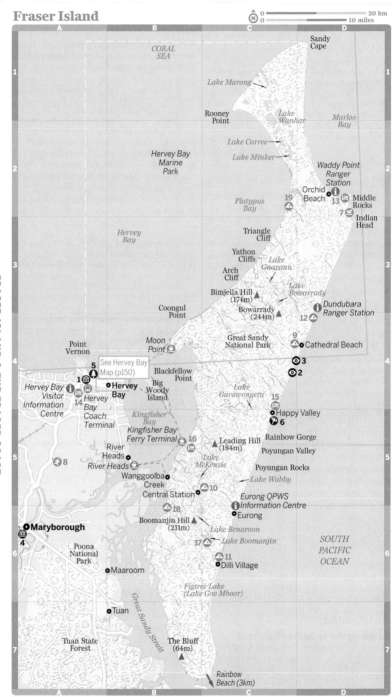

0   20 km
0   10 miles

CORAL SEA

Sandy Cape

Lake Marong

Rooney Point

Lake Wanhar

Marloo Bay

Hervey Bay Marine Park

Lake Carree

Lake Minker

Waddy Point Ranger Station

Platypus Bay

19

Orchid Beach

13

Middle Rocks

7

Indian Head

Hervey Bay

Triangle Cliff

Yathon Cliffs

Arch Cliff

Lake Gnarann

Bimjella Hill (174m)

Lake Bowarrady

Coongul Point

Bowarrady (244m)

12

Dundubara Ranger Station

Moon Point

Great Sandy National Park

9

Cathedral Beach

Point Vernon

5

See Hervey Bay Map (p150)

Blackfellow Point

3

1

Hervey Bay Visitor Information Centre

14

Hervey Bay

Big Woody Island

2

Lake Garawongera

Hervey Bay Coach Terminal

Kingfisher Bay

15

Happy Valley

Kingfisher Bay Ferry Terminal

16

Leading Hill (184m)

Rainbow Gorge

6

Poyungan Valley

River Heads

Lake McKenzie

Poyungan Rocks

River Heads

Lake Wabby

8

Wanggoolba Creek

Lake Boomanjin

Central Station

10

Eurong QPWS Information Centre

18

Eurong

Maryborough

Boomanjin Hill (211m)

Lake Benaroon

4

17

Lake Boomanjin

SOUTH PACIFIC OCEAN

Poona National Park

11

Dilli Village

Maaroom

Figtree Lake (Lake Goo Mboor)

Tuan

Great Sandy Strait

The Bluff (64m)

Tuan State Forest

Rainbow Beach (3km)

Fraser Island

120km by 15km), and is the only known place where rainforest grows on sand.

Inland, the vegetation varies from dense tropical rainforest and wild heath to wetlands and wallum scrub, with sandblows, mineral streams and freshwater lakes opening onto long sandy beaches. The island, most of which is protected as part of the Great Sandy National Park, is home to a profusion of bird life and wildlife, including the famous dingo, while offshore waters teem with dugong, dolphins, manta rays, sharks and migrating humpback whales.

⊙ Sights & Activities

Starting at the island's southern tip, where the ferry leaves for Inskip Point on the mainland, a high-tide access track cuts inland, avoiding dangerous Hook Point, and leads to the entrance of the Eastern Beach's main thoroughfare. The first settlement is Dilli Village, the former sand-mining centre; Eurong, with shops, fuel and places to eat, is another 9km north. From here, an inland track crosses to Central Station and Wanggoolba Creek (for the ferry to River Heads).

Right in the middle of the island is the ranger centre at Central Station, the starting point for numerous walking trails. From here you can walk or drive to the beautiful McKenzie, Jennings, Birrabeen and Boomanjin Lakes. Lake McKenzie is spectacularly clear and ringed by white-sand beaches, making it a great place to swim; Lake Birrabeen sees fewer tour and backpacker groups.

About 4km north of Eurong along the beach, a signposted walking trail leads across sandblows to the beautiful Lake Wabby, the most accessible of Fraser's lakes. An easier route is from the Lake Wabby Lookout, off Cornwell's Break Rd from the inland side. Lake Wabby is surrounded on three sides by eucalyptus forest, while the fourth side is a massive sandblow that encroaches on the lake at a rate of about 3m a year. The lake is deceptively shallow and diving is very dangerous.

As you drive up the beach, during high tide you may have to detour inland to avoid Poyungan and Yidney Rocks, before reaching Happy Valley, which has places to stay, a shop and a bistro. About 10km further north is Eli Creek, a fast-moving, crystal-clear waterway that will carry you effortlessly downstream. About 2km from Eli Creek is the rotting hulk of the Maheno, a former passenger liner which was blown ashore by a cyclone in 1935 as it was being towed to a Japanese scrap yard.

Roughly 5km north of the Maheno you'll find the Pinnacles, an eroded section of coloured sand cliffs, and about 10km beyond, Dundubara, with a ranger station and an excellent camping ground. Then there's a 20km stretch of beach before you come to the rock outcrop of Indian Head. Sharks, manta rays, dolphins and (during the migration season) whales can often be seen from the top of this headland.

Between Indian Head and Waddy Point, the trail branches inland, passing Champagne Pools, which offers the only safe saltwater swimming on the island. There are good camping areas at Waddy Point and Orchid Beach, the last settlement on the island. Many tracks north of here are closed for environmental protection.

FRASER ISLAND & THE FRASER COAST FRASER ISLAND

SAND SAFARIS

The only way to explore Fraser Island (besides walking) is with a 4WD. For most travellers, there are three transport options: tag-along tours, organised tours or 4WD hire; the fourth option is to stay at one of the island's accommodations and take day tours from there. This is a fragile environment; bear in mind that the greater the number of individual vehicles driving on the island, the greater the environmental damage. With an average of 1000 people per day visiting the island, Fraser can sometimes feel like a giant sandpit with its own peak hour and congested beach highway.

Tag-Along Tours

Popular with backpackers, tag-along tours see groups of travellers pile into a 4WD convoy and follow a lead vehicle with an experienced guide and driver. Travellers take turns driving the other vehicles, which can be great fun, but has also led to accidents. Rates hover around $400 to $430; be sure to check if your tour includes food, fuel, alcohol etc. Accommodation is often in tents.

Advantages You can make new friends fast; driving the beaches is exhilarating.

Disadvantages If food isn't included you'll have to cook; groups can be even bigger than on bus tours.

Operators include the following:

Dropbear Adventures (☎1800 061 156; www.dropbearadventures.com.au) Lots of departures from Hervey Bay, Rainbow Beach and Noosa to Fraser Island; easy to get a spot.

Fraser's on Rainbow (p154) Departs from Rainbow Beach.

Pippies Beach House (p155) Departs Rainbow Beach; well-organised, small convoys with high safety standards.

Organised Tours

Most organised tours cover Fraser's hot spots: rainforests, Eli Creek, Lakes McKenzie and Wabby, the coloured Pinnacles and the *Maheno* shipwreck.

Advantages Expert commentary; decent food and comfortable accommodation; often the most economical choice.

Disadvantages Day-tour buses often arrive at the same place at the same time; less social.

Operators include the following:

Cool Dingo Tours (☎07-4120 3333; www.cooldingotour.com; 2-/3-day tours from $360/415) Overnight at lodges with the option to stay extra nights on the island. The party option.

Fraser Explorer Tours (p151) Very experienced drivers; lots of departures.

Fraser Experience (p151) Small group tours offer greater freedom with the itinerary.

Remote Fraser (☎07-4124 3222; www.tasmanventure.com.au; tours $150) Day tours to the less-visited west coast.

4WD Hire

You can hire a 4WD from Hervey Bay, Rainbow Beach or on Fraser Island itself. All companies require a hefty bond, usually in the form of a credit-card imprint, which you will lose if you drive in salt water – don't even think about running the waves!

When planning your trip, reckon on covering 20km an hour on the inland tracks and 40km an hour on the eastern beach. Most companies will help arrange ferries, permits and camping gear. Rates for multiday rentals start at around $185 a day.

Advantages Complete freedom to roam the island and escape the crowds.

Disadvantages You may encounter beach and track conditions that even experienced drivers find challenging; expensive.

There are rental companies in Hervey Bay (p154) and Rainbow Beach (p156). On the island, **Aussie Trax** (☎07-4124 4433; www.fraserisland4wd.com.au) hires out 4WDs from $283 per person, per day.

Air Fraser Island (p166) has a terrific-value 'Day Away' tour ($150) for those looking to land on the island and explore a little on foot. Depart from Hervey Bay or Sunshine Coast.

Sleeping

Camping permits are required in order to camp at NPSR camping grounds and any public areas (ie along the beach). The most developed **NPSR camping grounds** (☎13 74 68; www.npsr.qld.gov.au; per person/family $6.15/24.60), with coin-operated hot showers, toilets and BBQs, are at **Waddy Point** (☎13 74 68; www.nprsr.qld.gov.au; per person/family $6.15/24.60), **Dundubara** (www.nprsr.qld.gov.au; per person/family $6.15/24.60) and **Central Station** (☎13 74 68; www.nprsr.qld.gov.au; per person/family $6.15/24.60). Campers with vehicles can also use the smaller camping grounds with fewer facilities at **Lake Boomanjin** (☎13 74 68; www.nprsr.qld.gov.au; per person/family $6.15/24.60), and at **Ungowa** (☎13 74 68; www.nprsr.qld.gov.au; per person/family $6.15/24.60) and **Wathumba** (☎13 74 68; www.nprsr.qld.gov.au; per person/family $6.15/24.60) on the western coast. Walkers' camps are set away from the main camping grounds, along the Fraser Island Great Walk trail. The trail map lists the camp sites and their facilities. Camping is permitted on designated stretches of the eastern beach, but there are no facilities. Fires are prohibited except in communal fire rings at Waddy Point and Dundubara – bring your own firewood in the form of untreated, milled timber.

Supplies on the island are limited and costly. Stock up well before arriving, and be prepared for mosquitoes and March flies.

Dilli Village Fraser Island CAMPGROUND $
(☎07-4127 9130; www.usc.edu.au; sites per person $10, dm/cabins $50/120) Managed by the University of the Sunshine Coast, which uses this precinct as a base for research purposes, Dilli Village offers good sites on a softly sloping camping ground. Great value for the space.

Cathedrals on Fraser CARAVAN PARK $
(☎07-4127 9177; www.cathedralsonfraser.com.au; Cathedral Beach; powered/unpowered sites $39/29, 2-bed cabins with/without bathroom $200/180; @) New owners have kept up the standard and lowered the prices at this spacious dingo-fenced park with abundant, flat, grassy sites. It's a hit with families.

★ **Kingfisher Bay Resort** RESORT $$
(☎1800 072 555, 07-4194 9300; www.kingfisherbay.com; Kingfisher Bay; d from $178, 2-bedroom villas $329; ❄@≋) This elegant eco-resort has hotel rooms with private balconies, and sophisticated two- and three-bedroom timber villas that are elevated to limit their environmental impact. There's a three-night minimum stay in high season. The Seabelle Restaurant is terrific (mains from $18), while the three bars are great fun in summer at sunset, especially the Dingo Bar.

Fraser Island Retreat CABIN $$
(☎07-4127 9144; www.fraserisretreat.com.au; Happy Valley; d/apt from $140/200; @🛜≋) Located in the relatively remote Happy Valley, halfway along the east coast of the island, this retreat's nine timber cabins (each sleeping up to four people) are great for a comfortable nature experience. The cabins are airy, nestled in native foliage and close to the beach. On-site there's a camp kitchen, a licensed restaurant and a shop that sells fuel.

★ **Eliza Fraser Lodge** LODGE $$$
(☎0418 981 610; www.elizafraserlodge.com.au; per person $375) Located at a stunning house up at Orchid Beach in the northeast of the island, Eliza Fraser is the finest lodging available by far. Serviced directly by Air Fraser (regular ferry transfers also available), the two-level house is exquisite for families or small groups. The hosts are expert guides and will organise fishing trips, nature hikes and 4WD adventures, or let you enjoy the run of the house and spectacular surrounds.

DON'T MISS

FRASER ISLAND GREAT WALK

The Fraser Island Great Walk is a stunning way to experience this enigmatic island. The trail undulates through the island's interior for 90km from Dilli Village to Happy Valley. Broken up into seven sections of around 6km to 16km each, plus some side trails, it follows the pathways of Fraser Island's original inhabitants, the Butchulla people. En route, the walk passes underneath rainforest canopies, circles around some of the island's vivid lakes, and courses through shifting dunes.

It's imperative that you visit www.npsr.qld.gov.au for maps, detailed information and updates on the track, which can close when conditions are bad.

ℹ Information

You must purchase permits from **NPSR** (☑13 74 68; www.npsr.qld.gov.au) for vehicles (less than a month $48.25) and to camp in the NPSR camping grounds ($6.15/24.60 per person/ family) before you arrive. Permits aren't required for private camping grounds or resorts. Buy permits online or check with visitor centres for up-to-date lists of where to buy them.

Eurong QPWS Information Centre (☑07-4127 9128) is the main ranger station. Others can be found at **Dundubara** (☑07-4127 9138) and **Waddy Point** (☑07-4127 9190). Offices are often unattended as the rangers are out on patrol.

ℹ Getting There & Away

Before crossing via ferry from either Rainbow Beach or Hervey Bay, ensure that your vehicle has suitably high clearance (if you're one of the few not visiting on a tour, that is) and, if camping, that you have adequate food, water and fuel.

AIR

Air Fraser Island (☑1300 172 706, 07-4125 3600; www.airfraserisland.com.au) charges from $150 for a return flight (30-minute round trip) to the island's eastern beach, departing Hervey Bay airport.

BOAT

Vehicle ferries connect Fraser Island with River Heads, about 10km south of Hervey Bay, or further south at Inskip Point, near Rainbow Beach. Ferries from Hervey Bay dock at Moon Point.

Fraser Venture Barge (☑1800 227 437, 07-4194 9300; www.fraserislandferry.com. au) Makes the crossing (pedestrian adult/child return $58/30, vehicle and four passengers return $175, 30 minutes) from River Heads to Wanggoolba Creek on the western coast of Fraser Island. It departs daily from River Heads at 8.30am, 10.15am and 4pm, and returns from the island at 9am, 3pm and 5pm.

Kingfisher Bay Ferry (☑1800 227 437, 07-4194 9300; www.fraserislandferry.com) Operates a daily vehicle and passenger ferry (pedestrian adult/child return $58/30, vehicle and four passengers return $175, 50 minutes) from River Heads to Kingfisher Bay, departing at 6.45am, 9am, 12.30pm, 3.30pm, 6.45pm and 9.30pm (Friday and Saturday only) and returning at 7.50am, 10.30am, 2pm, 5pm, 8.30pm and 11pm (Friday and Saturday only).

Manta Ray (☑07-5486 3935; www.mantaray-fraserislandbarge.com.au) Coming from Rainbow Beach, Manta Ray has two ferries making the 15-minute crossing from Inskip Point to Hook Point on Fraser Island, continuously from about 6am to 5.30pm daily (vehicle return $120).

ℹ Getting Around

A 4WD is necessary if you're driving on Fraser Island; you'll need a permit. Expensive fuel is available from stores at Cathedral Beach, Eurong, Kingfisher Bay, Happy Valley and Orchid Beach. If your vehicle breaks down, call the **tow-truck service** (☑0428 353 164, 07-4127 9449) in Eurong.

The 4WD **Fraser Island Taxi Service** (☑07-4127 9188; www.fraserservice.com.au) operates all over the island. Bookings are essential, as there's only one cab for the whole island!

If you want to hire a 4WD while on the island, Aussie Trax (p164) has a medium-sized fleet, from Suzuki Sierras to LandCruisers, available at the Kingfisher Bay Resort (p165).

ℹ DEALING WITH DINGOES

Despite its many natural attractions and opportunities for adventure, there's nothing on Fraser Island that gives a thrill comparable to your first glimpse of a dingo. Believed to be among the most genetically pure in the world, the dingoes of Fraser are sleek, spry and utterly beautiful. They're also wild beasts that can become aggressive at the drop of a hat (or a strong-smelling food sack). While attacks are rare, there are precautions that must be taken by every visitor to the island.

➡ However skinny they appear, or whatever woebegone look they give you, never feed dingoes. Dingoes that are human-fed quickly lose their shyness and can become combative and competitive. Feeding dingoes is illegal and carries heavy fines.

➡ Don't leave any food scraps lying around, and don't take food to the lakes: eating on the shore puts your food at 'dingo level', an easy target for scrounging scavengers.

➡ Stay in groups, and keep any children within arm's reach at all times.

➡ Teasing dingoes is not only cruel, but dangerous. Leave them alone, and they'll do same.

➡ Dingoes are best observed at a distance. Pack a zoom lens and practise some silence, and you'll come away with some brilliant photographs...and all your limbs intact.

Capricorn Coast & the Southern Reef Islands

Best Places to Eat

→ Getaway Garden Café (p170)

→ Ginger Mule (p175)

→ Lightbox (p172)

→ Megalomania (p177)

→ Sol Foods (p170)

Best Places to Sleep

→ Svendsen's Beach (p178)

→ Cool Bananas (p169)

→ Lady Elliot Island Eco Resort (p173)

→ Takarakka Bush Resort (p180)

Why Go?

The stretch of coastline that straddles the tropic of Capricorn is one of the quietest and most lovely lengths of the east coast. While local families flock to the main beaches during school holidays, the scene is uncrowded for most of the year, and even in high season you needn't travel far to find a deserted beach.

Agnes Water and Town of 1770 are twin towns with a glowing reputation, and many travelers head from here for some of the world's best snorkelling and diving on the Southern Reef Islands. Opportunities for wildlife spotting are plentiful.

Great Keppel National Park is another tourism commercial in the making. The stunning powdery white sand and turquoise waters of the Capricorn Coast fit the holiday-brochure image perfectly. Unspoiled and windswept national parks such as Deepwater and Byfield can be found along the entire coastline, and are almost never busy.

Inland, you'll find bustling Rockhampton – Capricornia's economic hub and the capital of cattle country, with the steakhouses, rodeos and gigantic hats to prove it.

When to Go
Rockhampton

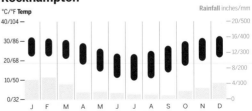

Feb The Agnes Blues & Roots Festival rocks the Discovery Coast.

May–Sep Warm winter temperatures are ideal for swimming and sunning.

Dec Nature puts on a stunning light show during the summer solstice at Capricorn Caves.

Capricorn Coast & the Southern Reef Islands Highlights

1 **Heron Island** (p173) and **Lady Elliot Island** (p173) Diving the spectacular underwater coral gardens.

2 **Great Keppel Island** (p178) Claiming a tropical beach for the day.

3 **Agnes Water** (p169) Surfing and chilling at

Queensland's most northerly surf beach.

4 **Carnarvon Gorge** (p179) Hiking to find aboriginal rock art.

5 **Rockhampton** (p174) Tucking into a huge steak in Australia's beef capital.

6 **Capricorn Caves** (p175) Crawling through black holes and tight tunnels.

7 **Gem Fields** (p180) Fossicking for a fortune-changing sapphire.

Agnes Water & Town of 1770

POP 1650

Not so long ago the twin coastal towns of Agnes Water and Town of 1770 were tipped by property speculators as Australia's next Noosa or Gold Coast. Thankfully for visitors to this lovely outpost 70km south of Gladstone, hemmed in by national parks, hidden red rock coves and the Pacific Ocean, little has changed and the tourism boom was more like a fizz.

Agnes Water is the east coast's most northerly surf beach, a long, glorious point break rolling into an idyllic shoreline by a friendly strip of shops. A 6km jaunt down the road is the site of Captain Cook's first landing in Queensland in, you guessed it, 1770. The short bluff walks are outstanding, and the camping site is one of the most dreamy in the state, a launching point for kayaking and paddleboarding and fishing excursions around the inlets of the 'Discovery Coast'.

⊙ Sights & Activities

Miriam Vale Historical Society Museum   MUSEUM

(☑ 07-4974 9511; www.agneswatermuseum.com; Springs Rd, near cnr Captain Cook Dr, Agnes Water; adult/child $3/free; ⊙ 1-4pm Mon & Wed-Sat, 10am-4pm Sun) The museum displays extracts from Cook's journal and the original telescope from the first lighthouse built on the Queensland coast.

★ Scooter Roo Tours   ADVENTURE SPORTS

(☑ 07-4974 7697; www.scooterrootours.com; 2694 Round Hill Rd, Agnes Water; 3hr rides $85) You don't need to be a petrolhead to absolutely love this hilarious and informative 50km-tour of the Agnes Water area. Better yet, you only need a car licence to get low and dirty on a real 'chopper' bike. Wear long pants and closed-in shoes; they'll supply the tough-guy leather jackets (with flames, of course).

1770 SUP   WATER SPORTS

(☑ 0421 026 255; www.1770sup.com.au; 1½/2hr tours $45/50) Explore the calm waters and sandy banks of 1770 with a top-notch stand-up paddleboarding (SUP) instructor. Tours include an intro lesson, or rent your own board for $25/30 for one/two hours. The roving SUP trailer can often be found on the 1770 waterfront across from Tree Bar.

1770 Liquid Adventures   KAYAKING

(☑ 0428 956 630; www.1770liquidadventures.com. au) Paddle off on a spectacular twilight kayak tour. For $55 you ride the waves off 1770, before retiring to the beach for drinks and snacks as the sun sets – keep an eye out for dolphins. You can also rent kayaks (from $20/30 per one/two hours). Family tours ($30 per person) focus on bird and marine life and will appeal to any child who is comfortable paddling alone.

1770 Larc Tours   TOURS

(☑ 07-4974 9422; www.1770larctours.com.au; day trips adult/child $155/95) 🕭 The ex-military Lighter Amphibious Resupply Cargo (LARC) vehicle makes a comfortable ride for exploring the natural joys of Bustard Head and Eurimbula National Park. Guides know their stuff and will entertain all ages. Aside from the signature seven-hour day trip (lunch included), they also run hour-long afternoon tours (adult/child $38/17) and sandboarding safaris ($120).

Hooked on 1770   BOATING

(☑ 07-4974 9794; www.1770tours.com; half-/full-day tours $175/250) Hooked on 1770 has full- and half-day fishing tours which come highly recommended by long-time locals and Australian repeat visitors alike.

★☆ Festivals & Events

Agnes Blues & Roots Festival   MUSIC

(www.agnesbluesandroots.com.au; SES Grounds, Agnes Water; ⊙ Feb) Top names and up-and-coming Aussie acts crank it up on the last weekend of February.

🛏 Sleeping

★ Cool Bananas   HOSTEL $

(☑ 07-4974 7660, 1800 227 660; www.coolbananas.net.au; 2 Springs Rd, Agnes Water; dm $29; @ 🕭) The young and free go bananas for this funky, open-minded backpacker hangout, with a questionable colour scheme but an irresistible vibe cultivated by the friendly owners. Roomy six- and eight-bed dorms are functional, and management does not allow rooms to be locked in order to encourage mingling. Funnily enough, it works (smiles all round when we visited!). It's only a five-minute walk to the beach and shops.

Backpackers @ 1770   HOSTEL $

(☑ 0408 533 851; www.backpackers1770.com. au; 22 Grahame Colyer Dve, Agnes Water; dm/d

$26/60) The most established hostel in 1770 is a beauty. The upsides are obvious: easy interactions between staff and guests, spotless dorms, three smart doubles at a good price point and a lush communal garden where meals are taken and stories are shared. For many young travellers, this hostel is an east coast must.

1770 Camping Ground
CARAVAN PARK $

(☑07-4974 9286; www.1770campingground.com. au; Captain Cook Dr, Town of 1770; powered/unpowered sites from $39/35, beachfront sites $44) This camping ground, 1770's favourite, must challenge for best location on the east coast. Fall into the shallow water from your tent strung among plenty of shady trees.

Workmans Beach
Camping Area
CAMPGROUND $

(Workmans Beach, Springs Rd, Agnes Water; sites per person $9) Workmans Beach is a council-run camping ground with spacious sites in gorgeous beachside surrounds. Facilities include cold-water showers, drop toilets and gas BBQs. If you're really smitten, you can stay up to 44 days. You can't book sites; just turn up, and good-humoured council staff will knock on your van/tent at an ungodly hour of the morning to sort out payment.

1770 Southern
Cross Backpackers
HOSTEL $

(☑07-4974 7225; www.1770southerncross.com; 2694 Round Hill Rd, Agnes Water; dm/d incl breakfast $25/85; @ ☎ ⬛) The large eucalypt-forest retreat of Southern Cross is 2.5km out of town and will suit the more mellow backpacker (or one in search of time out!). There's plenty of space to lie about the pool, play games, cook a BBQ or sling a hammock. A courtesy bus takes revellers and beach-goers into the 'action' of Agnes, but most guests just roam between their bare four-bed dorms, pleasant double rooms and the Buddha Bar come nightfall.

The Lovely Cottages
GUESTHOUSE $$

(☑07-4974 9554; www.thelovelycottages.com. au; 61 Bicentennial Dr, Agnes Water; cottages $155, 2 nights $300; P ✳ ☎ ⬛) New owners and a name change have boosted the creative energy at this eco-retreat and outdoor gallery, which is the epitome of Queensland casual bush chic. Each colourful cottage sleeps up to five people. There is an excellent lagoon-style pool, which makes for thrilling swimming in the bush scrub.

Agnes Water Beach Club
APARTMENT $$

(☑07-4974 7355; www.agneswaterbeachclub.com. au; 3 Agnes St, Agnes Water; 1-/2-bedroom apt from $180/280; ✳ @ ☎ ⬛) The Beach Club has the most convenient location for access to shops in Agnes and the patrolled beach. The apartments themselves are bright and comfortable, facing onto a good-sized pool. Very much a family atmosphere permeating the communal areas.

★ 1770 Getaway
RESORT $$$

(☑07-4974 9323; www.1770getaway.com.au; 303 Bicentennial Dve, Agnes Water; d from $170; P ☎ ☎ ⬛) The much-loved Getaway Garden Cafe (p170) has expanded its repertoire with a delightful series of villas running across 1.5 hectares acres of bush onto an empty stretch of beach. Each villa has an airy, open feel and luxury bathrooms. Breakfast by the pond can be included and there's a hip little boutique on-site.

✕ Eating

Sol Foods
VEGAN $

(☑07-4974 9039; 1 Round Hill Rd, Agnes Water; salads from $10, cakes from $6; ⊙8am-4.30pm) This wholefoods grocer doubles as a cafe and an enlightened source of local knowledge. The vegan cakes are unbeatable and the salads are hearty and good value.

Agnes Water Bakery
BAKERY $

(☑07-4974 9500; Round Hill Rd, Agnes Water; pies $5.50; ⊙6am-4pm Mon-Sat, to 2pm Sun) Don't dawdle if you want to get your mouth around one of this popular bakery's killer pies. Expect gourmet stuffings, including a couple of vegetarian selections. On the sweet side, the chocolate éclairs, jam scrolls and apple turnovers are usually gone by noon. Oh, and there's bread too.

★ Getaway
Garden Café
MODERN AUSTRALIAN $$

(☑07-4974 9323; 303 Bicentennial Dr, Agnes Water; breakfast $7-19, lunch $10-22, dinner $20-25; ⊙8am-4pm Sun-Thu, & 5.30pm-late Wed & Sun) The region's most revered eatery continues to impress due to its culinary simplicity using only local ingredients, impeccable family-oriented service and natural, waterside setting. Breakfasts are healthy and accompanied by fine coffee and juices. Lunch features pizza, fish and burgers. The lamb spit roasts on Wednesday and Sunday nights are very popular with locals (book ahead). Stop in for cake and coffee outside of main meal times.

Tree Bar MODERN AUSTRALIAN **$$**
(☑ 07-4974 7446; 576 Captain Cook Dr, Town of 1770; mains $16-34; ⊙ breakfast, lunch & dinner) This is the best outlook for a sundowner and a steak sandwich in 1770. This little salt-encrusted waterfront diner and bar is no award-winner, but it marvellously catches sea breezes from the beach through the trees. Prices are a little steep for the quality, but you couldn't paint a better view.

Agnes Water Tavern PUB FOOD **$$**
(☑ 07-4974 9469; 1 Tavern Rd, Agnes Water; mains $15-30; ⊙ from 11.30am) A broad snapshot of Australian life is found in the huge tavern just outside town, where you can drink, gamble, play games, watch sport, party, eat, meet and enjoy the sunshine in the ample outdoor seating. The backpacker set keep it lively some nights. Lunch and dinner specials daily.

ℹ Information

Agnes Water Visitors Centre (☑ 07-4902 1533; 71 Springs Rd, Town of 1770; ⊙ 9am-5pm Mon-Fri, to 4pm Sat & Sun) Staffed by above-and-beyond volunteers who even leave out information and brochures when it's closed, just in case a lost soul blows into town.

Discover 1770 (☑ 07-4974 7557; www. discover1770.com.au; next to Shell service station) With so many different operators plying the Discovery Coast – and often changing hands or merging businesses – the friendly folk at Discover 1770 can help to guide your decision making. At the time of research, it was the only outlet for arranging boats to Lady Musgrave Island.

ℹ Getting There & Away

A handful of **Greyhound** (☑ 1300 473 946; www. greyhound.com.au) buses detour off the Bruce Hwy to Agnes Water; daily services include Bundaberg ($28, 1½ hours) and Cairns ($210, 21 hours). **Premier Motor Service** (☑ 13 34 10; www.premierms.com.au) also goes in and out of town.

Eurimbula & Deepwater National Parks

Eight kilometres south of Agnes Water is **Deepwater National Park** (www.nprsr.qld. gov.au/parks/deepwater), an unspoiled coastal landscape with long sandy beaches, walking trails, freshwater creeks, good fishing spots and two camping grounds accessible only by 4WD. It's also a major breeding ground for loggerhead turtles, which dig nests and lay eggs on the beaches between November and February; hatchlings emerge at night between January and April.

The 78-sq-km Eurimbula National Park, on the northern side of Round Hill Creek, has a landscape of dunes, mangroves and eucalypt forest. Both offer delightful beaches, hikes and splendid, relatively accessible isolation in the Australian bush.

Camping permits are available from the **NPRSR** (☑ 13 74 68; www.npsr.qld.gov.au; permit per person/family $6.15/24.60). Wreck Rock Campground has a sizeable picnic area, rain and bore water and composting toilets.

Gladstone

POP 37,941

Gladstone is a middle-sized town known nationwide, for better or worse, as a major port for the mining industry, and an industrial town with a power station and an incongruous outlook on the Great Barrier Reef. You might want to head straight for the marina (Bryan Jordan Dr), the main departure point for boats to the southern coral cay islands of Heron, Masthead and Wilson on the Great Barrier Reef. If there's anything happening in town, it's on at the port end of Gondoon St.

Lake Awoonga Boat Hire (☑ 07-4975 0930; tinnies half-day $80, kayaks per hour $15) is an unofficial tourist guide and friendly boat hire place, or you can charter the **MV Mikat** (☑ 0427 125 727; www.mikat.com.au).

CURTIS ISLAND

Curtis Island, just across the water from Gladstone, can't be confused with a resort island. Apart from swimming, fishing and lolling about on the dunes, its main drawcard is the annual appearance of rare flatback turtles on its eastern shores between October and January. Camping permits can be booked via **NPRSR** (☑ 13 74 68; www.nprsr.qld.gov.au; permit per person/family $5.45/21.80) or you can stay with the friendly folks at **Capricorn Lodge** (☑ 07-4972 0222; capricornlodge@ bigpond.com; lodgings from around $80). They have a corner store and a liquor licence. Curtis Ferry Services (p172) connects the island with Gladstone every day bar Tuesday and Thursday.

🛏 Sleeping

Gladstone Backpackers   HOSTEL **$**
(☑ 07-4972 5744; www.gladstonebackpackers.
com.au; 12 Rollo St; dm/tw $28/66; @ 🛜 ❄) Set
inside a big blue Queenslander down by the
marina, Gladstone Backpackers has under-
gone a makeover. There's a large communal
kitchen and shared bathrooms, while dorm
rooms and twins feel brand new. Grey
nomads, itinerant miners and European
wanderers like to sit on the airy verandah
and find common ground. There's free use
of bicycles and free pick-ups from the all
transport depots.

🍴 Eating & Drinking

Gladstone Yacht Club   PUB FOOD **$$**
(☑ 07-4972 2294; www.gyc.com.au; 1 Goondoon
St; mains from $22; ☺ noon-2pm & 6-8.30pm
Mon-Thu, 11.30am-2.30pm & 5.30-9pm Fri & Sat,
11.30am-2pm & 6-8.30pm Sun) Clubs are a
mainstay of regional Australia. Hugely social
places where the beer flows, the yarns are
spun and the meals are generally massive
and good value. The Gladstone Yacht Club
is a welcoming place where burgers and sea-
food are the best bets. You can also eat on
the deck overlooking the water.

Tables on Flinders   SEAFOOD **$$$**
(☑ 07-4972 8322; 2 Oaka La; mains from $38;
☺ lunch Tue-Fri, dinner Tue-Sat) If you feel like a
Gladstone splurge, this is the place to do it,
with exquisite local seafood including fresh
mudcrab, bugs and prawns dominating the
menu.

Lightbox   WINE BAR
(☑ 07-4972 2698; 56 Goondoon St; ☺ 7am-late)
Indicative of Gladstone's maturing social
scene, this slick wine bar in the newly developed entertainment precinct also has a long
cocktail list and serves delicious charcuterie
(cured meat dishes). Breakfast and coffee
are also recommended.

ℹ Information

Visitor Centre (☑ 07-4972 9000; Bryan Jordan
Dr; ☺ 8.30am-4.30pm Mon-Fri, 9.30am-
4.30pm Sat & Sun) Located at the marina, the
departure point for boats to Heron Island, and
for free tours of the alumina refineries which
help drive the region's economy.

ℹ Getting There & Away

AIR

Qantas (☑ 13 13 13; www.qantas.com.au) and
Virgin (☑ 13 67 89; www.virginaustralia.com)
operate flights to and from Gladstone Airport,
which is 7km from the city centre.

BOAT

Curtis Ferry Services (☑ 07-4972 6990; www.
curtisferryservices.com.au; return adult/child
$30/18, family from $84) has regular services
to Curtis Island on Monday, Wednesday, Friday,
Saturday and Sunday. The service leaves from
the Gladstone marina and stops at Farmers
Point on Facing Island en route. Transport
to other nearby islands can be arranged on
request.

You can also access the islands with various
charter operators.

If you've booked a stay on Heron Island, the
resort operates a launch (one-way adult/child
$50/25, two hours), which leaves the Gladstone
marina at 11am daily.

BUS

Greyhound Australia (☑ 1300 473 946; www.
greyhound.com.au) has several coach services
from Brisbane ($154, 10 hours), Bundaberg
($47, three hours) and Rockhampton ($24, 1½
hours). The terminal is at the BP service station

ART DETOUR

Cedar Galleries (☑ 07-4975 0444; www.cedargalleries.com.au; Bruce Hwy, Calliope; ☺ 9am-
4pm Thu-Sat, 8am-4pm Sun) is a tranquil artists' bush retreat where you can watch painters
and sculptors at work in the rustic slab-hut studios. To unleash your creative genius you
can take art & craft classes with visiting artists (call ahead to book) or just browse the
gardens and the gallery. There's also a cafe, a beautiful handcrafted wedding chapel, kids'
jumping castle, a winery cellar door and a herd of friendly alpacas. The complex runs a
weekly farmers market every Sunday (from 8am to noon); the friendly bazaar is the ideal
spot for stocking up on gourmet goodies, freshly baked bread, local wines and handmade
gifts. Having too much fun to move on? Cedar Galleries has limited **farmstay accommodation** (studio $100 first night, $60 subsequent nights) available.

This old-school Aussie artists' colony (25km south of Gladstone) is signposted off the
Bruce Hwy, 7km southeast of Calliope.

on the Dawson Hwy, about 200m southwest of the centre.

TRAIN
Queensland Rail (☑ 07-3235 1122, 1800 872 467; www.queenslandrail.com.au) has frequent north- and southbound services passing through Gladstone daily. The Tilt Train stops in Gladstone from Brisbane (from $84, five hours) and Rockhampton (from $26, one hour).

Southern Reef Islands

While much fuss is made about the Great Barrier Reef's northern splendour, Southern Reef Island is the place of 'castaway' dreams: tiny coral atolls fringed with sugary white sand and turquoise-blue seas, and hardly anyone within flipper-flapping reach. From beautiful Lady Elliot Island, 80km northeast of Bundaberg, secluded and uninhabited coral reefs and atolls dot the ocean for about 140km up to Tryon Island. Lady Musgrave is essentially a blue lagoon in the middle of the ocean, while Heron Island is a discerning natural escape for adventurous families and world-class scuba diving.

Several cays in this part of the reef are excellent for snorkelling, diving and just getting back to nature – though reaching them is generally more expensive than reaching islands nearer the coast. Some of the islands are important breeding grounds for turtles and seabirds, and visitors should be aware of precautions to ensure the wildlife's protection.

Lady Elliot Island

Set on the southern rim of the Great Barrier Reef, Lady Elliot is a 40-hectare vegetated coral cay populated with nesting sea turtles and an impressive number of seabirds. It's considered to have the best snorkelling in the southern Great Barrier Reef and the diving is good too: explore an oceanbed of shipwrecks, coral gardens, bommies (coral pinnacles or outcroppings) and blowholes, and abundant marine life, including barracuda, giant manta rays and harmless leopard sharks.

Lady Elliot Island Eco Resort (☑ 1800 072 200; www.ladyelliot.com.au; r $175-420, child $95) has been around for a few decades now, but it has fortunately lost little of its ramshackle charm. The cabins are a great deal for groups of four on a budget, while the garden suites offer a little more protection from the wind and more space to stretch out at night.

Heron & Wilson Islands

Part of the smaller Capricornia Cays group, Heron Island is ranked among the finest scuba-diving regions in the world, particularly in terms of ease of access. Visitors to Heron generally know what they are coming for – underwater paradise – but the island's rugged beauty is reason enough to stay above the surface. A true coral cay, it is densely vegetated with pisonia trees and surrounded by 24 sq km of reef. There's a resort and research station on the northeastern third of the island; the remainder is national park. Note that 200,000 birds call the island home at different stages of the year, so there can be a lot of guano at times.

The island has excellent beaches, superb snorkelling and, during the season, turtle watching.

Heron Island Resort (☑ 1300 863 248; www.heronisland.com; d/ste from $330/572) is not particularly glamorous, despite the hefty price tag for a room, however the interaction with an incredible natural environment is difficult to find elsewhere in the world, and the resort itself should not be the reason you visit. Great deals are often available on its website. Meal packages are extra, and guests will pay $62/31 (one-way) per adult/child for launch transfer, $338 by seaplane from Gladstone.

The **Heron Islander** (☑ 1800 837 168; www.heronisland.com; adult/child one-way $62/31) departs Gladstone daily at 2pm (2½ hours).

For a more glamorous approach, take a **seaplane** (☑ 1300 863 248; www.heronisland.com; $338 one-way). Departures are daily subject to demand, and times can vary.

North West Island

North West is a spectacular 106-hectare coral cay, the second-biggest on the reef. Like much of the Capricornia Cays National Park, North West is a remote tropical haven, its walking and camping pedigree steadily growing in recent years. It is now an important site for nesting green turtles and birds; every October, hundreds of thousands of wedge-tailed shearwaters descend on the island to nest, squabble and scare the wits out of campers with their creepy nighttime howls. It's hard to imagine that North West was once a guano mine and home to a turtle-soup cannery. It really is paradise revisited.

Rockhampton & Around

POP 66.192

Welcome to Rockhampton ('Rocky' to its mates), where the hats, boots and utes are big...but the bulls are even bigger. With over 2.5 million cattle within a 250km radius of Rockhampton, it's called Australia's Beef Capital for a reason. This sprawling country town is the administrative and commercial centre of central Queensland, its wide streets and fine Victorian-era buildings (take a stroll down Quay St) reflecting the region's prosperous 19th-century heyday of gold and copper mining and beef-cattle industry.

Straddling the tropic of Capricorn, Rocky can be aptly scorching. It's 40km inland and lacks coastal sea breezes; summers are often unbearably humid. The town has a smattering of attractions but is best seen as a gateway to the coastal gems of Yeppoon and Great Keppel Island, and the Byfield National Park to the north.

◉ Sights

★ **Botanic Gardens**   GARDENS
(☑07-4932 9000; Spencer St; ⊘6am-6pm) FREE Just south of town, these gardens are a beautiful oasis, with tropical and subtropical rainforest, landscaped gardens and lily-covered lagoons. The formal Japanese garden is a zone of tranquillity, there's a cafe (⊘8am to 5pm), and the small, well-kept zoo (⊘8.30am to 4.30pm, admission free) has koalas, wombats, dingoes, monkeys, a walk-through aviary and tonnes more.

Dreamtime Cultural Centre CULTURAL CENTRE
(☑07-4936 1655; www.dreamtimecentre.com. au; Bruce Hwy; adult/child $15.50/7.50; ⊘10am-3.30pm Mon-Fri, tours 10.30am & 1pm) The story of the local Dharumbal people is well conveyed in this easily accessible insight into Aboriginal and Torres Strait Islander heritage and history. The excellent 90-minute tours are hands on – throw your own boomerangs! – and appeal to all ages. It's about 7km north of the city centre.

Kershaw Gardens   GARDENS
(☑07-4936 8254; via Charles St; ⊘6am-6pm) FREE Just north of the Fitzroy River, this excellent botanical park is devoted to Australian native plants. Its attractions include artificial rapids, a rainforest area, a fragrant garden and heritage architecture.

Mt Archer   MOUNTAIN
This mountain (604m) has walking trails weaving through eucalypts and rainforest abundant in wildlife. A brochure to the park is available from the visitor centres.

Rockhampton Art Gallery   GALLERY
(☑07-4936 8248; www.rockhamptonartgallery. com.au; 62 Victoria Pde; ⊘10am-4pm) FREE Boasting an impressive collection of Australian paintings, this gallery includes works by Sir Russell Drysdale and Sir Sidney Nolan. Contemporary Indigenous artists are also on display.

Archer Park Rail Museum   MUSEUM
(☑07-4936 8191; www.rockhamptonregion.qld.gov. au; 51-87 Denison St; adult/child/family $8/5/26; ⊘10am-3pm Mon-Thu, 10am-1pm Sun) This museum is housed in a former train station built in 1899. Through photographs and displays it tells the station's story, and that of the unique Purrey steam tram. Take a ride on the restored tram – the only remaining one of its kind in the world! – every Sunday from 10am to 1pm.

Heritage Village   MUSEUM
(☑07-4936 8688; www.heritagevillage.com.au; 296 Boundary Rd; adult/child/family $14/8.50/40; ⊘9am-4pm) A great place to break up a road trip, especially with kids, the Heritage Village is an active museum of replica historic buildings with townsfolk at work in period garb. The classrooms, garages and reconstructed shops will tickle all ages. There's also a visitor centre here. It's 10km north of the city centre, just off the Bruce Highway (A1).

🛏 Sleeping

Southside Holiday Village   CARAVAN PARK $
(☑07-4927 3013; www.sshv.com.au; Lower Dawson Rd; powered/unpowered sites $38/30, cabins $93, villas $98-125; ✳@🛜🏊) This is one of the city's best caravan parks, with neat, self-contained cabins and villas, large grassy camp sites and a good kitchen. Prices are for two people. It's about 3km south of the centre on a busy main road.

Rockhampton Backpackers   HOSTEL $
(☑07-4927 5288; www.rockhamptonbackpackers .com.au; 60 MacFarlane St; dm/d $23.50/60; ✳@🛜🏊) A very fluid, unpretentious YHA hostel that at times resembles an employment agency, Rocky Backpackers has an industrial-sized communal kitchen, open-plan living areas where travellers share

CAPRICORN CAVES

Capricorn Caves (☑ 07-4934 2883; www.capricorncaves.com.au; 30 Olsens Caves Rd; adult/child/family $30/15/75; ☺ 9am-5pm) are a rare acoustic and visual treat found deep beneath the Berserker Range 24km north of Rockhampton near the Caves township. The most popular one-hour tour includes a classical music recording and, around mid-morning, a sunlit refraction of stunning natural beauty. These ancient caves honeycomb a limestone ridge where you'll see cave coral, stalactites, dangling fig-tree roots and, less likely, little insectivorous bats.

In December, around the summer solstice (1 December to 14 January), sunlight beams directly through a 14m vertical shaft into Belfry Cave, creating an electrifying light show. If you stand directly below the beam, reflected sunlight colours the whole cavern with whatever colour you're wearing.

Daring spelunkers can book a two-hour 'adventure tour' ($75; reserve a day or more in advance) which takes you through tight spots with names such as 'Fat Man's Misery'. You must be at least 16 years old for this tour.

The Capricorn Caves complex has barbecue areas, a pool, a kiosk and accommodation (powered sites $35, cabins $150 to180).

information on cattle stations and fruit farms, and basic four-bed dorms. The pool is small but you'll take a cold puddle in Rocky's brutal summers.

Myella Farm Stay
FARMSTAY $$
(☑ 07-4998 1290; www.myella.weebly.com; Baralaba Rd; d/tr from $90/130, 2/3 days $250/390, powered sites $22; ❄ @ ☲) Myella Farm Stay, 125km southwest of Rockhampton, gives you a taste of the outback on its 10.6-sq-km farm. Lots of options are available, including comfortable camping and bush meals ($10 to $20) for those who are just passing through. The best experience though is engaging in the many activities on offer in a package deal. The package includes bush explorations by horseback, motorcycle and 4WD, all meals, accommodation in a renovated homestead with polished timber floors and a wide verandah, farm clothes and free transfers from Rockhampton.

Criterion
HOTEL $$
(☑ 07-4922 1225; www.thecriterion.com.au; 150 Quay St; pub r $65-90, motel r $130-160; ❄ ☎) The Criterion is Rockhampton's grandest old pub, with an elegant foyer, a friendly bar and a well-respected steakhouse. For travellers – or heavy drinkers – its top two storeys have dozens of dated period rooms, some in original heritage style, and all exceptional value for money. All rooms have showers, although the toilets are down the hall. If it's a little raw, or noisy, you can find a number of bland, though modern motel rooms next door.

Coffee House
MOTEL, APARTMENT $$
(☑ 07-4927 5722; www.coffeehouse.com.au; 51 William St; r $150-180; ❄ ☎ ☲) The Coffee House features small, tiled motel rooms, self-contained apartments and spa suites, all thoughtfully decorated and including darkwood writing desks. There's a popular and stylish cafe-restaurant–wine bar on-site.

★ Denison
Boutique Hotel
BOUTIQUE HOTEL $$$
(☑ 07-4923 7378; www.denisonboutiquehotel.com.au; 233 Denison St; d $200) The newest hotel in Rockhampton is also the finest: a gorgeous white building constructed in 1885. Surrounded by rose gardens and hedges, Denison rooms have king-sized four-poster beds, high ceilings and large plasma TVs. Discounts are available online, which make the experience very accessible.

✕ Eating & Drinking

Saigon Saigon
ASIAN $
(☑ 07-4927 0888; www.saigonbytheriver.com; Quay St; mains $12-28; ☺ lunch & dinner Wed-Mon; ☑) This two-storey bamboo hut overlooks the Fitzroy River and serves delicious pan-Asian food with local ingredients like kangaroo and crocodile served in a sizzling steamboat. Not up for reptile? The menu is as intricate as the restaurant exterior's neon light display. Lots of vegetarian options, too.

Ginger Mule
STEAK $
(☑ 07-4927 7255; 8 William St; mains from $10; ☺ noon-midnight Tue-Thu, noon-2am Fri, 4pm-2am Sat) Rocky's coolest eatery bills itself as a

tapas bar, but everyone's here for one thing: steak! The steak sandwich ($11) has to be among the best bargain meals in Queensland, while the $12 sirloin flies out of the busy kitchen late into the night. Morphs into a cocktail bar late in the evening.

Pacino's   ITALIAN $$
(☑07-4922 5833; cnr Fitzroy & George Sts; mains $25-40; ☺lunch & dinner) Run by the same family for 30 years, Pacino's is a riverside favourite and the best Italian for miles. Pricey, though consistently popular for enormous pasta dishes and many regional specialities. The lamb's brains and lobster ravioli are well above what you'd expect from such a small city, though avoid the pizza.

Restaurant 98   SEAFOOD $$
(☑07-4920 1000; www.98.com.au; 98 Victoria Pde; mains $18-46; ☺breakfast daily, lunch Mon-Fri, dinner Mon-Sat) Oysters, steak and flagons of fine red wine are the signature order at this licensed dining room attached to **Motel 98** (d from $124). Sit inside or on the terrace overlooking the Fitzroy River.

★ Great Western Hotel   PUB
(☑07-4922 1862; www.greatwesternhotel.com. au; cnr Stanley & Denison Sts; ☺10am-2am) The GWH is part country pub, part concert venue, and part of Rockhampton's social fabric. Try to time your visit to Rocky for a Wednesday or Friday night when you can watch brave cattlefolk being tossed in the air by bucking bulls and broncos. The pub is a jocular place with enough memorabilia to stuff a B-grade Western. Touring bands occasionally rock here, alongside bouts of Ultimate Fighting and stand-up comedy; you can get tickets online. The food is all about great steak.

ℹ Information
Tropic of Capricorn Visitor Centre (☑1800 676 701; Gladstone Rd; ☺9am-5pm) Helpful centre on the highway right beside the tropic of Capricorn marker, 3km south of the centre.

ℹ Getting There & Away
AIR
Qantas (☑13 13 13; www.qantas.com.au) and **Virgin** (☑13 67 89; www.virginaustralia.com) connect Rockhampton with various cities. The airport is about 6km from the centre of town.

BUS
Greyhound (☑1300 473 946; www.greyhound. com.au) buses run from Rockhampton to

Brisbane ($168, 12 hours) and Mackay ($65, four hours), among other destinations.

TRAIN
Queensland Rail (☑1800 872 467; www. queenslandrailtravel.com.au) runs a daily service to Brisbane ($135, 12 hours) and Gladstone ($39, three hours).

Yeppoon
POP 17,241

Yeppoon has slowly evolved from a tiny village known as a launching pad for trips to Great Keppel Island to today's more established seaside town. The long, beautiful beach serves as a holiday destination or residential highlight for many graziers, miners and other folk from nearby Rockhampton seeking to beat the heat. A hinterland of volcanic outcrops and pineapple patches and (a short drive north) the wonderful Byfield National Park, give Yeppoon a rich diversity often overlooked by travellers from other parts of Australia. The broad, quiet streets, sleepy motels and beachside cafes are the setting for a nightly migration of black-and-red flying foxes, which pass over the main beach and beyond in a startling sunset display.

☆ Activities
Sail Capricornia   CRUISE
(☑0402 102 373; www.sailcapricornia.com.au; full-day cruises incl lunch adult/child $115/75) Sail Capricornia offers snorkelling cruises on board the *Grace* catamaran, as well as sunset ($55) and three-day ($499) cruises.

Funtastic Cruises   CRUISE
(☑0438 909 502; www.funtasticcruises.com; full-day cruises adult/child/family $98/80/350) Funtastic Cruises operates full-day snorkelling trips on board its 17m catamaran, with a two-hour stopover on Great Keppel Island, morning and afternoon tea, and all snorkelling equipment included. It can also organise camping drop-offs to islands en route.

🛏 Sleeping & Eating
Beachside Caravan Park   CARAVAN PARK $
(☑07-4939 3738; Farnborough Rd; powered sites $31-34, unpowered sites $28) This basic, neat little camping ground, north of the town centre, commands a wonderful, totally beachfront location. It has good amenities and grassed

sites with some shade, but no cabins or on-site vans. Rates are for two people.

★Surfside Motel
MOTEL $$

(☑07-4939 1272; www.yeppoonsurfsidemotel.com.au; 30 Anzac Pde; r from $140; ❋@🛜💈) Location and service lift the Surfside to the top of the tree in Yeppoon. Across the road from the beach and close to town, this 1950s strip of lime-green motel units epitomises summer holidays at the beach. And it's terrific value – the rooms are spacious and unusually well equipped, complete with toaster, hair dryer and free wi-fi. Prices go down for three or more nights.

While Away B&B
B&B $$

(☑07-4939 5719; www.whileawaybandb.com.au; 44 Todd Ave; s $115, d $140-155, incl breakfast; ❋) Perenially popular B&B, While Away has good-sized, immaculately clean rooms with wheelchair access and a quiet location back from the beach. The bubbly owners offer complimentary nibbles, tea, coffee, port and sherry as well as generous breakfasts.

Coral Inn Yeppoon
HOSTEL $$

(☑07-4939 2925; www.coralinn.com.au; 14 Maple St; d/q from $129/149; ❋❋@🛜💈) Beautiful lawns and reef-bright colours in the rooms, all with bathrooms and mod-cons, make Coral Inn a great find, just back from the beach. Families and discerning groups in particular will enjoy the quad rooms, communal kitchen, and mini 'beach' area with hammocks and an inviting pool. Note that management does enforce a number of rules to deter rowdy backpackers.

Strand Hotel
PUB FOOD $

(☑07-4939 1301; www.thestrandyeppoon.com.au; 2 Normanby St; mains from $16; ⊙noon-2.30pm & 6-9pm Mon-Fri, 11.30am-2.30pm & 5.30-9pm Sat & Sun) There has been a welcome refurb in the form of glass frontage and faux-leather furniture at this grand old pub facing the sea. The food is dependable, ranging from pizzas ($16 to $24) to fantastic steaks ($29 to $42). There's live music most weekends, and the odd random weeknight.

★Megalomania
FUSION $$$

(☑07-4939 2333; www.megalomaniabarandbistro.com.au; cnr James & Arthur Sts; mains $26-40; ⊙noon-2pm & 6pm-late Tue-Sat) An Oz-Asian fusion beast, with a stylish ambience that's hard to replicate anywhere, let alone a small coastal town, by head chef Callan Crigan. Panko-crumbed tiger prawns and red sea salt soft-shell crab were our starters ($18 each), and Byron Bay pork belly and white miso barramundi came in for mains ($36 each). You get the idea. Loll beneath the fig tree with your stiff cocktail, or clink silverware in the indoor woodsy surrounds.

❶ Information

Capricorn Coast Information Centre (☑1800 675 785; www.capricorncoast.com.au; Ross

WORTH A TRIP

BYFIELD

Byfield is a village in Byfield National Park, 40km north of Yeppon, a well-concealed landscape of rare diversity: empty sand dunes running up to rocky pinnacles, wetlands and semi-tropical rainforests. A 4WD will get you to remote hiking paths and isolated beaches beautiful enough to warrant a much longer stay.

Nob Creek Pottery (☑07-4935 1161; www.nobcreekpottery.com.au; 216 Arnolds Rd; ⊙10am-4pm Thu-Mon) FREE is a working pottery and gallery nestled in leafy rainforest. The gallery showcases hand-blown glass, woodwork and jewellery; the handmade ceramics are outstanding. Take a boat trip through the rainforest with Waterpark Eco-Tours (☑07-4935 1171; www.waterparkecotours.com; 201 Waterpark Creek Rd; 2-3hr tour $27.50, cabins $150), keeping an eye out for bright blue kingfishers, baby turtles and big daddy eels.

There are five camping grounds (☑13 74 68; www.nprsr.qld.gov.au; per person/family $6.15/24.60) to choose from (prebook). Nine Mile Beach and Five Rocks are on the beach and you'll need a 4WD to access them.

Set on 26 hectares of richly scented, cacophonous rainforest splendour, Byfield Mountain Retreat (☑07-4935 1161; www.byfieldmountainretreat.com; 216 Arnolds Rd; per night/week $250/1300) is only a short drive from Byfield village and will suit anyone looking for a deep nature experience.

Creek Roundabout; ⊘9am-5pm) Has plenty of information on the Capricorn Coast and Great Keppel Island, and can book accommodation and tours.

ⓘ Getting There & Away

Yeppoon is 43km northeast of Rockhampton. **Young's Bus Service** (⌨07-4922 3813; www.youngsbusservice.com.au) runs frequent buses from Rockhampton ($6.70 one-way) to Yeppoon and down to the Rosslyn Bay Marina.

If you're driving, there's a free daytime car park at the marina. For longer, secure undercover parking, the **Great Keppel Island Security Car Park** (⌨07-4933 6670; 422 Scenic Hwy; per day from $15) is on the Scenic Hwy south of Yeppoon, by the turn-off to the marina.

Keppel Konnections and Funtastic Cruises (p176) both leave from Yeppoon daily to Great Keppel Island and the Great Keppel National Park.

Great Keppel Island

This jewel of the Capricorn Coast is synonymous with deserted island fantasies of the urban travel set. Once home to one of Australia's most iconic resorts, the 4-sq-km island – natural bushland covering 90% of the interior – has a total of 17 beaches, all in the category of 'bloody beautiful'. A new mega-resort, environmental research centre and golf course are on the way, so get here soon if you prefer to do your islands in solitude.

🏃 Activities

Freedom Fast Cats   CRUISE
(⌨07-4933 6888; www.freedomfastcats.com; Keppel Bay Marina, Rosslyn Bay; tours adult/child from $78/50) Operates a range of island tours, from glass-bottomed-boat reef-viewing to snorkelling and boom-netting.

Great Keppel Cruises   BOATING
(⌨0401 053 666; www.greatkeppelcruises.com.au; half-/full-day trips $65/125) *Keppel Dreams* departs from Fisherman's Beach for snorkelling forays around the island. Departures are scheduled to fit in with Keppel Konnections arrival from Yeppoon.

Watersports Hut   WATER SPORTS
(⌨0415 076 644; Putney Beach; ⊘Sat, Sun & school holidays) The Watersports Hut on the main beach hires out snorkelling equipment, kayaks and catamarans, and runs tube rides.

🛏 Sleeping & Eating

★ **Svendsen's Beach**   CABIN $$
(⌨07-4938 3717; www.svendsensbeach.com; d from $115) ✎ The three-night minimum stays are barely enough at this secluded boutique retreat on the 'other' side of Great Keppel. Run by knowledgeable Carl and Lindy, the retreat is an ecofriendly operation, run on solar and wind power; there's even a bush-bucket shower. It's the perfect place for snorkelling, bushwalking and romantic getaways. Guests can choose from luxury tent-bungalows (doubles $115) on elevated timber decks, plus a colourful studio ($150) and house (from $220; sleeps up to four people), all within a turtle shuffle of the beach.

Great Keppel Island Hideaway   RESORT $$
(⌨07-4939 2050; www.greatkeppelislandhideaway.com.au; safari tents $90 r $140-200, cabins $200-360) This hideaway is set across massive grounds on a sublime bend of Fisherman's Beach. The distance between the various cabins, houses and safari tents lends an air of rugged isolation to a family holiday. The reality is there's a beachfront restaurant (mains $12 to $25) nearby where guests compare their lodgings, sip on sundowners and half-contemplate a nature walk somewhere not too far away.

Keppel Lodge   GUESTHOUSE $$
(⌨07-4939 4251; www.keppellodge.com.au; Fisherman's Beach; d per person $65-75, houses $520-600; @🖲) Keppel Lodge is terrific value and sandy stumbling distance to Fisherman's Beach. The pleasant open-plan house has four large bedrooms (with bathrooms) branching from a large communal lounge and kitchen. It's available in its entirety – ideal for a group booking – or as individual suites.

Island Pizza   PIZZA $
(⌨07-4939 4699; The Esplanade; dishes $6-30; ⊘varies) You'll be doing better than us if you can figure out exactly when this incongruously located pizza house is open, but if you hang around long enough, someone will let you know. The pizzas are huge and delicious. Get anything with pineapple on it.

ⓘ Getting There & Away

Great Keppel is a 30-minute ferry trip from Roslyn Bay Marina in Yeppoon. **Keppel Konnections** (www.keppelkonnections.com.au)

Great Keppel Island

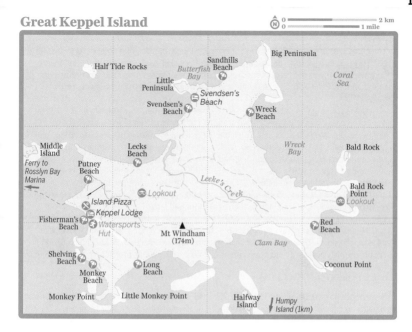

N   0   2 km
0   1 mile

Half Tide Rocks

Little Peninsula

Butterfish Bay

Sandhills Beach

Big Peninsula

Coral Sea

Svendsen's Beach

Svendsen's Beach

Wreck Beach

Middle Island

Ferry to Rosslyn Bay Marina

Putney Beach

Lecks Beach

Wreck Bay

Bald Rock

Leeke's Creek

Bald Rock Point

Lookout

Lookout

Island Pizza

Keppel Lodge

Fisherman's Beach

Watersports Hut

Mt Windham (174m)

Red Beach

Clam Bay

Shelving Beach

Monkey Beach

Long Beach

Coconut Point

Monkey Point

Little Monkey Point

Halfway Island

Humpy Island (1km)

has twice-daily services to the island departing Yeppoon at 9am and 3pm and returning at 10am and 4pm. **Freedom Fast Cats** (07-4933 6888; www.freedomfastcats.com; return adult/child/family $55/35/160) leave Yeppoon at 9.15am and return at 2.30pm or 3.45pm depending on the day and the season.

Capricorn Hinterland

The central highlands, west of Rockhampton, are home to two excellent national parks. Blackdown Tableland National Park is a brooding, powerful place, while visitors to Carnarvon National Park will be gobsmacked by the spectacular gorge.

At Emerald, 270km inland, try fossicking for gems in the heat and rubble – you'll be surrounded by the good people and vibe of the outback. Try to stick to the cooler months between April and November.

Carnarvon National Park

Carnarvon Gorge is a dramatic rendition of Australian natural beauty. The 30km-long, 200m-high gorge was carved out over millions of years by Carnarvon Creek and its tributaries twisting through soft sedimentary rock. What was left behind is a lush,

other-worldly oasis, where life flourishes, shielded from the stark terrain. You'll find giant cycads, king ferns, river oaks, flooded gums, cabbage palms, deep pools, and platypuses in the creek. Escaped convicts often took refuge here among ancient rock paintings. The area was made a national park in 1932 after defeated farmers forfeited their pastoral lease.

For most people, Carnarvon Gorge *is* the Carnarvon National Park, because the other sections – including Mt Moffatt (where Indigenous groups lived some 19,000 years ago), Ka Ka Mundi and Salvator Rosa – have long been difficult to access.

Coming from Rolleston the road is bitumen for 75km and unsealed for 20km. From Roma via Injune and Wyseby homestead, the road is good bitumen for about 215km, then unsealed and fairly rough for the last 30km. After heavy rain, both these roads can become impassable.

The main walking track also starts here, following Carnarvon Creek through the gorge, with detours to various points of interest. These include the Moss Garden (3.6km from the picnic area), Ward's Canyon (4.8km), the Art Gallery (5.6km) and Cathedral Cave (9.3km). Allow at least a whole day for a visit.

OFF THE BEATEN TRACK

GEM FIELDS

The gem fields of central Queensland are a tough landscape drawing prospectors who eke out a living until a jackpot (or sunstroke) arrives. Fossickers descend in winter – in the hot summers the towns are nearly deserted. Sapphires are the main haul, but zircons are also found and, very rarely, rubies. Sapphire and Rubyvale are two of the main towns on the fields.

To go fossicking you need a licence (www.dnrm.qld.gov.au; adult/family $7.75/11.15); they can be found at a few places in the area – the **Central Highlands Visitors Centre** (www.centralhighlands.com.au; 3 Clemont St,; ☉10am-4.30pm) in Emerald has a list – or online. If you just wish to dabble, you can buy a bucket of 'wash' (mine dirt in water) from one of the fossicking parks to hand-sieve and wash.

Bobby Dazzler Mine Tours (☎07- 4981 0000) will help you get your hands dirty in the right way, and throw in a fair whack of local history and colour to boot.

Pat's Gems (☎07-4985 4544; 1056 Rubyvale Rd, Sapphire; ☉8.30am-4pm) is a quirky shop and fossicking station where regular visitors and travelling prospectors can rent equipment and pick up tips on how to find that precious gem.

The super-clean and friendly **Sapphire Caravan Park** (☎07-4985 4281; www.sapphirecaravanpark.com.au; 57 Sunrise Rd, Sapphire; powered/unpowered sites $29/25, cottages $115), set on four hilly acres with sites and cabins tucked into the eucalyptus forest, is great for fossickers.

Sunrover Expeditions (☎1800 353 717; www.sunrover.com.au; safaris per person incl all meals $940) runs a five-day camping safari into Carnarvon Gorge between August and October.

🛏 Sleeping

There are national park camp sites at **Big Bend** (☎13 74 68; www.qld.gov.au/camping; sites per person/family $6.15/24.60) and **Mt Moffat** (☎13 74 68; www.qld.gov.au/camping; sites per person/family $6.15/24.60), as well as the excellent **Takarakka Bush Resort** (☎07-4984 4535; www.takarakka.com.au; Wyseby Rd; powered/unpowered sites from $45/38, cabins $195-228), with safari tents, cottages and cabins.

Carnarvon Gorge
Wilderness Lodge　　　　　　　LODGE **$$$**
(☎1800 644 150; www.carnarvon-gorge.com; Wyseby Rd; d from $220; ☉closed Nov-Feb; ☒) Glampers can wake to kangaroos chewing grass outside their attractive tented chalets. This is outback chic set deep in the bush. Excellent guided tours are available, plus a full-board package (from $155 to $300 per person).

Whitsunday Coast

Best Places to Eat

➜ Mr Bones (p196)

➜ Fusion 128 (p185)

➜ Harry's Corner (p195)

➜ Jochheims Pies (p200)

➜ Paddock & Brew Company
(p185)

Best Places to Sleep

➜ Qualia (p198)

➜ Kipara (p193)

➜ Stoney Creek Farmstay
(p183)

➜ Riviera Mackay (p183)

➜ Platypus Bushcamp (p187)

Why Go?

Many travellers to Australia, especially those with a sailing pedigree, head straight for the Whitsunday Islands and barely leave. This white-fringed archipelago, a stunning feature of the Coral Sea coast, can be easily seen from shore. Opal-jade waters and pure-white beaches fringe the forested isles; around them, tropical fish swarm through the world's largest coral garden in the Great Barrier Reef Marine Park. The gateway to the islands, Airlie Beach, is a backpacker hub with a parade of tanned faces zinging between boats, beaches and nightclubs. This is as close to the islands as some budget travellers will get.

South of Airlie, Mackay is a typical coastal Queensland town with palm-lined streets framed by a jumble of art-deco buildings. It's a handy base for trips to Eungella National Park – a lush hinterland oasis where platypuses cavort in the wild. North of Airlie Beach is cute little Bowen, a low-key alternative for backpackers working through their holiday.

When to Go
Mackay

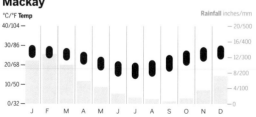

Jun–Oct The perfect time to enjoy sunny skies, calm days, mild weather and stinger-free seas.

Aug Sailing boats skim across the water and parties are held during Airlie Beach Race Week.

Sep & Oct Optimal conditions for kayaking around the islands.

Map labels:

Bowen • Hydeaway Bay • Stone Island • Dingo Beach • Gloucester Island • Cape Gloucester • Armit Island • Grassy Island • Hayman Island • Hook Island

Whitsunday Islands ②

Whitsunday Islands National Park ①

Great Barrier Reef ⑤

Airlie Beach ④ • Cannonvale • South Molle Island • Shute Harbour • Whitsunday Island • Whitehaven Beach ⑦

CORAL SEA

Cedar Creek Falls • Long Island • Hamilton Island ⑥

Proserpine • Conway • Conway National Park • Lindeman Island • Shaw Island

Cape Conway • Thomas Island • East Repulse Island • Blacksmith Island

Laguna Whitsundays • Midge Point • Goldsmith Island • Linne Island • Tinsmith Island • Wigton Island

Bloomsbury

Broken River

Bruce Hwy • Calen • Seaforth • Rabbit Island • Brampton Island • Carlisle Island • Cockermouth Island • Scawfell Island

Cameron's Pocket • Cape Hillsborough National Park ⑨ • Keswick Island • St Bees Island

Eungella National Park ③ • Mt Ossa • Kuttabul • Yakapari • Bucasia • Eimeo • Blacks Beach • Slade Point

Finch Hatton Gorge • Eungella • Marian • Broken River • Finch Hatton • Mirani • Walkerston • Mackay

Lake Kinchant • Bakers Creek • Eton • Homebush • Hay Point

Bowen River • Nebo Creek • Sarina • Sarina Beach

Elphinstone

Bruce Hwy

0 — 40 km
0 — 20 miles

Whitsunday Coast Highlights

① **Whitsunday Islands National Park** (p191) Camping under the stars and making like an island castaway.

② **Whitsunday Islands** (p189) Sailing through magnificent aquamarine waters.

③ **Eungella National Park** (p187) Waiting patiently for a glimpse of a shy platypus and walking in the misty rainforest.

④ **Airlie Beach** (p191) Swilling beer and partying hard in fun-lovin' Airlie Beach.

⑤ **Great Barrier Reef** (p189) Diving and snorkelling the outer fringing reefs.

⑥ **Hamilton Island** (p198) Hiking the steep forest trails.

⑦ **Whitehaven Beach** (p199) Being dazzled by the bright-white silica sand.

⑧ **Bowen** (p200) Picking fruit or swimming in empty coves in this laid-back town.

⑨ **Cape Hillsborough National Park** (p188) Exploring where bush meets the beach at this semi-remote spot.

Mackay

POP 82,500

Once home to opera star Dame Nellie Melba, this workaday, midsized Queensland city puts tourism a distant second to the machinations of the sugar and agricultural industries, but there's nonetheless plenty to like about Mackay's tropical suburbia. For starters, it's an incongruously impressive art-deco destination, and even better is its location between protected mangroves and a smart, beachy marina. Mackay is a convenient base for excursions out of town, but when the backpacker shuffle and island-hopping overwhelms, its alfresco cafes provide a quick urban fix. It's only a 1½-hour drive to Airlie Beach and boats to the Whitsundays, and a scenic jaunt past the sugar-cane fields to Eungella National Park.

◉ Sights

Mackay's impressive art-deco architecture owes much to a devastating cyclone in 1918, which flattened many of the town's buildings. Enthusiasts should pick up a copy of *Art Deco in Mackay* from the visitor centre.

There are good views over the harbour from Rotary Lookout in North Mackay and over the beach at Lampert's Lookout.

Mackay Marina (Mackay Harbour) is worth the trip to wine and dine with a waterfront view, while the artificial **Bluewater Lagoon** (⊙9am-5.45pm) **FREE** near Caneland Shopping Centre has water fountains, water slides, grassed picnic areas, free wi-fi and a cafe.

Mackay Regional Botanical Gardens   GARDENS
(Lagoon St) On 33 hectares, 3km south of the city centre, these gardens are a must-see for flora fans. Home to five themed gardens and the Lagoon cafe-restaurant (open Wednesday to Sunday).

Artspace Mackay   GALLERY
(⏲07-4961 9722; www.artspacemackay.com.au; Gordon St; ⊙10am-5pm Tue-Fri, 10am-3pm Sat & Sun) **FREE** Artspace Mackay is a welcoming regional art gallery showcasing works from local and visiting artists. Chew over the masterpieces at on-site noshery Foodspace (p185).

Beaches
Mackay has plenty of beaches, although not all are ideal for swimming. The best option near town is Harbour Beach, 6km north of the centre and just south of the Mackay Marina. The beach here is patrolled and there's

a foreshore reserve with picnic tables and barbecues.

⌕ Tours

Reeforest Adventure Tours   CULTURAL TOUR
(⏲07-4959 8360, 1800 500 353; www.reeforest. com) The Mackay region's most experienced operator offers a wide range of junkets, including a platypus and rainforest eco-safari, two-day Eungella tours, and a Cape Hillsborough expedition in the footsteps of the Juipera mob. In the cane-crushing season (June to December), you can see how sugar cane is turned into sweet crystals with its two-hour tour of the Farleigh Sugar Mill (adult/child $28/14); long pants and enclosed shoes are required.

Heritage Walk   WALKING
(⏲07-4944 5888; ⊙8.45am Tue & Wed May-Sep) **FREE** Weekly wandering (1½ to two hours) that takes in the sights and secrets of ye olde Mackay. Leaves from Paxton's Warehouse on the corner of River and Carlyle Sts.

✦ Festivals & Events

Wintermoon Folk Festival   MUSIC
(www.wintermoonfestival.com; ⊙Apr/May) Folk and world-music love-fest.

⌂ Sleeping

★**Stoney Creek Farmstay**   FARMSTAY $
(⏲07-4954 1177; www.stoneycreekfarmstay.com; Peak Downs Hwy; dm/stables/cottages $25/130/175) ⚑ This bush retreat 32km south of Mackay is a down 'n' dirty option in the best possible way. Stay in an endearingly ramshackle cottage, the rustic livery stable or the charismatic Dead Horse Hostel, and forget all about the mod-cons: this is dead-set bush livin'. Three-hour horse rides cost $105 per person and lots of other activities are available. Free dorm room if you ride for two consecutive days.

Mackay Marine Tourist Park   CARAVAN PARK $
(⏲07-4955 1496; www.mmtp.com.au; 379 Harbour Rd; powered/unpowered sites $35/32, villas $110-180; ❄@⚡🐕🏊) A step up from the usual caravan parks: all cabins and villas come with private patios and widescreen TVs, and you've gotta love anywhere with a giant jumping pillow.

Riviera Mackay   APARTMENT $$
(⏲07-4088 1459; www.rivieramackay.com.au; 5-7 Nelson St; 1-/2-bedroom apt $171/256) Mackay desperately need this light, stylish property, architecturally inspired by Palm Springs, and akin to a hip inner-city flat in a city further

Mackay

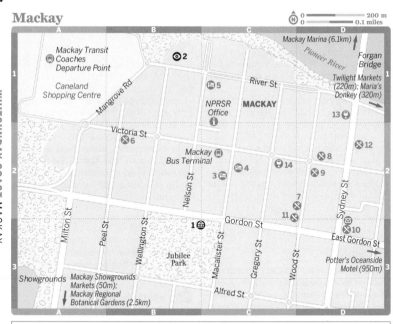

Mackay

◉ Sights
1 Artspace Mackay B3
2 Bluewater Lagoon B1

🛏 Sleeping
3 Coral Sands Motel C2
4 International Lodge Motel C2
5 Riviera Mackay C1

✕ Eating
6 Austral Hotel B2
7 Burp Eat Drink D2

Foodspace .... (see 1)
8 Fusion 128 .... D2
9 Kevin's Place D2
10 Oscar's on Sydney D3
11 Paddock & Brew Company C2
12 Woodsman's Axe Coffee D2

◐ Drinking & Nightlife
13 Ambassador Hotel D1
14 Cartel C2

south. Very good value too in an expensive city for accommodation.

Coral Sands Motel MOTEL **$$**
(☑ 07-4951 1244; www.coralsandsmotel.com.au; 44 Macalister St; r from $115; ✳ 🤖 🏊) One of Mackay's better midrange options, the Coral Sands boasts ultrafriendly management and large rooms in a central location. Popular with the transient workforce, it's a bit tropi-kitsch, but with the river, shops, pubs and cafes so close to your doorstep, you won't care. Great value.

Potter's Oceanside Motel MOTEL **$$**
(☑ 07-5689 0388; www.pottersoceansidemotel.com. au; 2c East Gordon St; d $149-169, f $269; ✳ 🤖 🏊) Near the unappealing Town Beach, Potter's is nonetheless an excellent temporary answer

to your travel woes. Very accommodating management will crack open a beer at check-in and point you to immaculate, modern rooms (some of which are wheelchair accessible) with garden views. The small restaurant does a pleasant breakfast; room service also available. Perfect for a dose of clean comfort if you've been taking the rough road too long.

International Lodge Motel MOTEL **$$**
(☑ 07-4951 1022; www.internationallodge.com.au; 40 Macalister St; r from $105; 🅿 ✳ 🤖) The ugly mustard building with a brown roof and a concrete garden is one of Mackay's better midrange motels. The rooms are clean, bright and cheerful, and your door is shouting distance from the city nightlife.

Clarion Hotel
Mackay Marina
LUXURY HOTEL **$$$**

(📞07-4955 9400; www.mackaymarinahotel.com; Mulherin Dr; d from $249; ❄@🔊🏊) This large chain hotel on the marina was the talk of the town when it opened, and it's still a professional operation and the pick for most corporate folk. There's an excellent on-site restaurant, kitchenettes, private balconies and an enormous swimming pool. It's located 6.5km northeast of the centre. To get there take Sydney St north across the Forgan Bridge. Online discounts make a mockery of the rack rates.

🍴 Eating

Woodsman's Axe Coffee
CAFE **$**

(41 Sydney St; coffee from $4.30; ⏰6am-2pm Mon-Fri, 7am-2pm Sat & Sun) The best coffee in town paired with light eats, from wraps to quiches to muffins.

Maria's Donkey
TAPAS **$**

(📞07-4957 6055; 8 River St; tapas $8-15; ⏰noon-10pm Wed & Thu, to midnight Fri-Sun) Quirky, energetic riverfront joint dishing up tapas, jugs of sangria, occasional live music and general good times. Service is erratic, but somehow, that's part of the charm.

Fusion 128
MODERN AUSTRALIAN **$$**

(📞07-4999 9329; 128 Victoria St; mains $13.50-33; ⏰11.30am-2pm & 5.30-10pm) Mackay is becoming quite the foodie destination. The latest instalment is Fusion 128, a superb, casual restaurant with a low-lit industrial design run by the effusive David Ming. It combines Asian flavours with Australian bush ingredients, and serves fine cocktails and desserts to match the mood.

Paddock & Brew Company
AMERICAN **$$**

(📞0487 222 880; 94 Wood St; mains $18-30) Mackay needed this upmarket, craft-beer-soaked, American home-style restaurant, which serves up amazing burgers ($25). Part of the new breed of north Queensland culinary creatives, the team at Paddock & Brew whiz between the wooden tables at this happening pre-party venue.

Oscar's on Sydney
FUSION **$$**

(📞07-4944 0173; cnr Sydney & Gordon Sts; mains $10-23; ⏰7am-5pm Mon-Fri, to 4pm Sat, 8am-4pm Sun) The delicious *poffertjes* (Dutch pancakes with traditional toppings) are still going strong at this very popular corner cafe, but don't be afraid to give the other dishes a go. Top spot for breakfast.

Kevin's Place
ASIAN **$$**

(📞07-4953 5835; 79 Victoria St; mains $16-27; ⏰11.30am-2pm & 5.30-8pm Mon-Fri, 5.30-8pm Sat) At Kevin's, housed in a marvellous deco building on Victoria St, large groups gather on round tables – square on the street – and share sizzling, spicy Singaporean dishes. Don't go past the classics such as mee goreng ($18). Lunch specials are a bargain from $12.

Austral Hotel
PUB FOOD **$$**

(📞07-4951 3288; www.theaustralhotel.com.au; 189 Victoria St; mains $19-36, steaks $24-47; ⏰noon-2.30pm & 6-9pm) So many steaks, so little time. The Austral is a red-meat specialist, but it's also a knockabout Aussie pub with timber interiors, the horses on the telly and plenty of old, single men sipping pots of beer.

Foodspace
CAFE **$$**

(www.artspacemackay.com.au; Gordon St; mains $16-26; ⏰9am-3pm Tue-Sun) You can graze on impressive salads, sandwiches and light meals prepared by beginning chefs at Foodspace, the licensed cafe inside Artspace Mackay (p183).

Burp Eat Drink
MODERN AUSTRALIAN **$$$**

(📞07-4951 3546; www.burp.net.au; 86 Wood St; mains from $33; ⏰11.30am-3pm & 6pm-late Tue-Fri, 6pm-late Sat) Run by the enterprising NE Food mob, this swish Melbourne-style restaurant in the tropics has a small but tantalising menu. Sophisticated selections include pork belly with scallops, Kaffir-lime-crusted soft-shell crab, plus some serious steaks.

🍷 Drinking & Nightlife

Cartel
CLUB

(99 Victoria St; ⏰10pm-4am Thu-Sat) Frenetic dance club hosting a mix of resident and guest-star DJs. Changes name as fast as music trends.

Ambassador Hotel
BAR

(📞07-4953 3233; www.ambassadorhotel.net.au; 2 Sydney St; ⏰5pm-late Thu, 4pm-late Fri-Sun) Both a social and historical landmark, the Ambassador is art deco outside, wild 'n' crazy inside. There's multilevel carousing on weekends, including Mackay's only rooftop bar. Remarkably, you will soon be able to sleep here in renovated dorms and double rooms.

🛍 Shopping

They like their markets in Mackay; try the **Mackay Showgrounds Markets** (Milton St; ⏰6.30am-10am Sat), **Twilight Markets**

(Northern Beaches Bowls Club; ⊙5pm-9pm 1st Fri of the month) and the Troppo Market (Mt Pleasant Shopping Centre car park; ⊙from 7.30am 2nd Sun of the month).

ⓘ Information

Mackay Visitor Centre (☑1300 130 001; www.mackayregion.com; 320 Nebo Rd; ⊙9am-5pm; ⓢ) About 3km south of the centre. Internet access and wi-fi.

NPRSR Office (☑07-4944 7818; www.nprsr.qld.gov.au; Level 5, 44 Nelson St; ⊙8.30am-4.30pm Mon-Fri) For camping permits.

Post Office (69-71 Sydney St)

ⓘ Getting There & Away

AIR

The airport is about 3km south of the centre of Mackay. **Jetstar** (☑13 15 38; www.jetstar.com.au), **Qantas** (☑13 13 13; www.qantas.com.au) and **Virgin** (☑13 67 89; www.virginaustralia.com) have flights to/from Brisbane.

BUS

Buses stop at the **Mackay Bus Terminal** (cnr Victoria & Macalister Sts), where tickets can also be booked. **Greyhound** (☑1300 473 946; www.greyhound.com.au) travels up and down the coast. Sample one-way adult fares and journey times: Airlie Beach ($33, two hours), Townsville ($72, 6½ hours), Cairns ($127, 13 hours) and Brisbane ($227, 17 hours).

Premier (☑13 34 10; www.premierms.com.au) is less expensive than Greyhound but has fewer services.

TRAIN

The Spirit of Queensland, operated by **Queensland Rail** (☑1800 872 467; www.queenslandrail.com.au), runs from Mackay to Brisbane ($199, 13 hours) and Cairns ($159, 14 hours). The train station is at Paget, 5km south of the city centre.

ⓘ Getting Around

Major car-rental firms have desks at Mackay Airport; see www.mackayairport.com.au/travel/car-hire for listings. **NQ Car & Truck Rental** (☑07-4953 2353; www.nqcartruckrentals.com.au; 6 Malcolmson St, North Mackay) is a reliable local operator.

Mackay Transit Coaches (☑07-4957 3330; www.mackaytransit.com.au) has several services around the city, and connects the city with the harbour and northern beaches; pick up a timetable at the visitor centre or look online.

For a taxi, call **Mackay Taxis** (☑13 10 08).

Mackay's Northern Beaches

There's a lot of gorgeous, winding coastline and not a lot of people north of Mackay to the wilds of Cape Hillsborough. A series of headlands and bays shelter small residential communities that blossom in summer with local holidaymakers and year-round with romantic weekenders.

At Blacks Beach, the beach extends for 6km, so stretch those legs and claim a piece of Coral Sea coast for a day. Blacks Beach Holiday Park (☑07-4954 9334; www.mackayblacksbeachholidaypark.com.au; 16 Bourke St; unpowered/powered sites $30/35, villas $150-180; ℗❋☀) has good beachfront facilities, while Blue Pacific Resort (☑07-4954 9090; www.bluepacificresort.com.au; 26 Bourke St; d $114-152, unit $209-220; ❋ⓢ☀) is also beautifully located.

North of Dolphin Heads is Eimeo, where the Eimeo Pacific Hotel (☑07-4954 6805; www.eimeohotel.com.au; Mango Ave; mains $18.50-32.50; ⊙10am-10pm) is a great place for a sunset drink. Bucasia is across Sunset Bay from Eimeo and Dolphin Heads. Bucasia Beachfront Caravan Resort (☑07-4954 6375; www.bucasiabeach.com.au; 2 The Esplanade; powered sites $30-45; ❋☀) has a selection of sites, some with absolute beachfront views.

Sarina

POP 5730

Sarina is a sugar heartland 34km south of Mackay. It's a quiet place to stop on the Bruce Hwy, however the nearby coastline is worth a longer detour, especially the area around Sarina Beach and Armstrong Beach, which buzzes on weekends.

The Sarina Tourist Art & Craft Centre (☑07-4956 2251; Railway Sq, Bruce Hwy; ⊙9am-5pm) showcases locally made handicrafts and assists with visitor information.

Sarina Sugar Shed (☑07-4943 2801; www.sarinasugarshed.com.au; Railway Sq; adult/child $21/11; ⊙9am-4pm, tours 9.30am, 11am, 12.30pm & 2pm Mon-Sat) is the only miniature sugar-processing mill and distillery of its kind in Australia. After the tour, enjoy a complimentary tipple at the distillery.

Armstrong Beach Caravan Park (☑07-4956 2425; www.caravanpark.wixsite.com/armstrong beach; 66 Melba St; powered site per couple $32) is a very laid-back place with spacious sites.

Whatever you order at The Diner (11 Central St; mains $5-12; ⊙ 4am-6pm Mon-Fri, to 10am Sat), you'll get a plateful. Grills, sandwiches and burgers are popular; shakes, coffee and spiders wash it all down. Breakfast is popular with truck drivers.

Sarina Beach

On the shores of Sarina Inlet, this laid-back coastal village boasts a gorgeous, wide, long beach, a general store/service station and a boat ramp at the inlet. It's one of the best-looking beaches in the area with excellent opportunities for relaxing, fishing, beachcombing and spotting wildlife such as nesting marine turtles – but there are also warning signs for crocs.

Fernandos Hideaway (☑ 07-4956 6299; www.sarinabeachbb.com; 26 Captain Blackwood Dr; s/d/ste $130/140/160; ✳ ✖) is a hacienda-style B&B perched on a rugged headland near Sarina. It offers magnificent coastal views and absolute beachfront. In the living room there's a stuffed lion, a suit of armour and an eclectic assortment of souvenirs from the eccentric owners' global travels.

Eungella

Pretty little Eungella (*young*-gulluh; meaning 'land of clouds') sits perched 600m above sea level on the edge of the Pioneer Valley. It's the best-known town in the region and is synonymous with the magnificent Eungella National Park.

Lively markets are held on the first Sunday of each month (April to December) from 9am at the town hall.

The three, neat, self-contained wooden cabins at **Eungella Mountain Edge Escape** (☑ 07-4958 4590; www.mountainedgeescape.com. au; North St; 1-/2-bedroom cabin $120/140; ✳) form a wonderful vantage point for appreciating Eungella.

Eungella Chalet (☑ 07-4958 4509; www. eungellachalet.com.au; Chelmer St; r from $90, 1-/2-bedroom cabin $115/155; ✖) has a certain fading charm with basic hotel rooms and larger cabins out back. The pub food at the chalet dining room (mains $17-28; ⊙ 12-2pm & 6-8pm) is satisfactory.

There's basic camping at the self-registration **Explorers' Haven** (☑ 07-4958 4750; 32 North St; unpowered/powered site $25/30; @ ⌂).

Eungella National Park

Mystical, mountainous Eungella National Park covers nearly 500 sq km of the lofty Clarke Range, but is largely inaccessible except for the walking tracks around Broken River and Finch Hatton Gorge. The large tracts of tropical and subtropical vegetation have been isolated from other rainforest areas for thousands of years and now boast several unique species, including the orange-sided skink and the charming Eungella gastric-brooding frog, which incubates its eggs in its stomach and gives birth by spitting out the tadpoles.

Finch Hatton Gorge

Finch Hatton Gorge is a remarkable, prehistoric place set in a rugged subtropical rainforest. Hills of farmland disappear into a lush gorge dotted with volcanic boulders and buzzing with bird and insect life. It can feel like you've stepped through a geographical black hole into another physical dimension.

A gorgeous 1.6km walking trail leads to Araluen Falls, with its tumbling waterfalls and swimming holes, and a further 1km hike takes you to the Wheel of Fire Falls, another cascade with a deep swimming hole. Both these falls tend to be busy with locals on weekends.

Rainforest Scuba (☑ 0434 455 040; www. rainforestscuba.com; 55 Anzac Pde, Finch Hatton) claims the dubious title as the world's first rainforest dive operator; submerge in crystal-clear creeks where eels, platypus, turtles and fish share the habitat.

A brilliantly fun and informative way to explore the rainforest here is to glide through the canopy with **Forest Flying** (☑ 07-4958 3359; www.forestflying.com; $60). The sky-high guided tours see you harnessed to a 350m-long cable and suspended up to 25m above the ground; you control your speed via a pulley system.

Platypus Bushcamp (☑ 07-4958 3204; www.bushcamp.net; Finch Hatton Gorge; sites/dm/ huts $7.50/25/75; ✖) ✎ is a true-blue bush retreat hand-built by Wazza, the eccentric owner. The three basic huts are surrounded by rainforest. A creek with platypuses and great swimming holes runs next to the camp, and the big, open-air communal kitchen and eating area is the heart of the place.

For a peaceful sleep, stay at Finch Hatton Gorge Cabins (07-4958 3281; www.finch hattongorgecabins.com.au; cabins $155;), set in enchanting subtropical surrounds, with a creek nearby.

Broken River

Cool and sometimes misty, Broken River is worth a detour inland from Mackay for its high-elevation rainforest where hilly cattle ranches house some very happy cows and prolific bird life. Broken River has some of the best walking tracks in the region and you may spot a few marsupials hiding in the brush.

Fern Flat Camping Ground (www.npsr. qld.gov.au/camping; sites per person/family $6.15/24.60) is a lovely place to camp, with shady sites adjacent to the river where the platypuses play. This is a walk-in camping ground and is not vehicle accessible but it's an easy 500m past the information centre and kiosk. Register online.

Crediton Hall Camping Ground (www.npsr.qld.gov.au; sites per person/family $6.15/24.60), 3km after Broken River, is accessible to vehicles. Turn left into Crediton Loop Rd and turn right after the Wishing Pool circuit track entrance.

Non-campers should head to the Broken River Mountain Resort (07-4958 4000; www.brokenrivermr.com.au; d $140-200;), with cosy cedar cabins, ranging from small, motel-style units to a large self-contained lodge sleeping up to six. There's a cosy guest lounge with an open fire and the friendly Possums Table Restaurant & Bar (mains $25-35; breakfast & dinner).

Getting There & Away

The park is 84km west of Mackay. There are no buses to Eungella or Finch Hatton, but Reeforest Adventure Tours (p183) runs day trips from Mackay and will drop off and pick up those who want to linger; however, tours don't run every day so your stay may wind up being longer than intended.

Cumberland Islands

There are about 70 islands in the Cumberland group, sometimes referred to as the southern Whitsundays. Almost all the islands are designated national parks. Brampton Island is well-known for its nature walks, and will soon be home to a 'seven-star' resort. Facilities on all islands, aside

from Keswick Island, are very limited and access can be difficult unless you have your own boat or can afford to charter one (or a seaplane); ask for more info at the Mackay visitor centre (p186).

Keswick Island Campground (1300 889 290; unpowered sites from $20, ste from $80) has a number of unpowered sites within a very easy walking distance of pristine Basil Bay and is a real secret among the camping community.

The Beach House (1300 889 290; www. keswickisland.com.au; 6 Coral Passage Dr, Keswick Island; houses $275) is a good way to enjoy Keswick's beauty without any hassle. The modern, stylish property sleeps six comfortably and has direct beach access to Basil Bay.

Cape Hillsborough National Park

Cape Hillsborough National Park would be a must-visit in many parts of the world, but around these parts, nature lovers are spoiled for choice. Still, this semi-remote bush scrub falling into the sea some 50km north of Mackay is worthy of more serious attention. On the marvellous walking trails through the headlands, you may spot kangaroos, wallabies and sugar gliders. Turtles are common close to shore, and roos might be seen on the beach in the evening and early morning.

The park features rough cliffs, a broad beach, rocky headlands, sand dunes, mangroves, hoop pines and rainforest. There are also the remains of Aboriginal middens and stone fish traps, accessible by good walking tracks. On the approach to the foreshore area there's also an interesting boardwalk leading out through a tidal mangrove forest. Recent renovations have made it easier to negotiate the area on your own.

Smalleys Beach Campground (www. nprsr.qld.gov.au; site per person/family $6.15/24.60) is a small, pretty and grassed camping ground hugging the foreshore and absolutely jumping with kangaroos. There's no self-registration here; book permits online.

Cape Hillsborough Nature Resort (07-4959 0152; www.capehillsboroughresort. com.au; 51 Risley Pde; unpowered/powered site $29/34, cabin $80-265;) is popular with families from Mackay and grey nomads from way further south.

THE WHITSUNDAYS

Seen from above, the Whitsundays are like a stunning organism under the microscope. Indigo, aqua, yellow and bottle-green cellular blobs mesmerise the senses. Sheltered by the Great Barrier Reef, the waters are particularly perfect for sailing. Seen from afloat in the Coral Sea, any of the 74 islands will hypnotise on approach and leave you giddy with good fortune.

Some of the oldest archaeological sites on the east coast are found here and you can only imagine the displeasure of the Ngaro people at losing such land to sawmills and force.

Five of the islands have resorts but most are uninhabited, and several offer back-to-nature beach camping and bushwalking. Whitehaven Beach is the finest beach in the Whitsundays and, many claim, the world. Airlie Beach, on the mainland, is the coastal hub and major gateway to the islands, where you can book myriad tours and activities, or just party hard.

Activities

Sailing & Cruising

Atlantic Clipper BOATING
(www.atlanticclipper.com.au; 2-day, 2-night trips from $460) Young, beautiful and boozy crowd...and there's no escaping the antics. Snorkelling (or recovering) on Langford Island is a highlight.

Derwent Hunter BOATING
(☑1800 334 773; www.tallshipadventures.com.au; day trips $195) A deservedly popular sailing safari on a beautiful timber gaff-rigged schooner. A good option for couples and those more keen on wildlife than the wild life.

SV Domino BOATING
(www.aussieyachting.com; day trips $180) Takes a maximum of eight guests to Bali Hai Island, a little-visited 'secret' of the Whitsundays. Includes lunch and a good two-hour snorkel. The boat is also available for custom, private charters.

Prima Sailing BOATING
(☑0447 377 150; www.primasailing.com.au; 2-day, 2-night tours from $390) Fun tours with a 12-person maximum. Ideal for couples chasing style and substance.

Whitehaven Xpress BOATING
(☑07-4946 1585; www.whitehavenxpress.com.au; day trips $160) Various boat excursions, but best known for its daily trip to Whitehaven Beach.

Diving

Most dives in this area visit the easy-to-reach fringing reefs around the Whitsundays, but you can also dive further afield on the Great Barrier Reef.

Costs for open-water courses with several ocean dives start at around $900. **Whitsunday Diving Academy** (☑1300 348 464; www.whitsundaydivingacademy.com.au; 2579 Shute Harbour Rd, Jubilee Pocket) is a good place to start.

A number of sailing cruises include diving as an optional extra. Prices start from $95 for introductory or certified dives. Ferry operator Cruise Whitsundays (p193) offers dives (from $119) on day trips to its reef pontoon.

Most of the island resorts also have dive schools and free snorkelling gear.

Kayaking

Paddling with dolphins and turtles is one of the best ways to experience the Whitsundays. **Salty Dog Sea Kayaking** (☑07-4946 1388; www.saltydog.com.au; Shute Harbour; half-/full-day trips $80/130) offers guided tours and kayak rental ($50/80 per half-/full day), plus a brilliant six-day kayak and camping expedition ($1650) that's suitable for beginners.

TOP BEACHES

The Whitsundays boast some of the finest beaches in a country full of them. Our top picks:

Whitehaven Beach (p199) With azure-blue waters lapping the pure-white, silica sand, Whitehaven on Whitsunday Island is absolutely stunning.

Chalkies Beach Opposite Whitehaven Beach, on Haslewood Island, this is another idyllic, white-sand beach.

Langford Island At high tide, Langford is a thin strip of sand on the rim of a ludicrously picturesque coral-filled turquoise lagoon.

Butterfly Bay On the northern side of Hook Island is this protected bay, which flutters with butterfly song each winter.

Catseye Beach (p198) Hamilton Island's Catseye Beach is a busy-ish spot by Whitsunday standards, but its palm-shaded sand and turquoise waters are social-media ready.

Whitsunday Islands

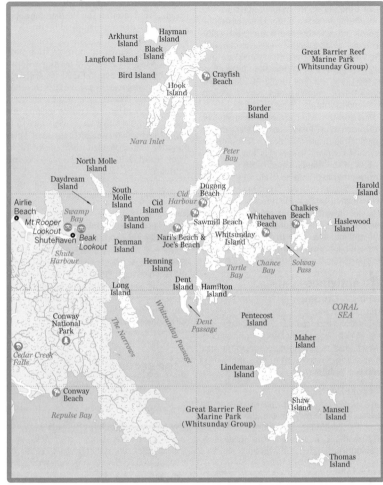

☞ Tours

Ocean Rafting
BOATING

(☎07-4946 6848; www.oceanrafting.com.au; adult/child/family from $134/87/399) Visit the 'wild' side of the islands in a very fast, big yellow speedboat. Swim at Whitehaven Beach, regain your land legs with a guided national park walk, or snorkel the reef at Mantaray Bay and Border Island.

Ecojet Safari
TOURS

(☎07-4948 2653; tours per person $195) Explore the islands, mangroves and marine life of the northern Whitsundays on these three-, hour, small-group jet-ski safaris (two people per jet ski).

Big Fury
BOATING

(☎07-4948 2201; www.magicwhitsundays.com; adult/child/family $130/70/350) Speed out to Whitehaven Beach on an open-air sports boat, and follow up with lunch and snorkelling at a secluded reef nearby. Great value and bookable through Airlie Beach travel agencies.

HeliReef
SCENIC FLIGHTS

(☎07-4946 9102; www.helireef.com.au) Scenic helicopter flights from $135.

📖 Sleeping

NPRSR (www.nprsr.qld.gov.au) manages the Whitsunday Islands National Park camping grounds on several islands for both independent campers as well as groups on commercial trips. Camping permits ($6.15/24.60 per person/family) are available online or at the **NPRSR booking office** (☑13 74 68; www. npsr.qld.gov.au; cnr Shute Harbour & Mandalay Rds; ⊙9am-4.30pm Mon-Fri) in Airlie Beach.

You must be self-sufficient and are advised to take 5L of water per person per day plus three days' extra supply in case you get stuck. You should also have a fuel stove as wood fires are banned on all islands.

Operated by **Whitsunday Island Camping Connections** (☑07-4946 6285; www.whit sundaycamping.com.au), the *Scamper* leaves from Shute Harbour and can drop you at South Molle, Denman or Planton Islands ($65 return); Whitsunday Island ($105 return); Whitehaven Beach ($155 return); and Hook Island ($160 return).

❶ Getting There & Away

AIR

The two main airports for the Whitsundays are at Hamilton Island and Proserpine (Whitsunday Coast). Airlie Beach is home to the small Whitsunday Airport, about 6km from town.

Jetstar (☑13 15 38; www.jetstar.com.au) flies to Proserpine from Melbourne and Brisbane, while Virgin flies to/from Brisbane. Tiger runs from Sydney to Proserpine; **Qantas** (☑13 13 13; www. qantas.com.au), Jetstar and Virgin all service Hamilton Island from major Australian cities.

BUS

Greyhound (☑1300 473 946; www.greyhound. com.au) and **Premier** (☑13 34 10; www. premierms.com.au) detour off the Bruce Hwy to Airlie Beach. **Whitsunday Transit** (☑07-4946 1800; www.whitsundaytransit.com.au) connects Proserpine, Cannonvale, Abel Point, Airlie Beach and Shute Harbour.

Whitsundays 2 Everywhere (☑07-4946 4940; www.whitsundaytransfers.com) operates airport transfers from both Whitsunday Coast (Proserpine) and Mackay Airports to Airlie Beach.

Proserpine

POP 3875

There's no real reason to linger in this industrial sugar-mill town, which is the turn-off point for Airlie Beach and the Whitsundays. However, it's worth stopping at the helpful **Whitsundays Region Information Centre**

(☑1300 717 407; www.whitsundaytourism.com; ⊙10am-5pm) just south of town for information about the Whitsundays and surrounding region.

If you do find yourself in Proserpine with time to spare, head to **Colour Me Crazy** (☑07-4945 2698; 2b Dobbins Lane; ⊙8.30am-5.30pm Mon-Fri, to 3.30pm Sat, 9.30am-2.30pm Sun), an eye-popping labyrinth of out-there jewellery, clothing and homewares. Who knew there were so many uses for sequins?

Airlie Beach

POP 9165

Aside from being the obvious departure point for most trips to the unparalleled Whitsunday Islands, Airlie Beach has long been a destination par excellence on the east coast road-trip and binge-drink adventure trail. Its multiple hostels and massive beer gardens sit opposite a lawn-surrounded swimming lagoon where nothing much happens but the passing of carefree youth.

Sure, there's the relatively new Port of Airlie marina, with its faux-sophisticated hotel and restaurant complex, as well as the town's impressive sailing pedigree, but the heart of Airlie still beats to the rhythm of unskilled sailors, taking to the sparkling seas and jungle-clad isles with bleary-eyed wonder.

🏊 Activities

Lagoon   SWIMMING
(Shute Harbour Rd) **FREE** Take a dip year-round in the stinger-croc-and-tropical-nasties-free lagoon in the centre of town.

Red Cat Adventures   BOATING
(☑1300 653 100, 07-4940 2000; www.redcatad ventures.com.au) Excellent family-owned operation with three distinct crafts and tours. Our pick is the Ride to Paradise ($569), a two-night adventure to a 'secret' resort, as well as many highlights of the Whitsundays.

Airlie Beach Skydivers   SKYDIVING
(☑1300 759 348; www.airliebeachskydivers.com. au; 2/273 Shute Harbour Rd; 4270m jumps from $249) The only beach landing in Airlie Beach is provided by this passionate team with a shopfront on Shute Harbour Rd.

Skydive Airlie Beach   SKYDIVING
(☑07-4946 9115; www.skydive.com.au/airlie-beach; skydives from $199) Jump out of a plane from 1830m, 2440m or 4270m and land in front of the cafe set on Airlie Beach. Fabulous group

Airlie Beach

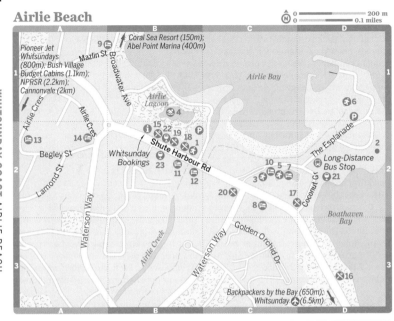

Airlie Beach

and there is not a more beautiful view in the world for a death-defying plummet.

Whitsunday Sailing Adventures BOATING
(07-4946 4999; www.whitsundayssailingadventures.com.au; The Esplanade) This well-connected agency can book seats on every sailing boat in town, plus a few decent dive operators.

Pioneer Jet Whitsundays BOATING
(1800 335 975; www.pioneerjet.com.au; Abel Point Marina; adult/child $69/49) The Ultimate

Bay Blast is a thunderous 30-minute spin in a jetboat. Fun and informative guides roundoff the experience. Expect to get very wet.

Just Tuk'n Around GUIDED TOUR
(www.justtuknaround.com.au; tours per person $30) Fun and informative 30-minute tours around the 'secrets' of Airlie Beach reveal more than you'd think possible in a small coastal town.

Lady Enid BOATING
(☎0407 483 000; www.ladyenid.com.au; boat trips from $225) High-end bespoke sailing trips for couples aboard a heritage yacht.

Illusions BOATING
(☎0455 142 021; www.illusion.net.au; day tours $125) A 12m catamaran that offers the least expensive, yet consistently good, sailing tours to the islands.

Solway Lass BOATING
(☎1800 355 377; www.solwaylass.com; 3-day, 3-night trips from $589) You get a full three days and nights on this 28m tall ship – the only authentic tall ship in Airlie Beach. Popular with backpackers.

Whitsunday Sailing Club BOATING
(☎07-4946 6138; www.whitsundaysailingclub.com.au; Airlie Point) The heart of the Airlie Beach Race Week is a family-friendly club and an authentic introduction to the town's nautical scene.

Explore Whitsundays SAILING
(☎07-4946 5782; www.explorewhitsundays.com; 4 The Esplanade; 2-day, 1-night trips from $359) Inexpensive but well-run trips with a variety of options offered across a few vessels, each with its own ambience. Generally geared towards the backpacker set.

Tours

Cruise Whitsundays CRUISE
(☎07-4846 70602; www.cruisewhitsundays.com; Shingley Dr, Abel Point Marina; full-day cruises from $99) As well as operating a ferry to the Whitsunday Islands, Cruise Whitsundays offers trips to Hardy Reef, Whitehaven Beach and islands, including Daydream and Long. Or grab a daily Island Hopper pass (adult/child $125/65) and make your own itinerary. It also operates a popular day trip aboard the *Camira* ($195).

Air Whitsunday SCENIC FLIGHTS
(☎07-4946 9111; www.airwhitsunday.com.au; Terminal 1, Whitsunday Airport) Offers a range of tours, including day trips to Whitehaven ($255) and scenic-flight-plus-snorkelling tours of the Great Barrier Reef ($375).

Whitsunday Crocodile Safari TOURS
(☎07-4948 3310; www.crocodilesafari.com.au; adult/child $120/60) Spy on wild crocs, explore secret estuaries and eat real bush tucker.

Courses

Maritime & Sailing Training Centre BOATING
(☎07-4946 6710; www.maritimetrainingcentre.com.au) Respected training provider offering sailing courses for those looking to explore further than the norm.

Festivals & Events

Airlie Beach Race Week SAILING
(www.airlieraceweek.com; ⊙Aug) The town's sailing pedigree is tested every August when sailors from across the world descend on Airlie for the town's annual regatta.

Airlie Beach Music Festival MUSIC
(www.airliebeachfestivalofmusic.com.au; ⊙Nov) This festival has really taken off since its inception into the Whitsunday social calendar back in 2012. Party to three days of Australian and international rock, folk and electronic music, with plenty of local talent on show.

Sleeping

Airlie Beach is a backpacker haven, but with so many hostels, standards vary and bedbugs are a common problem. There is also a remarkable variety of midrange accommodation particularly suitable for families. Not a lot at the very top end though.

★ **Kipara** RESORT $
(☎07-4946 6483; www.kipara.com.au; 2614 Shute Harbour Rd; r/cabins/villas from $85/105/130; ❄@🛜🏊) Tucked away in the lush, green environs of Jubilee Pocket, this budget resort makes it easy to forget you're only 2km from the frenzy of town (it's next to the bus stop so you don't need a car). It's mega-clean and offers outstanding value, with helpful staff, cooking facilities and regular wildlife visits – one of Airlie's best options. Huge discounts available online. There's a fab pool with surrounding deck.

★ **Sunlit Waters** APARTMENT $
(☎07-4946 6352; www.sunlitwaters.com; 20 Airlie Cres; studios from $95, 1-bedroom apt $115; ❄🛜🏊) Just so affordable for a tourist town like Airlie Beach! We expected the studio apartments to be tiny or rundown, but they are beautifully presented and have everything you need, including a self-contained kitchenette and stunning views from the long balconies. There's even a good swimming pool.

Flametree Tourist Village CARAVAN PARK $
(☎07-4946 9388; www.flametreevillage.com.au; 2955 Shute Harbour Rd; powered/unpowered sites

$40/30, cabins from $109; ✱@☎⛱) Our favourite camping ground and caravan park in the region has been thoroughly scrubbed up and is a top alternative to the chaos of Airlie Beach. Spacious sites are scattered through lovely, bird-filled gardens and there's a good camp kitchen and BBQ area. It's 6.5km west of Airlie.

Airlie Beach YHA   HOSTEL $

(☏ 07-4946 6312; www.yha.com.au; 394 Shute Harbour Rd; dm $33, d from $85; ✱@☎⛱) Trust YHA to provide a genuine alternative for young budget travellers to sordid hostels and inconvenient bush dumps. Central and reasonably quiet with a sparkling pool and great kitchen facilities, this is our favourite hostel in Airlie Beach, though the double rooms are pretty grim.

Airlie Waterfront Backpackers   HOSTEL $

(☏ 1800 089 000; www.airliewaterfront.com; 6 The Esplanade; dm/d from $22/74; ✱☎) Basic hostel, with coveted ocean views and a very central location. A little less hectic than other downtown options.

Bush Village Budget Cabins   HOSTEL $

(☏ 07-4946 6177, 1800 809 256; www.bushvillage. com.au; 2 St Martins Rd; dm from $33, d with/without bathroom from $97/82; P✱@☎⛱) Not for those looking for a party, this budget place suits travellers who have their own vehicle and enjoy having a village to return to after a long day on the reef or a night on the tiles. The dorms and doubles are in a clutch of self-contained cabins and it's licensed so you can sit and drink a beer by the pool. It's a five-minute walk to Abel Point Marina and about a half-hour stroll to central Airlie Beach. Reception closes early so communicate clearly.

Beaches Backpackers   HOSTEL $

(☏ 07-4946 6244; www.beaches.com.au; 356 Shute Harbour Rd; dm/d from $20/85; ✱@☎⛱) The hostel scene in Airlie is pretty fickle, but Beaches is consistent in its bubbly customer service and unwavering desire to crank the party to maximum (and fair enough given the awesomeness of the open-air bar). Dorms are sufficient, but could be cleaner.

Note that the hostel sustained some damage from Cyclone Debbie; check ahead that they are taking guests.

Backpackers by the Bay   HOSTEL $

(☏ 07-4946 7267; www.backpackersbythebay.com; 12 Hermitage Dr; dm $27, d & tw $83; ✱@☎⛱) About a 10-minute walk from Airlie's centre,

this hostel is very quiet, which will suit those who like to keep their party and their sleep separate. The small rooms are cleaned every second day, and there are hammocks strung around a good-sized pool. You'll need to head into Airlie to arrange tours.

Waterview   APARTMENT $$

(☏ 07-4948 1748; www.waterviewairliebeach.com. au; 42 Airlie Cres; studios from $140, 1-bedroom units from $155; ✱☎) Waterview's small units are an excellent choice for location and comfort. You can enjoy glimpses of the main street and gorgeous views of the bay. The rooms are modern, airy and spacious, and have kitchenettes for self-caterers. Top value for a couple in Airlie who can do without a pool.

Airlie Beach Hotel   HOTEL $$

(☏ 07-4964 1999; www.airliebeachhotel.com.au; cnr The Esplanade & Coconut Gr; motel r from $145, hotel r $195-295; ✱☎⛱) The ABH has seen it all in Airlie. The sea-facing hotel rooms are some of the best in town at this price point. With three restaurants and a bottle shop onsite and a perfect downtown location, you could do far worse than stay here.

The hotel was damaged during Cyclone Debbie and had to close temporarily: it is due to reopen in January 2018.

Coral Sea Resort   RESORT $$$

(☏ 07-4964 1300; www.coralsearesort.com; 25 Ocean View Ave; d from $275; ✱@☎⛱) Coral Sea Resort is an excellent option for families and older folk wanting quality service, spacious tiled rooms, and one of the best pool settings in Queensland. An easy stroll to the marina, it's located at the end of a low headland just west of the town centre. Many rooms have stunning views, but you'll save plenty of dosh by going for a garden view and then lingering poolside.

Airlie Waterfront B&B   B&B $$$

(☏ 07-4946 7631; http://airliewaterfrontbnb.com. au; cnr Broadwater Ave & Mazlin St; 1-/2-bedroom apt from $209/252; ✱@☎⛱) Karen and Malcolm are gregarious hosts at this misnamed property, which is more like a small resort. Views are superb from the position slightly above town, accessed by a five-minute stroll along the boardwalk. The two-bedroom apartments are the best value in town. Some rooms have a spa.

Heart Hotel and Gallery   BOUTIQUE HOTEL $$$

(☏ 1300 847 244; www.hearthotelwhitsundays. com.au; 277 Shute Harbour Rd; d $225-275, ste

DON'T MISS

SAILING THE WHITSUNDAYS

The Whitsundays are the place to skim across fantasy-blue waters on a tropical breeze. If you're flexible with dates, last-minute stand-by rates can considerably reduce the price and you'll have a better idea of weather conditions. Many travellers hang out in Airlie Beach for a few days for this exact purpose, although you may end up spending your savings in the pub!

Most vessels offer snorkelling on the fringing reefs, where the colourful soft corals are often more abundant than on the outer reef. Diving and other activities nearly always cost extra. Once you've decided, book at one of the many booking agencies in Airlie Beach.

Other than the superfast Camira, operated by Cruise Whitsundays (p193), sailing boats aren't able to make it all the way to destinations such as Whitehaven Beach on a day trip from Airlie Beach. Instead they usually go to the lovely Langford Reef and Hayman Island; check before booking.

Bareboat Sailing

Rent a boat without skipper, crew or provisions. You don't need formal qualifications, but you (or one of your party) have to prove that you can competently operate a vessel.

Expect to pay between $500 and $1000 a day in high season (September to January) for a yacht sleeping four to six people, plus a booking deposit and a security bond (refunded when the boat is returned undamaged). Most companies have a minimum hire period of five days.

There are a number of bareboat charter companies around Airlie Beach, including:

Charter Yachts Australia (☑ 1800 639 520; www.cya.com.au; Abel Point Marina; 4 people from $495)

Cumberland Charter Yachts (☑ 1800 075 101; www.ccy.com.au; Abel Point Marina)

Queensland Yacht Charters (☑ 1800 075 013; www.yachtcharters.com.au; Abel Point Marina)

Whitsunday Escape (☑ 1800 075 145; www.whitsundayescape.com; Abel Point Marina)

Whitsunday Rent A Yacht (☑ 1800 075 000; www.rentayacht.com.au; 6 Bay Tce, Shute Harbour)

Crewing

In return for a free bunk, meals and a sailing adventure, crewing will see you hoisting the mainsail and cleaning the head. Look for 'Crew Wanted' signs around the marina, and at restaurants and hotels. Your experience will depend on the vessel, skipper, other crew members (if any) and your own attitude. Be sure to let someone know where you're going, with whom and for how long. Aside from safety precautions, it may make them bitterly jealous.

$300-350) A brand-new luxury boutique hotel in the heart of Airlie. Architecturally inspired by early Queensland homes, the rooms are small but most are elegant. Good discounts online.

Eating

The strip facing the port at the new Port of Airlie is a good hunting ground for sophisticated, upmarket dining options, while downtown Airlie Beach has a mishmash of everything from cheap takeaway kebab shops to fancier restaurants with outdoor patios. There's a massive Woolworths supermarket (Shute Harbour Rd; ☺ 8am-9pm) conveniently located in the centre of town for self-caterers.

Harry's Corner CAFE **$**
(☑ 07-4946 7459; 273 Shute Harbour Rd; mains $7-18; ☺ 7am-3pm) Locals are wild about Harry's, which serves quaint European tea sets, Danish sandwiches, filled bagels and good-sized salads. The all-day breakfasts are a must for a hangover.

Wisdom Health Lab CAFE **$**
(1b/275 Shute Harbour Dr; toasties from $5.50, juices from $7; ☺ 7.30am-3.30pm; ☑) Mostly a takeaway place, this rightfully busy corner cafe does have a few indoor and outdoor tables. It serves healthy toasties, sandwiches (including lots of vegetarian options such as a tasty lentil burger), and a huge array of fresh smoothies and juices.

★ Mr Bones
PIZZA $$

(☑0413 017 331; Lagoon Plaza, 263 Shute Harbour Rd; shared plates $12-17, pizzas $15-23; ☺9am-9pm Tue-Sat) Carefully curated play lists and creative thin-based pizzas have made Mr Bones the coolest place to eat in Airlie since it opened six years ago. Overlooking the lagoon, the small, sunny restaurant also has an extensive 'not pizzas' menu of appetisers to play around with. Service is upbeat and interested. Great coffee, too.

Airlie Beach Treehouse
MODERN AUSTRALIAN $$

(☑07-4946 5550; www.airlietreehouse.com; 6/263-265 Shute Harbour Rd; mains $18-36; ☺8.30am-9.30pm) This new restaurant by the lagoon is making ripples for its uncomplicated service and quality food in a shady setting.

Denman Cellars Beer Cafe
TAPAS $$

(☑07-4948 1333; Shop 15, 33 Port Dr; tapas $10, mains $18-38; ☺11am-10pm Mon-Fri, 8am-11pm Sat & Sun) Regular live music and a convivial mood are found in this tapas bar that stocks more boutique beers – 700 brews! – than the rest of the town combined. The food – such as a shared seafood platter ($57), and 'beer bites' such as zucchini balls ($14) and duck pancakes ($17) – is decent. Larger meals are available.

Fish D'vine
SEAFOOD $$

(☑07-4948 0088; 303 Shute Harbour Rd; mains $17-33; ☺5pm-late) Pirates were definitely onto something: this fish-and-rum bar is shiploads of fun, serving up all things nibbly from Neptune's realm and lashings and lashings of rum (over 200 kinds of the stuff). Yo-ho-ho! Sport eaters can take on the 'Seafood Indulgence', a mountain of shells and claws for a whopping $149.

Village Cafe
CAFE $$

(☑07-4946 5745; 366 Shute Harbour Rd; mains $15-34; ☺7.30am-9.30pm) Interactive dining is a lot of fun at the very popular Village Cafe, where you sizzle your own meal on a volcanic slab. The massive breakfasts are popular with reef crews getting ready to set sail.

🍷 Drinking & Nightlife

It's said that Airlie Beach is a drinking town with a sailing problem. The bars at Magnums (☑07-4964 1199, 1800 624 634; www.magnums.com.au; 366 Shute Harbour Rd; camp sites/van sites $24/26, dm/d from $24/56; ❄@🛜) and Beaches (p194), the two big backpackers in the centre of town, are always crowded, and are popular places to kick off a ribald evening.

Mama Africa
CLUB

(263 Shute Harbour Rd; ☺9pm-5am) Mama's is a jumping African-style safari nightclub throbbing with a beat that both hunter and prey find hard to resist. Themed nights and all kinds of promotions aimed at the backpacker party set ensure spontaneous all-nighters any day of the week.

Just Wine & Cheese
WINE BAR

(Shop 8, 33 Port Dr; wines by the glass $7-18; ☺3-10pm) Run by two astute wine aficionados, this glamorous bottle shop and bar serves fine examples of what it promises, with a view of the Port of Airlie marina.

Paddy's Shenanigans
IRISH PUB

(352 Shute Harbour Rd; ☺5pm-3am) Live music every night, but otherwise the usual sports-watching, hard-drinking venue.

ⓘ CYCLONE WARNING

In Queensland's far north, between November and April each year, cyclones – known in the northern hemisphere as hurricanes – are a part of life, with an average of four or five forming each season. It's rare for these cyclones to escalate into full-blown destructive storms; however, in March 2017 Severe Tropical Cyclone Debbie made landfall near Airlie Beach, causing significant damage and flooding in South East Queensland and the Northern Rivers area of New South Wales. Airlie Beach and Bowen were affected as well.

Bringing torrential rain, strong winds and ferocious seas, the storm killed at least twelve people in Australia, primarily as a result of extreme flooding. At the time of writing the clean-up was in full swing. We recommend checking ahead before you travel to ensure that accommodation is available and confirm the state of the beaches.

During the season, keep a sharp ear out for cyclone predictions and alerts. If a cyclone watch or warning is issued, stay tuned to local radio and monitor the Bureau of Meteorology website (www.bom.gov.au) for updates and advice. Locals tend to be complacent about cyclones, but will still buy out the bottle shop when a threat is imminent!

ℹ Information

Whitsunday Bookings (🖉 07-4948 2201; www.whitsundaybooking.com.au; 346 Shute Harbour Rd) Tina has been helping travellers book the right tour for years. For a while this office was even the default tourist information office, although now it looks like many of the other information booking centres along the strip.

Whitsundays Central Reservation Centre (🖉 1800 677 119; www.airliebeach.com; 259 Shute Harbour Rd) can take the hassle out of finding the right accommodation.

ℹ Getting There & Away

AIR

The closest major airports are Whitsunday Coast (Proserpine) and Hamilton Island.

Whitsunday Airport (🖉 07-4946 9180) is a small airfield 6km east of Airlie Beach, midway between Airlie Beach and Shute Harbour.

BOAT

Transfers between the **Port of Airlie** (www.portofairlie.com.au) and Hamilton, Daydream and Long Islands are provided by Cruise Whitsundays (p193).

BUS

Greyhound (🖉 1300 473 946; www.greyhound.com.au) and **Premier Motor Service** (🖉 13 34 10; www.premierms.com.au) buses detour off the Bruce Hwy to Airlie Beach. There are buses between Airlie Beach and all of the major centres along the coast, including Brisbane ($248, 19 hours), Mackay ($31, two hours), Townsville ($49, four hours) and Cairns ($100, nine hours).

Long-distance buses stop on the Esplanade, between the sailing club and the Airlie Beach Hotel.

Whitsunday Transit (🖉 07-4946 1800; www.whitsundaytransit.com.au) connects Proserpine (Whitsunday Airport), Cannonvale, Abel Point, Airlie Beach and Shute Harbour. There are several stops along Shute Harbour Rd.

Conway National Park

There's enough diverse beauty in Conway National Park to lure travellers to Airlie Beach away from the Whitsundays, deep into the rainforest hills and remote beaches that were once the hunting grounds of the Giru Dala. The mountains of this national park and the Whitsunday Islands are part of the same coastal mountain range. Rising sea levels following the last ice age flooded the lower valleys, leaving only the highest peaks as islands, now cut off from the mainland.

Several walking trails start from near the picnic and day-use area. Further along the main road, towards Coral Point and before Shute Harbour, there's a 1km track leading down to Coral Beach and the Beak lookout.

About 1km past the day-use area, there's a 2.4km walk up to the Mt Rooper lookout, with good views of the Whitsunday Passage and islands.

To reach the beautiful Cedar Creek Falls, turn off the Proserpine–Airlie Beach road on to Conway Rd, 18km southwest of Airlie Beach. It's then about 15km to the falls; the roads are well signposted.

Long Island

Long Island has secluded, pretty white beaches, lots of adorable wild rock wallabies and 13km of walking tracks.

Camp at Long Island's Sandy Bay (www.nprsr.qld.gov.au; sites per person/family $6.15/24.60).

Palm Bay Resort (🖉 1300 655 126; www.palmbayresort.com.au; villas/bures/bungalows from $229/249/329) is Long Island's luxury self-catering resort where guests can choose from a variety of secluded housing options. The pool is huge and the camaraderie between guests is understated given there is no dining area. The resort store sells gourmet groceries and a rustic bar provides the booze. If you want your own supplies delivered, contact Whitsundays Provisions (🖉 07-4946 7344; www.whitprov.com.au). This is a model for sustainable tourism that could have some legs.

Cruise Whitsundays (🖉 07-4946 4662; www.cruisewhitsundays.com) connects Palm Bay Resort to the Port of Airlie by frequent daily services ($48 each way).

Hook Island

The 53-sq-km Hook Island, the second-largest island in the Whitsundays group, is mostly national park and rises to 450m at Hook Peak. There are a number of good beaches dotted around the island, and some of the region's best diving and snorkelling locations.

There are national park camping grounds (www.npsr.qld.gov.au; sites per person/family $6.15/24.60) at Maureen Cove, Steen's Beach, Curlew Beach and Crayfish Beach. Although basic, they provide some wonderful back-to-nature opportunities.

South Molle Island

The largest of the Molle group of islands at 4 sq km, South Molle is virtually joined to Mid and North Molle Islands. Apart from the private residence area and golf course at Bauer Bay in the north, the island is all national park and is criss-crossed by 15km of walking tracks, with some superb lookout points.

There are national park **camping grounds** (☏13 74 68; www.npsr.qld.gov.au; sites per person/family $6.15/24.60) at Sandy Bay in the south, and at Paddle Bay near the resort.

Daydream Island

Daydream Island is the closest resort to the mainland and perfectly located to attract the tourist hordes. At just over 1km long and 200m wide, the island can be explored in an hour or two; one strength is its marine biology program, which allows visitors to encounter much of the region's wildlife in a short space of time. Unfortunately, it does feel overwhelming at times, more sterile than natural. Recently sold to an investment group that plans to make it a 'luxury' destination, it will likely retain its popularity as a day-trip destination and is suitable for everybody, especially busy families, or travellers with little time to explore the 'real' Whitsundays. Damage from Cyclone Debbie in early 2017 has meant the redevelopment has been brought forward. The resort is expected to reopen in 2018.

Daydream Island Resort & Spa (☏1800 075 040; www.daydreamisland.com; d from $245; ❋ 🛜 🌊) has a monopoly on the accommodation on the island, so you might expect some shoddy efforts but they know their clientele – families with kids, cautious international travellers and time-poor holiday-makers – and understand the buzz generated by the location alone. Rooms are reasonably priced and many face out to the glorious Coral Sea. Tennis courts, a gym, catamarans, windsurfing, three swimming pools and an open-air cinema are all included in the tariff. There's also a club with constant activities to keep children occupied.

Hamilton Island

POP 1346

Welcome to a little slice of resort paradise where the paved roads are plied with golf buggies, steep, rocky hills are criss-crossed by walking trails, and the white beaches are buzzing with water-sports action. Though it's not everyone's idea of a perfect getaway, it's hard not to be impressed by the selection of high-end accommodation, restaurants, bars and activities – if you've got the cash, there's something for everyone.

Day trippers can use some resort facilities – including tennis courts, a golf driving range and a minigolf course – and enjoy the island on a relatively economical budget.

A few shops by the harbour organise dives and certificate courses, and just about everyone can sign you up for a variety of cruises to other islands and the outer reef.

If you only have time for one walk, make it the clamber up to Passage Peak (239m) on the northeastern corner of the island.

🛏 Sleeping & Eating

⭐ **Qualia**   RESORT $$$
(☏1300 780 959; www.qualia.com.au; d from $1100; ❋ @ 🛜 🌊) Stunning, ultraluxe Qualia is set on 30 secluded acres, with modern villas materialising like heavenly tree houses in the leafy hillside. The resort has a private beach, two restaurants, a spa and two swimming pools. It remains our favourite luxury resort for miles.

Reef View Hotel   HOTEL $$$
(☏02-9007 0009; www.hamiltonisland.com.au/reef-view-hotel; d from $370; ❋ @ 🌊) Aptly named, this hilltop resort has spectacular views over the green hills out to turquoise seas. It's central and popular with families and groups. It's a slightly more manageable price for long-ish stays, and the mood is more low-key.

Whitsunday Holiday Homes   APARTMENT $$$
(☏13 73 33; www.hihh.com.au; from $320; ❋ @ 🛜 🌊) Private accommodation ranging from three-star apartments to family-friendly houses and five-star luxury digs. Rates include your own golf buggy for highbrow hooning. There's a four-night minimum stay in some properties.

Popeye's Fish n' Chips   FISH & CHIPS $
(Front St; fish & chips $11.50; ⊙10am-9pm Sun-Thu, 11.30am-9pm Fri & Sat) Massive boxes of fish and chips that can comfortably feed two people. Also sells burgers, chicken...and fishing bait.

Manta Ray Cafe   CAFE $$
(☏07-4946 8213; Marina Village; mains $17-30; ⊙10.30am-9pm) Wood-fired gourmet pizzas are a favourite here, but you can also settle in for an afternoon of drinks and oysters. It's popular with families and day visitors.

Romano's ITALIAN $$$

(🖉 07-4946 8212; Marina Village; mains $33-40; ☺ 6pm-midnight Thu-Mon) Popular Italian restaurant with a large enclosed deck jutting out over the water.

Drinking & Nightlife

Marina Tavern PUB

(🖉 07-4946 8839; Marina Village; mains from $17.50; ☺ 11am-midnight) The food is not the reason to come here. Stick with the beer and cocktails and indulge in some people-watchng.

Getting There & Away

AIR

Hamilton Island Airport is the main arrival centre for the Whitsundays, and is serviced by **Qantas** (🖉 13 13 13; www.qantas.com.au), **Jetstar** (🖉 13 15 38; www.jetstar.com.au) and **Virgin** (🖉 13 67 89; www.virginaustralia.com.au).

BOAT

Cruise Whitsundays (🖉 07-4946 4662; www.cruisewhitsundays.com) Connects Hamilton Island Airport and the marina with the Port of Airlie in Airlie Beach ($48).

Hayman Island

The most northern of the Whitsunday group, little Hayman is just 4 sq km in area and rises to 250m above sea level. It has forested hills, valleys and beaches, and a luxury five-star resort. Hayman Island has long been a stage for the lifestyles of the rich and famous. It is Australia's most celebrated island resort, first conceived by an airline magnate, and ever since then the enviable playground of celebrities and dignitaries of every stripe. Sadly, the average punter will have to settle for the other 73 islands; Hayman is for resort guests only.

An avenue of stately date palms leads to the entrance of One&Only Hayman Island Resort (🖉 07-4940 1838; www.hayman.com.au; r incl breakfast $730-12,300; ❈ @ 🛜 ⛤) – one of the most gilded playgrounds on the Great Barrier Reef, with its hectare of swimming pools (open around the clock), landscaped gardens and exclusive boutiques. The rooms vary from well-appointed poolside cabins to deluxe three-bedroom suites and stand-alone villas; all are huge.

Resort guests must first fly to Hamilton Island Airport, before being escorted to Hayman's fleet of luxury cruisers for a pampered transfer to the resort.

Lindeman Island

Situated 15km southeast of the luxurious Hamilton Island, Lindeman was once a flashy resort but has since been returned to nature by liquidators. For the past decade, only nature photographers and hikers have provided any semblance of bustle, making independent treks for the varied island tree life and the sublime view from Mt Oldfield (210m). The mood is poised to change, however, as a $600 million redevelopment is set to commence in 2017. Lindeman is still mostly national park, with empty bays and 20km of impressive walking trails. Get here while you can.

Boat Port (sites per person/family $6.15/24.60) is an open camp site on a sandy beach area backed by rainforest. There are basic toilet and picnic facilities. It was once a bay used to clean sailing vessels, hence the name.

Whitsunday Island

Long proclaimed by talking heads of tourism as one of Australia's most beautiful beaches, Whitehaven Beach, on Whitsunday Island, is a pristine 7km-long stretch of blinding sand (at 98% pure silica, the sand is some of the whitest in the world), bounded by lush tropical vegetation and a brilliant blue sea. From Hill Inlet at the northern end of the beach, the swirling pattern of dazzling sand through the turquoise and aquamarine water paints a magical picture. There's excellent snorkelling from its southern end.

There are national park camping grounds (sites per person/family $6.15/24/60) at Dugong, Nari's and Joe's Beaches in the west; at Chance Bay in the south; at the southern end of Whitehaven Beach; and Peter Bay in the north.

Other Whitsunday Islands

The northern islands are undeveloped and seldom visited by cruise boats or water taxis. Several of these – Gloucester, Saddleback and Armit Islands – have national park camping grounds.

Bona Bay on Gloucester Island has the largest campground (🖉 13 74 68; www.npsr.qld.gov.au; sites per adult/family $6.15/24.60), with toilets, picnic tables and good shelter. Armit Island's basic campground has a toilet and picnic tables, while Saddleback's is modest, close to the mainland and has picnic tables.

Bowen

POP 9277

Bowen is a small coastal town set on a hill just north of Airlie Beach, and is famous for its mangoes – Bowen gets busy during fruit-picking season – but known locally for its secret bays and inlets. Its wide, quiet streets, wooden Queenslander houses and laid-back, friendly locals encourage a gentle pace of life. The foreshore, with its landscaped esplanade, picnic tables and BBQs, is a focal point, but there are some truly stunning – and little-visited – beaches and bays northeast of the town centre.

Keep an eye out for the 'Bowenwood' sign on the town's water tower; Baz Luhrmann's epic movie *Australia* was shot here in 2007 and the locals are still a little star-struck.

⌂ Sleeping & Eating

Bowen Backpackers   HOSTEL $
(☑ 07-4786 3433; www.bowenbackpackers.com.au; Herbert St; dm night/week from $40/190; ⌗@🛜) Located at the pretty beach end of Herbert St (past the Grandview Hotel), this is the place to stay if you're working in the surrounding fruit farms. New management has a stellar reputation around town. Rooms are neat and reasonably spacious.

Barnacles Backpackers   HOSTEL $
(☑ 07-4786 4400; www.barnaclesbackpackers.com; 18 Gordon St; dm from $30; 🛜) New management has taken over this 84-room hostel, which has close links to the fruit-picking industry. The communal areas have a clinical feel, but it's highly functional and quiet. Jury is out on the direction it will take, so listen to the backpacker grapevine for the latest.

Rose Bay Resort   RESORT $$
(☑ 07-4786 9000; www.rosebayresort.com.au; 2 Pandanus St; r $160-300; ⌗@🏊) Rose Bay is a seriously underrated beach, especially for snorkelling, and guests at this friendly resort have it pretty much all to themselves. Spacious studios and comfy units all sleep four guests comfortably. You'll need a car to reach the Bowen strip. Minimum two-night stay.

Jochheims Pies   BAKERY $
(49 George St; pies $5; ⊙5.30am-3.30pm Mon-Fri, to 12.30pm Sat) Jochheims has been keeping Bowen bellies full of homemade pies and baked treats since 1963. Try a Hugh Jackman (hunky beef) pie – the actor was a regular here during the filming of *Australia*.

Food Freaks   MODERN AUSTRALIAN $$
(☑ 07-4786 5133; mains $16-26; ⊙lunch & dinner) Bowen is not the coolest place in Queensland and this restaurant is not the hippest place you will eat in, but that's the way they like it – and the way we like it – eating mod-Oz creations overlooking the marina. Fresh, fast and delicious.

Cove   CHINESE, MALAY $$
(☑ 07-4791 2050; Coral Cove Apartments, Horseshoe Bay Rd; mains $17-28.50; ⊙lunch & dinner Tue-Sun) An unusually large Chinese and Thai restaurant with unbroken views of the Coral Sea from its timber deck. The menu features the usual Australian fusion entrees and mains; the service is excellent and there are extensive vegetarian and seafood dishes. Takeaway is available.

♟ Drinking & Nightlife

Grand View Hotel   PUB
(☑ 07-4786 4022; www.grandviewhotelbowen.com; 5 Herbert St) Recently renovated but still high on the hill, the grand old Grand View is a ripping Aussie pub with a rocking beer garden and loads of memorabilia (including from Baz Lurhman's *Australia*). The restaurant looks promising, but it's very easy to forget to eat when you're nursing a pint in the late afternoon sunshine.

ⓘ Information

There's a friendly **information booth** (Santa Barbara Pde; ⊙10am-5pm Mon-Fri, hours vary Sat & Sun) in town and a **visitor centre** (☑ 07-4786 4222; www.tourismbowen.com.au; ⊙8.30am-5pm Mon-Fri, 10.30am-5pm Sat & Sun) 7km south of Bowen on the Bruce Hwy (look for the humongous mango). Both sell big scoops of Bowen mango sorbet.

ⓘ Getting There & Away

Greyhound (☑1300 473 946; www.greyhound.com.au) and **Premier** (☑13 34 10; www.premierms.com.au) are two companies that have frequent bus services running to/from Airlie Beach ($26, 1½ hours) and Townsville ($29, four hours).

SUPERJOSEPH / SHUTTERSTOCK ©

The Great Barrier Reef

Each year, more than 1.5 million visitors come to this World Heritage–listed area that stretches across 2000km of coastline. Diving and snorkelling are just some of the ways to experience this wonderful and rich ecosystem. There's also sailing, scenic flights and idyllic days exploring the reef's gateway towns and stunning islands.

Contents
➡ **Gateways to the Reef**
➡ **Top Reef Encounters**
➡ **Nature's Theme Park**

Above Aerial view of the Great Barrier Reef

Gateways to the Reef

There are numerous ways to approach Australia's massive undersea kingdom. You can head to a popular gateway town and join an organised tour, sign up for a multiday sailing or diving trip exploring less-travelled outer fringes of the reef, or fly out to a remote island, where you'll have the reef largely to yourself.

Southern Reef Islands

For an idyllic getaway off the beaten path, book a trip to one of several remote reef-fringed islands on the southern edge of the Great Barrier Reef. You'll find fantastic snorkelling and diving right off the island.

Port Douglas

An hour's drive north of Cairns, Port Douglas is a laid-back beach town with dive boats heading out to over a dozen sites, including more pristine outer reefs, such as Agincourt Reef.

The Whitsundays

Home to turquoise waters, coral gardens and palm-fringed beaches, the Whitsundays offer many options for reef-exploring: base yourself on an island, go sailing, or stay on Airlie Beach and island-hop on day trips.

Townsville

Australia's largest tropical city is far from the outer reef (2½ hours by boat) but has some exceptional draws: access to Australia's best wreck dive, an excellent aquarium, marine-themed museums, plus multiday liveaboard dive boats departing from here.

Cairns

The most popular gateway to the reef, Cairns has dozens of boat operators offering day trips with snorkelling, as well as multiday reef explorations on liveaboard vessels. For the uninitiated, Cairns is a good place to learn to dive.

1. Clownfish 2. Port Douglas (p253) 3. Palm Cove (p246)
4. Townsville (p209)

GIVENWORKS / GETTY IMAGES ©

AUTAU / SHUTTERSTOCK ©

TANYA ANN PHOTOGRAPHY / GETTY IMAGES ©

1. Whitehaven Beach (p199) **2.** Helicopter flight (p190) over Whitsunday Islands **3.** Snorkelling, Cairns (p229)

Top Reef Encounters

Donning a mask and fins and getting an up-close look at this aquatic marvel is one of the best ways to experience the Great Barrier Reef. You can get a different take aboard a glass-bottomed boat tour, on a scenic flight or on a land-based reef walk.

Diving & Snorkelling

The classic way to see the Great Barrier Reef is to board a catamaran and visit several different coral-rich spots on a long day trip. Nothing quite compares to that first underwater glimpse, whether diving or snorkelling.

Semi-Submersibles & Boats

A growing number of reef operators (especially around Cairns) offer semi-submersible or glass-bottomed boat tours, which give cinematic views of coral, rays, fish, turtles and sharks – without you ever having to get wet.

Sailing

You can escape the crowds and see some spectacular reef scenery aboard a sailboat. Experienced mariners can hire a bareboat, others can join a multiday tour – both are easily arranged from Airlie Beach or Port Douglas.

Reef Walking

Many reefs of the southern Great Barrier Reef are exposed at low tide, allowing visitors to walk on the reef top (on sandy tracks between living coral). This can be a fantastic way to learn about marine life, especially if accompanied by a naturalist guide.

Scenic Flights

Get a bird's-eye view of the vast coral reef and its cays and islands from a scenic flight. You can sign up for a helicopter tour or a seaplane tour (particularly memorable over the Whitsundays).

Marine life

Nature's Theme Park

Home to some of the greatest biodiversity of any ecosystem on earth, the Great Barrier Reef is a marine wonderland. You'll find 30-plus species of marine mammals along with countless species of fish, coral, molluscs and sponges. Above the water, 200 bird species and 118 butterfly species have been recorded on reef islands and cays.

Common fish species include dusky butterfly fish, which are a rich navy blue with sulphur-yellow noses and back fins; large graphic turkfish, with luminescent pastel coats; teeny neon damsels, with darting flecks of electric blue; and six-banded angelfish, with blue tails, yellow bodies and tiger stripes. Rays, including the spotted eagle ray, are worth looking out for.

The reef is also a haven to many marine mammals, such as whales, dolphins and dugongs. Dugongs are listed as vulnerable, and a significant number of them live in Australia's northern waters; the reef is home to around 15% of the global population. Humpback whales migrate from Antarctica to the reef's warm waters to breed between May and October, and minke whales can be seen off the coast from Cairns to Lizard Island in June and July. Porpoises and killer and pilot whales also make their home here.

One of the reef's most-loved inhabitants is the sea turtle. Six of the world's seven species (all endangered) live on the reef and lay eggs on the islands' sandy beaches in spring or summer.

Townsville to Mission Beach

Best Places to Eat

➡ PepperVine (p225)

➡ Bingil Bay Cafe (p224)

➡ Oliveri's Continental Deli (p227)

➡ Longboard Bar & Grill (p212)

➡ Wayne & Adele's Garden of Eating (p213)

Best Places to Sleep

➡ Jackaroo Hostel (p223)

➡ Sejala on the Beach (p224)

➡ Civic Guest House (p211)

➡ Orpheus Island Lodge (p219)

➡ Base Backpackers (p216)

Why Go?

Spread out between the tourist darlings of Cairns and the Whitsunday Islands, this lesser-known, rainforested stretch of quiet, palm-edged beaches is where giant endangered cassowary graze for seeds, and koalas nap in gum trees on turquoise encircled islands. Oft-overlooked Townsville is the urban centre and offers pleasant, wide, modern streets, a landscaped seaside promenade, gracious 19th-century architecture, and a host of cultural venues and sporting events. It's also the jumping-off point for Magnetic Island, a great budget alternative to the Whitsundays and with far more wildlife – hand-feed wild wallabies, spot an incredible range of bird life on fantastic bushwalking trails, and look for koalas.

North of Townsville, beautiful Mission Beach is a laid-back village that ironically attracts thrill seekers by the busload, all eager to skydive over the reef and on to white-sand beaches, or go on an adrenalin-pumping white-water rafting trip along the Tully River.

When to Go
Townsville

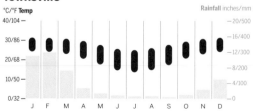

May–Oct Stinger-free seas make this the best time of year for water activities.

Aug Townsville shows off its cultural side during the Australian Festival of Chamber Music.

Sep Magnetic Island moves gently into second gear for the month-long Bay Dayz Festival.

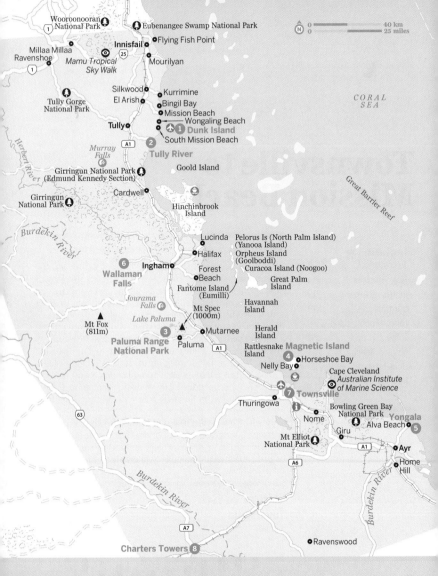

Townsville to Mission Beach Highlights

1 **Dunk Island** (p226)
Launching to this quintessential
tropical Queensland escape.

2 **Tully River** (p220)
Veering wildly around white-
water bends.

3 **Paluma Range National
Park** (p221) Searching for the
shy platypus in the winding
trails of this national park.

4 **Magnetic Island** (p214)
Spotting dozing koalas or
hand-feeding rock wallabies
on this paradisiacal island.

5 **Yongala** (p213) Scuba
diving at one of Australia's
greatest wreck dives.

6 **Wallaman Falls** (p218)
Admiring the view then
schlepping down to the

bottom of Australia's highest
single-drop waterfall.

7 **Townsville** (p209)
Cheering on the Cowboys,
North Queensland's revered
National Rugby League team.

8 **Charters Towers** (p215)
Watching a *Ghosts After Dark*
outdoor film screening in this
outback gold-rush town.

Townsville

POP 174,797

Northern Queensland's less-visited major city is easy on the eye: at Townsville's heart is its handsome, endless esplanade, an ideal viewing platform to fabulous Magnetic Island offshore. It's a pedestrian-friendly city, and its grand, refurbished 19th-century buildings offer loads of landmarks. If in doubt, join the throngs of fit and fabulous marching up bright red Castle Hill to gaze across the city's dry environs.

Townsville has a lively, young populace, with thousands of students and armed forces members intermingling with old-school locals, fly-in-fly-out mine workers, and summer-seekers lapping up the average 320 days of sunshine per year. Needless to say, the nightlife is often full throttle.

◎ Sights

★ Reef HQ Aquarium   AQUARIUM
(www.reefhq.com.au; Flinders St E; adult/child $28/14; ⊗9.30am-5pm) A staggering 2.5 million litres of water flow through the coral-reef tank here, home to 130 coral and 120 fish species. Kids will love seeing, feeding and touching turtles at the turtle hospital. Talks and tours (included with admission) throughout the day focus on different aspects of the reef and the aquarium.

★ Museum of
Tropical Queensland   MUSEUM
(☑07-4726 0600; www.mtq.qm.qld.gov.au; 70-102 Flinders St E; adult/child $15/8.80; ⊗9.30am-5pm) An absolute must for school-age children and grown-up science and history fans, the Museum of Tropical Queensland reconstructs scenes using detailed models with interactive displays. At 11am and 2.30pm you can load and fire a cannon, 1700s-style. Galleries include the kid-friendly MindZone science centre, and displays on North Queensland's history from the dinosaurs to the rainforest and reef.

Australian Institute
of Marine Science   RESEARCH INSTITUTE
(AIMS; ☑07-4753 4444; www.aims.gov.au) 🏊 Scheduled to re-commence free two-hour tours (10am Fridays from March through November) in mid-2017 after extensive renovations, this marine-research facility at Cape Ferguson conducts crucial research into issues such as coral bleaching and management of the Great Barrier Reef, and how it relates to the community; advance bookings are essential. The turn-off from the Bruce Hwy is 35km southeast of Townsville.

Billabong Sanctuary   WILDLIFE RESERVE
(www.billabongsanctuary.com.au; Bruce Hwy; adult/child $35/22; ⊗9am-5pm) 🏊 Just 17km south of Townsville, this eco-certified wildlife park offers up-close-and-personal encounters with Australian wildlife – from dingoes to cassowaries – in their natural habitat. You could easily spend all day at the 11-hectare park, with feedings, shows and talks every half-hour or so.

Botanic Gardens   GARDENS
(⊗sunrise-sunset) FREE Townsville's botanic gardens are spread across three locations: each has its own character, but all have tropical plants and are abundantly green. Closest to the centre, the formal, ornamental Queens Gardens (cnr Gregory & Paxton Sts; ⊗sunrise-sunset) FREE are 1km northwest of town at the base of Castle Hill.

Castle Hill   VIEWPOINT
FREE Much of Townsville's fit and fabulous hoof it up this striking 286m-high red hill (an isolated pink granite monolith) that dominates Townsville's skyline for stunning views of the city and Cleveland Bay. Walk up via the rough 'goat track' (2km one-way) from Hillside Cres. Otherwise, drive via Gregory St up the narrow, winding 2.6km Castle Hill Rd. A signboard up top details short trails leading to various lookout points.

Cultural Centre   CULTURAL CENTRE
(☑07-4772 7679; www.cctownsville.com.au; 2-68 Flinders St E; adult/child $5/2; ⊗9.30am-4.30pm) Showcases the history, traditions and customs of the local Wulgurukaba and Bindal peoples. Call for guided-tour times.

Maritime Museum of Townsville   MUSEUM
(☑07-4721 5251; www.townsvillemaritimemuseum.org.au; 42-68 Palmer St; adult/child/family $6/3/15; ⊗10am-3pm Mon-Fri, noon-3pm Sat & Sun) One for the boat buffs, with a gallery dedicated to the wreck of the *Yongala* and exhibits on North Queensland's naval industries. Tours of decommissioned patrol boat HMAS *Townsville* are available.

🏃 Activities

Strand   SWIMMING
Stretching 2.2km, Townsville's waterfront is interspersed with parks, pools, cafes and playgrounds – with hundreds of palm trees

TOWNSVILLE TO MISSION BEACH TOWNSVILLE

Townsville

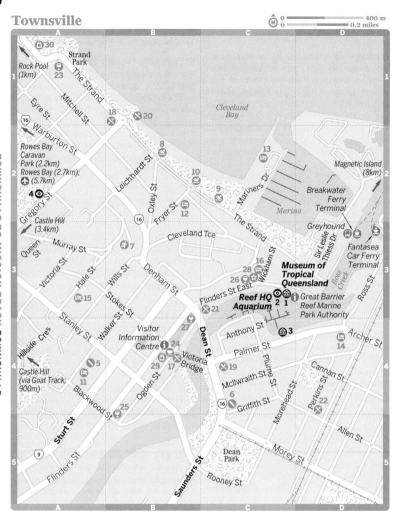

providing shade. Its sandy beach is patrolled and protected by two stinger enclosures.

At the northern tip is the **rock pool** (⊙24hr) **FREE**, an enormous artificial swimming pool surrounded by lawns and sandy beaches. Alternatively, head to the chlorinated safety of the heritage-listed, Olympic-sized swimming pool, **Tobruk Memorial Baths** (www.townsville.qld.gov.au; adult/child $5/3; ⊙5.30am-7pm Mon-Thu, to 6pm Fri, 7am-4pm Sat, 8am-5pm Sun). There's also a fantastic **water playground** (⊙10am-8pm Dec-Mar, to 6pm Sep-Nov, Apr & May, to 5pm Jun-Aug) **FREE** for the kids.

Skydive Townsville   SKYDIVING
(☑07-4721 4721; www.skydivetownsville.com.au; 182 Denham St; 3050/4270m tandem dives from $395/445) Hurl yourself from a perfectly good plane and land right on the Strand, or over on Magnetic Island.

☞ Tours

Townsville History Walking Tour   WALKING
(☑0400 560 471; www.townsvillehistorywalking tours.com.au; tours $20-80) New historical walking tours of Townsville are proving popular with locals and curious visitors. The City Day Tour ($50) and Palmer St

Townsville

Wine and Dine Tour ($80) are particularly recommended.

★ Festivals & Events

The city has a packed calendar of festivals and events, including the home games of its cherished North Queensland Cowboys (www.cowboys.com.au) National Rugby League team.

Townsville 500   SPORTS
(www.v8supercars.com.au; ☉ Jul) Racing cars roar through a purpose-built street circuit during the V8 Supercar Championship.

Australian Festival of Chamber Music   MUSIC
(www.afcm.com.au; ☉ Aug) Townsville gets cultural during this internationally renowned festival at various venues across the city.

⛱ Sleeping

★ Civic Guest House   HOSTEL $
(☑ 07-4771 5381; www.civicguesthousetownsville.com.au; 262 Walker St; dm/d from $20/56; @ ☎) This old-fashioned hostel respects the independent traveller's needs for cleanliness, comfort, security and easy company. The mustard-coloured, colonial-tinged Civic is a welcome change from the boisterous backpacker trend. Free transport to/from the ferry or bus station.

Orchid Guest House   GUESTHOUSE $
(☑ 07-4771 6683, 0418 738 867; www.orchidguesthouse.com.au; 34 Hale St; dm $28, d with/without bathroom $90/65; ☒) The Orchid has really bloomed since our last visit. In a quiet hillside location within walking distance of town, the old suburban inner-city home is now wonderfully kept in that quaint Queensland fashion, with a peaceful flow of guests looking for a place to make plans for Magnetic Island or find temporary work.

Reef Lodge   HOSTEL $
(☑ 07-4721 1112; www.reeflodge.com.au; 4 Wickham St; dm $23-35, d with/without bathroom $80/62; ☒ @ ☎) The only downtown hostel worth bothering with is a warren of room configurations, but the staff are very capable of creating a sense of community in the games room, chill-out zone and hammock-strewn garden area. Jobs can be found in the region here, if you've spent all your dough at the nearby nightclubs.

Rowes Bay Caravan Park   CARAVAN PARK $
(☑ 07-4771 3576; www.rowesbaycp.com.au; Heatley Pde; powered/unpowered sites $36/28, cabins with/without bathroom from $110/75, villas $115-140; ☒ @ ☎ ☒) Leafy park directly opposite Rowes Bay's beachfront. The villas are smaller than cabins, but spiffier.

GREAT BARRIER REEF TRIPS FROM TOWNSVILLE

The Great Barrier Reef lies further offshore from Townsville than it does from Cairns and Port Douglas; the extra fuel costs push up prices. On the upside, it's less crowded (and the reef suffers less from the effects of crowds). Trips from Townsville are generally dive-oriented; if you only want to snorkel, take a day trip that just goes to the reef – the *Yongala* wreck is for diving only. The *Yongala* is considerably closer to Alva Beach near Ayr than to Townsville, so if your main interest is wreck diving, you may want to consider a trip with Alva Beach–based Yongala Dive.

The visitor centre (p214) has a list of Townsville-based operators offering PADI-certified learn-to-dive courses with two days' training in the pool, plus at least two days and one night living aboard the boat. Prices start at $600, and you'll need to obtain a dive medical (around $60).

Operators include the following:

Adrenalin Dive (☑07-4724 0600; www.adrenalinedive.com.au; 252 Walker St) Day trips to the *Yongala* (from $264) and Lodestone Reef (from $229), both including two dives. Also offers liveaboard trips and dive-certification courses.

Remote Area Dive (RAD; ☑07-4721 4424; www.remoteareadive.com.au; 16 Dean St) Runs day trips (from $225) to Orpheus and Pelorus Islands. Also liveaboard trips and dive courses.

Historic Yongala Lodge Motel
MOTEL $

(☑07-4772 4633; www.historicyongala.com.au; 11 Fryer St; motel r $79-139, 1/2-bedroom apt $115/159; ❄️🛜🏊) Built in 1884, this lovely historic building with gingerbread-house-style balustrades is but a short stroll from the Strand and city centre. The rooms and apartments are small but good value. Long-term 'tenants' and noisy party-goers can detract from the overall feel of the place, but there's enough variety and space to make it work.

Oaks M on Palmer
BOUTIQUE HOTEL $$

(☑07-4753 2900; 81 Palmer St; d from $100; 🅿️❄️🛜🏊) Perfect for an after-party or pre-dinner in-room drinks, Oaks M is right at the end of the Palmer St shuffle. The rooms are small, but stylish and bright. Popular with single professionals. Parking is free, service is discreet, and there's a small gym.

Mariners North
APARTMENT $$$

(☑07-4722 0777; www.marinersnorth.com.au; 7 Mariners Dr; 2-/3-bedroom apt from $209/360; 🅿️❄️🛜🏊) The pick for families in Townsville is Mariners North, located in the newer section of the marina, with a sandy stretch out front and a delightful pool. The apartments are very good, particularly the ground-floor ones with direct pool and garden access; others may prefer views over Cleveland Bay.

🍴 Eating

Perpendicular to the Strand, Gregory St has a clutch of cafes and takeaway joints. The Palmer St dining strip offers a diverse range of cuisines: wander along and take your pick. Many of Townsville's bars and pubs also serve food.

Harold's Seafood
SEAFOOD $

(cnr The Strand & Gregory St; meals $4-10; ⊙8am-9pm Mon-Thu, to 9.30pm Fri-Sun) The big fish-and-chip joint on the corner whips up fish burgers ($12) and large-sized barramundi and salad ($11).

⭐Longboard Bar & Grill
MODERN AUSTRALIAN $$

(☑07-4724 1234; www.longboardbarandgrill.com; The Strand, opp Gregory St; mains $15-37; ⊙11.30am-3pm & 5.30pm-late) The coolest place in Townsville for a light meal and a light party overlooking the water is this surf-themed pub-restaurant, which does terrific nightly specials including tacos and buffalo wings. The regular steak, seafood and pasta menu is very reliable. Orders are taken at the bar, but that's not a problem as the vibe is right most nights, and staff are fast and efficient.

Jam
MODERN AUSTRALIAN $$

(☑07-4721 4900; 1 Palmer St; mains $15-30; ⊙7am-10pm) This neat midrange restaurant, on happening Palmer St, understands its casual northern Queensland clientele and serves a wide menu with celebratory breakfasts and desserts.

Wayne & Adele's
Garden of Eating   MODERN AUSTRALIAN **$$**
(☑07-4772 2984; 11 Allen St; mains from $19; ⊙6.30-10.30pm Mon, to 11pm Thu-Sat, noon-3pm Sun) Irreverence at every turn in this husband-and-wife-run gourmet restaurant situated in an Aussie backyard (well courtyard, at least). Those who like a side serving of quirky with their grub shouldn't miss mains including Safety Net (crocodile pattie with an eggnet Asian salad) or Bounce Back (tandoori kangaroo fillet with lime pickle yoghurt).

Summerie's Thai Cuisine   THAI **$$**
(☑07-4420 1282; www.summeriesthaicuisine.com.au; 232 Flinders St; lunch specials $13, dinner mains from $17; ⊙11.30am-2.30pm & 5.30-10pm) A wildly successful local Thai restaurant with a prime downtown location and a new branch in the suburbs, Summerie's adapts traditional dishes to the Aussie palate and incorporates Coral Sea produce in dishes such as Barrier Reef (fish sauce, coriander and chilli-jam-spiced seafood), Heaven on Earth (slow-cooked coconut prawns with crunchy greens) and Summer Sunset (sweet-and-sour pineapple sauce).

A Touch of Salt   MODERN AUSTRALIAN **$$$**
(☑07-4724 4441; www.atouchofsalt.com.au; 86-124 Ogden St; mains $35-37; ⊙noon-3pm & 6-11.30pm) Although the favoured high-end dining experience for Townsville's posh set doesn't look very stylish upon entry, the bar is slick, the service is fussy and the sophisticated Asian-fusion cuisine is ambitious (though can overreach at times).

🍷 Drinking & Nightlife

Townsville Brewery   BREWERY
(252 Flinders St; ⊙11.30am-midnight Mon-Sat) Brews are made on-site at this hopping, stunningly restored 1880s former post office. Soak up a Townsville Bitter or Bandito Loco.

Beach Bar   BAR
(Watermark Hotel, 72-74 The Strand) The place to be seen in Townsville. Well, if it's good enough for Missy Higgins and Silverchair, then it's good enough for the rest of us. Some serious Sunday sessions take place in the tavern bar with prime ocean views down the flash end of the Strand.

Coffee Dominion   CAFE
(www.coffeedominion.com.au; cnr Stokes & Ogden Sts; ⊙6am-5pm Mon-Fri, 7am-1pm Sat & Sun) An eco-conscious establishment roasting beans sourced from the Atherton tablelands to Mombasa. If you don't find a blend you like, invent your own and they'll grind it fresh.

Grand Northern Hotel   PUB
(☑07-4771 6191; 500 Flinders St) This historic 1901 pub in Townsville's bustling centre is not exactly a tranquil haven, but it's great for a beer at any time. For those who like to be in the thick of it all, the GN can't be beat.

Heritage Bar   BAR
(☑07-4724 1374; www.theheritagetownsville.com; 137 Flinders St E; bar snacks from $11; ⊙5pm-2am Tue-Sat) A surprisingly chic craft bar. Suave 'mixologists' deliver creative cocktails ($18) to a cool crowd looking for something more than a beer-barn swillfest. Also has a sophisticated bar menu for meals (think BBQ bourbon pork, and scallop and chorizo gnocchi), as well as tipsy nibbles such as coconut prawns.

☆ Entertainment

Flynns   LIVE MUSIC
(www.flynnsirishbar.com; 101 Flinders St E; ⊙5pm-late Tue-Sun) A jolly Irish pub that doesn't try too hard to be Irish. Wildly popular for its live music every night except Wednesdays, when karaoke takes over.

🔒 Shopping

Check out the weekly **Cotters Market** (www.townsvillerotarymarkets.com.au; Flinders St Mall; ⊙8.30am-1pm Sun) or monthly **Strand Night Market** (www.townsvillerotarymarkets.com.au; The Strand; ⊙5-9.30pm 1st Fri of month May-Dec).

DIVING THE YONGALA WRECK

Yongala Dive (☑07-4783 1519; www.yongaladive.com.au; 56 Narrah St, Alva Beach) offers dive trips ($259 including gear) out to the *Yongala* wreck from Alva Beach, 17km northeast of Ayr. It only takes 30 minutes to get out to the wreck from here, instead of a 2½-hour boat trip from Townsville. Book ahead for backpacker-style accommodation at its onshore **dive lodge** (dm/d $29/68; @), with free pick-ups from Ayr.

ℹ Information

Great Barrier Reef Marine Park Authority
(☑ 07-4750 0700; www.gbrmpa.gov.au) National body overseeing the Great Barrier Reef.

Visitor Information Centre (☑ 07-4721 3660; www.townsvilleholidays.info; 280 Flinders St; ⊙ 9am-5pm) Extensive visitor information on Townsville, Magnetic Island and nearby national parks. There's another branch on the Bruce Hwy 10km south of the city.

ℹ Getting There & Away

AIR

From **Townsville Airport** (www.townsvilleairport. com.au), **Virgin** (☑ 13 67 89; www.virginaustralia. com), **Qantas** (☑ 13 13 13; www.qantas.com.au), **Air North** (☑ 1800 627 474; www.airnorth.com. au) and **Jetstar** (☑ 13 15 38; www.jetstar.com.au) fly to Cairns, Brisbane, the Gold Coast, Sydney, Melbourne, Mackay and Rockhampton, with connections to other major cities.

BOAT

SeaLink (☑ 07-4726 0800; www.sealinkqld. com.au) runs an excellent ferry service to Magnetic Island from Breakwater in Townsville (return adult/child including all-day bus pass $35/17.50, 25 minutes). There's roughly one trip per hour between 5.30am and 11.30pm. All ferries arrive and depart Magnetic Island from the terminal at Nelly Bay.

BUS

Greyhound (☑ 1300 473 946; www.grey hound.com.au; The Breakwater, Sealink Travel Centre, Sir Leslie Thiess Dr) has three daily services to Brisbane ($249, 24 hours), Rockhampton ($129, 12 hours), Airlie Beach ($49, 4½ hours), Mission Beach ($44, 3¾ hours) and Cairns ($64, six hours). Buses pick up and drop off at the **Breakwater Ferry Terminal** (2/14 Sir Leslie Thiess Dr; lockers per day $4-6).

Premier Motor Service (☑ 13 34 10; www. premierms.com.au) has one service a day to/ from Brisbane ($184, 23 hours) and Cairns ($55, six hours), stopping in Townsville at the **Fantasea car ferry terminal** (Ross St, South Townsville).

TRAIN

Townsville's **train station** (Charters Towers Rd) is 1km south of the centre.

The Brisbane–Cairns Spirit of Queensland travels through Townsville five times a week. Journey time between Brisbane and Townsville is 25 hours (one-way from $189), while tickets to Cairns (6½ hours) start from $79. Contact **Queensland Rail** (☑ 1800 872 467; www. queenslandrail.com.au).

ℹ Getting Around

TO/FROM THE AIRPORT

Townsville Airport is 5km northwest of the city centre in Garbutt. A taxi to the centre costs about $22.

BUS

Sunbus (☑ 07-4771 9800; www.sunbus.com. au) runs local bus services around Townsville. Route maps and timetables are available at the visitor information centre and online.

TAXI

Taxis congregate at ranks across town, or call **Townsville Taxis** (☑ 13 10 08; www.tsvtaxi. com.au).

Magnetic Island

POP 2500

Sitting within shouting distance of Townsville, Magnetic Island is a verdant island and one of Queensland's most laid-back residential addresses. The local population, who mostly commute to Townsville or cater for the tourist trade, must pinch themselves as they come home to the stunning coastal walking trails, gum trees full of dozing koalas (you're likely to spot some), and surrounding bright turquoise seas.

Over half of this triangular-shaped, mountainous island's 52 sq km is national park, with scenic walks and abundant wildlife, including a large (and adorable) rock wallaby population. Inviting beaches offer adrenalin-pumping water sports, and the chance to just bask in the sunshine. The granite boulders, hoop pines and eucalyptus are a fresh change from the clichéd tropical-island paradise.

◉ Sights

There's one main road across the island, which goes from Picnic Bay, past Nelly and Geoffrey Bays, to Horseshoe Bay. Local buses ply the route regularly. Walking trails through the bush also link the main towns. Maps are available at the ferry terminal ticket desk.

◉ Picnic Bay

Picnic Bay is one of the most low-key spots on the island, dominated more by a community of friendly locals than anything else. There's a stinger net during the season (November to May) and the swimming is superb. There's also a fine jetty if you like to throw in a line.

RAVENSWOOD & CHARTERS TOWERS

Detour inland from the coast to taste a bit of Queensland's outback character at these two old gold towns.

Ravenswood (population 160) is a tiny gold-mining town whose fortunes have fluctuated over the past century. It's now best known for its two grand hotels, one of which supposedly houses one of Queensland's most active resident ghosts.

Accommodation, food and, of course, drinks can be found in the town's two pubs, the Imperial Hotel (07-4770 2131; 23 Macrossan St; s/d $39/65; P ⊖ ❄ ☎) and the Railway Hotel (07-4770 2144; 1 Barton St; s/tw/d $42/79/90; P ⊖ ❄ ☎).

The 19th-century gold-rush settlement of Charters Towers (population 8500) is about 140km southwest of Townsville on the Flinders Hwy. William Skelton Ewbank Melbourne (WSEM) Charters was the gold commissioner during the rush, when the town was the second-largest, and wealthiest, in Queensland. The 'towers' are its surrounding tors (hills). With almost 100 mines, some 90 pubs and a stock exchange, the town became known simply as 'the World'. Today, a highlight of a visit to the Towers is strolling past its glorious facades and recalling the grandeur of those heady days.

The Stock Exchange Arcade (07-3223 6666; www.nationaltrust.org.au/places/stock-exchange-building-and-arcade; 76 Mosman St; ⊙9am-5pm), with its barrel-vaulted portico, was the commercial hub in the late 19th century. Today it features a breezy, sun-filtered cafe and a fine art gallery.

Come nightfall, panoramic Towers Hill, the site where gold was first discovered, is the atmospheric setting for an open-air cinema showing the 20-minute film *Ghosts After Dark* – check seasonal screening times and buy tickets ($10) at the visitor centre.

Staying at the atmospheric and friendly old Royal Private Hotel (07-4787 8688; www.royalprivate-hotel.com; 100 Mosman St; r from $60; ❄ ☎) feels like something between time travel and visiting a museum. The creaky wooden beds and black-and-white-chequered bathroom tiles are charming or cheesy.

For those looking for a real-life cattle-station experience, contact friendly Rhonda at Bluff Downs (07-4770 4084; www.bluffdowns.com.au; dm $20, d $90-300, camp sites $20). The vast majority of guests are looking for medium-term employment, but passers-by are welcome. It's 110km northwest of Charters Towers.

Healthy Treat (07-4787 4218; 14 Gill St; meals $12-24) is an ever-popular eatery serving massive homemade burgers, sandwiches and meat dishes to a steady flow of families and professionals. The Mars Bar, Nutella and Salted Caramel thickshakes ($8) are intense.

The excellent Charters Towers Visitor Centre (07-4761 5533; www.charters towers.qld.gov.au; 74 Mosman St; ⊙9am-5pm) books all tours in town, including those to the reputedly haunted Venus Gold Battery, where gold-bearing ore was crushed and processed from 1872 to 1973.

◉ Nelly Bay

Magnetic Harbour in Nelly Bay is your first taste of life on the island. There's a wide range of busy but relaxing eating and sleeping options and a decent beach. There's also a children's playground towards the northern end of the beach, and good snorkelling on the fringing coral reef.

◉ Arcadia Bay

Arcadia village is a conglomerate of shops, eateries and accommodation. Its main beach, Geoffrey Bay, has a reef at its south-ern end (reef walking at low tide is discouraged). By far its prettiest beach is the cove at Alma Bay with huge boulders tumbling into the sea. There's plenty of shade here, along with picnic tables and a children's playground.

If you head to the end of the road at Bremner Point, between Geoffrey Bay and Alma Bay, at around 5pm you can have wild rock wallabies – accustomed to being fed at the same time each day – literally eating out of the palm of your hand. For those who make it out here, this can be a trip highlight.

◎ Radical Bay & the Forts

Townsville was a supply base for the Pacific during WWII, and the forts were designed to protect the town from naval attack. If you're going to do just one walk, then the forts walk (2.8km, 1½ hours return) is a must. It starts near the Radical Bay turn-off, passing lots of ex-military sites, gun emplacements and false 'rocks'. At the top of the walk is the observation tower and command post, which have spectacular coastal views, and you'll almost certainly spot koalas lazing about in the treetops. Return the same way or continue along the connecting paths, which deposit you at Horseshoe Bay (you can catch the bus back).

Nearby Balding Bay is Maggie's unofficial nude beach.

◎ Horseshoe Bay

Horseshoe Bay, on the north coast, is the best of Maggie's accessible beaches and attracts its share of young, hippie-ish nature lovers and older day trippers. You'll find water-sports gear for hire, a stinger net, a row of cafes and a fantastic pub. Bungalow Bay Koala Village has a wildlife park (☑07-4778 5577, 1800 285 577; www.bungalowbay.com.au; 40 Horseshoe Bay Rd; adult/child $29/13; ☺2hr tours 10am, noon & 2.30pm), where you can cuddle crocs and koalas. Pick up local arts and crafts at Horseshoe Bay's market (☺9am-2pm 2nd & last Sun of month), which sets up along the beachfront.

🏃 Activities

Big Mama Sailing   BOATING
(☑0437 206 360; www.bigmamasailing.com; full-day cruises adult/child $195/110) Hit the water on an 18m ketch with passionate boaties Stu, Lisa and Fletcher, who recently moved the Big Mama down from Mission Beach.

Pro Dive Magnetic   DIVING
(☑0424 822 450; www.prodivemagnetic.com; 43 Sooning St, Nelly Bay) This Nelly Bay dive school offers splashing Magnetic Island day trips for both snorkellers ($149) and scuba divers ($199). PADI courses cost $299.

Tropicana Tours   DRIVING
(☑07-4758 1800; www.tropicanatours.com.au; full day adult/child $198/99) Ziggy and Co run magnificent island tours that take in the island's best spots in their stretch 4WD. Prices include close encounters with wildlife, lunch

at a local cafe and a sunset cocktail. Shorter tours are also available, but the eight-hour version is a hit.

Horseshoe Bay Ranch   HORSE RIDING
(☑07-4778 5109; www.horseshoebayranch.com.au; 38 Gifford St; 2hr rides $120) Gallop dramatically into the not-so-crashing surf on this popular bushland-to-beach two-hour tour. Pony rides for littlies are available too (20 minutes, $20).

Magnetic Island Sea Kayaks   KAYAKING
(☑07-4778 5424; www.seakayak.com.au; 93 Horseshoe Bay Rd; morning/evening tours $85/60) 🐾 Magnetic Island is a perfect destination for sea kayaking, with plenty of launching points, secret beaches, marine life, and laid-back cafes to recharge in after your paddle. Join an eco-certified morning or sunset tour, or go it alone on a rented kayak (single/double per day $85/160).

Pleasure Divers   DIVING
(☑07-4778 5788; www.pleasuredivers.com.au; 10 Marine Pde, Arcadia; open-water courses per person from $300; ☺8.30am-5pm) A snorkel tour with these guys based in Arcadia is a good-value way to get an appreciation of the ecology around Geoffrey Bay. Deep-water thinkers can do three-day PADI open-water courses to kick-start their scuba skills, as well as advanced courses and *Yongala* wreck dives for regular plungers.

🛏 Sleeping

For holiday cottages check out www.best ofmagnetic.com or www.magneticisland tourism.com.

⭐**Base Backpackers**   HOSTEL $
(☑1800 242 273; www.stayatbase.com; 1 Nelly Bay Rd, Nelly Bay; camping per person $15, dm $32-37, d from $110; @🛜🏊) Away from any semblance of holidaymakers to disrupt your natural state, Base has to be one of the best-located hostels in Australia, situated between Nelly and Picnic Bays. It's famous for wild full-moon parties, and things can get raucous at any time at the infamous on-site Island Bar. Sleep, food and transport package deals are available.

Arcadia Beach Guest House   GUESTHOUSE $
(☑07-4778 5668; www.arcadiabeachguesthouse.com.au; 27 Marine Pde, Arcadia; dm from $35, safari tents $65, r with/without bathroom from $135/$75; ❄🛜🏊) Well-priced and staffed by effusive professionals, Arcadia Beach Guest House

does a lot right, including providing an enormous variety of sleeping quarters. Will you stay in a bright, beachy room (named after Magnetic Island's bays), a safari tent or a dorm? Go turtle-spotting from the balcony, rent a canoe, a Moke or a 4WD...or all of the above?

Magnetic Island B&B
B&B **$$**

(📞 07-4758 1203; www.magneticislandbedandbreakfast.com; 11 Dolphin Ct, Horseshoe Bay; d $150) The double rooms here book out quickly, but a new Bush Retreat ($190) sleeps four and is a great deal for some natural seclusion. Rooms are bright and breezy, and the hosts are astutely professional. There's a neat saltwater pool, and the inclusive breakfasts are wholesome and delicious. Minimum two-night stay applies.

Shambhala Retreat
BUNGALOW **$$**

(📞 0448 160 580; www.shambhala-retreat-magnetic-island.com.au; 11 Barton St, Nelly Bay; d from $105; ❄️🌐🏊) 🅿 With some of the best-value, self-contained, tropical units on the island, Shambhala is a green-powered property with distinct Buddhist influences evident in the wall hangings and water features. Two units have outdoor courtyard showers; all have fully equipped kitchens, large bathrooms and laundry facilities. Local wildlife is often drawn to the patios. Minimum stay is two nights.

Arcadia Village Motel
HOTEL **$$**

(📞 07-4778 5481; www.arcadiavillage.com.au; 7 Marine Pde, Arcadia; r from $120; ❄️🌐🏊) Situated down the quiet end of Marine Pde (which is saying something in a chilled-out place like Maggie), this family-friendly motel has an on-site bistro and bar, which can get a little rowdy on weekends. There are two awesome pools, and a great beach a short stroll across the street.

Island Leisure Resort
RESORT **$$**

(📞 07-4778 5000; www.islandleisure.com.au; 4 Kelly St; burés d/f from $197/247; ❄️🌐🏊) Self-contained, Polynesian-style cabins (burés) give this by-the-beach spot an extra-tropical feel. Private patios allow guests to enjoy their own piece of paradise: a lagoon pool and BBQ area beckon social souls.

Magnetic Sunsets
APARTMENT **$$**

(📞 07-4778 1900; www.magneticsunsets.com.au; 7 Pacific Dr; 1-/2-/3-bedroom apt $195/295/395, B&B s/d $115/159; ❄️🌐🏊) These great-value, self-contained apartments are just a literal stagger from the beach. Private balconies

overlook the bay; inside, they're cool, clean and welcoming. Smart, new B&B rooms are good alternatives.

Tropical Palms Inn
MOTEL **$$**

(📞 07-4778 5076; www.tropicalpalmsinn.com.au; 34 Picnic St, Picnic Bay; s/d $120/130; ❄️🌐🏊) With a terrific little swimming pool right outside your front door and superbly friendly hosts, the simple, self-contained motel units here are bright and comfortable. Prices drop if you stay two or more nights, and you can also rent 4WDs here. Good discounts for longer stays.

🍴 Eating & Drinking

⭐ Cafe Nourish
CAFE **$**

(📞 07-4758 1885; 3/6 Pacific Dr, Horsehoe Bay; wraps from $9; ⏰ 8am-4pm) Horseshoe Bay has become the hip cafe strip and our favourite cafe on the island does the small things well: fresh, healthy wraps, breakfasts, smoothies and energy balls. And don't even get us started on the coffee. Service is energetic and heartfelt.

Arcadia Night Market
MARKET **$**

(RSL Hall, Hayles Ave, Arcadia; ⏰ 5.30-8pm Fri) Small but lively night market with licensed bar and plenty of cheap eats to chow through.

Noodies on the Beach
MEXICAN **$**

(📞 07-4778 5786; 2/6 Pacific Dr, Horseshoe Bay; mains from $10; ⏰ 10am-10pm Mon-Wed & Fri, 8am-10pm Sat, 8am-3pm Sun; 🅿) An integral part of the Horseshoe Bay food scene, Noodies is an irreverent Mexican-themed cafe with a book exchange and a licence to serve killer margaritas.

Gilligan's Cafe
CAFE **$$**

(Arcadia Village; burgers $14-18; ⏰ 8am-4pm) Fun, licensed cafe in Arcadia that pumps out massive breakfasts and the finest burgers on Maggie. The owners have a *Gilligan's Island* thing going on. Get stranded while you enjoy the decent booze selection over lunch.

Marlin Bar
PUB FOOD **$$**

(📞 07-4758 1588; 3 Pacific Dr, Horseshoe Bay; mains $16-24; ⏰ 11am-8pm) Marlin Bar is popular with sailing crews dropping anchor in Horseshoe Bay and locals looking for some live music in the evenings. Meals are on the large side and (surprise!) revolve around seafood. Dogs are welcome.

Picnic Bay Hotel PUB FOOD **$$**
(☑07-4778 5166; www.picnicbayhotel.com.
au; 1 The Esplanade, Picnic Bay; mains $11-26;
☺9.30am-10pm) There are worse places to
settle in at for a drink than the very quiet
Picnic Bay, with Townsville's city lights spar-
kling across the bay. There's an all-day graz-
ing menu and huge salads.

❶ Getting There & Away

SeaLink (☑07-4726 0800; www.sealinkqld.
com.au) runs an excellent ferry service to Mag-
netic Island from Townsville (return adult/child
including all-day bus pass $35/17.50, 25 min-
utes). There's roughly one trip per hour between
5.30am and 11.30pm. All ferries arrive and de-
part Maggie from the terminal at Nelly Bay. Car
parking is available in Townsville.

Fantasea (☑07-4796 9300; www.magnetic
islandferry.com.au; Ross St, South Townsville)
operates a car ferry crossing eight times daily
(seven on weekends) from the south side of Ross
Creek, taking 35 minutes. It costs $178 (return)
for a car and up to three passengers, and $29/17
(adult/child return) for foot passengers only.
Bookings are essential and bicycles are trans-
ported free.

❶ Getting Around

Sunbus (www.sunbus.com.au/sit_magnetic_
island) ploughs between Picnic and Horseshoe
Bays, meeting all ferries and stopping at major
accommodation places. A day pass covering
all zones is $7.20, or you can include it in your
ferry ticket price. Be sure to talk to the bus
drivers, who love chatting about everything
Maggie.

Moke- ('topless' car) and scooter-rental places
abound. You'll need to be over 21 years old, have
a current driver's licence and leave a credit-card
deposit. Scooter hire starts at around $40 per
day, Mokes at about $75. Try **MI Wheels** (☑07-
4758 1111; www.miwheels.com.au; 138 Sooning
St, Nelly Bay) for a classic Moke, or **Roadrunner
Scooter Hire** (☑07-4778 5222; 3/64 Kelly St,
Nelly Bay) for scooters and trail bikes.

NORTH OF TOWNSVILLE

Heading north from Townsville, the
scorched-brown landscape slowly gives way
to sugar-cane plantations lining the high-
way and tropical rainforest shrouding the
hillsides.

Waterfalls, national parks and small vil-
lages hide up in the hinterland, including
Paluma Range National Park (part of the
Wet Tropics World Heritage Area). Visitor

centres in the area have leaflets outlining
walking trails, swimming holes and camp-
ing grounds.

Ingham & Around

POP 4681

Ingham is a cane-cutting centre with a
proud Italian heritage. It's also the guard-
ian of the 120-hectare Tyto Wetlands
(Tyto Wetlands Information Centre; ☑07-4776
4792; www.tyto.com.au; cnr Cooper St & Bruce
Hwy; ☺8.45am-5pm Mon-Fri, 9am-4pm Sat &
Sun), which has 4km of walking trails and
attracts around 230 species of birds, in-
cluding far-flung guests from Siberia and
Japan. The locals – hundreds of wallabies –
love it too, converging at dawn and dusk.
The town is the jumping-off point for the
majestic Wallaman Falls; at 305m, it's the
longest single-drop waterfall in Australia.

Mungalla Station (☑07-4777 8718; www.
mungallaaboriginaltours.com.au; 2hr tours adult/
child $70/35) ⏺, 15km east of Ingham, runs
insightful Aboriginal-led tours, including
boomerang throwing and stories from the
local Nywaigi culture, plus a traditional
Kupmurri lunch. Minimum of 10 needed, so
call ahead to check. Basic camping sites also
available.

In August the Australian Italian Festival
(www.australianitalianfestival.com.au) celebrates
the fact that 60% of Ingham residents are
of Italian descent. The motto is 'eat, drink
and celebrate'.

You can camp at Wallaman Falls Camp-
ground (www.npsr.qld.gov.au; sites per person/
family $6.15/24.60).

The poem that inspired the iconic Slim
Dusty hit 'Pub With No Beer' (1957) was
written in the Lees Hotel (☑07-4776 1577;
www.leeshotel.com.au; 58 Lannercost St; s/d
from $90/105, meals from $14; ☺lunch & dinner
Mon-Sat; ✳🐾) by Ingham cane-cutter Dan
Sheahan, after American soldiers drank the
place dry. The en-suite rooms here are very
comfortable, while the busy bistro does fine
steak and pasta dishes. Oh, and there's plen-
ty of beer.

The award-winning Hinchinbrook Ma-
rine Cove Resort (☑07-4777 8395; www.
hinchinbrook-marine-cove-resort.com.au; 54
Dungeness Rd; d $135, bungalows $150; ✳🐾) is
terrific value given the bright, spacious bun-
galows sleep up to five, management are
hands-on and there's easy access to Hinchin-
brook Island.

ORPHEUS ISLAND

Orpheus is a heavenly 1300-hectare island 80km north of Townsville, with a protected national park and surrounding ocean that is part of the Great Barrier Reef Marine Park. Its dry sclerophyll forest is a geographical anomaly this far north, where bandicoots, green tree frogs, echidnas, ospreys and a peculiar number of goats roam free, the latter as part of a madcap 19th-century scheme to provide food for potential shipwreck survivors. Visitors gravitate towards the eucalypt-scented hiking trails and crystal-clear snorkelling.

Part of the Palm Islands group, Orpheus is surrounded by magnificent fringing reef that's home to a mind-blowing collection of fish (1100 species) and a mammoth variety of both hard and soft corals. While the island is great for snorkellers and divers year-round (pack a stinger suit in summer), seasonal treats such as manta-ray migration (August to November) and coral spawning (mid-November) make the trip out here all the more worthwhile.

Orpheus Island Lodge (07-4839 7937; www.orpheus.com.au; d incl meals from $1500) is arguably the finest five-star resort in Queensland, rivalling the more famous Hayman Island for sheer tropical splendour, food, service and prestige.

Nautilus Aviation (07-4034 9000; www.nautilusaviation.com.au; one way from Townsville $275) runs helicopters from Townsville at 2pm daily for $275 one-way. The spectacular trip takes 30 minutes. Otherwise, ask around the town of Lucinda to arrange a boat ride over.

Cardwell

POP 1300

It's no wonder the truck drivers make Cardwell a must-stop destination. Given the Bruce Hwy runs inland for most of the east coast, it's a rare blessing to see and hear the sea lapping right outside your vehicle window; the uninterrupted views of Hinchinbrook Island don't hurt either. Most travellers merely linger here for seasonal fruit picking (check at the backpackers if you're looking for work), but there are worse places in the world to slow down.

Cardwell Forest Drive is a scenic 26km round trip chock-a-block with lookouts, walking tracks and picnic areas signposted along the way. There are super swimming opportunities at Attie Creek Falls, as well as at the aptly named Spa Pool, where you can sit in a rock hollow as water gushes over you. At **Girringun Aboriginal Art Centre** (www.art.girringun.com.au; 235 Victoria St; ⊗8.30am-5pm Mon-Thu, to 2pm Fri) traditional woven baskets, paintings and colourful wooden sculptures are among the works for sale.

Sleeping & Eating

Cardwell Beachcomber Motel & Tourist Park CARAVAN PARK $
(07-4066 8550; www.cardwellbeachcomber.com.au; 43a Marine Pde; powered/unpowered sites $38/29, motel d $98-125, cabins & studios $120-130;

With a very sweet location across from the sea, the Beachcomber has a good variety of options, though the camping sites are a little tight. Cute studios and modern oceanview villas by the pool will take the heat off your east coast adventure. The small **Beachcomber restaurant** (mains from $25; ⊗breakfast daily, lunch & dinner Mon-Sat) serves light meals and can whip up a yummy breakfast.

Cardwell Central Backpackers HOSTEL $
(07-4066 8404; www.cardwellbackpackers.com.au; 6 Brasenose St; dm $24;) Good feedback from the banana farm workers suggests Cardwell Central can both arrange regular work and host in a heartfelt, secure way. They also accept overnighters. Free internet and pool table.

Seaview Cafe FAST FOOD $$
(87 Victoria St; mains $12-25; ⊗24hr) The place with the giant crab on the roof, the cavernous Seaview is a famous stopover for hungry drivers. Trucker chefs dish up local flavours in the form of seafood sandwiches and a mammoth all-day breakfast ($17). It ain't fancy, but it gets the job done nicely.

Information

Rainforest & Reef Centre (07-4066 8601; www.greatgreenwaytourism.com; 142 Victoria St; ⊗8.30am-5pm Mon-Fri, 9am-1pm Sat & Sun) The Rainforest & Reef Centre, next to Cardwell's jetty, has a truly brilliant interactive rainforest display, and detailed info on Hinchinbrook Island and other nearby national parks.

Hinchinbrook Island

Australia's largest island national park (399 sq km) is a holy grail for walkers, but it's not easy to get to and advance planning is essential. Granite mountains rise dramatically from the sea and wildlife creeps through the foliage. The mainland side is dense with lush tropical vegetation, while long sandy beaches and tangles of mangrove curve around the eastern shore.

Hinchinbrook Island Cruises (☑07-4066 8601; www.hinchinbrookislandcruises.com.au) runs a service from Cardwell's Port Hinchinbrook Marina to Hinchinbrook's Ramsay Bay boardwalk (per person one way $99, 1½ hours). It also operates a four-hour, two-island tour (adult/child $110/99) that includes a cruise between Goold and Garden Islands spotting dolphins, dugongs and turtles, before docking at Ramsay Bay boardwalk for a walk on the 9km-long beach and a picnic lunch.

NPRSR camp sites (☑13 74 68; www.npsr.qld.gov.au; sites per person $6.15) are interspersed along the wonderful 32km Thorsborne Trail (or East Coast Trail)

Tully

POP 2350

Though it may look like just another sleepy sugar-cane village, Tully is a burg with a boast, calling itself the 'wettest town in Australia'. A gigantic golden gumboot at Tully's entrance is as high as the waters rose (7.9m) in 1950: climb the spiral staircase to the viewing platform up top to get a sense of just how much that is! And while boggy Babinda challenges Tully's claim, the fact remains that all that rain ensures plenty of raftable rapids on the nearby Tully River, and shimmering fruit farms in need of travelling labour.

The Golden Gumboot Festival (☉May) celebrates the soak with a parade and lashings of entertainment.

Book at the visitor centre for 90-minute tours of Tully Sugar Mill (adult/child $17/11; ☉daily late Jun-early Nov).

🏃 Activities

Ingan Tours TOUR
(☑07-4068 0189; www.ingan.com.au; 5 Blackman St) The Indigenous operators of Ingan Tours visit sacred story places on their full-day Spirit of the Rainforest tours (Tuesdays, Thursdays and Saturdays) and offer powerful, authentic insights into the lives of the area's first people and their relationship with the natural world. It's heady stuff and often the highlight of a trip to Australia for many visitors.

🛏 Sleeping & Eating

Banana Barracks HOSTEL $
(☑07-4068 0455; www.bananabarracks.com; 50 Butler St; 8-/4-bed dm weekly $135/165; @🛜🐕) Banana Barracks is the go-to backpackers for wannabe fruit pickers in the Tully region. The hostel is also the hub of Tully's nightlife, Rafters Bar, with an on-site nightclub.

Mount Tyson Hotel PUB $
(☑07-4068 1088; www.mttysonhotel.com.au; s/d $60/105) This newly renovated pub is a bit bland in terms of ambience, but the motel rooms are fresh and clean, and provide good value for a short stay.

★Redgates Steakhouse DINER $$
(☑0400 773 315; 99 Butler St) A top bloke runs this spacious diner on the way into town. The menu is long and changes often, but the mainstays are the burgers –

TULLY RIVER RAFTING

The Tully River provides thrilling white water year-round thanks to Tully's trademark bucket-downs and the river's hydroelectric floodgates. Rafting trips are timed to coincide with the daily release of the gates, resulting in Grade IV rapids foaming against a backdrop of stunning rainforest scenery.

Day trips with Raging Thunder Adventures (☑07-4030 7990; www.ragingthunder.com.au; full-day rafting $189) or R'n'R White Water Rafting (☑07-4041 9444; www.raft.com.au; full-day rafting from $179) include a BBQ lunch and transport from Tully or nearby Mission Beach.

PALUMA RANGE NATIONAL PARK

It's worth making time to venture off the Bruce Hwy via the Paluma Range National Park, southern gateway to the Wet Tropics World Heritage Area. The park is divided into two parts, the Mt Spec section and the northern Jourama Falls section, with both offering a variety of waterholes, inland beaches, hiking trails and a gentle entrée into tropical north Queensland. This glorious parallel universe, running alongside the Bruce Hwy from roughly Ingham to Townsville, is also prime platypus-spotting territory.

Mt Spec

The Mt Spec part of the park (61km north of Townsville or 40km south of Ingham) is a misty Eden of rainforest and eucalypt trees criss-crossed by a variety of walking tracks. This range of habitats houses an incredibly diverse population of birds, from golden bowerbirds to black cockatoos.

From the northern access route of the Bruce Hwy, take the 4km-long partially sealed Spiegelhauer Rd to Big Crystal Creek; from there, it's an easy 100m walk from the car park to Paradise Waterhole, a popular spot with a sandy beach and lofty mountain views.

The southern access route (Mt Spec Rd) is a sealed, albeit twisty, road that writhes up the mountains to Paluma Village. Beware: though you may have come up here 'just for a drive', the village's cool air and warm populace may change your mind.

En route to Paluma, be sure to stop off at Little Crystal Creek, a picturesque swimming hole with a cute stone bridge, picnic area and waterfalls.

In Paluma village the cool **Rainforest Inn** (☑ 07-4770 8688; www.rainforestinnpaluma. com; 1 Mt Spec Rd; d $125; ❋) has well-designed rooms and a nearby restaurant-bar.

Jourama Falls

Waterview Creek tumbles down these eponymous falls and other cascades past palms and umbrella trees, making this section a fine place for a picnic and a perambulation. It's a steep climb to the lookout; keep your eyes peeled for kingfishers, freshwater turtles and endangered mahogany gliders on the way up. The **NPSR camping ground** (www. npsr.qld.gov.au; sites per person/family $6.15/24.60) has cold showers, gas BBQs, water (treat before drinking) and composting toilets.

This part of the park is reached via a 6km sealed road (though the creek at the entrance can be impassable in the Wet), 91km north of Townsville and 24km south of Ingham. Be sure to fuel up before veering off the highway.

both the fish and beef ($12) get a massive thumbs up, while the thickshakes and coffee come in a close second. Wi-fi is fast and free.

❶ Information

Tully Visitor & Heritage Centre (☑ 07-4068 2288; Bruce Hwy; ⊙ 8.30am-4.45pm Mon-Fri, 9am-2pm Sat & Sun) The Tully Visitor & Heritage Centre has a brochure outlining a self-guided heritage walk around town, with 17 interpretative panels (including one dedicated to Tully's UFO sightings), and walking-trail maps for the nearby national parks. The centre also has free internet and a book exchange.

❶ Getting There & Away

Greyhound (☑ 1300 473 946; www.grey hound.com.au) and **Premier** (☑ 13 34 10; www.premierms.com.au) buses stop in town on the Brisbane–Cairns route; fares to Cairns/ Townsville are $28/$43. Tully is also on **Queensland Rail's** (☑ 1800 872 467; www. traveltrain.com.au) Brisbane–Cairns train line.

Mission Beach

The rainforest meets the Coral Sea at Mission Beach, a tropical enclave of beach hamlets that has long threatened to take the Australian getaway circuit by storm. Yet this Coral Sea bolt-hole has maintained a beautiful balance between yoga living, backpacker bravado and eco-escape, plus it has Australia's highest density of cassowaries. Hidden among World Heritage rainforest, a short 30km detour from the Bruce Hwy, this 14km-long palm-fringed stretch of secluded

Mission Beach

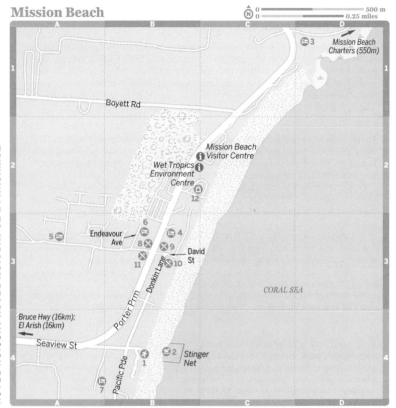

N 0 ——————— 500 m
0 ——————— 0.25 miles

Boyett Rd

Mission Beach
Visitor Centre

Wet Tropics
Environment
Centre

12

6

5

Endeavour
Ave

8

11

4

9

David
St

10

Mission Beach
Charters (550m)

3

CORAL SEA

Bruce Hwy (16km);
El Arish (16km)

Seaview St

Porter Prm

Donkin Lane

Pacific Pde

1

2

Stinger
Net

7

inlets and wide, empty beaches is one of the closest access points to the Great Barrier Reef, and is the gateway to Dunk Island.

Collectively referred to as Mission Beach, or just 'Mission', the area comprises a sequence of individual, very small and laid-back villages strung along the coast. Bingil Bay lies 4.8km north of Mission Beach proper (sometimes called North Mission). Wongaling Beach is 5km south; from here it's a further 5.5km south to South Mission Beach. Most amenities are in Mission proper and Wongaling Beach.

🏃 Activities

There's a stinger enclosure for swimming during stinger season (January through March).

Ingan Tours   WALKING
(📞1800 728 067; www.ingan.com.au; 4hr tours adult/child $130/70; ⊙Tue, Thu & Sat) Local

Aboriginal guides offer a unique insight into the ancient rainforest around Mission Beach. A fabulous new kayak tour along the Tully is also highly recommended (adult/child $100/65). Prices include pick-ups from Mission Beach and a light lunch.

Skydive Mission Beach SKYDIVING
(☑ 1300 800 840; www.skydivemissionbeach.com.au; 1 Wongaling Beach Rd; 1830/4270m tandem dives $199/334) Mission Beach is rightfully one of the most popular spots in Australia for skydiving, with views over gorgeous islands and blue water, and a soft landing on a white-sand beach. Skydive Australia, known locally as Skydive Mission Beach, runs several flights per day.

Altitude Skydivers SKYDIVING
(☑ 07-4088 6635; www.altitudeskydive.com.au; 4/46 Porter Promenade; 4270m $299) The new boys in town are a small, highly experienced and fun-loving jump team, with very competitive pricing.

Coral Sea Kayaking KAYAKING
(☑ 07-4068 9154; www.coralseakayaking.com; half-/full-day tours incl lunch $80/136) Knowledgeable full-day guided tours to Dunk Island; easygoing bob-arounds on the half-day option. Longer three-day journeys to the Barnard and Family Islands can be arranged.

Fishin' Mission FISHING
(☑ 0427 323 469; www.fishinmission.com.au; half-/full-day trips $160/260) Chilled-out reef-fishing charters with local pros. By far the most reputable operator in the area.

🛏 Sleeping

★ **Jackaroo Hostel** HOSTEL $
(☑ 07-4068 7137; www.jackaroohostel.com; 13 Frizelle Rd; sites $12-15, dm/d incl breakfast from $25/58; 🅿 @ 🛜 🌊) Oh to be young enough again to justify whiling away the days in a timber pole-frame retreat deep in the rainforest by a huge jungle pool overlooking the Coral Sea. Bugger it: just drive inland past Clump Mountain, find a quiet double room and wander around the communal areas granting silent, wise nods to those young rascals bronzing in the tropical sun.

Dunk Island View Caravan Park CARAVAN PARK $
(☑ 07-4068 8248; www.dunkislandviewcaravanpark.com; 21 Webb Rd; sites $30-32, 1-/2-bedroom units $105/135; 🌊 🛜 🌊 🌊) One of the best caravan parks we visited in northern Queensland; its views of Dunk Island are stupendous and the grounds are impeccably kept. The small pool is welcome in stinger season, and there's also an on-site cafe (fish and chips, $9).

Mission Beach Ecovillage CABIN $
(☑ 07-4068 7534; www.ecovillage.com.au; Clump Point Rd; d $119-150, 2-bedroom bungalows $180; 🌊 🛜 🌊) With its own banana and lime trees scattered around its tropical gardens, and a direct path through the rainforest to the beach, this 'ecovillage' makes the most of its environment. Clustered around a rocky pool, the bungalows are a little worn, but there's a licensed restaurant and bubbly enough service to compensate.

Mission Beach Retreat HOSTEL $
(☑ 07-4088 6229; www.missionbeachretreat.com.au; 49 Porter Promenade; dm $22-25, d $56; 🌊 @ 🛜 🌊) Bang in the centre of town, with the bonus of being beachfront, this is an easy, breezy backpacker spot that's hard not to like. YHA-accredited, it fills up quickly. Extras include a shuttle service to the supermarket and free wi-fi. Staff insist on friendly interaction with guests.

Rainforest Motel MOTEL $
(☑ 07-4088 6787; www.rainforestmotel.com.au; 9 Endeavour Ave; d/tw $95/105; 🌊 @ 🛜 🌊) Though not about to gain plaudits for contemporary luxury, this hidden motel off Mission's humble main street is nonetheless great value and is very well serviced. Rooms are cool and clean, and the communal sitting areas near the tiny pool feel like you've been dropped in a rainforest garden. Free bikes available.

Sanctuary CABIN $
(☑ 1800 777 012, 07-4088 6064; www.sanctuaryatmission.com; 72 Holt Rd; dm $40, huts s/d from $75/80, cabins $185; ⊘ mid-Apr–mid-Dec; @ 🛜 🌊) 🌱 This popular group retreat centre is reached by a steep 600m-long rainforest walking track from the car park (4WD pick-up available). At Sanctuary you can sleep surrounded only by flyscreen on a platform in a simple hut, or opt for an en-suite cabin whose shower has floor-to-ceiling rainforest views. Yoga, night walks and massage are all available to guests at a cost.

Scotty's Mission Beach House HOSTEL $
(☑ 07-4068 8676, 1800 665 567; www.scottysbeachhouse.com.au; 167 Reid Rd; dm $24-29,

d $71; ✳@🛜⛵) Dropped right on a quiet stretch of beach, Scotty's is a YHA hostel with modest rooms grouped around a grassy pool area. Management is tapped into the east coast circuit and is keen to help guests capitalise on their adventure. Out front, Scotty's Bar & Grill (mains $12-24; ⏱5pm-12am), open to nonguests, has something happening virtually every night, from fire-twirling shows to pool comps to live music.

Hibiscus Lodge B&B
B&B $$

(☑07-4068 9096; www.hibiscuslodge.com.au; 5 Kurrajong Cl; r from $145; 🛜) The main homestead of this charming Mission Beach property forms the backdrop for a local fauna roll-call. Hibiscus Lodge is a discerning choice; you can taste the self-satisfaction at the breakfast table. With only three (very private) rooms, bookings are essential. Generous online discounts are available. No kids.

Licuala Lodge
B&B $$

(☑07-4068 8194; www.licualalodge.com.au; 11 Mission Circle; d incl breakfast from $135; 🛜⛵) You'll need your own car and a willingness to sit still at this peaceful B&B located 1.5km from the beach and pretty much everything else. Guests alternate between the wonderful verandah, where breakfast can be taken overlooking landscaped gardens, and the swimming pool surrounded by a rock garden. Cassowaries pop by regularly to check out the scene.

Nautilus B&B
B&B $$

(1 Nautilus St; 2-bedroom apt from $180) While bookings are technically only available online, it's worth popping past Nautilus B&B and asking Dena if she can help you out. Two newly built, pristine white-tiled apartments sit side-by-side atop a hill overlooking the town, offering a smooth stay. The one large shared bathroom has a powerful shower, while each room has its own small courtyard.

The lounge and open-plan kitchen are great for enjoying your breakfast ($18 per person) and planning the day ahead. Look out for wallabies grazing nearby at sunset.

★ Sejala on the Beach
CABIN $$$

(☑07-4088 6699; www.sejala.com.au; 26 Pacific Pde; d $275; ✳⛵) Choose from 'Waves', 'Coral' and 'Beaches', three self-contained beach 'huts' within snoring sound of the coconut palms. Each one comes with rainforest shower, deck with private BBQ and loads of character. Perfect for hiding away with a partner.

Castaways Resort & Spa
RESORT $$$

(☑07-4068 7444; www.castaways.com.au; Pacific Pde; d $115-265 1-/2-bedroom units $290/360; ✳@🛜⛵) Stare longingly out to sea from your unit in this mainstay of the Mission Beach family holiday scene. Travellers on a budget can play it smart in a simple rainforest room ($115) and take advantage of the two elongated pools, a luxurious spa (www.driftspa.com.au; Pacific Pde) and stunning beach views from its tropical-style bar-restaurant (mains $12-32; ⏱breakfast, lunch & dinner). Come on Tuesdays for tropical high tea.

✗ Eating

Early Birds Cafe
CAFE $

(Shop 2, 46 Porter Promenade; mains $7-18; ⏱6am-3pm Thu-Tue; 🖉) The only joint open first thing in the morning, Early Birds wins return customers with its honest, cheap, cafe-style breakfasts (veggie $14) and famous, bigger-than-average fresh juices.

Fish Bar
SEAFOOD $

(☑07-4088 6419; Porter Promenade; mains $10-17; ⏱10am-midnight) Very affordable fish and other ocean creatures are served up in a casual atmosphere. A small courtyard has views of the sea. Takeaway available.

★ Bingil Bay Cafe
CAFE $$

(☑07-4068 7146; 29 Bingil Bay Rd; mains $14-23; ⏱6.30am-10pm; 🖉) Sunshine, rainbows, coffee and gourmet grub make up the experience at this lavender landmark with a great porch for watching the world drift by. Breakfast is a highlight, but it's open all day. Regular art displays and live music ensure a creative clientele.

Caffe Rustica
ITALIAN $$

(☑07-4068 9111; 24 Wongaling Beach Rd; mains $13-25, pizzas $10-25; ⏱5pm-late Wed-Sat, 10am-9pm Sun; 🖉) Traditional pizza and pasta are the staples at this evening haunt set inside a corrugated-iron beach shack; they also make their own gelato and sorbet. Bookings are encouraged as it's popular with locals year-round.

Garage Bar & Grill
MODERN AUSTRALIAN $$

(☑07-4088 6280; 41 Donkin Lane; meze plates $17; ⏱9am-late; ✳🖉) The hot spot in Mission with the twenty-something set, the Garage is famous for its delicious 'sliders' (mini

THE CASSOWARY: ENDANGERED NATIVE

Like something out of *Jurassic Park*, this flightless prehistoric bird struts through the rainforest. It's as tall as a grown man, has three razor-sharp, dagger-style clawed toes, a bright-blue head, red wattles (the lobes hanging from its neck), a helmet-like horn, and shaggy black feathers similar to an emu's. Meet the cassowary, an important link in the rainforest ecosystem. It's the only animal capable of dispersing the seeds of more than 70 species of trees whose fruit is too large for other rainforest animals to digest and pass (which acts as fertiliser). You're most likely to see cassowaries in the wild around Mission Beach, Etty Bay and the Cape Tribulation section of the Daintree National Park. They can be aggressive, particularly if they have chicks. Do not approach them; if one threatens you, don't run – give the bird right-of-way and try to keep something solid between you and it, preferably a tree.

It is estimated that there are 1000 or less cassowaries in the wild north of Queensland. An endangered species, the cassowary's biggest threat is loss of habitat, and most recently the cause has been natural. Tropical Cyclone Yasi stripped much of the rainforest around Mission Beach bare, threatening the struggling population with starvation. The cyclone also left the birds exposed to the elements, and more vulnerable to dog attacks and cars as they venture out in search of food.

Next to the Mission Beach visitor centre, there are cassowary conservation displays at the **Wet Tropics Environment Centre** (www.wettropics.gov.au), staffed by volunteers from the **Community for Cassowary & Coastal Conservation** (www.cassowary conservation.asn.au). Proceeds from gift-shop purchases go towards buying cassowary habitat. The website www.savethecassowary.org.au is also a good source of info.

burgers) and free-pour cocktails ($14). The hard-working chef mixes up the menu regularly and the management ensure there's a festive vibe in the beer garden with an eclectic playlist and tapas specials.

Millers Beach Bar & Grill   PUB FOOD $$
(☑07-4068 8177; www.millersbeachbar.com.au; 1 Banfield Pde; mains $14-38; ☺3pm-late Tue-Fri, noon-late Sat & Sun) Wongaling Beach's evening star, Millers is so close to the beach you'll be picking sand out of your beer. It's a popular function space, but the occasional crowd only adds to the ambience, especially at sunset with Dunk Island calling in the distance. The fish burger ($18) was a hit when we visited.

Zenbah   INTERNATIONAL $$
(☑07-4088 6040; 39 Porter Promenade; mains $12-28; ☺10am-1.30am Fri & Sat, to midnight Sun-Thu) The colourful chairs on the pavement mark Zenbah as the vibrant little eatery/hang-out that it is. The food ranges from Middle Eastern to Asian all the way back to pizza, and you can digest it all against a backdrop of live tunes on Fridays and Saturdays.

Sealevel   SEAFOOD $$
(☑07-4088 6179; 42 Donkin Lane; mains $15-30; ☺noon-9pm) The newest restaurant in Mission Beach village has the best location – beachfront and square – but is suffering a few teething problems due to poor layout

and an inconsistent menu. The line-caught jewfish was sensational ($17), but the barramundi ($18) was not fresh. A barren concrete area doubles as a beer garden. One to watch if they get it right.

★PepperVine   MODERN AUSTRALIAN $$$
(☑07-4088 6538; 2 David St; mains $16-32; ☺4.30-11pm) On the Village Green, PepperVine is an uncomplicated contemporary restaurant borrowing from Italian, Spanish and Mod-Oz culinary influences, but nailing the atmosphere and service. Wood-fired pizza and a glass of Australian wine is the early evening staple, but the fine dining announces itself after sunset as the crowd descends.

🛍 Shopping

Between them, **Mission Beach Markets** (Porter Promenade; ☺8am-1pm 1st & 3rd Sun of month) and **Mission Beach Rotary Monster Market** (Marcs Park, Cassowary Dr, Wongaling Beach; ☺8am-12.30pm last Sun of month Apr-Dec) operate three Sundays a month.

ℹ Information

Mission Beach Visitor Centre (☑07-4068 7099; www.missionbeachtourism.com; Porters Promenade, Mission Beach; ☺9am-4.45pm Mon-Sat, 10am-4pm Sun) The main visitor centre in town has reams of information in multiple languages.

WORTH A TRIP

PARONELLA PARK

Set beside a series of creeks and waterfalls 50km northwest of Mission Beach (with at least one resident croc), Paronella Park (07-4065 0000; www.paronellapark.com.au; Japoonvale Rd, Mena Creek; adult/child $44/23) is a whimsical tropical retreat and a romantic, Dali-esque escape from reality. Moss-covered steps, lush tropical foliage and huge palatial structures appear straight from some Victorian-Mayan movie set.

Self-made Spanish immigrant José Paronella built Paronella Park as a gift to his wife Margarita before opening it to the public. He died in 1948, and the park is now privately owned and National Trust listed.

Nearby camping and quaint on-site cabins ($90) are available.

Wet Tropics Environment Centre (07-4068 7197; www.wettropics.gov.au; Porter Promenade; ⊙10am-4pm) Next door to the Mission Beach Visitor Centre you'll find displays and movies about the local environment, including, of course, the cassowary.

❶ Getting There & Away

Greyhound (1300 473 946; www.greyhound.com.au) and **Premier** (13 34 10; www.premierms.com.au) buses stop in Wongaling Beach next to the 'big cassowary'. Fares with Greyhound/Premier are $25/19 to Cairns (two hours), $44/46 to Townsville (3½ hours).

Dunk Island

Dunk is known to the Djiru Aboriginal people as Coonanglebah (the island of peace and plenty). They're not wrong: this is pretty much your ideal tropical island, with lush jungle, white-sand beaches and impossibly blue water.

Walking trails criss-cross (and almost circumnavigate) Dunk: the circuit track (9.2km) is the best way to have a proper stickybeak at the island's interior and abundant wildlife. There's snorkelling over bommies (coral pinnacles or outcroppings) at Muggy Muggy and great swimming at truly beautiful Coconut Beach. On weekends in high season there are often special events such as bongo lessons or a ukulele band – check with the Mission Beach Visitor Centre.

Dunk Island was hammered by Cyclone Yasi in 2011, but has since mostly recovered, although part of the old resort remains off limits and a veritable eyesore.

Mission Beach Charters (07-4068 7009; adult/child return $35/18; 3hr tour $50) runs a shuttle as well as a range of fishing, diving and camping trips, or you can stay at the Dunk Island campground (0417 873 390; per person/family $6.15/24.60).

Innisfail & Around

POP 7500

Innisfail is a handsome, unhurried North Queensland town known for river fishing, farming and a remarkable collection of art-deco edifices. Only 80km south of Cairns, but not a tourist in sight, here you can join the locals on the wide Johnstone River, dodge tractors along the pretty main street, or discuss the fortunes of the Cowboys rugby league team.

Relaxing, beachside Flying Fish Point is some 8km northeast of Innisfail's town centre, while national parks, including the fun Mamu Tropical Sky Walk (a 2.5km, wheelchair-accessible walking circuit through the canopy), are within a short drive. Turn-offs out of town lead to different beach communities including exquisite Etty Bay, with its wandering cassowaries, rocky headlands, rainforest, large stinger enclosure and a simple but superbly sited caravan park.

In March, the Feast of the Senses (www.feastofthesenses.com.au) is a highlight of the northern Queensland culinary calendar.

❍ Sights

Mamu Tropical Sky Walk VIEWPOINT
(www.mamutropicalskywalk.com.au; Palmerston Hwy; adult/child/family $23/12/64; ⊙9.30am-5.30pm, last entry 4.30pm) About 27km along the Palmerston Hwy (signposted 4km northwest of Innisfail), this canopy-level rainforest walkway gives you eye-level views of the fruits, flowers and birds, and a bird's-eye perspective from its 100-step, 37m-high tower. Allow at least an hour to complete the 2.5km, wheelchair-accessible circuit.

The Palmerston Hwy continues west to Millaa Millaa, passing the entrance to the Waterfalls Circuit.

🛏 Sleeping & Eating

Backpackers Shack
HOSTEL $

(📞 0499 042 446, 07-4061 7760; www.backpackers shack.com; 7 Ernest St; dm per week $195; P ❄ @) Modest, dormitory-style accommodation awaits guests at the Shack, a locally operated, unofficial employment agency for seasonal fruit workers.

Flying Fish Tourist Park
CARAVAN PARK $

(📞 07-4061 3131; www.ffpvanpark.com.au; 39 Elizabeth St, Flying Fish Point; powered sites $32-39, cabins $50-99, villa $119-125; ❄ @ 🛜 🏊) Travellers with their own wheels (or camping gear), will love this laid-back park from where you can fish right off the beach across the road, or organise boat rental through the friendly managers. The cabins are spacious and fragrant. Call ahead for directions.

★ Barrier Reef Motel
MOTEL $$

(📞 07-4061 4988; www.barrierreefmotel.com.au; Bruce Hwy; s/d from $135/145; ❄ @ 🛜 🏊) More than a road-trip stopover, the Barrier Reef Motel is almost reason enough to hang out an extra day or so in Innisfail. The Barrier Reef has exceptional motel-style rooms, with soothing tiled floors and large bathrooms, and assured customer service. It is right next to the visitor centre and the on-site restaurant (mains $28-30.50; ⏱ breakfast & dinner; 🍴) serves great 'surf and turf' (steak and seafood). The saltwater pool and bar give it an extra tick.

★ Oliveri's Continental Deli
DELI $

(www.oliverisdeli.com.au; 41 Edith St; sandwiches $8.50-11; ⏱ 8.30am-5.15pm Mon-Fri, to 12.30pm Sat; 🍴) An Innisfail institution offering goodies including 60-plus varieties of European

cheese, ham and salami, and scrumptious sandwiches. Fantastic coffee, too.

Innisfail Seafood
SEAFOOD $

(51 Fitzgerald Esplanade; ⏱ 8am-6pm Mon-Fri, 9am-4pm Sat, 10am-4pm Sun) Fresh-as-it-gets fish to throw on the barbecue and organic cooked prawns by the bagful ($18 to $20 per kilogram).

Flying Fish Point Cafe
SEAFOOD $

(9 Elizabeth St, Flying Fish Point; mains $12-25; ⏱ 7.30am-8pm) Regulars enjoy the idyllic, breezy seaside setting and the huge seafood baskets of battered and crumbed fish, barbecued calamari, wonton prawns, tempura scallops and more.

ℹ Information

NPRSR (www.nprsr.qld.gov.au) Has details of campgrounds and walking trails.

Visitor Information Centre (📞 07-4061 2655; cnr Eslick St & Bruce Hwy; ⏱ 9am-4.30pm Mon-Fri, to 1pm Sat, to 12pm Sun) The helpful visitor centre gives out discount vouchers for many of the area's attractions and has a full list of accommodation options that can help with finding work.

ℹ Getting There & Away

Bus services operate once daily with **Premier** (📞 13 34 10; www.premierms.com.au) and several times daily with **Greyhound** (📞 1300 473 946; www.greyhound.com.au) between Innisfail and Townsville ($45 to $52, 4½ hours) and Cairns ($19 to $22, 1½ hours).

Innisfail is on the Cairns–Brisbane train line; contact **Queensland Rail** (📞 1800 872 467; www.queenslandrail.com.au) for information.

Cairns & the Daintree Rainforest

Best Places to Eat

➜ Vivo (p247)

➜ Coco Mojo (p248)

➜ Ganbaranba (p239)

➜ Prawn Star (p241)

➜ On the Inlet (p259)

Best Places to Sleep

➜ Peppers Beach Club (p258)

➜ Cape Trib Beach House (p265)

➜ Cedar Park Rainforest Resort (p250)

➜ Coral Beach Lodge (p257)

➜ Sarayi (p247)

Why Go?

Tropical, touristy Cairns is an unmissable stop on any east coast traveller's itinerary. Experienced divers and first-time toe-dippers swarm to the steamy city for its easy access to the Great Barrier Reef, while those more interested in submerging themselves in boozy good times are well served by a barrage of bars and clubs. The Atherton Tablelands – home to cooler climes, volcanic craters, jungly waterfalls and gourmet food producers – are a short, scenic drive inland.

The winding road north of Cairns hugs ludicrously scenic sections of shoreline en route to ritzy Port Douglas; keep going and you'll meet the mighty Daintree River's vehicular ferry. From here, profuse, protected rainforest stretches up to Cape Tribulation and beyond, tumbling on to long swaths of white-sand beaches; don't be so awestruck that you forget to keep an eye out for crocs!

When to Go
Cairns

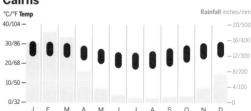

May Port Douglas pizazz at Carnivale. Stinger season ends.

Aug Milder temps and the Cairns Festival make this an ideal time to visit.

Nov Divers delight in the reef's annual coral spawning.

CAIRNS

POP 160,285

Cairns (pronounced 'cans') has come a long way since its beginnings as a boggy swamp and rollicking goldfields port. Heaving under the weight of countless resorts, tour agencies, souvenir shops and a million reminders of its proximity to the Great Barrier Reef, Cairns is unabashedly geared towards tourism.

Old salts claim Cairns has lost its soul, but it does have an infectious holiday vibe. The city centre is more boardshorts than briefcases, and you'll find yourself throwing away all notions of speed and schedules here, thanks to heady humidity and a hearty hospitality that can turn a short stroll into an impromptu social event. Fittingly, Cairns is awash with bars, clubs, eateries and cafes suiting all budgets. There's no beach in town, but the magnificent Esplanade Lagoon more than makes up for it; otherwise, the northern beaches are but a local bus ride or short drive away.

⊙ Sights

Cairns' newest attraction, the state-of-the-art **Cairns Aquarium** (⟋07-4044 7300; www.cairnsaquarium.com.au; 163 Abbott St; adult/child/family $42/28/126; ⊙9am-5.30pm), was due to open in mid-2017.

★**Cairns Esplanade, Boardwalk & Lagoon**   WATERFRONT
(www.cairns.qld.gov.au/esplanade; ⊙lagoon 6am-9pm Thu-Tue, noon-9pm Wed; 👬) **FREE** Sunseekers and fun-lovers flock to Cairns Esplanade's spectacular swimming lagoon on the city's reclaimed foreshore. The artificial, sandy-edged, 4800-sq-metre saltwater pool is lifeguard patrolled and illuminated nightly. The adjacent 3km foreshore boardwalk has picnic areas, birdwatching vantage points, free barbecues and fitness equipment. Follow the signposts for the excellent **Muddy's** (www.cairns.qld.gov.au/esplanade/facilities/playgrounds/muddys) **FREE**, which has playgrounds and water fun for little kids, and the skate ramp, beach volleyball courts, bouldering park and Fun Ship playground.

★**Flecker Botanic Gardens**   GARDENS
(⟋07-4032 6650; www.cairns.qld.gov.au/cbg; 64 Collins Ave; ⊙grounds 7.30am-5.30pm, visitor centre 9am-4.30pm Mon-Fri, 10am-2.30pm Sat & Sun) **FREE** These gorgeous gardens are an explosion of greenery and rainforest plants. Highlights include a section devoted to Aboriginal plant use, the Gondwana Heritage Garden, and an excellent conservatory filled with butterflies and exotic flowers. Staff at the made-of-mirrors visitor centre can advise on free guided garden walks (daily from 10am).

Follow the Rainforest Boardwalk to Saltwater Creek and Centenary Lakes, a birdwatcher's delight. Uphill from the gardens, **Mt Whitfield Conservation Park** (www.cairns.qld.gov.au/facilities-sport-leisure/sport-and-recreation/active-living/red-and-green-arrow-walking-tracks; Edge Hill) has walking tracks through the rainforest to city viewpoints.

★**Reef Teach**   CULTURAL CENTRE
(⟋07-4031 7794; www.reefteach.com.au; 2nd fl, Mainstreet Arcade, 85 Lake St; adult/child/family $23/14/60; ⊙lectures 6.30-8.30pm Tue-Sat) 🗲 Take your knowledge to new depths at this fun, informative centre, where marine experts explain how to identify specific species of fish and coral, and how to approach the reef respectfully.

CAIRNS GALLERIES

Cairns Regional Gallery (⟋07-4046 4800; www.cairnsregionalgallery.com.au; cnr Abbott & Shields Sts; adult/child $5/free; ⊙9am-5pm Mon-Fri, 10am-5pm Sat, 10am-2pm Sun) The permanent collection of this acclaimed gallery has an emphasis on local and Indigenous work.

Canopy Art Centre (⟋07-4041 4678; www.canopyartcentre.com; 124 Grafton St; ⊙10am-5pm Tue-Sat) Showcases prints, paintings, sculptures and weavings of Indigenous artists from Cairns and communities as far north as the Torres Strait.

Tanks Arts Centre (⟋07-4032 6600; www.tanksartscentre.com; 46 Collins Ave; ⊙9.30am-4.30pm Mon-Fri) Three gigantic, ex-WWII fuel-storage tanks have been transformed into art galleries; it's also an inspired performing-arts venue.

KickArts (www.kickarts.org.au; CoCA, 96 Abbott St; ⊙10am-5pm Mon-Sat) **FREE** Showcases cutting-edge local and regional artworks, plus touring exhibitions.

CAIRNS & THE DAINTREE RAINFOREST CAIRNS

Cairns & the Daintree Rainforest Highlights

1 Great Barrier Reef (p235) Diving, snorkelling and swimming among the fish, turtles and multicoloured corals.

2 Kuku-Yalanji Dreamtime Walks (p261) Walking alongside Mossman Gorge's crystal-clear waters.

3 Kuranda (p249) Riding the Skyrail above the rainforest to the markets, then returning to Cairns by the Kuranda Scenic Railway.

4 Palm Cove (p246) Indulging in the romantic restaurants and resorts of pristine Palm Cove.

CORAL SEA

40 km
25 miles

Cape Bedford

Hope Vale

Endeavour River National Park

Cooktown

Mt Cook National Park

Archer Point

Trevathan Falls

Black Mountain National Park

Rossville

Cedar Bay (Mangkal-Mangkalba) National Park

Bloomfield Lodge

Wujal Wujal

Ayton

Bloomfield Falls

Emmagen Beach

Bloomfield Track

10 Cape Tribulation

Myall Beach

Thornton Beach

Cow Bay

Daintree National Park (Cape Tribulation Section)

Daintree Village

Snapper Island National Park

Wonga Beach

Daintree National Park

Newell

9 Port Douglas

Four Mile Beach

1 Great Barrier Reef

Annan River

Annan River Gorge

Helenvale

Endeavour River

Endeavour Falls

81

Lakeland

Palmer River Roadhouse

Mulligan Highway

Peninsula Developmental Rd

Quinkan Reserve

81

81

Mossman Gorge 2

Mossman

Mulligan Highway

N

5 Hartley's Crocodile Adventures (p248) Getting up close to prehistoric predators.

6 Yungaburra Hotel (p253) Stopping for a coldie at Yungaburra's must-see pub.

7 Atherton Tablelands (p249) Cruising green hills and stopping for a swim along the Millaa Millaa Waterfalls Circuit.

8 Chillagoe (p256) Getting a taste of the outback and exploring 400-million-year-old caves.

9 Port Douglas (p253) Sunbathing on Four Mile Beach before hitting the bars and restaurants around Macrossan St.

10 Cape Tribulation (p262) Horse riding, kayaking, ziplining, snorkelling or lazing at laid-back Cape Trib.

Cairns

CAIRNS & THE DAINTREE RAINFOREST

500 m
0.25 miles

200 m
0.1 miles

Enlargement

Rondo Theatre (500m)

NORTH CAIRNS

Tanks Arts Centre (1.2km); Starry Night Cinema (1.5km); Flecker Botanic Gardens (1.5km); Mt Whitfield Conservation Park Walking Tracks (1.8km); Cairns Adventure Park (1.9km); Edge Hill (2km); GSL Aviation (2km); (4km); Smithfield (13km)

Cairns Colonial Club (1.1km)

Cairns Cemetery

MANUNDA

Little St

Smith St

James St

Martyn St

Grove St

Gatton St

Water St

Sheridan St

McLeod St

Thomas St

Charles St

McKenzie St

Digger St

The Esplanade

Lake St

Grove St

Grafton St

Sheridan St

Trinity Bay

Cairns Harbour

Pier Marina

Aplin St

Lake St

Shields St

Sheridan St

McLeod St

Abbott St

Spence St

Grafton St

Florence St

Minnie St

Upward St

Munro Martin Park

The Esplanade

Aplin St

Pierpoint Rd

CAIRNS

Mainstreet Arcade

City Arcade

Reef Teach

Cairns & Tropical North Visitor Information Centre

Cairns Esplanade, Boardwalk & Lagoon

17
60
19
56
39
4
46
8
63
54
57
44
52
41
36
37
16
40
29
61
30
38
42
51
18
49
24
21
5
32
59
28
22
20
48
35
15
26
6
3
25
23
1
55
45
11
12
53
2

Mangrove Boardwalk NATURE RESERVE

(Airport Ave) FREE Explore the swampier side of Cairns on this revelatory wander into the wetlands. Eerie snap-crackle-slop noises provide a fitting soundtrack to the spooky surrounds, which are signposted with informative guides to the weird life forms scurrying in the mud below you. Slather yourself in mosquito repellent. The boardwalk (and its car park) is just before Cairns Airport (p303).

Tjapukai Aboriginal
Cultural Park CULTURAL CENTRE

(☑07-4042 9999; www.tjapukai.com.au; Cairns Western Arterial Rd, Caravonica; adult/child/family $62/42/166; ☻9am-5pm) This award-winning cultural extravaganza is managed by the area's original custodians and tells the story of creation using giant holograms and actors. There's a dance theatre, a gallery, boomerang- and spear-throwing demonstrations and turtle-spotting canoe rides. The Nightfire dinner-and-show package (adult/child/family $123/75/321, from 7pm to 9.30pm) culminates in a fireside corroboree.

Australian Armour &
Artillery Museum MUSEUM

(☑07-4038 1665; www.ausarmour.com; 1145 Kamerunga Rd, Smithfield; adult/child/family $25/15/65; ☻9.30am-4.30pm) Military and history buffs will enjoy this, the largest display of armoured vehicles and artillery in the southern hemisphere. Go for a ride in a tank (adult/child $15/10) or fire off bolt-action rifles (including a WWII British 303 and German Mauser) in the underground bunker (from $80).

Crystal Cascades WATERFALL

(via Redlynch) About 14km from Cairns, the Crystal Cascades are a series of beautiful waterfalls and idyllic, croc-free swimming holes that locals would rather keep to themselves. The area is accessed by a 1.2km (30-minute) pathway. Crystal Cascades is linked to Lake Morris (the city's reservoir) by a steep rainforest walking trail (allow three hours return); it starts near the picnic area.

There is no public transport to the pools. Drive to the suburb of Redlynch, then follow the signs.

🏃 Activities & Tours

Innumerable tour operators run adventure-based activities from Cairns, most offering transfers to/from your accommodation.

CAIRNS & THE DAINTREE RAINFOREST CAIRNS

Cairns

An astounding 800-plus tours drive, chug, sail and fly out of Cairns daily, making the selection process almost overwhelming. We recommend operators with the benefit of years of experience, who cover the bases of what visitors are generally looking for, and then some.

★ **Cairns Zoom & Wildlife Dome**   ADVENTURE SPORTS, WILDLIFE
(☑ 07-4031 7250; www.cairnszoom.com.au; Wharf St; wildlife entry $24, wildlife & zoom $45; ⊙ 9am-6pm) Cards, croupiers and...crocodiles? Sitting on top of the Reef Hotel Casino (p243), this unusual park brings

the best of Far North Queensland's outdoors inside, with a native-creatures zoo, aviary and recreated rainforest. The complex is criss-crossed with ziplines, swings, obstacle courses and more; the truly adventurous can even venture outside for a nerve-testing dome climb.

★ **Behana Days Canyoning**   OUTDOORS
(✐0427 820 993; www.behanadays.com; tours $179) Give the salty stuff a break and join this fantastic freshwater expedition to beautiful Behana Gorge, a rainforest oasis of pools, waterfalls and canyons 45 minutes south of Cairns. The all-day tours include abseiling, ziplining, cliff jumping, snorkelling and swimming; you'll be shown the ropes (literally) on the day. Transfers and lunch included.

★ **Rapid Boarders**   WATER SPORTS
(✐0427 364 311; www.rapidboarders.com.au; tours $235) If you'd rather ride in the rapids than on them, this utterly exhilarating full-day adventure is for you. Thrill seekers ride riverboards down the mighty Tully, taking on pumping Grade 3 rapids at eye level. It's the only tour of its kind in Australia. This is not for the water-shy; participants must be good swimmers and relatively fit.

★ **Aussie Drifterz**   OUTDOORS
(✐0401 318 475; www.facebook.com/aussiedrifterz; adult/child $75/55) Scenic and serene (and virtually guaranteed to kick a hangover), a relaxing bob down the beautiful Behana Gorge on an inner tube is tough to beat. The crystal-clear river runs through natural tree tunnels, and you'll almost certainly catch glimpses of curious wildlife (don't fret; crocs not included).

Cairns Adventure Park   ADVENTURE SPORTS
(✐07-4053 3726; www.cairnsadventurepark. com.au; 82 Aeroglen Dr, Aeroglen; packages from $39; ⊙9am-5pm) Zipline, rock climb or abseil in rainforest surrounds with views to the sea as breathtaking as the high-energy activities themselves. For something a little more sedate, Cairns Adventure Park also offers bushwalks and birdwatching. Contact the office about pick-ups from your accommodation; if you're driving, get there by taking the Aeroglen turn-off opposite Cairns Airport (p303).

Flyboard Cairns   WATER SPORTS
(✐0439 386 955, 0487 921 714; www.flyboard cairns.com.au; 30/60min session $169/299) Billed as a combination of waterskiing, wakeboarding and snowboarding, flyboarding gives thrill seekers the chance to surf the sky while attached to a water jetpack – and cop some bird's-eye views while you're up there. It looks tricky, but the experienced instructors here guarantee even beginners will get airborne; no fly, no pay.

DIVE COURSES & TRIPS

Cairns, scuba-dive capital of the Great Barrier Reef, is a popular place to attain Professional Association of Diving Instructors (PADI) open-water certification. A staggering number of courses (many multilingual) are available; check inclusions thoroughly. All operators require you to have a dive medical certificate, which they can arrange (around $60). Reef taxes ($20 to $80) may apply.

Keen, certified divers should look for specialised dive opportunities such as night diving, annual coral spawning, and trips to Cod Hole, near Lizard Island, one of Australia's premier diving locations. Recommended dive schools and operators include the following:

Mike Ball Dive Expeditions (✐07-4053 0500; www.mikeball.com; 3 Abbott St; liveaboards from $1827, PADI courses from $395)

Cairns Dive Centre (CDC; ✐07-4051 0294; www.cairnsdive.com.au; 121 Abbott St; liveaboard 1-/2-nights from $435/555, day trips from $120, dive courses from $520)

Deep Sea Divers Den (✐07-4046 7333; www.diversden.com.au; 319 Draper St; day trips from $165)

Pro-Dive (✐07-4031 5255; www.prodivecairns.com.au; cnr Grafton & Shields Sts; day trips adult/child from $195/120, PADI courses from $765)

Tusa Dive (✐07-4047 9100; www.tusadive.com; cnr Shields St & Esplanade; adult/child day trips from $205/130) 🍃

AJ Hackett Bungy & Minjin ADVENTURE SPORTS
(☑07-4057 7188; www.ajhackett.com/cairns; McGregor Rd, Smithfield; bungee $169, minjin $129, combos from $259; ☺from 10am) Bungee jump from the 50m rainforest tower or drop 45m and swing through the trees at 120km/h in the Minjin harness swing. Pricing includes return transfers from Cairns.

Scenic Flights

**Great Barrier
Reef Helicopters** SCENIC FLIGHTS
(☑07-4081 8888; www.gbrhelicopters.com.au; Helipad, Pierpoint Rd; flights per person from $175) Offers a range of scenic helicopter flights, from a 10-minute soar above Cairns city to an hour-long hover over the reef and rainforest ($699).

GSL Aviation SCENIC FLIGHTS
(☑1300 475 000; www.gslaviation.com.au; 3 Tom McDonald Dr, Aeroglen; 40min flights per person from $179) Those wanting to see the reef from above would do well to consider these scenic flights; they are cheaper than chopper tours, and offer more time in the air.

White-Water Rafting

Raging Thunder ADVENTURE SPORTS
(☑07-4030 7990; www.ragingthunder.com.au; 59-63 Esplanade) These experienced folks offer rafting, canyoning ($169) and hot-air ballooning ($250) trips and tours. Foam-hounds can choose between full-day Tully River rafting trips (standard trip $209, 'xtreme' trip $250) and half-day Barron trips ($133). They also run transfers (adult/child/family $75/48/205) to/from and activities on Fitzroy Island.

Foaming Fury RAFTING
(☑07-4031 3460; www.foamingfury.com.au; half-/full-day trips from $138/200) Full-day trips on the Russell River, and half-day trips down the Barron. Prices include transfers. Family rafting and multiday package options are also available.

Ballooning & Skydiving

Hot Air Cairns BALLOONING
(☑07-4039 9900; www.hotair.com.au/cairns; Reef Fleet Terminal; 30min flights adult/child from $250/219) Balloons take off from Mareeba to float through dawn over the Atherton Tablelands. Prices include return transfers from Cairns. These trips are worth the 4am wake-up call.

Skydive Cairns ADVENTURE
(☑1300 663 634; www.skydive.com.au/cairns; 47 Shields St; tandem jumps from $334) Scream from 4270m up at otherwise serene views of the reef and rainforest.

City Tours

★ **Segway Tours** OUTDOORS
(☑0451 972 997; www.cairnsninebottours.com; tour $79; ☺tours 9.30am & 3.30pm) Glide through some of Cairns' most beautiful natural surrounds on an easy-to-master Segway. The 90-minute tours start at the Esplanade and run past mangroves, Centenary Lakes and the Botanic Gardens; they're a peaceful and immersive way to check out local flora and fauna (including the ever-present possibility of a croc or two).

Cairns Discovery Tours TOURS
(☑07-4028 3567; www.cairnsdiscoverytours.com; 36 Aplin St; adult/child $75/40; ☺Mon-Sat) Eye-opening afternoon tours that take in the sights of the city, Barron Gorge, the Botanic Gardens (p229) (includes a horticultural-ist-guided tour) and Palm Cove.

Fishing

Fishing Cairns FISHING
(☑0448 563 586; www.fishingcairns.com.au; half-day trips from $95) Choose from a burley-bucket-load of half- to multi-day fly, sports and game fishing tours and charters, on calm or open water. Prices vary accordingly.

Catcha Crab Tours FISHING
(☑07-4051 7992; www.cairnscatchacrab.com.au; adult/child $95/75) These long-running tours not only offer visitors the chance to catch some tasty tucker, but are a simultaneously thrilling and relaxing way to take in the mangroves and mudflats of Trinity Inlet. The four-hour tours, which include morning or afternoon tea plus a fresh crab lunch, depart at 8.30am and 1pm. There are free pick-ups if you're staying in the city centre.

🎊 Festivals & Events

Cairns Show CARNIVAL
(☺Jul) Three days of carnival rides, agricultural exhibits, enthralling events (think dancing diggers and wood-chopping competitions) and all the deep-fried delights you can stomach. The last day of the Show is a public holiday in Cairns.

Cairns Ukulele Festival MUSIC
(www.cairnsukulelefestival.net; ☺late Aug) Uke players from around the world descend on Cairns every August to plinka-plinka in paradise. Events include workshops, jams and parties.

SEX ON THE REEF

If you're a keen diver or just a romantic at heart, try to time your visit with the annual coral spawning, an all-in orgy in which reef corals simultaneously release millions of eggs and sperm into the water. The ejaculatory event has been described as looking like a psychedelic snowstorm, with trails of reproductive matter streaking the sea in rainbow colours visible from miles away.

The spawning occurs sometime in November or December; the exact date depends on factors including water temperature (must be 26°C or above), the date of the full moon, the stillness of the water and the perfect balance between light and dark (who doesn't appreciate a bit of mood lighting?). Most Cairns-based diving outfits offer special spawning night dives for those looking to get in on the action. Even if you're on land, you may notice an, um, 'amorous' aroma on the night of the mass love-in.

Cairns Festival　　　　　　　　FAIR
(www.cairns.qld.gov.au/festival; ⊘ end Aug-early Sep) The Cairns Festival takes over the city with a packed program of performing arts, visual arts, music and family events.

🛏 Sleeping

Cairns is a backpacker hot spot, with hostels ranging from intimate, converted houses to hangar-sized resorts. Holiday apartment complexes are dotted across the city. Dozens of nondescript, drive-in motels line Sheridan St.

Families and groups should check out **Cairns Holiday Homes** (📞07-4045 2143; www. cairnsholidayhomes.com.au). If you plan to stick around for a while, **Cairns Sharehouse** (📞07-4041 1875; www.cairns-sharehouse.com; 17 Scott St; per week from \$120-260; ❋🗻🖥) has around 200 long-stay rooms strewn across the city. The **Accommodation Centre** (📞1800 807 730, 07-4051 4066; www.accomcentre. com.au) has information on a wide range of sleeping options.

★**Bellview**　　　　　　　　HOSTEL **$**
(📞07-4031 4377; www.bellviewcairns.com.au; 85-87 Esplanade; dm/s/d \$22/35/55, motel units \$59-75; P❋🗻🖥) This low-key hostel has been on the radars of discerning backpackers since – seemingly – time eternal. There's little surprise it's lasted so long, thanks to a perfect position looming over the most bustling slice of the Esplanade, basic but well-maintained rooms and a staff that knows its stuff; the lovely pool helps too. Despite its central location, noise doesn't seem to travel to the rooms.

★**Cairns Coconut**
Holiday Resort　　　　CARAVAN PARK **$**
(📞07-4054 6644; www.coconut.com.au; cnr Bruce Hwy & Anderson Rd, Woree; powered sites/cabins/

units/villas/condos from \$43/115/135/155/245; P❋🗻🖥) If you're travelling with kids and don't mind being a bit (8km) out of town, this holiday park is a destination unto itself. It's got a massive water park, two pools with slides, playgrounds, a humungous jumping pillow, tennis courts, minigolf, spas, an outdoor cinema and much more, all spread over 11 immaculate hectares. Accommodation choices are as varied as the facilities.

★**Cairns Plaza Hotel**　　　　HOTEL **$**
(📞07-4051 4688; www.cairnsplaza.com.au; 145 Esplanade; d/studios/ste from \$124/150/170; P❋@🗻🖥) One of Cairns' original high-rise hotels, the Plaza is – thanks to a full makeover and professional staff – one of the best. Rooms have crisp, clean decor, and functional kitchenettes; many enjoy stunning views over Trinity Bay. A guest laundry, friendly round-the-clock reception staff and great rates make it an excellent choice. Kids will be thrilled by its location, directly across from Muddy's (p229).

★**Travellers Oasis**　　　　HOSTEL **$**
(📞07-4052 1377; www.travellersoasis.com.au; 8 Scott St; dm/s/d from \$28/57/68; P❋@🗻🖥) Folks love this little hippie hostel, hidden away in a side street behind Cairns Central Shopping Centre. It's intimate, inviting and less party-centric than many of Cairns' other offerings. A range of room types – from three-, four- and six-bed dorms, to single, twin and deluxe double rooms – are available. Air conditioning is \$1 for three hours.

★**Tropic Days**　　　　　　　HOSTEL **$**
(📞07-4041 1521; www.tropicdays.com.au; 28 Bunting St, Bungalow; camping per person \$14, tents \$18, dm/d from \$26/64; P❋@🗻🖥) Tucked behind the showgrounds (with a

courtesy bus into town), this popular hostel has a tropical garden with hammocks, pool table, bunk-free dorms, fresh linen and towels, free wi-fi and a relaxed vibe. Its Monday night croc, emu and roo barbecues are legendary. Air conditioning is $1 for three hours.

Tropic Days and the equally awesome Travellers Oasis are sister hostels.

★ Gilligan's Backpacker's Hotel & Resort
HOSTEL $

(☑07-4041 6566; www.gilligans.com.au; 57-89 Grafton St; dm/r from $24/120; ※@🛜☎) There's nothing quite like Gilligan's: a loud, proud, party-hardy flashpacker resort, where all rooms have bathrooms and most have balconies. Higher-priced rooms come with fridges and TVs. Guests get $4 dinners. The mammoth bar and adjacent lagoon pool is the place to be seen, and there's more nightly entertainment than you can poke a stick at. Pick-up central.

★ Lake Placid Tourist Park
CARAVAN PARK $

(☑07-4039 2509; www.lakeplacidtouristpark.com; Lake Placid Rd; powered sites from $37, bungalows from $60, en-suite cabins from $85, cottages from $110; P※🛜☎🏊) Just a 15-minute drive from the city centre, but far enough away to revel in rainforesty repose, this delightful spot overlooks the aptly named Lake Placid: it's an excellent alternative to staying downtown if you're driving. Camping and a variety of well-priced, tasteful accommodation options are available. It's within striking distance of a wide range of attractions and the northern beaches.

★ Northern Greenhouse
HOSTEL $

(☑07-4047 7200; www.northerngreenhouse. com.au; 117 Grafton St; dm/apt from $26/95; P※🛜☎) It fits into the budget category, but this friendly, relaxed place is a cut above, with tidy dorms and neat studio-style apartments with kitchens and balconies. The central deck, pool and games room are great for socialising. Free breakfast and Sunday BBQ seal the deal.

Cairns Central YHA
HOSTEL $

(☑07-4051 0772; www.yha.com.au; 20-26 McLeod St; dm/s/d from $27.50/59.50/71; ※@☎) Opposite Cairns Central Shopping Centre, this award-winning YHA is bright, spotlessly clean and professionally staffed. En-suite rooms are available and there are free pancakes for breakfast!

Floriana Guesthouse
GUESTHOUSE $

(☑07-4051 7886; www.florianaguesthouse.com; 183 Esplanade; s/d $79/89, studios $130-150; ※@🛜☎) The Cairns of old still exists at this quirky guesthouse, which retains its original polished floorboards and art-deco fittings. The swirling staircase leads to 10 individually decorated rooms; all have bathrooms.

Cairns Girls Hostel
HOSTEL $

(☑07-4051 2016; www.cairnsgirlshostel.com.au; 147 Lake St; dm/tw $20/48; 🛜) Sorry lads! This white-glove-test-clean, female-only hostel is one of the most accommodating budget stays in Cairns.

Cairns Colonial Club
RESORT $$

(☑07-4053 8800; www.cairnscolonialclub.com.au; 18-26 Cannon St, Manunda; r $95-175; P※🛜☎) A stalwart on the Cairns accommodation map since 1986, this Queenslander-style resort has a little something for everyone; families, businessfolk and solo travellers all love it here. Tucked away in a leafy suburb, the 11-acre complex boasts three pools, playgrounds, bars, a popular restaurant and gorgeous gardens. It's 4km from the centre of town; a shuttle bus runs regularly.

Bay Village Tropical Retreat
APARTMENT $$

(☑07-4051 4622; www.bayvillage.com.au; cnr Lake & Gatton Sts; d $135, apt $165-275; P※🛜☎) Sleek, shiny and ever-so-slightly removed from the Cairns hubbub, this complex offers large, cool apartments (one to three bedrooms) and spacious serviced rooms. It's a lovely place to hang your hat, and perhaps an even better spot for filling your stomach; it's attached to the award-winning Bayleaf Balinese Restaurant (p241).

Pacific Hotel
HOTEL $$

(☑07-4051 788; www.pacifichotelcairns.com; cnr Esplanade & Spence St; d from $144; P※🛜☎) In a prime location at the southern-end start of the Esplanade, this iconic hotel has been lovingly maintained and refurbished. There's a fun blend of original '70s features and woodwork, with fresh, modern amenities. All rooms have balconies. Friendly, helpful staff help to make this an excellent midrange choice. The fun **Bushfire Flame Grill** (☑07-4044 1879; www.bushfirecairns.com; steak from $38, churrasco per person $55; ⊙5.30pm-late) restaurant is attached.

Reef Palms
APARTMENT $$

(☑07-4051 2599; www.reefpalms.com.au; 41-47 Digger St; apt from $120; P※@🛜☎) Couples and families love the excellent value and friendly service at this quiet complex. The squeaky-clean apartments have cooking facilities and balconies or courtyards; larger apartments include a lounge area and spa.

★201 Lake Street
HOTEL $$$

(☑07-4053 0100, 1800 628 929; www.201lakestreet.com.au; 201 Lake St; r from $205, apt $270-340; ※🄿🛜🏊) Lifted from the pages of a trendy magazine, this gorgeous apartment complex has a stellar pool and a whiff of exclusivity. Grecian white predominates and guests can choose from a smooth hotel room or contemporary apartments with an entertainment area, a plasma-screen TV and a balcony.

Harbour Lights
APARTMENT $$$

(☑07-4057 0800; www.cairnsharbourlightshotel.com.au; 1 Marlin Pde; apt $215-325; 🄿※🛜🏊) This collection of slick, self-contained apartments overlooks the marina from its prime position above the Reef Fleet Terminal (p244). Take in the splendid views from your balcony (request one facing the water) or the glorious saltwater pool. There's a collection of excellent restaurants just down the stairs (on the boardwalk).

Shangri-La
HOTEL $$$

(☑07-4031 1411; www.shangri-la.com/cairns; 1 Pierpoint Rd; d/ste from $235/395; 🄿※🛜🏊) Towering over the marina, this is one of Cairns' most swish hotels. All rooms and suites have private balconies and original local artworks on the walls; if you have cash to splash, consider a Horizon Club suite, with wraparound views of the water and 74 sq metres of designer space. Service is as attentive as you'd expect from this luxury chain.

✖️ Eating

The **Night Markets** (www.nightmarkets.com.au; Esplanade; dishes $10-15; ⊙10am-11pm) have a cheap, busy Asian-style food court; despite the name, the eateries here are open all day.

For fresh fruit, veg and other local treats, hit Rusty's Markets (p243) on the weekend; for groceries, try **Cairns Central Shopping Centre** (☑07-4041 4111; www.cairnscentral.com.au; cnr McLeod & Spence Sts; ⊙9am-5.30pm Mon-Wed, Fri & Sat, to 9pm Thu, 10.30am-4pm Sun).

★Ganbaranba
JAPANESE $

(☑07-4031 2522; 12 Spence St; mains $8-12; ⊙11.30am-2.30pm & 5-8.30pm) You'll recognise this tiny place by the queues outside, and the beatific faces of the customers inside. This is a cult joint, and without a doubt the best place for ramen in Cairns. Slurpers can watch the chefs making noodles; if the view proves too tempting, you can ask for a refill for a mere $1.50. Absolutely worth the wait.

Cafe Fika
SWEDISH $

(☑07-4041 1150; www.swedishshop.com.au; 111-115 Grafton St; meals $9.50-15; ⊙7am-4pm Mon-Fri, 9am-2pm Sat) From meatballs with lingonberry jam to toast topped with *skagen* (prawn, dill and sour cream), this little Euro-haven serves up Swedish classics to hungry hordes of homesick Scandinavians and locals looking for something new. There's an excellent gourmet grocery store attached, stocked with treats from Sweden (of course), Germany, Hungary, Estonia, France and elsewhere.

Pineapple Cafe
HEALTH FOOD $

(www.facebook.com/pineapplecafecairns; 92 Lake St; mains $10-18; ⊙7am-3pm Mon-Sat) Healthy, fresh and creative cuisine is dished up by the ladleful at this adorable cafe; think acai and smoothie bowls, super-food salads, grass-fed beef burgers and all-day breakfasts that are actually good for you. The feel-good vibes don't end with what you put in your mouth: the cafe itself is adorned with happy-making murals and the staff always have a smile.

Bagus
INDONESIAN $

(☑07-4000 2051; www.baguscafe.info; 149 Esplanade; mains $10-20; ⊙6.45am-2.30pm & 5.30-8.30pm Mon, Tue, Thu & Sat, 6.45am-2.30pm Wed & Fri, noon-3pm & 5.30-8.30pm Sun) The heady aromas of traditional Indonesian street food waft from this friendly little hole in the wall; the nasi goreng could be straight from a beach cafe in Bali. Breakfasts ($4.50 to $11.50) are good value. Opposite Muddy's (p229) playground.

Tokyo Dumpling
JAPANESE $

(☑07-4041 2848; www.facebook.com/tokyodumpling46; 46 Lake St; dumplings from $4.50, bowls from $13.80; ⊙11.30am-9.30pm) Come to this spotless little takeaway for ludicrously moreish homemade dumplings and exceptional rice and noodle dishes. Lunch specials are between 11am and 2pm. We predict you won't be able to eat here just once.

Meldrum's Pies in Paradise
BAKERY $

(☑07-4051 8333; 97 Grafton St; pies $5.30-6.80; ⊙7am-4.30pm Mon-Fri, to 2.30pm Sat; 🌱) Multi-award-winning Meldrum's deserves the

DAY TRIPS FROM CAIRNS

Cairns is a great base for day trips to many destinations in the region.

Great Barrier Reef

Reef trips generally include transport, lunch, stinger-suits and snorkelling gear. When choosing a tour, consider the vessel type, its capacity, inclusions and destination: outer reefs are more pristine but further afield; inner reefs can be patchy and show signs of decay.

Most boats depart from the Marlin Wharf around 8am, returning around 6pm. Check-in and booking facilities are located inside the Reef Fleet Terminal (p244). Smaller operators may check-in boat-side at their berth on the wharf itself; check with your operator.

Falla Reef Trips (☑ 0400 195 264; www.fallareeftrips.com.au; D-Finger, Marlin Marina; adult/child/family from $145/90/420, intro dives $85) Reach the reef in inimitable style on this graceful 1950s pearl lugger. The tours, which spend time at Coral Gardens and Upolu Cay, have an exclusive feel. There's a maximum of 22 guests (who can help with the sailing), personalised snorkel tours and the old-school boat is the polar opposite of the sleek fibreglass vessels bobbing elsewhere on the reef.

Reef Magic (☑ 07-4031 1588; www.reefmagiccruises.com; Reef Fleet Terminal; adult/child/family day trips from $210/105/525) A long-time family favourite, Reef Magic's high-speed catamaran sails to its all-weather Marine World pontoon moored on the edge of the outer reef. If you're water shy, try a glass-bottomed boat ride, chat with the marine biologist or have a massage!

Reef Encounter (☑ 07-4037 2700; http://reefencounter.com.au; 100 Abbott St; 2-day liveaboards from $450) If one day isn't enough, try an overnight 'reef sleep' with Reef Encounter. Twenty-seven air-conditioned en-suite cabins accommodate a maximum of 42 guests; you don't even have to snorkel or dive to appreciate this floating hotel. A wide range of programs, including meals and daily departures from Cairns, make this excellent value for those wanting something a little different.

Cape Tribulation & the Daintree

Active Tropics Explorer (☑ 07-4031 3460; www.capetribulationadventures.com.au; day tours from $159) These fun all-day trips take in the sights and cultural highlights of Mossman Gorge, the Daintree and Cape Trib; overnight tours and add-ons including horse riding, sea kayaking and 'jungle surfing' are also available.

Billy Tea Safaris (☑ 07-4032 0077; www.billytea.com.au; day trips adult/child/family $220/165/665) This reliable bunch offers exciting small-group day trips to Cape Trib in purpose-built 4WD vehicles. They also run multiday safaris heading as far north as Cape York and over to the islands of the Torres Strait.

Atherton Tablelands

Barefoot Tours (☑ 07-4032 4525; www.barefoottours.com.au; tours $105) Backpackers love this fun, full-day jaunt around the Tablelands, with swimming stops at waterfalls and a natural water slide. Free pick-ups from central accommodation from 7am; tours arrive back in town by 7pm to 8pm. Minimum age 13.

On the Wallaby (☑ 07-4033 6575; www.onthewallaby.com; day tours $99, overnight tours $139-189) Excellent activity-based tours of the Tablelands' rainforests and waterfalls including swimming, cycling, hiking and canoeing. Daily pick-ups from Cairns at 8am.

Uncle Brian's Tours (☑ 07-4033 6575; www.unclebrian.com.au; 1-/2-day tours $119/219; ☺ Mon-Sat) High-energy, small-group day and overnight trips taking in the Babinda Boulders, Josephine Falls, Millaa Millaa, Yungaburra, the Crater Lakes and more. Bring your togs!

Food Trail Tours (☑ 07-4041 1522; www.foodtrailtours.com.au; adult/child/family from $195/115/570) Taste your way around the Tablelands, visiting farms producing macadamias, tropical fruits, wine, cheese, chocolate and coffee. Tours run on Monday, Tuesday, Thursday and Saturday; accommodation transfers from Cairns and northern beaches are included.

accolades bestowed upon its seemingly innumerable renditions of the humble Aussie pie; it's been at it since 1972, an achievement that speaks volumes in a transient tourist town like Cairns. For something different, try the chicken and macadamia satay or tuna mornay with spinach pies; the many vegetarian options are delicious, and sell out quickly.

Lillipad   CAFE $

(☑ 07-4051 9565; www.lillipadcafe.com; 72 Grafton St; dishes $12-22; ⊙ 7am-3pm; ⌨) With humongous feasts, from crêpes to wraps and a truckload of vegetarian options, this is one of the best-value options in town. It's a little bit hippie, and a whole lot busy: you'll probably have to wait a while. Don't miss the fresh juices.

★ Spicy Bite   INDIAN, FUSION $$

(☑ 07-4041 3700; www.spicybitecairns.com; cnr Shields St & Esplanade; mains $15.50-35; ⊙ 5-10pm; ⌨) Cairns has plenty of good Indian restaurants, but none are quite as innovative as this unassuming place, where fusion food has been turned into a write-home-about-it experience: where else on earth could you try crocodile masala or kangaroo tikka? The classic curries are divine, and there are loads of vegetarian and vegan options.

★ Prawn Star   SEAFOOD $$

(☑ 0456 421 172; www.facebook.com/prawn starcairns; E-Finger, Berth 31, Marlin Marina; seafood from $20; ⊙ 10am-8pm) Trawler restaurant Prawn Star is tropical dining perfection: clamber aboard and fill yourself with prawns, mud crabs, oysters and whatever else was caught that day, while taking in equally delicious harbour views. A second boat – Prawn Star Too – was added to the eat-fleet in mid-2017, but seating is still limited and much in-demand: get there early. Why the Cairns waterfront isn't lined with restaurants like this is a mystery for the ages.

★ Bayleaf Balinese Restaurant   BALINESE $$

(☑ 07-4051 4622; www.bayvillage.com.au/bayleaf; Bay Village Tropical Retreat, cnr Lake & Gatton Sts; mains $14-25; ⊙ noon-2pm Mon-Fri, 6pm-late nightly) One of Cairns' best restaurants isn't along the waterfront or in the lobby of a flash hotel, but rather, attached to a midrange apartment complex. It's completely unexceptional from the outside, but the Balinese food created inside by specialist chefs is outrageously good and wholly authentic. Order a ton of starters, go for the banquet or share a heap of mains.

★ Perrotta's at
the Gallery   MEDITERRANEAN $$

(☑ 07-4031 5899; www.perrottasatg.com; 38 Abbott St; breakfast $7-23, mains $19-37; ⊙ 6.30am-10pm; ⌨) This unmissable eatery, connected to the Cairns Regional Gallery (p229), tempts you onto its covered deck with splendid gourmet breakfasts – until 3pm! – fresh juices, barista coffees and an inventive Mediterranean-inspired lunch and dinner menu. It's a chic spot with an interesting crowd and ideal people-watching perches.

Bobby's   VIETNAMESE, CHINESE $$

(☑ 07-4051 8877; Oceana Walk Arcade, 62 Grafton St; mains from $12; ⊙ 7am-10pm) Authentic Vietnamese and Chinese food are the go at Bobby's, beloved by locals and visitors that make the effort to find it. It's reputed to do the best *pho* in town; if you're after a midday filler, the marinated Vietnamese beef rolls will certainly hit the spot.

Fetta's Greek Taverna   GREEK $$

(☑ 07-4051 6966; www.fettasgreektaverna.com. au; 99 Grafton St; mains $26.50-28.50, set menu $35; ⊙ 11.30am-3pm Mon-Fri, 5.30pm-late daily) The white walls and blue-accented windows do a great job evoking Santorini, but it's the classic Greek dishes that are the star of the show here. The set menu goes the whole hog – dip, saganaki, moussaka, salad, grilled meats, calamari, baklava and coffee. Yes, you can break your plate.

Marinades   INDIAN $$

(☑ 07-4041 1422; 43 Spence St; mains from $16, lunch thali from $10; ⊙ 11.30am-2.30pm & 5.30-9.30pm Tue-Fri, 5.30-9.30pm Sat & Sun; ⌨) One of Cairns' most popular Indian restaurants has a *long* menu of aromatic dishes, such as lobster marinated in cashew paste and Goan prawn curry. The lunch specials are great value.

★ Ochre   MODERN AUSTRALIAN $$$

(☑ 07-4051 0100; www.ochrerestaurant.com.au; Marlin Pde; mains $28-40; ⊙ 11.30am-2.30pm & 5.30-9.30pm) The menu at this innovative waterfront restaurant utilises native Aussie fauna (such as croc with native pepper, or roo with quandong-chilli glaze) and flora (try wattle-seed damper loaf or Davidson plum mousse). It also cooks Tablelands steaks to perfection. Can't decide? Order a tasting plate.

Dundees   SEAFOOD $$$

(☑ 07-4051 0399; www.dundees.com.au; Marlin Pde; mains $25-82; ⊙ 11.30am-late) This tried-and-true waterfront restaurant comes up trumps for ambience, generous portions and friendly service. The varied menu of appealing appetisers includes chunky seafood chowder, tempura soft-shell crab and lightly dusted calamari strips; main-meal highlights include barbecued lobster, wagyu eye fillets and enormous seafood platters.

🍷 Drinking & Nightlife

⭐ Three Wolves   BAR

(📞07-4031 8040; www.threewolves.com.au; Red Brick Laneway, 32 Abbott St; ⊙4pm-midnight Thu-Sat & Mon, 2-10pm Sun) Intimate, understated and bang on trend (think Edison bulbs, copper mugs and mixologists in old-timey barkeep aprons), this new laneway bar has delivered a very welcome dash of Melbourne. It's got an excellent selection of speciality spirits, cocktails and beers, plus a bar menu including hip faves like pulled-pork tortillas, sliders and New York–style hot dogs. Small but superb.

⭐ Green Ant Cantina   BAR

(📞07-4041 5061; www.greenantcantina.com; 183 Bunda St; ⊙4pm-late Tue-Sun) Behind the railway station (p244), this grungy, rockin' Tex-Mex bar is an ace and arty alternative hang-out. Smothered in bright murals and peopled by friendly folks, the Green Ant brews its own beers and hosts regular music events. It also does fab food, including pulled-pork quesadillas, jambalaya and the infamous, blistering Wings of Death.

⭐ Salt House   BAR

(📞07-4041 7733; www.salthouse.com.au; 6/2 Pierpoint Rd; ⊙11am-2am Mon-Fri, 7am-2am Sat & Sun) By the yacht club, Cairns' coolest, classiest bar caters to a hip and happy crowd. With killer cocktails, tremendous views, occasional live music and DJs, and a superb mod-Oz nibbles-and-mains menu, the Salt House is absolutely not to be missed.

⭐ Conservatory Bar   WINE BAR

(📞0467 466 980; www.theconservatorybar.com.au; 12-14 Lake St; ⊙4-10pm Wed-Thu, to midnight Fri & Sat, to 9pm Sun) Tucked away in a little room in a little laneway, this is Cairns' best wine bar, and one of the city's top places for a low-key tipple, whatever your flavour. It also makes fabulous cocktails and has loads of craft beers. It's relaxed, friendly and oozes a tropical sophistication all its own. The Conservatory regularly hosts exhibitions and live (mellow) music.

⭐ Lyquid Nightlife   CLUB

(📞07-4028 3773; www.lyquid.com.au; 33 Spence St; ⊙9pm-3am) Lyquid is the hottest ticket in town: dress to impress and party the night away with top DJs, professional bartenders and a happy, hyped-up young crowd.

⭐ Jack   PUB

(📞07-4051 2490; www.thejack.com.au; cnr Spence & Sheridan Sts; ⊙10am-late) The Jack is a kick-arse pub by any standards, housed in an unmissable heritage Queenslander with an enormous shaded beer garden. There are nightly events, including live music and DJs, killer pub grub, and an adjacent hostel (dorm from $26) for those who just can't tear themselves away.

Flying Monkey Cafe   CAFE

(📞0411 084 176; www.facebook.com/theflying monkeycafe; 154 Sheridan St; ⊙6.30am-3.30pm Mon-Fri, 7am-noon Sat) Fantastic coffee, ever-changing local art exhibitions, colourful buskers and a beyond-affable staff make the Monkey a must-do for caffeine-and-culture hounds.

Pier Bar   BAR

(📞07-4031 4677; www.thepierbar.com.au; Pier Shopping Centre, 1 Pierpoint Rd; ⊙11.30am-late) This local institution is much loved for its killer waterfront location and daily happy hour (5pm to 7pm). Its Sunday sessions are the place to see and be seen, with live music, food and drink specials and an always-happening crowd.

Grand Hotel   PUB

(📞07-4051 1007; www.grandhotelcairns.com; 34 McLeod St; ⊙10am-9pm Mon-Wed, to 11pm Thu, to midnight Fri & Sat, to 8pm Sun) Established in 1926, this laid-back haunt is worth visiting just to rest your beer on the bar – an 11m-long carved crocodile! There's usually live music on the weekend. It's a great place to loiter with the locals.

Woolshed   BAR

(📞07-4031 6304; www.thewoolshed.com.au; 24 Shields St; ⊙7pm-3am Sun-Thu, to 5am Fri & Sat) An eternal backpacker magnet and meat market, where young travellers, dive instructors and living-it-up locals get happily hammered and dance on tables. The classier Cotton Club speakeasy-style cocktail bar is downstairs.

PJ O'Briens   IRISH PUB

(www.pjobriens.com.au/cairns; cnr Lake & Shields Sts; ⊙11.30am-late) It has sticky carpets and reeks of stale Guinness, but Irish-themed PJs packs 'em in with party nights, pole dancing and dirt-cheap meals.

☆ Entertainment

Pop & Co Tapas & Music Bar   LIVE MUSIC
(✒ 07-4019 6132; 92 Abbott St; ⊙ 5pm-late Wed-Sun) Live jazz, blues and croony tunes share the limelight with a good nibbles menu and some of the cheapest on-tap beers in town. It's a diminutive diamond, and its local popularity means it sometimes gets crowded. You'll find it next to the giant jelly babies at the Centre of Contemporary Arts as you head north down Abbott St.

Rondo Theatre   THEATRE
(✒ 1800 855 835; www.therondo.com.au; 46 Greenslopes St) Community plays and musicals hit the stage regularly at this small theatre opposite Centenary Lakes. It's 4.5km northwest of the city centre (take Sheridan St to Greenslopes St).

Starry Night Cinema   CINEMA
(www.starrynightcinema.com.au; Flecker Botanic Gardens, Collins Ave, Edge Hill; adult/child from $13/5) Enjoy classic films amid the foliage and finery of the Botanic Gardens (p229). Check the website for upcoming showings (there are usually one or two a month).

Reef Hotel Casino   CASINO
(✒ 07-4030 8888; www.reefcasino.com.au; 35-41 Wharf St; ⊙ 9am-5am Fri & Sat, to 3am Sun-Thu) In addition to table games and pokies, Cairns' casino has four restaurants and four bars, including the enormous Casino Sports Arena bar.

Centre of Contemporary Arts   GALLERY, THEATRE
(CoCA; www.centre-of-contemporary-arts-cairns. com.au; 96 Abbott St; ⊙ 10am-5pm Mon-Sat) CoCA houses the KickArts (p229) galleries of local contemporary visual art, as well as the JUTE Theatre (www.jute.com.au). Look for the jelly babies out the front.

🛍 Shopping

★ Rusty's Markets   MARKET
(✒ 07-4040 2705; www.rustysmarkets.com.au; 57-89 Grafton St; ⊙ 5am-6pm Fri & Sat, to 3pm Sun) No weekend in Cairns is complete without a visit to this busy and vibrant multicultural market. Weave (and taste) your way through piles of seasonal tropical fruits, veggies and herbs, plus farm-fresh honey, locally grown flowers, excellent coffees, curries, cold drinks, antiques and more.

Doongal Aboriginal Art   ART
(✒ 07-4041 4249; www.doongal.com.au; 49 Esplanade; ⊙ 9am-6pm) Authentic artworks, boomerangs, didgeridoos and other traditional artefacts by local and central Australian Indigenous artists. Worldwide shipping available.

Crackerbox Palace   VINTAGE
(✒ 07-4031 1216; www.crackerboxpalace.com. au; 228 Sheridan St; ⊙ 10am-5pm Mon-Fri, to 3pm Sat) This treasure trove of all things vintage has been luring in the locals for over 20 years. It's crammed full of one-off clothes, furniture, records, knick-knacks and awesome oddities. Check your baggage weight allowances before stepping through the Palace doors; once you shop, it's hard to stop.

ℹ Information

MEDICAL SERVICES
Cairns 24 Hour Medical Centre (✒ 07-4052 1119; cnr Grafton & Florence Sts; ⊙ 24hr) Centrally located medical centre; it also does dive medicals.

Cairns Base Hospital (✒ 07-4226 0000; 165 Esplanade) Largest hospital in Far North Queensland.

POST
Post Office (✒ 13 13 18; www.auspost.com. au; 38 Sheridan St; ⊙ 8.30am-5.30pm Mon-Fri, 9am-12.30pm Sat)

TOURIST INFORMATION
Cairns & Tropical North Visitor Information Centre (✒ 07-4051 3588; www.tropicalnorth queensland.org.au; 51 Esplanade; ⊙ 8.30am-6pm Mon-Fri, 10am-6pm Sat & Sun) This is the only government-run visitor information centre in town offering impartial advice. Hundreds of free brochures, maps and pamphlets are available. Friendly staff can help with booking accommodation and tours. Look for the yellow 'i' on the blue background.

ℹ Getting There & Away

AIR
Qantas (✒ 13 13 13; www.qantas.com.au), **Virgin Australia** (✒ 13 67 89; www.virginaustralia. com) and **Jetstar** (✒ 13 15 38; www.jetstar. com.au), and a handful of international carriers, arrive in and depart from Cairns Airport (p303), located approximately 6km from the city centre, with direct services to all Australian capital

cities except Canberra and Hobart, and to regional centres including Townsville, Weipa and Horn Island. Direct international connections include Bali, Singapore, Manila, Tokyo and Port Moresby.

Hinterland Aviation (07-4040 1333; www.hinterlandaviation.com.au) has at least two flights daily from Cairns to Cooktown.

Skytrans (1300 759 872; www.skytrans.com.au) services Cape York communities and the Torres Strait islands.

BOAT

Almost all reef trips from Cairns depart the Marlin Wharf (sometimes called the Marlin Jetty), with booking and check-in facilities located inside the **Reef Fleet Terminal** (Pierpoint Rd). A handful of smaller operators may have their check-in facilities boat-side, on the wharf itself. Be sure to ask for the correct berth number.

International cruise ships and **SeaSwift** (1800 424 422, 07-4035 1234; www.seaswift.com.au; 41-45 Tingira St, Portsmith; one way/return from $650/1166) ferries to Seisia on Cape York dock at and depart from the **Cairns Cruise Terminal** (07-4052 3888; www.cairnscruiseinerterminal.com.au; cnr Wharf & Lake Sts).

BUS

Long-distance buses arrive at and depart from the **Interstate Coach Terminal** (Reef Fleet Terminal), Cairns Central Railway Station, the airport and the **Cairns Transit Mall** (Lake St). Operators include the following:

Cairns Cooktown Express (07-4059 1423; www.cairnsbuscharters.com/services/cairns-cooktown-express)

Greyhound Australia (1300 473 946; www.greyhound.com.au)

John's Kuranda Bus (0418 772 953)

Premier Motor Service (13 34 10; www.premierms.com.au)

Sun Palm (07-4087 2900; www.sunpalmtransport.com.au)

Tablelands Tours & Transfers (07-4045 1882; www.tablelandstoursandtransfers.com.au)

Trans North (07-4095 8644; www.transnorthbus.com; Cairns Central Railway Station)

CAR & MOTORCYCLE

Major car-rental companies have airport and downtown (usually on Sheridan St) branches. Daily rates start at around $40 for a compact auto and $80 for a 4WD. **Cruising Car Rental** (07-4041 4666; www.hirecarcairns.com; 196 Sheridan St; per day from $39) and **Rent-a-Bomb** (07-4031 4477; www.rentabomb.com.au; 144 Sheridan St; per day from $33) have cheap rates on older model vehicles. If you're looking for a cheap campervan, **Jucy**

(1800 150 850; www.jucy.com.au; 55 Dutton St, Portsmith; per day from $40), **Spaceships** (1300 132 469; www.spaceshipsrentals.com.au; 3/52 Fearnley St, Portsmith; per day from $40) and **Hippie Camper Hire** (1800 777 779; www.hippiecamper.com; 432 Sheridan St; per day from $44) have quality wheels at budget prices. **Bear Rentals** (1300 462 327; www.bearrentals.com.au; cars per day from $127) has top-notch Land Rover Defenders that make bush-bashing a breeze.

If you're in for the long haul, check hostels, www.gumtree.com.au and the big noticeboard on Abbott St for used campervans and ex-backpackers' cars.

If you prefer two wheels to four, try **Choppers Motorcycle Tours & Hire** (07-4051 6288; www.choppersmotorcycles.com.au; 150 Sheridan St; rental per day from $90) or **Cairns Scooter & Bicycle Hire** (07-4031 3444; www.cairnsbicyclehire.com.au; 47 Shields St; scooters/bikes per day from $87/11).

TRAIN

The Kuranda Scenic Railway (p250) runs daily; the Savannahlander (p309) offers a miscellany of rail journeys into the outback from **Cairns Central Railway Station** (Bunda St).

Queensland Rail (1300 131 722; www.queenslandrailtravel.com.au) operates services between Brisbane and Cairns.

ⓘ Getting Around

TO/FROM THE AIRPORT

The airport is about 6km north of central Cairns; many hotels and hostels offer courtesy pick-up. **Sun Palm** (07-4087 2900; www.sunpalmtransport.com.au) meets all incoming flights and runs a shuttle (adult/child $15/7.50) directly to your accommodation; its **Airport Connect Shuttle** ($4) runs between the airport and a Sunbus stop on Sheridan St just north of town. **Cairns Airport Shuttle** (0432 488 783; www.cairnsairportshuttle.com.au) is a good option for groups; the more passengers, the cheaper the fare.

Taxis to the city centre are around $25 (plus $4 airport surcharge).

Some travellers choose to walk between the airport and town to save on bus or taxi fares, but keep in mind, these are busy roads: a pedestrian was hit by a car and killed in 2015. Also, crocodiles have been known to cross Airport Ave, which is bordered by mangrove swamps, so...

BICYCLE

Cairns is criss-crossed with cycling paths and circuits; some of the most popular routes take in the Esplanade, Botanic Gardens and Centenary Lakes. There's a detailed list of routes and maps at www.cairns.qld.gov.au/region/tourist-information/things-to-do/cycle.

Cairns Scooter & Bicycle Hire (☑ 07-4031 3444; www.cairnsbicyclehire.com.au; 47 Shields St; scooters/bikes per day from $87/11)

Pro Bike Rental (☑ 0438 381 749; www.pro bikerental.com.au; bikes per day from $120)

BUS

Sunbus (☑ 07-4057 7411; www.sunbus.com.au/cairns; single/daily/weekly ticket from $2.40/4.80/19.20)

TAXI

Cairns Taxis (☑ 13 10 08; www.cairnstaxis.com.au)

AROUND CAIRNS

Islands off Cairns

Green Island

Showing some of the scars that come with fame and popularity, this pretty coral cay (45 minutes from Cairns) nevertheless retains much of its beauty. The island has a rainforest interior with interpretive walks, a fringe of white-sand beach, and superb snorkelling just offshore; it's great for kids. You can walk around the island (which, along with its surrounding waters, is protected by national- and marine-park status) in about 30 minutes.

The star attraction at family-owned aquarium, **Marineland Crocodile Park** (☑ 07-4051 4032; www.greenislandcrocs.com.au; adult/child $19/9; ⊙ 9.30am-4pm), is Cassius, the world's largest croc in captivity at 5.5m. Believed to be over 110 years old, he's fed daily at 10.30am and 1.30pm.

If you don't want to get your hair wet, **Seawalker** (www.seawalker.com.au; per person $172) allows you to don a helmet and simply go for a (guided) stroll on the sea floor, 5m below the surface.

Luxurious **Green Island Resort** (☑ 07-4031 3300; www.greenislandresort.com.au; ste from $580; ❈ @ ☎) maintains a sense of privacy and exclusivity despite having sections opened to the general public, including restaurants, bars, an ice-cream parlour and water-sports facilities. Spacious split-level suites feature tropical themes, timber furnishings and inviting balconies.

Big Cat (☑ 07-4051 0444; www.greenisland.com.au; adult/child/family from $90/45/225) has transfers and day-return tours to Green Island.

Fitzroy Island

A steep mountaintop rising from the sea, fabulous Fitzroy Island has clinking coral beaches, giant boulders and rainforest walking tracks, one of which ends at a now-inactive lighthouse. It's a top spot for swimming and snorkelling; one of the best places to lay your towel is Nudey Beach, which, despite its name, is not officially clothing-optional.

The **Cairns Turtle Rehabilitation Centre** (www.saveourseaturtles.com.au; adult/child $8.80/5.50; ⊙ tours 1pm & 2pm) looks after sick and injured sea turtles before releasing them back into the wild. Daily educational tours (45 minutes, maximum 15 guests) take visitors through the turtle hospital to meet recovering residents. Bookings through the Fitzroy Island Resort are essential.

Fitzroy Island Resort (☑ 07-4044 6700; www.fitzroyisland.com; studios/cabins from $185/445, ste/apt from $300/350; ❈ 🛜 ☎) has tropi-cool accommodation ranging from sleek studios, suites and beachfront cabins through to luxurious apartments. The restaurant, bar and kiosk are open to day trippers. Budgeteers can book here for a site at the **Fitzroy Island Camping Ground** (sites $35).

Fast Cat (www.fitzroyisland.com/getting-here; adult/child/family $78/39/205) departs Cairns' Marlin Wharf (berth 20) at 8am, 11am and 1.30pm (bookings essential) and whisks you to Fitzroy Island in just 45 minutes. It returns to Cairns at 9.30am, 12.15pm and 5pm.

Frankland Islands

If the idea of hanging out on one of five uninhabited, coral-fringed islands with excellent snorkelling and stunning white-sand beaches appeals, cruise out to the Frankland Group National Park. These continental islands are made up of High Island to the north, and Normanby, Mabel, Round and Russell Islands to the south.

Frankland Islands Cruise & Dive (☑ 07-4031 6300; www.franklandislands.com.au; adult/child from $169/99) runs excellent day trips that include a cruise down the Mulgrave River, snorkelling gear, tuition and lunch.

Cairns' Northern Beaches

Despite what some brochures may infer, Cairns city is sans swimmable beach. But a 15-minute drive (or a local bus ticket) will get you out to a string of lovely beach communities, each with their own character: Yorkeys Knob is popular with sailors, Trinity is big with families, Holloways is loved by locals (and their dogs) and Palm Cove is a swanky honeymoon haven.

Once you're there, **Northern Beaches Bike Hire** (📞 0417 361 012; www.cairnsbeachesbikehire.com; adult/child bikes per day from $20/14, per week $80/50) can deliver rental bikes to your digs, and collect them when you're done.

Yorkeys Knob

POP 2766

Yorkeys Knob is a laid-back beach community best known for its marina and **golf course** (📞 07-4055 7933; www.halfmoonbaygolf.com.au; 9/18 holes $26/42, clubs hire $25), and the cheeky crocs that frequent it. The 'Knob' part of the name elicits chortles from easily amused locals; others wonder where the apostrophe went. Yorkeys has a stinger net in summer.

Blazing saddles (📞 07-4055 7400; www.blazingsaddles.com.au; 154 Yorkeys Knob Rd; horse rides from $125) has half-day horse-riding tours that meander through rainforest, mangroves and sugar-cane fields.

For fresh seafood and delightful views of the marina's expensive floating toys from the expansive dining deck, **Yorkeys Knob Boating Club** (📞 07-4055 7711; www.ykbc.com.au; 25-29 Buckley St; mains $18-30; ⊙ 10am-midnight Mon-Thu, to 2am Fri & Sat, 8am-midnight Sun; 🚲) is worth the trip from Cairns.

Trinity Beach

One of the region's better-kept secrets, Trinity Beach, with its gorgeous stretch of sheltered sand, pretty esplanade and sensibly priced dining and accommodation, has managed to stave off the tourism vibe, despite being a holiday hot spot and popular dining destination for locals in the know. There's not much to do here except eat, sleep and relax, but Trinity Beach's central position makes it easy to get out and about if you're feeling active.

One of the most handsome blocks on the beachfront, **Sea Point on Trinity Beach** (📞 07-4057 9544; www.seapointontrinitybeach.com; 63 Vasey Esplanade; apt $165-230; 🅿🕸🛜🏊) offers indoor-outdoor balconies, tiled floors and breezy outlooks.

Don't let the easy-breezy beach-shack vibe fool you into thinking the food at **Fratelli on Trinity** (📞 07-4057 5775; www.fratelli.net.au; 47 Vasey Esplanade; mains $20-35; ⊙ 7am-10pm Wed-Sun, from 5.30pm Mon & Tue) is anything less than top-class. Pastas are superb, and dishes like pistachio prawns and soft-shell crab with pomegranate and saffron aioli might even distract you from the million-dollar views.

Blue Moon Grill (📞 07-4057 8957; www.bluemoongrill.com.au; Shop 6, 22-24 Trinity Beach Rd; mains $22-40; ⊙ 4-10pm Mon-Thu, 7-11am & 4-10pm Fri-Sun) wows with a creative, original menu presented with passion. Where else can you try crocodile popcorn?

Palm Cove

POP 1215

The best known of Cairns' northern beaches, Palm Cove has grown into a destination in its own right. More intimate than Port Douglas and more upmarket than its southern neighbours, Palm Cove is a cloistered coastal community with a beautiful promenade along the paperbark-lined Williams Esplanade. Its gorgeous stretch of white-sand beach and its sprinkling of fancy restaurants do their best to lure young lovers from their luxury resorts; inevitably, they succeed.

If you can drag yourself off the beach or poolside, Palm Cove has some excellent water-sports operators including **Beach Fun Co** (📞 0411 848 580; www.beachfunco.com; cnr Williams Esplanade & Harpa St), **Palm Cove Watersports** (📞 0402 861 011; www.palmcovewatersports.com; 149 Williams Esplanade; kayak hire per hour from $20) and **Pacific Watersports** (📞 0413 721 999; www.pacificwatersports.com.au; 41 Williams Esplanade), which offers turtle tours by SUP or kayak.

🛏 Sleeping & Eating

⭐ **Cairns Beaches Flashpackers**   HOSTEL $
(📞 07-4055 3797; www.cairnsbeachesflashpackers.com; 19 Veivers Rd; dm/d $45/120; 🅿🕸🛜🏊) Though technically a hostel – the first and only in Palm Cove – this splendid, spotless place 100m from the beach is more restful retreat than party palace. The bunk-free dorms are tidy and comfortable; the private rooms have bathrooms and

sliding-door access to the pool. Cook in the immaculate communal kitchen, or scout for restaurants further afield on a Piaggio scooter.

Palm Cove Holiday Park　　CAMPGROUND $
(☑ 07-4055 3824; www.palmcovehp.com.au; 149 Williams Esplanade; powered/unpowered sites from $36/29; P �) For cheap, alfresco Palm Cove accommodation, stake out your spot at this modern, well-run beachfront camping ground near the jetty. It has tent and van sites, a new camp kitchen, a barbecue area and a laundry.

★**Sarayi**　　BOUTIQUE HOTEL $$
(☑ 07-4059 5600; www.sarayi.com.au; 95 Williams Esplanade; d $115-240; P ❄ �rm ☎) White, bright and perfectly located among a grove of melaleucas across from the beach, Sarayi is a wonderful choice for couples, families and the growing number of visitors choosing to get married on its rooftop terrace. The name means 'palace' in Turkish, and it's an apt one: the laid-back but efficient management here does everything to ensure you're treated like royalty.

Reef Retreat　　APARTMENT $$
(☑ 07-4059 1744; www.reefretreat.com.au; 10-14 Harpa St; apt from $165; P ❄ ☎ ☎) This delightful property has a rightful reputation for excellent service. In a peaceful forested setting around a shaded pool, Reef Retreat's well-maintained one-, two- and three-bedroom apartments feature lots of rich timbers, durable high-quality furnishings, kitchenettes and wide, airy balconies.

★**Reef House**
Resort & Spa　　BOUTIQUE HOTEL $$$
(☑ 07-4080 2600; www.reefhouse.com.au; 99 Williams Esplanade; d from $300; P ❄ ☎ ☎) Once the private residence of an army brigadier, Reef House is more intimate and understated than most of Palm Cove's resorts. The whitewashed walls, wicker furniture and big beds romantically draped in muslin add to the air of refinement. The Brigadier's Bar works on an honesty system; complimentary punch is served by candlelight at twilight.

★**Chill Cafe**　　CAFE $$
(☑ 0439 361 122; www.chillcafepalmcove.com.au; 41 Williams Esplanade; mains from $19; ☉ 6am-late) The *primo* position on the corner of the waterfront Esplanade, combined with fun, friendly and attentive service, sexy tunes

and a huge airy deck are all great reasons to try the oversized, tasty treats (think fish tacos and chunky club sandwiches) offered by this hip cafe. You can also just soak up some sunshine with a juice or a beer.

Seafarer's Oyster Bar &
Restaurant　　SEAFOOD $$
(☑ 07-4059 2653; 45 Williams Esplanade; oysters per dozen from $20, mains from $19; ☉ noon-3pm & 5-8.30pm Mon-Thu, noon-8.30pm Fri-Sun) Come for the delicious oysters and the freshest seafood in town; stay for the beach breezes and social buzz.

★**Vivo**　　MODERN AUSTRALIAN $$$
(☑ 07-4059 0944; www.vivo.com.au; 49 Williams Esplanade; mains from $30; ☉ 7.30am-9pm) The most beautiful-looking restaurant on the Esplanade is also one of the finest. Menus (breakfast, lunch and dinner) are inventive and well-executed using fresh local ingredients, service is second to none, and the outlook is superb. Daily set menus are excellent value.

★**Beach Almond**　　SEAFOOD $$$
(☑ 07-4059 1908; www.beachalmond.com; 145 Williams Esplanade; mains from $27; ☉ 5-11pm Mon-Sat, noon-3pm & 5-11pm Sun) The rustic, ramshackle, beach-house-on-sticks exterior belies the exceptional fine-dining experience that awaits within. Black-pepper prawns, Singaporean mud crab and banana-leaf barramundi are among the fragrant innovations here, combining Asian flavours and spices.

Nu Nu　　MODERN AUSTRALIAN $$$
(☑ 07-4059 1880; www.nunu.com.au; 1 Veivers Rd; mains from $38, tasting menu per person from $70; ☉ 6.15am-late) Trendy Nu Nu uses fresh local produce to create Mod Oz masterpieces including poached prawns with candied bacon, apple, seed crumb and endive, and the stupendous wok-fried mud crab with sweet pork, chilli tamarind, ginger and market greens.

☕ Drinking & Nightlife

Apres Beach Bar & Grill　　BAR
(☑ 07-4059 2000; www.apresbeachbar.com.au; 119 Williams Esplanade; ☉ 8am-11pm) The most happening place in Palm Cove, with a zany interior of old motorcycles, racing cars, and a biplane hanging from the ceiling, plus regular live music. Big on steaks of all sorts, too.

Surf Club Palm Cove BAR
(📞07-4059 1244; www.surfclubpalmcove.com.au; 135 Williams Esplanade; ⊙11am-10pm Mon & Tue, to midnight Wed-Sat, 8am-midnight Sun) This local hang-out is great for a drink in the sunny garden bar, bargain-priced seafood and decent kids' meals.

Ellis Beach

Little Ellis Beach is the last – and arguably the best – of Cairns' northern beaches and the closest to the highway, which runs right past it. The long sheltered bay is a stunner, with a palm-fringed, patrolled swimming beach, and a stinger net in summer. Cairns' only (unofficial) clothing-optional beach, Buchans Point, is at the southern end of Ellis; there's no stinger net here, so consider your valuable assets before diving in in your birthday suit.

North of Ellis Beach towards Port Douglas, **Hartley's Crocodile Adventures** (📞07-4055 3576; www.crocodileadventures.com; Captain Cook Hwy, Wangetti Beach; adult/child/family $37/18.50/92.50; ⊙8.30am-5pm) 🐊 offers a daily range of squeal-inducing events including croc farm tours, feedings, 'crocodile attack' and snake shows, and croc-infested lagoon cruises.

Ellis Beach Oceanfront Bungalows (📞1800 637 036, 07-4055 3538; www.ellisbeach.com; Captain Cook Hwy; powered/unpowered sites from $41/34, cabins with shared bathroom from $115, bungalow d from $170, oceanfront bungalows from $190; 🅿️❄️😺) has camping, cabins and contemporary bungalows, the best of which have direct ocean views. Just try to drive past **Ellis Beach Bar 'n' Grill** (📞07-4055 3534; www.ellisbeachbarandgrill.com.au; Captain

---

THE CAIRNS OF CAIRNS

As if the natural scenery on the road to Port Douglas wasn't distracting enough, the comely Captain Cook Hwy now has another eye-catcher: hundreds upon hundreds of mysterious, precariously piled rocks. The stone stackers' identity and mission has puzzled and delighted locals: is it a play on 'cairns'? Conceptual art? Whatever's going on, you'll want to pull over for a peek and a ponder. You'll find the cryptic collection just north of Ellis Beach.

Cook Hwy; mains $10-30; ⊙8am-8pm) and not stop for a beer and a burger.

Clifton Beach

Cute Clifton is very much a locals' beach, with minimal development and long, oft-deserted stretches of palm-lined sands that run all the way to Palm Cove. If you're after privacy or a place to let the little ones run free, drop your bags.

Idyllic, private and hosted by a genuinely welcoming couple, **South Pacific B&B** (📞07-4059 0381; www.southpacificbnbcliftonbeach.com.au; 18 Gibson Cl; s/d from $100/120; 🅿️❄️📶😺) is everything a B&B should be with expansive, tropical rooms and cottages and exotic-fruit-laden breakfasts.

Even if you're not staying at Clifton, **Coco Mojo** (📞07-4059 1272; 14 Clifton Rd; mains $23-40; ⊙5.30-11.30pm Mon & Tue, noon-11.30pm Wed-Fri, 9am-11.30pm Sat & Sun) is worth a special trip. The extensive menu focuses on the wildly varying street foods of the world, covering cuisines from Nigerian to Texan, Indonesian to Lebanese; somehow, the experienced international chefs make it work.

South of Cairns

Babinda

Babinda is a small working-class town that leads 7km inland to the Babinda Boulders, where a photogenic creek rushes between 4m-high granite rocks. It's croc-free, but here lurks an equal danger: highly treacherous waters. Aboriginal Dreaming stories say that a young woman threw herself into the then-still waters after being separated from her love; her anguish caused the creek to become the surging, swirling torrent it is today. Almost 20 visitors have lost their lives at the boulders. Swimming is permitted in calm, well-marked parts of the creek, but pay careful heed to all warning signs. Walking tracks give you safe access for obligatory gasps and photographs.

There's free camping at Babinda Boulders Camping Area.

Wooroonooran National Park

Part of the Wet Tropics World Heritage Area, steamy, dreamy Wooroonooran National Park brims with stunning natural spectacles, including Queensland's highest peak (Mt Bartle Frere; 1622m), dramatic falls, tangled rainforest, unusual flora and fauna and blissfully cool swimming holes. It's heaven for hikers, or anyone looking to escape the (relative) rat race of bustling Cairns.

Contact **NPRSR** (☑13 74 68; www.nprsr. qld.gov.au/parks/wooroonooran; camping permits per person/family $6.15/24.60) about camping permits.

ATHERTON TABLELANDS

Climbing back from the coast between Innisfail and Cairns is the fertile food bowl of the far north, the Atherton Tablelands. Quaint country towns, eco-wilderness lodges and luxurious B&Bs dot greener-than-green hills between patchwork fields, pockets of rainforest, spectacular lakes, waterfalls, and Queensland's highest mountains, Bartle Frere (1622m) and Bellenden Ker (1593m).

The Tablelands make for a great getaway from the swelter of the coast; they're almost always a few degrees cooler than Cairns, and on winter nights things get downright chilly.

❶ Getting There & Away

Trans North (p244) has regular bus services connecting Cairns with various spots on the Tablelands, including Kuranda ($6.70, 30 minutes), Mareeba ($19.60, one hour), Atherton ($25.30, 1¾ hours) and Herberton/Ravenshoe ($32/37.40, two/2½ hours, Monday, Wednesday, Friday).

Kuranda

POP 2966

Tucked away in thick rainforest, arty, alternative Kuranda is one of Cairns' most popular day trips. During the day, this hippie haven swarms with tourists soaking up the vibe, visiting animal sanctuaries and poking around its famous markets; come evening, you can almost hear the village sigh as the streets and pubs are reclaimed by mellow locals (and the occasional street-hopping wallaby).

Just getting here is an experience in itself: choose between driving a winding forest road, chugging up on a train or soaring over the treetops on Australia's longest gondola cableway (p250).

⊙ Sights & Activities

⭐**Kuranda Original Rainforest Markets** MARKET
(☑07-4093 9440; www.kurandaoriginalrainforest market.com.au; Therwine St; ⊙9.30am-3pm) Follow the clouds of incense down to these atmospheric, authentic village markets. Operating since 1978, they're still the best place to see artists at work and hippies at play. Pick up everything from avocado ice cream to organic lingerie and sample local produce such as honey and fruit wines.

BatReach WILDLIFE RESERVE
(☑07-4093 8858; www.batreach.com; 13 Barang St; by donation; ⊙10.30am-2.30pm Tue, Wed, Thu & Sun) Visitors are welcome at this rescue and rehabilitation centre for injured and orphaned bats, possums and gliders. Passionate volunteers are more than happy to show folks around and explain the work they do. It's located next to the fire station.

Rainforestation PARK
(☑07-4085 5008; www.rainforest.com.au; Kennedy Hwy; adult/child/family $47/23.50/117.50; ⊙9am-4pm) You'll need a full day to properly explore this enormous complex, divided into three sections: a koala and wildlife park, the interactive Pamagirri Aboriginal Experience, and a river and rainforest tour aboard the amphibious Army Duck boat-truck.

The park is 3km east of Kuranda. Shuttles (one-way/return adult $7/12, child $3.50/6) run every half-hour between the park and Kuranda village.

Rainforestation is included in the Capta 4 Park Pass (www.capta.com.au), which offers discounted entry to four Far North Queensland attractions.

Heritage Markets MARKET
(☑07-4093 8060; www.kurandamarkets.com.au; Rob Veivers Dr; ⊙9.30am-3.30pm) This is Kuranda's more touristy market, hawking Australiana souvenirs – think emu oil, kangaroo-skin bow ties and Akubra hats – by the busload. It's also home to **Frogs** (www.frogsrestaurant.com.au; mains $12.40-35; ⊙9.30am-4pm; 🐾📶) cafe and a handful of wildlife sanctuaries, including **Kuranda Koala Gardens** (☑07-4093 9953; www.koalagardens.com; adult/child $18/9, koala photos extra; ⊙9am-4pm), **Australian Butterfly Sanctuary** (☑07-4093 7575; www.australianbutter flies.com; adult/child/family $19.50/9.75/48.75; ⊙9.45am-4pm) and **Birdworld** (☑07-4093

9188; www.birdworldkuranda.com; adult/child $18/9; ⊙9am-4pm).

Kuranda Riverboat
CRUISE

(☑07-4093 0082; www.kurandariverboat.com.au; adult/child/family $18/9/45; ⊙hourly 10.45am-2.30pm) Hop aboard for a 45-minute calm-water cruise along the Barron River, or opt for an hour-long interpretive rainforest walk in a secluded spot accessible only by boat.

You'll find Kuranda Riverboat on the jetty behind the train station; buy tickets (cash only) for the cruise on board, or book online for the walk.

🛏 Sleeping & Eating

Kuranda Rainforest Park
CARAVAN PARK $

(☑07-4093 7316; www.kurandarainforestpark.com.au; 88 Kuranda Heights Rd; powered/unpowered sites $32/30, s/d without bathroom $35/70, cabins $90-110; P❄🗢🏊) This well-tended park lives up to its name, with grassy camp sites enveloped in rainforest. The basic but cosy 'backpacker rooms' open onto a tin-roofed timber deck, cabins come with poolside or garden views, and there's an excellent restaurant serving local produce on-site. It's a 10-minute walk from town via a forest trail.

Fairyland House
B&B $

(☑07-4093 9194; www.fairylandhouse.com.au; 13 Fairyland Rd; r per person from $60; P) With a vegan raw-food restaurant, tarot readings, yoga classes, abundant fruit garden and wellness workshops, this bush retreat is about as 'Kuranda' as they come. All rooms are airy and open onto the garden. It's a 4km walk to the village; no cooked or animal food products, cigarettes, alcohol, pets or drugs allowed.

★Cedar Park Rainforest Resort
RESORT $$

(☑07-4093 7892; www.cedarparkresort.com.au; 250 Cedar Park Rd, Koah; s/d incl breakfast from $165/175; P❄🗢) 🕊 Set deep in the bush (a 20-minute drive from Kuranda towards Mareeba), this unusual property is part Euro-castle, part Aussie-bush-retreat. In lieu of TV, visitors goggle at wallabies, peacocks and dozens of native birds; there are hammocks aplenty, creek access, a fireplace, and a gourmet restaurant with well-priced meals and free port.

German Tucker
GERMAN $

(www.germantucker.com; Therwine St; sausages $7.50-9; ⊙10am-3pm) Fill up on classic *würste* or try the tasty emu and crocodile sausages at this amusing eatery, where they blast oompah music and splash out steins of top-notch German beer.

Petit Cafe
CRÊPES $

(www.petitcafe.com.au/kuranda; Original Kuranda Rainforest Markets, 7 Therwine St; crêpes $10-17; ⊙8am-3pm) Duck out the back of the Kuranda Original Rainforest Markets (p249) for a mouth-watering range of crêpes with savoury or sweet fillings. Winning combinations such as macadamia pesto and feta cheese will entice *le* drool.

Annabel's Pantry
BAKERY $

(15 Therwine St; pies $4.50-6.50; ⊙10am-3pm) Popular bakery offering around 25 pie varieties, including kangaroo and veggie.

★Kuranda Veranda
INTERNATIONAL $$

(www.kurandarainforestpark.com.au; Kuranda Rainforest Park, 88 Kuranda Heights Rd; mains $13-27; ⊙5.30-9.30pm Mon, Tue & Thu-Sat, 11.30am-9.30pm Sun; 🖉👶) Hidden away in the foliage at the Kuranda Rainforest Park, this superb restaurant serves up massive portions of steaks, stir-fries and salads. Kids will have fun ticking off the ingredients for their very own 'create-a-tayta' (loaded baked potato) and the build-your-own sundaes. The restaurant has a no-phones rule, so put 'em away and enjoy the sound of real tweets for a change.

ⓘ Information

Kuranda Visitor Information Centre (☑07-4093 9311; www.kuranda.org; Centenary Park; ⊙10am-4pm) The knowledgeable staff at the unmissable, map-laden visitor centre in Centenary Park are happy to dish out advice.

ⓘ Getting There & Away

Kuranda is as much about the journey (from Cairns) as the destination: choose between the **Skyrail Rainforest Cableway** (☑07-4038 5555; www.skyrail.com.au; cnr Cook Hwy & Cairns Western Arterial Rd, Smithfield; adult/child one way from $50/25, return $75/37.50; ⊙9am-5.15pm) and the **Kuranda Scenic Railway** (☑07-4036 9333; www.ksr.com.au; adult/child one way from $50/25, return from $76/38), or do both with a combination return ticket (adult/child from $109.50/54.75). Fares to Kuranda from Cairns are $6.70 with Trans North (p244), $16 on the Cairns Cooktown Express (p244) and $5 with John's Kuranda Bus (p244).

Kuranda is a 25km drive up the Kuranda Range from Cairns.

Mareeba

POP 10,181

Mareeba revels in a Wild West atmosphere, with local merchants selling leather saddles, handcrafted bush hats and the oversized belt buckle of your bronco-bustin' dreams; unsurprisingly, it hosts one of Australia's biggest rodeos (www.mareebarodeo.com.au; ☺Jul).

Once the heart of the country's main tobacco-growing region, Mareeba has since turned its soil to more wholesome produce, with fruit orchards, coffee plantations and distilleries in abundance. There is also a handful of unusual natural attractions in the region that differ dramatically from those found in the higher-altitude central Tablelands.

Mareeba Tropical Savanna & Wetland Reserve (☎07-4093 2514; www.mareeba wetlands.org; adult/child/family $10/5/25; ☺8.30am-4.30pm Apr-Dec) is a wonderful 20-sq-km reserve that includes woodlands, grasslands, swamps and the expansive Clancy's Lagoon, a birdwatchers' nirvana.

Granite Gorge Nature Park (☎07-4093 2259; www.granitegorge.com.au; adult/child $10/3), 12km from Mareeba, occupies an alien landscape of humungous granite boulders, caves, turtle-inhabited swimming holes and wildlife galore.

Campers can use the rodeo campgrounds (☎07-4092 1654; www.mareebarodeo. com.au; Kerribee Park; powered/unpowered sites for 2 people $18/15) year-round.

Atherton

POP 7287

The largest settlement and unofficial capital of the same-named Tablelands, Atherton is a spirited country town that makes a decent base for exploring the region's highlights.

Many backpackers head up to the Tablelands for year-round fruit-picking work; the Atherton Visitor Information Centre (☎07-4091 4222; www.itablelands.com.au; cnr Main & Silo Sts; ☺9am-5pm) can help with up-to-date work info.

Thousands of Chinese migrants came to the region in search of gold in the late 1800s. All that's left of Atherton's Chinatown now is corrugated-iron Hou Wang Miau Temple (☎07-4091 6945; www.hou-wang.org.au; 86 Herberton Rd; adult/child $10/5; ☺11am-4pm Wed-Sun). Admission includes a guided tour.

TABLELANDS MARKETS

As is seemingly obligatory for any quaint country region, the tiny towns of the Tablelands host a miscellany of monthly markets. Kuranda's blockbuster bazaars are legendary, but for something a bit more down-home, check out the following:

Malanda Markets (Malanda Showgrounds; ☺7am-noon 3rd Sat of month)

Yungaburra Markets (www.yungaburra markets.com; Gillies Hwy; ☺7.30am-12.30pm 4th Sat of month)

Atherton Undercover Markets (Merriland Hall, Robert St; ☺7am-noon 2nd Sun of month)

Tumoulin Country Markets (63 Grigg St; ☺8am-noon 4th Sun of month)

Crystal Caves (☎07-4091 2365; www.cry stalcaves.com.au; 69 Main St; adult/child/family $22.50/10/55; ☺9am-5pm Mon-Fri, to 4pm Sat & Sun; ⊕) is a gaudy mineralogical museum that houses the world's biggest amethyst geode (more than 3m high and weighing 2.7 tonnes).

Millaa Millaa

Evocatively nicknamed the 'Village in the Mist', charming Millaa Millaa is a small and gloriously green dairy community famous for its wonderful waterfalls. Surrounded by rolling farmland dotted with black-and-white cows, it's a picturesque spot to stop for lunch or to spend a few quaint and quiet nights.

There's accommodation at Millaa Millaa Tourist Park (☎07-4097 2290; www.millaa caravanpark.com.au; cnr Malanda Rd & Lodge Ave; powered/unpowered sites $29/24, cabins $65, with bathroom $75-110; P❄☎❄❄) and the Millaa Millaa Hotel (☎07-4097 2212; www.millaa millaahotel.info; 15 Main St; s/d $85/95; P❄☎). Stop in at the Falls Teahouse (☎07-4097 2237; www.fallsteahouse.com.au; 6 Theresa Creek Rd; meals from $10; ☺9am-4pm, closed Wed) for a Devonshire tea.

Malanda & Around

Malanda has been a byword for 'milk' in north Queensland ever since 560 cattle made the 16-month overland journey from New

DON'T MISS

TABLELANDS FOR FOODIES

The Atherton Tablelands is a popular place for produce, foodie festivals and other gourmet treats. Some of the best:

Rainforest Bounty (☑ 07-4076 6544; www.rainforestbounty.com.au; 66 Lindsay Rd, Malanda; courses from $220) Riverside slow-cooking school using local ingredients in its one-day courses.

Cheesemaking & More (☑ 07-4095 2097; www.cheesemakingandmore.com.au; Quinlan Rd, Lake Eacham) Twice-monthly, two-day cheesemaking classes, and one-day courses on bread and butter making and hard cheese.

Gallo Dairyland (☑ 07-4095 2388; www.gallodairyland.com.au; Atherton-Malanda Rd; ⊙ 9.30am-4.30pm; ⊞) Working farm outside Atherton with cheese factory and handmade chocolates.

Honey House (www.honeyhousekuranda.com; 7 Therwine St; ⊙ 9am-3pm; ⊞) Kuranda institution with high-quality raw local honeys, hives and a resident beekeeper.

Tastes of the Tablelands (www.tastesofthetablelands.com; ⊙ Oct) One-day festival showcasing the produce of the Tablelands with paddock-to-plate exhibitions, demonstrations and feasts.

Mt Uncle Distillery (☑ 07-4086 8008; www.mtuncle.com; 1819 Chewko Rd, Walkamin; ⊙ 10am-4.30pm; ⊞) Whiskies, seasonal liqueurs and spirits distilled from local bananas, coffee, mulberries and lemons.

South Wales in 1908. There's still a working dairy here, at the **Malanda Dairy Centre** (☑ 07-4095 1234; www.malandadairycentre.com; 8 James St; ⊙ 9am-3pm Wed-Sun) FREE, which has a kid-friendly museum highlighting the region's bovine history.

Rainforest-shrouded Malanda and its surrounds – including the other-worldly Mt Hypipamee crater – are also home to shy, rare Lumholtz's tree-kangaroos; be sure to bring a low-wattage torch to enjoy an evening of spotlighting.

Spot a platypus or fish for barramundi at the **Australian Platypus Park & Tarzali Lakes Aquaculture Centre** (☑ 07-4097 2713; www.tarzalilakes.com; Millaa Millaa-Malanda Rd, Tarzali; ⊙ 10am-4pm; ⊞).

Malanda Falls Visitor Centre (☑ 07-4096 6957; www.malandafalls.com; 132 Malanda-Atherton Rd; ⊙ 9.30am-4.30pm) has thoughtful displays and guided rainforest walks.

Yungaburra

Wee, winsome Yungaburra ticks every box on the country-cute checklist; within one lap of its tree-lined streets, you'll find 19 heritage-listed sites, a welcoming 1910 pub populated by local larrikins, boho-boutiques and cafes, and a dedicated platypus-watching platform. Its proximity to Lake Tinaroo and

some of the region's top natural attractions makes Yungaburra a contender for best base on the Tablelands.

The sacred, 500-year-old **Curtain Fig tree** (Fig Tree Rd, East Barron), signposted 3km out of town, is a must-see for its gigantic, other-worldly aerial roots that hang down to create an enormous 'curtain'. If you're very quiet, you might catch a glimpse of a timid monotreme at the **platypus-viewing platform** (Gillies Hwy) on Peterson Creek.

Explore the wilds around Yungaburra with **Alan's Wildlife Tours** (☑ 07-4095 3784; www.alanswildlifetours.com.au; day tours $90-500, multiday tours from $1790), led by a passionate local naturalist.

Tablelands Folk Festival (www.tablelands folkfestival.org.au; ⊙ Oct) is a fabulous community event held in Yungaburra and neighbouring Herberton featuring music, workshops, performances and a market.

🛌 Sleeping & Eating

★**On the Wallaby**   HOSTEL **$**
(☑ 07-4095 2031; www.onthewallaby.com; 34 Eacham Rd; sites per person $15, dm/d with shared bathroom $25/60; ⊚) This cosy hostel features handmade timber furniture and mosaics, spotless rooms and no TV! Nature-based tours ($40) include night canoeing; tour packages and transfers are

available from Cairns. Cook for yourself in the communal kitchen, or indulge in the nightly barbecue ($12).

★**Yungaburra Hotel** PUB FOOD **$$**
(Lake Eacham Hotel; ☑ 07-4095 3515; www.yung-aburrahotel.com.au; 6-8 Kehoe Pl; mains from $23; ☺ restaurant 11am-8pm, pub to 11pm) This wonderful, welcoming, original-timber country pub ranks as one of the best in the state, let alone on the Tablelands. It often hosts live jams and bands; even if there's nothing on, it's an ideal place to sink a schooner, meet the locals and soak up the old-school atmosphere. The restaurant does huge, wholesome meals.

❶ Information

Yungaburra Information Centre (☑ 07-4095 2416; www.yungaburra.com; Maud Kehoe Park; ☺ 9am-5pm Mon-Sat, 10am-4pm Sun) The utterly delightful volunteers at this immaculate centre can help recommend accommodation, provide info on walks and tours and generally yarn about all things Yungaburra.

Lake Tinaroo

Lake Tinaroo, also known as Tinaroo Dam, was allegedly named when a prospector stumbled across a deposit of alluvial tin and, in a fit of excitement, shouted 'Tin! Hurroo!' The excitement hasn't died down since, with locals fleeing the swelter of the coast for boating, waterskiing and shoreline lolling. Barramundi fishing (☑ 0438 012 775; www.tinaroobarra.com; full-/half-day fishing $600/350) is permitted year-round, though if you're not joining a charter, you'll need to pick up a permit from local businesses.

The 28km Danbulla Forest Drive winds its way through rainforest and softwood plantations along the north side of the lake. The unsealed but well-maintained road passes the pretty Lake Euramoo and the boardwalk-encircled Cathedral Fig, a gigantic 500-year-old strangler fig similar to the Curtain Fig in nearby Yungaburra; it's also accessible via a signposted road off the Gillies Hwy.

There are five Queensland Parks camping grounds (☑ 13 74 68; www.npsr.qld.gov.au/parks/danbulla; camping permits per person/family $6.15/24.60) in the Danbulla State Forest. All have water, barbecues and toilets; advance bookings are essential.

Lake Tinaroo Holiday Park (☑ 07-4095 8232; www.laketinarooholidaypark.com.au; 3 Tinaroo Falls Dam Rd, Tinaroo Falls; powered/unpowered sites $37/27, cabins from $90; P ❀ 🎧 ➳) is a modern, well-equipped and shady camping ground with tinnies, canoes and kayaks for rent.

Crater Lakes National Park

Part of the Wet Tropics World Heritage Area, the two mirrorlike, rainforest-fringed croc-free volcanic crater lakes of Lake Eacham and Lake Barrine are popular for swimming.

There's info at the Rainforest Display Centre (McLeish Rd, Lake Eacham; ☺ 9am-1pm Mon, Wed & Fri).

Spot water dragons and tortoises or simply relax and soak up the views on a 45-minute cruise (www.lakebarrine.com.au/cruises; adult/child/family $18/8/40; ☺ 9.30am, 11.30am & 1.30pm) around Lake Barrine; book and board at the excellent Lake Barrine Teahouse (☑ 07-4095 3847; www.lakebarrine.com.au; Gillies Hwy; mains from $8.50; ☺ 9am-3pm).

The pretty Lake Eacham Tourist Park (☑ 07-4095 3730; www.lakeeachamtouristpark.com; Lakes Dr; powered/unpowered sites $27/22, cabins $110-130; @ 🎧), 1km down from Lake Eacham, has shady sites, cosy cabins, a general store and a cafe.

PORT DOUGLAS

POP 3205

From its early days as a fishing village, Port Douglas has grown into a sophisticated and upmarket resort town that's quite a contrast to Cairns' hectic tourist scene. The outer Great Barrier Reef is less than an hour offshore, the Daintree Rainforest is practically in the backyard, and there are more resorts than you can poke a snorkel at: a growing number of flashpackers, cashed-up couples and fiscally flush families choose Port Douglas as their Far North base.

Apart from easy access to the reef and daily sunset cruises on the inlet, the town's main attraction is Four Mile Beach (p255), a broad strip of palm-fringed, white sand that begins at the eastern end of Macrossan St, the main drag for shopping, wining and dining. On the western end of Macrossan you'll find the picturesque Dickson Inlet and Reef Marina, where the rich and famous park their aquatic toys.

CAIRNS & THE DAINTREE RAINFOREST LAKE TINAROO

Port Douglas

0 500 m
0 0.25 miles

Low Isles (15km);
Great Barrier Reef

Anzac Park

Douglas Shire Historical Society

Coral Sea

35

1

3

28

Dixie St

31

25 33

34

Ashford Ave

29 Port Douglas Tourist Information Centre

Macrossan St

23

24

Murphy St

7

Island Point Rd

4

Magazine Island

10

Inlet St

27 22

26

11

Grant St

Warner St

Owen St

36

8

32 12

9 5 6

Reef Marina

Mowbray St

19

Mudlo St

15

21

16

Four Mile Beach

Esplanade

Davidson St

17

20

Swimming Enclosure

Beryl St

Reynolds Park

Oval

Garrick St

Sand St

Trinity Bay

Blake St

2

Packers Creek

Spinnaker Cl

Wharf St

Bally Hooley Railway

30

Dicksons Inlet

Port St

13 Craven Cl

14

Crimmins St

18

Davidson St / Port Douglas Rd

Mirage Country Club (1.3km);
QT Resort (1.5km);
Moonlight Cinema (1.5km)

Port Douglas

◎ Sights

Four Mile Beach   BEACH
Fringed by lazy palms, this broad stretch of squeaky sand reaches as far as you can squint. There's a patrolled swimming area in front of the surf life-saving club (with a stinger net in summer) and sun loungers available for hire.

★ Wildlife Habitat Port Douglas   ZOO
(☑ 07-4099 3235; www.wildlifehabitat.com.au; Port Douglas Rd; adult/child/family $34/17/85; ◎ 8am-5pm) This sanctuary endeavours to keep and showcase native animals in enclosures that mimic their natural environment, while allowing you to get up close to koalas, kangaroos, crocs, cassowaries and more. Tickets are valid for three days. For an extra special experience book for **Breakfast with the Birds** (adult/child/family breakfast incl admission $53/26.50/132.50; ◎ 8-10.30am) or **Lunch with the Lorikeets** (adult/child incl admission $56/28; ◎ noon-2pm). It's 5km from town ($5 by shuttle bus).

Trinity Bay Lookout   VIEWPOINT
(Island Point Rd) Head up to Flagstaff Hill for absolutely sensational views over Four Mile Beach and the Coral Sea. Drive or walk up via Wharf St, or there's a walking path leading up from the north end of Four Mile Beach.

Court House Museum   MUSEUM
(☑ 07-4098 1284; www.douglashistory.org.au; Wharf St; adult/child $2/free; ◎ 10am-1pm Tue, Thu, Sat & Sun) The 1879 Court House contains historical exhibits, including the story of Ellen Thompson, who was tried for murder in 1887 and the only woman ever hanged in Queensland.

St Mary's by the Sea   CHURCH
(☑ 0418 456 880; 6 Dixie St) **FREE** Worth a little peek inside (when it's not overflowing with wedding parties), this quaint, non-denominational, white timber church was built in 1911.

♣ Activities

Port Douglas is best known for its smorgasbord of activities and tours, both on water and land. For golfers the **Mirage Country Club** (☑ 07-4099 5537; www.miragecountryclub.com.au; 9/18 holes $55/85) and **Palmer Sea Reef** (☑ 07-4087 2222; www.palmergolf.com.au; 9/18 holes with cart $85/145) are two of north Queensland's top resort courses.

Several companies offer PADI open-water certification as well as advanced dive certificates, including **Blue Dive** (☑ 0427 983 907; www.bluedive.com.au; 32 Macrossan St; reef intro diving courses from $300). For one-on-one instruction, learn with **Tech Dive Academy** (☑ 0422 016 517; www.tech-dive-academy.com; 4-day open-water courses from $1290).

CAIRNS & THE DAINTREE RAINFOREST PORT DOUGLAS

WORTH A TRIP

CHILLAGOE

This charismatic former gold-rush town will fulfil your wildest, most romantic outback dreams. With a raw, unhurried quality, it's at the centre of an area that has impressive limestone caves, indigenous rock-art sites and the creepy-cool ruins of an early 20th-century smelting plant (www.nprsr.qld.gov.au/parks/chillagoe-caves). Chillagoe Observatory (07-4094 7155; www.coel.com.au; Hospital Ave; adult/child from 6 years $20/15; 7.30pm Easter-Oct) offers the chance to scan the clear outback skies through two huge telescopes.

Stop in at the Hub (www.qwe.com.au/chillagoe/the_hub.html; Queen St; 8am-5pm Mon-Fri, to 3pm Sat & Sun) for help with finding some of Chillagoe's more hidden highlights. The Chillagoe–Mungana Caves National Park (www.nprsr.qld.gov.au/parks/chillagoe-caves; 1-cave/2-cave/3-cave tours $26.30/41.75/52.45) website has information on walking tracks in the area.

Chillagoe's big annual events are the rodeo (www.chillagoerodeo.com.au; May) and Great Wheelbarrow Race (www.greatwheelbarrowrace.com; May).

⭐ **Wind Swell** WATER SPORTS
(0427 498 042; www.windswell.com.au; Barrier St; lessons from $50) Kitesurfing and stand-up paddleboarding for everyone from beginners to high-flyers. Kitesurfing lessons and paddleboarding tours from the beach start at $50, but there are also plenty of advanced options. Find them in action at the southern end of Four Mile Beach (p255).

Port Douglas Yacht Club BOATING
(07-4099 4386; www.portdouglasyachtclub.com.au; 1 Spinnaker Close; from 4pm Wed) Free sailing with club members every Wednesday afternoon: sign on from 4pm. Those chosen to go sailing are expected to stay for dinner and drinks in the club afterwards.

Aquarius Sunset Sailing CRUISE
(07-4099 6999; www.tropicaljourneys.com; adult/child $60/50; cruises depart 4.45pm) Twilight sailing is practically de rigueur in Port Douglas. This 1½-hour catamaran cruise includes canapés, and BYO alcohol is allowed.

Ballyhooley Steam Railway RAIL
(07-4099 1839; www.ballyhooley.com.au; 44 Wharf St; adult/child day pass $12/6; Sun; ♿) Kids will get a kick out of this cute miniature steam train. Every Sunday (and some public holidays), it runs from the little station at Reef Marina to St Crispins Station four times between 10am and 4pm. A round trip takes about one hour; discounts are available for shorter sections.

Port Douglas Boat Hire BOATING
(07-4099 6277; www.pdboathire.com.au; Berth C1, Reef Marina; rentals per hour $45; 8.30am-5.30pm) Rents canopied, family friendly pontoon boats that can carry up to six people. An excellent way to explore the calm inland estuaries or go fishing.

👉 Tours

The outer reef is closer to Port Douglas than it is to Cairns, and the unrelenting surge of visitors has had a similar impact on its condition here. You will still see colourful corals and marine life, but it is patchy in parts.

Most day tours depart from Reef Marina. Tour prices usually include reef tax, snorkelling, transfers from your accommodation, lunch and refreshments.

⭐ **Quicksilver** CRUISE
(07-4087 2100; www.quicksilver-cruises.com; Reef Marina; adult/child/family $238/119/535) Major operator with fast cruises to its own pontoon on Agincourt Reef. Try an 'ocean walk' helmet dive ($166) on a submerged platform or snorkelling with a marine biologist (from $60). Also offers 10-minute scenic helicopter flights ($175, minimum two passengers).

Reef Sprinter SNORKELLING
(07-4099 6127; www.reefsprinter.com.au; Shop 3, Reef Marina; adult/child from $130/110) The fastest way to the reef, this 2¼-hour snorkelling trip gets to the Low Isles in just 15 minutes for one to 1½ hours in the water. Half-day outer reef trips are also available (from $200).

Poseidon TOURS
(07-4087 2100; www.poseidon-cruises.com.au; Reef Marina; adult/child $240/171) This luxury

catamaran specialises in snorkelling trips to the Agincourt Ribbon Reefs, as well as scuba diving (one/two dives an additional $46/66).

Sail Tallarook
BOATING
(☑07-4099 4070; www.sailtallarook.com.au; adult/child half-day sails $120/100) Morning and afternoon half-day sailing adventures on a historic 30m yacht. Also sunset and full-day sails.

Sailaway
SAILING, SNORKELLING
(☑07-4099 4200; www.sailawayportdouglas.com; Shop 18, Reef Marina; adult/child $255/178; ♿) Runs a popular catamaran sailing and snorkelling trip to the Low Isles that's great for families. The afternoon and sunset cruises are for adults only.

★ Tony's Tropical Tours
TOURS
(☑07-4099 3230; www.tropicaltours.com.au; day tours from $185) This luxury, small-group (eight to 10 passengers) tour operator specialises in trips to out-of-the-way sections of the Mossman Gorge and Daintree Rainforest (adult/child $185/160), and Bloomfield Falls and Cape Trib (adults only $215 – good mobility required). A third tour heads south to the Tablelands. Highly recommended.

Bike N Hike
CYCLING
(☑0477 774 443; www.bikenhiketours.com.au; tours $120-128) Mountain bike down the aptly named Bump Track on a cross-country bike tour, or take on an action-packed berserk night tour. Also does half-day cycling and hiking trips.

Back Country Bliss Adventures
ADVENTURE
(☑07-4099 3677; www.backcountryblissadventures.com.au; tours $99-249) Go with the flow as you drift-snorkel down the Mossman River. Also small-group sea-kayaking, hiking and mountain-biking trips.

Lady Douglas
BOATING
(☑0408 986 127; www.ladydouglas.com.au; Reef Marina, Wharf St; 1½hr cruises adult/child/family $35/15/90; ⊗ cruises 10.30am, 12.30pm, 2.30pm & 4.30pm) Lovely paddle steamer running four daily crocodile-spotting river tours (including a sunset cruise) along the Dickson Inlet.

✦✦ Festivals & Events

Port Douglas Carnivale
CARNIVAL
(www.carnivale.com.au; ⊗May) Port Douglas is packed for this 10-day festival, which

includes a colourful street parade featuring live music, and lashings of good food and wine.

Portoberfest
BEER
(Reef Marina; ⊗late Oct) The tropical take on Oktoberfest, with live music, German food and, *natürlich*, beer is held at Lure Restaurant in the Reef Marina.

🛏 Sleeping

Although it has a few backpacker resorts and caravan parks, Port Douglas isn't a true budget destination like Cairns – five-star resorts and boutique holiday apartments are more a part of the PD experience. Much of the accommodation is some distance from town off the 5km-long Port Douglas Rd, while most restaurants, bars, pubs and the marina are around the main drag, Macrossan St.

★ Coral Beach Lodge
HOSTEL $
(☑07-4099 5422; www.coralbeachlodge.com; 1 Craven Close; dm $25-39, d $114; ❄@🖥♿) 🖉 A cut above most backpacker places, this fabulous, chilled-out hostel has well-equipped en-suite dorms (with four or five beds) and double or triple rooms that put many motels in the shade – flat-screen TVs, new bathrooms and comfy beds. Each room has an outdoor area with hammocks, and there's a lovely pool, games room, kitchen and the owners are helpful. Highly recommended.

Dougies
HOSTEL $
(☑1800 996 200, 07-4099 6200; www.dougies.com.au; 111 Davidson St; tent s/tw $25/40, sites per person $25, dm/d $30/75; ❄@🖥♿) It's easy to hang around Dougies' sprawling grounds in a hammock by day and move to the bar at night. If you can summon the energy, bikes and fishing gear are available for rent and the beach is a 300m walk east. Free pick-up from Cairns on Monday, Wednesday and Saturday.

Port Douglas Backpackers
HOSTEL $
(☑07-4099 5011; www.portdouglasbackpackers.com.au; 37 Warner St; dm $20-28, d $85; ❄♿) For a cheap bed close to the centre of town, this brand-new place will suit travellers looking for action. There's a lively bar at the front, clean four- to eight-bed dorms, a few private rooms at the rear and a pool in-between. Free transfer to Cairns Tuesday, Thursday and Sunday.

Tropic Breeze Caravan Park CARAVAN PARK $
(🖉07-4099 5299; www.tropicbreeze.com.au; 24 Davidson St; powered/unpowered sites $48/37, cabins $120; ❋ ≋) This small park is beautifully located a short walk to the beach and town. Grassy sites, and units with kitchenette but no bathroom.

★**Pink Flamingo** BOUTIQUE HOTEL $$
(🖉07-4099 6622; www.pinkflamingo.com.au; 115 Davidson St; d $145-205; ❋ @ 🛜 ≋) Flamboyantly painted rooms, private walled courtyards and a groovy alfresco pool-bar make the Pink Flamingo Port Douglas' hippest gay-friendly digs. With just two studios and 10 villas, it's an intimate stay in a sea of mega-resorts. Heated pool, a gym and bike rental are also on offer.

Mantra Aqueous on Port APARTMENT $$
(🖉07-4099 0000; www.mantraaqueousonport.com.au; 3-5 Davidson St; d from $180, 1-/2-bed apt from $280/415; ❋ 🛜 ≋) You can't beat the location of this unique resort with four individual pools. The pricier ground-floor rooms have swim-up balconies, and all rooms have outdoor Jacuzzi tubs! Studio and one- and two-bedroom apartments are available. Longer stays attract cheaper rates.

Birdsong Port Douglas B&B $$
(🖉07-4099 1288; www.portdouglasbnb.com; 6188 Captain Cook Hwy; d from $165; P ❋ 🛜 ≋) Posh open-plan B&B set on sprawling tropical grounds back from the highway 5km from Port Douglas. Induce delusions of grandeur as you ogle the private helipad and gawp at the in-house movie theatre. Rates go down the longer you stay. Custom breakfasts to order and cooking classes available.

Martinique on Macrossan APARTMENT $$
(🖉07-4099 6222; www.martinique.com.au; 66 Macrossan St; apt $215; ❋ 🛜 ≋) Martinique is a terracotta boutique block that contains lovely tiled one-bedroom apartments, each with a small kitchen, a private balcony, colourful accents and plantation shutters. Wonderful hosts and an excellent mainstreet location near the beach seal the deal. The pool has six coves and is supervised by a lavish elephant and dolphin shrine. Good value.

★**Peppers Beach Club** RESORT $$$
(🖉1300 737 444; www.peppers.com.au/beach-club; 20-22 Davidson St; spa ste from $309, 1-/2-bedoom ste from $409/566; ❋ 🛜 ≋) A killer location and an exceptional, enormous, sandy lagoon pool, combined with luxurious, airy apartments with high-end furnishings and amenities, put Peppers right up there with Port Douglas' best. Some rooms have balcony spas, others swim-up decks or full kitchens. Family friendly, but recommended for young romantics.

Thala Beach Nature Reserve RESORT $$$
(🖉07-4098 5700; www.thalabeach.com.au; Captain Cook Hwy; d $255-668; ❋ 🛜 ≋) On a private coastal headland 15km south of Port Douglas, Thala Beach is an upmarket eco-retreat so relaxing that even locals come here to chill for the weekend. Luxurious treehouse-style bungalows are scattered throughout the jungle with easy access to a private stretch of beach, two pools, walking trails and a quality restaurant.

QT Resort RESORT $$$
(🖉07-4099 8900; www.qthotelsandresorts.com/port-douglas; 87-109 Port Douglas Rd; d $279-299, villas $329-439; ❋ @ 🛜 ≋) Fresh, fun and funky, this one is aimed at a trendy, twenty-to thirty-something crowd. There's a lagoon pool and swim-up bar, retro-kitsch rooms with free wi-fi, chic staff, and DJs spinning lounge beats in Estilio, the cocktail bar. The breakfast buffet rates as one of the best in Port Douglas.

✖ Eating

Port Douglas' compact centre is awash with sophisticated cafes and restaurants, many with a tropical alfresco setting. All of the resorts also have restaurants.

Self-caterers can stock up on supplies at the large **Coles Supermarket** (11 Macrossan St; ⏱7am-6pm) in the Port Village shopping centre.

Cafe Fresq CAFE $
(🖉07-4099 6111; 27 Macrossan St; mains $6-19; ⏱7am-3pm) Cafe Fresq is always busy at breakfast with tables spilling out onto the footpath. Good coffee, gourmet breakfasts, pancakes and lunch items such as soft-shell crab burgers.

Cafe Ziva FRENCH $
(20 Macrossan St; mains $7.50-22; ⏱12.30-10pm; 🛜) Ziva specialises in French-style pancakes with a range of savoury galettes (such as ham and cheese) and sweet crêpes, along with sandwiches, smoothies and fresh juice. The open-fronted cafe is good for people-watching.

Mocka's Pies
BAKERY $

(☑07-4099 5295; 9 Grant St; pies $4.50-6; ⊙8am-4pm) Local institution serving classic Aussie pies with exotic fillings such as crocodile, kangaroo and barramundi.

★ Yachty
MODERN AUSTRALIAN $$

(☑07-4099 4386; www.portdouglasyachtclub. com.au; 1 Spinnaker Close; mains $22-34; ⊙noon-2.30pm & 5.30-8pm) One of the best-value nights out is the local yacht club, where well-crafted meals, from Moroccan spiced lamb to lobster tail, are served nightly with sunset views over Dickson Inlet. The lunch menu is similar but cheaper.

★ On the Inlet
SEAFOOD $$

(☑07-4099 5255; www.ontheinlet.com.au; 3 Inlet St; mains $26-42; ⊙noon-11.30pm) You'll feel like you're floating over Dickson Inlet here, with tables spread out along a huge deck from where you can await the 5pm arrival of George, the 250kg groper that comes to feed most days. Take up the bucket-of-prawns-and-a-drink deal ($18 from 3.30pm to 5.30pm) and enjoy watching the reef boats come in.

Seabean
TAPAS $$

(☑07-4099 5558; www.seabean.com.au; 3/28 Wharf St; tapas $9-15, paella from $35; ⊙3-9pm Mon-Thu, noon-9pm Fri-Sun) This cool little tapas bar with bright red stools and attentive staff brings quality Spanish plates and paella to PD.

Little Larder
CAFE $$

(☑07-4099 6450; Shop 2, 40 Macrossan St; mains $10-19; ⊙7.30am-3pm) Brekky until 11.30am then gourmet sandwiches and killer cocktails from noon. Good coffee, or try freshly brewed and super-healthy kombucha tea.

Beach Shack
MODERN AUSTRALIAN $$

(☑07-4099 1100; www.the-beach-shack.com. au; 29 Barrier St; mains $26-31, pizza $21-26; ⊙4-10pm; 🖉) It's quite a hike down to the southern end of Four Mile Beach (p255), but this locals' favourite is worth the trip for sublime pizzas, tapas and tasty dishes like macadamia-encrusted barramundi. The lantern-lit garden completes the beach theme with its sandy floor. Saturday is $20 pizza night.

★ Harrisons Restaurant
MODERN AUSTRALIAN $$$

(☑07-4099 4011; www.harrisonsrestaurant.com. au; 22 Wharf St; lunch $19-26, dinner mains from $38; ⊙noon-2pm & 5-10pm) Marco Pierre White–trained chef-owner Spencer Patrick whips up culinary gems that stand toe-to-toe with Australia's best. Fresh locally sourced produce is turned into dishes such as smoked duck breast and tamarind beef cheeks. Possibly the only place in Port where diners bother ditching their thongs for shoes.

Sassi Cucina e Bar
ITALIAN $$$

(☑07-4099 6744; www.sassi.com.au; cnr Wharf & Macrossan Sts; mains $30-48; ⊙noon-10pm) It's quite a splurge on an authentic Italian feast at this legendary local eatery but it remains a favourite in Port Douglas. The brainchild of owner-chef Tony Sassi, from Abruzzo, the spin on seafood and *spuntini* (small dishes) is world renowned: the balanced flavours of each dish should linger longer than your Four Mile Beach (p255) tan.

2 Fish Restaurant Port Douglas
SEAFOOD $$$

(☑07-4099 6350; www.2fishrestaurant.com.au; Shop 11, 56 Macrossan St; mains $32-44; ⊙noon-10pm) In a town where seafood is plentiful, 2 Fish stands out for its upmarket innovative dishes, over a dozen types of fish, from coral trout to red emperor and wild barramundi, along with locally caught oysters, prawns and sea scallops. Between lunch and dinner, tapas plates are available.

★ Flames of the Forest
MODERN AUSTRALIAN $$$

(☑07-4099 3144; www.flamesoftheforest.com.au; Mowbray River Rd; dinner with show, drinks & transfers from $219; ⊙Tue, Thu & Sat) This unique experience goes way beyond the traditional concept of 'dinner and a show', with diners escorted deep into the rainforest for a truly immersive night of theatre, culture and gourmet cuisine. Transport provided from Port Douglas or Cairns (no self-drive). Bookings essential.

🍷 Drinking & Entertainment

Pubs turn into clubs later in the night and Port has a **Moonlight Cinema** (www.moonlight.com.au/port-douglas; QT Resort, 87-109 Port Douglas Rd; adult/child $17.50/13; ⊙Thu-Sun Jun-Oct) in season.

★ Hemingway's
MICROBREWERY

(☑07-4099 6663; www.hemingwaysbrewery.com; Reef Marina, 44 Wharf St) Port Douglas deserves its own brewery and Hemingway's makes the most of a fabulous location on the Reef Marina with a broad deck, a long bar and

Dickson Inlet views. There are currently six brews on tap, including Hard Yards dark lager and Pitchfork Betty's pale ale. Naturally, food is available, but this is one for the beer connoisseurs.

Tin Shed   CLUB
(📞07-4099 5553; www.thetinshed-portdouglas. com.au; 7 Ashford Ave; mains $22-29; ⊗10am-10pm) Port Douglas' Combined Services Club (sign in as a guest member) has gone a bit fancy since its days of being dubbed the Tin Shed, but the over-water deck, good-value meals and reasonably priced drinks make this an inviting spot at any time of day.

Iron Bar   PUB
(📞07-4099 4776; www.ironbarportdouglas.com. au; 5 Macrossan St; ⊗11am-3am) Wacky outback meets Wild West decor of corrugated iron and old timber, setting the scene for a wild night out. Don't miss the nightly 8.30pm cane-toad races ($5).

Court House Hotel   PUB
(📞07-4099 5181; cnr Macrossan & Wharf Sts; ⊗9am-late) Elegant and unmissable, the old 'Courty' holds court on the street corner. It's a lively local, with live music on weekends and reasonable meals.

🛍 Shopping

The weekly **Reef Marina Sunset Market** (Reef Marina, Wharf St; ⊗noon-6.30pm Wed) and **Port Douglas Markets** (Anzac Park, Macrossan St; ⊗8am-2pm Sun) are both good for crafts, souvenirs and local produce.

ℹ Information

There are many tour booking agents in PD masquerading as tourist information offices, but no official tourist office.
Douglas Shire Historical Society (📞07-4098 1284; www.douglashistory.org.au; Wharf St; ⊗10am-1pm Tue, Thu, Sat & Sun) Download do-it-yourself historical walks through Port Douglas, Mossman and Daintree, or chat with a local at the on-site Court House Museum (p255).
Port Douglas Tourist Information Centre (📞07-4099 5599; www.infoportdouglas.com. au; 23 Macrossan St; ⊗8am-6.30pm) Not a government tourist office, but a reliable private booking agency; pick up brochures here and book tours.
Post Office (📞07-4099 5210; 5 Owen St; ⊗8.30am-5pm Mon-Fri, 9am-noon Sat)

ℹ Getting There & Away

Port Douglas Bus (📞070-4099 5665; www. portdouglasbus.com.au) and **Sun Palm** (📞07-4087 2900; www.sunpalmtransport.com.au; adult/child $35/17.50) operate daily between Port Douglas, Cairns and the airport.

Trans North (📞07-4095 8644; www.trans northbus.com.au) picks up in Port Douglas on the coastal drive between Cairns and Cooktown.

ℹ Getting Around

Hire bikes at the **Bicycle Centre** (📞07-4099 5799; www.portdouglasbikehire.com.au; 3 Warner St; half-/full-day from $16/20; ⊗8am-5pm).

Minibuses, such as those run by **Coral Reef Coaches** (📞07-4098 2800; www.coralreef-coaches.com.au), shuttle between town and the highway for around $5.

Major car-rental chains have branches here, or try **Comet Car Hire** (📞07-4099 6407; www. cometcarhire.com.au; 3/11 Warner St) and keep it local.

MOSSMAN
POP 1733

Surrounded by sugar-cane fields, the workaday town of Mossman, 20km north of Port Douglas, is best known for beautiful Mossman Gorge, part of Daintree National Park. The town itself is worth a stop to get a feel for a Far North Queensland working community and to stock up if you're heading further north.

◉ Sights & Activities

⭐**Mossman Gorge**   GORGE
(www.mossmangorge.com.au) In the southeast corner of Daintree National Park, 5km west of Mossman town, Mossman Gorge forms part of the traditional lands of the Kuku Yalanji people. The gorge is a boulder-strewn valley where sparkling water washes over ancient rocks. It's 3km by road from the **visitor centre** (📞07-4099 7000; www.moss mangorge.com.au; ⊗8am-6pm) to a viewpoint and refreshing swimming hole – take care as the currents can be swift. You can walk the 3km but visitors are encouraged to take the **shuttle** (adult/child return $9.10/4.55, every 15 minutes).

There are several kilometres of walking trails on boardwalks and a picnic area at the gorge, but no camping.

★ Kuku-Yalanji
Dreamtime Walks OUTDOORS
(adult/child $62/31; ☺10am, 11am, noon, 1pm & 3pm) These unforgettable Indigenous-guided walks of Mossman Gorge last 1½ hours and include a smoking ceremony, bush tea and damper. Book through the Mossman Gorge Centre.

🛏 Sleeping & Eating

Mossman Motel Holiday Villas VILLA $$
(☎07-4098 1299; www.mossmanmotel.com.au; 1-9 Alchera Dr; villas $140-200; P ✶ @ 🜄 ≋) These great-value, spacious villas occupy lovely landscaped grounds complete with rock waterfall and pool.

★ Silky Oaks Lodge RESORT $$$
(☎07-4098 1666; www.silkyoakslodge.com.au; Finlayvale Rd; treehouses $440-698; ste $898-998; ✶ @ 🜄 ≋) This international eco-resort on the Mossman River woos honeymooners and stressed-out execs with amazing architecturally designed treehouses, riverside lodge suites, luxury hammocks, rejuvenation treatments and polished-timber interiors and private spa baths. Activities include tennis courts, gym, yoga classes and canoeing. Its stunning **Treehouse Restaurant & Bar** (☎07-4098 1666; Finlayvale Rd; mains $36-50; ☺7-10am, noon-2.30pm & 6-8.30pm) is open to interlopers with advance reservation.

THE DAINTREE

The Daintree represents many things: Unesco World Heritage–listed **rainforest** (www.daintreerainforest.com), a river, a reef, laid-back villages and the home of its traditional custodians, the Kuku Yalanji people. It encompasses the coastal lowland area between the Daintree and Bloomfield Rivers, where the rainforest tumbles right down to the coast. It's a fragile, ancient ecosystem, once threatened by logging, but now protected as a national park.

Part of the Wet Tropics World Heritage Area, the spectacular region from the Daintree River north to Cape Tribulation features ancient rainforest, sandy beaches and rugged mountains. North of the Daintree River, electricity is supplied by generators or, increasingly, solar power. Shops and services are limited, and mobile-phone reception is patchy at best. The **Daintree River Ferry** (www.douglas.qld.gov.au/community/daintree-ferry; car one-way/return $14/26, motorcycle $5/10, pedestrian & bicycle $1/2; ☺6am-midnight) carries wanderers and their wheels across the river every 15 minutes or so.

Daintree Village

For wildlife lovers and birdwatchers, it's well worth taking the 20km each-way detour from the Mossman-Daintree Rd to tiny Daintree village, set on a plateau of farmland on the Upper Daintree River. Croc-spotting cruises are the main event. Try long-running **Crocodile Express** (☎07-4098 6120; www.crocodileexpress.com; 1hr cruises adult/child/family $28/14/65; ☺cruises 8.30am); **Daintree River Wild Watch** (☎0447 734 933; www.daintreeriverwildwatch.com.au; 2hr cruises adult/child $60/35), which has informative sunrise birdwatching cruises and sunset photography

---

CONSERVATION, CONTROVERSY & CONTROL OF THE DAINTREE

The greater Daintree Rainforest is protected as part of Daintree National Park, but this protection is not without controversy. In 1983, despite conservationist blockades, what's now the Bloomfield Track was bulldozed through lowland rainforest from Cape Tribulation to the Bloomfield River. Ensuing publicity led to the federal government nominating Queensland's wet tropical rainforests for World Heritage listing, generating state government and timber industry opposition. In 1988 the area was inscribed on the World Heritage List and commercial logging here was banned.

Unesco World Heritage listing (www.whc.unesco.org) doesn't affect ownership rights or control. Since the 1990s the Queensland government and conservation agencies have attempted to buy back and rehabilitate freehold properties in the area, adding them to the Daintree National Park. Sealing the road to Cape Tribulation in 2002 triggered the buy back of even more land, which, coupled with development controls, now bears the fruits of forest regeneration. Check out **Rainforest Rescue** (www.rainforestrescue.org.au) for more information.

nature cruises; or **Daintree River Cruise Centre** (⌨07-4098 6115; www.daintreeriver cruisecentre.com.au; 2914 Mossman-Daintree Rd; adult/child $28/14; ⊙9.30am-4pm).

The boutique 'banyans' (treehouses) of **Daintree Eco Lodge & Spa** (⌨07-4777 7377; www.daintree-ecolodge.com.au; 3189 Mossman-Daintree Rd; treehouses $325-425; ✳@🛜🏊) 🏊 sit high in the rainforest a few kilometres south of the village. Nonguests are also welcome at its superb **Julaymba Restaurant** (⌨07-4098 6100; www.daintree-ecolodge.com.au; 3189 Mossman-Daintree Rd; mains $28-32; ⊙dinner from 4.30pm), where the menu makes expert use of local produce.

In the village, **Big Barramundi Garden** (⌨07-4098 6186; www.bigbarra.daintree.info; 12 Stewart St; mains $18-22, burgers from $9; ⊙10am-4pm) serves exotic burgers (barra, crocodile and kangaroo) and smoothies or fruit juices (black sapote, pawpaw) as well as Devonshire teas.

Cow Bay & Around

Tiny Cow Bay is the first community you reach after the Daintree ferry crossing. On the steep, winding road between Cape Kimberley and Cow Bay, the **Walu Wugirriga Lookout** (Alexandra Range Lookout) offers sweeping views beyond the Daintree River inlet; it's especially breathtaking at sunset.

The white-sand Cow Bay Beach, at the end of Buchanan Creek Rd, rivals any coastal paradise.

The award-winning **Daintree Discovery Centre** (⌨07-4098 9171; www.discover-thedaintree.com; Tulip Oak Rd; adult/child/family $32/16/78; ⊙8.30am-5pm) features an aerial walkway leading you high into the forest canopy. A theatre screens films on cassowaries, crocodiles, conservation and climate change.

Get closer to nature on a boat trip with **Cape Tribulation Wilderness Cruises** (⌨0457 731 000; www.capetribcruises.com; Cape Tribulation Rd; adult/child from $30/22) or a walking tour with **Cooper Creek Wilderness** (⌨07-4098 9126; www.coopercreek.com.au; 2333 Cape Tribulation Rd; guided walks $60-170).

🛏 Sleeping & Eating

⭐**Epiphyte B&B**　　　　　　　B&B $
(⌨07-4098 9039; www.rainforestbb.com; 22 Silkwood Rd; s/d/cabins from $80/110/150) This lovingly built, laid-back place is set on a lush 3.5-hectare property. Individually styled rooms are of varying sizes, but all have their own verandah. A spacious, private cabin features a patio, kitchenette and sunken bathroom. Minimum two-night stay.

Lync-Haven
Rainforest Retreat　　　　　CAMPGROUND $
(⌨07-4098 9155; www.lynchaven.com.au; Lot 44, Cape Tribulation Rd; camp sites per person $14, powered sites $32, d from $150; ✳) This family-friendly retreat is set on a 16-hectare property on the main road, about 5km north of Cow Bay, and has walking trails, hand-reared kangaroos, well-grassed sites and comfy en-suite rainforest cabins. The restaurant serves robust steaks, good pasta and fish.

⭐**Heritage Lodge & Spa**　　　　LODGE $$$
(⌨07-4098 9321; www.heritagelodge.net.au; Lot 236/R96 Turpentine Rd, Diwan; cabins $330; ✳🛜🏊) The friendly, accommodating owners of this wonderful retreat will do their best to make sure you feel at home. Their cute but comfortable renovated cabins are well spaced and ensconced in rainforest. A highlight is swimming in the crystal-clear waters of their gorgeous croc-free Cooper Creek swimming hole. On-site **dining** (mains $26-37; ⊙12-2pm & 5.30-9pm) and day spa are superb.

Daintree Ice Cream Company　ICE CREAM $
(⌨07-4098 9114; www.daintreeicecream.com. au; Lot 100, Cape Tribulation Rd; ice creams $6.50; ⊙11am-5pm) We dare you to drive past this all-natural ice-cream producer with a palette of flavours that changes daily. You might get macadamia, black sapote and wattleseed – they're all delicious.

Cow Bay Hotel　　　　　　PUB FOOD $$
(⌨07-4098 9011; 1480 Cape Tribulation Rd; mains $18-24; ⊙noon-2pm & 6-8pm, bar 10am-10pm) If you're craving a decent counter meal, a coldie and that Aussie country pub atmosphere, the Cow Bay is the only real pub this side of the Daintree River.

Cape Tribulation
POP 330

Cape Trib is at the end of the winding sealed road from the Daintree River and, with its two magnificent beaches, laid-back vibe, rainforest walks and compact village, it's a little slice of paradise.

WORTH A TRIP

LIZARD ISLAND

The five islands of the Lizard Island Group are located 33km off the coast about 100km north of Cooktown. Lizard, the main island of the group, has rocky, mountainous terrain, glistening white beaches and spectacular fringing reefs for snorkelling and diving. Most of the island is national park and teeming with wildlife. Sumptuous accommodation and dining epitomise five-star luxury at the ultra-exclusive **Lizard Island Resort** (☑1300 863 248; www.lizardisland.com.au; Anchor Bay; d $1900-2900; ❄@☎☒), decimated by Cyclone Ita in April 2014 and exquisitely rebuilt and refurbished in 2015. There's limited bush camping at the island's **camp site** (☑13 74 68; www.npsr.qld.gov.au/parks/lizard-island/camping.html; Watsons Bay; per adult/family $6.15/24.60) ✐. There are no shops on the island. Book air transfers to/from Cairns through the resort.

Daintree Air Services (☑07-4034 9300; www.daintreeair.com.au; day tours from $740) offers spectacular full-day tours from Cairns including gourmet lunch, snorkelling gear, transfers and a local guide to take you to some of the most magnificent spots in this pristine ecosystem.

Despite the backpacker bars and tour operators (jungle surfing, anyone?), Cape Trib still retains a frontier quality, with road signs alerting drivers to cassowary crossings, and croc warnings making evening beach strolls a little less relaxing. The fact that there's no reliable mobile-phone reception or network internet adds to the remoteness – and freaks a few travellers out!

The rainforest skirts beautiful Myall and Cape Tribulation beaches, which are separated by a knobby cape. The village here marks the end of the sealed road: beyond, the strictly 4WD-only Bloomfield Track continues north to Wujal Wujal.

◉ Sights & Activities

Good access points for Cape Trib and Myall beaches are the signposted Kulki and Dubuji boardwalks, respectively.

Bat House   WILDLIFE RESERVE
(☑07-4098 0063; www.austrop.org.au; Cape Tribulation Rd; $5; ☺10.30am-3.30pm Tue-Sun) A nursery for injured or orphaned fruit bats (flying foxes), run by conservation organisation Austrop.

Mt Sorrow Ridge Walk   WALKING
Mt Sorrow is a demanding day hike for fit walkers. The ridge-walk trail starts about 150m north of the Kulki picnic area car park, just off the Bloomfield Rd. The strenuous walk (7km, five to six hours return, start no later than 10am), offers spectacular views over the rainforest and reef.

☞ Tours

Most tours offer free pick-ups from local accommodation.

★ Ocean Safari   TOURS
(☑07-4098 0006; www.oceansafari.com.au; Cape Tribulation Rd; adult/child/family $139/89/415; ☺8am & noon) Ocean Safari leads small groups (25 people maximum) on morning and afternoon snorkelling cruises to the Great Barrier Reef, just half an hour offshore. Wetsuit hire ($8) available.

Paddle Trek Kayak Tours   KAYAKING
(☑07-4098 1950; www.capetribpaddletrek.com.au; Lot 7, Rykers Rd; half-day guided trips $75-85) Guided sea-kayaking trips (morning/afternoon 2½/3½ hours) depart from Cape Trib Beach House (p265).

Mason's Tours   WALKING, DRIVING
(☑07-4098 0070; www.masonstours.com.au; Mason's Store, Cape Tribulation Rd) Long-timer Lawrence Mason conducts enlightening rainforest walks (groups of up to five people two hours/half day $300/500), including a night walk; 4WD tours up the Bloomfield Track to Cooktown are also available (groups up to five people half/full day $800/1250).

Jungle Surfing Canopy Tours   OUTDOORS
(☑07-4098 0043; www.junglesurfing.com.au; ziplines $95, night walks $45, combo $130; ☺7.45am-3.30pm, night walks 7.30pm) Get right up into the rainforest on an exhilarating two-hour flying-fox (zipline) surf

Cape Tribulation Area

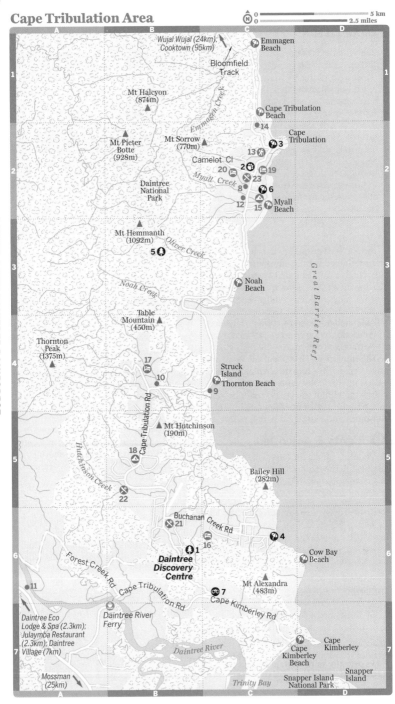

N
0 ———————————————— 5 km
0 ———————————————— 2.5 miles

CAIRNS & THE DAINTREE RAINFOREST

Emmagen Beach

Wujal Wujal (24km);
Cooktown (95km)

Bloomfield Track

Mt Halcyon (874m)

Emmagen Creek

Cape Tribulation Beach

14

Cape Tribulation

Mt Pieter Botte (928m)

Mt Sorrow (770m)

13

Camelot Cl

3

Myall Creek

20
2
23
19

8
6

Daintree National Park

12
15

Myall Beach

Mt Hemmanth (1092m)

Oliver Creek

5

Noah Creek

Noah Beach

Great Barrier Reef

Table Mountain (450m)

Thornton Peak (1375m)

17

10

Struck Island

Thornton Beach

9

Cape Tribulation Rd

Mt Hutchinson (190m)

18

Hutchinson Creek

Bailey Hill (282m)

22

Buchanan Creek Rd

21

16

4

Cow Bay Beach

1

Daintree Discovery Centre

7

Mt Alexandra (483m)

Forest Creek Rd

Cape Tribulation Rd

Cape Kimberley Rd

11

Daintree River Ferry

Daintree Eco Lodge & Spa (2.3km);
Julaymba Restaurant (2.3km); Daintree Village (7km)

Daintree River

Cape Kimberley

Cape Kimberley Beach

Mossman (25km)

Trinity Bay

Snapper Island National Park

Snapper Island

Cape Tribulation Area

through the canopy. Guided night walks follow biologist-guides who shed light on the dark jungle. Rates include pick-up from Cape Trib accommodation (self-drive not permitted).

D'Arcy of the Daintree DRIVING
(📞0402 849 249; www.darcyofdaintree.com. au; 116 Palm Rd, Diwan; tours adult/child from $146/108) Local Mike D'Arcy offers entertaining small-group 4WD trips up the Bloomfield Track to Wujal Wujal Falls (half day) and as far as Cooktown (full day).

Cape Trib Horse Rides HORSE RIDING
(📞07-4098 0043; www.capetribhorserides.com. au; rides per person from $99; ⏰8am & 2.30pm) Leisurely morning and afternoon rides along the beach and into the forest.

🛏 Sleeping & Eating

Restaurants at Cape Trib's resorts are all open to nonguests. There's a **supermarket** (📞07-4098 0015; Cape Tribulation Rd; ⏰8am-6pm) stocking basic supplies for self-caterers.

★**Cape Trib Beach House** HOSTEL, RESORT $
(📞07-4098 0030; www.capetribbeach.com. au; 152 Rykers Rd; dm $29, cabins $150-180; ❄@🛜🏊) The Beach House is everything that's great about Cape Trib – a secluded patch of rainforest facing a pristine beach and a friendly vibe that welcomes backpackers, couples and families. Clean dorms and romantic almost-beachfront cabins make the most of the location. The open-deck licensed **restaurant** (mains $18-30) and bar is so good many locals eat and drink here. HI affiliated.

Cape Tribulation Camping CAMPGROUND $
(📞07-4098 0077; www.capetribcamping.com.au; Lot 11, Cape Tribulation Rd; adult/child powered sites $20/10, unpowered sites $15/10) Myall Beach is just steps away from this lovely laid-back camping ground. Grassy sites are reasonably well spaced, facilities are good (unless you want a pool) and the Sand Bar is a sociable verandah restaurant serving Cape Trib's best wood-fired pizzas.

PK's Jungle Village HOSTEL $
(📞07-4098 0040; www.pksjunglevillage.com; Cape Tribulation Rd; unpowered sites per person $15, dm $25-32, cabin d $70-125; ❄@🛜🏊) With the giant **Jungle Bar** (mains $11-25; ⏰7.30am-10pm) restaurant-pool area, a boardwalk to Myall Beach and a range of budget accommodation, PK's has long been a favourite with backpackers. Camp sites and dorms are a little cramped but the place is well-maintained and sociable.

Rainforest Hideaway B&B $
(📞07-4098 0108; www.rainforesthideaway.com; 19 Camelot Close; d $135-149) 🏳 This colourful B&B, consisting of one room in the main house and a separate cabin, was single-handedly built by its owner, artist and sculptor 'Dutch Rob' – even the furniture and beds are handmade. A sculpture trail winds through the property.

★**Whet** AUSTRALIAN **$$**
(✆07-4098 0007; www.whet.net.au; 1 Cape Tribulation Rd; mains $16.50-33; ⊙11am-4pm & 6-8.30pm) Whet is regarded as Cape Trib's most sophisticated place to eat, with a loungy cocktail-bar feel and romantic, candlelit, alfresco dining. Tempura wild barramundi and house chicken-curry grace the menu; all lunch dishes are under $20. You'll often find locals at the bar.

★**Mason's Store & Cafe** CAFE **$$**
(✆07-4098 0016; 3781 Cape Tribulation Rd; mains $9-18, tasting plates from $29; ⊙10am-4pm) Everyone calls into Mason's for tourist info, the liquor store, or to dine out on exotic meats. Pride of place on the menu at this laid-back alfresco cafe goes to the croc burger, but you can also try camel, emu and kangaroo in burgers or tasting plates. A short walk away is a crystal-clear, croc-free swimming hole ($1).

ℹ **Information**

Mason's Store (✆07-4098 0070; Cape Tribulation Rd; ⊙8am-6pm) The best place for regional info including Bloomfield Track conditions.

Understand Queensland

Queensland Today

The vast state of Queensland has always been a land of boom, bust and opportunity. There's been a bit more 'bust' here of late, with mass climate-change damage to the Great Barrier Reef, political upheaval, Australia's mining boom grinding to a halt and real-estate prices reaching insane levels. But the sun still shines on Queensland: Brisbane can rightly claim its mantle as 'Australia's New World City', and the 2018 Gold Coast Commonwealth Games are shaping up to be a huge event.

Best on Film

The Proposition (2005) – Directed by John Hillcoat and written by Nick Cave (!), this gritty Western was filmed around Winton.

Muriel's Wedding (director PJ Hogan; 1994) Comedic misadventures of awkward dreamer Muriel (Toni Collette).

Australia (director Baz Luhrmann; 2008) Sweeping epic filmed around Bowen on the Whitsunday Coast.

Dead Calm (director Phillip Noyce; 1989) Nicole Kidman gets nervous on a yacht in the Great Barrier Reef.

The Coolangatta Gold (director Igor Auzins; 1984) Critically derided '80s Gold Coast surf-life-saving saga.

Best in Print

Carpentaria (Alexis Wright; 2006) Indigenous writer Alexis Wright's tale of the fictional town of Desperence.

Johnno (David Malouf; 1975) Coming-of-age tale set in 1940s Brisbane.

He Died with a Felafel in his Hand (John Birmingham; 1994) Grungy share-house life in Brisbane.

Mango Country (John van Tiggelen; 2003) Gonzo, guffaw-inducing take on the far-out folks of Far North Queensland.

The White Earth (Andrew McGahan; 2005) A not-so-darling family epic set in the Darling Downs.

The Reef in Strife?

Climate change is a hot topic in Queensland (no pun intended) – particularly when it comes to the state's biggest attraction, the Great Barrier Reef. In 2016, unusually elevated sea temperatures caused a disastrous 'bleaching' event, where sensitive corals perished en masse. Similar events happened in 1998 and 2002, but never to this extent: an estimated 22% of the reef died, including 26% of corals in the reef's northern reaches and 67% in the far north. Mercifully, a cyclonic weather system cooled the ocean before further damage was done, and the reef's central and southern sections were largely unaffected.

If climate change continues at present rates and such bleaching events become more regular – especially in conjunction with wave damage from more-frequent cyclones, the scourge of the coral-eating crown of thorns starfish, and environmentally menacing port-expansion and dredging activities along the Queensland coast – some estimates place the reef's near-total devastation within the next 50 years. This destruction is unthinkable on many fronts – not least of which are the catastrophic economic consequences: the reef generates an estimated $4 billion in annual tourism revenue for Australia.

The Sporting Life

Queenslanders love sport: watching it, talking about it and playing it. On the 'watching' front, in the annual best-of-three State of Origin rugby league clash between the Queensland 'Maroons' and New South Wales 'Blues', normality has been restored, with Queensland winning in 2015 and 2016. Other than a momentary lapse in 2014, when NSW were victorious, Queensland has won the series every time since 2006.

In the 2016 Rio de Janeiro Olympics, a slew of Queenslanders won medals, including gold-medal winners Evania Pelite, Shannon Parry, Emilee Cherry and Charlotte Caslick in the Rugby 7s (...and Gemma Etheridge, an adopted Queenslander from NSW). In the swimming pool, Brisbanites Brittany Elmslie and sisters Cate and Bronte Campbell won gold in the 4x100m women's freestyle race, knocking off their American arch-rivals.

Meanwhile, the Brisbane Lions women's team, competing in the Australian Football League's new women's competition (www.afl.com.au/womens), has made a bright start, winning its first few games. Down on the Gold Coast, preparations are in full swing for the April 2018 Commonwealth Games. With 6600 athletes and officials representing 70 countries, this will be the largest sporting event held in Australia since the 2000 Sydney Olympics. See www.gc2018.com for updates.

Political Upheaval

After 20-plus years of left-wing Labor government, Queenslanders elected Campbell Newman's conservative Liberal National Coalition to office in a landslide 2012 election victory. Newman brought swagger and confidence to the position, befitting a state on the rise, but he immediately caused ructions. Sinking rapidly in the polls, he signed off on a 42% pay rise for members of parliament, decided not to introduce daylight-savings time in Queensland, and wound-back laws protecting the Wild Rivers area in Far North Queensland.

By the time the 2015 election rolled around, Newman had become grossly unpopular. His conservatives fell to Labor in a close result, with Newman losing his own seat in the process. Annastacia Palaszczuk was sworn in as the new premier, just the second woman to hold the top job in Queensland. Meanwhile, renegade north Queensland federal MP Bob Katter has been ruminating about north Queensland seceding to become Australia's seventh state – interesting times!

Unreal Real State

When the global financial crisis bit hard in 2008, economists and bankers across the Western world very sensibly said, 'Whoops! We've been lending people money they can't afford to pay back, and they've been blowing it on home loans that are too expensive' – and real-estate prices tumbled. But not in Australia. There was a mining boom in full swing: nobody worried about ridiculous housing prices when there was always another chunk of Queensland or Western Australia waiting to be exhumed and sold to China. Australians just kept on buying pricey houses, driving the market skywards.

Now – with the mining boom over and society reaching a tipping point where the median house price is more than five times the median annual household income – Australian real-estate prices are among the least affordable on the planet. Buying a house in Brisbane is now all but unattainable for young first-home buyers.

Fears of a property 'bubble' about to burst are rife, but as long as interest rates remain low and the perception that Australia is the 'lucky country' and somehow immune to global strife endures, Queensland's real-estate addiction will be hard to break.

POPULATION: **4.84 MILLION**

AREA: **1,730,620 SQ KM**

GDP: **AUD$314 BILLION**

INFLATION: **1.5%**

if Queensland were 100 people

48 would live in Brisbane
13 would live on the Gold Coast
6 would live on the Sunshine Coast
4 would live in Townsville
3 would live in Cairns
26 would live in other places

belief systems
(% of population)

66 — Christian
19 — no religion
12 — other
1 — Buddhist
1 — Hindu
1 — Muslim

population per sq km

QUEENSLAND   AUSTRALIA   USA

ⓘ ≈ 3 people

History

Human settlement in Queensland dates back 60,000 years, with Aboriginal inhabitants thriving in these fertile tropics for millennia prior to Captain James Cook's arrival in 1770. Since then, the state has been shaped by pastoral expansion, gold rushes, workers strikes, wars, depression, mining booms, a rise in nationalism and, most recently, a growing global outlook and landmark legal recognition of Australia's first peoples.

First Australians

Before Europeans arrived, Queensland contained more than 200 of Australia's 600 to 700 Aboriginal nations. Among them, they spoke at least 90 Indigenous languages and dialects.

Human contact with Australia is thought by many to have begun around 60,000 years ago, when Aboriginal people journeyed across the straits from what is now Indonesia and Papua New Guinea. Aboriginal people, however, believe they have always inhabited the land. Undoubtedly, Indigenous life in Australia marked the beginning of the world's longest continuous cultural history.

Across the continent, Aboriginal peoples traded goods, items of spiritual significance, songs and dances, using routes that followed the paths of ancestors from the Dreaming, the complex system of country, culture and beliefs that defines Indigenous spirituality. An intimate understanding of plant ecology and animal behaviour ensured that food shortages were rare. Even central Australia's hostile deserts were occupied year-round, thanks to scattered permanent wells. Fire-stick farming was practised in forested areas, involving the burning of undergrowth and dead grass to encourage new growth, to attract game and reduce the threat of bushfires.

At the time of European contact the Aboriginal population was grouped into 300 or more different nations, with distinct languages and land boundaries. Most Aboriginal people did not have permanent shelters but moved within their territory and followed seasonal patterns of animal migration and plant availability. The diversity of landscapes in Australia meant that each nation varied in their lifestyles; although they were distinct cultural groups, there were also many common elements, and each nation had several clans or family groups who were responsible for looking after specific areas. For thousands of years Aboriginal people lived within a complex kinship system that tied them to the natural environment. From the desert

TIMELINE

60,000 BC	**6000 BC**	**3000 BC**
Although the exact start of human habitation in Australia is still uncertain, according to most experts this is when Aboriginal people settled on the continent.	Rising water levels due to global warming force many Indigenous groups off their fertile flatland homes along the coast. Vast sections of land disappear into the sea.	The last known large migration to the continent from Asia occurs (at least until about 1970). Humans introduce the dingo which, along with hunting, drives some native species to extinction.

to the sea Aboriginal people shaped their lives according to their environments and developed skills and a wide body of knowledge on their territory.

Intruders Arrive

In April 1770, Aboriginal people standing on a beach in southeastern Australia saw an astonishing spectacle out at sea. It was an English ship, the *Endeavour*, under the command of then-Lieutenant James Cook. His gentleman passengers were English scientists visiting the Pacific to make astronomical observations and to investigate 'new worlds'. As they sailed north along the edge of this new-found land, Cook began drawing the first British chart of Australia's east coast. This map heralded the beginning of conflicts between European settlers and Indigenous peoples.

A few days after that first sighting, Cook led a party of men ashore at a place known to the Aboriginal people as Kurnell. Though the Kurnell Aboriginal people were far from welcoming, the *Endeavour's* botanists were delighted to discover that the woods were teeming with unfamiliar plants. To celebrate the edge of this new-found land, Cook renamed the place Botany Bay.

As his voyage northwards continued, Cook strewed English names the entire length of the coastline. In Queensland, these included Hervey Bay (after an English admiral), Dunk Island (after an English duke), Cape Upstart, the Glass House Mountains and Wide Bay.

One night, in the seas off the great rainforests of the Kuku Yalanji Aboriginal people, in what is now known as Far North Queensland, the *Endeavour* was inching gingerly through the Great Barrier Reef when

Robert Hughes' bestseller *The Fatal Shore* (1987) is a highly readable, if sometimes harrowing, portrait of Australian history, told through the experiences of convicts, free settlers and the Indigenous peoples they displaced.

STORYTELLING IN ABORIGINAL CULTURE

Indigenous Australians historically had an oral culture, so storytelling was an important way to learn. Stories gave meaning to life and were used to teach the messages of the spirit ancestors. Although beliefs and cultural practices vary according to region and language groups, there is a common world-view that these ancestors created the land, the sea and all living things. This is often referred to as the Dreaming.

Through stories, knowledge and beliefs are passed on from one generation to another, setting out the community's social mores and recording events from the past. Today artists have continued this tradition with new media such as film and literature. In 1927, David Unaipon, a Ngarrindjeri man from South Australia became the first published Indigenous Australian with *Aboriginal Legends* – you can see Unaipon's portrait on the $50 note.

Other early published writers include Queensland poet Oodgeroo Noonuccal, and authors Kevin Gilbert and Jack Davis. Contemporary writers of note include Alexis Wright, Kim Scott, Anita Heiss and Ali Cobby Eckerman. Award-winning novels to read are Kim Scott's *Deadman Dancing* (2010) and *Benang* (1999); Alexis Wright's *Carpentaria* (2006); and Ali Cobby Eckerman's *Little Bit Long Time* (2009) and *Ruby Moonlight* (2012).

AD 1607	1770	1823	1840
Spanish explorer Luis Torres manages to sail between Australia and New Guinea and not notice the rather large continent to the south. The strait bears his name today.	English Captain James Cook maps Australia's east coast in the scientific ship *Endeavour*. He runs aground near the Great Barrier Reef near a place he names Cape Tribulation.	Government explorer John Oxley surveys Redcliffe for a convict settlement. It is established the following year and becomes known as a place of blood, sweat and tears.	Squatters from New South Wales establish sheep runs on the Darling Downs; it proves to be some of the most fertile agricultural land in the country.

A classic biography is *The Life of Captain James Cook* (1974), by JC Beaglehole. Another fascinating read is Tony Horwitz's *Blue Latitudes: Boldly Going Where Captain Cook Has Gone Before* (2002), equal parts travelogue and biography.

Raymond Evans' award-winning *A History of Queensland* (2007) is a good single-volume work covering the major events and power shifts in Queensland, from precontact Aboriginal times up to the present.

the crew heard the sickening sound of ripping timbers. They had run aground near a cape which today is a tourist paradise. Cook was in a glowering mood: he named it Cape Tribulation, 'because here began all our troubles'. Seven days later Cook managed to beach the wounded ship in an Aboriginal harbour named Charco (Cook renamed it Endeavour), where his carpenters patched the hull.

Back at sea, the *Endeavour* finally reached the northern tip of the Cape York Peninsula. On a small, hilly island (Possession Island), Cook raised the Union Jack and claimed the eastern half of the continent for King George III. His intention was not to dispossess the Indigenous peoples, but to warn off other European powers – notably the Dutch, who had already charted much of the coastline.

The Beginnings of Colonisation

In 1788 the English were back. On 26 January, 11 ships sailed into a harbour just north of Botany Bay. The First Fleet was packed with supplies, including weapons, tools, building materials and livestock, as well as 751 convicts and around 250 soldiers, officials and their wives, all under the command of a humane and diligent officer named Arthur Phillip. Under Phillip's leadership, the settlers cut down trees, built shelters and laid out roadways. They were building a prison settlement in the lands of the Eora people. Phillip called the place Sydney.

In the early years of the settlement, both the convicts and the free people of Sydney struggled to survive. Their early attempts to grow crops failed and the settlement relied on supplies brought by ship. Fortunate or canny prisoners were soon issued with 'tickets of leave', which gave them the right to live and work as free men and women on the condition that they did not attempt to return home before their sentences expired.

The convict system could also be savage. Women (who were outnumbered five to one) lived under constant threat of sexual exploitation. Female convicts who offended their jailers languished in the depressing 'female factories' (women's prisons). Male offenders were cruelly flogged and could be hanged even for such crimes as stealing. In 1803, English officers established a settlement to punish reoffenders at Port Arthur, on the wild southeast coast of Tasmania.

The impact of these settlements on the Aboriginal people was devastating. The effects of colonisation started immediately after the Europeans arrived. It began with the appropriation of land and water resources and an epidemic of diseases – smallpox killed around half of the Indigenous people who were native to Sydney Harbour. A period of resistance occurred as Aboriginal people fought back to retain their land and way of life; as violence and massacres swept the country, many were pushed away from their traditional lands.

1844–45	1846	1859	1860s
The first guidebook to Australia is written in the form of a journal by Ludwig Leichhardt. It chronicles his party's expedition from Brisbane almost to Darwin. In 1848 he vanishes without a trace.	Sole survivor of a shipwreck off Queensland, Jemmy Morrill is rescued by Aboriginal people. He lives with them for 17 years, and later plays a key role in improving European–Aboriginal relations.	Queen Victoria gives approval to establish the new colony of Queensland, which formally separates from NSW and is named in her honour (rather than 'Cooksland', another proffered option).	Queensland becomes a pioneer in the nation's education system when the government subsidises municipalities to set up grammar schools – the first free education in Australia.

Convicts to Queensland

By the 1820s, Sydney was a busy port, teeming with soldiers, merchants, children, schoolmistresses, criminals, preachers and drunks. The farms prospered, and in the streets children were chatting in a new accent that we would probably recognise today as 'Australian'.

The authorities now looked north to the lands of the Yuggera people, where they established another lonely penal colony at Redcliffe. Here, men laboured under the command of the merciless Captain Patrick Logan, building their own prison cells and sweating on the farms they had cleared from the bush. These prisoners suffered such tortures that some welcomed death, even by hanging, as a blessed release.

Logan himself met a brutal end when he was bashed and speared while riding in the bush. Soon after, a group of soldiers reported that they had seen him on the far bank of a river, screaming to be rescued. But as they rowed across to investigate, his tormented ghost melted into the heat...

Logan's miserable prison spawned the town of Brisbane, which soon became the administrative and supply centre for the farmers, graziers, loggers and miners who occupied the region. But the great hinterland of Queensland remained remote and mysterious – in the firm control of its Aboriginal owners.

Vestiges from a Convict Past

St Helena Island, Moreton Bay

Commissariat Store Museum, Brisbane

Old Windmill & Observatory, Brisbane

The Barracks (former Petrie Terrace Gaol), Brisbane

Heritage Centre, Maryborough

Explorers & Settlers

The hinterland frontier was crossed in 1844, when an eccentric Prussian explorer named Ludwig Leichhardt led a gruelling 15-month trek from Brisbane to Port Essington (near today's Darwin). His journal – the first European travel guide to Australia's Top End – would have secured his place in Australian history, but today he is remembered more for the manner of his death. In 1848 his entire party vanished in the desert during an attempt to cross the continent. Journalists and poets wrote as if Leichhardt had been received into a silent mystery that lay at the heart of Australia. It might seem strange that Australians should sanctify a failed explorer, but Leichhardt – like two other dead explorers, Burke and Wills – satisfied a Victorian belief that a nation did not come of age until it was baptised in blood.

As Queensland formally separated from NSW in 1859, graziers, miners and small farmers were pushing further west and north. Some European settlers established cooperative relations with local tribes, sharing the land and employing Aboriginal people as stockmen or domestics. Others saw settlement as a tough Darwinian struggle between the British race and a primitive Stone Age people – a battle the Europeans were destined to win. Indeed, settlers who ran sheep on the vast grasslands of the Darling Downs sometimes spoke as if they had taken possession of a great park where no other humans had ever lived. Today, Aboriginal people across the country

The Commissariat Store Museum in Brisbane was built in 1829 by convicts; the original section of the building is the second-oldest structure in Queensland (the oldest being the 1828 stone windmill in Brisbane's Wickham Park).

1870s	1872	1884	1891
Thousands of Chinese people arrive to work in the goldfields. In 1877 the government imposes restrictions on Chinese immigration and access to the goldfields.	The gold rush sweeps into Charters Towers, funding the construction of magnificent homes and public buildings. Queensland is connected to Europe by telegraph.	In a tragic last stand, the defiant Kalkadoon Indigenous nation is defeated in a massacre at Battle Mountain, near Mt Isa.	A violent shearers' strike around Barcaldine, where 1000 men camp around the town, establishes a labour legend. The confrontation leads to the birth of the Australian Labor Party.

A LAST STAND

The Kalkadoon (also known as Kalkatungu) people of the Mt Isa region in western Queensland were known for their fierce resistance to colonial expansion. As pastoralism and mining concerns pushed into their country in the 1860s, some of the Kalkadoon initially worked for the settlers as labourers and guides. However, competition for land and resources eventually led to conflict, and the Kalkadoon waged guerrilla-style warfare against settlers and their stock. They soon gained a reputation as ferocious warriors who seemingly melted away into the bush. In 1883 they killed five Native Police and a prominent pastoralist – an incident that turned the tide of the conflict against them.

In September 1884, some 600 Kalkadoon retreated to a defensive site known as Battle Mountain, where they fought one last battle against the Native Police and armed settlers. Despite heroic resistance, which included a charge against cavalry positions, the Kalkadoon warriors were mercilessly slain, their spears and clubs no match for guns. In all, an estimated 900 Kalkadoon were killed between 1878 and 1884.

tell stories of how European settlers shot whole groups of their people or killed them with poisoned food. Some Aboriginal tribes fought back, but the weapons of the white people were formidable – including the notorious Native Police, a government-backed squad made up of Aboriginal people recruited from distant tribes who violently suppressed any uprisings.

Meanwhile, on the tropical coast, growers were developing a prosperous sugar-cane industry that relied on the sweat of thousands of labourers from the Solomon Islands, Vanuatu and other Pacific islands. Known as 'kanakas', these workers endured harsh and sometimes cruel conditions that were considered intolerable for white workers.

By the late 1800s most of the fertile land had been taken by the European arrivals and most Indigenous Australians were living in poverty on the fringes of settlements or on land unsuitable for settlement. Aboriginal people had to adapt to the new culture, but had few to no rights. Employment opportunities were scarce and most worked as labourers or domestic staff. Over a century, the Aboriginal population was decimated by 90%.

River of Gold (Hector Holthouse; 1994) is a high-spirited novel set in the wild days of Queensland's Palmer River gold rush.

Gold & Revolution

In 1871 an Aboriginal stockman named Jupiter spotted gold glinting in a waterhole near Charters Towers. His find triggered a gold rush that attracted thousands of prospectors, publicans, traders, prostitutes and quacks to the diggings. For a few exhilarating years, any determined miner, regardless of class, had a real chance of striking it rich. By the 1880s, Brisbane itself had grown prosperous on wool and gold but, by then, life on the

1901	1902	1908	1915
The new federal government removes kanakas from Queensland, in line with the White Australia policy. Mortality figures for these Pacific Islanders were almost five times those of whites.	The first trans-Pacific cable between Australia and Canada is completed, terminating on the Gold Coast. The cable also allows Australia to join the England cable link.	Queensland's first national park is established on the western slope of Tamborine Mountain. Today, the national park stretches on to the Tamborine plateau and into surrounding foothills.	In line with Australia's close ties to Britain, Australian and New Zealand troops (the Anzacs) join the Allied invasion of Turkey at Gallipoli.

goldfields was changing radically. The easy gold was gone. The free-for-all had given way to an industry in which the company boss called the shots.

As displaced prospectors searched for work, the overheated economy of eastern Australia collapsed, throwing thousands of labouring families into the miseries of unemployment and hunger. The depression of the 1890s exposed stark inequalities as barefoot children scavenged in the streets. But this was Australia, 'the working man's paradise' – the land where the principle of 'a fair day's pay for a fair day's work' was sacred. As employers tried to drive down wages, a tough Queensland working class began to assert itself. Seamen, factory workers, miners, loggers and shearers organised themselves into trade unions to take on Queensland's equally tough bosses and shareholders.

The result was a series of violent strikes. The most famous of these erupted in 1891 after angry shearers proclaimed their socialist credo under a great gum tree, known as the 'Tree of Knowledge', at Barcaldine in central Queensland. As the strike spread, troopers, right-wing vigilantes and union militants clashed in bitter class warfare. The great radical poet Henry Lawson expected revolution: *'We'll make the tyrants feel the sting/O' those that they would throttle/They needn't say the fault is ours/If blood should stain the wattle!'*

The striking shearers were defeated and their leaders jailed by a government determined to suppress the unrest. Despite this loss, trade unions remained a powerful force in Australia and the Barcaldine strike contributed to the formation of a potent new force in Australian politics: the Australian Labor Party.

The Australian Stockman's Hall of Fame and Outback Heritage Centre at Longreach shamelessly celebrates Queensland's bush legends – explorers, pastoralists, Aboriginal people and cattlemen. See www.outback heritage.com.au.

Nationalism

Whatever their politics, many Queenslanders still embody the gritty, independent outlook that was so potent in colonial thinking. At the end of the 19th century, Australian nationalist writers and artists idealised the people of 'the bush' and their code of 'mateship'. The most popular forum for this 'bush nationalism' was the *Bulletin* magazine, whose pages were filled with humour and sentiment about daily life, written by a swag of writers, most notably Henry Lawson and AB 'Banjo' Paterson.

While these writers were creating national legends, the politicians of Australia were forging a national constitution.

A Queensland classic, Tom Petrie's *Reminiscences of Early Queensland* (1904) is the story of a white bushman who lived with Indigenous people around Moreton Bay and the Bunya Mountains.

Federation & WWI

On 1 January 1901, Australia became a federation. When the bewhiskered members of the new national parliament met in Melbourne, their first aim was to protect the identity and values of a European Australia from an influx of Asians and Pacific Islanders. Their solution was the

1918	1923	1928	1929
The Great War ends. Out of a country of 4.9 million, 320,000 were sent to war in Europe and almost 20% were killed. Cracks appear in Australian–British relations.	Vegemite, a savoury, yeasty breakfast spread, is invented. Given it is a by-product of brewing that had previously gone to waste, it is a modern marketing triumph.	Reverend John Flynn starts the Royal Flying Doctor Service in Cloncurry – an invaluable service that now has networks around the country.	The Great Depression: thousands go hungry and one in three households experiences unemployment. Irene Longman becomes the first woman elected to Queensland's parliament.

ONCE A JOLLY SWAGMAN

Written in 1895 by AB 'Banjo' Paterson (1864–1941), *Waltzing Matilda* is widely regarded as Australia's unofficial national anthem. While not many can sing the entire official anthem, *Advance Australia Fair*, without a lyric sheet, just about every Aussie knows the words to the strange ditty about a jolly swagman who jumped into a billabong and drowned himself rather than be arrested for stealing a jumbuck (sheep). But what does it mean?

For the song's origins to be understood, it has to be seen in the political context of the 1890s, a period of political change in Queensland. Along with nationalistic calls for federation, economic crisis, mass unemployment and severe droughts dominated the decade. An ongoing battle between pastoralists and shearers led to a series of strikes that divided the state and led to the formation of the Australian Labor Party to represent workers' interests.

In 1895 Paterson visited his fiancée in Winton, and together they travelled to Dagworth Station south of Kynuna, where they met Christina Macpherson. During their stay they went on a picnic to the Combo Waterhole, a series of billabongs on the Diamantina River, where Paterson heard stories about the violent 1894 shearers' strike on Dagworth Station. During the strike rebel shearers burnt seven woolsheds to the ground, leading the police to declare martial law and place a reward of £1000 on the head of their leader, Samuel Hoffmeister. Rather than be captured, Hoffmeister killed himself near the Combo Waterhole.

Paterson later wrote the words to *Waltzing Matilda* to accompany a tune played by Macpherson. While there is no proof he was writing allegorically about Hoffmeister and the shearers' strikes, a number of prominent historians have supported the theory that the song was a political statement. Others maintain it's just an innocent, catchy tune about a hungry vagrant, but the song's undeniable anti-authoritarianism and the fact that it was adopted as an anthem by the rebel shearers weigh heavily in favour of the historians' argument.

infamous 'White Australia' policy. Its opposition to nonwhite immigrants would remain a core Australian value for the next 70 years.

Peter Weir's epic film *Gallipoli* (1981) shows the utter brutality and senselessness of WWI through the eyes of two young mates (played by Mark Lee and a young Mel Gibson).

For European settlers, this was to be a model society, nestled in the skirts of the British Empire. Just one year later, in 1902, white women won the right to vote in federal elections. In a series of radical innovations, the government introduced a broad social-welfare scheme and protected Australian wage levels with import tariffs. This mixture of capitalist dynamism and socialist compassion became known as the 'Australian Settlement'.

When war broke out in Europe in 1914, thousands of Australian men rallied to the Empire's call. They had their first taste of death on 25 April 1915, when the Anzacs (the Australian and New Zealand Army Corps) joined an Allied assault on the Gallipoli Peninsula in Turkey. Eight months later, the British commanders acknowledged that the tactic had failed. By then, 8141 young Australians were dead. Soon, Australians were fighting in the killing fields of Europe. When the war ended, 60,000 Australian men

1937	1941	1942	1950s–1960s
Thousands of cane toads are released into the wild in an effort to control pests damaging Queensland's sugar-cane fields. The action proves disastrous to Australian biodiversity.	The Japanese bomb Townsville – a strategic centre for defence, with a major base for US and Australian military forces.	The Battle of the Coral Sea is fought off northern Queensland between Japan and US–Australian forces. Although there is no clear winner, the USA loses the carrier USS *Lexington*.	The postwar boom is on as Queensland experiences strong growth in manufacturing and other industries. Affordable housing is the norm with rampant construction in the suburbs.

had died. Ever since, on 25 April, Australians have gathered at the country's many war memorials for the sad and solemn services of Anzac Day.

Turbulent '20s

Australia careered wildly into the 1920s, continuing to invest in immigration and growth. In Queensland, breathtakingly rich copper, lead, silver and zinc deposits were discovered at Mt Isa, setting in motion a prosperous new chapter in the history of Queensland mining.

This was also the decade in which intrepid aviators became international celebrities. For Queensland, a state that felt its isolation profoundly, the aeroplane was a revolutionary invention. The famous airline Qantas (Queensland and Northern Territory Aerial Services) was founded at Longreach, in the centre of the state, in 1920. Eight years later, veteran Queensland aviator Bert Hinkler flew solo from England to Darwin in just 16 days.

It was not just aeroplanes that linked Australia to the rest of the world. Economics, too, was a global force. In 1929 the Wall St crash and high foreign debt caused the Australian economy to collapse into the abyss of the Great Depression. Once again, unemployment brought shame and misery to one in three households, but for those who were wealthy or employed, the Depression made less of a dent in day-to-day life. In the midst of this hardship, sport diverted a nation in love with games and gambling.

WWII & Growth

As the economy began to recover, the whirl of daily life was hardly dampened when Australian servicemen and -women sailed off to Europe to fight in a new war in 1939. Though Japan was menacing, Australians took it for granted that the British navy would keep them safe. In December 1941, Japan bombed the US fleet at Pearl Harbor. Weeks later, the 'impregnable' British naval base in Singapore crumbled, and soon thousands of Australians and other Allied troops were enduring the savagery of Japan's prisoner-of-war camps.

As the Japanese swept through Southeast Asia and into Papua New Guinea, the British announced that they could not spare any resources to defend Australia. But the legendary US general Douglas MacArthur saw that Australia was the perfect base for US operations in the Pacific and established his headquarters in Brisbane. As the fighting intensified, thousands of US troops were garrisoned in bases the length of Queensland: Australians and Americans got to know each other as never before. In a series of savage battles on sea and land, Australian and US forces gradually turned back the Japanese advance. The days of the Australian–British alliance were numbered.

As the war ended, a new slogan rang through the land: 'Populate or Perish!' The Australian government embarked on an ambitious scheme

HISTORY TURBULENT '20S

Historic Places

Queensland Maritime Museum, Brisbane

Cobb & Co Museum, Toowoomba

Jondaryan Woolshed Complex, Darling Downs

Queensland Museum, Brisbane

Avian Cirrus, Bert Hinkler's tiny plane that made the first England-to-Australia solo flight, is on display at the Queensland Museum in Brisbane.

1962	1965	1968	1970s
Indigenous Australians gain the right to vote in federal elections – but they have to wait until 1967 to receive full citizenship.	Merle Thornton and Rosalie Bogner chain themselves to a Brisbane bar to protest public bars being open to men only. Their action marks the beginnings of the feminist movement in Australia.	Setting the political scene in Queensland for the next 19 years, Joh Bjelke-Petersen becomes premier. His political agenda was widely described as development at any price.	Inflation, soaring interest rates and rising unemployment bring the golden postwar days to an end. As house prices skyrocket, home ownership slips out of reach for many.

to attract thousands of immigrants. With government assistance, people flocked from Britain and non-English-speaking countries. They included Greeks, Italians, Slavs, Serbs, Croatians, Dutch and Poles, followed by Turks, Lebanese and others.

This was the era when Australian families basked in the prosperity of a 'long boom' created by skilful government management of the economy. Manufacturing companies such as General Motors and Ford operated with generous tariff support. The social-welfare system became more extensive and included generous unemployment benefits. The government owned many key services, including Qantas, which it bought in 1947. This was the high point of the 'Australian Settlement' – a partnership of government and private enterprise designed to share prosperity as widely as possible.

At the same time, there was growing world demand for the type of primary products produced in Queensland: metals, coal, wool, meat and wheat. By the 1960s, mining dominated the state's economy and coal was the major export. That same decade, the world's largest bauxite mine roared into life at Weipa on the Cape York Peninsula.

This era of postwar growth and prosperity was dominated by Robert Menzies, the founder of the modern Liberal Party of Australia, and Australia's longest-serving prime minister. Menzies had an avuncular charm, but he was also a vigilant opponent of communism. As the Cold War intensified, Australia and New Zealand entered a formal military alliance with the USA – the 1951 Anzus security pact. It followed that when the USA became involved in a civil war in Vietnam more than a decade later, Menzies committed Australian forces to the conflict. In 1966 Menzies retired, leaving his successors a bitter legacy: an antiwar movement that divided Australia.

A Question of Tolerance

In the 1960s, increasing numbers of Australians saw that Indigenous Australians had endured a great wrong that needed to be put right. From 1976 until 1992, Aboriginal people won major victories in their struggle for land rights. As Australia's imports from China and Japan increased, the White Australia policy became an embarrassment. It was officially abolished in the early 1970s, and soon thereafter Australia was a little astonished to find itself leading the campaign against the racist apartheid policies of white South Africa.

By the 1970s more than one million migrants had arrived from non-English-speaking countries, filling Australia with new languages, cultures, food and ideas. At the same time, China and Japan far outstripped Europe as Australia's major trading partners. As Asian immigration increased, Vietnamese communities became prominent in Sydney and Melbourne. In both those cities a new spirit of tolerance known as multiculturalism became a particular source of pride.

It's not widely known within Australia, but in 1942 there were three Japanese air raids on Townsville and one on Mossman. There were also nine raids on Horn Island in the Torres Strait between 1942 and 1944: 190 Australian and Allied personnel were killed in the Torres.

1974	1975	1980	1981
The audacious Beerburrum mail robbery is pulled off in southeast Queensland – the most lucrative mail robbery in Australian history at the time.	The Great Barrier Reef Marine Park is proclaimed, protecting 2000km of reef – the most extensive reef system in the world.	Queensland wins the first of the annual all-star 'State of Origin' rugby league series against southern rivals NSW. As of 2013, the ledger stands at 20 wins to Queensland, 12 to NSW, with two drawn series.	The Great Barrier Reef becomes a Unesco World Heritage Site, a move furiously opposed by Queensland Premier Joh Bjelke-Petersen, who intended to do exploratory mining for oil on the reef.

STOLEN GENERATIONS

In 1901, a government policy known as the 'White Australia policy' was put in place. It was implemented mainly to restrict non-white immigration to Australia, but the policy also had a huge impact on Indigenous Australians. Assimilation into the broader society was encouraged by all sectors of government, with the intent to eventually 'fade out' the Aboriginal race. A policy of forcibly removing Aboriginal and Torres Strait Islander children from their families was official from 1909 to 1969, although the practice happened both before and after those years. Although accurate numbers will never be known, it is estimated that around 100,000 Indigenous children – or one in three – were taken from their families.

A government agency, the Aborigines Protection Board, was set up to manage the policy, and had the power to remove children from families without consent or even a court order. Many children never saw their families again; those who did find their way home often found it difficult to maintain relationships. They became known as the Stolen Generations.

In the 1990s the Australian Human Rights Commission held an inquiry into the practice of removing Aboriginal children. Bringing Them Home, a nearly 700-page report that was tabled in parliament in May 1997, told of the devastating impact these policies had had on the children and their families. Government bureaus, church missions and welfare agencies all took part in the forced removal, and sexual and physical abuse and cruelty was found to be common in many of the institutions where children were placed. Today many of the Stolen Generations still suffer trauma associated with their early lives.

On 13 February 2008 Kevin Rudd, then prime minister of Australia, offered a national apology to the Stolen Generations. For many Indigenous people it was the start of a national healing process, and today there are many organisations working with the survivors of the Stolen Generations to bring healing and, in some cases, to seek compensation.

To learn more about the Stolen Generations and its impact upon countless Indigenous lives, the film Rabbit-Proof Fence (2002) and Archie Roach's classic song 'Took the Children Away' are good places to start.

The impact of postwar immigration was never as great in Queensland, and the values of multiculturalism made few inroads into the state's robustly old-time sense of what it means to be Australian. This Aussie insularity was well understood by the rough-hewn and irascible Joh Bjelke-Petersen, premier of Queensland for 19 years from 1968 to 1987. New Zealand–born Bjelke-Petersen was the longest-serving and longest-lived (1911–2005) premier of Queensland. He was described as a paradox of piety, free enterprise and political cunning or, more succinctly, as 'a Bible-bashing bastard' by Prime Minister Gough Whitlam in 1975.

Kept in office by malapportionment (which gave more voting power to his rural base – he never won more than 39% of the popular vote), he established a policy of development. Forests were felled to make way for dams, coal mines, power stations and other burgeoning infrastructure projects.

1982	1988	1990s	1992
Brisbane hosts the Commonwealth Games. Australia tops the medal tally, winning 107 medals overall. Matilda, a 13m-high winking kangaroo, was the mascot for the Games.	Over a six-month period between April and October, Brisbane hosts a World Fair called Expo '88. The theme is 'Leisure in the Age of Technology'.	Queensland experiences rapid population growth – mostly from domestic migration – even while a full-blown recession is under way, with high unemployment and huge bank and corporate collapses.	After 10 years in the courts, the landmark Mabo decision is delivered by the High Court. Effectively, this gives recognition to Indigenous land rights across the country.

Bjelke-Petersen's administration strongly encouraged the development of the Gold Coast. There were few environmental restrictions as hotels and high-rise apartment blocks transformed quiet seaside towns into burgeoning holiday resorts. Among many projects under his term was the building of a highway through the Daintree rainforest and the demolition of historic or heritage buildings to make way for new developments (Brisbane's Bellevue Hotel, dating from the 1880s, was demolished – in the middle of the night – despite public attempts to save it). His plans to drill for oil in the Great Barrier Reef came to nothing when the reef was declared a World Heritage Site in 1981. Meanwhile, Queensland spent less on social infrastructure than any other state in Australia.

David Malouf's novel *Johnno* (1975) is a beautifully written coming-of-age story set in post-war Brisbane.

In the 1970s, there were widespread reports of police brutality against student demonstrations at the University of Queensland, a well-known haven for anti–Bjelke-Petersen sentiment. In 1977, street marches were banned.

Things took a turn in the late 1980s, when a series of investigations revealed that Bjelke-Petersen presided over a compromised system. His police commissioner was jailed for graft (bribery), and in 1991 Bjelke-Petersen faced his own criminal trial (for perjury; allegations of corruption were also incorporated into the trial). Although the jury was deadlocked and didn't return a verdict, the tide had turned against him, and most Queenslanders were eager to put the Bjelke-Petersen days behind them.

TERRA NULLIUS TURNED ON ITS HEAD

In May 1982, Eddie Mabo led a group of Torres Strait Islanders in a court action to have traditional title to their land on Mer (Murray Island) recognised. Their argument challenged the legal principle of *terra nullius* (literally 'land belonging to no one') and demonstrated their unbroken relationship with the land over a period of thousands of years. In June 1992, the High Court of Australia found in favour of Eddie Mabo and the islanders, rejecting the principle of *terra nullius* – this became known as the Mabo decision. The result has had far-reaching implications in Queensland and the rest of Australia, including the introduction of the Native Title Act in 1993.

Eddie Mabo accumulated more than 20 years' experience as an Indigenous leader and human-rights activist. He had 10 children, was often unemployed, established a Black Community School – the first institution of its kind in Australia – and was involved in Indigenous health and housing. In the late 1960s, he worked as a gardener at James Cook University, returning there in 1981 for a conference on land rights, where he delivered a historic speech that culminated in the landmark court case.

Eddie Mabo died of cancer six months before the decision was announced. After a customary period of mourning, he was given a king's burial ceremony on Mer, reflecting his status among his people – the ritual had not been performed on the island for some 80 years.

1997	2001–03	2006	2007
Warning of being 'swamped by Asians', Queenslander Pauline Hanson founds the anti-immigration One Nation party. A 2003 fraud charge sees her lose popularity for over a decade, but she returns to parliament in 2016.	The Brisbane Lions win three Australian Football League championships in a row: dazzling success in a state dominated by rugby league.	The legendary 'Crocodile Hunter' Steve Irwin is killed by a stingray while shooting the wildlife documentary *Ocean's Deadliest*. His conservation work continues via the Steve Irwin Foundation.	Peter Beattie, the longest-serving Labor premier in Queensland history, retires. His deputy, Anna Bligh, becomes the state's first female premier. She is ousted by conservative Campbell Newman in 2012.

Recent Challenges

Since the 1970s, Australia has been dismantling the protectionist scaffolding that allowed its economy to develop. Wages and working conditions, which used to be fixed by an independent authority, are now much more uncertain. Two centuries of development have also placed great strains on the environment – on water supplies, forests, soil, air quality and the oceans. Australia is linked more closely than ever to the USA (exemplified by its involvement in the 21st century's Afghanistan and Iraq wars). Some say this alliance protects Australia's independence; others insist that it reduces Australia to a fawning 'client state'.

In Queensland, old fears and prejudices continue to struggle with tolerance and an acceptance of Asia, and Indigenous issues seem as intractable as ever. The history of forced resettlement, removal of children, and the loss of land and culture can never be erased: there is still great disparity between Indigenous Australians and the rest of the population, including lower standards of education, employment, health and living conditions; high incarceration and suicide rates; and a lower life expectancy. Current policies focus on 'closing the gap' and better delivery of essential services to improve lives. In the Cape York Peninsula, Aboriginal leaders, cattle ranchers, the government and mining companies displayed a new willingness to work with each other on land issues when they signed the Cape York Heads of Agreement in 2001. In late 2007, worrying reports of child sexual abuse in the Cape York Aboriginal communities highlighted the enormous social problems faced by Indigenous communities in Queensland and across the country. Aboriginal people continue to have very limited access to political or economic wealth, but communities across Queensland and the country have continued to make hard-won gains, keeping their struggle for legal and cultural rights at the forefront of politics.

In 2008 then-prime minister Kevin Rudd issued a formal apology to Indigenous Australians for the injustices they had suffered over the past two centuries. Though his government promised sweeping reforms in environment and education, it found itself faced with a crisis when the world economy crashed in 2008; by 2010 it had cost Rudd his position. Incoming prime minister Julia Gillard, along with other world leaders, now faced three related challenges: climate change, a diminishing oil supply and a shrinking economy. Queensland's economic and cultural dependence on both mining and tourism to the threatened Great Barrier Reef have been at the centre of this difficult landscape, as Gillard and subsequent Prime Ministers have faced shrinking popularity and ongoing agitations from their own parties. 2013 saw Gillard toppled and Rudd reinstated; not three months later Rudd lost government to Tony Abbott's conservative Liberal-National Coalition in the 2013 federal election. With his own poll numbers slipping, Abbott fell to his Liberal Party colleague Malcolm Turnbull in 2015.

For more on one of Queensland's most controversial politicians, read Lunn's *Joh: The Life and Political Adventures of Johannes Bjelke-Petersen* (1978) – written halfway through his tenure, but insightful nonetheless.

2008	2011	2011	2017
On behalf of parliament, Australian prime minister Kevin Rudd (a Queenslander) delivers a moving apology to Indigenous Australians for laws and policies that 'inflicted profound grief, suffering and loss'.	Powerful floods inundate vast areas of Queensland (including Brisbane), killing 35 people and causing billions of dollars in damages. Cyclone Yasi follows weeks later, devastating parts of north Queensland.	The Gold Coast wins its bid to host the 2018 Commonwealth Games, beating the Sri Lankan city of Hambantota for the privilege, 43 votes to 27.	Severe Tropical Cyclone Debbie makes landfall near Airlie Beach, causing significant damage in South East Queensland. Torrential rain, strong winds and ferocious seas kill at least twelve people in Australia.

Climate Change & the Great Barrier Reef

The Great Barrier Reef (GBR) is one of the world's most diverse coral-reef ecosystems. It is also the world's largest, an archipelagic edifice so vast that it can be viewed from space. But, like coral reefs all around the world, the GBR is facing some big environmental challenges.

The Reef

The reef's ecosystem includes the sea-floor habitats between the reefs, hundreds of continental islands and coral cays, and coastal beaches, headlands and estuaries. The 2900 reefs (ranging from less than 1km to 26km in length) that make up the GBR system support truly astounding biological diversity, with over 1500 species of fish, over 400 species of reef-building coral, and hundreds of species of molluscs (clams, snails, octopuses), echinoderms (sea stars, bêches-de-mer, sea urchins), sponges, worms, crustaceans and seaweed. The GBR is also home to marine mammals (dolphins, whales, dugongs), dozens of species of birds and six of the planet's seven species of sea turtles. The GBR's 900-or-so islands range from ephemeral, unvegetated or sparsely vegetated sand cays to densely forested cays and continental islands.

At the Crossroads

These are tough times in which to be a coral reef. In the last three decades the GBR has endured more severe cyclones than in the whole of the last century, recurrent outbreaks of coral-devouring crown-of-thorns starfish, three major coral-bleaching events caused by unusually hot water temperatures, and record-breaking floods that washed huge volumes of fresh water, sediments, fertilisers and other farm chemicals into

GREAT BARRIER REEF MARINE PARK

Established in 1975, the 360,000-sq-km Great Barrier Reef Marine Park (about the same size as Italy) is one of the best-protected large marine systems on the planet. About 30% of the park is closed and the remainder is open to commercial and recreational fishing. There are a handful of coastal cities along the reef's southern half (notably Cairns, Townsville, Mackay and Gladstone), some with ports to service cattle and sugar export, and mineral export and import. Shipping lanes traverse its length and breadth, and ore carriers, cargo ships and cruise liners must use local marine pilots to reduce the risk of groundings and collisions.

Australia is internationally recognised for its leading management and protection of the Great Barrier Reef – the marine park is inscribed on the World Heritage List and has an envied program of management led by the Great Barrier Reef Marine Park Authority. But still, there is an aura of pessimism across the reef-science world. For comprehensive information and educational tools at all levels, see www.gbrmpa.gov.au and www.coralwatch.org.

the sea, triggering blooms of light-blocking plankton and disrupting the ecological relationships that keep coral reefs vibrant and resilient.

With all this going on, it's no surprise that a bit of web surfing could give the impression that the GBR is suffering more than other reefs around the world. But the plethora of information about risks to the reef simply reflects the amount of research, government investment and national commitment to tackling the challenge rather than pretending that everything is OK. It is an unfortunate reality that damaged reefs are easier to find now than they were 30 years ago, but the GBR is still one of the best places in the world to see coral reefs, especially if you have one of the hundreds of accredited tourism operators show you around. Like every reef around the world, the GBR is in trouble, but in this case scientists, reef managers, coastal residents and even visitors are joining forces to help the reef through the challenges of the century ahead.

Eroding the Foundation

Overshadowing the future of coral reefs is climate change. Global warming is a serious problem for these iconic ecosystems, even though they have evolved in warm water and thrive in clear, shallow seas along the equator and as far north and south as the Tropics of Cancer and Capricorn.

The main building blocks of coral reefs are 'stony' or 'hard' corals, and about 400 of the world's 700-or-so species occur on the GBR. The secret of their success as reef builders – and their Achilles heel in a warming world – is symbiosis between the coral and tiny single-celled plants called zooxanthellae that live within their tissues. Thanks to bright sunlight and warm waters, the zooxanthellae are photosynthetic powerhouses that produce sugars and other carbohydrates needed by the coral (a colony of polyps) to grow its tissues, produce sperm and eggs and build the colony's communal limestone skeletons. These skeletons, occupied by thousands of polyps and capable of growing several metres high and across in many different shapes, are an evolutionary bonanza in that they provide a rigid framework to orient the polyps to best utilise the sunlight and to use their stinging tentacles to catch passing pinhead-sized crustaceans that corals need nutritionally. Over thousands of years, the corals produce the reef framework, lagoon sands, coral beaches and coral islands that are the foundation for the entire coral-reef ecosystem. But now, as temperatures approach levels not seen for thousands of years, these foundations are at risk.

Changing Environments & Coral Bleaching

The idyllic symbiosis between coral and zooxanthellae evolved to perfectly match the environmental conditions of the past. But corals don't like change, and they are currently being hit with rates of change unparalleled for at least 400,000 years.

Bright sunlight and warm waters are required to support coral reefs, but it's a fine line between warm enough and too warm. Around the turn of the last century (1998 and 2002) and again in 2016, spikes in water temperature around the GBR caused the densely packed zooxanthellae to go into metabolic overdrive, producing free radicals and other chemicals that are toxic to the coral host. The corals' response was to expel their zooxanthellae, to rid themselves of the damaging toxins. Water temperatures must return to normal before the small numbers of remaining zooxanthellae start to reproduce and thus reinstate the corals' live-in food factory. But if the heat wave persists for more than a few weeks, the highly stressed corals succumb to disease and die, their skeletons soon becoming carpeted with fine, shaggy algal turfs. This is known as coral bleaching. The 2016 bleaching event was unprecedented and catastrophic, with coral mortality

REEF GEOLOGY

Unlike mainland Australia, today's Great Barrier Reef (GBR) is relatively young, geologically speaking. Its foundations formed around 500,000 years ago, with northern Australia by then surrounded by tropical waters as Australia drifted gradually northward from the massive South Pole land mass that was Gondwana. The GBR grew and receded several times in response to changing sea levels. Coastal plains that are now the sea floor were occupied by Indigenous Australians only 20,000 years ago, when the ice-age sea level was 130m lower than it is today. As the icecaps contracted, seas flooded continental shelves and stabilised near their current levels about 6000 to 8000 years ago. Corals settled atop high parts of the Queensland shelf, initiating the unique combination of biological and geological processes that have built the reef ecosystem we see today.

rates estimated at 67% in the far northern section of the reef (offshore reefs north of Cape Melville) and 26% in the northern section (inshore reefs north of Port Douglas). Critically, central and southern reef areas south of Cairns remained largely unaffected, with just 6% and 1% coral deaths reported.

An important reality is that these bleaching events aren't occurring in isolation: storm waves and outbreaks of the coral-eating crown-of-thorns starfish are also big killers of corals. The effects are cumulative, and with projections of an increase in the severity of cyclones and the frequency of coral-bleaching events, we are likely to see more incidents of broad-acre coral death under a changing climate.

It takes one to two decades for a healthy coral reef to bounce back after being wiped out. So far, damaged GBR sites have shown remarkable resilience to damaging events, but the future might not be so rosy, as more frequent events driven by climate change repeatedly decimate reefs before they can fully recover. In other parts of the world, some reefs have suffered the added insults of decades of pollution and overfishing. By those means, former coral areas have become persistent landscapes of rubble and seaweed.

Worry Globally, Act Locally

Floating in the warming waters of the GBR, feeling the immensity of the reef and the issues presented by a changing climate, it's easy to feel that action is futile. But science is showing that local efforts can make a difference. Reducing the amount of nutrients (from fertilisers) that enter GBR waters may increase the tolerance of corals to warmer seas, decrease crown-of-thorns outbreaks and help corals maintain dominance over seaweeds. State and federal governments are therefore working with farmers to improve practices and reduce the losses of chemicals and valuable soil into the reef, and their efforts have already begun to deliver encouraging results.

Science also suggests that those fishing practices that maintain abundant herbivorous fish on the reefs may also be vital in keeping corals in the ascendancy. Fishing is carefully regulated, making the GBR a rare example of a coral-reef system that maintains a healthy coral-seaweed balance while still delivering sustainable seafood. There is no commercial use of fish traps or spears, and responsible fishing practices adopted by most fishers in the GBR also mean that sharks are still a common sight (although more work needs to be done to secure the future of these important predators). Bottom trawling for prawns (shrimp) has been dramatically scaled back over recent decades, with associated improvements in the health of the soft-seabed communities between reef outcrops. Other issues on the radar for the GBR include ship groundings, dredging and port expansions, with several ports along the reef, including Abbot Point, Gladstone, Hay Point, Mackay and Townsville, slated for development.

The GBR tourism industry is a world leader in sustainable, ecofriendly and climate-friendly practices. Visiting the reef with an eco-accredited tourism business is not only a great way to experience the beauty and wonder of coral reefs, it's also one of the best things you can do to help the GBR, with a small part of your fare directly supporting reef research and management.

Beyond the Corals

Coral reefs are more than just corals – a multitude of critters call these ecosystems home. Green and loggerhead turtles bury their eggs at the back of coral-island beaches, where the warm sand incubates the developing embryos. The sex of the hatchlings is determined by the temperature the eggs experience: cooler temperatures cause eggs to develop into male hatchlings; warmer eggs become females. Turtle researchers are worried that a warmer world could create an imbalance in the sex ratio, putting extra strain on already depleted turtle populations. For turtles, the risks don't stop there. Rising sea levels (some predictions are as much as 1.1m higher by the end of this century) put many nesting areas at greater risk of deadly flooding. Turtles will need to find higher ground for nesting, but in many coastal areas natural barriers or urban development limit their options.

For coral-reef fish, sea-level change might not be a big issue, but changes in ocean temperature have the potential to affect the timing and success of important processes such as reproduction. There is also growing evidence that fish might be prone to the effects of ocean acidification, which is the direct result of increased absorption of carbon dioxide by the world's seas. The upside to this process is that it has kept the atmosphere from warming even faster. But the pH of seawater is important to a wide range of chemical and biological processes, including the ability of fish to find their home reef and to avoid predators.

Changing ocean currents also have the potential to make life difficult for animals that rely on the timing and location of water movements for their survival. Seabird chicks become vulnerable when their parents have to travel too far to find the schools of fish they need to feed their flightless young. Plankton, too, are vulnerable to changing chemistry and currents, with potential flow-on effects through entire food chains. Corals don't escape the effects of ocean acidification, either. More acidic water makes it more difficult for corals to build their skeletons, leading to slower growth or more fragile structures.

GET INVOLVED

You can help the reef in practical ways during your visit. You can report sightings of important reef creatures, or send in information about any problems you encounter directly to the Great Barrier Reef Marine Park Authority by contributing to the Eye on the Reef Program (go to www.gbrmpa.gov.au or get the free Eye on the Reef app). If you're around for long enough (or time your visit right), you could undertake some training and become a Reef Check volunteer (see www.reefcheckaustralia.org). If turtles are your passion, see www.seaturtlefoundation.org for opportunities to volunteer with them. If you're a resident, look out for www.seagrasswatch.org, and if you like fishing, combine your fishing with research at www.info-fish.net.

The Future

In the best traditions of good science, its practitioners are a sceptical lot, but most coral-reef experts agree that climate change is a serious issue. Where scientists may differ is about the rate at which and the extent to which reefs and their mind-boggling biodiversity may adjust or adapt.

You might have heard it said that 'the climate has changed before and we still have corals'. While this is true, previous episodes of rapid climate change caused mass extinctions from which the world took millions of years to recover. The solid body of science indicates that climate change is happening, and that coral reefs are right in the firing line. Energetic debate is required on the best ways of tackling this problem, with action at local, national and global levels needed if we are to give coral reefs a fighting chance of providing future generations with the wonderful experiences we can still enjoy.

If humans continue to pollute the atmosphere with greenhouse gases at present rates, we will likely overtax any realistic capacity of coral-reef ecosystems to cope. All around the world, coral reefs are proving themselves to be the 'canary in the coal mine' of climate change. The worldwide reduction in reef assets that occurred when heatwaves swept equatorial regions in 1998 provided a wake-up call to reef scientists, reef managers and the community at large about what the future holds, with the 2016 event providing further impetus for action. Like polar zones, coral reefs are sentinel systems that will continue to show us the impacts of climate change on the natural world (and the millions of humans who depend on these ecosystems). But the ending to the climate-change story is still being written. Any action to reduce sources of pressure on corals and other reef creatures buys coral reefs important time to adapt – and, hopefully, to cope – until society takes the necessary action to control its impacts on the climate.

The Arts in Queensland

Artists from Queensland – and Brisbane in particular – can certainly claim a substantial contribution to Australia's artistic heritage. Traditionally, ancient Aboriginal rock-art galleries in remote locations showcased this landscape and its inhabitants, a role now assumed by Queensland's burgeoning film industry. Local musicians, writers, painters and photographers also continue to chronicle life in this part of Australia.

The Arts: Brisbane & Beyond

Following the fall of the National Party in the 1990s, the new Labor government did much to stimulate and encourage artistic and cultural development in Queensland. Brisbane, in particular, has since experienced a cultural renaissance with the building of world-class art museums and exhibition spaces. Home to one of Australia's biggest arts festivals – the Brisbane Festival (p69) in September – it's also a town where you can get your artistic rocks off every night of the week: live music, theatre, opera, poetry readings, and art-house and international cinema are all accessible and affordable.

Outside of the capital, you'll find simmering arts scenes in Cairns and Townsville, both of which have a mix of galleries and cultural centres that showcase the best of north Queensland and beyond. Cairns also has a lively arts and culture festival to rival Brisbane's, though on a smaller scale – the Cairns Festival (p237) in August.

The Aboriginal art scene in Queensland is vibrant, though you have to know where to look. The state has some captivating rock-art sites, where you can connect to ancient art traditions dating back tens of thousands of years. You can also encounter fine works by living Aboriginal artists at galleries scattered around the state, though Brisbane is still the best place to begin the cultural journey.

In 1964 Oodgeroo Noonuccal (1920–1993) from North Stradbroke Island became the first Aboriginal woman to be published (under the name of Kath Walker), with her collection of verse *We Are Going*. The publication sold out in three days and during the 1970s and '80s her subsequent work received international acclaim.

Queensland on Film

Although Australia's film industry was founded in Victoria and New South Wales (with no small input from South Australia), Queensland has made significant inroads in recent decades, which in turn has fostered new growth in the artistic wing of the industry.

The commercial industry here is based around the Village Roadshow Studios at Warner Bros Movie World on the Gold Coast – one of two world-class movie studios in Australia (the other being Fox Studios Australia in Sydney). Village Roadshow has produced a string of films targeting the family market including *Scooby Doo* (2002), *Peter Pan* (2003) and *The Chronicles of Narnia: The Voyage of the Dawn Treader* (2011). Other commercial films produced here include the horror thriller *Ghost Ship* (2002) and *The Great Raid* (2002), which tells the story of a WWII rescue mission of Americanin a Japanese prisoner-of-war camp in the Philippines. More recently, Village Roadshow was the filming site for Angelina Jolie's WWII epic *Unbroken* (2014), and the latest Marvel superhero epic, *Thor: Ragnarok* (2017), starring Chris Hemsworth and several of his muscles.

DAVID MALOUF

Lebanese–Australian author and poet David Malouf (b 1934 in Brisbane) is one of Queensland's most internationally recognised writers, having been nominated for the Booker Prize in 1993 and winning the Neustadt International Prize for Literature in 2000. Among other titles, he is well known for his evocative tales of an Australian boyhood in Brisbane – *Johnno* (1975); for his memoir *12 Edmondstone Street* (1985); and for *The Great World* (1990), his Australian epic that spans two world wars. Set on the Gold Coast, his 1982 novel *Fly Away Peter* tells the poignant story of a returned soldier struggling to come to terms with ordinary life and the unjust nature of social hierarchy. His collection of short stories *Every Move You Make* (2006) dissects Australian life across the continent, including Far North Queensland. His most recent novel is *Ransom* (2009), an ambitious recount of books 16 to 24 of Homer's epic *Iliad*.

Other titles filmed in the state include the following:

The Brisbane Writers Festival (p71) is a chance to hobnob with writers and editors from around the globe. Over a week in early September, the festival features seminars, master-classes, round-table discussions and plenty of wordsmithing tips from the pros.

***Flammable Children* (2017)** Directed by Stephan Elliott and filmed on the Gold Coast, starring Neighbours alumni Guy Pearce, Radha Mitchell and Kylie Minogue. A teen coming-of-age story in an archetypal '70s beach burb.

***Australia* (2008)** – Baz Luhrmann's epic was partly filmed in Bowen. The second-highest-grossing Australian film of all time (after *Crocodile Dundee*) relates the adventure of an English aristocrat (played by Nicole Kidman) in northern Australia against the backdrop of WWII.

***Ocean's Deadliest* (2007)** – The last documentary Steve Irwin made before his untimely death features Philippe Cousteau, grandson of renowned oceanographer Jacques Cousteau.

***The Proposition* (2005)** – Directed by John Hillcoat and written by Nick Cave, this gritty Western was filmed around Winton.

***Gettin' Square* (2003)** – Directed by Jonathan Teplitzky is this exquisitely funny and dark story about two low-grade criminals trying to extricate themselves from their past.

***Undead* (2002)** A horror flick shot in southeast Queensland, about a town that becomes infected with a zombie virus.

***Swimming Upstream* (2002)** – The autobiographical story of Anthony Fingleton, a Queensland swimmer. It captures the hardship of his life with his alcoholic father (played by Geoffrey Rush) in gritty 1960s Brisbane.

***The Thin Red Line* (1998)** – Terrence Malick's critically acclaimed tale of WWII soldiers in the Pacific.

***Praise* (1998)** – Adapted from the novel by Andrew McGahan, this is a toothy, honest tale of mismatched love in down-and-out Brisbane.

***Muriel's Wedding* (1994)** – A hit comedy that strips the lino off the suburban dream as Muriel attempts to escape a monotonous life.

***Dead Calm* (1989)** – A taut, underrated thriller-on-a-yacht starring Nicole Kidman, Sam Neill and Billy Zane, filmed around the Great Barrier Reef.

***Crocodile Dundee* (1986)** – Paul Hogan's record-breaking vehicle to stardom, as well as its two sequels, were partially shot in Queensland.

***The Coolangatta Gold* (1984)** – Fabulously B-grade surf life-saving film about two brothers at odds on the Gold Coast.

Music

Indigenous music has been one of the Australian music industry's great success stories of recent years, and Queensland has produced some outstanding indigenous musicians. Christine Anu is a Torres Strait Islander who was born in Cairns. Her debut album, *Stylin' Up* (1995), blends Creole-style rap, Islander chants and traditional languages with English, and was followed by the interesting *Come My Way* (2000) and *45 Degrees* (2003) – highly recommended listening.

Ever evolving, she even released a colourful children's album *Chrissy's Island Family* (2007). In 2015 she released *ReStylin' Up 20 Years*, a live take on her 1995 album.

Brisbane's pub-rock scene has produced a couple of Australia's all-time greatest bands. The Saints, considered by many to be one of the seminal punk bands (and oft quoted as a founding inspiration for the Seattle grunge movement of the early 1990s), began performing in Brisbane in the mid-1970s before moving on to bigger things in Sydney and, later, London. Their 1976 single, *I'm Stranded,* was a high-water mark for the band.

More recently, the iconic Brisbane band Powderfinger – a five-piece melodic rock outfit – played a dominant role in the Australian music industry from the 1990s until their breakup in 2010. Sing-along anthems and angelic-but-grunty guitar riffs define their classic albums such as the breakthrough *Double Allergic* (1996); *Odyssey Number Five* (2000); *Vulture Street* (2003); their best-of album, *Fingerprints* (2004); and their last hurrah, *Golden Rule* (2009). They played their final concert in Brisbane in late 2010 before a crowd of 10,000. Critics were left scratching their heads as to why the band failed to harness a broader international audience. Lead singer Bernard Fanning has also released three solo albums: *Tea and Sympathy* (2005), *Departures* (2013) and *Civil Dusk* (2016).

The Australian Recording Industry Association (ARIA) award-winning debut album *Polyserena* (2002) by Queensland band George is deliciously haunting. Katie Noonan (George's acclaimed lead singer) went on to release her first solo album, *Skin*, in 2007. She's worked on myriad collaborative recordings and performances since then, including projects with jazzy trio Elixir.

Another star hailing from the Sunshine State is Pete Murray. He looks more like a rugby player than a sensitive lyricist, but his beachy acoustic licks and chocolate-smooth voice have earned him national and international acclaim. His debut, *Feeler* (2003), and more recent offerings *See the Sun* (2005), *Summer at Eureka* (2008) and *Blue Sky Blue* (2011) are all summer-sweet listens.

More recently, Brisbane rockers Violent Soho have been cutting a swathe through the nation's alt-rock radio waves, their albums *Hungry Ghost* (2013) and *WACO* (2016) garnering new hirsute listeners around the country.

Another Queensland success story is The Veronicas, made up of twins of Sicilian descent whose pop style is a hit with teenagers. More interesting is Kate Miller-Heidke, a classically trained singer who channels the likes of Björk, Kate Bush and Cyndi Lauper in her works. Chase down a copy of *Little Eve* (2007), *Curiouser* (2008), *Night Flight* (2012) or *O Vertigo!* (2014). *The Last Day on Earth,* from *Curiouser,* was a top-10 single.

Flying the flag for Far North Queensland, the McMenamins are a talented brother-and-sister folk duo who are receiving increased airplay and have performed around the country. Their self-titled debut (released in 2003), as well as *In this Light* (2006), *Long Time Gone* (2010) and *Sand and Stone* (2013) are all worth a spin.

For a dose of 100% Australian music talent, tune in to the national radio station Triple J (www.abc.net.au/triplej) for 'Home and Hosed', from 9pm Monday to Thursday.

THE ARTS IN QUEENSLAND MUSIC

BERNARD FANNING

Through the 1990s and 2000s, Brisbane band Powderfinger where everywhere, their melodic rock songs galvanising Australian listeners like a home-grown Pearl Jam. Floppy-haired front man Bernard Fanning was their charismatic talisman: at once impassioned, grizzled, handsome and witty. When Powderfinger dissolved in 2010, Fanning's solo career took off. Three albums later and with a 2017 tour supporting James Taylor under his belt, Fanning continues to wow the crowds. See www.bernardfanning.com for more.

Painting & Photography

Queensland's Aboriginal painters have been creating brilliant works – particularly rock art galleries – for millennia, but post colonisation a painting scene founded in European aesthetics was slow to emerge here. Paintings by early settlers first appeared in the second half of the 19th century. In the 20th century a few seminal figures helped put Queensland on the map.

Ian Fairweather (1891–1974) is described by some critics and fellow artists as Australia's greatest painter. He used muted colours and shied away from typical Australian themes (such as gum trees, and pastoral and rugged landscapes), instead incorporating Asian elements (gouaches of villages and market scenes), influenced by his years living in China from 1930 to 1933. An enigmatic figure, he spent the last years of his life as a recluse on Bribie Island.

The long-lived Lloyd Rees (1895–1988) has an impressive body of work and is one of Queensland's best-known artists of the 20th century. A master of light and texture, he was obsessed with capturing a spiritual element in the landscapes he painted. He was born in Brisbane and painted right up until his death in Hobart in 1988.

One of Queensland's most successful living artists is William Robinson (b 1936) who has won Australia's esteemed Archibald Prize for portraiture twice (1987 and 1995). He has worked in a variety of styles and completed some of his most successful work after moving from Brisbane to a large property in the Gold Coast hinterland. His paintings capture the magical quality of the rainforest and the awe-inspiring power of the mountains near Springbrook. His work is on display in Brisbane's Old Government House.

Brisbane-based Richard Bell (b 1953) is an Aboriginal artist who creates provocative works that examine politics, religion and race (words over one of his controversial, prize-winning pieces read, 'Aboriginal art – it's a white thing'). Many of his works involve large Lichtenstein-like cartoon tableaux.

Tracey Moffatt (b 1960), who also hails from Brisbane, blends cinema, photography and visual arts in carefully constructed 'film stills' with underlying themes of poverty and violence. Her work hangs in galleries all over the world and she has been described as one of Australia's '50 most collectable artists'.

For a first-hand look at some of the best contemporary painting and photography being produced in Queensland, swing by Brisbane's deliciously subversive Institute of Modern Art (p53) in Fortitude Valley.

Top Art Galleries

Gallery of Modern Art, Brisbane

Stanthorpe Regional Art Gallery

Tanks Arts Centre, Cairns

Institute of Modern Art, Brisbane

Perc Tucker Regional Gallery, Townsville

Aboriginal Rock Art

Rock art – engravings, stencils, drawings and paintings, often found in broad cave or cliff galleries – is a diary of human activity by Australia's Indigenous peoples stretching over tens of thousands of years. Queensland has plenty of sites, especially hidden around the Far North. Try to see some while you're here – the experience of viewing rock art in the surroundings in which it was painted is far more profound than seeing it in a gallery.

Carnarvon Gorge, in Carnarvon National Park, houses rock engravings, freehand drawing and over 2000 mouth-sprayed stencils, which are of deep spiritual significance to the present-day Bidjarra people of the area.

The Kuku Yalanji sites, in Mossman Gorge, feature Dreaming legends depicted in cave paintings. The Kuku Yalanji community offers excellent guided walks to see and understand the art.

Survival
Guide

Deadly & Dangerous

If you're the pessimistic type, you might focus on the things that can bite, sting, burn or drown you in Queensland: bushfires, treacherous surf, blazing heat, jellyfish, snakes, spiders, sharks, crocodiles, ticks... But chances are the worst you'll encounter are a few pesky flies and mosquitoes. So splash on some insect repellent and boldly venture forth!

Out & About

At the Beach

Around 80 people per year drown on Australia's beaches, where pounding surf and rips (strong currents) can create serious hazards. If you happen to get caught in a rip and are being taken out to sea, swim parallel to the shore until you're out of the rip, then head for the beach – *don't* try to swim back against the rip; you'll only tire yourself.

Bushfires

Bushfires happen regularly in Queensland. In hot, dry and windy weather and on total-fire-ban days, be extremely careful with naked flames (including cigarette butts) and don't use camping stoves, campfires or barbecues. Bushwalkers should delay trips until things cool down. If you're out in the bush and you see smoke, take it seriously: find the nearest open space (downhill if possible). Forested ridges are dangerous places to be. Always heed the advice of authorities.

Coral Cuts

Coral can be extremely sharp; you can cut yourself by merely brushing against the stuff. Thoroughly clean cuts and douse with antiseptic to avoid infection.

Heat Sickness

Hot weather is the norm in Queensland and can lead to heat exhaustion or more severe heatstroke (resulting from extreme fluid depletion). When arriving from a temperate or cold climate, remember that it takes two weeks to acclimatise.

Unprepared travellers die from dehydration each year in remote areas. Always carry sufficient water for any trip (driving or hiking), and let someone know where you're going and when you expect to arrive. Carry communications equipment and if in trouble, stay with your vehicle rather than walking for help.

Sunburn & Skin Cancer

Australia has one of the highest rates of skin cancer in the world. Monitor exposure to direct sunlight closely. Ultraviolet (UV) radiation is greatest between 10am and 4pm, so avoid skin exposure during these times. Wear a wide-brimmed hat and a long-sleeved shirt with a collar. Always use SPF 30+ sunscreen; apply it 30 minutes before exposure and reapply regularly to minimise sun damage.

Things That Bite & Sting

Crocodiles

The risk of a crocodile attack in tropical Far North Queensland is real, but with some common sense it is entirely avoidable. 'Salties' are estuarine crocodiles that can grow to 7m. They inhabit coastal waters and are mostly seen in the tidal reaches of rivers, though on occasion they're spotted on beaches and in freshwater lagoons. Always heed any advice, such as crocodile warning signs, that you might come across. Don't assume it's safe to swim if there are no signs: if you're not sure, don't swim.

If you're away from popular beaches anywhere north of Rockhampton, avoid swimming in rivers, waterholes and in the sea near river outlets. Don't clean fish or prepare food near the water's edge, and camp at least 50m away from waterways. Crocodiles are particularly mobile and dangerous during the breeding season (October to March).

Jellyfish

Jellyfish – including the potentially deadly box jellyfish and Irukandji – occur in Queensland's tropical waters. It's unwise to swim north of Agnes Water between November and May unless there's a stinger net. 'Stinger suits' (full-body Lycra swimsuits) prevent stinging, as do wetsuits. Swimming and snorkelling are usually safe around Queensland's reef islands throughout the year; however, the rare (and tiny) Irukandji has been recorded on the outer reef and islands.

Wash stings with vinegar to prevent further discharge of remaining stinging cells, followed by rapid transfer to a hospital. Don't attempt to remove the tentacles.

Marine Animals

Marine spikes and poisonous spines – such as those found on sea urchins, catfish, stingrays, scorpionfish and stonefish – can cause severe local pain. If you're stung, immediately immerse the affected area in hot water (as hot as can be tolerated) and seek medical care.

Contact with blue-ringed octopuses and Barrier Reef cone shells can be fatal, so don't pick them up. If someone is stung, apply a pressure bandage, monitor breathing carefully and conduct mouth-to-mouth resuscitation if breathing stops. Seek immediate medical care.

Mosquitoes

'Mozzies' can be a problem just about anywhere in Queensland. Malaria isn't present, but dengue fever is a danger in the north of the state, particularly during the wet season (November to April). Most people recover in

A BIT OF PERSPECTIVE

Australia's plethora of poisonous and biting critters is impressive, but don't let it put you off. There's approximately one shark-attack and one croc-attack fatality per year here. Blue-ringed-octopus deaths are rarer – only two in the last century. Jellyfish do better – about two deaths annually – but you're still more than 100 times more likely to drown. Spiders haven't killed anyone in the last 20 years. Snake bites kill one or two people per year, as do bee stings, but you're about a thousand times more likely to perish on the nation's roads.

a few days, but more severe forms of the disease can occur.

To minimise bites:

➡ Wear loose, long-sleeved clothing.

➡ Apply repellent with minimum 30% DEET on exposed skin.

➡ Use mosquito coils.

➡ Sleep under fast-spinning ceiling fans.

Sharks

Despite extensive media coverage, the risk of shark attack in Queensland is no greater than in other countries with extensive coastlines. Check with surf life-saving groups about local risks.

Snakes

There's no denying it: Australia (and especially Queensland) has plenty of venomous snakes. Few species are aggressive: unless you are messing with or accidentally stand on one, you're unlikely to be bitten. About 80% of bites occur on the lower limbs: wear protective clothing (such as gaiters) when bushwalking.

If bitten, apply an elastic bandage (or improvise with a T-shirt). Wrap firmly around the entire limb – but not so tightly that you cut off the

circulation – and immobilise with a splint or sling; then seek medical attention. Don't use a tourniquet, and don't try to suck out the poison.

Spiders

Australia has poisonous spiders, although the only species to have killed anyone recently, the Sydney funnel-web, isn't a Queenslander. Common species:

Redback Bites cause increasing pain followed by profuse sweating. Apply ice and transfer to hospital.

Whitetail Blamed for causing slow-healing ulcers. If bitten, clean bite and seek medical assistance.

Huntsman A disturbingly large spider that's harmless, though seeing one can affect your blood pressure (and/or underpants).

Ticks

Common bush ticks can be dangerous if lodged in the skin and undetected. When walking in tick-prone areas, check your body every night (and those of children and dogs). Remove a tick by dousing with methylated spirits or kerosene and levering it out intact. See a doctor if bites become infected (tick typhus cases have been reported in Queensland).

Directory A–Z

Accommodation

Camping & Holiday Parks

If you want to explore Queensland on a shoestring, camping is the way to go. Better yet, book a campervan you can sleep in and explore this state's *loooong* east coast. Caravan parks are often close to the beach and town centres, and are great bang for your family-friendly buck.

Camping in national parks can cost from nothing to $15 per person. Tent sites at private camping and caravan parks usually cost between $22 and $32 per couple per night (slightly more with electricity). Many of these outfits also hire out cabins with kitchenettes, running from $70 to $170 per night sleeping one to six people.

National parks and their camping areas are administered by Queensland's Department of National Parks, Sport & Racing (www.nprsr.

qld.gov.au), with bookings online.

If you intend to do a lot of caravanning or camping, joining a major chain will save you some dollars:

Big 4 (www.big4.com.au)

Discovery Holiday Parks (www.discoveryholidayparks.com.au)

Top Tourist Parks (www.top touristparks.com.au).

Hostels

Backpacker hostels are highly social, low-cost Queensland fixtures, ranging from family-run places in converted houses to huge, custom-built resorts replete with bars, nightclubs and party propensity. Standards range from outstanding to awful, and management from friendly to scary.

Dorm beds typically cost $28 to $35, with single rooms sometimes available (around $70) and doubles costing $80 to $110. Chain organisations include the following:

Base Backpackers (www.stayatbase.com)

Global Backpackers (www.globalbackpackers.com.au)

Nomads (www.nomadsworld.com)

VIP Backpackers (www.vip backpackers.com)

YHA (www.yha.com.au) YHA offers dorms, as well as twin and double rooms, plus cooking and laundry facilities. The vibe is generally less 'party' than in independent hostels...but there's always plenty of cutlery. Nightly charges start at $27 for members; hostels also take non-YHA members for an extra $3. Australian residents can become YHA members for $25 for one year, $45 for two. Join online or at any YHA hostel. Families can also join: just purchase the adult memberships, then kids under 18 can join for free. The YHA is part of Hostelling International (www.hihostels.com): if you already have HI membership in your own country, you're entitled to YHA rates in Australian hostels.

Pubs, Hotels & Motels

Hotels in Queensland – the ones that serve beer – are commonly known as pubs (from the term 'public house'). Generally, rooms are small and weathered, with a long amble down the hall to the bathroom. They're usually central and cheap – singles/doubles with shared facilities from $60/80, more if you want a private bathroom – but if you're a light sleeper, avoid booking a room above the bar and check whether a band is playing downstairs that night.

Hotels in Queensland (other than resorts) are often of the business or luxury-chain variety (midrange to top end): comfortable, anonymous, mod-con-filled rooms in multistorey blocks. Expect to pay more than $150 a night per double, though significant discounts may be offered when business is quiet.

More interesting (and more expensive), boutique hotels offer quirky, luxurious experiences, and are often brilliantly located (arty inner-city suburbs, remote tropical peninsulas). Expect to pay upward of $250 per night, but you definitely get what you pay for.

Drive-up motels offer comfortable midrange accommodation and are found all over the state. They rarely offer a cheaper rate for singles, so are better value for couples or small families. You'll mostly pay between $100 and $150 for a simple room with kettle, fridge, TV, air-con and bathroom...and that inexplicably romantic on-the-road motel vibe.

B&Bs

Bed-and-breakfast options around Queensland include restored cottages, rambling old houses, upmarket country manors, beachside bungalows and simple bedrooms in family homes.

Tariffs are typically in the midrange bracket ($150 to $250 per night including breakfast) but can be much higher. Some B&B hosts may also cook dinner for guests (usually 24 hours' notice is required).

Local tourist offices can generally give you a list of options. Good online information:

B&B and Farmstay Far North Queensland (www.bnbnq.com.au)

Bed & Breakfast Site (www.babs.com.au)

Hosted Accommodation Australia (www.australian bedandbreakfast.com.au)

OZ Bed and Breakfast (www.ozbedandbreakfast.com)

Farmstays

Many coastal Queensland and hinterland farms offer a bed for the night and the chance to see rural Australia at work. At some you sit back and watch other people raise a sweat, while others like to get you involved in day-to-day activities. Check out B&B Australia (www.babs.com.au, under family holidays/farmstays) and Willing Workers on Organic Farms (www.wwoof.com.au). Regional and town tourist offices should also be able to tell you what's available in their area.

Resorts

There are plenty of islands in Queensland, and plenty of them have resorts. Here's your chance to either ditch the kids and sleep for a week (with the odd dip in the pool and cocktail), or bring the family along for a fun-filled tropical holiday full of activities (snorkelling, kayaking, bushwalking, windsurfing, swimming, sailing...). Most resorts are at the pricey end of the scale – at least $250 a night, often a lot more – but some offer good family rates, particularly out of peak season.

Rental Accommodation

If you're in Queensland for a while or just want to base yourself in a city or surf town for a week or two, then a rental apartment will be an economical option – particularly if you're travelling with kids, a group of mates or just want to cook dinner once in a while. Most of the towers on the Gold Coast are apartment buildings – you'll have

plenty of choice here! Expect to pay upwards of $150 a night. Beachside and country cottages are pricier, starting at around $200 per night, and often include breakfast provisions.

Customs Regulations

➡ For comprehensive information on customs regulations, contact the Australian Customs & Border Protection Service (www.customs.gov.au).

➡ There's a duty-free quota of 2.25L of alcohol, 50 cigarettes and dutiable goods up to the value of $900 per person.

➡ Prohibited imports include drugs (all medicines must be declared), wooden items and food – Australia is very strict on this, so declare all food items, even leftover edibles taken from the plane.

Discount Cards

Senior Cards Travellers over 60 with some form of identification (eg a Seniors Card – www.australia.gov.au/content/seniors-card) are often eligible for concession prices. Most Australian states and territories issue their own versions of these, which can be used Australia-wide.

Student & Youth Cards The internationally recognised International Student Identity Card (www.isic.org) is available to full-time students aged 12 and over. The card gives the bearer discounts on accommodation, transport and admission to various attractions. The same organisation also produces the International Youth Travel Card (IYTC), issued to people under

26 years of age who are not full-time students, and has benefits equivalent to the ISIC. Also similar is the International Teacher Identity Card (ITIC), available to teaching professionals. All three cards are available online or from student travel companies ($30).

Electricity

Type I
230V/50Hz

Embassies & Consulates

The Department of Foreign Affairs & Trade (www.dfat.gov.au) lists all foreign missions in Australia. Most are in Canberra; many countries also have consular offices in Sydney and Melbourne.

Food & Drink

Eating in Queensland, with its endless coastline and immense swaths of farming country, often involves seafood or steak (or a combination of the two, known as 'surf 'n' turf' or 'reef 'n' beef'). You'll find cafes and restaurants almost everywhere, with vegetarians well catered for in the cities and larger towns. Booking on the day of your meal is usually fine; top-end restaurants should be booked a couple of weeks in advance.

Cafes Queensland cafes are the hubs of local life – meeting places, conversation backdrops and breakfast/lunch stalwarts. And the coffee here – along the coast at any rate – is usually pretty great.

Pubs & Clubs Head to the pub or the local surf life-saving club for a quick-fire steak/schnitzel/seafood lunch or dinner, plus a couple of beers and maybe some ice cream for the kids.

Restaurants The restaurant experience here ranges from reliable bistro encounters to amazing high-end gourmet experiences using organic local fare. Seafood is the standout ingredient.

GLBTI Travellers

Historically, Queensland has a poor reputation when it comes to acceptance of gays and lesbians. Homosexuality was only decriminalised in Queensland in 1991, after the fall of the long-term National Party government.

Brisbane has a small but lively gay and lesbian scene centred on the inner-city suburbs of New Farm and Fortitude Valley, with a few nightclubs, pubs and guesthouses. There are also gay- and lesbian-only accommodation options in some of the more popular tourist centres, including Brisbane and Cairns. Elsewhere in Queensland, however, there can be a strong streak of homophobia, and violence against homosexuals is a risk, particularly in rural communities.

Resources

Gay and lesbian magazines include *DNA*, *Lesbians on the Loose* (LOTL) and *Queensland Pride*. Other resources:

Gay & Lesbian Counselling Brisbane (☑1800 877 924; www.gayandlesbiancounselling.com) Counselling appointments.

Gay & Lesbian Tourism Australia (www.galta.com.au) General info.

Gay News Network (www.gaynewsnetwork.com.au)

Same Same (www.samesame.com.au) News, events and lifestyle features.

Health
Before You Go
HEALTH INSURANCE

Health insurance is essential for all travellers. You may prefer a policy that pays doctors or hospitals directly rather than requiring you to pay on the spot and claim later. If you have to claim later make sure you keep all documentation. Check that the policy covers ambulances and emergency medical evacuations by air.

VACCINATIONS

If you're travelling to Australia from overseas, visit a physician four to eight weeks before departure. Ask your doctor for an International Certificate of Vaccination (aka the 'yellow booklet'), which will list the vaccinations you've received.

Upon entering Australia, you'll be required to fill out a 'travel history card' detailing any visits to Ebola-affected regions within the last 21 days.

If you're entering Australia within six days of having stayed overnight or longer in a yellow-fever-infected country, you'll need proof of yellow-fever vaccination. For a full list of these countries visit Centers for Disease Control & Prevention (www.cdc.gov/travel).

The World Health Organization (www.who.int) recommends that all travellers be covered for diphtheria, tetanus, measles, mumps, rubella, chicken pox and polio, as well as hepatitis B, regardless of their destination. While Australia has high levels of childhood vaccination coverage, outbreaks of these diseases do occur.

In Queensland

Although there are plenty of hazards (p292) in Australia, few travellers should experience anything worse than sunburn or a hangover. If you do fall ill, health-care standards are high.

AVAILABILITY & COST OF HEALTH CARE

The Medicare system covers Australian residents for some health-care costs. Visitors from countries with which Australia has a reciprocal health-care agreement are eligible for benefits specified under the Medicare program. Agreements are currently in place with Belgium, Finland, Italy, Malta, the Netherlands, New Zealand, Ireland, Norway, Slovenia, Sweden and the UK – check the details before departing these countries. For further details, visit www.humanservices.gov.au/customer/subjects/medicare-services. Even if you're not covered by Medicare, a short consultation with a local GP will usually set you back only $60 or $70.

ENVIRONMENTAL HAZARDS

In remote locations there may be a significant delay in emergency services reaching you. Don't underestimate the vast distances between most major rural towns; an increased level of self-reliance and preparation is essential. Consider taking a wilderness first-aid course, such as those offered by Wilderness Medicine Institute (www.wmi.net.au).

Take a comprehensive first-aid kit and ensure that you have adequate means of communication. Australia

has extensive mobile-phone coverage, but additional radio communication is important for remote areas. The Royal Flying Doctor Service (www.flyingdoctor.net) provides a backup for remote communities.

TAP WATER

Tap water in Queensland is generally safe to drink. Water taken from streams, rivers and lakes should be treated before drinking.

Insurance

A good travel insurance policy covering theft, loss and medical problems is essential. Some policies specifically exclude designated 'dangerous activities' such as scuba diving, surfing, white-water rafting and even bushwalking. Make sure the policy you choose fully covers you for your activity of choice, and covers ambulances and emergency medical evacuations by air.

Worldwide travel insurance is available at www.lonelyplanet.com/travel-insurance. You can buy, extend and claim online anytime – even if you're already on the road.

Internet Access

In our Queensland listings we have allocated the internet icon where a venue provides terminals for guest/public use, and the wi-fi icon where wireless internet is available.

Wi-Fi & Internet Service Providers

Wi-fi is still rare in remote Queensland, but the norm in urban accommodation, with cafes, bars, libraries and even some public gardens also providing wi-fi access (often free for customers/guests).

Telstra, Optus, Vodafone and other big carriers sell mobile broadband devices with a USB connection that work with most laptops

and allow you to get online just about anywhere in the country. Prices are around $80 for 30 days of access (cheaper for long-term fixed contracts). If you're travelling here from overseas you might be better off buying a local SIM card with a data allowance you can top up.

Internet Cafes

No one goes to internet cafes any more, do they? You can still find them in the big cities if you ask around, and most public libraries have internet terminals (generally provided for research, not for travellers to check Facebook).

If you're bringing your palmtop or laptop, check with your Internet Service Provider (ISP) for access numbers you can dial into in Australia. Some major Australian ISPs:

Dodo (www.dodo.com)

iinet (www.iinet.net.au)

iPrimus (www.iprimus.com.au)

Optus (www.optus.com.au)

Telstra BigPond (www.bigpond.com)

Legal Matters

Most travellers will have no contact with Australia's police or legal system; if you do, it's most likely to be while driving.

Driving There's a significant police presence on Queensland's roads. Police have the power to stop your car, see your licence (you're required to carry it), check your vehicle for roadworthiness, and insist that you take a breath test for alcohol (and sometimes illicit drugs). The legal limit is 0.05 blood-alcohol content. If you're over you'll be facing a court appearance, a fine and/or suspension of your licence.

Drugs First-time offenders caught with small amounts of illegal drugs are likely to receive a fine rather than go to jail, but the recording of a conviction against you may affect your visa status.

Visas If you remain in Australia beyond the life of your visa, you'll officially be an 'overstayer' and could face detention and then be prevented from returning to Australia for up to three years.

Arrested? It's your right to telephone a friend, lawyer or relative before questioning begins. Legal aid is available only in serious cases; for Legal Aid office info see www.nationallegalaid.org. However, many solicitors do not charge for an initial consultation.

Money

The Australian dollar comprises 100 cents. There are 5c, 10c, 20c, 50c, $1 and $2 coins, and $5, $10, $20, $50 and $100 notes.

ATMs & Eftpos

ATMs Common in Queensland cities and towns, but don't expect to find them everywhere, certainly not off the beaten track or in small towns. Most ATMs accept cards issued by other banks (for a fee) and are linked to international networks.

Eftpos Most service stations, supermarkets, restaurants, cafes and shops have Electronic Funds Transfer at Point of Sale (Eftpos) facilities, allowing you to make purchases and even withdraw cash with your credit or debit card.

Fees Remember that withdrawing cash via ATMs or Eftpos may incur significant fees – check the costs with your bank first.

Credit & Debit Cards

Credit cards such as MasterCard and Visa are widely accepted for most accommodation and services, and a credit card is essential (in lieu of a fat wad of cash) when hiring a car. They can also be used to get cash advances over the counter at banks and from many ATMs, depending on the card – but be aware that these withdrawals incur immediate interest. Diners Club and American Express cards are not as widely accepted.

Lost credit-card contact numbers:

American Express (☑1300 132 639; www.americanexpress.com.au)

Diners Club (☑1300 360 060; www.dinersclub.com.au)

MasterCard (☑1800 120 113; www.mastercard.com.au)

Visa (☑1800 450 346; www.visa.com.au)

For international travellers, debit cards connected to the international banking networks – Cirrus, Maestro, Plus and Eurocard – will work fine in Queensland ATMs. Expect substantial fees. A better option may be prepaid debit cards (such as MasterCard and Travelex 'Cash Passport' cards) with set withdrawal fees and a balance you can top up from your bank account while on the road.

Money Changers

Changing foreign currency is usually no problem at banks throughout Australia, or at licensed money changers such as Travelex or AmEx in airports and cities. Expect substantial fees.

Taxes & Refunds

Australia has a flat 10% tax on all goods and services (GST), included in quoted/shelf prices. A refund is sometimes possible under the Tourist Refund Scheme (TRS): see www.border.gov.au/trav/ente/tour/are-you-a-traveller.

Tipping

Tipping isn't traditionally part of Australian etiquette, but it's increasingly the norm to tip around 10% for good service in restaurants, and a few dollars for porters (bellhops) and taxi rides.

Opening Hours

Business hours sometimes vary from season to season, but use the following as a guide:

Banks 9.30am to 4pm Monday to Friday; some also 9am to noon Saturday

Bars 4pm to late

Cafes 7am to 5pm

Nightclubs 10pm to 4am Thursday to Saturday

Post Offices 9am to 5pm Monday to Friday; some also 9am to noon Saturday

Pubs 11am to midnight

Restaurants noon to 2.30pm and 6pm to 9pm

Shops 9am to 5pm Monday to Saturday

Supermarkets 7am to 8pm

Post

Australia Post (www.auspost.com.au) is the nationwide provider. Most substantial towns have a post office, or an Australia Post desk within a bank. Services are reliable, but slower than

---

PRACTICALITIES

DVDs Australian DVDs are encoded for Region 4, which includes Mexico, South America, Central America, New Zealand, the Pacific and the Caribbean.

Newspapers Leaf through Brisbane's *Courier-Mail* or the national *Australian* newspapers.

Radio Tune in to ABC radio (www.abc.net.au/radio).

TV The main free-to-air TV channels are the government-sponsored ABC and multicultural SBS, plus the three commercial networks – Seven, Nine and Ten. There are also numerous additional channels from these main players.

Weights & Measures Australia uses the metric system.

they used to be (recent cost-saving cutbacks are to blame). Express Post delivers a parcel or envelope interstate between Australia's urban centres by the next business day; otherwise allow four days for urban deliveries, longer for country areas.

Public Holidays

New Year's Day 1 January

Australia Day 26 January

Easter (Good Friday to Easter Monday inclusive) March or April

Anzac Day 25 April

Labour Day First Monday in May

Queen's Birthday Second Monday in June

Royal Queensland Show Day (Brisbane only) Second or third Wednesday in August

Christmas Day 25 December

Boxing Day 26 December

Safe Travel

Queensland is a relatively safe place to visit – in terms of crime and war, at any rate – but take reasonable precautions. The Gold Coast and Cairns get dishonourable mentions when it comes to theft: don't leave hotel rooms or cars unlocked, or valuables visible through car windows.

➜ Beware undertows (rips) at surf beaches. Swim parallel to the shore to escape the current, then head for the sand.

➜ Bushfires, floods and cyclones regularly decimate parts of Queensland: pay attention to warnings from local authorities.

➜ Use sunscreen and cover up to avoid sunburn and heat sickness.

➜ Crocodiles, jellyfish and stinging marine animals inhabit Australia's tropical northern waters: always heed warnings.

GOVERNMENT TRAVEL ADVICE

The following government websites offer travel advisories and information on current hot spots.

Australian Department of Foreign Affairs & Trade (www.smarttraveller.gov.au)

British Foreign & Commonwealth Office (www.gov.uk/fco)

Government of Canada (www.travel.gc.ca)

US State Department (www.travel.state.gov)

➜ Sharks occur right along the Queensland coast: seek local advice about risks.

➜ Cover up at dusk and wear insect repellent to deter mosquitoes and ticks.

➜ Snakes are active in summer and common on bushwalking trails: wear boots, socks and long trousers (ideally gaiters).

Telephone

Regular Australian phone numbers have a two-digit area code followed by an eight-digit number. Drop the initial '0' if calling from abroad.

Australia's main telecommunications companies:

Telstra (www.telstra.com.au) The main player – landline and mobile phone services.

Optus (www.optus.com.au) Telstra's main rival – landline and mobile phone services.

Vodafone (www.vodafone.com.au) Mobile phone services.

Virgin (www.virginmobile.com.au) Mobile phone services.

Mobile Phones

European phones will work on Australia's network, but most American or Japanese phones will not. Use global roaming or a local SIM card and prepaid account.

Numbers Local numbers with the prefix 04xx belong to mobile phones.

Network Australia's digital network is compatible with GSM 900 and 1800 (used in Europe),

but generally not with networks in the USA or Japan.

Reception Queensland generally gets good mobile-phone reception, but service can be haphazard or nonexistent in the interior and far north (eg the Daintree Rainforest).

Connections To get connected, buy a starter kit, which may include a phone or, if you have your own phone, a SIM card (under $10) and a prepaid charge card. Pick up starter kits and SIM cards at airport mobile-phone shops or outlets in the big cities. Purchase recharge vouchers at convenience stores and newsagents.

Local & International Calls

➜ Local calls from private phones cost 30c and are untimed.

➜ Local calls from public phones cost 50c and are untimed.

➜ Calls to mobile phones attract higher rates and are timed.

➜ When calling overseas you need to dial the international access code from Australia (☑0011), the country code, then the area code (without the initial 0).

➜ When dialling Queensland from overseas, the country code is ☑61, and you need to drop the zero in the 07 area code.

Long-Distance Calls & Area Codes

➜ STD (long-distance) calls can be made from

private, mobile and virtually any public phone and are cheaper during off-peak hours (7pm to 7am).

➡ When calling from one area to another area within the same area code, there's no need to dial the area code before the local number. If these calls are long-distance (more than 50km away), they're charged at long-distance rates, even though they have the same area code. Area codes within Australia:

STATE/TERRITORY	AREA CODE
Queensland	☑07
New South Wales, Australian Capital Territory (ACT)	☑02
South Australia, Western Australia, Northern Territory	☑08
Victoria, Tasmania	☑03

Information & Toll-Free Calls

➡ Toll-free numbers (prefix 1800) can be called free of charge, though they may not be accessible from certain areas or from mobile phones.

➡ Calls to numbers beginning with 13 or 1300 are charged at the rate of a local call.

➡ To make a reverse-charge (collect) call within Australia, dial 1800-REVERSE (☑1800 738 3773) from any public or private phone.

➡ Telephone numbers beginning with either 1800, 13 or 1300 cannot be dialled from outside Australia.

Phonecards

➡ A variety of phonecards can be bought at newsagents, hostels and post offices for a fixed dollar value (usually $10, $20 etc) and can be used with any public or private phone. Shop around.

➡ Most public phones use phonecards; some also accept credit cards. Old-fashioned coin-operated public phones are becoming

increasingly rare (and if you do find one, chances are the coin slot will be gummed up or vandalised beyond function).

Time

Australia is divided into three time zones:

Eastern Standard Time (Greenwich Mean Time + 10 hours) Queensland, New South Wales, Victoria and Tasmania

Central Standard Time (30 minutes behind Eastern Standard Time) Northern Territory, South Australia

Western Standard Time (two hours behind Eastern Standard Time) Western Australia

Note that Queensland remains on Eastern Standard Time all year, while most of Australia switches to daylight-saving time over the summer (October to early April) when clocks are wound forward one hour.

Tourist Information

Tourist information is provided in Queensland by numerous regional and local info centres in key tourist spots, often staffed by volunteers (chatty retirees). Keep in mind that some tourist info outlets are also booking agents and will steer you towards the tour/accommodation that pays them the best commission.

Australian Tourist Commission (www.australia.com) National organisation charged with luring foreign visitors.

Department of National Parks, Sport & Racing (www.nprsr.qld.gov.au) Information on national parks throughout Queensland, including campsite bookings.

Tourism Queensland (www.queenslandholidays.com.au) Official Queensland government-run website stacked with information, from accommodation to diving the Great Barrier Reef.

Travellers with Disabilities

Disability awareness in Queensland is reasonably high. Legislation requires that new accommodation must meet accessibility standards and tourist operators must not discriminate. Facilities for wheelchairs are improving in accommodation, but there are still many older establishments where the necessary upgrades haven't been made: call ahead to confirm.

Download Lonely Planet's free Accessible Travel guide from http://lptravel.to/AccessibleTravel.

Resources

Australian Tourist Commission (www.australia.com) Publishes detailed, downloadable information for people with disabilities, including travel and transport tips and contact addresses of organisations in each state.

Deaf Australia (www.deafau.org.au)

Disability Information Service (www.communities.qld.gov.au/disability) Queensland government's Department for Communities, Child Safety & Disability Services; support throughout Queensland.

National Disability Services (www.nds.org.au) The national industry association for disability services.

National Information Communication & Awareness Network (Nican; ☑1300 655 535, 02 6241 1220; www.nican.com.au) Australia-wide directory providing information on access, accommodation, sports and recreational activities, transport and specialist tour operators.

Spinal Life Australia (www.spinal.com.au) In Brisbane, Townsville and Cairns.

Vision Australia (www.visionaustralia.org)

Wheelie Easy (www.wheelieeasy.com.au) Runs specialised tours in Far North Queensland for travellers with impaired mobility.

Visas

All visitors to Australia need a visa. Apply online through the **Department of Immigration and Border Protection** (☑1300 363 263, 02-6275 6666; www.border.gov.au).

Visitor Visa

➡ Many European passport holders are eligible for a free eVisitor visa, allowing stays in Australia of up to three months within a 12-month period.

➡ eVisitor visas must be applied for online. They are electronically stored and linked to individual passport numbers, so no stamp in your passport is required.

➡ It's advisable to apply at least 14 days prior to the proposed date of travel to Australia.

Electronic Travel Authority

➡ Passport holders from those European countries eligible for eVisitor visas, plus passport holders from Brunei, Canada, Hong Kong, Japan, Malaysia, Singapore, South Korea and the USA, can apply for either a visitor Electronic Travel Authority (ETA) or business ETA.

➡ ETAs are valid for 12 months, with stays of up to three months on each visit.

➡ ETA visas cost $20.

Work Visa

➡ Nationals from Argentina, Bangladesh, Chile, China, Indonesia, Israel, Malaysia, Poland, Portugal, Slovakia, Slovenia, Spain, Thailand, Turkey, the USA and Uruguay aged between the ages of 18 and 30 can apply for a Work and Holiday visa prior to entry to Australia.

➡ Once granted, this visa allows the holder to enter Australia within three months of issue, stay for up to 12 months, leave and re-enter Australia any number of times within

those 12 months, undertake temporary employment to supplement a trip, and study for up to four months.

➡ Application fee: $440.

Working Holiday Scheme

➡ Young (aged 18 to 30) visitors from Belgium, Canada, Cyprus, Denmark, Estonia, Finland, France, Germany, Hong Kong, Ireland, Italy, Japan, the Republic of Korea, Malta, the Netherlands, Norway, Sweden, Taiwan and the UK are eligible for a Working Holiday visa, which allows you to visit for up to 12 months and gain casual employment.

➡ Holders can leave and re-enter Australia any number of times within those 12 months.

➡ Holders can only work for any one employer for a maximum of six months.

➡ Apply prior to entry to Australia (up to a year in advance) – you can't change from another tourist visa to a Working Holiday visa once you're in Australia.

➡ Conditions include having a return air ticket or sufficient funds ($5000) for a return or onward fare.

➡ Application fee: $440.

➡ Second Working Holiday visas can be applied for once you're in Australia, subject to certain conditions.

➡ Note that New Zealanders entering Australia are automatically granted a Special Category Visa, allowing them to live, work and stay in Australia without restrictions.

Volunteering

Lonely Planet's *Volunteer: A Traveller's Guide to Making a Difference Around the World* provides useful information about volunteering.

Conservation Volunteers Australia (www.conservation-volunteers.com.au) Nonprofit organisation involved in tree

planting, walking-track construction, and flora and fauna surveys.

Go Volunteer (www.govolunteer.com.au) National website listing volunteer opportunities.

Greening Australia (www.greeningaustralia.org.au) Helps volunteers get involved with environmental projects in the bush or in plant nurseries.

Lizard Island Research Station (www.australianmuseum.net.au/lizard-island-research-station) Opportunities to help researchers studying marine ecology and seabirds.

Reef Check (www.reefcheckaustralia.org) Train to monitor the health of the Great Barrier Reef (not so healthy of late...).

Sea Turtle Foundation (www.seaturtlefoundation.org) Volunteer opportunities in sea-turtle conservation.

Volunteering Australia (www.volunteeringaustralia.org) Support, advice and volunteer training.

Volunteering Qld (www.volunteeringqld.org.au) Volunteering info and advice across Queensland.

Willing Workers on Organic Farms (www.wwoof.com.au) WWOOFing is where you do a few hours' work each day on a farm in return for bed and board. Most hosts are concerned to some extent with alternative lifestyles, and have a minimum stay of two nights. Join online for $70. You'll get a membership number and a booklet listing participating enterprises ($5 overseas postage). There's also an app available ($20).

Women Travellers

Queensland is generally a safe place for women travellers, although the usual sensible precautions apply. Sexual harassment is rare, though some macho Aussie males still slip – particularly in rural areas when they've been drinking. Hitch-hiking isn't such a great idea anywhere in Australia these days, even when travelling in pairs.

Work

If you come to Australia on a tourist visa then you're not allowed to work for pay. You'll need either a Work & Holiday (462) or Working Holiday (417) visa: see www.border. gov.au for details.

➜ If you're in Brisbane and happy with bar work or waiting on tables, the best advice is to go knocking on doors in Fortitude Valley or New Farm. Many places want staff for longer than three months, though, so it may take a bit of footwork to find a willing employer. The *Courier-Mail* newspaper has daily employment listings – Wednesday and Saturday are the best days to look.

➜ Backpacker magazines and hostel noticeboards are also good options for sourcing local work. Casual work can often be found during peak season in tourist hubs such as Cairns, the Gold Coast and the resort towns along the Queensland coast.

➜ Harvest work is popular elsewhere in Queensland (just don't expect to make a fortune). The main spots are Bundaberg, Childers, Stanthorpe, Bowen, Tully and Innisfail, where everything from avocados to zucchinis are harvested throughout the year, and hostels specialise in finding travellers work.

➜ People with computer, secretarial, nursing and teaching skills can often find work temping in the cities (via employment agencies).

Resources

Australian Job Search (www. jobsearch.gov.au) Government-run website listing myriad jobs around the country.

Career One (www.careerone. com.au) General employment site; good for metropolitan areas.

Harvest Trail (www.harvesttrail. gov.au) Harvest job specialists.

National Harvest Telephone Information Service (☎1800 062 332) Advice on when and where you're likely to pick up harvest work.

Seek (www.seek.com.au) General employment site; good for metropolitan areas.

Travellers at Work (www.taw. com.au) Excellent site for working travellers in Australia.

Workabout Australia (www. workaboutaustralia.com.au) Gives a state-by-state breakdown of seasonal work opportunities.

Income Tax

➜ If you're earning money in Australia, you'll be paying tax in Australia and will have to lodge a tax return. See the website of the Australian Taxation Office (www.ato. gov.au) for info on how to do this, including getting a payment summary from your employer, timing and dates for lodging returns, and receiving your notice of assessment.

➜ As part of this process you'll need to apply for a Tax File Number (TFN) to give your employer. Without it, tax will be deducted at the maximum rate from your wages. Apply online via the Australian Taxation Office; it takes up to four weeks to be issued.

Transport

GETTING THERE & AWAY

Entering Australia

Unless you're travelling from within Australia, getting to Queensland usually involves a long-haul flight. Flights, tours and rail tickets can be booked online at lonelyplanet.com/bookings.

Air

High season (with the highest prices) for flights into Australia is roughly over the country's summer (December to February); low season generally tallies with the winter months (June to August), though this is actually peak season in tropical Far North Queensland.

Many international flights head to Sydney or Melbourne before flying to Queensland, but Brisbane receives a growing number of direct international flights. Cairns, the Gold Coast and the Sunshine Coast also receive some international flights.

Australia's international carrier is Qantas (www.qantas.com.au), which has an outstanding safety record (...ask anyone who saw Dustin Hoffman in *Rainman*).

International airports include the following:

Brisbane Airport (www.bne.com.au; Airport Dr)

Cairns Airport (07-4080 6703; www.cairnsairport.com; Airport Ave)

Gold Coast Airport (www.goldcoastairport.com.au; Longa Ave, Bilinga) In Coolangatta, 25km south of Surfers Paradise.

Sunshine Coast Airport (Maroochydore Airport; 07-5453 1500; www.sunshinecoastairport.com; Friendship Ave, Marcoola) Air New Zealand flights direct to/from Auckland between July and October.

Land

Travelling overland to Queensland from elsewhere in Australia is an education in how big this country is. The journey from Brisbane to the nearest state capital, Sydney, is a convoluted 1030km, while the journey from Brisbane to Cairns in Queensland's north covers 1700km!

➡ The Pacific Hwy is the main access point into Queensland from the south, crossing the New South Wales (NSW) border at Tweed Heads. A lesser-used route from the south is the New England Hwy, crossing the border at Tenterfield. The inland Newell Hwy is the most direct route to Brisbane from Melbourne or Adelaide.

➡ The other major route into southern Queensland is the Mitchell Hwy. It crosses the border at Barringun and links Bourke in outback NSW with Charleville in outback Queensland.

➡ The main road from the west is the Barkly Hwy, which crosses the Northern Territory–Queensland border around 15km west of Camooweal and cuts across to Mt Isa.

Sea

It is possible (if not straightforward) to travel between Queensland and Papua New Guinea, Indonesia, New Zealand and the Pacific islands by hitching rides or crewing on yachts – usually you have to at least contribute towards food. Ask around at marinas and sailing clubs in places like Great Keppel

QANTAS PASS

Qantas offers a discount-fare Walkabout Pass for passengers flying into Australia from overseas with Qantas or American Airlines. The pass allows you to link up around 80 domestic Australian destinations for less than you'd pay booking flights individually. See www.qantas.com.au for more information.

Island, Airlie Beach, the Whitsundays and Cairns.

➡ P&O Cruises (www.pocruises.com.au) operates holiday cruises between Brisbane and destinations in New Zealand and the Pacific.

➡ Alternatively, some cargo ships allow passengers to travel on board as they ship freight to/from Australia: see websites such as www.freighterexpeditions.com.au and www.freightercruises.com for options.

GETTING AROUND

Air

Queensland is well serviced by airlines, big and small.

Hinterland Aviation (www.hinterlandaviation.com.au) Flies between Cairns and Cooktown.

Jetgo (www.jetgo.com) Flights between Essendon Airport in Melbourne's northern suburbs and Brisbane, and between the Gold Coast, Rockhampton and Townsville.

Jetstar (www.jetstar.com.au) Budget offshoot of Qantas; has extensive services, including flights to Hamilton Island.

Qantas (www.qantas.com.au) Australia's main player; flies to many locations in Queensland, including Brisbane, Cairns, Townsville and Hamilton Island.

Regional Express (www.regionalexpress.com.au) Connects Brisbane, Cairns and Townsville with small regional airports.

Skytrans (www.skytrans.com.au) Serves northern Queensland and the Torres Strait, flying from Cairns to Bamaga (tip of Australia), among other obscure locations.

Tiger Airways (www.tigerair.com) Budget offshoot of Singapore Airlines. Services Brisbane, the Gold Coast and a few other Queensland destinations.

Virgin Australia (www.virginaustralia.com.au) Services throughout Queensland and Australia.

Bicycle

Queensland can be a good place for cycling, although you need to choose your areas: roads such as the Bruce Hwy between Brisbane and Cairns can be long and hot with limited verges and heavy traffic. The best areas for touring are the Gold Coast hinterland, the Sunshine Coast secondary roads, and the area north of Cairns. Many touring cyclists carry camping equipment but it's feasible to travel from town to town staying in hostels, hotels or caravan parks.

➡ Summer in Queensland isn't a great time for cycling. It can get very hot and incredibly humid here, with daily torrential downpours. Drink plenty of water: dehydration can be life-threatening.

➡ Bicycle helmets are compulsory, as are front and rear lights for night riding.

➡ Within Australia you can load your bike on to a bus or train to skip the less interesting bits of road. Note that some bus companies require you to dismantle your bike, and don't guarantee that it will travel on the same bus as you. Trains are easier: supervise the loading if you can.

➡ See Lonely Planet's *Cycling Australia* or contact Bicycle Queensland (www.bq.org.au) for detailed information. Additionally, the Queensland government has an informative website, including road rules, maps and other resources: www.tmr.qld.gov.au/travel-and-transport/cycling.

Hire

Rates charged by most rental outfits for road or mountain bikes range from $10 to $15 per hour and $25 to $50 per day. Security deposits can range from $50 to $200, depending on the rental period.

Buying a Bike

For a new road or mountain bike in Queensland, your bottom-level starting price will be around $600. With all the requisite on-the-road equipment (panniers, helmet, lights etc) you're looking at upwards of $1700.

To sell your bike (or buy a secondhand one), try hostel noticeboards or online:

Bike Exchange (www.bikeexchange.com.au)

Gumtree (www.gumtree.com.au)

Trading Post (www.tradingpost.com.au)

CLIMATE CHANGE & TRAVEL

Every form of transport that relies on carbon-based fuel generates CO_2, the main cause of human-induced climate change. Modern travel is dependent on aeroplanes, which might use less fuel per kilometre per person than most cars but travel much greater distances. The altitude at which aircraft emit gases (including CO_2) and particles also contributes to their climate change impact. Many websites offer 'carbon calculators' that allow people to estimate the carbon emissions generated by their journey and, for those who wish to do so, to offset the impact of the greenhouse gases emitted with contributions to portfolios of climate-friendly initiatives throughout the world. Lonely Planet offsets the carbon footprint of all staff and author travel.

Brisbane Bike-Share

Brisbane has an inexpensive public bike-sharing scheme that allows speedy access to bikes across town. Basically you subscribe online and can then borrow a bike for up to 24 hours, and return it to any of the dozens of bike stations around the city. Sometimes a helmet will accompany the bike, but it's a good idea to have your own (and a lock). For details see **CityCycle** (☎1300 229 253; www.citycycle.com.au; hire per hr/day $2.20/165, 1st 30min free; ⏱24hr).

Boat

There are no scheduled ferry services along the Queensland coast (other than those out to various islands...and the MV *Trinity* which is a regular passenger/cargo boat between Cairns and Seisia on Cape York), but cruising the coastline on a yacht is certainly an idyllic way to explore the state. Ask about the possibility of crewing on board a yacht at marinas in places like Cairns, Airlie Beach, Great Keppel Island, the Whitsundays and Manly in Brisbane.

Bus

Queensland's bus network is reliable, but not the cheapest for long hauls. Most buses have air-con and toilets; all are smoke-free. Small towns eschew formal bus terminals for an informal drop-off/pick-up point, usually outside a post office or shop.

Reservations

Over summer, school holidays and public holidays, you should book well ahead on the more popular routes – even if you're using a bus pass. At other times you should have few problems getting a seat on your preferred service.

There are no distinct seating classes on buses (very democratic).

BUS FARES

ROUTE	FARE ($)	DURATION (HR)
Airlie Beach–Townsville	49	5
Brisbane–Cairns	344	29
Brisbane–Hervey Bay	74	6
Brisbane–Noosa	25	3
Hervey Bay–Rockhampton	93	6½
Mackay–Airlie Beach	33	2
Rockhampton–Mackay	54	3¾
Townsville–Cairns	65	5½

Bus Passes

Bus passes are a good option for getting to Queensland, and also handy if you plan on making multiple stop-overs within the state. Both Greyhound (www.greyhound.com.au) and Premier Motor Service (www.premierms.com.au) offers passes – check the websites for comprehensive info.

Bus Companies

Bus Queensland (www.busqld.com.au) Toowoomba based, and the new long-haul operator for inland Queensland, running the major daily routes through outback Queensland from Townsville and Brisbane to Mt Isa.

Cairns Cooktown Express (www.cairnscooktownexpress.com.au) Cairns to Cooktown via Kuranda and Mareeba.

CON-X-ION (www.coachtransonline.com.au) Connects Brisbane, Gold Coast and Sunshine Coast airports with surrounding areas.

Coral Reef Coaches (www.coralreefcoaches.com.au) Runs between Cairns and Port Douglas.

Crisps Coaches (www.crisps.com.au) Services inland from Brisbane to Toowoomba, Stanthorpe and south to Tenterfield in NSW.

Greyhound (www.greyhound.com.au) Extensive network across Queensland, continuing interstate.

Murrays (www.murrays.com.au) Long-distance bus company with routes including Brisbane–Toowoomba.

Premier Motor Service (www.premierms.com.au) Greyhound's main competitor: has fewer daily services and usually costs a little less.

Sun Palm (www.sunpalmtransport.com.au) Services between Cairns and Port Douglas.

Trans North (www.transnorthbus.com.au) Cairns to Cooktown via the inland route (Kuranda, Mareeba) or the coast (Port Douglas, Daintree).

Car & Motorcycle

Queensland is a big, sprawling state – for the locals, driving is the accepted means of getting from A to B. For travellers too, the best way to explore much of the state is with your own wheels – it's certainly the only way to access interesting, out-of-the-way places without taking a tour.

Motorcycles are also popular here: between April and November the climate is ideal for bikes. A fuel range of 350km will easily cover fuel stops along the coast. The long, open roads here are really made for large-capacity bikes (750cc and up).

The Department of Transport and Main Roads (www.tmr.qld.gov.au) is the Queensland government body responsible for roads.

It provides a wealth of free information on Australian road rules and conditions, and downloadable brochures including the extremely useful *Guide to Queensland Roads,* which includes distance charts, road maps and other helpful information.

Driving Licences

To drive in Australia you'll need to hold a current driving licence issued in English from your home country. If the licence isn't in English, you'll also need to carry an International Driving Permit, issued in your home country.

Fuel

Diesel and unleaded fuel are available from all service stations. LPG (gas) is also available in populated areas but not always at more remote service stations. On main Queensland highways there's usually a small town or petrol station every 50km or so.

Prices vary from place to place, but at the time of writing unleaded was hovering between $1.40 and $1.60 per litre in the cities. Out in the country, prices soar – in outback Queensland you can pay as much as $2.20 per litre.

Hire

There are plenty of car-rental companies in Queensland, big and small, ready to put you behind the wheel. The main thing to remember is distance – if you want to travel far, you'll need unlimited kilometres.

Larger car-rental companies have drop-offs in major cities and towns; smaller local firms are sometimes cheaper but may have restrictions. The big firms sometimes also offer one-way rentals, which may not cost extra. Most companies require drivers to be over the age of 21, though in some cases it's 18 and in others 25. Typical rates are from $40/60/80 per day for a small/medium/large car.

The usual big international companies all operate in Queensland (Avis, Budget, Europcar, Hertz, Thrifty), but smaller companies often have better deals:

Abel Rent A Car (www.abel.com. au) Good for vans, as well as cars; based in Brisbane.

Apex Car Rentals (☑1800 558 912; www.apexrentacar.com. au; 400 Nudgee Rd, Hendra) Outlets at Brisbane, Cairns and Gold Coast airports.

East Coast Car Rentals (www. eastcoastcarrentals.com.au) Some of Queensland's best prices; offices in Brisbane, Cairns and the Gold Coast.

The following websites offer rate comparisons and last-minute discounts:

Bargain Wheels (www.bargain-wheels.com.au)

Carhire.com (www.carhire. com.au)

Drive Now (www.drivenow. com.au)

Webjet (www.webjet.com.au)

Campervan

Once the preserve of meandering grey nomads, campervanning has exploded in Australia in recent years, and nowhere more so than in Queensland. The advantages are obvious: a weather-proof home on wheels, providing transport, accommodation, cooking gear (usually), and no mucking around with tents. Most towns have at least one caravan park where you can park and plug into power. National parks usually have self-registration or prebooked campsites. There are also lots of off-track free camping options – with a good map and a bit of planning you can always find a secluded spot.

Campervans start with budget two-berth vans. Seating folds down to a double bed and there's generally room for a basic gas stove and hand-pump sink. But there's usually no fridge, so storing food is a pain, and they're too cramped for extended trips. Next up are pop-top or hi-top campervans that can sleep three or four, have a gas stove, a water tank and a fridge, and plug into 240V power – economical and brilliant for a couple or a small family. From there you can go to a four- or five-berth campervan.

Companies for campervan hire – with rates from around $90 (two-berth) or $150 (four-berth) per day, usually with minimum five-day hire and unlimited kilometres – include the following:

Apollo (☑1800 777 779; www. apollocamper.com)

Britz (☑1300 738 087; www. britz.com.au)

Camperman (☑1800 216 223; www.campermanaustralia. com.au)

Hippie Camper (☑1800 777 779; www.hippiecamper.com)

Jucy Rentals (☑1800 150 850; www.jucy.com.au)

Maui (☑1800 827 821; www. maui.com.au)

TOLL ROADS

There are a handful of toll roads around Brisbane with electronic toll-pass detection. Regardless of whether you're travelling in your own vehicle or in a rental, you'll be in for a hefty fine if you don't pay the tolls (all of which are under $5 for cars and campervans). You can organise a toll pass ahead of time (most rental companies can supply you with one for a daily charge), or you can pay tolls online within three days of driving on the toll roads: see www.govia.com.au for payment and pass details.

Mighty Campers (☎1800 821 824; www.mightycampers. com.au)

Spaceships (☎1300 132 469; www.spaceshipsrentals.com.au)

Travelwheels (☎0412 766 616; www.travelwheels.com.au)

ONE-WAY RELOCATION

Relocations (where you pick up a vehicle in one location and return it to another) are usually cheap deals, although they don't allow much time flexibility. Most of the large hire companies offer deals, or try the following operators:

Drive Now (www.drivenow. com.au)

imoova (www.imoova.com)

Relocations2Go (www.facebook. com/relocations2go)

Transfercar (www.transfercar. com.au)

Ride-Sharing

Ride-sharing is a good way to split costs and environmental impact with other travellers. As with hitching, there are potential risks: meet in a public place before hitting the road, and if anything seems off, don't hesitate to back out. Hostel notice-boards are good places to find ads; also check these online classifieds:

Catch a Lift (www.catchalift. com)

Coseats (www.coseats.com)

HopHop Ride (www.hophopride. com.au)

Share Ur Ride (www.shareur ride.com.au)

4WD

Having a 4WD enables you to get right off the beaten track and revel in the natural splen-dour that many travellers miss. Something midsize like a Nissan X-Trail costs around $100 to $150 per day; for a Toyota Land Cruiser you're looking at around $150 up to $200, which should include unlimited kilometres. Check insurance conditions carefully, especially the excess, as they can be onerous.

The major car-hire compa-nies have 4WD rentals, or try **Apollo** (☎1800 777 779; www. apollocamper.com) or **Britz** (☎1300 738 087; www.britz. com.au). Alternatively, **Bear Rentals** (☎1300 462 327; www.bearrentals.com.au; cars per day from $127) is a small 4WD drive hire company in Cairns that rents affordable old Land Rovers fitted out as campers for driving to Cape York.

Insurance

Third-Party Insurance In Australia, third-party person-al-injury insurance is included in the vehicle-registration cost, ensuring that every registered vehicle carries at least minimum insurance. We recommend extending that minimum to at least third-party property insurance – minor collisions can be amazingly expensive.

Rental Vehicles When it comes to hire cars, understand your lia-bility in the event of an accident. You can pay an additional daily amount to the rental company that will reduce your liability in the event of an accident from upwards of $3000 to a few hundred dollars.

Exclusions Be aware that if you're driving on dirt roads you may not be covered by insurance (even if you have a 4WD); if you have an accident you'll be liable for all costs. Also, many insur-ance policies don't cover damage to windscreens or tyres – always read the small print.

Purchase

Australian cars are not cheap, but if you plan to stay several months and do plenty of driving, buying a car will probably work out to be cheaper than renting one. You can buy from a car deal-er or a private vendor (pri-vate sales are often cheaper). Hostel noticeboards are good places to start looking. On-line, have a look at Car Sales (www.carsales.com.au) and Trading Post (www.trading-post.com.au).

Road Hazards

➡ Be wary of driver fatigue; driving long distances (particularly in hot weather) can be utterly exhausting. Falling asleep at the wheel is not uncommon. On a long haul, stop and rest every two hours or so – do some exercise, change drivers or find a decent coffee.

➡ Unsealed road conditions vary wildly and cars perform differently when braking and turning on dirt. Don't exceed 80km/h on dirt roads; if you go faster you won't have time to respond to a sharp turn, livestock on the road or an unmarked gate or cattle grid. If you're in a rental car, check your contract to ensure you're covered for driving on unsealed roads.

➡ Queensland has few multilane highways, although there are stretches of divided road (four or six lanes) in busy areas such as the toll roads and freeways around Brisbane. Two-lane roads, however, are the only option for many routes. Be aware that you can only overtake other vehicles when there is a dotted white line down the middle or on your side of the road. Never overtake on full double lines as these are placed along high-risk, low-visibility stretches of road.

➡ Many rural Queenslanders avoid travelling after dark because of the risks posed by nocturnal animals on the roads. Kangaroos are common on country roads, as are cows and sheep in the unfenced outback. Kangaroos are most active around dawn and dusk and often travel in groups: if you see one hopping across the road, slow right down, as its friends may be just behind it. Despite the obvious implications for the poor creature involved, hitting a 2m-tall, 90kg kangaroo will do untold damage to your vehicle! If you do hit and kill an animal, pull it off the road, potentially preventing the next car from having an accident. If the animal is injured, wrap it in a towel or blanket and contact the **RSPCA Queensland** (☎1300 264 625; www.rspcaqld.org.au).

➜ With Queensland's heavy tropical rains, flooding can occur with little warning, especially in outback areas and the Far North (and, more recently, in downtown Brisbane!). Roads can be cut off for days during floods, and floodwaters sometimes wash away whole sections of road.

Road Rules

Australians drive on the left-hand side of the road; all cars are right-hand drive.

Give Way If an intersection is unmarked (unusual) and at roundabouts, you must give way to vehicles entering the intersection from your right.

Speed Limits The general speed limit in built-up and residential areas is 50km/h (sometimes 60km/h). Near schools, the limit is usually 25km/h around school drop-off and pick-up times. On the highway it's 100km/h or 110km/h. Police have speed radar guns and cameras and are fond of using them in strategic locations.

Seat Belts & Car Seats Seatbelt usage is compulsory. Children up to the age of seven must be belted into an approved safety seat.

Drink Driving Random breath tests are common. If you're caught with a blood-alcohol level of more than 0.05%, expect a court appearance, a fine and the loss of your licence. Police can randomly pull any driver over for a breathalyser or drug test.

Mobile Phones Using a mobile phone while driving is illegal (excluding hands-free technology).

Local Transport

Bus, Train & Ferry

Brisbane has a comprehensive public transport network with buses, trains and river ferries run by **Translink** (☎13 12 30; www.translink.com.au), with services extending to the Sunshine Coast, Gold Coast and parts of the Darling Downs.

Larger cities such as Toowoomba, Mt Isa, Bundaberg, Rockhampton, Mackay, Townsville and Cairns all have local bus services. There are also local bus services throughout the Gold Coast and Sunshine Coast.

The new Gold Coast Rapid Transit tram (www.goldlinq.com.au) is now operational, linking 16 stops over 13km between Southport and Broadbeach.

Taxi

Brisbane, Cairns and the Gold Coast have plenty of taxis, but outside of these centres taxi numbers diminish. Taxi fares vary throughout the state, but shouldn't differ much from those in Brisbane, where a 5km cross-town jaunt costs about $25.

Black & White (☎13 32 22; www.blackandwhitecabs.com.au) In Brisbane.

Cairns Taxis (☎13 10 08; www.cairnstaxis.com.au)

Gold Coast Cabs (☎13 10 08; www.gccabs.com.au)

Suncoast Cabs (☎13 10 08; www.suncoastcabs.com.au) On the Sunshine Coast.

Townsville Taxis (☎13 10 08; www.tsvtaxi.com.au)

Yellow Cab Co (☎13 19 24; www.yellowcab.com.au) In Brisbane.

Train

Queensland has a sizeable intra-state rail network that services the coast between Brisbane and Cairns, with several routes heading inland to Mt Isa, Longreach and Charleville. There are eight main service routes, including the Kuranda Scenic Railway, which is primarily a tourist route in northern Queensland. All services are operated by **Queensland Rail Travel** (☎1300 131 722; www.queenslandrailtravel.com.au).

Classes & Costs

Travelling by rail within Queensland is generally slower and more expensive than bus travel, although some economy fares are comparable. Where sleeping berths are available they cost from around $70 extra per night in economy and approximately $230 more for 1st class.

Half-price concession fares are available to kids under 16 years of age, and students with an International Student Identity Card (ISIC) can get discounts of up to 40%. There are also discounts for seniors and pensioners.

Reservations

Book online or by phone via **Queensland Rail Travel** (☎1300 131 722; www.queenslandrailtravel.com.au). There are also Queensland Rail travel centres throughout the state. These booking offices can advise on rail travel, sell tickets and put together rail-holiday packages: see the website for locations.

Train Services
GULFLANDER

The Gulflander is a strange, snub-nosed little train that travels once a week along the 152km line connecting the remote Gulf of Carpentaria towns of Normanton and Croydon – a unique and memorable five-hour journey. Fares are $69/115 one-way/return. Departs Normanton on Wednesday; departs Croydon on Thursday. See www.gulflander.com.au for more info.

INLANDER

The Inlander runs from Townsville 977km east to Mt Isa (economy seat $179, 21 hours) on Wednesday and Saturday. Returns from Mt Isa Sunday and Thursday. No sleeper carriages; good advance-purchase discounts.

KURANDA SCENIC RAILWAY

One of the most popular tourist trips out of Cairns is the fabulous **Kuranda Scenic Railway** (☎07-4036 9333; www.ksr.com.au; adult/child one way from $50/25, return from $76/38) – a spectacular 1½-hour trip on a historic steam train through the rainforest to Kuranda, 34km west of Cairns. Runs daily.

SAVANNAHLANDER

A classic 1960s train, the **Savannahlander** (☎07-4053 6848; www.savannahlander. com.au) makes the relatively short 229km trip between Cairns (departs Wednesday) and Forsayth (departs Friday) over two days in each direction, with stops en route for morning tea and lunch, and to look at various sights and museums. Trains run between March and December. The journey costs $250/426 for a single/return trip.

SPIRIT OF QUEENSLAND

The Spirit of Queensland service runs 1681km from Brisbane to Cairns (24 hours, departing Monday, Tuesday, Wednesday, Friday and Saturday), with flashy reclining 'railbed' seats and premium economy seats. Fares are $369/519 for premium economy seat/railbed. Railbed fares include food. Returns from Cairns on Monday, Wednesday, Thursday, Friday and Sunday.

SPIRIT OF THE OUTBACK

The Spirit of the Outback travels 1325km northwest from Brisbane to Longreach via Rockhampton (economy seat $235, twin/1st-class sleeper per person $315/529, 24 hours) on Tuesday and Saturday. A connecting bus service operates between Longreach and Winton. Returns from Longreach

Monday and Thursday; 1st-class fares include meals.

TILT TRAIN

The Tilt Train, a high-speed, business-class train, makes the 351km trip from Brisbane to Bundaberg (business seat $89, 4½ hours) on Monday and Thursday (returning Tuesday and Friday); and 639km from Brisbane to Rockhampton ($135, 7½ hours) on Tuesday, Friday and Sunday (returning Monday, Thursday and Saturday).

WESTLANDER

The Westlander heads 777km inland from Brisbane to Charleville via Toowoomba (economy seat $149, 17 hours) on Tuesday and Thursday. From Charleville there are connecting bus services to Cunnamulla and Quilpie. Return from Charleville is on Wednesday and Friday. No sleeper carriages.

TRANSPORT TRAIN

Behind the Scenes

SEND US YOUR FEEDBACK

We love to hear from travellers – your comments keep us on our toes and help make our books better. Our well-travelled team reads every word on what you loved or loathed about this book. Although we cannot reply individually to your submissions, we always guarantee that your feedback goes straight to the appropriate authors, in time for the next edition. Each person who sends us information is thanked in the next edition – the most useful submissions are rewarded with a selection of digital PDF chapters.

Visit **lonelyplanet.com/contact** to submit your updates and suggestions or to ask for help. Our award-winning website also features inspirational travel stories, news and discussions.

Note: We may edit, reproduce and incorporate your comments in Lonely Planet products such as guidebooks, websites and digital products, so let us know if you don't want your comments reproduced or your name acknowledged. For a copy of our privacy policy visit lonelyplanet.com/privacy.

OUR READERS

Many thanks to the travellers who used the last edition and wrote to us with helpful hints, useful advice and interesting anecdotes:

Barbara Kendal, Hugh Cookson, Kevin Callaghan, Kieran Bayl, Wes Jeffries

WRITER THANKS

Paul Harding

Thanks to all those travellers and locals who helped with company and advice on my journey through Queensland's most remote corners, especially the helpful guys who got me out of vehicular trouble at Elliot Falls. Thanks to Tamara for coffee and a chat in Cairns, and to Tasmin at LP. But mostly to Hannah and Layla for being there.

Cristian Bonetto

First and foremost, an epic thankyou to Drew Westbrook for his hospitality and generosity. Sincere thanks also to Craig Bradbery, Tim Crabtree, Amy Ratcliffe, Leanne Layfield, Terese Finegan, Michael Flocke, Simon Betteridge, Annabel Sullivan, Garry Judd and the many locals who offered insight and insider knowledge along the way. At Lonely Planet, a huge thanks to Tasmin Waby for her support and encouragement.

Charles Rawlings-Way

Huge thanks to Tasmin for the gig, and to all the helpful souls I met and friends I reconnected with on the road who flew through my questions with the greatest of ease. Biggest thanks of all to Meg, who held the increasingly chaotic fort while I was busy scooting around in the sunshine ('Where's daddy?') – and made sure that Ione, Remy, Liv and Reuben were fed, watered, schooled, tucked in and read to.

Tamara Sheward

Sweaty Cairns hugs and hearty thanks to my friends, family, local experts and random ring-ins who helped me delve ever deeper into the wonders of my hometown and surrounds; it's always an eye-opener being a traveller/travel writer in one's own backyard. At LP, mega-thanks to Tasmin Waby for the gig, and for your eternal encouragement; and to chapter co-author Paul Harding. The biggest clink of the coconuts goes, as ever, to my favourite FNQers: my crazy crocodiles Dušan and Masha.

Tom Spurling

To Tasmin for choosing me to go around again! To Goose for riding shotgun to Rockhampton and making me go for a jog. To Lucy for sleeping in the backseat and showing no interest in cryptic crosswords. To the bar staff in Ravenswood for reminding me why I wanted this job in the first place. To the Whitsundays for being discovered. To the Town of 1770 for providing so many openings at dinner parties ('A number? Really?'). To my children for not missing me very much (I will never forget that slight, O and P).

Donna Wheeler

Love and gratitude to Juliette Claire for her inspiration and incredible regional knowledge. Thanks to ex-locals Peter Maclaine and Debbie Wheeler, especially for Pete's surfing expertise. Thanks to Harry in Broadbeach, to the Byron skydivers and to Amanda and Simon in Brunswick Heads for great hospo insights. Thanks also to Nic Wrathall for your company during some long research days and Brigid Healy and Andrew King, Kate Dale, and Darryn Devlin for Sydney homecoming love. Finally thanks to Joe Guario, for everything.

ACKNOWLEDGEMENTS

Climate map data adapted from Peel MC, Finlayson BL & McMahon TA (2007) 'Updated World Map of the Köppen-Geiger Climate Classification', *Hydrology and Earth System Sciences*, 11, 163344.

Cover photograph: Green turtle hatchling, Jason Edwards/Getty ©

BEHIND THE SCENES

THIS BOOK

This 8th edition of Lonely Planet's *Coastal Queensland & the Great Barrier Reef* guidebook was researched and written by Paul Harding, Cristian Bonetto, Charles Rawlings-Way, Tamara Sheward, Tom Spurling and Donna Wheeler.
This guidebook was produced by the following:

Destination Editor
Tasmin Waby

Product Editors Heather Champion, Joel Cotterell

Senior Cartographer
Julie Sheridan
Book Designer
Mazzy Prinsep
Assisting Editors
Sarah Bailey, Andrew Bain, Imogen Bannister, Michelle Bennett, Laura Crawford, Melanie Dankle, Andrea Dobbin, Gabrielle Innes, Sandie Kestell, Ali Lemer, Jodie Martire, Anne Mulvaney, Rosie Nicholson, Lauren O'Connell, Susan Paterson, Chris Pitts, Gabrielle Stefanos, Saralinda Turner, Simon Williamson

Cartographer
Julie Dodkins
Assisting Book Designer
Lauren Egan
Cover Researcher
Campbell McKenzie
Thanks to
Jennifer Carey, Hannah Cartmel, Daniel Corbett, Megan Eaves, Bruce Evans, Benjamin Little, Bruce McDonald, MaSovaida Morgan, Claire Naylor, Karyn Noble, Doug Rimington, Jessica Ryan, John Taufa, Angela Tinson, Clifton Wilkinson, Amanda Williamson

Index

EMMA NEUVONEN

Map Legend

Sights
- Beach
- Bird Sanctuary
- Buddhist
- Castle/Palace
- Christian
- Confucian
- Hindu
- Islamic
- Jain
- Jewish
- Monument
- Museum/Gallery/Historic Building
- Ruin
- Shinto
- Sikh
- Taoist
- Winery/Vineyard
- Zoo/Wildlife Sanctuary
- Other Sight

Activities, Courses & Tours
- Bodysurfing
- Diving
- Canoeing/Kayaking
- Course/Tour
- Sento Hot Baths/Onsen
- Skiing
- Snorkelling
- Surfing
- Swimming/Pool
- Walking
- Windsurfing
- Other Activity

Sleeping
- Sleeping
- Camping

Eating
- Eating

Drinking & Nightlife
- Drinking & Nightlife
- Cafe

Entertainment
- Entertainment

Shopping
- Shopping

Information
- Bank
- Embassy/Consulate
- Hospital/Medical
- Internet
- Police
- Post Office
- Telephone
- Toilet
- Tourist Information
- Other Information

Geographic
- Beach
- Gate
- Hut/Shelter
- Lighthouse
- Lookout
- Mountain/Volcano
- Oasis
- Park
- Pass
- Picnic Area
- Waterfall

Population
- Capital (National)
- Capital (State/Province)
- City/Large Town
- Town/Village

Transport
- Airport
- Border crossing
- Bus
- Cable car/Funicular
- Cycling
- Ferry
- Metro station
- Monorail
- Parking
- Petrol station
- Subway station
- Taxi
- Train station/Railway
- Tram
- Underground station
- Other Transport

Note: Not all symbols displayed above appear on the maps in this book

Routes
- Tollway
- Freeway
- Primary
- Secondary
- Tertiary
- Lane
- Unsealed road
- Road under construction
- Plaza/Mall
- Steps
- Tunnel
- Pedestrian overpass
- Walking Tour
- Walking Tour detour
- Path/Walking Trail

Boundaries
- International
- State/Province
- Disputed
- Regional/Suburb
- Marine Park
- Cliff
- Wall

Hydrography
- River, Creek
- Intermittent River
- Canal
- Water
- Dry/Salt/Intermittent Lake
- Reef

Areas
- Airport/Runway
- Beach/Desert
- Cemetery (Christian)
- Cemetery (Other)
- Glacier
- Mudflat
- Park/Forest
- Sight (Building)
- Sportsground
- Swamp/Mangrove

Tom Spurling

Coastal Queensland Tom is an Australian LP guidebook author and high school teacher currently based in Hong Kong in search of the long-lost expatriate package. He's worked on 13 LP titles, including *Japan*, *China*, *Central America*, *Turkey*, *India*, *South Africa* and *Australia*. When not chasing his tail, he enjoys tucking it under his crossed legs for minutes on end.

Donna Wheeler

The Gold Coast Donna has written guidebooks for Lonely Planet for ten years, including the Italy, Norway, Belgium, Africa, Tunisia, Algeria, France, Austria and Melbourne titles. She is the author of *Paris Precincts*, a curated photographic guide to the city's best bars, restaurants and shops and is reporter for Italian contemporary art publisher My Art Guides. Donna's work on contemporary art, architecture and design, food, wine, wilderness areas and cultural history also can be found in a variety of other publications. She became a travel writer after various careers as a commissioning editor, creative director, digital producer and content strategist.

OUR STORY

A beat-up old car, a few dollars in the pocket and a sense of adventure. In 1972 that's all Tony and Maureen Wheeler needed for the trip of a lifetime – across Europe and Asia overland to Australia. It took several months, and at the end – broke but inspired – they sat at their kitchen table writing and stapling together their first travel guide, *Across Asia on the Cheap*. Within a week they'd sold 1500 copies. Lonely Planet was born.

Today, Lonely Planet has offices in Franklin, London, Melbourne, Oakland, Dublin, Beijing and Delhi, with more than 600 staff and writers. We share Tony's belief that 'a great guidebook should do three things: inform, educate and amuse'.

OUR WRITERS

Paul Harding

Curator, Port Douglas & the Daintree As a writer and photographer, Paul has been travelling the globe for the best part of two decades, with an interest in remote and offbeat places, islands and cultures. He's an author and contributor to more than 50 Lonely Planet guides to countries and regions as diverse as India, Iceland, Belize, Vanuatu, Iran, Indonesia, New Zealand, Finland, Philippines and – his home patch – Australia.

Cristian Bonetto

Brisbane, Noosa & the Sunshine Coast Cristian has contributed to over 30 Lonely Planet guides to date, including *New York City*, *Italy*, *Venice & the Veneto*, *Naples & the Amalfi Coast*, *Denmark*, *Copenhagen*, *Sweden* and *Singapore*. Lonely Planet work aside, his musings on travel, food, culture and design appear in numerous publications around the world, including The *Telegraph* (UK) and *Corriere del Mezzogiorno* (Italy). When not on the road, you'll find the reformed playwright and TV scriptwriter slurping espresso in his beloved hometown, Melbourne. Instagram: rexcat75.

Charles Rawlings-Way

Charles is a veteran travel writer who has penned 30-something titles for Lonely Planet – including guides to Singapore, Toronto, Sydney, Tasmania, New Zealand, the South Pacific and Australia – and numerous articles. After dabbling in the dark arts of architecture, cartography, project management and busking for some years, Charles hit the road for LP in 2005 and hasn't stopped travelling since. 'What's in store for me in the direction I don't take?' (Kerouac). Charles wrote the Plan Your Trip and Understand sections of this book.

Tamara Sheward

Cairns & Around After years of freelance travel writing, rock'n'roll journalism and insalubrious authordom, Tamara leapt at the chance to join the Lonely Planet ranks in 2009. Since then, she's worked on guides to an incongruous jumble of countries including Montenegro, Australia, Serbia, Russia, the Samoas, Bulgaria and Fiji. She's written a miscellany of travel articles for the BBC, the *Independent*, *Sydney Morning Herald* et al; she's also fronted the camera as a documentary presenter for Lonely Planet TV, Nat Geo and Al-Jazeera. Tamara's based in far northern Australia, but you're more likely to find her roaming elsewhere, tattered notebook in one hand, the world's best-travelled toddler in the other.

OVER PAGE MORE WRITERS

Published by Lonely Planet Global Limited
CRN 554153
8th edition – November 2017
ISBN 978 1 78657 155 7
© Lonely Planet 2017   Photographs © as indicated 2017
10 9 8 7 6 5 4 3 2 1
Printed in China

Although the authors and Lonely Planet have taken all reasonable care in preparing this book, we make no warranty about the accuracy or completeness of its content and, to the maximum extent permitted, disclaim all liability arising from its use.